Overtaken by the Night

Pitt Series in Russian and East European Studies

JONATHAN HARRIS, EDITOR

Overtaken by the Night

ONE RUSSIAN'S JOURNEY THROUGH PEACE, WAR, REVOLUTION, & TERROR

Richard G. Robbins Jr.

UNIVERSITY OF PITTSBURGH PRESS

Published by the University of Pittsburgh Press, Pittsburgh, Pa., 15260

Manufactured in the United States of America
Printed on acid-free paper
10 9 8 7 6 5 4 3 2 1

Cataloging-in-Publication data is available from the Library of Congress

ISBN 13: 978-0-8229-4516-1
ISBN 10: 0-8229-4516-9

Jacket art: Vladimir Dzhunkovsky in the Preobrazhensky Guards. From Anastasiia Dunaeva, *Reformy politsii v Rossii nachala XX veka i Vladimir Fedorovich Dzhunkovskii.*
Jacket design by Alex Wolfe

For Lily, Jackson, and Piper

Contents

Preface

Vladimir Fedorovich Dzhunkovsky, the subject of this book, was a witness to his country's unfolding tragedy—the decay of the tsarist autocracy, world war, revolution, the rise of a new regime, and its descent into terror. But Dzhunkovsky was not just a passive observer, he was an active participant in the troubled and turbulent events of his time, often struggling against the tide. This is his story; it is Russia's story.

Russians such as Dzhunkovsky seldom get their stories told. Biographers, especially those in the West, prefer the four "Rs"—Royals, Revolutionaries, Writers, and Rogues. At the height of his career, Dzhunkovsky was an important tsarist official. But of the many men who served the state only a relative few, mostly those who reached the very top, have caught a writer's eye. Yet Dzhunkovsky's life deserves our attention. It was long and rich in experiences and in its course intersected with many of the most important events and people of the age. It offers the fresh perspective of a man who was near the apex of power but not part of the inner circles of government; of someone who mixed with political and cultural elites but knew workers and peasants better than many radicals did. Dzhunkovsky's administrative career provides insights into the ways that the character and style of Russian governance were changing in the last years of the old regime and into the struggle between reformers and the forces working to block that transformation. An account of his experiences in combat and of the revolution at the front provides a more nuanced picture of Russia's Great War and the ultimate collapse of the Russian armies. Dzhunkovsky's life after the revolution does more than show the quotidian troubles faced by "former people" under the new regime. It tells us much about early Soviet justice, police practices, cultural politics, and the long night of terror that overtook Dzhunkovsky and so many of his countrymen. As we observe the centennials of the Great War and the revolution in Russia that the conflict unleashed, the narrative of Dzhunkovsky's life may have special value. Because it spans both the years before and the years that followed these great cataclysms, his journey reminds us once more of the positive prospects that late imperial Russia held and of the negative energies that were generated during the crisis years from 1914 to 1921.

This work is an exercise in biographical history, an attempt to link Dzhunkovsky's life to the larger currents that flowed around him, tracing their mutual interaction. This is an uncomplicated, some would say old-fashioned approach, but it offers the reader the advantage of bringing complex and truly titanic events down to a human scale. When I was contemplating various ways of crafting a biography, a wise friend, apparently tired of my musings and mutterings said: "Just tell the story." It seemed like good advice then—and now. To the best of my ability, I have followed it.

Acknowledgments

Research for this book was made possible by financial support from the University of New Mexico, a grant from the International Research and Exchanges Board, and a Fulbright-Hays Fellowship. That generosity enabled me to travel to Russia and utilize the collections in libraries and archives there.

I am grateful to the staffs of the various archives where I worked: The Bakhmeteff Archive at Columbia University, the State Archive of the Russian Federation, the Manuscript Division of the Central State Theater Museum, the Manuscript Division of the Russian State Library, the Russian Military-Historical Archive, the Russian State Archive of Social and Political History, and the Hoover Institution Archives. Their skill and courtesy made my research pleasant and profitable.

My greatest intellectual debt is to the late Marc Raeff, who was both mentor and friend. By his teaching and exemplary scholarship he stimulated and sustained my interest in the institutions and officials of imperial Russia. His wise advice and generous support made possible my earlier scholarly efforts and his encouragement for this project helped push me to complete it.

Many academic colleagues, some no longer living, read portions of this book and made thoughtful suggestions on matters of style and substance: Abraham Ascher, Jonathan Daly, Gary Hamburg, Robert Kern, Semion Lyandres, Samuel Ramer, Jake Spidle, and Ferenc Szasz. They have my gratitude and thankful memory. I am also profoundly indebted to members of the Institute for Historical Study's Writers Group: Ann Harlow, Ellen Huppert, Joanne Lafler, Elizabeth Nakahara, Carol Sicherman, Autumn Stanley, Elizabeth Thacker-Estrada, and Louis Trager. Most of them read the entire manuscript and all asked innumerable questions and offered invaluable ideas for improvements. If this book is at all readable, it is in large part due to their efforts.

I owe a special and substantial debt to my Russian colleague Anastasia Dunaeva for her scholarship and generosity. Her excellent book on

Dzhunkovsky is frequently cited here, and she also shared material that had been denied me during my research in Russia. I am very grateful for her willingness to permit me to reproduce some of the pictures that appeared in her book. Thanks, too, to Koninklijke Brill Publishers for their permission to include material contained in two articles I wrote for the *Journal of Modern Russian History and Historiography*: "Was Vladimir Dzhunkovskii the Father of the 'Trust'? A Quest for the Plausible," in volume 1 (2008) and "Building Vladimir Dzhunkovskii's Memory Palace: The Curious Fate of His Archive and Memoir," in volume 4 (2008). I also wish to thank Peter Kracht, the director of the University of Pittsburgh Press and Jonathan Harris the editor of its Russian and East European Series for their enthusiastic support of this project and for their patience in answering my innumerable and often ill-informed questions. Pippa Letsky did a thorough and careful job of copyediting the text. I am grateful to Edward Kasinec, for his sage advice about pictures, and to Jonathan Lee, for scanning some of the images presented in this book.

My greatest debt is to my wife, Catherine, friend, colleague, and critic, whose affection has sustained me for so many years. No words can even begin to express my gratitude.

Note on Dates and Spelling

All dates are given in accordance with the calendar used in Russia. Until February 1, 1918, this was the Julian calendar, which was twelve days behind the Gregorian calendar used in Europe and America in the nineteenth century and thirteen days behind in the twentieth century. In cases where both Julian and Gregorian dates seem to be required, they are written with the Julian date first, thus: January 1/14, 1917.

The spelling of names and places generally follows a modified form of the Library of Congress system of transliteration. Exceptions are made for familiar names and the names of rulers. Diacritical marks are not used in the text although they appear in the notes and in Russian words presented in italics. Names of people are modified to make pronunciation easier (for example, Muravyov instead of Murav'ev); surnames ending in "skii" and "aia" are transliterated "sky" and "aya."

Prologue

Butovo, 1938

BLACK "RAVENS" FLY SOUTH FROM MOSCOW: THE MURDER vans of the NKVD, the Soviet secret police. On the sides of their locked compartments they often display a camouflage—the words "Bread" or "Meat." But their freight is human: prisoners destined for the killing ground at Butovo.

In the terrible winter of 1937–1938, Stalin's seemingly endless war against the subjects of his empire strained the capacities of the Soviet regime to dispose of his victims. Mass arrests clogged the jails. "Troikas," three-man tribunals under the control of the secret police, worked overtime to speed the flow, passing thousands of summary judgments on "enemies of the people." Soon boxcars and the holds of the NKVD's ships-of-the-line bulged with consignments of wretched men and women headed for slave labor on the hellish islands of the "Gulag Archipelago," while across the country unflinching death squads performed their bloody rituals of societal cleansing. The familiar cellars where the executioners had dispatched so many, and the grounds where they regularly dumped remains, quickly proved insufficient for the job at hand. From the Moscow region alone, a single order (and there would be others) demanded five thousand death sentences in a four-month period of late 1937. Clearly, the Soviet capital required new sites of murder and burial, preferably on the fringes of the city.

In the early 1920s, the "organs"—a term consistently applied to the frequently renamed repressive agencies of the Communist regime—had acquired a sizeable estate at Butovo, about fifteen miles to the south of

Moscow. It had once been a stud-farm, but when it passed into the hands of the secret police, the property became a firing range and was used in weapons training for about a decade. Now the execution overload of the late 1930s required its conversion to other, darker purposes. For these, the Butovo location was perfect—far enough from the center of the capital to be secret, but easily and quickly accessible by road. High wooden fences rendered the field largely invisible, and the residents of the nearby village had long been used to hearing shots. At first, they gave little thought to firing in the night that continued for hours.

In time, the neighbors suspected what was going on. Denizens of Butovo, walking home after arriving late by train from Moscow, saw the "ravens" flying over dimly lit forest roads. Soon parents sent their children off to school with the warning to avoid the "awful place," and the youngsters, for once, listened to their elders and gave the firing range a wide berth. Pervasive fear silenced the locals. Even today, when questioned, the very few who can recall those years usually reply that they saw nothing, heard nothing, knew nothing.

The men and women crammed into the vans bound for Butovo were told neither their destination nor their fate. Some, no doubt, realized that this would be their final trip; many may have hoped that their lives would be spared, if only for long years of penal servitude. Now, tightly packed in lots of twenty, thirty, or even fifty, they sped into the dark, usually reaching the shooting range in the first hours after midnight.

At Butovo, the condemned stepped out and entered a barracks, ostensibly for medical examination, a ruse that may have been designed to calm them. Prisoners learned the sentence of the tribunal only moments before they were taken out to be shot. At that point, the guards made a careful identity-check to see that the persons they held matched the names on the death list. Verification accomplished, prisoners were led individually from the barracks and handed over to one of the executioners, who marched his charge to the interior of the firing range where a trench had already been dug. Death usually came with a bullet fired into the back of the skull at close range; bodies either fell directly into the pit or were thrown there shortly afterwards. For most executioners, the weapon of choice was the "Nagan" pistol, familiar from the days of the Civil War. Employing a 7.63-mm slug, it was powerful, handled easily, and seldom jammed.

Given the size of the task assigned to them, the death squads were surprisingly small—often no more than three or four persons—unless the group to be dispatched was especially numerous. In 1937 and 1938, executions took place, on average, three days a week, and rarely did the number of the condemned fall below one hundred. Mass murder is not an easy business; the teams had to work fast if they hoped to finish in good time. Most executions took place at night, often in cold weather. The killers' spirits required fortification. This they got from copious quantities of vodka, brought to Butovo especially for the occasion, and which they regularly consumed throughout the slaughter. As the work wore on to morning, most were thoroughly intoxicated.

The carnage complete, white-handed clerks carefully filled out all the required documents. The drunken murderers prepared to depart, but not before they threw into the pits containing their night's work all kinds of rubbish: tree branches, old barrels, empty bottles, items of clothing belonging to the victims, and their own bloody gloves. Later, as the next evening approached, a local employee of the NKVD drove a bulldozer over the now-deserted field and covered the corpse-laden trenches with dirt in preparation for a new night of homicide. According to recent estimates, the soil of the firing range conceals the remains of over fifteen thousand souls.

In the early hours of February 26, 1938, 387 people died at Butovo. This was a sizeable group, but nothing out of the ordinary in the frenzied months when the "Great Terror" reached its peak. They were processed and dispatched quickly, and for half a century lay nameless and forgotten. Only in recent years has the horror of Butovo become known, the dead and their deeds remembered.

One of those who died that night had led an uncommon life, worthy of recall: Vladimir Fedorovich Dzhunkovsky. An extraordinary journey had brought him to this killing ground. It followed the tragic arc of his country's history, from the hopeful era of Tsar Alexander II's Great Reforms into the dark days of Stalin's Great Terror. Born to privilege, educated at the elite Corps of Pages, enrolled in the storied Preobrazhensky Guards, Dzhunkovsky had enjoyed the favor of the royal family. He achieved high office and public acclaim first as governor of Moscow and, later, as the empire's reform-minded security chief. In the Great War he had fought in the trenches as a frontline commander and won the affection of his men. But he knew failure and tragedy as well—abruptly dismissed from service by the emperor he revered, imprisoned after the revolution, and then consigned to an obscure and painful existence as a "former person," a despised remnant of a lost world. In his last years, Dzhunkovsky's life had taken an ironic turn, and for a time, the erstwhile head of the tsar's secret police became a valued consultant for Stalin's.

Yet through all these vicissitudes and ironies, Dzhunkovsky preserved his honor and remained true to his country and his Orthodox Christian faith. Now, at the edge of a pit and an unmarked common grave, he could stand unbroken.[1]

Part One

From Page to Public Man, 1865–1904

Chapter 1

Youth and the Corps of Pages

NOTHING LIKE THE HARSH CAWING OF STALIN'S "RAVENS" could be heard in Russia at the time of Vladimir Dzhunkovsky's birth. In a land where political winters are long and dark, 1865 was a bright, almost summery moment. The repressive reign of Nicholas I lay ten years in the past, and the country was in the midst of an era of reforms more profound than any since the time of Peter the Great.[1]

In 1861 Tsar Alexander II had abolished serfdom, at once breaking the chains binding man to master and giving the newly free the promise of land. Major changes followed the emancipation in rapid succession. In 1864 the tsar established institutions of local self-government, the zemstvos, in thirty-four Great Russian provinces. Elected by nobles, townsmen, and peasants, these institutions dealt with the economic problems of the rural areas and furnished services that the state had failed to provide. Russians gained an arena where they could publicly examine local needs and find solutions with minimal bureaucratic interference. In that same year came a new judicial system that promised to enshrine the rule of law with a more rational court structure, irremovable judges, open adversarial proceedings, citizen juries, and an easily accessible network of small-claims tribunals. The emancipation and the two reforms of 1864 marked the beginning of a freer and more pluralistic Russia. An empire of subjects seemed on the path to becoming a nation of citizens.

Still, the changes failed to satisfy everyone. Nobles lost free labor and a significant portion of their lands. Many mourned their diminished position in rural affairs. The peasants got their freedom but most of them tilled fewer acres than they had in bondage and often lost access to the nobles' forests and pastures. Their land came at a price, with "redemption payments" that were a heavy burden. They dreamed of "black repartition" that would bring the domains of the nobility, the state, and the imperial family into their possession.

The zemstvo and new court reforms also had flaws. Self-government institutions were limited in their scope and in their powers. Dominated by nobles, they imposed taxes that were resented by the peasants. They existed only at the province (*guberniia*) and county (*uezd*) levels, and there was neither a small zemstvo unit able to address village problems directly nor a national body that could voice local needs to the tsar and his officials in St. Petersburg. The new courts might be independent, but important areas such as family law lay beyond their reach. They barely touched the lives of the newly emancipated *muzhiki*, living in rural land communes and effectively segregated from the rest of society. There peasant tribunals were guided by local customary law, rendering decisions that were often arbitrary, corrupt, and cruel.

Despite disappointments and misgivings, most Russians in the mid-1860s were prepared to wait; many expected the government to extend the reforms and correct the shortcomings of earlier legislation. But following an attempt on the life of the tsar in 1866, the pace of reform slowed, and the social and political limits to further transformation became more and more visible. Still, the vast majority of Russians revered their anointed autocrat, accepted the measures he decreed, and believed what holy writ and the laws of the empire declared—that they should obey his will "not only out of fear, but for conscience sake."[2]

At the dimly lit edges of the political stage hovered impatient men and women—mostly young, usually educated, often born to privilege—for whom no reform would suffice. They dreamed of a new order "unknown even in America," to be achieved by peaceful means if possible, by violence if necessary.[3] A few eagerly welcomed the prospect of shedding the blood of royalty and of others as well. "The day will soon come," the early extremist Petr Zaichnevsky predicted, "when we will unfurl the great banner of the future, the red banner . . . and move against the Winter Palace to wipe out all who dwell there." The goal was a "Russian Social and Democratic Republic," and, Zaichnevsky proclaimed, "anyone who is not with us is against us and an enemy, and . . . every method is used to destroy an enemy."[4]

Who should lead this revolution? In 1862, the dissident journalist Nikolai Chernyshevsky completed a novel that would inspire generations of radicals, *What Is to Be Done?* He traced a vision of socialism and introduced his "perceptive readers" to the character of Rakhmetov. Disciplined, physically and mentally tough, this "rigorist" was devoted completely to science and the people's cause.[5] Later, Mikhail Bakunin and Sergei Nechaev advocated a tightly knit, underground conspiracy dominated by supermen whose dedication to the task of building a better world freed them from normal moral limits. Their *Catechism of the Revolutionary* presented a new hero: "a doomed man," wholly absorbed by "a single thought, a single passion—the revolution." His credo was simple: "everything that promotes the revolution is moral; everything that hinders it is immoral." In the struggle for that glorious goal, he would "always be prepared to . . . destroy with his own hands everything that hinders its attainment."[6] The few men and women who espoused such views believed that their revolution would solve all problems and usher in a bright future for mankind. They could not foresee where their dreams were going to lead and would have recoiled in horror before the global tragedy that, in time, their ideas and methods helped bring to pass.

Not even the faintest echo of the young radicals' overheated rhetoric sounded in the comfortable St. Petersburg home of the Dzhunkovskys where, on September 7, 1865, Fedor Stepanovich and his wife, Maria Karlovna, welcomed Vladimir, their seventh child and fourth son. Theirs was a deeply religious household, devoted to the emperor and the dynasty. Vladimir's father, a major general with a distinguished career, headed the chancellery of the inspector general of the cavalry, Grand Duke Nikolai Nikolaevich, brother of Alexander II. The Dzhunkovsky family was noble but not a princely house or a clan that could trace its origins to the ancient Muscovite boyars. Still, its members had served both God and tsar since the late seventeenth century.

According to family legend, its progenitor was a Mongol prince, Murza-Khan Dzhunk, who had come to Moscow in the early sixteenth century as part of an embassy sent to Vasilii III. Later, it was said, one of Dzhunk's descendants, a local military leader (*voevoda*) named Ksendzovsky, held an estate in Galich—"Dzhunkovka," from which the family name derived.

At some point, two major branches of the clan emerged: one Galician and Polish, the other Ukrainian, gravitating toward Russian service.[7] This early genealogy is probably a mix of fact and fancy. In nineteenth-century Russia, it was fashionable to claim Mongol or Tatar ancestry, much as Americans today take pride in the grandmother who was one-eighth Choctaw, Cherokee, or Nez-Perce.[8] The first clearly identifiable figure of the Ukrainian-Russian line was Kondratii Dzhunkovsky, a colonel from Chernigov, who lived at the end of the seventeenth century.

Kondratii's son Stepan entered the priesthood and during the early eighteenth century, his descendants—Semen Stepanovich and Semen Semenovich—served in the "white" or married parish clergy. Thus, despite long-standing claims, the Dzhunkovskys did not firmly establish their status as members of the nobility (*dvorianstvo*) until the 1840s. It would be based not on ancient lineage but on the career of Vladimir's grandfather, Stepan Semenovich Dzhunkovsky, a man of great ability and remarkable achievements, who put the priesthood behind him in favor of state service.[9]

Stepan Semenovich was born in 1762; he was educated in Kharkov and eventually specialized in agronomy. His clerical background and academic interest brought him to the attention of Father A. A. Samborsky, the very secular Orthodox priest Catherine II had placed in charge of her grandchildren's religious education. Samborsky, who had once studied agronomy in Britain, understood its importance, and in 1784 he convinced the empress to send Dzhunkovsky abroad so that he might deepen his knowledge of scientific agriculture.[10] The young man spent the next seven years traveling and studying in England, France, and Flanders, not only increasing his technical expertise but also mastering foreign languages. Upon his return to Russia, Stepan Semenovich was enrolled as a sergeant in the Preobrazhensky Guards, but his chief assignment seems to have been teaching English to members of the royal family.

When Paul I came to the throne in 1796, he promoted Stepan to captain and shortly thereafter permitted his transfer to the civil service with the corresponding rank of titled counselor. Dzhunkovsky's career quickly flourished, and he also began to play a significant role in the scientific life of the country. Under Alexander I, he occupied important positions in the newly formed Ministry of Internal Affairs and in 1811 took command of its Economic Department. Stepan became a leading figure in the influential Free Economic Society, serving as permanent secretary and editing its journal. The tsar regularly assigned Dzhunkovsky challenging tasks:

standardizing the empire's weights and measures, draining swamps on the outskirts of St. Petersburg, settling colonists, and solving a food supply crisis in the Baltic region. He accomplished all these successfully, while continuing to write scholarly articles on economics and agriculture as well as religious-philosophical works that showed the heavy influence of Enlightenment thought. Stepan Dzhunkovsky died in 1839, having gained the title of privy counselor, a rank that conferred nobility on him and his descendants, a status that was soon duly recognized by the Heraldry Office.[11]

Stepan Semenovich pointed his four sons toward state service. The eldest, Alexander, became a high postal official in St. Petersburg. Petr, the second, also served in the postal department in the province of Poltava. The third, Fedor (Vladimir's father), pursued a military career that led steadily upward and brought him into close contact with members of the imperial family. But the youngest son, Stepan, achieved the greatest fame or, more accurately, notoriety.

Deeply religious, Stepan's life became a spiritual quest that led him to Rome where he embraced Catholicism, joined the Jesuit Order, and entered the priesthood. But by 1853 Stepan had already left the Jesuits and moved to Paris where he embarked on an effort to bring about the unity of the Christian churches and reform Catholicism by, among other things, abolishing clerical celibacy. He spent a number of years as a missionary to the Eskimos, and in the early 1860s, his reform proposals rejected, he broke with Catholicism. In 1861 Stepan married an English woman in an Anglican ceremony, and five years later he reconverted to Orthodoxy. He returned to Russia and entered state service, employed in the educational committee of the Holy Synod.[12]

Stepan died in 1870, but many years later his specter would come back to haunt his nephew. In 1915 Vladimir, then the head of the empire's internal security apparatus, sought to warn Tsar Nicholas II of the danger that Grigorii Rasputin posed to the dynasty, only to be abruptly dismissed from office. Soon his enemies spread rumors of disloyalty, and one of them, citing as a kind of proof the strange career of his long-dead uncle, implied that the Dzhunkovsky family harbored a traitorous tendency.[13]

Neither treason nor nonconformity were to be found in the atmosphere surrounding Vladimir from his earliest days. Family circumstances breathed loyalty and faith and were, at the same time, both secure and loving. Shortly after Vladimir's birth, his mother and father moved their large brood to a spacious apartment on the second floor of the barracks of the Horse Guards, directly above the chancellery where Fedor Stepanovich presided. Their new quarters were in the center of the city, close to major palaces and the offices from which the vast Russian empire was governed. Young Vladimir, called "Vadya" by his parents and siblings, spent his first thirteen years in this pleasant home and fondly remembered its high ceilings, large windows, bright commodious rooms, and enormous kitchen.[14]

Because Fedor Dzhunkovsky worked and lived in the same building, he was not a distant patriarch but a vital presence for his children. Vladimir remembered the door to his father's office always standing open except when important committees were meeting. Fedor Dzhunkovsky became ill as Vadya entered his teens and did not live to influence him as he grew to manhood. But his son always recalled him as the main pillar of the family, whom "we all adored, believed, and revered."[15]

Vadya and his siblings were equally devoted to their mother, Maria Karlovna (née Roshet), who played a central part in their moral and religious development. Although born a Lutheran, a faith she never renounced, she went regularly to Orthodox mass, knew well the liturgy and rituals of the church, and helped her children to master them.[16] But among the Dzhunkovskys, religion was not merely a matter of attending church or performing rituals, it was a genuine spirituality that suffused their being and dictated a code of behavior. Both Fedor and Maria cherished the family motto, *Deo et proximo*, and what it proclaimed: devotion to God and a concern for the needs of others. Vadya, together with his brothers and sisters, had a lifelong respect for the efforts of their mother and father to inculcate these beliefs. "If any of us did not strictly follow [the motto]," he recalled somewhat ruefully years later, "then it was not the fault of our parents, but of ourselves."[17]

Vladimir never wrote much about his religious ideas or the role of faith in his life. But, clearly, the spiritual and moral principles instilled in his youth lay at the center of his character and found expression both in his commitment to treating others well and in his genuine concern for decent behavior. His religiosity was strong and sincere, not colored by superstition, fanaticism, or narrow prejudice. Dzhunkovsky believed that his life was at all times in God's hands, that larger events unfolded for a purpose not always clear to any human, and that he must try to do the right thing according to His lights, regardless of the personal consequences.

As the youngest in a large family, Vadya may have been something of a favorite, and he displayed a genuine fondness for all his siblings. He revered the oldest, Stepan, twelve years his senior, who graduated from the Corps of Pages and served in Warsaw as a cavalry officer. Vadya remembered that, after Stepan departed St. Petersburg, he would often go to his brother's room, try on some of the military gear he had left behind, and looking in the mirror, "dream of that time when I, too, would be an officer."[18] Even closer were his ties to Fedor, five years older, whose death from cholera in 1872 struck him a painful blow. "I greatly mourned my brother," Vladimir recalled, "in a childish way, of course, and for a long time could not adjust to the idea that he was no more. This was my first sorrow."[19] Many other family losses would follow.

In recalling his youth, Vladimir wrote less about his sisters, Evdokiia and Olga, and his brother Nikolai (Kolya). But this reticence belies their importance in his life. Since Kolya was just three years older than Vadya, there may have been something of an early rivalry between them, but later they would be devoted to one another, although often separated by distance. For his sisters, Vladimir always had deep affection, especially for Evdokiia, eight years his senior, who was almost a second mother to him. In the years to come, she would be her brother's most ardent and loyal supporter, a moral guide, and physical protector through difficult and dangerous days.

Vadya's early life experiences were fairly typical for a boy of his time and class: a wet-nurse who remained close for many years, a beloved nanny, a series of governesses and tutors he remembered almost as family members, despite the fact that, "far from being indulgent, [they] were very demanding."[20] Vadya possessed a robust constitution and was not greatly troubled by childhood illnesses, except that, as the result of a youthful accident, he broke a finger, and it was left bent and hard to move, a deformity sufficiently visible that during his imprisonment after the revolution doctors at his jail would note it as a distinguishing physical feature.[21]

Vadya obtained his earliest education at home from family and tutors, but his parents intended him to go to the Corps of Pages, an elite military school attached to the Imperial Court. Founded in 1801, the Corps was open to the sons and grandsons of those who had attained the rank of lieutenant general or its civilian equivalent, privy councilor. All admissions required an imperial order, and prospective cadets also had to pass tests in a variety of academic subjects. In 1872 Vadya received the required permission from the tsar and so, much to his delight, could wear the uniform of the Corps of Pages, but without epaulets. The school's entrance examinations, however, turned out to be no easy matter; their rigor demanded substantial effort. Accordingly, in 1874 Vadya began a period of formal preparation at a small academy on Vasily Island, but two years later his sister Evdokiia took charge. He proved to be a poor pupil: "I made slow progress in my studies," he recalled, "and quickly exhausted my sister, who, despite my good behavior, became angry at me and began to despair." In May 1876 Vadya took the exams and did poorly, failing Russian language and natural history. He was allowed to re-test, however, and after a summer of further work, finally passed.[22]

The Corps of Pages had not been a serious educational institution in its early years, but by Vadya's time it provided a level of instruction equal to that at any gymnasium or *realschule* in the country.[23] The school was a strictly regimented place where cadets rose at six to drumbeat or bugle call and then proceeded to prayers, breakfast, and study hall. Lessons started at eight and continued until eleven; then came a break for exercise and lunch. Classes resumed between twelve and two in the afternoon, followed by physical activities—gymnastics, fencing, dancing, and singing—lasting until four. Chapel and dinner were next, succeeded by a two-hour study hall that began at six. At half past nine, the cadets retired for the night.[24]

The approximately 330 students in the school were divided into forms; the third through the seventh provided the regular programs, with two special senior forms above them. The number of cadets in each form did not exceed forty or fifty, and academic classes were small. Rigorous lessons emphasized rote learning as opposed to open discussion, and the general atmosphere of the school was hardly intellectual. Pages did not see high marks as the measure of success and usually disliked students they considered grinds. Living conditions, while comfortable, were spare. The mess hall provided decent food, but as one former page remembered, "cutlets and macaroni played a big role."[25]

Education at the Corps sought to shape young men for service as officers in the army and navy. Graduates enjoyed the right to enroll in any guards' regiment they chose, even if there were no vacancies, a privilege that guaranteed more rapid promotions than could be obtained in regular units. Yet the training that pages received did not drum into them loyalty to the empire or devotion to the principle of autocracy. Reflecting on his years in the Corps of Pages, Dzhunkovsky's contemporary Petr Petrovich Stremoukhov marveled at the school's liberal atmosphere and the absence of anything resembling political propaganda.[26] Even the selection of teachers did not indicate a determination to instill "pure Russian values." History instruction was in the hands of a Pole, Rudolf Ignatievich Menzhinsky, whose son Viacheslav became the second head of the Soviet secret police. In his dry, pedantic style, the elder Menzhinsky even engaged in what might be considered a wry bit of subversion. When students referred to Catherine II as "the Great," he brought them up short. With legalistic precision Rudolf Ignatievich informed his charges that the empress (in Polish eyes the chief culprit in the criminal partitions that destroyed their country) was not entitled to the epithet, *Velikaia*—the Governing Senate had not formally bestowed it upon her![27]

Given the family background of the pages, political indoctrination was unnecessary; the moral tone of the institution was far more important. Located in the former Vorontsov Palace, which housed the Knights of Malta during the reign of Paul I, the school had assumed many of the trappings of that order, most notably the white Maltese cross. Graduates received a bimetallic ring engraved with the words "hard as steel, pure as gold." Pages took the oath of the Knights to love the fatherland, defend the church and its teachings, protect the weak, show generosity to all, and everywhere, and always be fighters for good against injustice and evil.[28] Not all graduates embraced these chivalric values, but Dzhunkovsky did, since they conformed closely to those he had learned at home.

Vadya made a quick and successful adjustment to the Corps. The hazing of lowerclassmen by those above them did not trouble him much. The severity of this practice had greatly diminished by his time, and the more exotic forms of punishment prevalent earlier seem to have disappeared.[29] Vadya blended in easily. He was not a brilliant student, his classmate Stremoukhov recalled, but good looks coupled with charm and tact made it easy for him to get along well with others.[30] He developed a passion for gymnastics and excelled at the sport, acquiring an athletic build that would last a lifetime. Vadya's singing, on the other hand, was so bad that his teachers excused him from class altogether once they determined that he could neither carry a tune nor hold a single true note.[31]

In many ways Dzhunkovsky was a model cadet, in one instance literally so, when he was chosen to model a new Corps uniform for Emperor Alexander III.[32] School officials also asked him to serve as a mentor for the son of the emir of Bukhara.[33] Still, Vadya did, on several occasions, breach discipline and wound up in the school's equivalent of the brig. Once he stood up to a tutor who was notorious for being angry and abusive to students; another time he helped a classmate on an examination.[34] In both cases, it seems he was motivated by his own sense of honor and fairness or by his sympathy for a comrade in trouble.

The empathy that Vadya frequently displayed for others was rooted not only in the religious and moral teachings of home and school but also in the pain and loss he and his family experienced during his formative years. Sickness and death had long haunted the Dzhunkovsky household. By the time he entered school, Vadya had already lost two siblings, and in the late 1870s his father began to suffer from an increasingly debilitating disease that forced him to retire from the army. In February 1879 Fedor Dzhunkovsky finally succumbed to his illness. At home at the time, Vladimir remembered being roused at five in the morning and coming to his parents' bedroom where his father lay. His mother and sisters knelt at the bedside. The young boy broke down: "I . . . could not bear to believe that all was at an end. My father wheezed . . . , the wheezing became slower and slower, then there was complete stillness—[he] . . . was no more."[35]

Shortly afterward, another blow fell; Vadya's beloved eldest brother, Stepan, also became sick and died unexpectedly. These two losses, coming in quick succession, had a profound impact on Vadya, who became so seriously depressed and unable to study that he failed his final exams.[36] Although Vadya's healthy disposition enabled him to recover eventually, these tragedies left their mark. They deepened his appreciation for the suffering of others, and this sympathy for those in distress would strongly influence his personal relations and, later, his practice as an administrator.

Dzhunkovsky's memoirs tell nothing of the books he read or the ideas that influenced him. As an early teenager he could not comprehend the rise of the revolutionary movement that shook the country in the late 1870s.

His loyal and conservative family and the atmosphere of the Corps gave him little basis for understanding the emerging political conflict. He had limited contact with workers and peasants and did not feel a sense of guilt toward "the people" that motivated so many of the radicals.

A year before his father died, terrorism first intruded in Vadya's life. On January 28, 1878, a young revolutionary, Vera Zasulich, tried to assassinate Fedor Trepov, the St. Petersburg city commandant (*gradonachal'nik*), shooting him at point blank range. Vadya was at home eating dinner with his family when his father, pale and shaken, came in with the news. Fedor Dzhunkovsky was close to Trepov, and although it was Trepov's flogging of a disrespectful student prisoner that had prompted Zasulich's attack, Vadya's father did not see the city commandant as a monster. The acquittal of the young terrorist at the end of her sensational trial came to all the Dzhunkovskys as a shock, "something completely unintelligible."[37]

Zasulich's shot triggered a volley of assassinations and other terrorist acts, most of them carried out by the People's Will (*Narodnaia volia*), an increasingly bold and determined band of revolutionaries. As these violent outrages escalated, ultimately focusing on the tsar, Vadya and the other pages watched in horror. Even if the goal of the radicals—a democratic, socialist regime—had been explained to them, it would have made little or no sense. To their minds, monarch and nation were virtually identical, and the terror campaign was an attack on the fatherland itself. Thus Dzhunkovsky was chagrined when, after repeated attempts on his life, Alexander II began to travel through St. Petersburg accompanied by armed guards. That diminished the prestige of the emperor, he felt, and lowered the standing of the country as a whole.[38] The terrorists' explosion of a bomb at the Winter Palace in February 1880 left fifteen-year-old Vadya and his classmates stunned, their patriotic feelings deeply offended.[39]

On the terrible day, March 1, 1881, when suddenly news came of a terrorist assault on the tsar's person, Vadya and his family were visiting Evdokiia, by then a lady-in-waiting at the court, living in an apartment at the Mariinsky Palace. They rushed to the Winter Palace Square, joining a large, anxious throng. There they learned that the assassins had been successful and heard the fateful announcement: "The Sovereign Emperor rests with God. Alexander III has ascended the throne." The people fell to their knees as one. Then, after about ten minutes, an unaccompanied sleigh, drawn by two horses, and bearing a tall, upright figure, sped from the Winter Palace, across the square, toward the arch of the General Staff building and the waiting crowd. Dzhunkovsky remembered vividly the scene that ensued:

> We looked. Yes: it was HE! Alexander III. . . . A kind of electric spark seemed to course through the crowd. Someone shouted: "The Emperor!" "Hurrah" sounded, and, in an instant, the multitude raced after the sleigh; hats flew into the air. My brother and I, drawn by the throng, ran as fast as we could to Nevsky Prospect. It was a wonderful, inspiring moment. A deafening "Hurrah" carried along the whole route to the Anichkov Palace. The lack of ceremony with which the sovereign, having just assumed the throne, in his first minutes as tsar, rode, completely alone, in an open sleigh, produced an enormous impression.[40]

What the young Dzhunkovsky saw in the traumatic hours following the assassination of Alexander II would have a lasting impact. On more than one occasion, he sought to emulate the new emperor's sangfroid in the face of danger, and he always maintained the greatest respect for the ruler known as the "tsar-peacemaker." In his eyes Alexander III was "a real autocrat in the ideal sense of the word," who showed that the essence of monarchy was "the subordination of [personal] interests and desires to a higher truth."[41] In 1894 fate placed him near the scene of the emperor's death, one of the few permitted to view him immediately after his passing. Kissing the still warm hand of the monarch he revered, Dzhunkovsky was unable to hold back his sobs. He felt a sense of loss akin to that he had suffered when his own father died.[42]

In the course of his life Dzhunkovsky undoubtedly came to know many of the great works of literature with which Russia has so generously endowed the world. He had a large personal library, and his memoirs clearly indicate a high degree of familiarity with important writers and their lives. But apart from a stated fondness for the poetry of Nikolai Nekrasov, Vladimir is silent as to his tastes. About the theater, however, he was unabashedly enthusiastic. His passion developed early and proved enduring. It became his chief entree into the world of the cultural elite, the basis of both solid friendships and life-saving support.

The play was not the thing that made the young Dzhunkovsky a theater lover. Rather, it was the face, figure, and talent of the great actress Maria Savina. Vadya was thirteen when he first saw the artist who would dominate the stage of St. Petersburg's Alexandrinsky Theater for decades.

He was smitten; soon all his spare cash went to buying tickets to her performances, although the cheapest seats were all he could afford. Obsessed with Savina, he hung about the stage doors whenever she performed. He found out where she lived and wandered nearby. Vadya learned where Savina went to church and attended services there, praying for a glimpse. When she appeared, his delight was indescribable.[43]

On the night Savina played in Viktor Krylov's comedy "The Prank" (*Shalost'*), she scored a complete triumph. "The public went wild," Vadya remembered, "and I almost hurled myself over the footlights in ecstasy." After the performance he waited with a large crowd at the stage door. At last Savina appeared, carrying an enormous bouquet, and seated herself in a carriage. Standing close by, Vadya took courage, pressed forward, and asked his idol for one of the flowers. "She pulled out a pale yellow rose and gave it to me," he wrote later. "I seized the rose in trembling hands and kissed it. I was boundlessly happy." He took his treasure home and carefully put it away. Years later, he rediscovered the petals of that rose, tenderly preserved in paper amid the jumbled souvenirs of a lifetime. Dzhunkovsky's memoirs do not tell us what emotions this encounter with his past evoked, only that he burned "those dear witnesses of my first, pure, selfless love."[44]

In 1882 Dzhunkovsky finished the seventh form and with it the regular academic program of the Corps. He felt both relief and a sense of accomplishment. Now "an educated person," he looked forward to the two special forms where he would concentrate on military science and advanced mathematics. Under teachers from the Academy of the General Staff, he studied fortification, tactics, artillery, military administration and history, as well as law.[45]

As graduation approached, Dzhunkovsky began to consider carefully his military career. At first he inclined toward the artillery, but many friends urged him to enter the Preobrazhensky Guards, a prospect that seemed attractive, since service in the guards meant more rapid promotions. The Preobrazhensky regiment was expensive, however, and Dzhunkovsky had limited financial resources. The pension his mother received after his father's death was far from lavish, and the family had no landed property. Eventually, with some misgivings, Vladimir convinced himself

Grand Duchess Elizabeth in bridal attire. Hoover Institution Archive (HIA), Russian Pictorial Collection, envelope A(1).

that he could afford the regiment and requested assignment there.[46] This proved to be an important decision; it strengthened his ties with the ruling dynasty and opened unimagined opportunities.

Before he put off the court uniform of a page for good, a final duty remained. In June 1884 Dzhunkovsky was called upon to serve at the wedding of Grand Duke Sergei Alexandrovich, Alexander III's brother, and Princess Elisabeth of Hesse-Darmstadt, a granddaughter of Britain's Queen Victoria. Later he recalled the brilliant ceremonies that surrounded the event as symbolic of a golden time, "when Russia was in the fullness of her power, [and] when the West not only paid attention . . . but trembled before her, feeling the extraordinary moral force of her monarch."[47] It was a fateful moment for Dzhunkovsky as well. In the course of these celebrations he first encountered two women who would have enormous consequences for his life: Sergei's new bride and her sister Alix, the future empress Alexandra. Elisabeth who, upon her conversion to Russian Orthodoxy in 1891, took the name Elizaveta Fedorovna, immediately attracted him with her beauty and charm. The younger Alix, however, left a different and much less favorable impression. Vladimir remembered that during the modest Lutheran wedding service that followed the elaborate Orthodox ceremony, the twelve-year-old "cried and sobbed hysterically, tears flowed from her eyes and there was no way anybody could calm her."[48] In the succeeding years, Dzhunkovsky and Elizaveta Fedorovna became extremely close, bound by faith, mutual affection, and respect. Alexandra, on the other hand, emerged as Vladimir's nemesis, and decades later her hysterical tendencies, noted at first sight, brought his administrative career to an end.

Chapter 2

Guardsman and Courtier

DZHUNKOVSKY ENTERED THE PREOBRAZHENSKY GUARDS with enthusiasm and found service there entirely to his satisfaction. "I liked everything, found everything interesting, and plunged headlong into regimental life."[1] He encountered little of the corruption and incompetence that characterized much of the tsarist officer corps.[2] But military duties were not the only thing that absorbed his attention and energies. The social whirl of the capital beckoned.

At twenty years old Vladimir, now often called "Dzhun" by friends and regimental comrades, was an attractive young man. Not strikingly handsome, perhaps, but standing about five feet nine inches tall, with reddish hair, gray eyes, an athletic build, and military bearing, he would not disgrace a lady's arm. He danced well and often, spending so much time at the many St. Petersburg balls that, looking back, he wondered how he had combined successfully his active social life and military obligations. His abilities on the dance floor gained him considerable attention, even from members of the royal family, and within a few years, Dzhun found himself being asked to serve as director (*dirizher*) at regimental balls. Organizing and lubricating these events, leading the dancers through quadrilles, cotillions, and mazurkas and determining their configurations, were tasks that required terpsichorean skills, stamina, and, as one memoir writer recalled, both "imagination and administrative talent."[3]

Vladimir Dzhunkovsky in the Preobrazhensky Guards. From Anastasiia Dunaeva, *Reformy politsii v Rossii nachala XX veka i Vladimir Fedorovich Dzhunkovskii.*

Dzhunkovsky's memoirs reveal next to nothing about his romantic life or his sexuality. Certainly the young guardsman was attracted to beautiful women, and he enjoyed physical contact on the dance floor and while skating. Still, he was apparently rather shy and restrained in his relationships with girls. St. Petersburg was famous for its extensive demimonde, a world often visited by officers of the guards, but Vladimir does not mention encounters of this kind. He was modest, even prudish, as an amusing incident recounted in his reminiscences reveals. Shortly after his sister Olga, living in Grodno, gave birth to a daughter, she wrote asking her brother to find a wet nurse, a task for which his service in the military had not prepared him. He made inquiries at a lying-in hospital and was invited to visit, whereupon he was confronted with a choice of eight candidates eager for the job. "They showed all of them to me," he wrote, "lined them up and asked me to choose. I was flustered; [then] they started to talk about [the girls'] 'yield' [*molochnost'*], and asked me to check them out more carefully." In the end, Dzhun passed up the chance for a closer inspection and simply asked the directress of the hospital to select the healthiest young woman, a good choice it turned out.[4]

Dzhunkovsky thought about marriage; both Olga and his brother Nikolai had wed happily.[5] Vladimir considered several young women as possible brides, but he proved unable to act on his intentions. He recalls being strongly attracted to a certain Baroness Vinnikin. Yet he hesitated; she was very rich, and he had no means other than his officer's pay. Should he propose? In the end his delay proved fatal to the romance. As Vladimir pondered, a more decisive cavalry officer swept in, requested the baroness's hand, and was accepted.[6] This story may reveal more about him than that he was somewhat faint of heart; it suggests he was often drawn to women who either were, or appeared to be, unattainable.

Still, military duties remained his central focus. In late nineteenth-century Russia, service in a guards regiment was often little more than "a pleasant and sociable finishing school for wealthy young aristocrats."[7] But Dzhunkovsky, who was neither wealthy nor an aristocrat, approached his obligations in a different manner. Frivolity and simple routine could never satisfy him for long. He threw himself into training new recruits and in 1891 published under the pseudonym "Lieutenant D.," *A Detailed Program for Training Young Soldiers for Infantry Duty* in three thousand copies.[8] He became chief clerk of the regimental court and after a time was able, he believed, "to bring a new, fresh approach into this dry, formal business."[9]

Even as Dzhunkovsky worked to define himself as a military professional, dynastic ties and loyalties became more central to his life. Family tradition had been reinforced by his father's close connection to Grand Duke Nikolai Nikolaevich (the elder).[10] Alexander II's brother had shown a great fondness for his head of chancellery, and as Dzhun's father became increasingly incapacitated, the grand duke eased his retirement, seeing to it that the general's pension equaled his regular salary. Nikolai Nikolaevich visited Fedor Dzhunkovsky's sickbed during his final illness and, after his death, made arrangements for the family's well-being. Vladimir's own service as a page, his sister's appointment as a lady-in-waiting, and the awe inspired by Alexander III's personal courage further strengthened his emotional bond to the Romanovs.

In 1887 the heir to the throne, Nicholas Alexandrovich, joined the Preobrazhensky Guards, becoming a brother officer and creating for Dzhunkovsky an even greater sense of loyalty and connection to the dynasty. Writing many years later, after having suffered cruel treatment at the monarch's hands, Vladimir could still recall his positive first impression of the future emperor. "I was astounded by his good manners, kindness and delicacy. He behaved without affectation and clearly enjoyed the absence of court etiquette in the regiment. He was, one could say, a good comrade, and tried never to stand out among the [other] officers, but immersed himself in their ranks."[11] Still, Dzhunkovsky noted the way the tsar-to-be was infantilized, held in check by his tutor, General Danilovich. The latter behaved in a pedantic and demanding way, interrupting Nicholas even when he was chatting with his fellow officers, telling the tsarevich when it was time to go to bed, an order that he always obeyed.[12]

It was Grand Duke Sergei Alexandrovich and his wife, Elizaveta Fedorovna, who most strengthened Dzhunkovsky's connection to the ruling family. When Vladimir joined the Preobrazhensky Guards, the grand duke served as chief of the first battalion, and in 1887 he assumed command of the entire regiment. Dzhun entered a circle of young officers who enjoyed the favor of Sergei and his wife, beginning an association that would endure for decades and greatly influence the course of his life.

For much of the Russian public (especially its more liberal elements) the grand ducal couple seemed a strange, even tragic pair. Sergei Alexandrovich was one of the most thoroughly disliked of the Romanovs. Even many

Tsarevich Nicholas Alexandrovich. General Research Division, New York Public Library, Astor, Lenox and Tilden Foundations.

members of the royal family saw him as a cold fish, distant, hypersensitive, quick to anger, an arch-conservative, and a harsh anti-Semite. Sergei strongly supported Alexander III's "counter-reforms," cutting back many of the liberalizing measures that had been adopted in the previous reign, limiting the autonomy of the zemstvos and urban self-government, establishing tighter controls over education and the press, and subjecting peasants to the authority of newly created officials, the "land captains." Later, the grand duke pushed Nicholas II to reject any changes that might diminish royal power.[13] Sergei's assumption of the post of Moscow governor-general in 1891 would be preceded by the expulsion of a large number of the city's Jews, followed by continued harassment of those who were permitted to remain.[14]

Within court circles, among the St. Petersburg elite, and also abroad, rumors circulated that the grand duke was a homosexual and that his marriage to Elizaveta Fedorovna was a sham—gossip well illustrated by an entry in the diary of Alexandra Bogdanovich, who presided over one of St. Petersburg's most frequented salons. On January 22, 1888, she wrote breathlessly of having just learned from a friend living in Tsarskoe Selo "that . . . Sergei Alexandrovich lives with his adjutant Martynov, [and] . . . has often proposed to his wife that she choose a husband from among her entourage."[15] Many noted the detached condescension with which the grand duke treated his lovely young spouse, and some members of the dynasty were roused to indignation. "I would have given ten years of my life to stop her from entering the church on the arm of haughty Sergei," Grand Duke Alexander Mikhailovich wrote.[16] Feelings like these almost certainly fostered additional speculations.

In sharp contrast to her husband, Elizaveta Fedorovna enjoyed nearly universal affection and respect. Her great beauty stunned those she encountered. It was "a marvelous revelation," her cousin Marie, later queen of Romania, recalled. "Her eyes, her lips, her smile, her hands, the way she looked at you, the way she talked, the way she moved, all was exquisite beyond words."[17] Upon seeing her shortly after her marriage, Grand Duke Konstantin Konstantinovich (the poet K. R.) wrote:

> I gazed on you, and loved you in an instant,
> You are so inexpressibly fair!
> It must be that beneath such surface beauty,
> Lies a soul equally sublime.

Like an angel, you are quiet, chaste and perfect,
As a woman, modest and demure.
Let none of this world's many pains and sorrows
Mar your unsullied purity.
And all who see you will praise God,
For creating such beauty![18]

Elizaveta Fedorovna (Ella to her family and friends) combined physical allure with an equally striking personal charm. Where Sergei put forward an icy, forbidding face, she exuded gentleness and warmth and was at ease with people of all ranks and classes. In this she outshone her sister, the future empress, who was painfully shy and uncomfortable both at court and among the larger public.

Because what we know about Sergei and Ella and their life together is composed of layers of scandalous rumor and impenetrable discretion, a true picture is probably impossible. But we can say that the image of the grand duke was, to some degree, distorted. He did, without question, often appear stern and forbidding; he was a rigid conservative and an anti-Semite. But to those who knew him well, he could be warm, gracious, even loving. Sergei was deeply religious and well educated with diverse intellectual interests including literature, history, and archeology. He strongly supported the arts and during his tenure as governor-general of Moscow would do much to encourage the cultural growth of the city. Ella, on the other hand, while fully deserving of her glowing reputation could at times be cold, haughty, and vain.[19]

As for the grand duke's alleged homosexuality, evidence is largely non-existent. Although Sergei seemed, to outsiders at least, unfeeling and over-bearing in his treatment of Ella, in private correspondence neither spouse indicated unhappiness; on the contrary, the letters express both affection and respect.[20] About the sexual dimension of their relationship, we have no reliable information, save that they shared the same bed throughout their life together. Even those who believe that Sergei was gay can cite no proof of any kind.[21]

As he served contentedly in the Preobrazhensky Guards, Vladimir either knew nothing about these concerns and speculations or, more likely,

Grand Duchess Elizaveta Fedorovna. General Research Division, New York Public Library, Astor, Lenox and Tilden Foundations.

Grand Duke Sergei Alexandrovich. General Research Division, New York Public Library, Astor, Lenox and Tilden Foundations.

refused to countenance them. Regimental solidarity and starry-eyed dynastic loyalty drew him toward the grand duke and his wife. Sergei had assumed his position in the regiment with some trepidation but soon felt he had found a home there; and despite being a strict commander, he developed a genuine camaraderie with many of his officers, Dzhunkovsky among them. In their company, the grand duke could set aside some of his extreme reserve.[22] Ella on occasion appeared at regimental dinners and functions, where her beauty, openness, and lack of formality won many hearts. "You could not look on her other than with rapture," Dzhun recalled.[23]

Dzhun soon found himself playing cards with the grand duke in a circle of regimental officers, losing more money than he could afford. He desperately wanted to escape this danger but feared that refusing to play might displease Sergei. Timid about approaching his commander directly, Dzhunkovsky asked Sergei's close friend Alexander Evreinov to speak for him. The grand duke readily understood the young officer's dilemma and was not in the least offended. Shaking Vladimir's hand warmly, Sergei said: "[Evreinov] told me about your circumstances. You really have had extremely bad luck and are completely right in your wish to give up playing cards for a while. I'm personally sad to lose you as a partner, but I hope it won't be for long."[24]

Dzhunkovsky did not rejoin the card players but continued to enjoy the grand duke's favor. In August 1886 Sergei invited him to visit his estate at Ilinskoe, a rural retreat about forty miles to the west of Moscow. There he received a warm welcome from the grand duke and duchess and other members of the royal family as well. Dzhunkovsky was struck by the beautiful, rather rustic home with its splendid setting and wonderful views. But even more impressive was the complete informality that prevailed in these circumstances, an atmosphere that charmed and surprised him. "I was amazed by the simplicity with which their highnesses behaved," he recalled. "From the very first evening, I felt no trepidation or inhibition; everything was simple and familial. No one stood up when the grand duke and duchess came [into the room]; it was all just as in an ordinary family home, even more informal than in other aristocratic houses."[25] The next day, Dzhunkovsky went riding with Ella and Grand Duke Pavel Alexandrovich; that evening, he was drawn into the various games and pranks that these members of the royal family played on each other as they strolled through the grounds after supper.

Dzhun was utterly enchanted by Sergei and Ella's hospitality. But then, quite unexpectedly, a somber note intruded. Professor V. P. Bezobrazov, who had earlier taught Sergei, arrived to visit his former student, and at one point, he and Dzhunkovsky found themselves alone. Bezobrazov asked him if he were going to be the grand duke's new adjutant, a post that had just become vacant. But without waiting for a reply, he continued, advising Dzhun not to take the job. "In essence," he said, "it is an unpleasant, servile [*lakeiskaia*] duty." Vladimir stammered that he would be honored by such an offer and did not consider the work beneath him. "All the same," Bezobrazov cautioned, "I would not like to see you in that position, it would not be in line with your character; you could not adjust to it."[26]

Dzhunkovsky subsequently learned that the grand duke had, indeed, planned to ask him to be his new adjutant. At the last moment, however, Baroness Tizengausen prevailed upon Sergei to take instead her relative, Felix Sumorokov-Elston. Later, Dzhun reflected on his good fortune. "I think that I was saved," he wrote. "Had I [become adjutant] . . . at the young age of twenty-one, nothing good would have come of it . . . court life would have taken hold of me completely. I would not have been able to understand its negative sides, and I would have been swallowed up."[27]

Dzhun happily returned to the regiment, pursuing his regular duties, active social life, and intellectual interests. The theater continued to be a major passion, but not all performances proved equally satisfying. Exposure to a portion of Wagner's "Ring" puzzled and tortured him. "I really suffered sitting in the theater from 8 to 12 at night with only one intermission," he recalled. "I did not regret having gone . . . [and] was glad to have gotten an idea of Wagner, an idea, to be sure, of some kind of chaos, but all the same something unusual."[28] On the other hand, the perfection of Tchaikovsky's "Sleeping Beauty" simply dazzled: "I had never seen anything better and more beautiful; the music, the acting on stage, the dances, everything was utterly extraordinary. I left the theater full of impressions, thoroughly charmed."[29]

Dzhunkovsky was a frequent guest at the Sergievsky Palace in St. Petersburg. There Sergei and Ella presided over gatherings of regimental officers, where everything was intimate and pleasant, and as always, "the grand duchess was enchanting in her simplicity and attentiveness."[30] Then in February 1891, Tsar Alexander III appointed Sergei governor-general of Moscow. At first Dzhun worried that he might be chosen one of the grand duke's adjutants as had his friend Vladimir Gadon and several other officers of the regiment, and he was relieved when it seemed the lot would not fall to him. He hoped to be left in the guards where he felt comfortable and successful. But shortly the grand duke did ask him to join his entourage, and Dzhun felt he could not refuse.

Although his Preobrazhensky comrades gave him an enthusiastic and affectionate send-off, leaving the regiment was hard. On the night of December 25, 1891, Dzhun boarded the train to Moscow in a somber mood. As the engine started, he stood by the window gazing at the friends who had accompanied him to the station, wondering what lay ahead: "How things would work out in my new life, in a new city and in new and unknown circumstances, I could not imagine. [Later], I sat sadly in my compartment; I felt that I had betrayed the regiment, betrayed all those in St. Petersburg who loved me. It was very painful."[31]

Dzhunkovsky's concerns soon dissipated upon his arrival in Moscow. After first praying before the icon of the wonder-working Iberian Virgin in her small chapel at the entrance to Red Square, he went straight to the Alexander Palace in the Neskuchny Gardens on what were then the outskirts of the city. The grand duke and duchess greeted him affectionately, and almost from the start he felt himself to be in familiar, familial circumstances. He quickly slipped into his job as adjutant, helping to organize the governor-general's reception (*priem*), regular official gatherings where Sergei would receive petitions and persons who wished to speak to him. Dzhunkovsky had just begun to take the measure of the administrative situation when he was caught up in a larger event that would take him far from Moscow, into the hinterlands of the Russian empire.

In the spring and early summer of 1891, much of agricultural Russia, particularly the Volga and Central Black Earth regions, experienced a serious drought, triggered by an El Niño weather pattern affecting harvests worldwide.[32] Fertile fields turned to dust, and by autumn crop failure and general peasant poverty raised the specter of starvation in a vast area inhabited by about thirty-six million people. Previous poor harvests had exhausted peasant reserves and provincial capital relief funds; at year's end, the Ministry of Internal Affairs estimated that over twelve million souls required some form of supplemental assistance.

The Russian government moved quickly. Even before the full dimensions of the crisis had become clear, the Ministry of Finance altered shipping rates on the railroads to facilitate movement of the grain that was normally intended for export back into the regions threatened by famine. The Ministry of Internal Affairs began to systematize the requests for aid received from the provinces and ordered the creation of local food supply commissions to coordinate the activities of government officials and zemstvo workers in the relief effort. The Committee of Ministers authorized outlays from the treasury of about 150,000,000 rubles. These funds were disbursed to the zemstvos in stricken areas, which then purchased grain in regions of the empire where sufficient supplies existed. Once acquired, the food was delivered to peasant communities for distribution to the needy. When toward the end of 1891 massive shipments of grain began to create logjams on the nation's railroads, the government appointed a special agent armed with extraordinary authority to eliminate the bottlenecks and push the needed supplies through. These jerry-built arrangements did not always work smoothly; the link between the agencies of the autocracy and local self-government was often uneasy and, on occasion, marred by conflict. But in the end, they proved sufficient to avert what could have been an enormous disaster. While many rural areas experienced great misery and in 1892 death rates rose, thanks to official measures Russia escaped the mass starvation that took place during the Soviet-era famines of 1921 and 1932–1933.[33]

In the face of great human suffering, individuals and private charitable groups rushed into the countryside to help the needy. On November 17, 1891, in an attempt to mobilize, organize, and focus (some said control) private efforts, Alexander III ordered the creation of the Special Committee on Famine Relief and put the heir to the throne at its head. In the months that followed, the Special Committee developed a network of local agencies throughout the stricken provinces and ultimately dispensed some twelve million rubles' worth of aid under its auspices.

In Moscow Ella set up her own independent relief organization but coordinated its efforts with those of the Special Committee. The grand duchess raised considerable sums to be funneled into the famine zone, and Sergei put his adjutants at his wife's disposal. They could be dispatched as field agents to see that the funds being sent out by the Moscow committee were properly spent and relief well managed.[34] At the end of February 1892, after fewer than two months at his new post, Dzhunkovsky received orders to serve as the committee's representative in Saratov, one of the most hard-hit provinces.

Dzhun did not get detailed instructions concerning his mission. He was told to meet with Saratov's governor and learn from him the overall situation in the region. He was then to visit areas that had experienced difficulties and oversee the distribution of aid sent out by the committee. Dzhunkovsky received three thousand rubles to manage directly and had the right to request additional sums. Even these straightforward tasks posed many problems, however, not least the difficulty of travel in a large province with only one transecting railway and extremely poor roads. As the train sped him toward Saratov, Dzhun studied a map of the area, trying to figure out where and how he could spend his time there to the best effect. He considered what lay ahead and fretted about his own inexperience. He had never had such a serious responsibility before and was uncertain whether he was up to the assigned task.[35]

Upon his arrival he obtained an audience with Governor Boris Meshchersky, who struck him as competent and hardworking. Food supply matters seemed well in hand, although Dzhun soon came to understand that this was the result of the efforts of Meshchersky's predecessor, General Alexander Kosich, who had foreseen difficulties and had taken measures to stockpile grain.[36] Dzhun then turned to the countryside, where the greatest need was felt. Here, for the first time, the city boy, born to privilege, encountered the depths of rural poverty and the misery and squalor in which so many peasants lived.

Dzhunkovsky began his work in the area surrounding the town of Elan, where charitable efforts were poorly organized and many landowners ignored peasant need. At a local soup kitchen (*stolovaia*) Dzhun was moved by what he saw, and years later he vividly recalled the scene: "The pale, emaciated children produced . . . a horrible, awful, distressing impression as they sat at the table, looking about fearfully, while they wolfed down the hot, nourishing soup."[37] Joining forces with one of the competent land captains in the district, he pulled together a group of public-spirited nobles and set up a committee to address the problems at hand. He placed nine hundred rubles and a carload of grain at their disposal. Dzhunkovsky then pushed on to Serdobsk county where he traveled extensively, covering more than two hundred miles on horseback or by sleigh.[38]

Dzhun devoted much of his attention to the situation in Khvalinsk county on the northern fringe of the province where food stocks were low and the roads poor. He immediately established contact with the leaders of local charitable efforts, Otto Medem and his wife. They proved to be the driving spirits in the region, displaying a genuine love for their fellow men. What struck Dzhunkovsky most about the couple, however, were their relations with the peasantry, "marked by reasoned concern, without any effort to gain popularity [and] devoid of sentimentality." To his surprise "the peasants looked on [the Medems] as their own, like their mother and father."[39] But despite the Medems' best efforts, some officials and landowners refused to use their own resources to meet peasant needs. The leading figures of the town of Khvalinsk were particularly unhelpful, and the mayor had the effrontery to ask Dzhunkovsky for money to support a soup kitchen there. At this, Dzhun exploded, berating the mayor and telling him to have the town council come up with the needed funds themselves. This brusque treatment had positive results, and the local leaders soon produced one thousand rubles to establish their own *stolovaia*.[40]

In his travels Dzhunkovsky found many examples of extreme need, but the most troubling scenes he witnessed were in some of the Tatar villages of the province. There the desperation was complete, and as he moved from one wretched hut to the next, it seemed as if each new hovel presented a still more tragic scene. Most distressing of all was the behavior of one of the mullahs, who insisted on providing tea and cakes to the visitors in the midst of such general suffering. The lack of concern that this religious leader showed for the feelings of those in dire need, his slavish desire to please a guest he obviously believed to be an important representative of "authority," left Dzhunkovsky sickened and angry.[41]

After a month in Saratov Dzhun returned to Moscow at the end of March 1892. He presented his findings to the grand duchess's committee, which received them enthusiastically and readily accepted all his requests for further aid to local charitable groups.[42] In mid-April, he traveled to St. Petersburg to make another report to the tsarevich's Special Committee, where the future emperor greeted him warmly and recalled their service together in the guards.[43] Following a brief visit with his mother and sister Evdokiia, Dzhun resumed his service as adjutant to the grand duke.

For Russia the hungry years 1891–1892 were a turning point. Although the imperial government had been largely successful in its struggle against the famine, the crisis became a public relations disaster. State officials did little to make known the size, scope, and effectiveness of the relief operations, and the cooperation between the government, zemstvos, and charitable groups fostered by their common effort faded. The educated public was horrified and humiliated that their country, a mighty European empire, suffered the mass hunger and disease associated with lesser, colonial lands. Many felt that the tax burdens imposed on the peasants and the state's policy of encouraging grain exports caused the catastrophe. Opposition groups began to stir, enemies of the autocracy took heart, some sensed the beginning of the end of the tsarist regime.

Russians drew many different lessons from the famine experience. In Samara a young radical, Vladimir Ulianov, watched with contempt the efforts of the tender-hearted to alleviate suffering.[44] Good deeds would not bring change, the future Lenin reasoned coldly; the worse, the better. But in nearby Nizhnii Novgorod, Alexander Guchkov, later a leading figure in the liberal Octobrist party, worked closely with the provincial governor in the struggle against both hunger and unresponsive local officials. He came away with optimistic expectations concerning future cooperation between government and the public.[45] For Dzhunkovsky, the time spent in Saratov gave him insight that later influenced his administrative style. He had seen peasant poverty at first hand, and he realized that individuals could make a difference. But to be effective, foresight and direct personal involvement were essential. The example of the Medems showed, moreover, that sympathy should be tempered with cool reason, and that a straightforward and unsentimental approach to the needs of the lower classes was likely to produce the best results.

As Dzhunkovsky resumed his duties in Moscow, he began to notice deficiencies in the governor-general's administration. Sergei had no governmental experience. The enormous challenge posed by Russia's second city and its environs proved beyond his grasp, and the problem was compounded by the ineptitude of the grand duke's assistants. The provincial governors, first V. M. Golitsyn and later D. S. Sipiagin, were weak; the police chief was an obtuse and abusive figure, who caused more harm than good. V. K. Istomin, Sergei's head of chancellery, lacked the intellect and personality needed in this important post. "He was not an administrator," Dzhunkovsky recalled sadly, and he could not help Sergei realize "that the people were not created for the governor-general, but the governor-general for the people."[46] In time, the grand duke would adjust, but it took him years to grow into the job. By then, Dzhun concluded sadly, "much had been lost and many things could not be undone."[47]

Dzhunkovsky had no power to rectify the administrative problems he saw. Professor Bezobrazov had been right: the adjutant's job was essentially "servile" with little meaningful responsibility. Vladimir passed much of his time attending to the grand duke and duchess and enjoying their relaxed private life. In their company he visited the field at Borodino, site of the momentous battle between Napoleon's Grand Army and General Kutuzov's Russian legions. Dzhun marveled at the fact that in such a small space—barely three miles in length—two mighty hosts had joined in a struggle that determined the fate of Europe. When it came time to leave, he was loath to go. He felt a strong bond to that place where so many of his countrymen had given their lives in defense of tsar and fatherland.[48]

Dzhun found himself called to serve as a "director" at balls given by the grand duke and duchess. Initially he shared this task with his fellow adjutant Vladimir Gadon, but in time it fell mostly on his shoulders. Soon he was tapped to direct at the ceremonial ball marking the emperor and empress's visit to Moscow to lay the cornerstone of the monument to Alexander II in the Kremlin. Dzhunkovsky skillfully managed the event, and even the tsar, who had little interest in dancing, was suitably impressed.[49]

All this was pleasant duty, but highly unsatisfying after his experience in the regiment and the serious work he had undertaken during the famine crisis. Dzhun felt trapped in a "monotonous, idle life." He sensed that he could not fulfill what centuries before Baldesar Castiglione had deemed the essential duties of a courtier: "to tell the prince whom he serves the truth about everything he needs to know . . . [and to] dissuade him of every evil intent and bring him to the path of virtue."[50] Dzhunkovsky believed that he lacked sufficient courtliness, that his passionate nature made him too blunt. "I always spoke the truth," he later recalled, "but I could not present it in the proper form; it always came out sounding harsh." Dzhun felt that his suggestions often had an effect opposite from what he intended; they angered the grand duke and produced negative results.[51]

Yet Dzhun knew he could not simply abandon his position as adjutant. To leave the service of a member of the dynasty without clear permission would appear ungrateful and was certain to damage a man's career. Moreover, his intense loyalty to the Romanovs and his personal affection for the grand duke and duchess made such a decision unthinkable. He valued Sergei as a kind and supportive patron, even as he recognized his limitations as an administrator. Of still greater importance was his positive attraction to Ella, a fondness that had romantic, even erotic undertones.

Dzhunkovsky's memoirs provide clear evidence of this. Decades after his service as adjutant had ended, he felt compelled to put on paper numerous observations of her beauty, charm, and kindness. His recollections contain details about her dress and the way she looked and behaved that betray his intense fascination and devotion to her person. Writing in full knowledge of her tragic death in 1918, he seemed determined to create and preserve for himself and for posterity a glowing picture of her as she had been in life. Nor was he alone in this; the memoirs and writings of others also reveal similar feelings.

Elizaveta Fedorovna is now listed among the saints of the Russian Orthodox Church, and her statue holds a place above the West Door of Westminster Abbey alongside those of other twentieth-century martyrs, including Martin Luther King Jr.[52] In her younger days, however, she was something of an innocent seductress, able to stimulate in men chivalric feelings, the desire to be her "cavaliere servente."[53] Ella was by no means oblivious to her magnetic qualities. She dressed with care, in a manner designed to enhance her attractiveness. Her elaborate, almost ritualistic toilette, described in detail by her niece Maria Pavlovna, reveals a woman well aware of her beauty and sexual power.[54] Ella was, of course, a proper Victorian, who had spent much of her youth at her grandmother's court; the thought of an inappropriate liaison probably never crossed her mind. Yet she displayed a special warmth toward Dzhun, engaging him in lengthy conversations and painting his portrait on two occasions.[55] (She was, among other things, a talented artist.) Identical in age, the two would find that they had similar religious values and intellectual interests; a genuine and long-lasting friendship developed, marked by a degree of condescension on Ella's side and reverence on Dzhun's. It is altogether likely that the grand duchess inspired in Dzhunkovsky the same chivalric and protective feelings that she did in so many others. Their closeness did not go unnoticed, and at some point—we cannot be certain when or whence—a rumor circulated that the two were lovers.[56] This was most certainly false; still, it is testimony to the visible bond that had formed between them.

Thus, despite growing frustration, which showed from time to time, Dzhunkovsky remained in the service of Sergei and his wife for over ten years. He realized that initially his patrons were puzzled by his disquiet, and he was touched when they tried to occupy him with various small assignments. Still, he believed that, in the end, their highnesses understood and accepted his feelings and the reasons for them: "They accustomed themselves to the idea that I could never become a real courtier, [and] that I would always be gazing out into the forest."[57]

Yet Dzhun did not simply languish in comfortable captivity. He was too intelligent and energetic, and too receptive to the vital, rapidly changing city that surrounded him. He developed a network of friends and associations, and Moscow became a school where he learned and refined his political and administrative skills. The Moscow years would educate not just his head but his heart as well. Unexpectedly, painfully, love entered Dzhunkovsky's life.

Chapter 3

Love, Labor, Loss

Antonina Vasilievna Evreinova was easy to fall in love with; many did. Strikingly good-looking, she had a tall statuesque figure and a face dominated by deep-set, almost violet eyes. Nina, as she preferred to be called, possessed a fine mind, sharpened by a splendid home education. She was talented; her skill at the piano so remarkable that, shortly before his death, Nikolai Rubenstein, the distinguished pianist and founder of the Moscow Conservatory, had proposed to take her on as a student.[1] Nina combined her gifts of beauty and musical ability with great personal charm. Outwardly quite reserved, she drew people to her by some special, almost ineffable quality. "Everybody loved her," a friend recalled, "the aged general, the little old bee-keeper . . . the young zemstvo doctor. . . . No one ever said a bad word about her."[2]

Nina was rich, too. Her father, Vasilii Nikitich Sabashnikov, a wealthy Siberian merchant and entrepreneur, had moved to Moscow with his wife, Serafima, and their family in the late 1860s. Sabashnikov's commerce prospered, but in 1876 Serafima died and, three years later, he passed away as well. Nina, then aged eighteen, her older sister, Ekaterina, and three younger brothers, Fedor, Mikhail, and Sergei, became orphans, joint heirs to a substantial fortune.[3] Not surprisingly, Nina had numerous admirers, gentlemen callers and suitors, among them Anatolii Koni, the distinguished liberal jurist and presiding judge at the Zasulich trial. Although seventeen years Nina's senior, Koni seriously contemplated making a proposal, only to reconsider because, as he said later (quoting Pushkin), "it was impossible to harness 'a warhorse [*Kon'*] and a trembling doe' to the same cart." Many others, bolder or less reflective, ventured to ask for her hand without success.[4]

Nina won the hearts of women as well. Katya Andreeva became her devotee at the age of ten when, during a ball given by the Andreevs, Nina arrived, accompanied by her sister and their English governess, Miss Besson. To Katya it seemed that the hall fell silent as the elegant Sabashnikovas swept in, making a deep bow to their hostess. Sixteen-year-old Nina shimmered, a "princess," an "enchantress," who cast an even stronger spell when she gave Katya her fan to hold while she danced and begged Katya's mother to let the girl stay longer at the ball. From that moment, a bond began to form, and as the two grew to womanhood, they became lifelong soul mates and confidantes.[5] Years later, Andreeva recalled that while her affection for Nina would change with time "from ecstatic adoration and devotion in childhood, to fierce, passionate friendship in youth, to firm love in old age," it never weakened.[6]

After their father's death, the Sabashnikov children continued to live in their parental house in Moscow's comfortable Arbat district under the loose guardianship of relatives and friends. In 1880, however, Ekaterina, the older sister, married Alexander Ivanovich Baranovsky, a man eighteen years her senior, who took up residence with his new wife in the family home. Alexander and his brother Egor quickly assumed control of the Sabashnikov finances and began treating Ekaterina and her siblings in a high-handed manner. Fedor, the eldest of the brothers, attempted suicide, while Nina, Mikhail, and Sergei became increasingly estranged from the Baranovskys.[7]

Nina searched for an escape from her untenable situation and seemed to find it through the help of Anna Mikhailovna Evreinova, an early feminist and Russia's first woman jurist. Anna introduced Nina to a group of people in St. Petersburg looking for funds to finance a new journal. The result was *Severnyi vestnik* (The Northern Herald), which came out in 1885 with Nina as publisher and Anna as editor.[8] It quickly won a respected place in the ranks of the "fat journals," those bulky periodicals that every month provided educated Russians with a wide variety of news, social commentary, and literature. *Severnyi vestnik* featured the works of such luminaries as the socialist philosopher Nikolai Mikhailovsky, and the popular writer Vladimir Korolenko. In 1888 it published "The Steppe" by a young Anton Chekhov, the short story that made his name.[9]

To assist her in some of the legal work connected with bringing out the new publication, Anna enlisted her nephew Aleksei Vladimirovich Evreinov, a recent graduate of law school. He fell in love with Nina almost as soon as they met and, only days later, asked her to marry him.[10] Nina was shocked and at first refused. But Aleksei pressed his suit relentlessly, and Nina, who may have seen marriage as a way to escape the oppressive Baranovsky brothers and acquire greater financial independence, agreed. Once she became engaged, however, Nina had serious doubts about her decision and sought to back out, only to be dissuaded by the always confident Evreinov. Although Nina agreed to proceed, her misgivings continued. On the eve of the wedding she suffered a serious fainting spell, first sign of the psychological problems that would plague her for years to come.[11]

After her marriage in May 1885 Nina's doubts were not dispelled, and returning from her honeymoon she seemed subdued and glum.[12] Despite her misgivings and unhappiness, however, she settled into married life, and four children followed. She gained considerable renown as a hostess; her intellect, talent, and charm gathered around her a diverse society. Nina, her brother Mikhail recalled, "had an exceptional ability to become close to people of varied backgrounds. . . . Writers, musicians, artists, performers, public and political figures came to her home in St. Petersburg in the winter and at Borshchen [the Evreinov estate in Kursk province] during the summer."[13] Still, troubles continued as Aleksei tightened his grip on Nina's property. In 1890 he forced her to give up her work as publisher of *Severnyi vestnik* and later made questionable investments that caused serious financial difficulties, bringing additional stress into their marriage.[14]

At the same time, other events intruded on Nina's world. By the end of the 1880s the marriage of Ekaterina and Alexander Baranovsky was falling apart, and in 1890, Nina's sister took the unusual step of making a request to the tsar, sent through the Chancellery for the Receipt of Petitions Submitted to the Emperor, for the right to live apart from her husband while retaining custody of her children.[15] In Russia at the time, divorce was a matter handled exclusively by the ecclesiastical courts and granted only on the strictly construed grounds of adultery, abandonment, sexual incapacity, and penal exile. Civil courts could not issue what was called an *otdel'nyi vid na zhitel'stvo*, the separate internal passport that a wife would need to live legally more than thirty miles distant from her husband. To circumvent these restrictions, the Chancellery for the Receipt of Petitions had, after 1884, begun to deal with a wide variety of women's appeals that could (or would) not be adjudicated by regular courts, civil or ecclesiastic.[16]

In 1892, despite vigorous opposition from Baranovsky who had powerful and influential connections, Ekaterina prevailed and gained the right to live separately from her husband.[17] The favorable resolution of her sister's problems may have had an impact on Nina's thinking. Aleksei was hardly an overbearing tyrant like Baranovsky; still, by then, he must have lost much of whatever respect he had earlier enjoyed in his wife's eyes.

If her sister's success in emancipating herself and her children from an unloved, oppressive husband suggested to Nina a path toward freedom, the adventures of her close friend Katya Andreeva opened a window on romance. In the late 1880s Katya, now an extremely attractive young woman, passed through several intense emotional relationships with older, married men. In these romantic dramas Nina played the role of a wise older advisor, steering the passionate and impulsive Katya away from what were clearly dangerous liaisons. But in 1893 Andreeva met her great love, Konstantin Dmitrievich Balmont, a flamboyant charter member of the Russian symbolist movement then at the threshold of his fame, handsome, and looking every inch the poet he was. While also married, Balmont soon embarked on the process of obtaining a divorce.[18] The romance that ensued, and the feelings that Katya shared with her friend, may have awakened in Nina emotions that had long slumbered or been denied.

By the beginning of the 1890s Nina, now in her early thirties, was becoming increasingly desperate. Deeply religious, a loving mother fiercely devoted to her children, she confronted both an empty marriage and, despite her intellect, talent, and social success, a life that seemed narrowly circumscribed. The sense of being trapped in what she saw as a tragic situation caused the symptoms of her psychological distress to become more pronounced. Bad dreams tormented her sleep, and she suffered panic attacks accompanied by frightening visions.[19] At this troubled moment, Vladimir Dzhunkovsky entered her life.

Dzhunkovsky met Nina in 1893, at a time when he was still in the process of getting his bearings and adjusting to his new life in Moscow. Thanks in part to his close friend and fellow adjutant Vladimir Gadon, he had begun to encounter people in the city's intellectual and cultural worlds. He became friendly with Gadon's brother Sergei, and through him met the artist Alexander Benois, who amazed him by his drawing skill and musical ability.[20] Later, Gadon urged Dzhun to make the acquaintance of the Evreinovs, commenting on Nina's talent and charm. Unimpressed at first, he quickly changed his mind. Writing years afterwards, he blandly recalled that "the Evreinov home became the dearest, closest home to me, and all their friends became my friends."[21]

From 1893 to 1896 a romance developed between Vladimir and Nina, but we cannot say with confidence when it began or how it proceeded. Undoubtedly, they first became friends on the basis of common interests and views. Dzhunkovsky had no musical talent himself, but he was able to appreciate Nina's abilities at the keyboard; they loved the theater, and Evreinova was a gifted amateur actress. Both were politically conservative and deeply religious, yet they shared a liberal disposition that made them able to accept as friends people who had very different outlooks and beliefs.[22]

The chemistry that turns friendship into love is something inexplicable. But in the case of Nina and Vladimir, the mystery is deepened because many of the sources that might shed light on the relationship are either missing or stubbornly silent. Three people who were privy to all or part of the story wrote memoirs—Dzhunkovsky himself, Nina's brother Mikhail Sabashnikov, and Katya Andreeva, Nina's close friend and confidante—yet none of them says a word about the romance. We also know that Nina and Vladimir wrote to each other. But while Dzhunkovsky was extremely careful to preserve the letters he received over the course of his lifetime (his archive holds correspondence from roughly four hundred different people), almost nothing from Nina survives. Presumably, he destroyed her messages. What evidence we have—chiefly letters from Dzhun's sister Evdokiia and his friend Konstantin Balmont—only lets us view their relationship indirectly, as "through a glass, darkly."

Silent sources can speak, of course, although often in words both indefinite and obscure. In this case, their deafening stillness cries out that a subject both painful and significant is being hidden. At the very least, it implies that the romantic episode in the lives of Nina and Vladimir was something both parties felt they needed to keep forever secret. Although the bond of affection between Evreinova and Dzhunkovsky would be strong and enduring, the two evidently came to regard the emotions they felt at the high point of their love with a measure of embarrassment, if not shame, something that imposed discretion on their friends and on each other.[23]

Between 1893 and 1896 Dzhunkovsky became a fairly regular visitor to the Evreinov estate at Borshchen, where his admiration and affection for Nina grew steadily. There Dzhunkovsky also formed a close bond with Katya Andreeva and her love interest, Konstantin Balmont. His growing awareness of the troubled state of Nina's marriage and the pain it caused her aroused his sympathy. Initially, Vladimir—true to the knightly values acquired at the Corps of Pages, his chivalric sensibilities primed by long association with Grand Duchess Elizaveta Fedorovna—may have seen Nina as a lady in distress for whom he should assume the role of *cavaliere servente*. But soon, still stronger emotions would come into play with painful, even tragic consequences.

Both Nina and Dzhun became involved with the Andreeva-Balmont romance and its problems.[24] Balmont, pursuing Katya with ardor and determination, faced a difficult situation because of complications arising from his divorce from his first wife. The ecclesiastical court dissolved the marriage in early 1896 but ruled that, while Balmont's ex-wife could wed again, he was forever forbidden to do so.[25] Katya demanded legal wedlock, however; her family would never permit her to enter into an illicit union or one unsanctioned by the church.[26] Balmont had to find his way around the prohibition that the religious authorities had imposed on his taking a new wife.

Nina and Vladimir tried to advise and console their two friends. Dzhun and Balmont often met to converse and commiserate, and later Vladimir helped the poet surmount the barriers he faced and marry the woman he loved.[27] But involvement in the love affair of others carried its own dangers. Romance can be contagious; as Nina and Dzhunkovsky witnessed the passion developing between Balmont and Katya, their mutual affection deepened.

Meanwhile, Dzhunkovsky suffered a loss that appears to have accelerated his infatuation with Evreinova or at least his willingness to act upon it. In May 1895 his adored mother died after a long illness. While her death came as a heavy blow, it removed an impediment to his pursuit of Nina. Vladimir knew that his mother could never have approved anything he might do to disrupt Nina's marriage or encourage her to seek a divorce.[28] With his mother's passing, however, he now had choices to ponder, and at the time of her funeral Dzhunkovsky struck his sister as both sorrowing and distracted.[29] By late 1895 or early 1896, the growing love between Nina and Vladimir, combined with her continued marital unhappiness, pushed matters toward a decision point. But then another event intervened: the coronation of Emperor Nicholas II and the accompanying tragedy at Khodynka field that cost the lives of more than a thousand people, casting a terrible pall over the ceremonies and the entire reign of the last tsar.

The lavish ceremonies that attended the enthronement of Nicholas II were deliberately contrived to allay fears that Alexander III's young and inexperienced successor was not equal to the task of ruling the vast Russian empire. The designers of the coronation spectacle packed it with powerful symbolism intended to exalt the autocracy, consecrate the emperor as the Lord's chosen instrument, and affirm the unity of the tsar and his people, demonstrating, in the words of one historian, "the vitality of a monarchy with mass democratic support."[30] Extravagant display sparing no expense enveloped the crowning of Russia's new ruler to such an extent that even those devoted to the Romanov dynasty questioned such a squandering of national wealth.[31]

As an adjutant to Sergei Alexandrovich, Dzhunkovsky observed the solemnities and festivities firsthand, and his memoirs, presumably based on a diary he wrote at the time, are filled with details of the coronation on May 14, 1896, and other aspects of the enormous celebration.[32] Dzhun recalled with a special vividness the gala performance of Glinka's patriotic opera *A Life for the Tsar* at the Bolshoi Theater on May 17, and the reaction of the audience as the curtain fell:

> The performance ended at exactly eleven. Their majesties had just risen from their seats, when the hall resounded with a thunderous "Hurrah!" Their majesties graciously bowed and left the [imperial] box. In the hall a fervent cry went up: "The Hymn! The Hymn!" The curtain rose, the musicians of the orchestra again turned to face the imperial box, and the hall of the theater sounded with the strains of "God Save the Tsar." The emperor and empress came back into the box and once more bowed to the glittering crowd that had come from all corners of the Russian lands. "Hurrah!" echoed through

> the theater and its waves rolled outward and were taken up by the tens of thousands in the streets, and the storm [of cheers] carried to the [Kremlin] Palace.[33]

The following day, however, Dzhunkovsky watched in sorrow and despair as an unexpected event forever tarnished the glitter of the coronation and the genuine outpouring of joy and popular support for the monarchy it had called forth.

A "public entertainment" (*narodnoe gulianie*) was scheduled to take place on Khodynka field at the northern edge of Moscow. There, in the name of the tsar, peasants and common folk could receive souvenir mugs and biscuits bearing the date of the coronation. Later, the emperor and empress would appear to accept the adulation of their loyal subjects. More than half a million Russians from all parts of the empire had been gathering at the site for several days, throngs larger by far than any that had ever appeared at earlier coronations. The Ministry of Court, charged with organizing the entertainment, made minimal plans for crowd control, however, naively assuming that Russia's commoners, disciplined and devoted to their sovereign, would maintain an exemplary order.[34] The ministry failed to provide enough stalls for dispensing the souvenirs. Numerous trenches had been dug on a portion of the field. Designed to help keep the multitude in check, they would become death traps.

The distribution of the tsar's gifts was to begin at ten o'clock in the morning of May 18. But the huge crowd that had waited through the night was restive; the weather was sweltering, and the people tightly pressed. At about six o'clock in the morning, in the face of great demand, several stalls started to give out the mementos. That news spread swiftly, and the agitated mass stampeded toward the proffered gifts. In ten minutes, more than thirteen hundred people died, trampled or suffocated after falling into the trenches; at least an equal number were hurt. Suddenly, celebration turned into horror, and by day's end it seemed to one observer that "an Egyptian night" had descended on the city. The gay decorations celebrating the coronation looked out of place; "sorrow and dejection were everywhere," he recalled. "Moscow stood like a bride prepared to be wed, whose groom had [just] refused her."[35]

Dzhunkovsky, like many others, placed considerable blame for the tragedy and its aftermath on Sergei Alexandrovich. Insulted when St. Petersburg authorities assigned the Ministry of Court the chief responsibility for organizing the "public entertainment" at Khodynka, the grand duke had indignantly refused to have anything to do with the task of crowd control at the field. Now for the first time, Dzhunkovsky saw clearly Sergei's limitations as an administrator. The grand duke had not met one of the chief obligations imposed on the high post of governor-general—to maintain order everywhere in the territory entrusted to his care—and this was a dereliction that contributed mightily to the disaster.[36]

Dzhunkovsky also felt that Sergei failed to properly advise his sovereign. As news of the tragedy spread through the city, he did not urge Nicholas to go at once to the field and order a memorial service to be conducted. "That would have been an act worthy of a tsar," Dzhun believed, and would have quieted much of the criticism subsequently heaped upon the new emperor. Dzhun and the rest of the grand duke's entourage fully expected such a gesture, only to be sorely disappointed.[37] That evening, when the tsar attended the ball given by the French ambassador, Dzhunkovsky was even more downcast. As a member of Sergei's suite, he had to be present, but dark thoughts enveloped him: "I did not dance, I just hung about the hall, and all the luxury and gaiety at the ball only made my mood worse."[38]

In the days that followed, Dzhunkovsky continued to witness a disturbing mix of mourning and celebration. On May 23, he attended another grand ball held at the Alexander Hall of the Kremlin Palace. The evening proved painful as he listened to the constant talk about the tragedy and the grand duke's failings.[39] The public would soon cast Sergei as the primary culprit, branding him with the enduring epithet "Prince of Khodynka." Dzhunkovsky always maintained affection and respect for Sergei and believed that some of the criticism was exaggerated. But the often cruel barbs directed toward the grand duke must have caused him to reflect upon the dire consequences of a detached, hands-off style of governance, combined with excessive pride and an indifference to public opinion. These were mistakes Dzhun would avoid when, a decade later, real administrative power was thrust into his hands.

The traumatic events associated with the coronation probably had no direct impact on relations between Nina Evreinova and Vladimir, but they undoubtedly contributed to Dzhunkovsky's unsettled mood. They also produced a hiatus in his correspondence with his sister, something that caused her considerable worry. A letter dated June 9, shows that Evdokiia was already concerned about the affection between her brother and Nina. Now Vadya's silence led his sister to suspect that things might be getting out of hand, and she began to inject herself into the situation. From this point on, Evdokiia became both a witness to her brother's romance and, increasingly, a participant.

Evdokiia, called "Dodo" by her family (not a reference to the extinct bird, but a nickname like "Dotty"), was deeply devoted to Vladimir, and he to her. Still, his memoirs fail to provide a clear and detailed picture of the sister who was his greatest friend and supporter. Fortunately, we possess a revealing portrait drawn by someone who knew her well: Grand Duchess Maria Pavlovna, the daughter of Grand Duke Pavel Alexandrovich and Princess Alexandra of Greece. Maria was born in 1890, and a year later her mother died giving birth to a son, Dmitrii. Shortly after Maria turned six, she and her brother passed from the care of nannies into the hands of a governess, called in her memoirs "Mlle Hélène," but who was, in fact, Evdokiia Dzhunkovskaya.[40] Because Maria's mother was dead and her father often absent, the relationship between the governess and her charge became closer than it might otherwise have been, marked by great affection but filled with conflict as well. Evdokiia would, in Maria's words, "instruct, love, and torment me for . . . twelve years . . . until my marriage."[41]

Evdokiia was determined to instill in Maria Pavlovna, a rather spoiled and very willful young person, respect for people beneath her on the social scale and concern for those who had to endure poverty and ill health. Once, Evdokiia insisted that Maria give alms to a beggar and punished the girl for her presumed selfishness when she refused.[42] Later, she forced the grand duchess to apologize to a footman at whom she had made a face.[43] Maria recalled that her governess, who was very active in the Red Cross, frequently took her to hospitals and "taught me to gaze on suffering humanity and not be afraid."[44] Evdokiia constantly strove to inculcate in her charge "good manners and humility" and often repeated the maxim that Nicholas I was supposed to have impressed upon his sons: "Always act so that you will be forgiven for having been born grand dukes."[45]

Maria bridled at Evdokiia's strictures; there would be bitter words and many tearful scenes. Still, the grand duchess could not deny that her governess's principles were honest and rooted in a deeply held Orthodox faith.

Evdokiia Dzhunkovskaya. From Anastasiia Dunaeva, *Reformy politsii v Rossii nachala XX veka i Vladimir Fedorovich Dzhunkovskii.*

Nina Evreinova. From Anastasiia Dunaeva, *Reformy politsii v Rossii nachala XX veka i Vladimir Fedorovich Dzhunkovskii.*

Evdokiia was, Maria wrote, "good and charitable and excessively devoted to religion. Every morning after she said her prayers she read a chapter in her Bible, which was worn out and filled with signatures and the yellowed photographs of dead members of her family. . . . She had lost her parents and an older brother, and in spite of our quarrels, I had much sympathy for her loneliness."[46] In time, Maria understood that Evdokiia acted out of genuine love and concern. Childhood disputes and grievances were forgiven if not forgotten, and a mature, true friendship emerged.[47]

The portrait provided by Grand Duchess Maria Pavlovna supplements and supports the impressions gleaned from Dodo's letters to her brother sent during the crisis caused by his love for Nina. Dzhun's sister was highly moral and deeply religious, capable of strong affection and profound sympathy for those in pain. But she was also an extremely controlling person, skillful at using both love and guilt to guide others toward the ends that she considered right.

In her letter of June 9, 1896, Dodo chided her brother for failing to write and expressed her concern for his troubled mood. "You are suffering because of N[ina]V[asilievna]," she lamented. "Vadya, darling, this crush will not be helpful either to her or to you. . . . There should be limits to everything." Dodo urged her brother to recognize the dangers posed by the affection he and Nina had for each other. "Don't count on your strength. Don't think that you and N.V. will never go beyond honorable feelings," she warned. "If you respect N.V., then you must stop. She is married and has children. Your [mutual] passion will give her more sorrow than joy! . . . Come to your senses," she pleaded, "restrain your feelings." Dodo told her brother that she was praying that God would give him and Nina the strength to subdue their mutual attraction. "Friendship I recognize," she concluded, "but without [romantic] passion—with passion it is not friendship."[48] In a letter sent the next day, Dodo asked that Nina also write, hoping to become a support and guide to her as well.[49]

Shortly after Evdokiia posted her letter of June 9, Vadya broke his silence, and a clearer picture of the situation began to emerge. He and Nina were well aware of the dangers. Nina understood that she might lose her children, and Dzhun knew that a scandal could destroy his career. As a consequence, the two had decided to step back and declared their intention simply to remain friends. Making this decision was painful; but sticking to it would prove even harder and cause genuine torment.[50]

From early June until late August 1896, Dzhunkovsky experienced physical illness—cough and fever—plus bouts of depression, marked by despair, self-pity, and sharp mood swings.[51] In one letter he told Dodo that since his life to date had been so bright, suffering might do him good.[52] Later he wrote that it would not matter to anyone if his life were ruined.[53] Dzhun thought about resigning his post but then pulled back, because he felt he could not desert Grand Duke Sergei in the difficult days following the coronation and the Khodynka tragedy.[54] At one point, he became angry and read into his sister's letters negative sentiments that were not there.

He accused Evdokiia of criticizing Nina in notes she had sent to her.[55] Nina, too, was in a highly agitated state, suffering from terrible dreams and frightening visions that made her nervousness and depression even worse.[56] Terribly distraught, Nina traveled abroad in the fall hoping to pull herself together. At Biarritz, in southern France, she rented a villa close to the Spanish border.

Meanwhile, Dzhunkovsky became distracted from his own troubles as he helped his friend Balmont in his struggle to marry Katya Andreeva. The decree of the Holy Synod dissolving Balmont's marriage denied him the right to take a new wife, but if a priest could be induced to perform a wedding ceremony, it would be possible to circumvent that official ruling. Marriage was a *sacrament* that, if duly administered to two single people, created a bond that the church would have to recognize. What Balmont needed was an official paper that stated he was a bachelor, not a divorcé, so that a priest, kept ignorant of the Synod's prohibition, might unite Katya with him in matrimony. Luckily, Balmont's brother obtained the necessary document and found a priest in a small parish outside the city of Tver who agreed to hear and sanctify the wedding vows. In the stress-filled months prior to the marriage, Dzhunkovsky and Balmont had been giving each other moral support in the face of their romantic difficulties. Now, with Balmont's problems solved, Dzhun journeyed from Moscow to stand as one of his friend's groomsmen at the ceremony.[57]

The marriage of Katya and Balmont took place on September 27, 1896, and the next day the newlyweds hurriedly departed the country via St. Petersburg. From the Warsaw Station, Balmont sent Dzhun a note of thanks. "Were it not for you," he wrote, "I would probably still be separated from Katya and we would both be suffering terribly." Then he offered his friend words of solace: "God grant that your life will be happier than it is right now. God grant that that soul, . . . dearer to you than your own, will be closer, that she will join with you in the harmony of happiness—that she will be yours forever."[58]

Katya and her new husband soon joined Nina in Biarritz. In early November Balmont wrote Dzhun again, recalling past good times and bringing him up to date on Nina's situation:

> [H]ow is your apartment . . . where things were good and cozy; where we would get together after a difficult day and forget all unpleasantness in friendly conversation? Katya and I are together with Nina . . . in the same

villa, and we both find that she is feeling better, is happier and stronger. . . . I am so sorry that it is not [now] possible for her to give to the one she loves all the tenderness and beauty of the love of which she is capable.[59]

Balmont mentioned plans to visit Paris and the prospect that Dzhun might meet them and Nina there, imagining how much happiness that would give his friend.

Dzhunkovsky had hoped to join Nina and the newlyweds at year's end.[60] But his plans were disrupted when, in late November, Sergei Alexandrovich appointed him to the Moscow provincial commission for the first all-Russian census, scheduled for April 1897. He was glad to have serious work and an escape from stifling court duties.[61] But Dzhun confessed to his sister that he was of two minds about the assignment and highly agitated.[62] In the end, Dzhun's sense of duty prevailed, but he deeply regretted his inability to go abroad and shared this disappointment with his friends. A Christmas letter Balmont sent from Paris makes it clear that the feelings were mutual:

I think of you often and am very sorry that fate has prevented you from coming here. . . . But God grant that other times will come—brighter and more joyous. It is terrible to see N.V. when she is so upset; she was so eager for the chance to see you. I don't know when you two will see each other now. But we are not separated from you in our thoughts, and not a day goes by that we do not remember you and feel sad that you are alone. . . . May fate smile upon . . . [you and Nina] and may you meet [again] with gentle caresses and feelings of mutual tenderness.[63]

Toward the end of the year Nina returned to Russia with her children, and shortly after Christmas Vladimir journeyed to St. Petersburg to meet her. There they discussed the prospect of Nina's getting a divorce or of their breaking off their relationship. Vadya wrote to his sister that the thought of breaking up was "terrible," but despite her sympathy, Dodo advised caution. She warned her brother that even should Aleksei grant Nina a divorce, the consequences might be tragic. "Won't you both have constant pangs of conscience?" she wrote plaintively. "You know, after all, that he is the father of the children. Other divorced people might not have these pangs, but you are both so religious. Will you be fully happy?"[64]

Such reservations and the resistance of Nina's husband—who in a divorce would almost certainly demand custody of the children—caused the lovers to reconsider and to hold off for a year before proceeding, however painful that might be. A relieved Dodo wrote Vadya on January 18: "Thank God that you are a little calmer and that hope for a good outcome in the future sustains you. May the Lord grant both of you the strength to endure this ordeal. It seems to me that the decision is for the best—a year will make it all clear, and the Lord will arrange everything for the best."[65]

Nina and Vladimir would spend the rest of 1897 apart. Nina took her children and went abroad for medical treatment, evidently intended to help her overcome the extreme anxiety and depression from which she was suffering. Dzhunkovsky continued in his adjutant's duties and worked on the census. Then in late spring, he was called to a new adventure, helping to organize and manage a Russian medical mission being sent to the Ottoman side in a war that had just broken out between the Greeks and the Turks.

The Greco-Turkish war of 1897 was a brief, nasty affair, harbinger of the larger struggles that would shortly convulse the Balkans and, within two decades, drive Europe to catastrophe.[66] Despite strong sympathy for their Greek co-religionists, the Russians sought to maintain strict neutrality in the conflict, hoping to play the honest broker at the end. As a token of this even hand, the Russian Red Cross dispatched a medical unit to each of the belligerents. A detachment from St. Petersburg went to aid the Greeks, while in Moscow Ella funded a medical team from the society of the Iberian Sisters of Mercy to treat the Turkish wounded. On April 21, 1897, Grand Duke Sergei, chairman of the local governing board of the Red Cross, asked Dzhunkovsky to assume the task of directing the unit.

Dzhun eagerly accepted the assignment as a welcome respite from his stultifying duties as adjutant and, we must assume, a diversion from his romantic trials as well. But the unanticipated nature of the appointment and the difficulty of the task ahead surprised and troubled him. With no medical experience, he had to preside over a sizeable group consisting of five doctors, ten nurses, and assorted support personnel.[67] Many times in the days to come he wondered if he had bitten off more than he could chew.

Dzhunkovsky's mission lasted from late April to mid-July and involved just one major engagement, the battle of Domokos. Despite its brief duration and limited scope, however, the assignment was a significant learning experience, providing lessons that would influence many of his later actions. From the outset, Dzhun had to confront and surmount a number of organizational and administrative challenges. He assumed the task of gathering equipment—tents, stretchers, cooking equipment, and canned goods—needed to sustain the medical detachment in the field. Once the team reached the war zone in Thessaly, Dzhun had to unload and store these necessities, plus the doctors' and nurses' own gear and supplies, and later transport them to the battle site. At the height of the engagement, with medical personnel fully occupied treating the wounded, he distributed medicines, bandages, and other supplies as they were called for. When the fighting subsided, he organized the feeding of over two hundred of the injured and their caregivers. Later, with military operations ended, Dzhun oversaw the transfer of the wounded from the field hospital to more permanent and better equipped facilities. Finally, he had to arrange for the medical team's departure from Greece to Constantinople and then their travel back to Russia.

The medical mission to Turkey also taught Dzhunkovsky valuable lessons in diplomacy and "people management." On numerous occasions, he had to confront suspicious and recalcitrant low-level Turkish officials. His attempts to reason with them sometimes failed, and he had to bluster and threaten. On the other hand, dealing with Turkish army leaders posed few difficulties. Dzhunkovsky's military standing and experience along with his natural charm and tact gained him quick acceptance and willing cooperation.

Even more important were the lessons he learned from dealing with the medical personnel. Doctors were among the testier members of the notoriously testy Russian intelligentsia, with a prickly sense of their own importance and self-worth, honed by decades of struggle against bureaucratic interference and class prejudice.[68] Unsurprisingly, at the beginning, Chief Doctor I. P. Lang and Head Nurse L. K. Pivorovich confronted Dzhun with a barrier of distrust. They resented his appointment and worked to turn the entire staff against him. In their eyes, a military man and an adjutant to an unpopular grand duke was a disagreeable presence, a representative of authority, and worse yet, someone just along for the ride who should not be taken seriously. Dzhun was undeterred, however, and ignoring their hostility, showed them every respect.[69] He tried to involve Lang and Pivorovich in the work of obtaining needed supplies, but they rebuffed his effort. Dzhun persisted. When he went to meet with Turkish military authorities to negotiate the team's travel to the battle site and its quartering there, he made sure to bring Dr. Lang along on the arduous journey.

Still it was not until the battle of Domokos had begun and the wounded started to pour in that Dzhunkovsky achieved a breakthrough. With doctors and nurses working under intense pressure, often sagging with fatigue, Dzhun made himself indispensible, taking on every manner of menial but important task called for in the crisis. By the time the team's work wound down, he was accepted as one of its valued members, and a man-to-man talk with Dr. Lang removed the last remnants of distrust. Dzhun's experience with the medical staff taught him techniques of coping with members of the intelligentsia that he would apply to advantage in his later governmental career. A straightforward, honest, approach and a refusal to take offense could overcome their ingrained distrust and lay the basis for amicable relations and mutual tolerance, if not agreement.

The assignment in Thessaly also gave Dzhun his first experience of the unromantic realities of war. After Domokos, as the Russian field hospital began to fill, Dzhunkovsky, who had never been in battle, saw firsthand its terrible results. "I will never forget the depressing scene," he wrote years later. "The largest room in the house was filled with wounded. When there was no place left . . . [inside], they were deposited in the garden and then right on the street. . . . The wounded lay fast upon each other; one had his leg torn off, another had been bandaged, but his dressing had simply turned into a red mass. Pools of blood quickly spread over the floor. Many [wounds] already give off the stench of gangrene." But in the midst of the squalor, suffering, and disorder, Dzhun was amazed by the stoicism of the men.[70]

He learned something about treating soldiers as well. Dzhunkovsky was genuinely appalled by what he saw as the Turks' attitude toward their troops—useful as cannon fodder but neglected after battle was done. Two decades later, when he was a frontline commander in the Great War, Dzhun would struggle to put the needs of his men first, to see that they were treated with dignity and not squandered in the field. It was an approach that would win him the loyalty of those he led and make it possible for him to maintain discipline in his units even as revolution spilled into the trenches.

Upon his return from Turkey, Vladimir quickly found himself lionized in court circles. He traveled to St. Petersburg, where Nicholas, Alexandra, and the dowager empress Maria Fedorovna received him graciously and the tsar thanked him for the "brilliant fulfillment" of his assignment. While pleased by his sovereign's praise, Dzhunkovsky sought to call the emperor's attention to the splendid work of the doctors and other medical personnel.[71] In his official report, he praised the entire medical team not only for its professional achievements but also for the symbolic value of its work—the display of Christian charity to the Moslems who got aid and comfort under the Russian flag and the sign of the Red Cross.

The applause he received made him uneasy, even a bit ashamed: "It seemed to me that I was completely unworthy of all this," he recalled. "I felt that my fame was exaggerated. . . . Going over in my heart what I had done, I found inadequacies that had been hidden; it seemed as if I had deceived people."[72] When, several months later, Dzhunkovsky presented a final accounting to the Moscow branch of the Red Cross, the chair of the meeting asked the whole assembly to join in expressing their thanks. Everyone rose and gave Vladimir an ovation that left him nonplussed. "I lost my composure," he wrote later. "I made a clumsy parting bow, but did not quite know how to get away [gracefully]."[73]

Back in Russia, Vladimir picked up the thread of his romance. Letters from his sister had informed him that Nina was still in Europe, undergoing medical treatment.[74] Dzhun had plans to visit, but the press of work in Moscow prevented him. It may have been just as well. In August, Evdokiia met Nina vacationing at St-Jean-de-Luz in southern France. There she learned that Nina was convinced that her husband would never give her custody of the children in a divorce and that she was determined never to be separated from them. She told Evdokiia that she would seek instead the special passport (*otdel'nyi vid*) which would give her the right to live on her own with her daughter and three sons.[75]

When Dodo wrote to inform her brother about Nina's intentions she sought to console him saying "the marriage of divorced persons cannot be pleasing to God." She added that the children of divorce would never accept their mother's new husband but would constantly make comparisons between him and their real father.[76] In a letter dated a week later, Dodo told Vadya that Nina had expressed concerns similar to her own regarding the reaction of the children. "N.V. is frightened that . . . [they] will not forget their real father and will make you unhappy. Knowing you, she understands that you will suffer if the [older] boys start to blame her. For the younger . . . [children] it is another matter, but the older boys will really be between two fires."[77] All Dodo could do was offer words of support and hope, mixed with gentle admonition: "Ach, Vadya, I hurt for you and pray that God will console you and give you strength. . . . I know this is hard, I grieve, grieve that things have gone this far. You should have thought everything through earlier; now you need to stop in time. My heart aches for you, knowing how you are."[78]

At this point, it appears that matters were put on hold as Nina sought to resolve her marital situation with her husband. Dzhunkovsky remained depressed and anxious, Nina's request for an *otdel'nyi vid* had not been satisfied, and both suffered the pain of uncertainty.[79] On December 30, Dodo sent her brother a picture of Christ calming the waters, saying that if the Lord could quiet the seas, then surely he could quell the storms in Vadya's heart.[80]

At the beginning of 1898 things became even more complicated. Evdokiia learned from one of Nina's friends that Aleksei had told his wife he was willing to let her live separately and have the children and full charge of their upbringing, but he demanded one condition: that the children not be allowed to see Vladimir. Still, this strange stipulation gave Dodo momentary hope. "This is, of course, a terribly hard condition for N.V. and you," she wrote, "but I think that, in the end, he will back down. God help us!"[81]

Aleksei's demands created considerable turmoil, and Dzhunkovsky was unsure how to proceed. Meanwhile, Nina was receiving letters from her husband in which he vacillated daily on the question of divorce or separation and combined these confusing signals with harsh words about Vladimir. Evdokiia's letters indicate that Dzhunkovsky considered both a direct approach to Nina's husband and a mediated solution employing his brother Nikolai as negotiator. For a time, Dodo thought that Aleksei might be prepared to give Nina a divorce and the children, but these hopes were soon disappointed.[82]

Difficulties increased in February when Katya Balmont fell gravely ill after a terribly painful labor and the stillbirth of a daughter.[83] Nina turned her attention to her close friend and, as a result of her efforts, fell sick herself. Dzhun, meanwhile, suffered great emotional distress, and his sister urged him to be reasonable, to look at things straight on, and not to give in to depression.[84] Nikolai Dzhunkovsky also wrote, strongly advising his brother against pushing for Nina's divorce and the prospect of marriage, since this would bring no happiness, only problems.[85]

In an apparent effort to resolve the issue, Dzhunkovsky left Russia in April and headed for Paris.[86] Dodo was gravely worried, fearing that what had been, as far as she knew, a passionate but chaste romance might now be consummated in the city whose name was practically synonymous with love. In the wake of her brother's departure she wrote words of caution: "My dear Vadya, don't create an abnormal situation for yourself. I pray, in the memory of Mama, look at matters honestly and help N. V. to see things sensibly—If N. V. cannot give up anything and cannot overcome pangs of conscience and terrible fears for the future, then, surely, no matter how painful, it is best for you to part."[87] Dodo's warning was apt, for once in the French capital Dzhunkovsky encountered severe disappointment.

Evdokiia's letter of May 1 gives the impression that Nina and Vladimir had worked matters out. "I am happy that you are satisfied, that the difficult negotiations are over and you are satisfied that you have clarified everything," Dodo wrote in a relieved tone.[88] Still, a subsequent note shows that she was uncertain just what had been decided and how.[89] As for Vladimir and Nina, they worried that others might find out they had been together. Evdokiia's letter of May 6 had been carried to Paris by a friend, and his arrival threw Nina into panic. Dodo tried to reassure her brother that even should her friend encounter Nina he would attach no significance to it. Still, she added: "I know that this was hard on N.V. and that she was frightened and that you suffered for her. Such situations are terribly painful and your nerves cannot bear being constantly under the burden of fear." Once more, Dodo pushed the two to resolve matters: "May the Lord help you to look at reality straightforwardly and without self-deception . . . [so that you can] find a way out and discover a direct path to spiritual peace. Of course, this is difficult to find, but gradually."[90]

Shortly after receiving his sister's letter of May 20, Vladimir returned to Russia, passing through St. Petersburg to see her on the way to Moscow. He spoke little and seemed greatly upset. Dodo did not dare question him about what had transpired in Paris, fearing to cause him still greater hurt.[91] Letters from Konstantin Balmont indicate that Nina was also in pain, but recovering.[92] The exact nature of the decision the two lovers had taken cannot be known, but everything suggests that Nina had abandoned the idea of divorce and remarriage. Dzhun may have entertained for a time the faint hope that happiness might be his, but to his sister he indicated that he was resigned and at peace.[93] That summer Evdokiia met Nina in western Europe and found that she, too, was calm, in good spirits, and had her children with her. By late August and early September Dodo's letters make it clear that the peak of Dzhunkovsky's romantic crisis had passed.[94]

Neither Dzhunkovsky's memoirs nor his sister's letters disclose his thoughts and emotions at this time. His love for Nina remained; but he also must have understood that love had led him into a moral swamp. What had begun as a chivalric impulse to comfort a lady who was in pain caused him in the end to violate deeply held religious principles and his own family code of honor. He had entered Aleksei Evreinov's home as a guest and friend. But he betrayed the trust that his host's invitation imposed. In pursuing Nina and encouraging her to leave her husband, Dzhun inflicted further damage on an already fragile marriage and ultimately increased the sorrow of both parties. In spite of his deep Christian faith, he had broken the Lord's commandment not to covet that which was his neighbor's. It must have been a contrite Dzhunkovsky who now accepted the fact that at present there was nothing he could do but follow his sister's council and leave matters to God. For the next few years he would have to seek solace in work, even in the stagnant routines of his adjutant's job. Sergei and Ella, who knew a great deal, but perhaps not all, about his romance, gave him sympathy and support in the midst of his trials.[95]

Dzhunkovsky's involvement in the activities of Sergei's court may have produced some comfort and satisfaction, but it could also lead to some painful (albeit amusing) moments. In October 1899, the grand duke staged a rabbit hunt at Ilinskoe during which Vladimir, whose vision may not have been particularly sharp, mistook a cat for a hare and shot it. When Ella learned of this, she flew into a rage. Displaying that peculiarly English hypocrisy that gladly sets the hounds upon deer and fox but cannot abide the mistreatment of a domestic animal, she bitterly denounced Dzhun despite his efforts to explain that it had all been a terrible mistake. Three days had to pass before she would so much as speak to him. Nor was the incident quickly forgotten or forgiven. At Christmas Sergei presented his adjutant with a silver Fabergé rabbit in memory of the hunt. Someone, attempting humor, quipped that it would have been better to have given Dzhun a silver cat instead. Ella exploded again, and everyone fell silent. When, several years later, Dzhunkovsky once more joined Sergei and his friends in a similar outing, Ella made a point of standing by Vladimir's side while he fired."That time, I did not disgrace myself," he recalled. "The grand duchess brought me luck, and I killed a rabbit before her eyes."[96]

The vibrant cultural life of Moscow also helped Dzhunkovsky find other, healthy distractions. His interest in the theater continued, and he readily joined Sergei and Ella, also lovers of the dramatic arts, in regularly attending performances on all the major stages of the city. The grand duke was a strong backer of Moscow's theaters, proudly singing their praises every time he visited St. Petersburg. In the company of his patrons, Vladimir became acquainted with many of the important actors and actresses of the day.[97] Later, these contacts would become more extensive, and strong bonds developed with the actor and dramaturge Alexander Ivanovich Sumbatov-Iuzhin and members of the theatrically oriented Bakhrushin family.

Satisfying though these diversions were, they failed to provide Dzhunkovsky with the serious and independent work he craved. Things changed decisively, however, in early 1901, when the grand duke appointed Dzhun as assistant chairman of the soon-to-be-created Moscow Guardianship of Public Sobriety (*Moskovskoe popechitel'stvo o narodnoi trezvosti*), the local branch of a national institution designed to assist the government in managing the impact of the state vodka monopoly, introduced in 1896. The Guardianship's goal was to develop a substantial program of outreach to the urban lower classes that would encourage moderation in the consumption of alcohol.

Dzhunkovsky felt that this assignment marked the real beginning of his administrative career. Formally, he would be second to the chair, General Alexander Bilderling, but Sergei made it clear that because of the general's military duties his role in the new organization would be confined only to broad oversight. "The whole work will fall to you," he assured his adjutant. Initially, the grand duke believed that Dzhun could combine his activities in the Guardianship with his regular obligations; but almost at once it became obvious that many of his court functions would have to make way for this large-scale undertaking. The task of designing and running the Guardianship turned Dzhun's attention from Sergei, Ella, and the heights of society toward the problems of Moscow's working class and those at the city's lower depths. He would encounter not only urban poverty and the proletariat but also the revolutionary forces that were making themselves felt in the ancient capital and throughout the country.[98] Soon the courtier would become a public man.

Chapter 4

Green Snake, Red Flag

THE CITY THAT NOW INCREASINGLY ABSORBED DZHUNKOVSKY'S attention and energies was, like the man himself, in rapid transition. Forty years after the reform era began, Moscow could no longer be called a "big village." With more than a million people, the second city of the tsar's empire was already the world's tenth largest, rapidly gaining on St. Petersburg. Its growth rate was the fastest in Russia, and at 4 percent per year, equaled or perhaps exceeded New York City's.

People came because there were jobs to be had and money to be made. The empire's industrialization drive of the late nineteenth century had borne spectacular fruit in Moscow and the surrounding provinces. Textiles, a key industry in Russia's economic expansion, did extremely well here, doubling profits between 1890 and 1900. At the beginning of the new century, the value of the output of Moscow's textile enterprises was nearly 60 percent of the nation's total, and the Moscow region accounted for one-quarter of the sales of all the factories in European Russia. Industrial production was only part of the picture. Located at the center of the empire's rail network, Moscow was a hub for domestic commerce of every sort; its trade in a wide variety of goods and services generated enormous wealth.

By 1900 the rapid expansion of industry and commerce enabled Moscow's merchant elite to push aside the nobility as the dominant economic force, yet its undisputable wealth and importance had not always brought social respect. Leading businessmen gained access to Moscow's exclusive clubs, where they now sat alongside members of the *dvorianstvo.* Still, they often found it difficult to escape the earlier stereotype—of the narrow-minded sharp trader, engaged in questionable deals, the petty tyrant who ruled his family and employees with a heavy hand but whose mental horizons did not extend beyond the end of the bolt of cloth he held or the doors of his shop.

This gap between wealth and status caused the younger generations of many of the leading business families—Morozovs, Mamontovs, Guchkovs, Riabushinskys, Tretiakovs, Bakhrushins, Sabashnikovs, and others—to turn toward civic and cultural matters. Scions of the merchant elite began to focus on the city's governance and to develop various programs, private and public, designed to improve the well-being of its population. More visibly, they contributed much of their acquired wealth to found museums, theaters, artists' colonies, and educational institutions. They established newspapers, journals, and publishing houses that disseminated their political views and the fruits of the new culture they were fostering. Their achievements propelled Moscow forward and presaged an even brighter future.

But the elegant, exciting world of the Muscovite haute bourgeoisie, nobility, and educated elite rested on the back of an impoverished and increasingly restive working class. Moscow was a city of laboring immigrants, chiefly peasants who poured in from the rural hinterland looking for jobs and a better life. Some found what they sought, severed their village ties, and became permanent residents whose children acquired education and upward mobility. Not all of them were so lucky. Many workers migrated with the seasons between rural and urban worlds, never fully at home in either. Others, while staying longer in the city, failed to rise and were trapped in its lower depths, employed as day laborers when times were good but cast into destitution and beggary when jobs dried up.

Whatever their status, most members of Moscow's growing proletariat faced on-the-job conditions that were demeaning and dangerous—long hours, exposure to poisonous fumes, deafening noise, machines that might maim or kill—for miserly wages. And after their day's toil, workers often returned to dwellings that were barely fit for habitation. The influx of new residents strained Moscow's housing stock to the limit. Some workers slept at their place of employment, while others took their rest in barracks supplied by their bosses, who often crammed in as many people as they could. For those who lived away from the workplace, squalid basement apartments were common, marked by crowding, dirt, and limited sanitation.

The workers' diets intensified their general misery. Low pay limited most laborers to the poorest quality foodstuffs, and because many factory owners forced their employees to buy at company stores, workers often had to settle for questionable goods. In self-defense, some formed collectives to buy and prepare food. But the resulting meals were often monotonous and unpalatable. A worker with a steady job might not starve, but the diet sustaining him and his family lacked essential nutrients, especially protein, contributing to ill health, injuries, and high infant mortality.

Although most of Moscow's toilers lived on its outer fringes, they made their presence felt on its streets. Wage workers, domestic servants, day laborers, and apprentices comprised at least 40 percent of the population. And at the very heart of the city, not far from the upscale Arbat and Prechistenka neighborhoods, lay the infamous Khitrovo market and the squalid slum that surrounded it. "Khitrovka" was a pit of almost limitless degradation that came to symbolize the plight of the urban poor in industrializing Russia. Wretched flophouses provided "homes" for those on the lowest rung of Moscow society. Sordid dens flourished, lairs for criminals of every stripe: pimps, thieves, murderers. Khitrovka's filthy alleys swarmed with prostitutes, child beggars, the unemployed desperately seeking any kind of work, and those so broken that they were good for nothing.

Narcotics were readily available, but it was alcohol that spawned and sustained Khitrovka's depravity. The quarter seemed to float on it; its fumes poisoned the air. In Khitrovka, as in other working-class areas, the ancient "joy of the Russes" showed itself to be a national curse—fostering moral decay and crime, endangering public health, and threatening the good order of society. But for many it was the only relief from the pain that life had heaped upon them.[1]

When drunkenness—"the green snake"—was chiefly a feature of the village world, associated with weddings, feast days, and local celebrations, it had not greatly troubled state officials. But as peasants poured into the cities, the ill effects of vodka became increasingly visible. As early as the reign of Alexander II, the government considered introducing a vodka monopoly in order to better control alcohol production and consumption. Signed into law by Alexander III and implemented gradually after 1896, the monopoly was supposed to enable officials to monitor and control the amount and quality of spirits. Its powerful proponent, Minister of Finance Sergei Witte, believed that the measure would restrain drunkenness and promote the health and prosperity of the nation. A more sober workforce would increase the country's productivity and strengthen its position in the world.[2]

Russians and foreign observers furiously debated whether Witte's brainchild decreased vodka consumption or instead soaked the nation in spirits. But one thing is certain—the vodka monopoly fathered a host of unexpected consequences. It confined alcohol sales to state stores and closed down bars, but imbibers took to drinking on the streets and brought their vodka with them to tearooms and eating places. Bootlegging increased dramatically. Most embarrassing of all, the revenues generated by the vodka monopoly helped fill the state's coffers. The government vigorously denied that this was an intended result of the reform, but critics scoffed. Soon the issues of drinking, temperance, and prohibition became politicized, firing up public controversy as the empire entered the twentieth century.[3]

Perhaps anticipating the criticism of its vodka monopoly, the government created a national Guardianship of Public Sobriety designed to educate people about the dangers of excessive drinking and to encourage moderation, though not total abstinence. Plans called for guardianships in every province, with subordinate groups in the counties and bigger towns, while the empire's major cities, including Moscow and St. Petersburg, were to have their own special guardianships. The institutions spread rapidly. Within five years, there were 364 of them with a membership of some 15,000 persons, mostly state officials, church leaders, and prominent members of the local establishments.[4] Guardianships fostered the creation of "people's houses" (*narodnye doma*) as alternatives to taverns, places where workers and peasants could gather in an alcohol-free environment to eat, drink tea, and enjoy popular entertainments.[5]

Almost from the outset, the intelligentsia attacked the guardianships. The aim of encouraging only moderation ran counter to the "all-or-nothing" mentality of the more radical elements of the cultural elite. Devoted temperance advocates accused these organizations of subordinating the health of the people to the financial needs of the state, and because the guardianships used cheap food and popular entertainments to win people over, their foes reproached them for corrupting the lower classes with "bread and circuses." Finally, detractors noted that some of the tearooms set up by the guardianships often began to resemble the bars they were supposed to replace. The facts justified many (but by no means all) of the accusations, for the performance of most of these institutions fell far short of their stated aims. The government adamantly rejected the charges, however, and sought to make the guardianships in St. Petersburg and Moscow showcases for the program, ripostes to the regime's opponents in a struggle to win the hearts and minds of the public.[6]

But the significance of the guardianships was far greater than either temperance or propaganda. They were part of a larger effort by both government and the educated public to "civilize" urban life at the start of the new century. The impulse behind the guardianships did not differ substantially from that which drove the cultural elite to establish museums, charitable societies, literacy committees, and a variety of other organizations designed to reach and educate the people. The rapid influx of peasants forced Moscow, St. Petersburg, and many other Russian towns to confront men and women whose ways and mentalities ill suited them to an urban environment. These new residents suffered the effects of poverty and dislocation; unaltered, their manners and mores would undermine the quality of city life for all inhabitants; unmet, their discontents could threaten the state. Government officials and members of the civic-minded public, although often in apparent competition or conflict, sought a common goal: to accommodate and integrate the newcomers, to help them adjust to a different world, and to provide access, however slight, to the nation's higher culture.[7]

Whether Dzhunkovsky understood fully the importance being attached to the guardianships is uncertain, but he eagerly began his new assignment. Frustrated by years of semi-servile duty as the grand duke's adjutant, he was like a coiled spring suddenly released. The government scheduled the opening of Moscow's Guardianship for the summer of 1901, timed to coincide with the introduction of the liquor monopoly in that city, but well before this Dzhunkovsky started to develop his ideas for the organization.[8] As soon as he became assistant chairman, he asked his nominal superior,

General Bilderling, for leave to go to St. Petersburg where a guardianship had opened three and a half years earlier. There he could gain useful information to assist his own planning.

With Bilderling's permission, Dzhunkovsky left at once. In the capital he inspected the large "people's house" named in honor of Emperor Nicholas II and toured the theaters and soup kitchens the guardianship had opened throughout the city. The scale of the operation impressed him, but he saw serious flaws: too much time was spent entertaining the public, too little educating it; meals at the soup kitchens were priced beyond the means of laboring people. He decided that the Moscow organization should operate differently and, in addition to alcohol abuse, confront directly the problems of joblessness, poor diet, urban anomie, and the lack of cultural and educational opportunities.[9] Returning home, Dzhun pulled together the Moscow Guardianship's guiding committee, which included the chief of police, the head of the local gendarmes, the chairman of the Moscow Literacy Committee, the mayor, and two members of the city duma. He found an excellent director for the Guardianship's chancellery in Vasilii Sheremetev, and located its offices near the city's center, only ten minutes away from the governor-general's mansion.

General Bilderling and his second-in-command forged a genuine partnership, but one that allowed Dzhunkovsky to assume the dominant role, free from close day-to-day supervision. While deeply interested in the work of the Guardianship, Bilderling recognized Dzhunkovsky's talents and readily deferred to him. The letters he sent to his vice-chairman show him as fully supportive, eagerly encouraging his efforts.[10] Staff appointments were the only source of disputes. The general, Dzhun recalled, "was an extremely kind and tolerant person, he was unable to refuse, [a quality] that many people exploited, often recommending to him individuals who were unsuitable. In these cases, I attempted to oppose, which was . . . unpleasant for him. But he always gave in to me in the end."[11]

Bilderling and Dzhunkovsky agreed on the Moscow Guardianship's mission. "Love and concern for laboring people should be the foundation of the Guardianship's work," the general declared at its opening session on June 26, 1901, "and enlightenment should be the means by which that love is expressed." Workers would get cheap, wholesome entertainment, and reading rooms, libraries, and auditoria where they could gain access to knowledge. The Guardianship's "people's houses" would be places where they could eat and drink tea and develop "feelings of sociability" while refreshing themselves and enjoying human contact. They would draw workers away from bars and help to moderate alcohol consumption.[12]

These aims were fairly standard for guardianships throughout the country, but Dzhunkovsky designed an approach that gave the Moscow Guardianship its special character. He focused first of all on the material needs of the workers, and one of his early efforts was to open a much-needed soup kitchen in the dismal Khitrovo slum. In short order, he founded a "people's house" in the Gruziny district, complete with tearoom, library, and auditorium and subsequently opened another tearoom on Sukharnaia Square. These new establishments were instantly popular; within the first month of operation each drew over two hundred thousand client visits.[13] Dzhunkovsky rapidly expanded the Guardianship, and within a year he had opened thirteen "people's houses," mostly in working-class districts on the outskirts of town.[14] The dining rooms were spare but clean, and some even displayed a touch of elegance with white tablecloths. Dzhun regularly sampled the food to make sure it was not only inexpensive but good tasting and nutritious. Determined that these places maintain an exemplary order, he put army officers in charge, with good results.[15] Writing years later, he recalled that at the soup kitchen in Khitrovo, surrounded by slums and every conceivable vice, women employees worked in complete safety. When the soup kitchen closed for the night, male patrons escorted them through the tough neighborhood, and in the twelve years Dzhunkovsky worked with the Moscow Guardianship, not one of the women was assaulted or injured.[16]

Within a year Dzhunkovsky had made such a remarkable beginning that Edith Sellers, a visiting British journalist whose reportage focused on the conditions of the poor throughout Europe, pronounced his work "a brilliant success" in an article she wrote for the *Contemporary Review.* With Dzhun as her guide, Sellers toured the Guardianship's facilities, impressed by his enormous energy, which, she wrote, "carried everything before it." "Thanks to him," Sellers maintained, "the Moscow workers are to-day better catered for than any other workers in the Empire—far better than the London workers—and . . . in some respects they are provided for more generously." She praised the cleanliness and pleasant ambience of the soup kitchens, lauding the quality and "marvelously low" cost of the food they served. But Sellers informed her readers that the Guardianship did much more than simply fill the workers' stomachs. In the Khitrovo district it had set up a labor bureau "where what can be done is done that men may not stand idle in the market place because no man hireth them, while there is work to be done."[17]

Sellers highlighted the Guardianship's educational role, particularly its libraries and reading rooms that Margarita Sabashnikova, a Dzhunkovsky appointee, skillfully managed. They were "charming resorts," Sellers wrote, nicely decorated "with quite the air of a gentleman's study," well supplied with newspapers and able to lend books. The Guardianship also sponsored concerts, lectures, and theatrical presentations. The British journalist could barely contain her enthusiasm for this aspect of the project: "It would be difficult . . . to over-estimate the value of the work the Moscow Committee is doing in bringing instruction within the reach of all classes," she gushed, "trying to give at least a touch of interest and pleasure, sweetness and light, to lives fraught with hardship and gloom."[18]

Sellers may have developed a mild crush on the dynamic "Captain Djounkovsky"; he is the only figure whose individual work for the guardianships she discussed in her article. But her infatuation, if such it was, did not prevent Sellers from being an observant journalist. She was keenly interested in an "experiment" several of the people's houses were undertaking, which she felt might "pave the way for a solution of one of the most difficult problems with which Russia is today face to face."[19]

Sellers wrote that city authorities, at the behest of Grand Duke Sergei Alexandrovich, had permitted workers from several of the city's factories to gather at the restaurants of four people's houses to "take council together" and to listen to lectures and discussions about the labor question. In the eyes of some, Sellers noted, these meetings appeared "quite revolutionary and dangerous" and had become "a sharp thorn in the flesh of the whole capitalist community."[20]

Sellers attended two gatherings (probably accompanied by Dzhunkovsky) but saw nothing threatening. At the first, several hundred workers listened, "with an eagerness that was almost painful," to a lecture on the history of English trade unionism. Many of them were "terribly dirty," the air in the hall "simply appalling," yet the men understood and clearly approved of the speaker's emphasis on the law-abiding character of the English labor movement. They applauded "to the echo" when the lecturer urged them to follow the British example. A second meeting focused on improving the conditions of workers in Russia. Here "the quite surprising intelligence of the men" struck Sellers, as did their "moderation and sound common sense." She witnessed no expressions of "class-animosity" or "extravagance" in their opinions. "All that they asked," the journalist reported, "was that labour might be allowed to organize itself into unions so as to be able to treat with capitalists on more equal terms than at present." True, one of the men, who "by his face . . . might have been a poet," raised the issue of expanding education. Another asked that the government supply workers with information "as to the wages their employers could afford to pay them, to tell them when the said employers were clearing, as they sometimes do, a profit of 30 per cent., while doling out to their employés perhaps a shilling a day." To Sellers, the whole exercise seemed entirely benign. She wrote that by letting their facilities be used for such meetings the members of the Guardianship had "given a strong proof of their sympathy with the workers and of their determination to help them in all possible ways."[21]

Sellers's account of the workers' gatherings was both generally accurate and delightfully naive, for it missed "the story behind the story." The British journalist had witnessed something much more than a well-intentioned effort to help Moscow's laborers better their lot. It was a small bet in a high-stakes gamble by progovernment forces designed to win the working class, now seen as increasingly dangerous, and lead it in a loyal, nonviolent direction. Dzhunkovsky and the Moscow Guardianship had enlisted in a fateful struggle with a rising revolutionary movement through what became known as *zubatovshchina*, the Zubatov experiment.

Until the late 1870s the imperial government largely ignored the problems posed by a growing urban workforce, convinced that Russia was on a special path, certain to avoid the class conflict and political turmoil currently shaking and transforming Western Europe. Russia would not have a proletariat; those who labored in her factories were and would remain peasants, linked to the land, devoted to the tsar, ardent in their Orthodox faith. But the last two decades of the nineteenth century rapidly undercut such sanguine assumptions. A distinct industrial working class was forming; its manifest discontents demanded action.[22]

As early as 1882 Russian legislation timidly began to regulate factory conditions. Still, authorities denied workers the right to organize or strike, and by the end of the 1890s an increasingly disgruntled labor force proved more and more receptive to propaganda spread by small revolutionary groups. The hopes of radicals, thwarted during the 1880s, revived after the famine of 1891. Those who would raise the world on new foundations now focused on the growing proletariat.[23]

Despite a present and rapidly clarifying danger, the imperial government failed to develop a unified approach. The powerful Ministry of Finance, eager to foster Russia's industrialization, urged policies that, while not indifferent to the workers' needs, favored their employers. It sanctioned the suppression of strikes, by force if necessary, and resisted calls for government intervention in labor disputes. But the Ministry of Internal Affairs (MVD), charged with maintaining public order, took a different stand. Local police frequently criticized management whose treatment of workers seemed to provoke their discontent. Provincial governors, drawn from the landed gentry, were often appalled by the unfamiliar factory conditions they saw when trying to end strikes and labor violence. The MVD's gendarmes regularly arrested radicals who spread seditious propaganda among the workers, but some of their leaders proposed to keep factory hands and other laborers loyal by more paternalistic means.[24]

One of these was Sergei Zubatov, the brilliant chief of the Moscow Security Bureau. A former radical who had become a sincere, even fanatical monarchist, Zubatov believed that the autocracy stood above classes and was the only force able to bring both peace and progress to the empire. During the 1890s Zubatov reformed the security police, increased the effectiveness of its surveillance techniques, and nurtured a small but potent cadre of secret informants within the revolutionary parties. The Moscow bureau became the nerve center of the tsar's security forces, and Zubatov extended the methods he had developed there to other parts of the country. Government agents were soon delivering powerful blows to radical organizations.

Zubatov knew that these measures alone could not end sedition. Radical groups would regroup and continue to gain influence in the ranks of the working class whose illegal strikes and demonstrations increased as the century waned. But Zubatov believed that the workers were instinctively loyal to the monarchy. Properly enlightened, they would see that the tsar and his government had their best interests in mind and could assist them in gaining fair treatment from their employers. They would then spurn the radicals and become a force for stability.[25]

Zubatov carefully studied the labor movement in Western Europe where developments in Germany particularly impressed him. Otto von

Bismarck's policies showed that the state could reduce the workers' discontent by social welfare measures. The growing appeal of the socialist Eduard Bernstein's ideas further suggested that the workers' economic struggle might lead them away from revolution and toward peaceful change. In the mid-1890s Zubatov developed plans to apply these observations to Russia. Backed by Grand Duke Sergei Alexandrovich, he began an experiment in Moscow.

Zubatov's audacious and innovative program had three distinct features. First, it created a few officially sanctioned workers' organizations. These were not real trade unions, but they could enable the workers to pressure their bosses for economic gains while the security police carefully monitored their activities. Second, the program tried to educate workers, providing them with lectures of a broad cultural nature as well as ones specifically focused on the reformist labor movements abroad. Third, the Zubatov experiment mobilized labor in support of the autocracy, inculcating the idea that the tsar was the true protector of working people.

In this latter effort, Zubatov gained his most dramatic and visible success. On February 19, 1902, the labor organizations he had helped to form brought out between 30,000 and 80,000 workers in a peaceful demonstration honoring the memory of Emperor Alexander II and the peasant emancipation of 1861. Led by Grand Duke Sergei, they gathered reverently before the tsar-liberator's statue in the Kremlin. Church dignitaries performed a requiem mass while the crowd laid wreaths, said prayers for the imperial family, and listened respectfully to the national hymn "God Save the Tsar." At the end of the ceremonies, the grand duke thanked the workers and their thunderous "hurrahs" echoed off the stones of the ancient seat of Russia's government.[26]

Zubatov's accomplishments alarmed both ends of the political spectrum. For the radicals, especially the Social Democrats, they raised the specter of a labor movement captured by the defenders of autocracy. But the spectacle of workers freed to organize and struggle for economic goals, albeit under government auspices, frightened Russia's industrialists and political conservatives who believed Zubatov was conjuring uncontrollable forces that threatened the empire's social and political order. In response to Zubatov's challenge, the revolutionaries, not least among them the young Vladimir Lenin, sought to increase organizational discipline, to perfect conspiratorial techniques, and to heighten the revolutionary consciousness of workers.[27] For their part, conservatives soon made their concerns about

Zubatov known to the tsar and his ministers in St. Petersburg and lobbied hard to bring him down.

Zubatov's conservative enemies proved to be the greatest threat. Indeed, only the strong support of Grand Duke Sergei allowed the experiment in Moscow to continue as long as it did. At the end of 1902 the MVD transferred Zubatov to a higher post in St. Petersburg where he tried to develop programs like those he had pioneered in the ancient capital. By this time, however, Zubatov's foes had grown too powerful. Within a year they engineered his dismissal, but the empire would feel the impact of his efforts for years to come.[28]

Zubatovshchina is usually discussed in the context of the imperial government's struggle against the revolutionary movement. But it should also be seen as one more effort by the educated classes to uplift and "civilize" newly urbanized social groups. These educative and integrative features of the Zubatov experiment created a natural link with the work of the Moscow Guardianship and its "people's houses." The demonstration on February 19, 1902, that Zubatov helped to engineer impressed Dzhunkovsky.[29] Like Sergei Alexandrovich, he believed workers' organizations could be a positive force if they were guided by those who sought to strengthen government authority. Initially, he was willing to let "people's houses" of the Guardianship be used for lectures that made workers aware of developments in the labor movement abroad and for discussions of their conditions at home. He continued this practice well after Zubatov had left Moscow. But he felt that these programs should always be secondary to broader goals: raising the intellectual and cultural level of workers and improving the material quality of their lives.

Consequently, Dzhunkovsky concentrated the Guardianship's efforts on the soup kitchens, teahouses, and educational ventures that always enjoyed the greatest popularity with the public. In 1904 clients of the canteens and tearooms made 6.5 million visits while workers' meetings drew fewer than 20,000. Visits to the Guardianship's reading rooms and libraries were just over 240,000; while 127,000 spectators watched its theatrical performances, 26,000 attended lectures with slides, and 6,000 studied at Sunday schools and evening classes.[30] Nor did the Moscow Guardianship neglect the medical aspects of alcoholism. Beginning in 1903 it set up an ambulatory clinic to treat those addicted to drink and began to gather information on the reasons for dependency. By 1912 more than 15,000 people had obtained care under its auspices.[31]

Although Dzhunkovsky focused the Moscow Guardianship on meeting the material and purely cultural needs of the workers, the steady growth of political radicalism inevitably intruded on its activities. Theatrical performances sponsored by the Guardianship, designed to arouse patriotic feelings in their audiences, brought large numbers of working people together and gave revolutionaries the chance to agitate. Upon leaving the theater, attendees sometimes gathered to listen to radical orators and occasionally formed tight circles around the speakers, protecting them from arrest.[32]

Similar developments ultimately led Dzhunkovsky to curtail the workers' meetings at the Guardianship's facilities. He regularly attended these gatherings, and as Sellers's article suggests, his initial attitude was favorable. Over time, however, Dzhun grew disenchanted by what he saw. The positive messages most speakers offered seemed lost on the majority of the audience who listened without real understanding. Dzhunkovsky did not specifically mention workers' radicalism, but he noted in his memoirs that the meetings started to display less "honesty . . . [and] began to produce a different and more unpleasant impression on me than they had at first." By the end of 1904 he concluded that "nothing sensible" was likely to result and decided to end the experiment gradually.[33] Events that would soon occur in St. Petersburg showed that his caution was fully justified.

Dzhunkovsky's work at the Moscow Guardianship gave him new purpose and a solid understanding of the working class and its needs. But it soon began to strain his relations with Grand Duke Sergei. Dzhun had long chafed in his largely empty court role, but now that real, meaningful work was at hand his unhappiness grew. While his affection for Sergei and Ella remained undiminished, being de facto head of the Moscow Guardianship made him feel more independent. This became clear in the fall of 1902, when an incident affecting both the Romanov and Dzhunkovsky families led Vladimir to take an action that could have had disastrous results.

In October 1902 Sergei's brother, Grand Duke Pavel Alexandrovich, married Olga Pistolkors, a divorced woman, not of a European ruling house. This morganatic union, undertaken without prior permission, caused Nicholas II to strip his uncle of all his offices, put his properties in a trusteeship, and banish him from Russia. The emperor appointed Sergei and Ella guardians of Pavel's children, Maria and Dmitrii, who had been living for the most part in St. Petersburg under the care of Dzhunkovsky's sister Evdokiia. This stunning development alarmed Dzhun who feared a serious mismatch. Evdokiia, he thought, "could not get along with the despotic character of Sergei Alexandrovich."[34]

Dzhunkovsky now did something he quickly came to regret, an act that would have been unthinkable without his newly acquired self-confidence. On October 26, he wrote the grand duke, then traveling in Italy, expressing his concerns about the situation. He suggested that Sergei not transfer Pavel's children from their familiar circumstances to new quarters and new situations. Given the trauma caused by their father's marriage, he argued, a sudden change might have undesirable consequences. He urged the grand duke to leave Maria and Dmitrii undisturbed in his sister's care.

Dzhunkovsky's letter provoked a sharp response: "Children *ought not* and *cannot* live *outside the family*," the grand duke replied sternly. "In the present painful situation, only my wife and I, albeit partially, can take the place of their parents. This is so *entirely* clear and understandable that there can be no two opinions about it. You, of course, did not think about all this when you wrote me. Permit me, however, to give you one piece of advice: Never interfere in the *family* affairs of others."[35]

Dzhunkovsky realized he had made a mistake that might forever spoil his relations with the grand ducal couple. Even as he considered what to do, he received a letter from Vladimir Gadon who had accompanied Sergei and Ella abroad. Gadon advised his friend to write at once to make amends. Letting matters stand would do neither Dzhun nor his sister any good.

Dzhunkovsky quickly sent the grand duke an abject apology: "What is especially painful to me," he lamented, "what now gives me no peace, is that in this terribly difficult time for you, I could have . . . added more bitterness to what you are [now] living through. I cannot forgive myself for this and it hurts me terribly." He told Sergei that he impatiently awaited his return, hoping that his misstep had not destroyed the goodwill the grand duke had always shown him. "You know, Your Highness, how tightly my spiritual happiness is bound to my good relations with you and the grand duchess. Once again, Your Highness, forgive me for my letter and, if it is possible, forget it."[36]

Sergei's affection for Dzhunkovsky was such that he let the matter pass. The duke's reply reassured him that the bond between them had not been ruptured, and Dzhun soon found that his fears about Sergei's imperious nature were groundless. Although the grand duke and duchess moved Maria and Dmitrii to Moscow, Sergei's relations with Evdokiia were "delicate and courteous to the highest degree." He gave her virtually complete independence, and the children's upbringing proceeded along the lines she set without interruption.[37]

In his memoirs Dzhunkovsky does not reflect on the lessons learned from this incident, but his detailed account suggests its importance. Certainly it made him aware of how jealously members of the Romanov dynasty guarded those things they believed belonged solely to the family. That Dzhunkovsky knew of their extreme sensitivity only heightens our understanding of the desperation he must have felt when, in the summer of 1915, he again risked intervening in Romanov family matters, this time to attack a trusted "friend." It was an act he hoped might save the monarchy, but which, instead, brought his government career to an end.

As Dzhunkovsky made a satisfying transition from courtier to administrator, he suffered painful changes in his personal life. Although 1898 marked the end to any immediate hopes he had of Nina Evreinova obtaining a divorce from her husband, his love and concern for her endured. In the years that followed, Nina was often unwell, and then, shortly after Dzhunkovsky had begun his work at the Guardianship, he learned that Aleksei Evreinov was gravely ill with cancer. A letter from Nina's brother Sergei Sabashnikov, dated December 2, 1902, informed him that both Evreinovs were sick; but while Nina was in the hospital recovering, the prospects for her husband were grim. Aleksei's "organism," Sergei wrote, "is extremely exhausted, and cannot long continue its struggle with death."[38]

By midsummer 1903 Evreinov's end was fast approaching, and his impending death seems to have called up a mixture of emotions in his wife: sorrow tinged, one suspects, with a measure of guilt. Katya Balmont, who was with Nina at this time, must have conveyed to her husband some of the feelings her close friend expressed, and the poet, in turn, inquired how Dzhun was faring: "You, of course, can imagine what is taking place in N.V.'s soul," he wrote. "I would like to know what is going on in yours. Life plays strangely with us, and I, as an artist, gaze with *a stern sympathy* on the pale faces of the players."[39]

Evreinov died in 1903, and next year Dzhunkovsky asked Nina to be his wife. But, for reasons that remain unclear, she refused. One source claims that Nina's oldest son, Vladimir, opposed the union, although it seems unlikely that the resistance of a seventeen-year-old would have prevented a marriage Nina truly wanted.[40] Her health, both emotional and physical, was frail; the prospects of a second marriage, following quickly in the wake of one that had been so unhappy, may not have been attractive to her. Religious scruples likely influenced Nina's decision. Her romantic involvement with Dzhunkovsky, even if never physically consummated, had been an act of infidelity for which she may have had serious regrets. Denying herself, and the man who loved her, the joys of matrimony would be a way to assuage that guilt.

No matter what reasons she may have had or given, Nina's rejection of Dzhunkovsky's proposal left him crushed. He tried to conceal his pain from Evdokiia, confiding it in a letter to his brother Nikolai. But Kolya passed Vadya's note on, and as she had done so often, Dodo poured out her affection: "May God help you. My dear, have no doubt that your sorrow is my sorrow, and if it is easier for you to be silent then we will be silent. But when you want to open your soul, you will find in me sincere and heartfelt sympathy."[41]

For a while, Dzhunkovsky simply withdrew, staying in Moscow on his name day in 1904, which he might otherwise have celebrated on the Evreinov estate at Borshchen. Balmont, who was there at the time, expressed his own sadness: "Dear Dzhun, I congratulate you on the day of your Angel and with all my heart wish you greater joy and happiness than that which a niggardly fate has sent you. . . . I am sorry that you will not come here. Maybe it's wrong for me to talk about it, but you know how I look on former circumstances, and I am truly sorry that the person who more than any other deserves happiness, is deprived of it."[42] In the end, Dzhunkovsky's wounds healed. Always drawn to women he could not have, he slipped into the familiar and comfortable role of "cavaliere servente," a constant friend, patron, and protector of Nina and her children. His deep Christian faith undoubtedly helped him to accept his disappointment, and it is almost certain that he felt a measure of guilt. By entering another man's house as a friend and then pursuing his wife, Dzhunkovsky had broken more than one of the Ten Commandments, failed to follow the family motto, *Deo et proximo*, and had proved untrue to the knightly values he learned at the Corps of Pages. How could this devout

Christian not realize that he had committed adultery in his heart, if not in the flesh?

Dzhunkovsky's memoirs and papers tell us almost nothing about these strictly private matters, however. Nor do they reveal much about another painful event taking place during the same time: the breakdown of his relations with Konstantin Balmont. The bond between the two men had always been an unlikely one. The brilliant, volatile poet with radical leanings seems mismatched with the stable, pedestrian, deeply religious courtier, whose loyalty to tsar and fatherland was ardent and unshakable. Yet the friendship was real, based not on intellectual equality or common views but on the love they felt for the two women who were lifelong soul mates. The trials Balmont and Dzhunkovsky shared in the 1890s as they pursued their romantic hopes had created strong affection between them. This is obvious in the tone of the letters Balmont sent to Dzhun over the course of a decade. The notes were warm and concerned, although a bit condescending; the writer did not share his poetry or his ideas. And while correspondence from Vladimir is lacking, it is hard to believe that the poet would have maintained the feelings he expressed had they not been reciprocated.

But the rise in antigovernment sentiment in the first years of the twentieth century led to the friends' estrangement. On March 4, 1901, police broke up a demonstration at the Kazan Cathedral in St. Petersburg, killing several students and provoking nationwide indignation. Balmont shared the outrage, and on March 14, publicly read his thinly veiled satirical lyric "The Little Sultan," aimed at the tsar. "It was in Turkey, where conscience is an empty thing," the poem began, "there rule the fist, the whip, the scimitar, / two or three zeros, four bastards / and one stupid little sultan." The defenders of "freedom, faith and knowledge," who gathered only to be dispersed by a gang of "bashi-bazouks," called upon a poet to show them the way out of "their dark sorrows." The poet's reply—"He who can speak, let his word breathe the spirit, / and he who is not deaf, let him attend, / or if not—the dagger"—threatened violence.[43] In response, the police forbade Balmont to reside in the capitals, major cities, or university towns for three years.[44]

Balmont repaired to Kursk province where he wrote verses for one of his most famous volumes, "We Will Be Like the Sun" (*Budem kak solntse*). But he realized that his act of lese majesty had offended Dzhunkovsky, and at year's end the poet tried to make amends:

O dear Dzhun! We have been too very close for anything to change between us, because of me or because of you. I love you the same, as always; and I cannot accept the thought that you have changed your feelings toward me. Aren't we the same people . . . ? Everywhere and always you will be the same, and everywhere and always I will be true to you. In the name of that loyalty—without you and with you and completely alone—I drink to your health. . . .

P.S. It was always good for me when I was with you. . . . I am happy that I have known you. I am happy in the knowledge that you exist. All the rest is nonsense.[45]

A few days later, the poet sent Dzhun best wishes for the New Year in the same vein: "I only know one thing—I truly loved and love you. I am glad that in difficult moments . . . I inevitably remember you. . . . Everything, almost everything, connected to you in my memory is good."[46]

It appears that Balmont's efforts to mend the rupture with Dzhun were successful for a time. In early 1902, shortly before a brief trip abroad, the poet felt free to write his friend asking for help in regard to some problems he was having with the police who were blocking his attempt to visit Moscow.[47] After his return to Russia Balmont invited Dzhunkovsky to some of the literary gatherings he regularly held at his Moscow apartment. The poet and novelist Andrei Belyi remembered the dark-haired, ruddy, youthful-looking soldier with the red cap band and silver braid who sat against the wall and did not utter a word.[48] Still the breach continued to widen.

On February 23, 1903, Dzhunkovsky attended a meeting of the Moscow University Society of the Lovers of Russian Literature (Obshchestvo liubitelei rossiiskoi solvesnosti pri Moskovskom universitete). Balmont was speaking at a session honoring the memory of Nikolai Nekrasov, whose marvelous lyrics celebrated the Russian people and the beauties of nature but who also saw the country's darker side. In one of his most famous works, "Vcherashnyi den,' chasu v shestom," he proclaimed that a peasant girl, beaten with the knout, was the true sister of his Muse. Balmont's talk emphasized Nekrasov's radicalism. "The unavoidable injury, the feel of the branding irons—that is the key to the poetry of Nekrasov," he announced. "For the sake of the many he took upon himself a great burden . . . and disrupted the crystal world of poetic feelings to give forth a cry that both warns and threatens. Life wounded him, and he consciously deepened that wound. It left him with an irremovable scar, and he intentionally kept the pain of that scar alive in order to remember those who were and would be wounded again and again." Nekrasov stood in the ranks of the nation's greatest poets—Pushkin, Lermontov, Tiutchev, Fet, Koltsov, and Baratynsky—Balmont concluded, but he possessed a special voice: "his is a ceaseless shout of pain and indignation. Through him we learn from our earliest days that there are prisons and hospitals, garrets and cellars; down to this day he tells us that now, in this very moment, as we breathe here, there are people out there who suffocate."[49]

Dzhunkovsky was offended. "[Balmont] spoke nervously and in an extremely provocative manner," he wrote in his memoirs. "He treated Nekrasov in a condescending and silly way. Many of his phrases strained for effect . . . ; without any need at all he repeatedly spoke of the lash that whistled through the air, raining blows on a helpless woman." Dzhun found Balmont's concluding peroration about those out in the world who were suffocating "completely stupid," and he remembered: "These words even called forth a smile from many [listeners] since the air in the hall was unbearable due to the heat." He left the lecture filled with "very unpleasant impressions."[50]

Dzhunkovsky's growing disenchantment with his friend certainly stemmed from his own conservatism and his anger at the poet's attacks on the tsar. But it also reflected his increased self-confidence and the condescension that a man of action can sometimes feel for a man of letters. Balmont lamented the conditions of the poor, but all he could offer was the balm of words. Dzhunkovsky believed that his own work in the Guardianship had already bettered conditions for those who suffocated in the garrets and the cellars that Nekrasov had depicted and Balmont had decried.

Both men struggled to keep their friendship alive. Balmont's sympathetic letters to Dzhun at the time of Nina's rejection of his marriage proposal are a clear sign that the poet's feelings were still warm. And as late as August 1905, Balmont believed their relationship was strong enough to support a serious request.[51] But when Russia's first revolution erupted, Balmont would cast his lot with the rebellion and even played a small role during the armed uprising that shook Moscow in December. Shortly thereafter, threatened with arrest, he went abroad and wrote poems that heaped abuse on the tsar and his minions.[52] He did not return home until 1913. Through it all, Balmont seems to have retained much of his fondness for Dzhun; in 1919, when Vladimir was on trial for his life, the poet would stand in his corner. For Dzhunkovsky, however, the breach was final. His memoir's account of his former friend is cold, referring to him always as "The poet Balmont." Despite his strong Christian moral sense, it seems Dzhun could not forgive Balmont his trespasses. Writing in the 1920s, when he knew that the poet had abandoned his revolutionary enthusiasm and had publicly supported him, Dzhunkovsky chose not to recall in any detail the closeness and affection they had once shared.[53]

The rupture of Dzhunkovsky's friendship with Balmont reflected the conflicts rending the society around them. Russia had entered an age of violence, a kind of civil war that would continue, with brief interruptions, for almost half a century. In February 1901, a radical student shot to death Nikolai Bogolepov, the minister of education; a year later Dmitrii Sipiagin, the minister of internal affairs, died at an assassin's hand. In the spring of 1902, peasant uprisings rocked the provinces of Poltava, Kharkov, and Saratov; authorities used soldiers and beatings to suppress them. Student disturbances and strikes erupted, and in March 1903 government troops fired on workers in Zlatoust, killing more than forty. A month later, the Bessarabian city of Kishinev exploded in a savage anti-Semitic pogrom; rampaging mobs raped and slaughtered.

Foreign policy blunders made things worse. Russia's push into Manchuria and Korea provoked hostility in Japan, and on January 27, 1904, a Japanese attack on Port Arthur, a Russian naval base in China, plunged the empire into a conflict it was ill equipped to fight. Some in the tsar's government may have hoped that a "victorious little war" would silence dissent. But as defeat followed defeat, the social and political tensions that had been building began to boil over, energizing political opposition of all stripes. In a nationwide "banquet campaign," foes of the existing order called for a constitutional regime, and radicals unleashed a wave of terrorist attacks. The Socialist Revolutionary Party's Combat Organization sent out a team headed by Boris Savinkov and on July 15 succeeded in assassinating Viacheslav Pleve, the harsh and unpopular minister of internal affairs. Shaken, Nicholas II offered the public broad reforms. But his ukase of December 12 did not provide for some form of national representation and so did little to calm the growing opposition.[54]

Dzhunkovsky watched these developments with increasing concern. He hoped that war with Japan could be avoided, but when it came he had no doubts about the justice of the Russian cause. More disturbing than the war, however, was the reaction of Moscow's lower classes to its outbreak. Initially, enthusiastic throngs greeted the event and gathered before the governor-general's house to shout "Hurrah." But soon things took a dangerous turn and signs of class warfare appeared. "Crowds went about the streets forcing all [they met] to take off their caps [and] get down on their knees, in a word, they behaved like hooligans, many were drunk."[55]

The sight of troops heading off to war made Dzhunkovsky want to join them. He envied those who "would share all the work, hardships and dangers of our front lines." Still, he felt that he could not leave the service of the grand duke in such perilous times.[56] He helped organize medical assistance for the soldiers, and soon his responsibilities at the Guardianship increased when General Bilderling was mobilized and his replacement proved even more detached from the work of the institution than his predecessor. Then in October, Vladimir Gadon took command of the Preobrazhensky Guards regiment. His final departure from the grand duke's service saddled Dzhun with still greater obligations to Sergei and Ella.[57]

News from the front became worse; tensions rose in Moscow. Opposition groups announced major demonstrations for December 5 and 6, 1904, and the Socialist Revolutionaries threatened to assassinate officials who used force against them.[58] At that moment, Sergei was in St. Petersburg, and Dzhunkovsky assumed responsibility for security at the governor-general's house. He handled the assignment carefully, and fortunately when the police broke up demonstrations in front of the mansion only a few student participants were hurt.[59]

Toward the end of December, Sergei asked the tsar to let him retire as governor-general, while retaining command of the Moscow military district. He strongly opposed the reformist policies of Prince Sviatopolk-Mirsky, Pleve's successor at the Ministry of Internal Affairs and was alarmed by the prospect of terrorist attacks.[60] The grand duke's relief at laying down the burdens of office was understandable; still, Dzhunkovsky was disappointed in his patron. "I felt it showed faint-heartedness on his part to quit his post at such a serious moment, under the pressure of threats," he recalled. "I felt badly for him . . . but could not bring myself to say anything—his life was in danger."[61] Not surprisingly, Vladimir was both honored and troubled when Sergei asked him to continue as his personal adjutant.

Dzhunkovsky made his feelings clear in a personal letter. He thanked Sergei for his trust and apologized for not being the adjutant that the grand duke needed because other duties pulled him away. "I constantly think about this and it always distresses me," he wrote. Dzhun agreed to remain "in the full knowledge of my uselessness" but asked the grand duke's indulgence: "It grieves me even now to realize that in the future I will not be able to meet your needs. [Please] understand that to serve exclusively as an adjutant is not for me. . . . I cannot live without serious work." He had to be free to devote himself to the Guardianship.[62]

Sergei agreed to Dzhunkovsky's conditions, and it seemed that things would go on almost as before. But in the gathering political and social storm, Dzhun must have sensed that the tumultuous events rapidly changing the nation would soon envelop him. He could not have anticipated how suddenly and with what explosive force they would transform his life.

Part Two

Alarms and Civil Strife, 1905

Chapter 5

Storm Signals

THE PLATFORM OF MOSCOW'S NICHOLAS RAILROAD STATION was crowded the evening after New Year 1905, as travelers hastened to catch the night train for St. Petersburg while families and friends gathered to see them off. Dzhunkovsky was there together with a large group of officials that included Dmitrii Trepov, the recently retired chief of police. They were accompanying Grand Duke Sergei Alexandrovich who was headed to the capital for a brief visit.

The grand duke had hardly entered his wagon-lit, when a shot exploded. Dzhunkovsky spun around to see Trepov doing what appeared to be a kind of jig, dancing first left, then right. Three paces in front of him stood a young man, wearing a student's cap, revolver in hand. Dzhun and the other officials froze, dumbfounded, as the youth fired two more rounds point blank. Then an alert gendarme rushed over, grabbed the shooter's arm, and quickly subdued him.[1] The bullets meant for Trepov buried themselves in a wall, and he escaped unhurt. But the incident could not easily be dismissed. Dangerous days lay ahead, and the singular event Dzhun had just witnessed soon became a terrifying commonplace.

The Russian empire appeared anything but calm. "You could feel a powerful turbulence," Dzhunkovsky remembered, "and although the government had already of its own accord moved . . . toward . . . reforms, in the eyes of the Russian public they were not enough. Step by step society was becoming revolutionized."[2] The decision of Grand Duke Sergei to relinquish the governor-generalship of Moscow reflected the ominous mood: unease gripped the country's rulers and splits had developed within the government. For the most part, however, life in the ancient capital was proceeding normally. On January 4, 1905, a party at the Grand Moscow Hotel honored the zemstvo doctors of the province; on January 8, a gathering at the Hotel Prague celebrated V. K. Lavrov, the respected editor and publisher of the journal *Russkaya mysl'* (Russian Thought), on his twenty-fifth year in journalism, while at Moscow University, preparations were under way to commemorate its sesquicentennial.[3] But in St. Petersburg troubles were escalating, outrage over the unsuccessful war with Japan and long-simmering worker discontent produced an explosive situation, with as many as a hundred thousand men and women on strike. Then on January 9, Sergei Zubatov's "police socialism," which a few years before had brushed by Dzhunkovsky and the Guardianship, gave rise to a fateful tragedy.

After his transfer to St. Petersburg in 1902, Zubatov tried to re-create the kind of workingmen's associations that had been so successful in Moscow. He soon discovered Gregorii Gapon, a young Orthodox priest whose own plebian background gave him a strong affinity for the workers, great concern for their welfare, and the ability to guide their behavior. Deeply religious and fanatically loyal to the tsar, Gapon seemed the ideal figure to put at the head of a police-sponsored labor organization. Before his sudden dismissal in August 1903, Zubatov had already made Father Gapon his protégé, and the fall of the priest's patron did little damage to his standing with either the workers or government officials. Authorities permitted Gapon to found the St. Petersburg Assembly of Factory and Mill Workers, which quickly gained considerable independence and influence. During the brief liberal "spring" that followed the assassination of Pleve, his successor, Prince Sviatopolk-Mirsky, gave Gapon and his organization further latitude.

In the strained circumstances of early January 1905, Gapon tried to bring workers and the tsar together. He organized a march on the Winter Palace to present Nicholas with a petition expressing, in loyal and humble tones, the needs and hopes of his toiling subjects. On Sunday, January 9, some thirty thousand workers accompanied by their wives and children, surged along various routes toward the Winter Palace. "Sovereign! . . . We are impoverished; our employers oppress us, overburden us with work, insult us, consider us inhuman," their plea began. "We have reached that terrible moment when death is preferable to the continuance of unbearable suffering."[4] They hoped they would not meet resistance but were prepared to face it if it came.

Government forces sought to bar the workers' way. At several points soldiers fired into the crowds and disrupted processions, but the workers pressed on. Large numbers reached the vicinity of Palace Square, where around two o'clock, troops of the Preobrazhensky Guards, commanded by Dzhunkovsky's close friend, Vladimir Gadon, unleashed several volleys followed by cavalry attacks. As many as forty men, women, and children died on the spot, while across the city government forces took similar steps to "restore order." By evening "Bloody Sunday," as the day would be forever called, had claimed between 150 and 200 lives and left perhaps 800 wounded. The image of Tsar Nicholas was irreparably tarnished, and shock waves rolled across the country.[5]

Dzhunkovsky was horrified by the disaster, but he did not blame the tsar. *Zubatovshchina* had gone off the rails in St. Petersburg, and the massacre was the result. The experiment with "police socialism" had begun in Moscow, but there its dangers had been recognized and, as he put it, "quickly liquidated, or more accurately rendered harmless." Dzhun sympathized with the St. Petersburg workers but felt that they had been victimized by Gapon, "a cunning, aggressive man." Gapon had used "deceptive means" to manipulate them into undertaking a "provocative march" that led to the tragedy. "As a result," he believed, "Gapon got what he wanted—the events of January 9 were transmitted to all corners of Russia in the most distorted form, everywhere these rumors inspired the circles of the discontented, increased them, revolutionized them."[6]

In the wake of Bloody Sunday, the response of the tsar and his chief officials was hopelessly muddled and inconsistent. Nicholas accepted the resignation of Prince Sviatopolk-Mirsky and replaced him as head of the Ministry of Internal Affairs with Alexander Bulygin, who seemed likely to continue his predecessor's conciliatory policies. At about the same time, however, Nicholas appointed Dmitrii Trepov, a fierce hard-liner, governor-general of St. Petersburg and later made him assistant minister of internal affairs with nationwide authority over the police. Bulygin and Trepov had both served in Moscow under Grand Duke Sergei but were of decidedly different stamps. The differences between these men showed the government to be of two minds in the face of Russia's rapidly growing crisis.

The tsar revealed himself to be equally uncertain in dealing with the labor unrest that now spread from the capital across the country, at one point involving as many as four hundred thousand workers. Orders from the capital demanded that local authorities take "decisive measures" against strikers, and many arrests followed. Simultaneously, Nicholas clumsily attempted conciliation, meeting with a carefully selected delegation of workers and "forgiving" them for Bloody Sunday. On a more hopeful note, the government pressed employers to make significant concessions to their employees and established two commissions to investigate the "labor question" and suggest reforms.[7]

Uncertainty at the top was reflected in Moscow, where the first months of 1905 found its administration in disarray. When Grand Duke Sergei stepped down at the beginning of January, the tsar left the post of governor-general unfilled and a bewildering series of changes followed. Nicholas placed the city of Moscow under the control of a special city commandant (*gradonachal'nik*), a situation similar to that which existed in St. Petersburg. The city commandant had powers equal to a governor's and the right to report directly to the tsar. But his responsibilities were primarily of a police character, with great emphasis on the maintenance of "good order," broadly construed.[8] The rest of Moscow province remained in the hands of the governor, G. I. Kristi. The confusion caused by this administrative reshuffling was increased by the fact that General Evgenii Volkov, the designated city commandant, could not immediately assume his post. For the moment General Rudnev, slated to be Volkov's assistant, held the reins, but he was in Dzhunkovsky's words "weak-willed, inefficient, and completely unsuited to any kind of administrative office."[9]

Rudnev quickly proved unable to deal with the wave of strikes that followed Bloody Sunday, and his failure prompted Dzhunkovsky to act: "I decided to involve myself in something that was not my business and use my influence among the workers." He suggested that the Guardianship issue a proclamation to the workers calling for calm. Rudnev gladly accepted Dzhun's idea, and within a matter of days the disturbances subsided and the workers returned to their factories. Writing about these events years later, Dzhunkovsky claimed no credit saying only "at least . . . [the proclamation] did not pour fat on the fire and maybe had a sobering influence on some of the workers."[10]

General Volkov arrived in mid-January but did little to stabilize the situation. "He went around Moscow not in uniform, but in a frock coat like an ordinary civilian," Dzhun recalled. "During his time . . . [in office] he failed to prove his worth, and his subordinates paid no attention to his orders."[11] Volkov's administration was further discredited by a horrific event. On February 4, a team of Socialist Revolutionary terrorists led by Boris Savinkov, who had been stalking Grand Duke Sergei Alexandrovich for months, assassinated him with a bomb as he rode in his carriage inside the Kremlin. The explosion decapitated Sergei and reduced his body to a shapeless mass. Bloody pieces of flesh and bone scattered, fragments blown onto the roofs of nearby buildings. Sergei's gravely wounded driver died a few days later, but his assassin, Ivan Kaliaev, though injured, survived and was taken into custody. Savinkov and the others in his squad quietly slipped away from Moscow and vanished.[12]

Within moments of the attack the telephone rang in Dzhunkovsky's office at the Guardianship. Picking up he heard the words: "The grand duke has just been killed." Stunned, he raced to the street, hailed the first available cab, and sped to the Kremlin. "It would be difficult to describe the melancholy picture that unfolded before my eyes," he recalled. "There was complete quiet, few people; some soldiers and officers were carrying something covered with a military greatcoat." He saw Ella, who upon hearing the explosion, had run to the scene of the bombing and tried desperately to gather parts of her husband's body. She now followed behind the small detachment, her face unnaturally calm. "I rushed up, took the hand of the grand duchess and kissed it," Dzhun remembered. He grabbed hold of the stretcher and joined the somber little procession that carried Sergei's mangled remains to the Alekseevsky Cathedral in the Chudov Monastery for the first of many requiem services. Later, Dzhunkovsky went with Ella to the hospital where her husband's driver lay dying. She wore no sign of mourning. Dzhunkovsky recalled a poignant, tragic encounter: "Andrei Rudinkin touchingly, forgetting his own great pain, asked the grand duchess about the grand duke, and she, just as bravely, took it upon herself not to disclose her own sorrow and distress." She assured the driver that Sergei had escaped harm.[13]

Several days later Dzhunkovsky marveled as Ella visited Kaliaev in Butyrka prison. "What conversation took place between the grand duchess and Kaliaev is unknown," his memoir records, "no one else was present. From the brief words of the grand duchess you could only conclude that the meeting satisfied . . . [her] Christian feelings and that Kaliaev's heart was touched: he took from her a small icon and kissed her hand."[14] But if the assassin was moved, he soon repented: "I fully recognize my mistake," he wrote Ella afterwards. "[A]t the time of our meeting, I hid the hatred I naturally feel for you."[15] Dzhun remembered that many criticized Ella for displaying kindness to her husband's murderer, but he felt differently: "Anyone acquainted with the grand duchess would know very well that she could not act otherwise."[16] Despite Ella's plea to Nicholas not to execute Sergei's assassin, Kaliaev was hanged. Thus began an extraordinary journey in which Queen Victoria's granddaughter freed herself from the things of this world and took up God's work among men, a path that led to sainthood.

For Dzhunkovsky the assassination of Sergei Alexandrovich was a deep and painful loss. But it opened the door to a much more independent life and an increasingly successful governmental career. Initially, however, it did not appear that way. "My personal situation at the time was extremely uncertain," he recalled. "From the moment of the grand duke's death, I should have been ordered to the Preobrazhensky Regiment where I was still enrolled." But until his orders arrived, he continued to live at the Nikolaevsky Palace and work as the de facto head of the Moscow Guardianship of Public Sobriety. Then on Good Friday, April 15, Dzhun got an unexpected telephone call from his longtime friend Alexander Bulygin, the newly appointed minister of internal affairs. "Congratulations!" Bulygin exclaimed excitedly. "Buy a white cap for Easter." Dzhunkovsky knew at once the meaning of this cryptic remark: the tsar had just made him an aide-de-camp, one of 119 members of the Imperial Suite, his chosen entourage.[17]

The appointment rewarded Dzhun for almost fifteen years of loyal service to the grand duke and duchess. With it came important perquisites and privileges. Aides-de-camp in the military received promotions strictly on the basis of seniority, regardless of the availability of positions, and had the right to present themselves to the tsar at any of his regular receptions without prior permission. In exceptional circumstances, they could even gain an unscheduled audience with the emperor.[18]

The responsibilities of an aide-de-camp were not arduous. The emperor might call on him to carry out special assignments, chiefly in the provinces, such as supervising recruitment and investigating peasant disturbances or ask him to escort foreign dignitaries and military delegations. During regular duty, his chief obligation was to present to the emperor persons appearing at his reception, to maintain proper order when officials reported to the sovereign, and to attend the tsar on parades, inspections, and even at the theater. On average, an aide-de-camp could expect to be on regular duty once every sixty days, although members of the Suite stationed in St. Petersburg might serve a three-week rotation. Dzhunkovsky's schedule normally took him to the capital once a month.[19]

Immediately after Easter Sunday, Dzhunkovsky left for St. Petersburg to thank the emperor for his appointment. Nicholas gave him an especially warm reception, telling him that he could remain in Moscow, continue his work with the Guardianship, and come to the capital only when on duty. Nicholas then led Dzhun to his wife's apartments and presented him to her. Next came a visit to the dowager empress, Maria Fedorovna. The day ended with the traditional Easter reception of the Suite in the Grand Palace where, together with his fellow members, Dzhun greeted their majesties and received an Easter egg from the hand of Empress Alexandra.[20]

Dzhunkovsky spent the next two weeks in St. Petersburg visiting members of the imperial family and meeting with others in the Suite. Then he returned to Moscow and settled into a pleasant three-room apartment in the Cavalier House of the Kremlin Palace. During his regular attendance on the tsar, his connection to the imperial family became closer, and he often lunched with Nicholas in the company of Alexandra and the "most august children." The atmosphere was loose and friendly, with the tsar chatting amiably about Moscow and various happenings. Later they all repaired to the empress's rooms where they enjoyed coffee and liqueurs. Sometimes the emperor invited Dzhun to have dinner in the intimate circumstances of Alexandra's quarters. There they would eat at a small table set for three. "You could talk with complete freedom," he remembered, "since their majesties behaved very informally and were wonderfully hospitable and kind." If in the evening the tsar and tsarina went to the theater, Vladimir accompanied them and they sat together in the imperial box.

In the ensuing months Nicholas continued to show his favor. On May 6, he made his new aide-de-camp a colonel, and on June 2, appointed him chairman of the Moscow Guardianship of Public Sobriety. Dzhunkovsky was especially delighted by this second assignment: "My hands were now unbound, and I could give myself to work . . . that provided me complete satisfaction." The Guardianship's activities embraced almost all the districts of Moscow, and Dzhun and his coworkers formed a close association. "I dare say that all the employees comprised a single family," he recalled, "working shoulder to shoulder for a common goal: the real good of the people."[21] But as Dzhunkovsky labored contentedly in his beloved Guardianship, the political situation in the country deteriorated rapidly.

The central government's confusion had become clearly evident in the aftermath of Sergei's assassination. On February 18, the tsar issued a manifesto that reasserted his commitment to autocracy and denounced those who would replace it by a regime based on "alien" principles, but at the same time he instructed the Committee of Ministers to consider proposals from both individuals and institutions for the reform of the state. Finally, Nicholas announced that he had just ordered Minister of Internal Affairs Bulygin to draft a law creating an elected body with the right to consult on future legislation. This marked a dramatic policy reversal, for the tsars and their advisors had long resisted such a measure as the first step on the road to a parliamentary system.[22]

The government's wavering made it appear vulnerable, and a spring and summer of mounting discontent followed. Strikes grew more numerous and more violent. Peasants plundered nobles' granaries, seized livestock, and destroyed records of their debts. Students demonstrated repeatedly, turned classrooms into radical forums, and made learning virtually impossible. The zemstvos, the elected institutions of local self-government, produced lengthening lists of demands for reform. Even the nobility, long unshakable in its support of the throne, began to desert the autocracy. Events simply moved too fast for Nicholas and most of his officials to grasp. The tsar's pledge to let elected representatives of the people have a say in the legislative process—something that a few months before seemed an impossible dream—now failed to satisfy an aroused public. Everywhere calls for change grew louder.

In Moscow, too, the government seemed unstable. On April 15, the tsar had restored the traditional administrative system and appointed a new governor-general, the sixty-eight-year-old cavalry officer General Alexan der Kozlov, and subordinated the city commandant to him. Kozlov accepted the position reluctantly and exacted a promise from the tsar that, if within three months his work proved unsatisfactory, he would be relieved. The ineffectual Volkov resigned and General P. P. Shuvalov, Kozlov's close friend, took his place. Shuvalov did not last long, however. On June 28, a former member of Savinkov's attack squad, Petr Kulikovsky, pumped three bullets into the new city commandant; he died a few hours later.[23]

St. Petersburg authorities now cast about for men who might be able to establish firmer control in the ancient capital. Thus it was that in early July, Dzhunkovsky, returning from a brief vacation abroad, found an unexpected letter from Alexander Bulygin that eloquently expressed the confusion and uncertainty of the time:

> Deeply esteemed Vladimir Fedorovich, my letter may surprise you, but please do not be angry, and be as open with me as I am with you. As the result of the death of poor Shuvalov, the post of Moscow city commandant is vacant. By the way, I proposed you to the Sovereign as a candidate [for that job], and he liked my idea *very much*. But of course I made a proviso, adding that I in no way shared the opinion that a service position is a duty, and that anyone to whom it is offered is *bound* to accept. I myself feel just how impossibly difficult, unjust, etc. such a thing would be, and I . . . am completely convinced that service is *possible* only when the duty is accepted *freely and without condition*. Do you want to be acting Moscow commandant? Yes or no? The whole thing depends entirely on your free will. If yes, His Majesty will be very pleased; if for some reason you do not wish [to take the position], your refusal will not be ill received, and will not have [a negative] impact on your future career. Act as God dictates to your heart. I feel that I do not have the right to give you any kind of advice. Pray to God and decide; let me know by a brief dispatch, yes or no. My heart is with you. Sincerely yours, A. Bulygin. Saturday, 2 July 1905.[24]

Bulygin's letter surprised Dzhunkovsky and confronted him with a serious dilemma. His friend's flattering proposal touched him deeply. "I did not want to refuse him," he recalled, "but on the other hand, a purely police position like that of city commandant did not suit me at all." Dzhunkovsky knew that under a governor-general the city commandant would have little independence. But he also wondered if he deserved this trust, and the obvious disarray in the city administration gave him further pause. Still, mindful of the Russian adage "Never seek an office, but never refuse an offer" (*Na sluzhbu ne naprashivaisia i ot sluzhby ne otkazivaisia*), he was torn and, in an effort to resolve his uncertainty, went to St. Petersburg to confer with Bulygin. Their conversations convinced him to turn down the post, and with a feeling of relief, he journeyed back to Moscow.

Back home, Dzhunkovsky wavered: "It seemed to me that, perhaps, I had acted dishonorably and timidly, refusing to take on combat duty." Shortly after his return, he asked the advice of Governor-General Kozlov. "Kozlov tried to convince me to take the position, explaining that it was not as complicated as I had imagined and tempted me with all the good that I could, in his opinion, undoubtedly accomplish." Vladimir vacillated once more. He wired Bulygin again to say that he had changed his mind and would accept the post.[25] But the matter did not end there.

On July 8, a new letter from Bulygin arrived. He had spoken to the emperor. "Your reservations were not just understood, but very well received," he reassured Dzhun. More important, Bulygin told him that the whole question of the city commandant's position was now up in the air. Kozlov had asked to retire, and as Bulygin put it, "a governor-general is being born. Who—I do not know, negotiations are underway." General Petr Pavlovich Durnovo was a strong candidate, and should he get the job, the new city commandant would have to be someone to his liking. Bulygin closed by saying that if Vladimir still wanted to be considered for the post, he would propose his name to Durnovo. Failing receipt of Dzhun's request, however, the minister promised to say nothing.[26]

"When I received this letter I calmed down," Dzhunkovsky recalled. "It was not my fate to be city commandant." But less than a week later, he opened yet another letter from the minister containing a new proposal: the vice-governorship of Moscow province. The current holder of the office had put in for retirement, and Bulygin felt that Dzhunkovsky was perfect for the job. To be sure, he would have to act as governor immediately since Kristi was on leave, but the current head of chancellery, A. M. Poliansky, was very competent and would bring him up to speed. "How God determines everything for the best!" Bulygin exclaimed in conclusion.

Dzhunkovsky was delighted: "The job suited me completely." This time he did not hesitate but wired his acceptance at once. On July 30 the imperial order confirming his appointment arrived.[27] For the first time in his life, Vladimir assumed a real governmental post.

On the surface Dzhunkovsky's selection as Moscow vice-governor (*vitse-gubernator*) appears to be a glaring example of favoritism in administrative appointments. He had gained the position as a reward for long service to the royal family and because both the emperor and the minister of internal affairs knew and liked him. He had held none of the offices normally seen as providing the necessary preparation for a job that had many complex administrative duties and required those who held it to manage the province during the frequent absences of their superiors.[28]

But Dzhunkovsky's qualifications for his new post were far stronger than they appeared on paper. Service to Sergei Alexandrovich had taught him much about the operations of provincial administration. At the grand duke's "court" he had gained valuable contacts with the cultural, social, and political elite of Moscow. The small assignments he carried out over the years—famine relief in Saratov, work on the 1897 census, management of the medical team in Greece—and the more substantial achievement of building the Moscow Guardianship from scratch, all provided rich experience. He had a solid appreciation of the conditions and needs of the lower classes and of the importance of a straightforward, patriarchal approach in handling them. Service in the Preobrazhensky Guards gave Dzhunkovsky a feeling for command, but in Thessaly he had seen just enough of the horrors of war to make him cautious in the use of force.

A character formed by family tradition, education, and religious and moral principles acquired over the course of four decades determined the way that Dzhunkovsky utilized his practical experience. The ideals of service to God, country, and fellow man were deeply ingrained. He saw the world through the twin lenses of Orthodox Christian piety and the chivalric code learned at the Corps of Pages. He possessed a positive self-image tempered by a tendency toward self-criticism and a sense of his own limitations and moral failings. He did not exaggerate his own intelligence or consider himself to be an intellectual; but he felt that the virtues of energy and hard work could compensate for his deficiencies.

Now extraordinary events would test both Dzhunkovsky's skills and principles. As a newly appointed vice-governor, he could reasonably expect advice and instruction from his immediate superior, Governor Kristi. But Kristi was currently abroad. He would resume his duties with visible reluctance and, when troubles escalated, desperately sought retirement. As a consequence Dzhunkovsky had to take up immediately the burden of managing Moscow province even as he learned the finer details of the lesser job he had just acquired. Fortunately, Bulygin's positive assessment of A. M. Poliansky was correct. He proved invaluable, skillfully handling the day-to-day paperwork and a wide range of correspondence and secret matters. Dzhun found most of the Standing Committees to be in good order, their members quite competent. The local police, too, were generally good and, in some counties, excellent. Only the Provincial Board posed a serious problem. By law it was "the highest institution in the province," and through it passed a huge volume of government business. Unfortunately, Dzhun recalled, "the councilors were not up to snuff, work went according to routine, and there was a large backlog of papers."[29]

The continuing disarray in other parts of the state administration in Moscow further complicated Dzhunkovsky's tasks. Just as he stepped into his position, the new governor-general, P. P. Durnovo, arrived with his hand-picked city commandant, Baron Georgii Petrovich fon Medem. Events would soon show that neither of these men was equal to the challenges that lay ahead. Durnovo, a vigorous seventy-year-old, reveled in the prestige of his office but displayed interest only in superficialities, pomp, and petty detail. His tenure, rendered brief by his incompetence, would be, in Dzhunkovsky's estimation, "tragicomic." Baron Medem likewise proved ill suited to his new post. "He was not a bad person, extremely well meaning, who tried to satisfy the people of the capital," Dzhun wrote later, "but he did not pay attention to what was going on around him." When disorders broke out, Medem "simply gave up, never left his house, and the police did not get the necessary directives." In Dzhunkovsky's eyes, the saving grace of these two men was their willingness to leave him alone. Durnovo, who had once been governor of Moscow province, informed Dzhunkovsky at the outset that he had no intention of meddling in his administration: "You may rest assured," he told the new vice-governor, "I will not get involved in your affairs, since I remember how unpleasant it was for me during my governorship when the then governor-general . . . interfered with my orders."[30]

The rapid pace of events gave Dzhunkovsky little time to catch his breath or to orient himself in his new position. The month of August clearly showed that government efforts to meet the demands of an aroused public had simply whetted its appetite for even more concessions. On August 6, Nicholas II made good on his decree of February 18 and published a manifesto establishing the State Duma, a consultative assembly to be elected by a small number of voters that was to advise the tsar on future legislation. This body, popularly called the "Bulygin Duma," would not be able to make law; but for the first time Russians had an institution through which they could formally make their wishes known to the sovereign.[31] Many moderates joined in praising the tsar's decision, but a chorus of critics quickly drowned out their voices. "Russian society would have been completely satisfied with a consultative Duma and the electoral law of August 6 when it still believed that the government was ready to make immediate reforms and that the government was armed with full power," Dzhunkovsky maintained. "But by August 6, that confidence did not exist . . . the power of the government was diminished, and the authority of the state wavered."[32] A concession that a year before would have provoked broad satisfaction now seemed a fraud.

Ten days later the wires delivered what for Dzhunkovsky and most Russians was "joyous news": the war against Japan had ended with the Treaty of Portsmouth. Given the extent of Russia's military defeat, the terms of the agreement were lenient and the empire salvaged a considerable portion of its honor. Russia lost her ports in China, accepted Japanese preeminence in Korea, and surrendered the southern half of Sakhalin Island. But Japan backed down from some of its more extravagant demands and Russia paid no war indemnity. Still, Nicholas II got little credit as a peacemaker, and when he awarded the title of Count to Sergei Witte, his chief negotiator at Portsmouth, who had skillfully extracted the best from a very bad situation, many made a sour face. Ill-disposed wags whispered that Count Witte deserved to have his title augmented with the sobriquet "*Polusakhalinskii*" (Half of Sakhalin) to commemorate his loss of Russian soil to Japan.

Finally, on August 27, a decree of the Imperial Senate restored to the nation's universities the autonomy they had lost during the reign of Alexander III. Faculty members could again elect their rectors and deans, and councils of professors could permit students to hold meetings on the grounds of their institutions. But the measure failed to cool the troubled campuses. To Dzhunkovsky's disgust, students interpreted "autonomy" as the right to turn lecture halls into platforms for antigovernment propaganda.[33]

In his memoirs Dzhunkovsky gives the impression that he was fully aware of the storm that was now gathering. But the facts suggest that this was hindsight gained by the passage of twenty years and the memory of three revolutions. At the end of August, Governor Kristi returned from abroad to assume the duties of his office, and Dzhun turned briefly to the task of familiarizing himself with the obligations of his vice-governorship. But he did not feel the situation in Moscow to be so threatening that he could not afford to take a ten-day Crimean vacation in early September. The extent of the danger became clear to him only after he came back in mid-month. Kristi once more stepped aside and repaired to a rural retreat, leaving his new "*vitse*" in charge of the province.

Tensions in the city of Moscow were rising steadily. Strikes closed more and more shops and industries; violence escalated. By early October the crisp autumn air crackled with revolutionary energy, and the people's willingness to obey the established authorities seemed about to end. Meanwhile Dzhunkovsky watched anxiously as petty squabbles between the governor-general and the city commandant weakened their ability to respond to the unfolding crisis.[34]

On October 3, the arrival of a train from St. Petersburg set in motion events that forged a link between Moscow's restive workers and the city's alienated liberal intelligentsia. It carried the body of Prince Sergei Trubetskoi, the respected exponent of moderate reform recently elected rector of Moscow University, who had died suddenly while on a visit to the capital. A huge crowd of students, professors, and representatives of various professional unions greeted the return of his remains. After a funeral service at the University Chapel, the mourners headed for the Donskoi Monastery where Trubetskoi was to be interred, students bearing the coffin along. From the outset, the event took on a radical tone; marchers sang both religious and revolutionary hymns.

Outside the cemetery several thousand students listened to antigovernment speeches and then turned back toward the university singing revolution's anthem, "La Marseillaise." Before they could reach the campus, however, they met a detachment of Cossacks. Fights broke out, authorities arrested twenty-three students, and Cossack whips injured many more. This unprovoked attack and the arrests shocked Moscow and the nation. Anti-autocratic solidarity grew and gave powerful impetus to an empire-wide general strike that saw the emergence of a new generation of revolutionary leaders.[35]

The railroad workers of Moscow took the lead. On October 6, the engineers on the Moscow-Kazan line walked out, halting traffic on this crucial east–west route. Soon workers on other lines joined them, and a nationwide shutdown followed. From railheads across the country, the strike spread to industries and businesses, halting commercial activity in major towns and cities. Workers curtailed and even stopped vital services, the cost of food rose sharply; many goods could not be had at any price. Doctors, lawyers, actors, and students joined the workers. Government offices and banks closed; utilities shut down. In St. Petersburg, factory hands created a new institution, the Soviet (Council) of Workers' Deputies, to represent their interests and voice their demands. Formed on October 13, gathering strength and importance as the general strike continued, the Soviet raised the curtain on things to come, and a twenty-six-year-old firebrand, Leon Trotsky, emerged as its tribune. Pressured from all sides, the tsar and his ministers soon had to choose between unwanted reforms and main force.[36]

In Moscow, as the prospect of violence and the breakdown of social services loomed, authorities seemed paralyzed. On October 13, a delegation of factory owners and businessmen urged the governor-general to take strong measures to deal with the strike. On the same day similar—if more forcefully expressed—orders came down from St. Petersburg. But Durnovo simply issued a proclamation denying the existence of shortages in the city and urged all Muscovites to go about their normal activities. One of the few institutions that continued to function during the strike was the Moscow Guardianship. "There were attempts to lure workers away from the 'people's houses,' but my personal intervention paralyzed this effort," Dzhunkovsky recalled proudly.[37] Meanwhile, the city duma debated and considered various resolutions but, as one historian aptly put it, "refused to break with the hallowed tradition of administrative inertia."[38]

The general strike soon thrust a technically complex and politically sensitive problem into Dzhunkovsky's hands. Of all the services provided by a modern city, perhaps the most vital is water. On October 9, Muscovites briefly panicked when water from the taps flowed with a brownish tinge and rumors flew that workers had poisoned the reservoirs. That alarm proved false, but the mayor asked authorities to station guards at the waterworks.[39] Then on October 14 word emerged from the Moscow Strike Committee that reservoir and pumping station workers were walking out and would cut off the water supply. Again there was general panic. Vladimir Malinin, an engineer newly elected to the duma who would play an important role in the struggle to keep Moscow from going dry, recalled that "people began to store water energetically, filling spare pots of all sizes and filling bathtubs in apartments." As pressure in the pipes fell and water flowed from the taps in weak streams or stopped altogether, public alarm rose.[40]

The prospects of a water stoppage that threatened the health and well-being of up to a million people terrified city leaders. Dr. N. N. Alekseev, the chief physician at the Morozov Children's Hospital, rushed to the Strike Committee, meeting within the confines of Moscow University, to plead on behalf of sick children, newborns, and their mothers for the maintenance of the water supply, to no avail. Malinin remembered the committee as being in the grip of "revolutionary ecstasy . . . completely deaf to the prayers of the selfless doctor." It recommended that he drag water by the barrelful from the polluted Moscow River. Later, militant workers on the committee informed a delegate from the city duma who appeared before them that they would end their strike only if all power was transferred into their hands. Under the pressure of events, the mayor of Moscow, Prince V. M. Golitsyn, collapsed, and the duma's acting chairman turned to Malinin, asking him to do what he could to keep the water flowing. Malinin agreed to take up the task and soon contacted Vice-Governor Dzhunkovsky.[41] Together, they confronted the crisis head-on.

Moscow's water came from two separate sources, both well beyond the city limits and therefore Dzhunkovsky's responsibility as acting head of the provincial administration. The first station, at the village of Mytishcha, gathered high-quality groundwater and brought it in via a pumping station at Aleksandrovsk. The second, a larger facility at Rublevo, completed just two years before, drew water directly from the Moscow River, purified it, then pumped it to a reservoir at Sparrow Hills whence it flowed into the city's mains. The extensive network of pipes this required was vulnerable to sabotage. Responding to the city duma's concerns for the system's safety, Dzhunkovsky had already assigned infantry detachments to guard the reservoirs and pumping stations and ordered cavalry units to patrol the pipelines. On October 11 and 12, even before the water workers announced their strike, he toured the facilities to survey their operations and inspect the troops assigned to protect them.[42]

Malinin hoped that as an engineer himself he might enlist the aid of the specialists who ran the waterworks. Many were old colleagues from the Imperial Moscow Technical School and the Polytechnic Society. But when Malinin turned to them, they refused to help. "The engineers were practically hypnotized, by the power of the . . . strike committee's resolutions," he recalled, "and did not consider it possible not to be in solidarity with . . . [their workers]."[43] In the meantime Dzhunkovsky had developed a clear picture of the number of technicians and other personnel that he would need to get the water flowing again. He concluded that the Rublevo installation required about thirty-three specialists, and he believed that he could count on some forty men drawn from detachments of combat engineers (sappers) and a government-controlled electric station.[44]

Malinin and Dzhunkovsky decided to concentrate their efforts on Rublevo, which normally supplied two-thirds of the city's water. Malinin, however, expressed doubts about the wisdom of relying entirely on sappers and other military personnel. The operations that had to be performed were delicate, and he recommended that they find someone with a high level of the relevant expertise. Dzhunkovsky agreed, and the two men soon discovered the right specialist—an engineer at the Bromley metalworks. The factory's owner readily gave leave for his employee to help restore the city's water, and the engineer took on the job, asking only that his name and those of his helpers be kept secret.[45]

Dzhunkovsky and Malinin presented their plans to a skeptical city duma. When the vice-governor boldly announced that water supply would be restored by the administration, N. P. Zimin, a delegate and the engineer who had built Rublevo waterworks, voiced grave concerns. "He feared that [our] intervention would be fatal for the integrity of the entire [complex]," Malinin wrote later. The strikers might inflict damage that would take a long time to repair. Malinin did not share those anxieties. He felt that Zimin did not know the workers who, as he put it, "were so attached to their machines and boilers that they loved them like living beings." Ultimately the duma yielded to Dzhunkovsky's firm resolve and Malinin's confident assurances. With some trepidation, it gave their engineers and sappers free access to all installations of the waterworks.[46]

Dzhunkovsky now took command. On the morning of October 15, he gathered his technicians and sappers to survey the field and plan their attack. They set two clear objectives: first, take charge of the Rublevo pumping station and get it working; second, gain complete control of the reservoir at Sparrow Hills and the network of pipes bringing water to the city and see that the flow, once started, was not disrupted. In some ways, the second assignment was the more difficult, since it involved many complicated tasks. "All this needed to be done quickly," Dzhunkovsky recalled, "and I was greatly worried whether the men I sent out could handle this complex specialized work." When news came that his team had carried out its mission, Dzhun's relief was enormous.

Meanwhile at the Rublevo station, Dzhunkovsky's squad faced daunting obstacles. The facility's engineer and his assistant flatly refused to help, citing threats from the workers to kill them. Undeterred, the vice-governor's team pushed ahead, and by 4:30 in the afternoon they had the plant's boilers operating and its electricity restored. Some of the operational "mysteries" of the station posed difficulties, but the Bromley engineer soon proved his worth, working around the problems. "Still the flow of water was held up for several hours," Dzhun remembered, and the machines worked poorly at first because several pieces of equipment were missing. But a careful search turned them up, and soon the machinery began to function properly. Around five o'clock in the morning on October 16, Dzhunkovsky learned that water was pouring into the reservoir at Sparrow Hills. "I breathed easy; all through the night I had received phone calls informing me that the work was not going well and I was greatly alarmed." Now it was clear: Moscow would not thirst.[47]

There remained the question of what to do about the workers. When Dzhun's team had first arrived at Rublevo, the strikers were confident that his men could never restore operations without their help. "But when on the evening of the fifteenth the station was suddenly lit by electricity and the arc lights blazed up, illuminating the surrounding area, their spirits fell," he recalled. On the evening of October 16, the workers met and announced that they were ready to resume their duties. Dzhunkovsky brusquely rejected the offer, his resolve strengthened by the fact that the employees at the Mytishcha and Aleksandrovsk facilities had ended their strike.

The next day Dzhunkovsky returned to the Rublevo station. The workers once more offered to end the strike, but he demanded that they guarantee they would not resume the walkout. When the workers replied that they could not do this without the permission of the Moscow Strike Committee, Dzhun stood firm: "I advised them to consider the circumstances and the position the . . . [Strike Committee] had put them in; I had no need of their work." Not until the evening of October 18, when the workers appeared before him in Moscow and gave the required assurances, did he consent to let them return to the job the next day. That morning, the vice-governor toured the Rublevo station and, after a prayer service, withdrew his men and fully restored normal operations.[48] Dzhunkovsky had won without resorting to force, but larger events had already swallowed up his achievement. On October 17, the tsar issued the fateful manifesto that radically transformed the empire's political system, ended the general strike, and began a new period in Russian history.

Chapter 6

Moscow Explodes

As the general strike spread nationwide, Nicholas II and his advisors faced a number of choices, all of them dangerous. They might do nothing and wait for the strike to subside, as indeed it showed some signs of doing. But this would merely delay resolution of the much deeper crisis. Force was an option, but risky; the number of troops available was barely sufficient, the loyalty of the men uncertain. Resort to violence, so soon after Bloody Sunday, could provoke a full-scale civil war. The aroused public demanded new concessions, but the government had made many already and they had failed to satisfy. How much further should the tsar go? Would any reforms work at this point?

The emperor turned to Sergei Witte, fresh from his successful negotiations with Japan. Nicholas disliked and feared the intelligent and forceful former minister of finance, and Witte, despite his devotion to the principle of autocracy, had little regard for the tsar. Nicholas's lack of resolve stood in sharp contrast to the decisive style of Alexander III, with whom Witte had worked so well. But the storm that now threatened to sweep away the monarchy and the state forced the two men to act together.

Witte believed that the severity of the crisis made delay impossible, and he presented Nicholas with a stark choice: either appoint a military "dictator" empowered to restore "order" by any means or grant to the nation what so many voices were demanding. In that case, the tsar would have to guarantee his subjects a broad spectrum of civil rights—inviolability of person and freedom of speech, conscience, assembly, and association—

and give to the State Duma (created by the decree of August 6) a broader electoral base and the right to legislate, not merely to consult on proposed measures. Witte added that although the decision was the emperor's alone, he would not serve in any government that chose the path of violence.

Nicholas may have preferred force, but who would serve as dictator? His uncle, Grand Duke Nikolai Nikolaevich, an imposing soldier and firm devotee of the autocracy, seemed the logical choice. Yet when the tsar proposed that he accept the task of suppressing the revolt, the grand duke (legend has it) flatly stated that if he were given such an order he would shoot himself rather than carry it out. With profound misgivings, Nicholas accepted the necessity of reform and on October 17 issued a manifesto, written by Witte, that read in part:

> We impose upon the Government the obligation to carry out Our inflexible will:
>
> (1) To grant to the population the unshakable foundations of civic freedom based on the principles of real personal inviolability, freedom of conscience, speech, assembly and union.
> (2) Without halting the scheduled elections to the State Duma, to admit to participation in the Duma . . . those classes of the population which at the present are altogether deprived of the franchise, leaving the further development of the principle of universal suffrage to the new legislative order, and
> (3) To establish it as an unbreakable rule that no law can become effective without the approval of the State Duma and that the elected representatives of the people should be guaranteed an opportunity for actual participation in the supervision of the legality of the actions of the authorities appointed by us.

Unlimited autocratic rule in Russia had come to an end.[1]

The October Manifesto caught the nation by surprise. State officials had no warning, and the suddenness and extent of the reform stunned a public that for a year had watched concessions wrung drop by drop from a reluctant government. As the tsar's loyal servitors struggled to make sense of the news, ecstatic crowds spilled into the streets to celebrate the dawn of a new era. Many radicals dismissed the manifesto as a fraud and tried to continue the general strike, but this quickly proved impossible. Still, once the euphoria of the moment passed, all Russians realized that the changes it wrought would require significant, often painful, readjustments. In his official report, published together with the emperor's decree, Count Witte proclaimed a firm belief in "the political tact" of the Russian people. "It is unthinkable," he wrote, "that the people should desire anarchy, which, in addition to all the horrors of civil war, holds the menace of the disintegration of the very State."[2] But the heady "Days of Liberty" that now ensued put Witte's faith to a severe test.

In the two months following October 17, Russia witnessed a kaleidoscopic series of events that almost defies accurate recounting or rational analysis. Throughout the country demonstrations in favor of what many took to be a constitution met counterdemonstrations of the so-called Black Hundreds, proclaiming loyalty to the tsar and the traditional autocratic order. As violence erupted with casualties on both sides, authorities often stood by or intervened on behalf of reactionary forces. In the escalating disorder Russia's baser elements, filled with passionate hatreds, organized pogroms that set howling mobs upon Jews and suspected radicals, inflicting mayhem, death, and destruction. Conflict in urban areas spilled into the countryside, where peasants interpreted the manifesto both as a sign that the authority of the state had weakened and as proof that the tsar had, at last, given them "freedom," the right to burn the homes of the nobles and seize their land. Mutinies shook army garrisons and naval bases.

Amid the tumult, political parties sprang up overnight or leapt from the shadows of illegality. Left-leaning liberals organized a Constitutional Democratic Party (KDs or Kadets) that expressed the aspirations of members of the "free professions" and the still small urban middle class. The Socialist Revolutionary Party (SRs) would claim to speak for the peasants but also enjoyed strong support among the workers, as did the two-headed Social Democratic Party (RSDRP), already dividing between Bolshevik and Menshevik factions. Monarchists formed the Union of the Russian People with the goal of undermining the constitutional experiment and restoring unlimited autocracy. Liberals of a more conservative stamp created the Union of 17 October (Octobrists) pledged to defend the political arrangements that flowed from the tsar's manifesto. Smaller nationalist and religious parties also emerged to fill out the picture. In a startling profusion of publications of every stripe, these movements announced their goals and programs.

During the "Days of Liberty," men dreamed the improbable, if not the impossible. Witte, now prime minister, aspired to form a new government that would include political figures drawn from the liberal opposition, but he insisted that the minister of internal affairs be Petr Nikolaevich Durnovo (not to be confused with the Moscow's hapless governor-general), a man whom educated society considered a reactionary with dubious morals. Liberals refused to serve with such an odious person and conjured their own vision of a full-fledged constitutional monarchy on the Western model. Socialists of every coloration thought they saw in the swirl of events the possibility of a sweeping transformation of the existing order. Leon Trotsky, a leading force in the St. Petersburg Soviet, began to contemplate a "permanent revolution" yet to come that would see the rapid transition from a "bourgeois" stage to a "proletarian" one. This would bring the Russian working class to power and place it in the vanguard of the European struggle for socialism.

For Nicholas II the events of October and the months that followed were simply a nightmare. He felt enormous guilt for betraying the autocratic principle he had pledged to uphold, hated the manifesto he had promulgated, and despised Witte as the man who had set him in the wrong direction. He yearned for a return to the past. Yet of all the dreams that were dreamt in the days after October 17, those of the tsar were closest to realization. His manifesto broke the united front of liberal and radical elements that had emerged during the general strike. Peace with Japan, however humiliating, brought troops back from the East, and by late November the balance of power tipped in favor of the forces of order.[3]

Like all state officials Dzhunkovsky was unprepared for the October Manifesto, and the explosion of demonstrations shook him: "Everywhere you felt great excitement," he remembered. "Oppositional and revolutionary circles were not sleeping and tried to create disorder all over. Processions in the streets appeared, one with the portrait of the sovereign, the other with red flags, skirmishes took place between them; one group sang the national anthem, the other revolutionary songs. . . . The police, not having directives, looked on but took no measures, and the rampage of the crowds spread panic among peaceful citizens." The failure of Durnovo, fon Medem, and the police to uphold the dignity and authority of the state filled Dzhunkovsky with disgust. When celebrants decorated the entrance to the governor-general's house with red flags and Durnovo did nothing about it, Dzhun could barely contain his outrage. "Order the removal of the red flags," he objected to the governor-general, "it's embarrassing, the crowds are laughing." To which Durnovo replied carelessly, "It's nothing. Don't get upset, at night the janitors will take them away."[4] Dzhunkovsky soon had little time to worry about such matters. Almost immediately he had to confront the question about what to do with the political detainees held in the Moscow prisons, institutions directly under the control of the provincial administration.

To the jubilant crowds now filling the streets, the October Manifesto's promise of the inviolability of person and other civil rights meant liberation for those held in jail. Governor-General Durnovo himself appeared on the balcony of his mansion to announce that authorities would soon free those arrested in connection with recent events. Many called for immediate amnesty, however, and on October 18, large bands of demonstrators headed in the direction of the Butyrka and Taganka prisons hoping to bring about the release of the "politicals" held there. Along the routes of both marches, fights broke out. An agitated throng approached the area of the Taganka, but its progress halted when a reactionary fanatic shot and then bludgeoned to death one of the procession's leaders, the Bolshevik Nikolai Bauman. The next day, crowds formed again demanding that the gates of the city's jails be opened.

Dzhunkovsky ordered the release of all political prisoners except those who had been charged with murders. At Butyrka, things proceeded smoothly, and those jailed there quickly exited to freedom. But at Taganka, delays occurred, and a large and volatile crowd gathered near the jail shouting for those held there to be let go. Determined to avoid further violence, Dzhun sped to the scene. "When I drove up to the prison," he recalled, "I saw that Malye Kamenshchiki Street was literally flooded with people bearing red flags. Seeing that I could go no further, I got out and started to work my way through the crowd." A few people recognized the vice-governor and called on their comrades to make way. The throng parted, and Dzhunkovsky finally reached the prison gates. He turned to the demonstrators, quieted them with the promise that he would straighten everything out, and entered Taganka's confines.

He found the prison corridor in complete chaos; and in the warden's office, a huge bearded figure wearing a Caucasian fur cap, red flag in hand, stood defiantly flanked by three representatives of the crowd come for the "politicals." Dzhun ordered the men to remove their hats and place the red flag in the corner, and they instantly obeyed. He then tried to make sense of the confused situation.

Several members of the judiciary were present, including District Procurator fon Klugen, and a number of officers of the gendarmes in charge of political matters. They told Dzhunkovsky that legal technicalities prevented the release of the prisoners. The ukase on amnesty referred to specific articles in the penal code, but these articles did not correspond to what was actually intended. Neither Dzhunkovsky nor fon Klugen felt he could resolve the issue on his own authority, so they decided to telephone Prime Minister Witte and ask him to settle the matter. "Fortunately," his memoirs record, "we were able to connect with Count Witte who solved the question sensibly."

Soon some sixty or seventy "politicals" slated for release stood ready to depart; only eleven charged with killings would remain behind bars. But now a new problem arose. Those being released were nervous. Shots had sounded outside, and they feared that upon leaving the prison they, too, might be attacked. Dzhun's initial efforts to reassure them had little effect, and he finally agreed to lead them out himself. As the vice-governor and the newly freed emerged from the prison together, a cheering crowd engulfed them. When the throng began to sing revolutionary songs, Dzhunkovsky ordered them to stop and they complied. He accompanied the demonstrators as far as his carriage, got in and drove away in the direction of the nearby Taganka Square. The celebrants and the released prisoners headed toward the center of the city.

Once he reached the square, Dzhunkovsky turned back to the prison. He feared that the detained radicals not entitled to amnesty might try to leave. But when he arrived, he encountered a curious scene. In one of the cells stood a festive table, covered by a cloth and complete with a candelabra, piled with snacks and fruit. Taganka's warden had given the remaining "politicals" permission to hold a small celebration in honor of their liberated comrades, and one of their number now politely asked the vice-governor to let the party proceed. After determining that all the prisoners who should be held were present, Dzhunkovsky consented, requiring only that they agree to return to their cells by midnight. Then as he prepared to leave the jail, a group of men being held for ordinary crimes stopped him. "How is it," they asked, "that we, loyal subjects, are not freed while those who went against the tsar are being let go?" They begged the vice-governor to intercede on their behalf, but Dzhunkovsky managed only embarrassed platitudes: "I calmed them as best I could, and left."[5]

Dzhunkovsky's account of the prisoners' release contains a major discrepancy. Moscow newspapers show clearly that the events he described took place on October 19.[6] But Dzhunkovsky states that he acted *after* receiving the ukase on amnesty.[7] This was a decree not issued until October 21,[8] and there is no evidence to suggest that government officials had obtained an advance text of the document. It appears then, that confronted by street demonstrations and with the threat of violence exacerbated by Bauman's murder, Dzhunkovsky acted on his own, taking his cue from the governor-general's announcement, and certain that amnesty would soon be proclaimed. While the confusion at Taganka, the concerns expressed by members of the judiciary, and the telephone call to Witte may well have taken place, what Dzhunkovsky and the others sought was not clarification regarding articles in the criminal code but permission to proceed with an action that, while technically illegal, the exigencies of the moment required.

In time Dzhunkovsky's actions would come back to haunt him. The story of how he had liberated prisoners and paraded with them under the red flag—a distorted account of the events of Octobe 19—regularly appeared in the writings of his critics who would question his loyalty to tsar and fatherland.[9] But for the moment, Dzhunkovsky's decisiveness and willingness to take risks when other representatives of authority in Moscow wavered seem to have pleased the tsar and high officials in St. Petersburg. On October 28, he unexpectedly received a coded telegram from Prime Minister Witte that read: "His Majesty has expressed the wish to appoint you Moscow city commandant, but ordered [me] to determine in advance your willingness to take the post."[10]

The dispatch confronted Dzhunkovsky with a dilemma he thought he had already resolved. Six months earlier he had refused the same assignment, and he was now immersed in gubernatorial duties that were both important and extremely satisfying. Kristi, determined to retire, was unwilling to resume his position, and Dzhun was eager for the job.

Supported by Kristi and Governor-General Durnovo, Dzhunkovsky wired Witte requesting an interview, and with the prime minister's consent traveled to St. Petersburg. There he informed Witte of the situation in Moscow, his reservations about being city commandant, and of Kristi's plan to retire. Witte was prepared to back Dzhun's gubernatorial ambitions but urged him to consult with Petr Nikolaevich Durnovo, whom the emperor had just appointed acting minister of internal affairs.

Meeting with Durnovo, Dzhunkovsky again explained his unwillingness to take the post of Moscow commandant, and Durnovo agreed that a governorship better suited his abilities. But the new minister added that for him to propose this in a report to the sovereign would be embarrassing. Dzhun should go directly to the emperor and personally clarify the situation. Accordingly, next morning, Dzhunkovsky took an early train to Peterhof for an audience with the tsar.

He arrived at the Alexander Palace at precisely 9:30. At first, the emperor's valet told him that their majesties were about to have coffee and that he would have to wait until they finished. But not five minutes had passed when the valet swung wide the door to the tsar's study and announced that the sovereign would receive him at once. When Dzhun entered the room, Nicholas extended his hand in greeting: "Have you come to present yourself on the occasion of being chosen Moscow city commandant?"

Again Dzhunkovsky was taken aback. But he quickly recovered his balance and made clear to the tsar his concerns about the post being offered. He then informed the emperor of Kristi's plan to retire, which would open up the gubernatorial position that he had been filling for the past three months.

"Kristi's leaving, is that so?" Nicholas asked, clearly surprised. "I didn't know. In that case, of course, it would be better for you to be governor, and I would prefer to see you in that post. I would be upset if you refused [a position] altogether, but since you would be glad to serve as governor, I am very pleased. Go to Count Witte and tell him, in my name, to draw up the decree for your appointment."

Returning to St. Petersburg, Dzhunkovsky informed Durnovo and Witte of the tsar's decision, and both men expressed their satisfaction with the way things had worked out. Happy and greatly relieved, he boarded the train for Moscow.[11] On November 11, an imperial ukase placed Dzhunkovsky in command of Moscow province with the title of "acting governor."[12]

The year 1905 now hurtled toward its bloody climax. Strikes, demonstrations, and sporadic violence continued throughout the country making the situation fluid and precarious, but by mid-November the government had gained strength and begun to assert its authority. In the capital, forces loyal to the tsar took the offensive. On November 26, army and Cossack units surrounded a meeting of the St. Petersburg Soviet and arrested its chairman together with several delegates. In response the Soviet elected a new presidium that included Leon Trotsky and adopted a resolution calling on workers to prepare for armed resistance. Together with other radical organizations and socialist parties, the Soviet issued a manifesto that urged the people to withhold all further payments due the state, withdraw their money from banks, and accept only gold as legal tender. But the police promptly jailed the editors of the newspapers that printed the manifesto, and on December 3, they arrested the Soviet's leaders and two hundred members, among them a defiant Leon Trotsky.[13]

While St. Petersburg seemed to stabilize, Moscow took an increasingly dangerous direction. The population was tense, and revolutionary forces continued to score dramatic, albeit minor, successes. But here, too, authority was firming up. Dzhunkovsky's appointment as acting governor, replacing the ineffective and clearly terrified Kristi, was a first step; others would soon follow. On November 20, Governor-General Durnovo received orders to report to the capital where he was abruptly dismissed.[14] In his place the tsar chose a man made of sterner stuff: Fedor Vasilievich Dubasov.

At the time of his appointment on November 24, Dubasov was an admiral with little governmental experience and in poor health. But he had just successfully suppressed agrarian disturbances in Kursk and Chernigov provinces. After a brief trip to the capital to consult with officials there, the new governor-general took up his post in Moscow on December 4. The next day, speaking at a gathering of state officials and representatives of public institutions, Dubasov told his listeners that the "moral pressure and determination" of the "best social forces of the country," not bayonets and bullets, would ultimately overcome the current wave of "sedition." But the present situation, he continued, was intolerable. Revolutionaries were putting forth "impudent demands" addressing the legal government "with raised fists." He boldly asserted that he was ready to meet this challenge, prepared to employ "the harshest and most forceful measures."[15] The governor-general's words delighted Dzhunkovsky: "Everyone felt that firm authority had at last been established in Moscow."[16]

"Sedition" was not slow to display its raised fists. On December 6, the newly formed Moscow Soviet of Workers' Deputies announced a general political strike as a first step in overthrowing the "criminal" tsarist government; by the next day some radicals were calling for "the great Russian Revolution" to begin.[17] On December 7, Dubasov responded by proclaiming the city and the province to be in a state of "maximum security" (*chrezvychainaia okhrana*), a special legal status akin to martial law under which the governor-general assumed near dictatorial powers. The next day he appealed to St. Petersburg for more troops, and that evening government forces encircled the Aquarium Theater where some six thousand persons were meeting. The aim of the soldiers was to seize weapons, but the revolutionary militiamen (*druzhinniki*) in the crowd escaped and took most of the arms with them. By now many of Moscow's store owners had boarded up their shops, public transportation had stopped, and the city was without electricity. Indignation over the Aquarium incident brought tensions to a flash point.

At ten o'clock on the night of December 9, government troops surrounded the Fiedler Academy where about one hundred members of the revolutionary militia had gathered and gave the radicals two hours to surrender their weapons, promising to free them once they disarmed. When the *druzhinniki* refused, troops stormed the building. Both sides exchanged fire, and the revolutionaries hurled a bomb that killed one officer and wounded another. The soldiers pulled back but several hours later resumed their advance using light artillery. Superior force compelled the militiamen to yield, and when survivors of the melee began to walk out of the academy, the soldiers fell upon them with drawn swords. In all, about twenty *druzhinniki* suffered wounds, seven died, and authorities took a hundred or so into custody. Later, SRs bombed secret police headquarters. The battle for Moscow had now begun in earnest.[18]

On the morning of December 10, Dzhunkovsky left the governor's house on the Tverskaia and rode on horseback to survey the scenes of the previous night's conflicts. "The weather was marvelous," he remembered, "light frost, the sun bright and clear, the streets seemed calm, and it was impossible to foresee that in a few hours the uprising would begin." Dzhunkovsky rode past the badly damaged Fiedler Academy and the bombed office of the secret police and then headed homeward. But when he approached Strastnaia Square, he encountered a substantial crowd. The governor asked the people to let him pass; they reluctantly complied, and he reached his residence at around ten o'clock.

Shortly after hearing the day's report from his head of chancellery and just as he was beginning to go through the business papers on his desk, Dzhunkovsky started; gunfire sounded close by, the windows rattled violently. Looking out onto the Tverskaia, he saw a throng running in panic from the direction of Strastnaia Square; two corpses lay in the street. Dzhun raced upstairs to another window that gave him a good view of the square. "[O]n all corners you could see groups of people in Caucasian caps taking shelter," he recalled, "one by one they ran around the corner and fired somewhere. In the square there were guns, infantry, shooting in all directions."

The telephone rang. Dubasov was asking him to come at once to the governor-general's mansion, about a half a mile away down the Tverskaia. Dzhunkovsky immediately ordered a sleigh brought round, but before he could leave, a police officer arrived to tell the governor that he was now cut off. Armed militiamen had blocked the Tverskaia and occupied all the side streets that led from his house.

Again the phone; again it was Dubasov. This time he told Dzhun that he had just dispatched a detachment of dragoons to provide escort. But no sooner had they arrived and Dzhunkovsky settled into his sleigh, than he was called to the phone once more; the director of a nearby girls' gymnasium faced a crisis. The school was holding a conference with the parents, and the disturbances in the streets had thrown them all into panic, not knowing how they would get home. Could the governor help? Dzhunkovsky answered that he would come right away and arrived surrounded by the dragoons. Drawing the troops up in a line, he asked the parents to come out and, under the soldiers' protection, go quickly to Strastnoi Boulevard and from there head home. The rescue complete, Dzhunkovsky drove to his meeting with Dubasov.

The governor-general had gathered his head of chancellery, fon Medem, the chief of staff of the Moscow military district, Baron E. A. Raush fon Traubenberg, and Dzhunkovsky to consider the increasingly dangerous situation. They decided to form a committee composed of representatives from the main state and public institutions so that they would all know about the measures that were going to be taken. Dzhunkovsky helped draw up the list of the membership. Meanwhile, alarming reports poured in from police and military units. Bloody fighting had erupted on many of Moscow's main streets.

At four o'clock in the afternoon, Dzhunkovsky headed home. He went without escort, certain that the troops had cleared the Tverskaia and Strastnaia Square. But as he approached their intersection, he saw that fighting there was still going on. He tried to reach the governor's house by means of side streets without success. Some of the *druzhinniki* caught sight of him: "An officer!" they shouted, and they raced after his sleigh. Bullets whistled, but none hit. The governor drove into Stoleshnikov Alley, then turned on to Kozmodemiansky Street, where he encountered a protective line of police and soon made it back to the relative safety of the governor-general's mansion. Dzhun remained there until around ten o'clock at night and then returned to his residence accompanied by a detachment of horse. The next day Dubasov assigned a squad of fifteen dragoons to protect the governor while the disturbances continued, and four of their number regularly accompanied him on his travels through the city. In the course of the uprising, his residence suffered considerable damage. Powerful shocks from artillery fire blew out some of its front windows, stray bullets shattered others. Dzhunkovsky moved into rooms toward the back of the building; two watchmen stood guard there, even at night. He had a policeman at his disposal, as well as six men from the gendarmes, two of whom were mounted and employed to carry dispatches.[19]

To this day an aura of heroism and martyrdom surrounds the Moscow armed uprising. In reality it was a foolhardy, hopeless affair with almost no chance of overthrowing the tsarist regime or even attaining the revolutionaries' immediate goal—control of the ancient capital. But in the heat of events it did not appear that way, and Dubasov, a man of iron will and great self-confidence, believed for a time that he faced a dire, even desperate situation. The number of soldiers at his disposal seemed insufficient, and the insurgents' tactics of urban guerrilla warfare made the task of suppression extraordinarily difficult. On December 11, the governor-general reported by telephone to Durnovo that barricades had gone up everywhere, unhindered by his forces who considered the cause lost. "I do not know what will come next." Later that day he told the minister, "the struggle is becoming hopeless" and called on St. Petersburg to send more troops.[20]

On December 12, the situation of those supporting the government was still uncertain, and the rebellion seemed to be gaining strength. The Presnia district, a squalid working-class quarter not far from the center of town, became its stronghold. Prefiguring "Soviet Power," radical partisans began to govern the area, maintained order, arrested known police officers, and established "people's tribunals." In several cases they engaged in a form of "Red Terror," delivering summary "justice" to figures hated for their strong counterrevolutionary actions.[21] But the strength of the partisan forces was far more apparent than real, and by December 13 the tide of the battle began to turn against them. On December 15, units of the Semenovsky Guards Regiment, under the command of Colonel Georgii Min arrived from the capital. They soon drove the insurgents back and surrounded them in the Presnia district, now the rebels' last redoubt.

Beginning on December 16 and continuing for three days, government troops under Min's control bombarded the Presnia, determined to destroy rebel forces. Well before the battle for the district started, officials in St. Petersburg and the tsar himself had directed civil and military authorities to crush all resistance decisively and without restraint. Although most of the insurgent leaders had already escaped, Min's artillery pounded the area causing enormous destruction and loss of life. Some workers held out until December 19, but for the most part the struggle was over before then. A hideous coda to the whole event played out on the Moscow-Kazan railroad, which had been in insurgent hands for some time. Min dispatched his subordinate Colonel Nikolai Riman to take control of the line using whatever means were necessary. Between December 16 and 20, Riman achieved his goal, but in the process far exceeded any appropriate force. His orders were simple: "Take no prisoners, act mercilessly," and he obeyed them to the letter. He executed sixty-eight *druzhinniki*, some by his own hand. Dzhunkovsky felt that Riman's actions were a "dark page" in the history of the struggle against the uprising.[22]

Statistics and "body counts" are hard to come by, but one sober estimate puts the number killed during the entire December uprising at 1,059, mostly civilians, more than 200 of them women and children. Govern-

Moscow Barricades in 1905. From *Dekabr'skoe vosstanie v Moskve 1905g.*

ment losses were comparatively small, 25 policemen and 9 soldiers.[23] At this terrible blood-price, "White-Stoned Moscow" returned to the hands of the tsar.

From the moment Dubasov arrived, Dzhunkovsky strongly supported the new governor-general, a bracing contrast to the ineffectual Durnovo. Dzhun recognized Dubasov's shortcomings, particularly his terrible temper and violent rages that spread panic among his subordinates. Still, in his eyes, Dubasov was "a noble soldier" with solid common sense, "able to distinguish between the honorable and the dishonorable," and at heart "a good, humane person." Although many would charge Dubasov with excessive cruelty in the suppression of the uprising, Dzhunkovsky felt that the challenges of those difficult December days demanded decisive action. Much of the problem lay with the governor-general's subordinates, "various people who understood . . . [his orders] in different ways, and [given that] . . . , mistakes and excesses were inevitable."[24] But in the hour of victory, Dzhunkovsky was quick to note, Dubasov did not wreak vengeance on the defeated foe. He insisted that civil rather than military courts try the captured insurgents, and no death sentences resulted. Immediately after the fighting ceased, moreover, the governor-general sought to bind up the city's wounds, organizing charitable relief for the innocent victims of the battle.

Dubasov's assessment of Dzhunkovsky was equally high, and the two men developed a close, mutually beneficial working relationship. Dzhunkovsky understood that Dubasov was a man of action, not an administrator, someone with little patience or talent for the regular run of government business. For his part the governor-general quickly grasped that this kind of work was Dzhunkovsky's strong suit. "He showed extraordinary confidence in me," Dzhun recalled, "and during the armed uprising when he did not have time to take care of day-to-day . . . business, he turned these matters over to me for decision, giving me authority to sign papers for him; this was not entirely legal, but the demands of the moment required it."[25]

Throughout the revolt, Dzhunkovsky went twice daily to the governor-general's mansion to attend to affairs and traveled about the city on various assignments.[26] These missions involved many perils, despite the fact that dragoons always rode with him. Nikolai Kisel-Zagoriansky, a future governor who lived through the turbulent time, recalled Dzhunkovsky in a heroic light: "Risking his life and every minute exposed to danger . . . [he] traveled through the city attempting, by appeals to reason and conscience, to restrain wavering workers and factories that had not yet gone over to the revolution, and to prevent the uprising from spreading into the counties."[27] On December 13, insurgents fired upon Dzhunkovsky as he left his house on the way to Dubasov's, and although his guards were especially careful thereafter, he came under attack on at least one other occasion.[28]

The task of suppressing the armed uprising fell chiefly to Dubasov, the police, and the military; but Dzhunkovsky's position as governor conferred a number of specific responsibilities. Within the city limits his obligations included managing and securing the main prisons, a focus of insurgent activity from the very beginning of the rebellion. The defense of most of the jails proved relatively easy, but in the case of Butyrka, the largest and most important in Moscow, serious threats arose both from without and within its walls. For the better part of six days, barricades cut the prison off; *druzhinniki* besieged it, firing from all sides. Dzhunkovsky directed the defense and resupply of this important installation as determined militiamen attacked it from the streets and rebellious prisoners inside struggled to escape. Despite some moments of real peril, his men carried out their mission with courage and determination. The defenders held, and by December 15, the danger had passed.[29]

Dzhunkovsky's main duties concerned the large expanse of Moscow province outside the city limits. Here he was fortunate, because the last months of 1905 passed with relatively few disturbances. Most of the factories continued to operate, and local forces proved able to handle the minor difficulties that arose. In several areas, notably Bogorodsk and Mytishcha, the population seemed restive, but a few well-timed arrests scotched the threat of uprisings.[30] The most serious problem occurred due north of the city at the Liamin factory. Since November workers there had engaged in a long, stubborn strike, and on several occasions, Dzhunkovsky dispatched soldiers to patrol the area. On December 20, however, the directors sent the governor word that, in violation of an earlier agreement, the workers had seized control of the factory, driven out the legal administration, and elected their own.[31] He also received information that agitators had appeared on the scene and tried to prevent workers from going back to the job, threatening to destroy the machines and burn the factory if they did.

Dzhunkovsky decided that the situation called for the use of troops. He turned to Dubasov and received permission to deploy a battalion from the Semenovsky regiment. But when he learned that the soldiers would be commanded by Colonel Riman, just back from his brutal suppression of the insurgents on the Moscow-Kazan line, Dzhun became alarmed: "Fearing that he might go overboard and repeat what had happened on the Kazan RR, I gave . . . [Riman] the strictest instructions not to resort to the use of arms since the Liamin factory was known for its patriarchal character, and I could not believe that the workers would offer any kind of resistance." He told the colonel simply to arrest the strike leaders and bring them back to him in Moscow. Riman obeyed. (Whatever blood lust he may have had was apparently satiated.) The Semenovtsy surrounded the factory; the workers surrendered their leaders and returned to the job.[32]

Once again Dzhunkovsky had achieved his ends with minimal force and no loss of life. And although he could not know it, his actions at this time may well have saved his own. Fourteen years later, Dzhun would stand before the Moscow Revolutionary Tribunal accused of crimes against the workers, with the prosecution calling for the death penalty. His dispatch of the Semenovtsy to the Liamin factory was on the list of charges against him; but the court viewed the fact that no blood was shed during that episode as exculpation, and the former governor's sentence was unexpectedly mild (see chapter 21).

The peasants, too, remained calm for the most part, and Dzhunkovsky did not confront any major disturbances. He was concerned, however, about the dangerous influence of propaganda coming from the radical Peasant Union that had emerged during the revolution, and he decided to counter it with some propaganda of his own. Toward the end of December, he issued a proclamation, posted throughout the province, explaining to the peasants the meaning of the governor-general's decree on "maximum security" and the penalties they would face if they violated its provisions. He warned against any actions directed at the private property of others—land seizures, illegal timbering, and interference with agricultural labor. He made it clear that the government would arrest all agitators and that any meetings they might attempt to organize were strictly forbidden.

At the same time Dzhunkovsky assured the peasants that all applications presented to him in the proper manner would receive due consideration: "Satisfaction of the legitimate requests of the peasants will always have my full support," the governor stated. He also wrote optimistically about the new legislature: "The interests of the peasants [will be] sufficiently protected in the State Duma," he declared, and he urged them to participate in the elections. Dzhunkovsky ended his proclamation stating that he was counting on "the good sense of the majority of the population" to make any resort to harsh measures unnecessary.[33]

Soon Dzhunkovsky could turn to more congenial tasks. Immediately after the fighting ended in Moscow, Dubasov appealed to the tsar for aid to the victims of the tragedy. The emperor granted one hundred thousand rubles for that purpose, and Dubasov set up a commission to oversee the dispersal of relief, appointing Dzhunkovsky its chairman. As private and institutional donations also poured in, the governor called on all those in need to turn directly to him either by writing or in person during receptions that would be held daily from ten o'clock in the morning to two o'clock in the afternoon. He requested that those having information about persons requiring assistance bring it to his attention so that the commission could meet their needs.

Dzhunkovsky also helped the families of those who had been arrested during the uprising to locate their loved ones. He ordered the Prison Inspectorate to draw up a list of all those in custody with information as to where, when, and why they had been detained and to give petitioners the documents they needed in order to see them. Workers of the Inspectorate gave out these papers at the governor's residence, and from early morning his reception hall was filled with people seeking information and permission for visits. "Everyone received what they asked for that very day," he remembered proudly.[34]

The needy and the wives and families of prisoners were not the only people who turned to Dzhunkovsky. On December 23, he learned that Grand Duchess Elizaveta Fedorovna had indirectly appealed to him in order to obtain permission to come down from St. Petersburg. Ella had left Moscow shortly before the uprising, intending a brief holiday visit with family in the capital. But now, even after the fighting had stopped, Dubasov feared for her safety and blocked her return. The grand duchess was eager to resume her charitable activities, work made more pressing by the privations caused by the rebellion and its suppression. In considerable vexation she asked the manager of the imperial court, Count Mengden, to pass word of her wishes on to "'Dzhun'—a man devoted to duty, who, I think, knows Moscow," so that he might intercede with the governor-general on her behalf. Immediately upon receipt of a note from Mengden with Elizaveta Fedorovna's request appended, Dzhun did as he was asked, and based on his assurances Dubasov authorized Ella's return. On December 26, the grand duchess arrived in Moscow to take up once more her service to God and neighbor.[35]

As 1905 came to an end, Dzhunkovsky looked back on days "filled with alarming and extraordinary events" and, like many of his countrymen, harbored deep concerns about the future.[36] Still, the preceding year had given him a good measure of personal satisfaction and prompted, perhaps, a sense of wonder. In January he had been a captain, adjutant to the former governor-general, assistant head of a small but important public service organization; by December he was a colonel, an aide-de-camp to the tsar, member of the Imperial Suite, and governor of one of the empire's most important provinces. The fires of revolution had consumed many prominent officials, but he had survived, even flourished. He believed he had done his duty and accomplished his work in an honorable manner. Radicals and a large segment of educated society viewed the men who had led government's struggle with sedition in 1905 as monsters, and they would suffer accordingly. Dubasov sustained serious injuries in several assassination attempts; an SR terrorist gunned down Min in a railway station before the eyes of his wife and daughter. Riman briefly fled the country and lived in obscurity after his return. In 1917 victorious revolutionaries arrested and shot him. Dzhunkovsky was not associated with harsh measures, however, and continued to enjoy public respect, even affection.

Nor did this approval damn him in the eyes of his superiors. On December 24, Governor-General Dubasov wrote to the emperor asking that Dzhun be made a major general. "Dzhunkovsky is a wonderfully gifted man imbued with the feeling of self-sacrifice and devotion to duty," he wrote. "In the terrible days of the rebellious uprising, I found in aide-de-camp Dzhunkovsky an assistant [who] always accurately evaluated the circumstances and was always well informed about the conditions we had to confront. Thanks to this, I could, in every instance, rely on him with complete confidence, and his participation in the work was always to my mind a firm guarantee of success. In the person of . . . Dzhunkovsky," Dubasov concluded, "Your Imperial Majesty has not only a selfless subject, but also an extraordinarily gifted servant."[37]

Part Three

Master of the Province, 1906–1912

Chapter 7

Learning the Ropes

Despite Dubasov's impassioned appeal, the emperor did not make Dzhunkovsky a major-general (much to Dzhun's own relief). It was far too early, he believed. Just promoted to colonel, he lacked the time in rank required for another advance. Being raised to general would have been extraordinary, certain to cause envy and unfriendly gossip. He was content with the award of the Order of Saint Vladimir (third class) for outstanding civil or military service.[1] Elevation in rank would come soon enough—in 1908—but meanwhile, Dzhunkovsky did not need the hostility of others. The political situation and the governmental tasks ahead would prove daunting for him and for all those who served the tsar.

The suppression of the December armed uprising in Moscow ended the most dramatic phase of the first Russian revolution. But tumult continued for two more years as rulers and ruled grappled with the legacy of 1905. In that span the empire received a new constitution, held two national elections, and witnessed two failed parliaments. A new national leader arose and put forward a broad program for social and institutional change; then in order to implement these reforms, he carried out a coup d'état. And through it all, came terror—Red and White—as the revolutionaries spread havoc and death with bombs and bullets while government forces used brutal means to impose order on a fractured, troubled country.

If the defeat of the Moscow revolt ended hopes for the immediate overthrow of tsarism, events of the two years that followed dashed other hopes as well. The expectations of liberals for a quick transition to a parliamentary regime ended with the electoral statute of December 11, 1905, and the constitutional arrangements embodied in the revised Fundamental Laws issued in April 1906. Suffrage was extended to twenty-five million people, but voting was indirect and the law favored the propertied element and the supposedly conservative peasantry. A reformed State Council became a second legislative chamber, equal to the Duma, half its members chosen by the tsar. Although no law could be passed without the consent of parliament, the monarch retained much of his autocratic power. He appointed all ministers, commanded the army and navy, determined foreign policy, and could veto any legislation. He had the right to dissolve the Duma and the elected portion of the State Council, but he had to call for new elections within four months. Parliamentary prerogatives were sharply limited even in budgetary matters, and the emperor was able to bypass the legislative bodies altogether. Article 87 of the Fundamental Laws permitted the tsar and his ministers to issue emergency laws when the legislative institutions were not in session. These could not alter the Fundamental Laws, change the electoral statute, or abolish the Duma or Council, and when the legislature reconvened, had to be submitted for its approval within two months. If either house rejected them they would lapse. Still, Article 87 opened the way for the tsar to stage a coup d'état against the institutions he had created and to change by unconstitutional means even those areas declared to be off limits.[2]

But government hopes for a conservative and submissive legislature were also dashed when the First State Duma convened on April 24, 1906. Peasant voters returned many radical delegates, and the Constitutional Democrats (KDs or Kadets), seen by the tsar and his ministers as dangerous revolutionaries, dominated. Their demands for a responsible ministry, full civil liberties, and extensive land reform were unacceptable, and after forty stormy sessions, Nicholas dissolved the Duma on July 9, 1906.

By this time Tsar Nicholas had found a man capable of managing the situation: Petr Arkadevich Stolypin, who had distinguished himself as the tough and effective governor of the turbulent province of Saratov. Well-educated, highly intelligent, a forceful personality and a brilliant speaker, Stolypin was prepared to undertake significant reforms in order to stabilize the country and build a great and revitalized Russia. Just before dissolving the First State Duma, the tsar made Stolypin minister of internal affairs; after the dissolution, Nicholas appointed him prime minister as well. The dynamic Stolypin quickly seized the initiative and would dominate the empire's political scene until his assassination in 1911.

Before undertaking reforms, Stolypin sought to restore order in a country shaken by a wave of political terrorism. Between October 1905 and September 1906, assassins killed 3,611 government officials, from lowly policemen to generals and provincial governors. In August the prime minister himself narrowly escaped death when three members of the Maximalists, an ultra-radical branch of the Socialist Revolutionary Party, entered his dacha and blew themselves up, killing twenty-seven people and injuring seventy others, including two of his children.[3] Using Article 87, Stolypin proposed and the emperor decreed the creation of field courts-martial that subjected terrorists and their supporters to swift, summary "justice." Closed-door trials before panels of five specially selected military officers delivered harsh sentences—death or long prison terms—that were to be imposed at once and were not subject to appeal. In the space of eight months, they sentenced 1,144 people to death. Simultaneously, regular military and civil courts handed down roughly 1,150 death sentences, although only about one-third of these were actually carried out. Government troops also resorted to massive repressions of peasant disturbances that took the lives of many more. In a nation where for the entire nineteenth century executions had only numbered in the hundreds, the ferocity of these measures shocked the public. But they broke the back of the terrorist threat, and after 1907 violence declined steadily. Order began to return; peaceful change became possible.

Stolypin linked repression with a program of reform. It included strengthening civil and religious freedoms, improving local government and the courts, expanding and enhancing university and secondary education, reworking the tax laws and the system of workers' insurance. Most important, Stolypin envisioned a far-reaching land reform that, he believed, would reduce communal tenure, improve agricultural productivity, and turn peasants into prosperous landowning citizens. On November 9, 1906, during the hiatus between the First and Second Dumas, he introduced this reform using Article 87. It permitted peasants to withdraw from their communes—the rural institutions that governed their lives, gathered taxes and dues, and collectively controlled planting, sowing, and reaping. Peasants could take their land allotments, usually divided into small strips, and consolidate them into individual farmsteads. Taken together Stolypin's reform projects sketched a revolution that would transform many of the country's major institutions. But this revolution would come from above, through the medium of an elected parliament.

Stolypin hoped that the Second State Duma would support his broad program for change. But when it opened on February 20, 1907, it proved even more radical than its predecessor. The socialist parties that had boycotted the first elections now had decided to participate, and they elected a sizeable number of delegates. By mid-May it was clear that the Duma would reject the land reform, and the tsar and his chief minister resolved on another dissolution. This time, however, they would carry out what amounted to a coup d'état, an unconstitutional change in the electoral law designed to produce a conservative and cooperative legislature.

Stolypin found a pretext for the dissolution in an alleged conspiracy by some of the fifty-five Social Democrats in the Duma to foster an uprising in the army. Using information gathered by a secret police agent, Ekaterina Shornikova, the government proclaimed a threat to national security and demanded that the SD deputies be expelled and arrested. Evidence for these allegations was flimsy, but on June 1 Stolypin went before the Duma to call for the SDs' removal. The Duma tried to investigate the government's charges, but the prime minister gave it little time. On June 3, 1907, the tsar dissolved the Duma and authorities arrested the accused deputies.

Simultaneously, Nicholas issued a new electoral law weighted even more heavily in favor of the propertied classes and sharply reducing the representation of peasants, workers, and non-Russians. The political arrangements that now emerged have been called "The Third of June System." Unquestionably illegal, a violation of the Fundamental Laws and Stolypin's proclaimed goal of a law-based state, they endured until the empire's collapse in 1917. Thanks to the modified suffrage, when the Third State Duma met in November, parties of the Right and the Center held sway. The Third Duma would serve out its full five-year term and be more tractable and productive. It adopted and subsequently augmented Stolypin's agrarian reform. But dominated by a nobility made warily conservative by the revolutionary events of 1905–1906, the Third Duma would frustrate many of the prime minister's other efforts to bring about broad social and institutional change.[4]

As Russia moved fitfully and uncertainly along the path toward something resembling a constitutional order, Dzhunkovsky began to immerse himself in his job as Moscow governor, a post that admirably suited both his energies and his talents. In the administrative structure of the Russian empire, few offices were as important or as difficult as the one Dzhunkovsky now held. Governors were the most powerful officials outside the capital, the personal representatives of the tsar. Sometimes called "master of the province" (*khoziain gubernii*) or more often "provincial chief" (*nachal'nik gubernii*), a governor wielded great authority. He was responsible for the peace, good order, and welfare of the territory entrusted to him and was supposed to see that all institutions and administrative personnel carried out their duties in the proper manner.

Governors occupied a special place in the hierarchy of state offices. Appointed by the emperor, with the right to report directly to him, they were "extra-departmental," outside the established ministerial system. At the same time, however, governors stood in the Ministry of Internal Affairs' chain of command, subject to its orders and discipline. Governors worked in a "paper rain" of official circulars and requests for information that poured ceaselessly from St. Petersburg chancelleries. They chaired as many as fifteen standing committees and handled official correspondence that alone could take up to four hours a day. Still, governors were not and never thought of themselves as simple bureaucrats; their personal link to the sovereign gave them a sense of independence as well as considerable real autonomy. Much of the public, too, saw them as emperor surrogates with the power to influence matters both great and small. Industrial disputes or peasant disturbances often required their intervention. At regular receptions or through the mail, ordinary citizens turned to governors for help in finding a job, obtaining a railroad ticket, or simply to request a small handout.

A governor's duties were both practical and ceremonial. Opening the triennial assembly of the provincial nobility or the annual meeting of the zemstvo were public events with considerable political significance. But His Excellency might also have to cut a ribbon at a museum exhibit, attend a prayer service at a local school, be present at the unveiling of a statue, inaugurate a charitable lottery, or even look in on student examinations. In addition, governors were leading figures in provincial society, expected to give or attend a variety of parties, dinners, formal banquets, and balls.

By the beginning of the twentieth century the governors were far from being the satraps often described in literature and in oppositional polemics. They were, rather, harried administrators with an important, burdensome, and complex job requiring a range of political, managerial, and personal skills. A governor needed to show the Ministry of Internal Affairs that he was an effective and responsive factotum. At the same time he had to use his personal connection to the tsar to maintain a degree of autonomy. A governor's status as the sovereign's representative and his extra-departmental position helped him deal with a bewildering variety of institutions and officials not all of whom were under his direct control.

Power in the provinces was highly fragmented. The governor might be the titular chief of the *gubernia* administration, but this position did not guarantee him the obedience or cooperation of local elites. The provincial agents of the central ministries—Finance, War, Agriculture, Education, Justice—were subject to the governor's overall supervision and obliged to carry out his lawful commands, but they usually looked to their superiors in St. Petersburg for guidance and support. At the very least they demanded that the governor show them proper respect and deference. Then there were the elected institutions and their officers: the assemblies and marshals of the nobility, the provincial and county zemstvos and their executive boards, the urban dumas and city mayors. These were not fully part of the state machine, but they carried out important governmental or quasi-governmental functions. Provincial marshals were independent influential spokesmen for the nobility who could, if offended, make a governor's life miserable. County marshals headed the administration at that level. Both provincial and county marshals had to be handled with care. In the case of the zemstvos and urban dumas, a governor might exercise considerable authority, but it was mostly of a negative character—challenging particular decisions or appointments. To attain positive goals, he had to seek accommodation, using persuasion rather than command.

Even those institutions and officials unquestionably subordinated to the governors posed problems. The men who staffed the provincial bureaucracy were usually undereducated, badly paid, frequently incompetent, and generally demoralized. Arbitrary behavior and corruption were constants. Governors could do little to change this; they had to work with the human material at hand. They needed to determine who among their officials they could reasonably count on and then treasure and inspire the capable. Here, too, simple command would not suffice; an effective governor led by lifting spirits, inspiring his staff by personal example.

To keep the gears of provincial government moving, governors needed to apply liberal amounts of a lubricant Russians called "service tact," a substance not always visible or palpable but whose absence could cause senseless personal conflict, bureaucratic confusion, institutional deadlock, or even violent bloodletting. In some cases service tact might simply be palaver, massaging the ego of an important person or official, or displaying the proper courtesy in arranging a meeting, seeing that the invitation was issued in the appropriate manner. In other instances, it meant finding the right words to buck up a discouraged official or showing appreciation for good work by means of a dinner invitation. A governor could employ service tact in worker and peasant disturbances: a ready ear to hear grievances and an appropriate touch of bonhomie might defuse a potentially volatile situation. A willingness to go along to get along was necessary in a variety of situations, but it could not be seen as spinelessness. Service tact was a balancing act: it required the ability to display and maintain authority while giving the minimum of offense. The style with which a governor exercised his power often had a greater impact than the substance of his decisions.

In the early 1800s the great Russian writer and historian Nikolai Karamzin claimed that by finding "fifty good governors" to preside over the provinces the emperor could solve the country's problems. But this search proved long and frustrating. By the beginning of the twentieth century, however, the tsar and the Ministry of Internal Affairs were having better luck. Something resembling a "gubernatorial corps" drawn from a pool of qualified candidates had started to form and a process of limited professionalization was under way. Educational levels of governors rose; the number of those who possessed the local administrative experience needed for the job increased. A cohort of new model governors, legally trained and more respectful of proper procedures and the rights of the tsar's subjects, was emerging, one that might be called a "Stolypin generation." Like the prime minister, they had been born into the Great Reform era and were receptive to the ideas and principles it generated. At the beginning of a new century they had begun to change the character of provincial rule.[5]

Dzhunkovsky belonged to that cohort. Although his career path differed substantially from that of many newer governors, his varied experiences had given him the skills the office required. His long service as a courtier—page, adjutant, and member of the tsar's Suite—refined the natural tact that his schoolmates had noted early. He had enormous energy and the capacity for hard work. During fifteen years in Moscow, Dzhunkovsky had come to know the city and the province well. His association with Grand Duke Sergei had revealed many administrative pitfalls he was determined to avoid. His attitude toward the duties he assumed differed markedly from that of his late patron. "The chief obligation of the administrator," Dzhun wrote, "is not to seek popularity, but to [obtain] the trust of the people; and to do that you must instill in yourself the sense that the people do not exist for the government, but the government for the people. . . . [You] must convey this sense to your subordinates . . . , not by words, but by deeds; you need to provide them with an example of *how* to work, *how* to approach their responsibilities. Not strictness, but example is, in my opinion, the most important thing."[6] These principles would guide Dzhunkovsky throughout his governorship, but it would be some time before he could apply them systematically. Echoes of the recent revolution made his first years in office turbulent and dangerous.

Dzhunkovsky's memoirs, drawn from his archive and the diary he kept for much of his life, contain a long list of assassinations and assassination attempts that makes it clear that the new governor was well aware of the perils surrounding him. Early in 1906, sheer chance spared his life when terrorists attacked Governor-General Dubasov. On April 23, the governor-general drove to the Kremlin to attend a service at the Uspensky Cathedral celebrating the name day of Empress Alexandra. Dzhunkovsky had often accompanied Dubasov on such occasions, but that day the governor-general chose to honor his orderly, Count Konovnitsyn, by inviting him on the ride. On the way back from the service, a bomb blew Dubasov's carriage apart; he survived, but Konovnitsyn died on the spot.[7] Dzhun's lucky escape does not seem to have frightened him and may even have strengthened his fatalistic sangfroid. A year later he learned from the Department of Police that he was the target of an assassination plot and was advised not to go out on horseback. On the day he received this warning, Dzhunkovsky had a lunch date with some friends at Yar, a popular Moscow restaurant. Urged to stay home, he went ahead. His only "precaution" was to go by streetcar.[8]

Nor did the dangers of the immediate postrevolutionary situation deter Dzhunkovsky from carrying out one of his most important duties: regular inspections ("revisions") of the institutions and population of the counties of the province. These tours were arduous, time-consuming, and often frustrating, but they were the only way the governor could get a picture of local conditions, assess the capabilities of officials who worked outside Moscow, and keep abreast of the needs and mood of the people. Dzhunkovsky wanted to know just about everything. This excerpt from a report on his inspection of the town of Klin gives a clear sense of his approach:

> The governor visited in the following order: the local church school, the municipal executive board, the girls' progymnasium, the city parish school, and the city bank; he looked over the vehicles of . . . the fire department, during which time the firemen conducted a drill. [The governor] noted that the girls' progymnasium was well housed and had exemplary instruction. The governor attended several classes in Russian language, arithmetic, geography, and French.
>
> Then he visited the zemstvo executive board [and] the county conference where the governor talked with . . . five headmen from neighboring cantons and nineteen elders from nearby villages. [He also visited] the zemstvo jail, which he found to be in proper order, the zemstvo agricultural storage house (where he noted there was only a small amount of seed oats on hand), the chancellery of the draft board, the county police department, and the treasury; the latter had an excellent safe.[9]

Dzhunkovsky continued in this style during his three-day tour of Bronitsy and Kolomna counties in mid-June 1906. Traveling mostly on horseback, he visited a host of small towns, interviewed officials, and inspected hospitals, schools, fire departments, military units, factories, and peasant and zemstvo institutions. All along the route he met large groups of peasants who asked many questions that often required lengthy answers so that the governor soon fell far behind schedule. On the second day, instead of getting to the village of Verkhovlian at six o'clock, Dzhun arrived at eleven at night. He reached Boiarkino, his next stop, an hour after midnight, and Gory at three in the morning. He got to Ozery, his planned destination, at four in the morning, caught a bit of sleep, and was up and running three hours later. He ended his tour at Kolomna and returned to Moscow.[10]

Dzhunkovsky's first "revisions" went well. The peasants and workers he met, while demanding, were mostly friendly, and the governor never felt himself to be in danger. This would not be the case when he visited Volokolamsk county. Three of its cantons (*volosts*)—Markovo, Kulpino and Iaropolets—were highly agitated and hostile. In late October 1905, the peasants of Markovo had proclaimed a "republic," elected a "president," and announced that they would not pay taxes, provide recruits, or obey government orders. The peasants initiated a rent strike and seized timber belonging to local landowners, including the county marshal of the nobility, Prince S. B. Meshchersky. Influenced by the SR-dominated Peasant Union and a popular local agronomist, the inhabitants of the "Markovo Republic" issued a list of political demands: direct elections to the Duma, free universal education, full civil rights for all, a general amnesty for political prisoners, and a progressive taxation system. For a time, local authorities had been unwilling to take punitive actions, fearing that they might further inflame the peasants. But now, with the revolution on the wane, the forces of order began to assert themselves. In late April, the local land captain had ordered the removal of the Markovo canton's elected "elder," Ivan Ryzhov, a leader of the "republic," but the peasants refused.[11] When Dzhunkovsky arrived in Volokolamsk toward the end of July, he sent a telegram to Ryzhov summoning him to the county seat. Ryzhov, believing he would be arrested upon arrival, wired back that he would await the governor at Markovo.[12] Not one to avoid a difficult situation, Dzhun headed straight for the rebellious canton.

He arrived accompanied by the captain of the local police and drove to the office of the canton board. In front of the building a large crowd of peasants had gathered with Ryzhov at their head, holding the traditional gift of bread and salt as a sign of welcome. If the governor accepted this offering it would imply that relations between the peasants and the authorities were on a normal footing, but Dzhunkovsky immediately made it clear that this was not the case. Without getting out of his carriage, he rejected the peasants' gift. He then drove to Lotoshino, the estate of Prince Meshchersky. Shortly thereafter, a delegation from Markovo appeared and asked Dzhunkovsky why he had insulted them by refusing to stop and speak. He responded that they knew very well what the reason was. He would return only when Ryzhov surrendered his office, and the peasants recognized their error.

This is how Dzhunkovsky described things in his memoirs and in a report to the minister of internal affairs.[13] The peasants remembered things differently. One of those present claimed that the governor came in with a mounted detachment of police. When he got to the canton office, he shouted: "You, Markovo peasants, are rebels, I won't come to you!" and sped away. Whereupon the peasants called after him: "We don't need you. Go back where you came from!" Their story contains no mention of a delegation making a later visit to the governor at Lotoshino.[14]

Although details of the event are in dispute, it is clear that Dzhunkovsky left Markovo with matters unresolved. He next drove with Meshchersky to the canton of Kulpino where the peasants were also in a rebellious mood. There a more threatening scene unfolded. When he arrived at the canton office, the governor was surprised to encounter only the local leaders; most of the peasants were absent. But as Dzhunkovsky began to go over the canton's records, a large agitated crowd of peasants gathered and started to push their way into the room where he sat. The governor told the peasants that he would not speak to a mob and asked them to select representatives with whom he could discuss things. For a while the crowd backed off; representatives came forward, and a conversation began. Then the peasants pressed in again, clearly contemptuous, shouting questions in an insulting tone. Many were drunk.[15]

Realizing that the situation was likely to get worse, Dzhun decided to retreat. Turning to the peasants he said: "Since you won't listen to me and continue to push in here, I will leave you. Let me through at once." Grudgingly, the crowd opened slightly, permitting the governor and the marshal to reach their carriage. But people clustered tightly around the vehicle, making it impossible for them to move ahead. The peasants began to pepper Dzhunkovsky with questions which he answered as best he could, seeking to maintain an air of calm. But the number of boisterous drunks grew alarmingly.

At this point the governor tried to defuse the situation, edging toward stand-up comedy. Rising in his carriage, Dzhun engaged the crowd: "I see it's impossible to talk to you today. You're very excited and don't know what you are saying. But I forgive this behavior." Then, alluding to the drunks in the audience, he struck a jocular tone: "It's the feast of the Virgin of Kazan, and clearly you have been celebrating a bit too sincerely." A few voices replied: "Yes, yes, the Virgin of Kazan!" and the peasants broke into laughter. Dzhun quickly took advantage of this momentary change of mood. "Make way!" he shouted. The throng parted; he and Meshchersky swiftly drove off.

Dzhunkovsky came next to Iaropolets, where at the canton office he encountered another crowd, better-mannered than the last but still expressing their concerns in hostile tones. After hearing them out, the governor returned to Moscow convinced that the situation in Volokolamsk county required prompt action lest more serious agrarian disturbances develop. He dispatched a company of Cossacks and quartered them in Iaropolets. He ordered the arrest of Ryzhov and all those agitating among the peasants. This display of force restored order. The peasants in the county submitted, and the "Markovo Republic" that had lasted for eight months collapsed.[16]

Dzhun did not let things end here, however. When he sent out the troops and ordered the arrests, he posted a circular throughout the county calling on the peasants to obey established authorities and to reject the counsel of agitators who "did not have . . . [their] best interests at heart." Though warning that he would use all necessary means to maintain law and order, he also tried to strike a conciliatory note: "Let the peasants understand and believe that I and my subordinate officials will meet all their lawful requests and will protect their interests as we would those of any other estate. I am personally willing to listen to any peasant and to help him in any legitimate matter."[17]

Sometime later Dzhunkovsky learned that during his tour of Volokolamsk county he had been at greater risk than he realized. Ryzhov, he was told, had planned to take him captive when he visited Markovo and force him to agree to a series of revolutionary demands. Dzhun's swift departure had scotched that scheme, but when the peasants of Kulpino heard of this they decided to catch the governor on his way to them with a similar aim in view. They gathered on the road at some distance from the village hoping to intercept him, which explained why so few of Kulpino's inhabitants were on hand when he arrived at the canton office by another route.[18] Once again, Dzhunkovsky had come through a dangerous situation unscathed. This escape may have strengthened his tendency to face future threats believing his life was in God's hands.

Despite continued disturbances Dzhunkovsky quickly assumed command of the provincial administration and steadily mastered its operations. By February 1906 he had taken so much of the gubernia's affairs in hand that

A. M. Poliansky, the head of chancellery who had managed things during Governor Kristi's tenure, began to feel superfluous; he resigned, accepting a new and more lucrative post in the city. The two men parted on good terms and Dzhun fondly remembered Poliansky's vital help during his first days in office. Still, the speed with which the new governor marginalized this experienced official reveals not only his competence but also his determination to run the show himself.[19]

The rapid flow of events made it difficult for Dzhunkovsky to establish a settled routine immediately, but in time one emerged. The governor began his day early: he rose at seven and was in his office by eight. At nine he started hearing reports from department chiefs and other officials, usually beginning with his head of chancellery. These could last until one o'clock, but ended at eleven on the three days a week when the governor held a reception for petitioners and others wishing to see him. Between reports, he sometimes met with marshals of the nobility and the chairmen of zemstvo and city duma executive boards who had come to him on matters of business.[20]

Dzhunkovsky easily grasped the material that his subordinates presented. Fedor Shlippe, who served as head of the Moscow Land Settlement Commission, gave this highly flattering description of his chief's style: "I recall, with a feeling of special thankfulness, the kind, good, always fair governor, V. F. Dzhunkovsky," he wrote in his memoirs. "Weekly reports to him were always a joy for me. He loved openness, and you never had to play politics but [could] speak God's honest truth. He understood things very rapidly and read with unbelievable speed. Sometimes it seemed that he signed my papers [after] looking over them superficially, not even reading them; but in fact it turned out that he had carefully examined both their contents and the form in which they were expressed."[21]

Dzhunkovsky attached great significance to the receptions he held three days a week, usually meeting fifty or more persons each time. An informal atmosphere prevailed, and in his reception hall one could see all kinds of people: Moscow workers, rural merchants wearing old fashioned knee-length jackets, peasants in sheepskin coats. Peasant women were often present as well, sometimes accompanied by their children when there was no one to care for them at home. The governor accepted all comers without appointment but asked his duty officers to find out if papers relating to a petitioner's business had previously been sent to the chancellery or to one of the standing committees. Should this be the case, Dzhunkovsky insisted that the documents be brought to him so he could consider the matter at once and, where possible, decide it. In the meantime the governor went around the room, patiently and attentively listening to all those who were there, trying to understand their concerns and deal with them on the spot. If visitors wished to speak to him in private, Dzhunkovsky asked them to wait until the general reception was over, then he would usher each person into his office individually. The receptions usually lasted for two hours, sometimes more, after which the governor broke for lunch.[22]

Meetings of the various standing committees took up most of the afternoon. Usually these began at three, but some started as early as one o'clock, and one began as late as nine at night. Dzhun chaired the most important ones, leaving others to the vice-governor. Sessions continued until six or seven, after which the governor had dinner. Dzhunkovsky enjoyed some free time in the evenings and often went to the theater, although it was not unusual for him to spend from two to three hours looking over petitions and reviewing and signing decisions that had been taken by gubernia agencies.[23] Even after he retired for the night, Dzhun remained on duty. He slept with a telephone at his bedside so that, should an emergency arise, he could be awakened to the situation and act immediately. (Some years later, when Stolypin—something of a workaholic himself—visited the governor's mansion, he pronounced this arrangement "too much," but Dzhunkovsky assured the prime minister that he had seen to it that only important calls came through.)[24]

Governors' jobs involved routine, some of it quite mind-numbing, and it was not unusual for them to delegate a portion of it to subordinates and staff. Dzhunkovsky, too, relied on his vice-governor, head of chancellery, and various committee heads for assistance. Still, Dzhun's energy and intellectual curiosity led him to confront perplexing administrative mysteries such as the workings of the Standing Committee on Commercial Taxation that handled complaints about taxes levied on businesses. The operations of this committee were complex, and many unresolved questions had accumulated in its files. Dzhunkovsky recalled that at first his ignorance of these matters forced him to "look blank" and sign the papers thrust in front of him. But a passive approach was not his style, and after considerable study he was ready to take things in hand and make informed decisions; in the process he considerably reduced the committee's backlog of paper.[25]

Dzhunkovsky took a strong interest in the work of the Medical Board, a standing committee that oversaw matters of public health. Given the rapid rise in the population and the expansion of industry in both the city of Moscow and the surrounding province, the governor felt that the delivery of medical services deserved high priority. But he found that the committee in charge worked poorly because of inadequate leadership and the low pay its members received. The board's operations were painfully slow, and bribery exercised undue influence on important matters such as decisions regarding the opening of drugstores in the province. Dzhun was particularly concerned about the pharmacies and made them the special responsibility of the vice-governor. The governor himself chose to give personal attention, time, and energy to another important and delicate medical issue: the certification and treatment of the mentally ill.

When he first became governor Dzhun was shocked by the careless manner with which the tragedy of insanity was being treated by a special subcommittee of the Medical Board. Composed of doctors as well as administrative and judicial officials, this body met irregularly and often delayed making the decisions that had profound consequences, for both the disturbed individual and his or her family. Mental illness was something Dzhunkovsky knew about firsthand. Alexander Mikhalkov, the widowed husband of a woman with whom he had been in love during his youth, had descended into madness and was eventually institutionalized. Dzhun became a guardian of his two small children and in 1899 had taken Mikhalkov to Germany for treatment.[26] Consequently, the governor quickly took charge of the mental health subcommittee and made sure that it held meetings every Thursday and decided all business received during the previous week. Meetings were long and often required the committee members to travel to various hospitals because not all those who had to be examined for possible certification could be brought to the Medical Board's offices. When travel was necessary, Dzhunkovsky was at great pains to arrange transportation, sometimes with comic results. On one occasion, Dzhun and the committee members rode in a "paddy wagon" normally used to cart prisoners to the Moscow jails. In his memoirs he recalled that travel in this less-than-elegant vehicle with barred windows caused his fellow passengers considerable embarrassment, but that they put a good face on the whole business. Then he added: "I could not know then that twelve years later I would again ride in this [same] conveyance, not as governor, but as a prisoner being transferred from the Cheka to Butyrka prison, arrested for having been a governor."[27]

Dzhunkovsky focused considerable attention on the conditions of those confined to mental institutions. He inspected all the hospitals throughout the province, both public and private, visiting violent and nonviolent wards, and he was profoundly affected by what he encountered.[28] He did his best to see that the family members of those who were declared insane would not suffer unduly. Final approval of certification required a ruling of the Senate, the empire's highest judicial institution, and until that time the assets of the person adjudged mentally ill were frozen and could not be used by his family and relatives; interest payments and even pensions stopped. Dzhunkovsky did all he could to speed Senate decisions, using personal connections and influence. In violation of the law he often saw to it that the loved ones (usually wives and children) of mentally ill persons whose status had not been finalized received portions of the sequestered capital and pensions. "I recognized that I was guilty of exceeding my authority and might have to face a civil suit," he recalled, "but there was no other way."[29]

Dzhunkovsky's direct involvement with the problems of the mentally ill and their families also reflected his larger concern for the rights and dignity of all people regardless of their condition or station in life, an attitude rooted in his Christian faith and moral principles. As governor Dzhunkovsky sought to treat all those living in the province with respect. He always viewed peasants and workers as rational human beings, and the frequent proclamations and circulars he addressed to them on a wide range of questions—from Duma elections to measures against cholera or the attacks of crop-killing snails—showed his belief that appeals to their intelligence, common sense, and decency were likely to elicit a positive response. His approach to the *narod* was straightforward and hardheaded, devoid of any kind of sentimental "populism," but he was deeply offended when his subordinates behaved in an abusive manner. During an inspection of Dmitrov county in the fall of 1907, Dzhun became outraged when a local police official, Snytko by name, sought to curry favor with him by forcing a group of peasants into a display of enthusiasm. After Dzhunkovsky had spoken with them and was in the process of driving off, he heard Snytko yell at the peasants: "Shout hurrah, you bastards!" The governor reprimanded Snytko and called on the police officials of the province to refrain from such tactless acts. His decree was not readily obeyed, however, and he would have to repeat it two years later.[30]

Dzhunkovsky's concern and protection extended even to those whose political actions and opinions he did not favor. In early 1906 a mounted police officer struck S. I. Chetverikov, a factory owner and vocal critic of the government, with a whip. Chetverikov had supported his workers in their oppositional activities, and the assault provoked a scandal. But Dzhunkovsky moved quickly to prevent things from getting out of hand. He immediately ordered the officer's arrest and personally went to the Chetverikov family to express his condolences and beg their pardon. The whole thing was "terribly painful and embarrassing" for the governor, but he felt he could do no less. For their part, the Chetverikovs graciously asked Dzhunkovsky not to punish the offending policeman. He complied and did not bind the man over for trial. But he reprimanded the officer and transferred him to another district.[31]

Respect for human dignity and devotion to proper procedures caused Dzhunkovsky to question the value of Stolypin's field courts-martial. In judicial matters Dzhun was not a "bleeding heart." In the fall of 1906 he complained to the prime minister that the judges who tried the leaders of the Moscow uprising—and found most of them not guilty—were far too liberal.[32] He had no sympathy for the terrorists the field courts were designed to combat, and he held Stolypin in the highest regard. Still he felt that the drumhead tribunals caused more harm than good: "They promoted the arbitrary abuse of authority and increased the ranks of the discontented," he wrote years later. "Some governors-general turned over to these courts not only those who had carried out attacks on state officials but also those who had simply committed armed robberies. . . . The field courts, made up not of jurists but of rank-and-file officers, were not bound by any limits; for identical offences they might hand down completely different sentences. . . . ; everything depended not on legal statutes, but on the character and views of those who chanced to be members of the tribunal. . . . It seemed to me that the introduction of the field courts-martial had the character of a sort of vengeance, a feeling unworthy of a government."[33]

Doubts about the field courts and a determination to go by the law spawned a series of conflicts between Dzhunkovsky and his superior, General S. K. Gershelman, Dubasov's successor as governor-general of Moscow and the brother-in-law of Dzhun's sister Olga. Gershelman intervened in the decisions of the tribunals, despite the strict rule that their decisions could not be altered. In one case a field court had sentenced two brothers to life in prison for killing a policeman. The governor-general felt that the decision was too lenient, so he ordered the men retried before another field court that condemned them to death. Dzhunkovsky argued passionately that the law did not permit the governor-general to void the original decision and obtain a harsher judgment. But he failed to convince Gershelman, and the brothers were hanged. Dzhun and Gershelman also clashed over the place where those sentenced to die could be executed. The governor-general ordered hangings held in Moscow's provincial prisons, which were under Dzhunkovsky's control, making him, in effect, responsible. Dzhun cited a law that required executions to be carried out at locations determined by the city commandant. Initially Dzhun had to yield to Gershelman but he protested the governor-general's orders, and the minister of justice eventually overturned them.[34]

Chapter 8

A Governor con Brio

DZHUNKOVSKY'S MEMOIR OF HIS YEARS AS GOVERNOR reveals a man who truly loved his job with all its challenges and dangers. The energy he displayed, his attention to detail, and his eager involvement with all aspects of the work amazed his contemporaries. His desire to be where the action was puts an American in mind of Theodore Roosevelt and Fiorello La Guardia. When fires broke out in the villages of the province, the governor was, whenever possible, quick to get to the scene, to oversee the work of those combating the blaze, and to assess the population's need for assistance. On one occasion he used his aide-de-camp status to secure immediate, direct help from the tsar for peasants who had been burned out.[1] In late July 1912 major forest and peat bog fires ravaged the province. The scope of the disaster required the full-scale mobilization of the police, fire brigades, local military units, and the general population. For five days and nights Dzhunkovsky went from one burning area to another, on horseback and by automobile, personally directing the forces engaged in the struggle with the conflagration, seeking to save threatened villages. In the dark the burning forest took on a hellish aspect; trees suddenly exploded and fell, consumed from within by fires coming from their roots; flames burst from pits in the earth. Ultimately, Dzhun and the firefighters were successful; the villages were spared, but only at the cost of an enormous collective effort.[2]

In early April 1908 colossal floods swept through Moscow province. The week before Easter, rain and several warm days melted the snow and broke up river ice. But while it was clear that the rivers would rise, no one expected what came—the worst floods in over half a century. On the night of Thursday, April 10, Dzhun first received word that the Moscow River had breached its banks and flooded the village of Mnevnika, fewer than five miles from the city. The torrent spread rapidly, inundating the neighboring village of Terekhove. As soon as morning came, the governor gathered life-saving equipment and raced to the scene where, together with the local police chief and land captain, he plunged into the work of pulling people and cattle out of the water. But this was only the beginning; the deluge soon reached Moscow itself. By Good Friday, April 11, one-third of the city was submerged; waves lapped the Kremlin's walls. The ground floors of many buildings flooded, their inhabitants caught unexpectedly, and the waters engulfed the central electric station causing a widespread power outage.[3]

As the rising tides flowed from the Moscow and Oka Rivers and their tributaries, calls for help poured in from people and villages all over the province. The governor dispatched rescue teams to the far reaches of the *gubernia*, and he came personally to stricken communities providing not just aid but on occasion spiritual comfort as well. On Easter Sunday, Dzhun arrived at Belopesotskaia Sloboda to supervise relief efforts. He brought hundreds of traditional cakes and eggs for the peasants huddled forlornly together with their cattle and few salvaged belongings on a hill not far from their completely submerged settlement. "When they saw me," he recalled, "the women began to keen and the old men crossed themselves." As soon as the eggs and cakes had been unloaded, the village priest said a mass and blessed the gifts the governor had brought. In the week that followed, Dzhun continued to travel throughout the province, sometimes by train but often by boat and on horseback, visiting the afflicted villages and organizing on-the-spot relief. Then as the waters started to recede, he began to put the work of dispensing aid on a more systematic basis.

On April 15, Dzhunkovsky called a conference of the provincial and county marshals of the nobility, the chairmen of the zemstvo governing boards, and key members of his administration to organize long-term assistance. After determining which areas had been the hardest hit, they established a provincial relief committee, chaired by the governor, with subordinate committees in six stricken counties, chaired by their marshals. The conference authorized the solicitation of contributions in both cash

Moscow Flood of 1908. Wikimedia commons.

and kind and opened a bank account to hold relief funds that did not have to be dispensed immediately. It requested the Metropolitan of Moscow to gather collections in the churches and to disburse sums from the capital that had been raised to aid those who had suffered during the 1905 uprising. The conference also sought the most accurate data on the number of those who required aid and asked the local land captains to look into the question of making loans of seed to peasants in need. Soon donations poured in from many quarters, and within the space of a month and a half the flood committees received over 130,000 rubles, enough to meet the initial costs of assistance. They handed out more relief in the following months, and Dzhunkovsky was delighted to learn that very few potential recipients exaggerated their needs.[4]

Dzhunkovsky's efforts earned him the gratitude of those whom he had helped: "Your Excellency's great and tireless concern for those of us who suffered from the flood was obvious in that you, from the first, came to aid the suffering residents, both personally at the site of the former flood, and also by your . . . [subsequent] measures," wrote the denizens of the village of Zakharovo. The peasants of Lokhino praised him as a "real true chief, like a father concerned for his children, who plunged into the work of aiding us, the poor, with all his heart . . . We have been able to put the misfortune behind us thanks to . . . [your] energy and labor."[5]

Dzhunkovsky's work on behalf of Moscow's population went beyond helping the victims of fire and flood and embraced even those held in the province's jails, including political prisoners. The health, safety, and moral well-being of these men and women concerned him deeply. He took measures to check the spread of infectious disease among the convicts, to see that prisoners had opportunities for work and education while behind bars and prospects for employment after their release.[6]

Dzhunkovsky's good intentions and enlightened policies did not prevent incidents of resistance and even rebellion in the jails, however. Moscow's prisons had been flash points during the 1905 revolution. Afterwards they held many who had joined the uprising and whose defiant spirit remained unbroken. In mid-April 1906, "politicals" in the Taganka prison declared a hunger strike. With the onset of spring, guards had opened some of the jail's windows and this gave prisoners the chance to sing revolutionary songs and converse with their comrades. When they refused the warden's orders to stop and resisted efforts to close the windows, the warden suspended visitation privileges, and the prisoners began their strike. In addition to the resumption of visits, the "politicals" demanded longer walks, more baths, open windows, and a change of rules that would permit the families of imprisoned workers to visit them on Sundays and holidays instead of Tuesdays and Fridays. Troops and gendarmes surrounded the jail, and as the strike persisted, anxious families of the strikers appealed to the governor. After four days, Dzhun went to Taganka.

He gathered the "politicals" and told them that he was prepared to change immediately the workers' visitation days and to consider other requests as well. But he insisted that they end their hunger strike and refrain from singing and conversing through the open windows. Once normal conditions had been restored, he continued, he would do all that the currently overcrowded facilities allowed to extend the time for exercise and increase the number of baths. With that the governor left and a few hours later learned that the strike had ended. He ordered the windows opened and visitation rights restored.[7]

Political prisoners were relatively easy to deal with. For the most part they were educated, and while their aims might be subversive, their behavior was, from the governor's perspective, normal and rational. But Moscow's jails were full of hardened criminals, desperate men with little or nothing to lose, whose families and associates frequently supplied them with files, chisels, knives, and vodka.[8] This made Taganka and Butyrka dangerous places where convicts regularly attacked prison staff, wounding and even killing some of the guards.[9] Dzhunkovsky's memoirs provide a dramatic account of a tragic prison disturbance that forced him to put his own life at risk.[10]

On January 21, 1911, Dzhun was chairing a meeting of marshals of the nobility, preparing for the celebration of the fiftieth anniversary of the peasant emancipation. Less than half an hour into the session, the telephone suddenly summoned him to his office. An agitated A. A. Zakharov, the inspector of Moscow's prisons, was calling to tell him that some prisoners at Butyrka had tried to break out and had injured several guards in the process. They had seized part of the jail and barricaded themselves inside. The governor ordered the inspector to go to the scene at once and report the details, while he returned to his meeting, fearing the worst. Considerable time passed before Zakharov called again with a still more disturbing picture: the prisoners had disarmed several guards and were holding them hostage. Dzhunkovsky's initial response was to order those guards still at liberty to break down the prisoners' barricade and restore order; but Zakharov replied that this could result in the murder of the hostages. Sensing irresolution on Zakharov's part, the governor told him to do nothing—he would come to the jail himself. Dzhunkovsky ended the meeting with the marshals, boarded a sleigh, and drove to Butyrka.

Dzhunkovsky knew he was heading into danger, and before leaving the governor's mansion he prayed. Soon the familiar feeling that his life was in God's hands took hold, and as he drove toward the prison many of his fears began to recede. He would later recall that a growing sense of calm and confidence enveloped him, and by the time he arrived his anxieties had vanished completely. Butyrka's warden greeted the governor with a report that clarified the now desperate situation. The attempted breakout had started in the prison's third-floor carpentry shop where about forty-seven men were working. Only three convicts took part in the attack, but they held the premises brandishing pistols they had seized from the guards. From a peephole in the locked shop door, they had fired at some of those who tried to climb the stairs leading toward it. Worse still, all the hostages were presumed dead. Dzhun thanked the warden and headed toward the scene of the riot. As he approached the stairwell, he looked up and saw Prison Inspector Zakharov, four assistant wardens, an assistant prosecutor, several guards, and a few soldiers pressed against the wall in a corner of the wide landing just outside the shop entrance. The barrel of a gun protruded ominously through an opening in the door.

Ignoring the threat, Dzhunkovsky strode up the stairs. No one fired, and he immediately sensed that the rebel prisoners had begun to understand the gravity of their situation and that the crisis might be ended without further bloodshed. Upon reaching the landing, he briefly joined Zakharov and the others along the wall. In a loud voice, the prison inspector announced that the governor had arrived.

"We saw that ourselves," the mutineers shouted back insolently.

Taking no further precautions Dzhunkovsky approached the barricaded workshop.

Looking through their peephole, the convicts could see the governor: powerfully built and broad shouldered, balding and clean-shaven save for a substantial moustache. His words and tone of voice conveyed confidence and resolve.

"How many guards have you killed?" he demanded of the convict standing at the door.

"Four."

"How many revolvers do you have?"

"Three."

"Where's the fourth?"

"The old man [we killed] had a sword but no revolver."

The cold-bloodedness of this response horrified Dzhunkovsky but did not shake his determination.

"Open the door at once and give me the revolvers," the governor barked. "You have three minutes to consider; then we'll break down the door and the blood of your comrades will be on your hands!"

The prisoners briefly whispered together, then asked anxiously: "Will they beat us? Will they torture us?"

"Of course we won't beat or torture you," Dzhun reassured them. "You'll be handed over to a court."

The mutineers conferred again and then announced that they would give the revolvers directly to the governor.

"In that case, open up and let me in," he commanded.

The door swung wide; Dzhunkovsky stepped inside. At that moment the convicts could have seized him, but instead they meekly surrendered their weapons, and the governor turned them over to the warden. The guns held eleven unfired rounds.

With the three desperados locked in solitary confinement, Dzhunkovsky took stock. He quickly understood that the forty-four other prisoners, found cowering under tables and benches in the workshop, were innocent bystanders. Despite the fact that they had witnessed and failed to stop the brutal murders of the guards, whose bodies lay on the floor surrounded by pools of blood, he did not charge them as accomplices or inflict any punishment. The convicts remembered this fair treatment; eight years later two of them would speak in defense of the former governor when he stood on trial for his life before the Moscow Revolutionary Tribunal.

Dzhunkovsky's bold decisiveness ended a serious crisis without further loss of life. But to some his behavior seemed unnecessarily reckless. A personal representative of the sovereign emperor had deliberately placed himself in harm's way and risked being killed or captured by murderous insurgents. Soon after the Butyrka incident, Pavel Kurlov, the assistant minister of internal affairs overseeing the police, sent the governor a secret letter of reprimand stating that when prisoners murdered guards, force, not negotiation, was required. From his memoir it is clear that Dzhunkovsky continued to think he had been right. Duty and a concern for the safety of others demanded that he act as he did. Ultimately, he believed, the issue was in the hands of God. This time, his Christian convictions had not played him false.[11]

Terrorist attacks, peasant resistance, fire, flood, and riot, all came with Dzhunkovsky's territory. But public life also offered many pleasures, and Dzhun enjoyed them thoroughly. In the years after the 1905 revolution, Moscow recovered its nerve and spirit; its social and cultural scene, already vibrant, became livelier still. The number of voluntary organizations—charitable, artistic, educational, and economic—grew rapidly, all clear signs of an emerging civil society. The city's theaters hummed with excitement and experiment while new technological marvels, the automobile and the airplane, appeared to thrill and charm the Muscovites, who looked forward to a new century with optimism even as they commemorated the heroes and achievements of the past. The turbulent, sharp-edged culture of Russia's "Silver Age," revolutionizing music, dance, art, and literature, was perhaps most evident in St. Petersburg, but it echoed in the ancient capital as well.

The city's political life also demonstrated considerable dynamism as the city fathers sought to put the revolution behind them. During the crisis of 1905 they had supported the suppression of the armed uprising, but now, with the danger past, a more liberal mood prevailed. In that spirit the Moscow duma took up a host of pressing issues: education, infrastructure, transportation, and most important of all, the working-class grievances that had fueled the late turmoil. Some of these efforts brought elected city leaders into conflict with the autocratic state, which had long exercised an assertive tutelage over urban institutions. But these conflicts became intense only after 1912, when opposition in the country exploded after the massacre of striking workers at the Lena goldfields in Siberia. In the disputes between the city duma and state authority that did arise, it was chiefly the Moscow city commandant who assumed the role of enforcer. Yet neither the accommodating but corrupt commandant Anatolii Reinbot nor his honest and somewhat stricter successor, Alexander Adrianov, relished that aspect of the job. The initiative for government opposition to the liberal policies of the city fathers came mostly from St. Petersburg.[12]

In rapidly changing postrevolutionary Moscow, Dzhunkovsky occupied a uniquely favorable position. His administrative writ did not extend to the city, so he was seldom involved directly in municipal politics and the conflicts that emerged from it. This remained true even after March 1909 when Gershelman stepped down as governor-general and was not replaced. Dzhunkovsky continued to govern the province, while the city commandant oversaw urban affairs.[13] Dzhun was, however, an active and welcome presence in Moscow's public life. Thanks to his long residence in the city, he knew most of the main figures in local government. He loved the theater, particularly the Malyi with its more traditional repertoire, and his regular attendance and close friendships with some of the leading artists gave him a valuable entree into the world of the cultural elite. Membership in the posh and conservative English Club (*Angliiskii klub*), just across the street from his official residence, assured him regular access to the upper crust of society. His extensive involvement with the work of the Moscow Practical Academy of Commercial Science helped him form and sustain ties with leading businessmen. Dzhunkovsky's continuing friendship with Grand Duchess Elizaveta Fedorovna and his highly visible support for her charitable efforts associated him in the public's mind with this increasingly popular figure. Perhaps most important of all, Dzhunkovsky had come through the crisis of 1905–1907 largely unmarked by the stigma of repression. An intelligent and attractive figure, an engaging conversationalist and raconteur, a man of visible goodwill, he was persona grata almost everywhere.

Dzhunkovsky's ready sociability reflected his friendly and outgoing nature. But it may have served to mask the emptiness of his personal life. His love for Nina Evreinova continued, but her refusal to remarry after the death of her husband consigned him to a bachelor's existence in which his devoted, dutiful, but domineering sister Evdokiia assumed many of the social and household duties a wife might perform. While Nina hovered at the edges of his life, important and sustaining, she was largely unnoticed by those outside his intimate circle. Her estate at Borshchen served as a refuge that Dzhun visited often, especially at the year-end holidays. But discretion shrouded their relationship, and it appears that many in the public believed he took regular trips to Kursk because he owned landed property there.[14] He derived considerable comfort from Nina's children, and as her sons grew to maturity he helped them get established in their service careers. For all that, the lack of a complete family created an emotional hole and the need to fill it. His constant engagement both with society and with the tasks of governance appears to have been a substitute for married life although, perhaps, not a fully satisfying one.

Dzhunkovsky's continued chairmanship of the Guardianship of Public Sobriety was especially important in maintaining his contacts with the various groups in Moscow society. While his duties as governor necessarily limited the amount of work he could do there, he always regarded the Guardianship with a special affection. He followed its activities closely and participated when and where he could. The Guardianship united many disparate elements. It drew its governing board from the city's "establishment," but it employed the services of many less august volunteers. The plays, operas, lectures, Sunday educational programs, and entertainments that took place under the auspices of the Guardianship involved prominent artists and intellectuals; the alcohol-treatment clinics it operated called on the skills of the medical profession. Daily, thousands of workers came to the Guardianship's "peoples' houses" for healthful food and a wholesome environment, a welcome escape from the dirt and noise of the factory floor and the often squalid quarters where they lived. Here they could meet others for quiet conversation, while the books and newspapers found in the reading rooms opened up a wider world. It might even be said that after 1905 the Guardianship embodied *zubatovshchina* without Zubatov: it continued the mission of civilizing and integrating the working class while abandoning the efforts to organize labor for economic gain that had so antagonized the business community. For Dzhunkovsky it was a useful way to keep a finger on the pulse of Moscow's proletariat.

Although he might not have recognized the term, Dzhunkovsky was an intuitive and skilled practitioner of public relations. His thrice-weekly receptions made him highly visible and accessible to Muscovites of all classes, but he did not restrict himself to government offices. He was regularly out and about, walking, riding in common cabs, or taking the streetcar, stopping to shop at various stores throughout the city, mixing with crowds at the theater. If it is true that "80 percent of success is showing up," then Dzhunkovsky's governorship was successful indeed: he showed up almost everywhere and was present at an extraordinary number of significant civic events.[15] What is more, Dzhunkovsky's presence was not simply that of a dutiful representative of state authority, a bored ex officio member of various committees and commissions. He was actively engaged in many dimensions of municipal life—and happily so.

Dzhunkovsky's diary-based memoir is perhaps the best index to his civic involvement. It contains long lists of dedications, openings, jubilees, and other events that the governor was asked to attend, and did. He notes some events just in passing, but he covers many extensively, a clear indication of his intellectual interest and emotional connection. It comes as little surprise to learn that Dzhunkovsky was an active member of the committee working to raise a statue in honor of the great writer Nikolai Gogol on Prechistensky Boulevard, or that he treasured the menu of the celebratory meal that followed the laying of the monument's foundation in 1907, a bill of fare that featured the favorite dishes of Gogol's characters.[16] Nor does it seem unusual that the memoirs also recount his deep chagrin at the botched festivities for the unveiling and dedication of the statue two years later, for which the governor felt he was largely responsible.[17] More remarkable is the obvious pleasure he derived from his role as the lifetime honorary guardian and chairman of the governing board of the Izmailovskii Experimental Bee-Keeping Station, which he first visited in 1906 to take part in an examination of graduating students. He was pleased to meet the scientists who joined him on the examining committee and was fascinated by the entire operation of the apiary. "Familiarizing myself in detail with the bee-garden, I took away astonishingly delightful impressions," he recalled. "[Later] I came to the apiary often, involved myself with all its needs and took its interests to heart. Every visit . . . [there] was pure recreation for me."[18]

In October 1909 the Moscow Practical Academy of Commercial Science, the highly respected educational institution of great importance to the city's business community, asked Dzhunkovsky to serve as its guardian. He agreed with considerable trepidation but was determined that his guardianship would not be simply a formal one. He devoted much time and effort to the job, familiarizing himself with the school's supporters, leadership, teaching staff, and program. He went often to the Academy to sit in on classes, and since some pupils then boarded at the school, he visited during the evenings as well. With the approach of the Academy's hundredth anniversary in 1910, Dzhunkovsky plunged into the work of preparing for the celebration. He traveled to St. Petersburg several times to secure official decorations for key figures at the school, and for the institution itself he gained the prestigious designation "Imperial" (*Imperatorskaia*). He supervised the composition of the lavish volume on the Academy's history and achievements.[19] He oversaw planning for an exhibition of student work. He supported a substantial reform of the curriculum and even introduced new uniforms for the pupils whose dress, he thought, had become so sloppy that, *horribile dictu*, they started to look like university students. Dzhunkovsky proudly opened the ceremonial gathering honoring the Academy's centennial that pulled together leading figures in commerce and the city administration. At its conclusion, the governor believed that he had cemented his ties with the school and its supporters. "I felt that for the Academy I had become someone close, one of their own, and that they had begun to listen to my voice not out of curiosity, as it had first seemed to me, but in recognition of my authority."[20] Dzhunkovsky's connection and concern for the Academy would continue for many years. Long after his governorship in Moscow ended, he remained the Academy's guardian. Even in the midst of his service in the front lines of the

Great War, he found the time and energy to involve himself in questions concerning the leadership and direction of the institution. Only the fall of the monarchy in February 1917 would cause him to resign from his guardianship.[21]

Dzhunkovsky enthusiastically joined his fellow Muscovites in welcoming the arrival of the automobile. After 1905 motor cars appeared more and more often on the streets and roads in and around Moscow, and auto racing became popular. Both developments produced thrills and dangers. In Russia as elsewhere, the advent of cars caused unfamiliar disruptions and the frequency of accidents required Dzhunkovsky to establish rules of the road. At the same time some peasants, resentful of the well-to-do, attacked the newfangled contraptions and their drivers. This led the governor to issue one of his frequent proclamations promising that motorists who violated traffic laws would be punished just as would those who deliberately damaged cars. But while he acknowledged peasant concerns, Dzhunkovsky stoutly defended the noisy harbinger of the modern age. "The automobile is one of the greatest and most useful inventions of recent times," he wrote; "it replaces and preserves the live power of man and horse. Not only should we not hinder the spread of this invention, but, on the contrary, we should encourage it in every way."[22]

Dzhunkovsky's memoirs show his excitement about the many automobile races he attended. He described in detail drivers, machines, and recorded speeds. But the governor was more than just a delighted spectator at these events and on at least one occasion became involved in the details, putting safety first. At a short local speed trial that was part of a much longer St. Petersburg–Kiev–Moscow–St. Petersburg race, Dzhunkovsky noticed that there was no first-aid team on-site. He refused to let the trial proceed until one arrived (by horse-drawn conveyance). This delayed the start for more than an hour, while drivers and their fans grumbled about the governor's excessive "formalism."[23]

Dzhunkovsky's enthusiasm for the airplane was even keener. He was an active charter member of the Moscow Aviation Society and in 1912 became its president, a position he held until he left government service in 1915. He quickly saw the civil and military potential of the new technology and was eager for Russia to overcome her backwardness in this field and catch up with the West. Nor was he content just to watch. In late April 1910, at an aviation exhibit on Khodynka field, the governor took to the air. His pilot was the legendary Sergei Utochkin, who combined the qualities of Jim Thorpe (he was a champion of many sports) and (as his later daredevilry and crashes would show) Evel Knieval. When, with great difficulty, Dzhunkovsky squeezed into Utochkin's bi-plane, he found himself perched atop a narrow bicycle seat with just some fragile poles to hold on to. Only the prospect of being shamed before the pilot and the watching crowd prevented panic from forcing him to climb back down. (His fear might have been even worse had he known that Utochkin had flown for the first time only a month before.) A white-knuckle flyer *avant le mot*, Dzhun firmly grasped the poles as the flimsy craft bounced painfully over the ground; but then the pounding stopped and suddenly the earth fell away. "The hellish noise of the motor and the terrible wind made it difficult to concentrate," he recalled, "but the feeling was surprisingly pleasant; it no longer seemed that I would go head-over-heels, and I felt steady and confident. The further we flew, the greater became my confidence, and I even took my hands off the poles I had been gripping. We circled and then set down." The flight over, Dzhunkovsky's only regret was that it had not been longer, and with a note of mild envy his memoir records that Utochkin gave his next passenger, a beautiful young woman, a higher and more thrilling ride.[24]

Dzhunkovsky's active and highly visible participation in the civic life of Moscow does much to explain his popularity. The seemingly endless public events that he attended brought him into contact with people from every walk of life, while his positive attitude toward the initiatives of civil society made it clear he was aligned with culture, science, education, and modernity itself. He formed close ties with people whose political ideas he did not share, including the left-leaning actor and dramaturge Alexander Sumbatov-Iuzhin, and on occasion these friendships may have led him to take actions seemingly at odds with his own conservative views.

Toward the end of 1918, over one hundred artists of the main Moscow theaters would address a petition to Vladimir Lenin on behalf of their former governor, then languishing in the Lubianka Prison. In it they claimed that during 1905 Dzhunkovsky, responding to a request from

Sumbatov-Iuzhin, had freed a large number of arrested Georgians (Sumbatov was a Georgian prince) being sent north via Moscow and gave them the means to return home. They also stated that he had intervened on behalf of another artist's brother who was being mistreated in jail.[25] The petitioners did not invent these stories, but Dzhunkovsky does not mention either incident in his memoirs.[26] He probably omitted them because they ran counter to his strongly held self-image as a conservative who went by the book.

Dzhunkovsky's public persona, associations, and some of his actions made him suspect in the eyes of the extremists on the political Right. The stigma that attached to him for releasing the Taganka prisoners in 1905, the legend that he had paraded under the red flag, did not fade. Even before the first Russian revolution had run its course, Pavel Bulatsel, a leading right-wing journalist was denouncing him for being "weak-willed, 'compromising' and ever so polite to the Jews and the dear little Kadets [*kadiukam*]."[27] Charges and rumors of secret disloyalty and even traitorous tendencies would follow Dzhunkovsky for the rest of his service career and into the years after 1917. Yet he never leaned politically toward the Kadets, whose views he continued to regard as dangerously radical.

His attitude toward the Jews was more complex. Nothing in his papers and memoirs indicates that Dzhunkovsky had any significant contact with Jews or that he was in any way sympathetic toward them. On the contrary, he seems to have shared the negative attitudes typical of his class, faith, and time: Jews were outsiders, economically aggressive, and because of their greater intelligence, able to deceive and cheat gullible Russian peasants. Still, despite his long association with Grand Duke Sergei Alexandrovich, whose antipathy to the Jews was well known, Dzhun never mentions this aspect of his patron's thought. Moreover, it seems clear that he felt none of the visceral anti-Semitism so often found in right-wing circles, nor did he look with favor on pogroms and extralegal measures directed against Jews. The murder of Mikhail Gertsenshtein, a converted Jew and a founder of the Kadet Party, saddened him, although his memoirs do not state that terrorists from the Union of the Russian People carried out the assassination.[28] His memoirs cite, with obvious disapproval, scandalous incidents in the Duma where speakers hurled anti-Jewish diatribes and insults.[29] Yet it remains unclear whether it was the ethnic slurs or the breaches of parliamentary decorum that shocked and appalled him; probably both. In his account of the murder of Prime Minister Stolypin in 1911, Dzhunkovsky identifies the assassin, Dmitrii Bogrov, using his Jewish name and patronymic, Mordko Gershevich (actually Gershkevich), and notes that his brother was baptized and married to a Russian woman. He makes no further comment on Bogrov's ethnicity.[30] And he does not link the assassination to the machinations of "World Jewry" as did extremists on the Right.[31] But his memoirs are uncharacteristically silent on one of the biggest anti-Semitic scandals of his day, the Beilis case.

That said, as governor, Dzhunkovsky vigorously and rigorously enforced laws that limited certain Jewish activities. In his annual report for 1910, he deplored attempts by Jews to rent parcels of land that peasants had obtained outside the communes. He felt that "the passing of a portion of peasant land into Jewish hands was a profoundly lamentable development, destructive of the basic goal laid out in the great [Stolypin] land reform." Dzhunkovsky told the emperor that Jews needed gubernatorial permission to make such rentals, and that he was denying all their applications.[32] The next year he issued strict orders designed to block Jews who were illegally trading in the villages of Moscow province. He demanded that police officials limit Jewish merchants to the county seats where their commerce was permitted. At the same time, however, he confronted a dilemma over the purchase of land outside the towns by industrial firms that had many Jewish stockholders, perhaps even a majority. Such purchases could put rural lands into Jewish hands; but to prevent businesses from buying land that they needed for growth would threaten the economic development of the province. He decided that until laws were issued forcing Jews to divest themselves of shares in companies that purchased land outside city limits he would continue to permit the practice.[33] Dzhunkovsky was certainly not the philo-Semite his enemies accused him of being. But whatever his personal *feelings* about Jews—and he never openly expressed them—his *actions* were always taken in the interest of state policy and limited by the law. He clearly disapproved when officials robbed Jews of rights they had been granted, and in his memoirs strongly criticized his friend N. A. Maklakov who, when governor of Chernigov, ordered Jews removed from a village where they had lived legally since 1881.[34]

Dzhunkovsky had absolutely no sympathy for those who were determined to turn back the clock to the days before the October Manifesto. As early as 1907 he tangled with one of their chief representatives, Vladimir Purishkevich, a Duma member and vocal exponent of unlimited autocracy. Purishkevich demanded to know why the governor had not confirmed a member of the reactionary Union of the Russian People for a school board post in one of the counties of Moscow province. Dzhun refused to answer the question and replied that the decision was the governor's alone and only the Senate could require any explanation. When Purishkevich sent back an insulting response, Dzhunkovsky charged him with violating the statute that made addressing an official in a demeaning manner a punishable offence. In April 1908 the governor won his case in court, and Purishkevich had to pay a twenty-five-ruble fine.[35] Somewhat later, Dzhun supported a local police chief and the chairman of a county zemstvo board who had refused to let what he called "base agents and blackmailers" from the extreme right-wing Union of the Archangel Michael interfere in administrative matters. This led the chauvinistic and monarchist daily newspaper *Kolokol* to publish a vicious diatribe against the two men, and by implication the governor himself, for allegedly aiding and abetting revolutionary forces.[36]

The reactionaries who regularly attacked Dzhunkovsky for "playing at liberalism" confused style and spirit with substance. To be sure, the governor had what could be called a "liberal" personality: he was open and accessible, and did not base his friendships and associations on political views. Still, his monarchist credentials were impeccable, his devotion to the dynasty clear, and his conservatism unquestionable. Indeed, it was his *conservatism* that separated him from the Purishkeviches of the world, proto-fascists, in their own way as radical as Lenin. Both Bolsheviks and members of the Union of the Russian People rejected the increasingly diverse, pluralistic society with strong commercial and "bourgeois" overtones that was steadily emerging because of the Great Reforms of the 1860s. Dzhunkovsky, however, embraced this new world, not in every detail, but in the main, and accepted the prospect of orderly change and the rule of law. He would display this "liberal conservatism" (as opposed to conservative liberalism) both in his handling of political struggles in Moscow province and in his response to the policies of Prime Minister Stolypin.

Chapter 9

Provincial Politics

THUMBING THROUGH THE PAGES OF RUSSIAN NEWSPAPERS and "fat" journals published before 1905, a modern reader is struck by the fact that the sections marked "politics" contain almost exclusively news of foreign countries. On reflection, this is not terribly surprising. Before its first revolution, the empire had no politics as practiced in most of Europe and the United States. In the years that followed, however, there was an abundance of it—for many Russians, entirely too much. It took some time and effort to adjust to the sudden appearance of national elections, political parties, strident propaganda, a Duma with parliamentary maneuvering and shifting coalitions, and elected representatives claiming to speak for social classes, national minorities, or the people as a whole. Some could not even try to accept this change. Dzhunkovsky was one of those who made the attempt, and to a considerable degree he succeeded.

Dzhunkovsky's personality made him a natural for politics. Intelligent, outgoing, likeable, not afraid of a crowd, he was able to talk with people of all classes. In another country it would be easy to imagine him as a successful candidate for office. But Dzhunkovsky was a Russian, a firm monarchist who believed in the tsar as an anointed ruler whose legitimacy could not be questioned. His ideal sovereign was Alexander III, who imposed peace at home and pursued it abroad. Yet Dzhun realized that the rigidly conservative political ideas that dominated the reign of the "tsar peacemaker" no longer fit the times.[1] Change was inevitable and necessary. He also revered the memory of Alexander II, the "tsar liberator," and those statesmen who shaped the "Great Reforms" that advanced personal freedom and the rule of law. Dzhun clearly abhorred the excesses of the recent revolution, but he was too perceptive to think it had been simply a conspiracy of evil men. His attitude toward the Duma shows he believed that those who wished to have a hand in shaping the laws of the empire should be accommodated.

Dzhunkovsky's hero was Stolypin, "a Russian in the fullest sense of the word," who "so firmly believed [in Russia] that by the strength of that faith he could repulse the forces of disintegration in the country and change the public mood."[2] Yet Dzhunkovsky was not uncritical in his admiration. While he embraced Stolypin's broad program of modernizing reform and a law-based state, over time he found that he could not support all of Stolypin's proposals. He strongly disapproved of the field courts martial and later opposed other aspects of the prime minister's plans.

Like Stolypin, Dzhun accepted the Duma as a useful instrument for achieving the goal of a great Russia. Rebuilding a stable polity in the wake of the revolution would require a degree of public participation; an arbitrary style of rule would no longer serve. He urged the citizens of Moscow province to participate in the national elections of 1906 and 1907, and he did not try to influence the vote by bribery or undue pressure.[3] But like the prime minister, he was deeply disappointed by the parliaments that emerged from the people's ballots. He welcomed the dissolution of the unproductive First State Duma and believed the legend of the Social Democratic conspiracy used to justify terminating the Second. Only years later would he learn the truth about its origins as an Okhrana "provocation" (see below). He embraced the "Third of June System" created by Stolypin's coup and the new electoral law as a necessary means to end political gridlock.

Despite his support for the government Dzhunkovsky was reluctant to participate in its effort to influence the elections for the Third Duma by, among other things, outright bribery. Indeed, if his memoirs are to be believed on this point, Dzhun was hopelessly naive in his estimation of government policy. While the governor was visiting St. Petersburg prior to the voting, Assistant Minister of Internal Affairs Sergei Kryzhanovsky, Stolypin's right-hand man and the author of the new electoral law, invited him to his office. Kryzhanovsky spoke about the need to get an acceptable Duma delegation from Moscow province and offered whatever monies

P. A. Stolypin. Hoover Institution Archive (HIA), Russian Pictorial Collection, envelope AA.

that might require. Going over to a cabinet, the assistant minister opened a drawer filled with bank notes, pulled out a handful, and asked the startled governor if fifteen thousand rubles would be sufficient. Thinking that Kryzhanovsky meant these sums to cover chancellery expenses and the costs of paperwork and printing connected with the election, Dzhunkovsky said that five thousand would do, and as it turned out, he needed just a little over two. The clueless Dzhun finally got the message when he returned the unused portion of the money with a written account about how the rest had been spent. Kryzhanovsky chided him for exposing a conspiracy, and only then did Dzhunkovsky realize that the money's purpose had been to buy votes. Still, he was pleased with the results of the elections in Moscow and nationwide because the new, restricted franchise brought to the Third Duma "representatives who had experience in local self-government and were accustomed to calm, peaceful work."[4]

In the province of Moscow, the chief political arenas were the zemstvos, institutions of self-government created during the Great Reforms to meet local needs in the areas of public health, education, infrastructure, agronomy, fire protection, famine relief, and the like. Delegates for the zemstvo assemblies were chosen at the county level every three years by nobles, urban property owners, and peasant communes voting in separate electoral curiae. The county zemstvo assemblies selected from their membership delegates to the provincial assemblies. Zemstvos at both levels met annually to develop programs and policies, levy taxes to pay for them, and issue "binding regulations" enforcing the measures they adopted. Elected executive boards managed the institutions' affairs between assembly sessions. Over the years, zemstvos assumed ever greater responsibilities, and in order to meet these obligations they hired large numbers of specialists. These doctors, paramedics, teachers, statisticians, and agronomists were called "the Third Element"; many held "advanced" views.

Although originally conceived as apolitical institutions, the zemstvos have been portrayed, with considerable justification, as the seedbeds of a nascent Russian democracy. Still, they were for the most part the domain of the well-born, the well educated, and the well-off. This was particularly true at the provincial level. County zemstvos, to be sure, had significant numbers of peasant members, but these were usually from the wealthier strata and were often quite passive. The delegations the counties chose and sent to the province assemblies came overwhelmingly from the nobility, the most active and vocal element.

In Moscow this was clearly the case. At the province level nobles and wealthy urban property holders dominated completely; the number of peasant delegates could be counted on one hand.[5] The provincial zemstvo assembly usually met in the elegant circumstances of the House of the Nobility and conducted business in a reasonably decorous manner. Normally, the issues were those that occupy local governments everywhere: concrete matters of immediate interest, a road, a school, measures to protect public health. Finances and levies were often at the center of discussions, and where money was concerned, disputes were frequent. Tempers flared and debates could become heated, but for the most part, civility prevailed.

In the galaxy of Russian institutions, the zemstvos were relative newcomers and even at the beginning of the twentieth century were still struggling to define their proper powers and spheres of activity. This task was made more difficult because zemstvos had to depend on agencies that were controlled by the governors—especially the police—to enforce their regulations. For their part, many governors watched suspiciously and resentfully as zemstvos began to acquire authority at the local level that seemed to challenge theirs; they distrusted the radical Third Element employed by the zemstvos. At the same time, governors needed the cooperation of these elected institutions to foster economic development and promote the general welfare of the provinces entrusted to them.

These complicated circumstances produced tensions and conflicts that, while natural and not altogether unhealthy, made governor-zemstvo relations edgy, even volatile. Usually governors did not become directly involved with the details of zemstvo work but often tried to influence its direction. In speeches at the opening of their annual assemblies, governors proposed economic and social programs for the zemstvos to consider. But governors regularly blocked or delayed zemstvo appointments they believed were undesirable and sometimes refused to confirm elected officers. They could also prevent the implementation of zemstvo measures they believed were "contrary to general state interests" or that "clearly violated" the interests of the local population and refer them to the Standing Committee on Zemstvo and Urban Affairs. Composed largely of state officials, this committee normally upheld the governors' rulings. But matters did not always end there. Zemstvos could protest the rulings of the governors and the standing committee to the Governing Senate, the highest appellate instance, which frequently supported the elected institutions.[6]

At the same time, a significant number of zemstvo figures craved a larger stage. They felt that the zemstvo "house" with its county and provincial assemblies ought to be given a proper "roof" in the form of a national representative institution. Zemstvo constitutionalism was muted in the 1870s and 1880s, but it became increasingly vocal following the famine of 1891. The years leading up to 1905 saw the radicalization of the nobility, and many zemstvos across the country began to lean decidedly to the left, the Moscow zemstvo among them. National political issues began to take precedence over local economic concerns, and the Moscow zemstvo took the lead. Speaking in the name of what many saw as the "Heart of Russia," rich from revenues generated by the province's growing industries, it exercised great influence. One of the Moscow zemstvo's longtime leaders, Dmitrii Shipov, was the chief organizer of the first national zemstvo congress in 1902, and he enjoyed enormous prestige in the broad-based movement against the status quo. Shipov's successor as chairman of the Moscow provincial zemstvo executive board, Fedor Golovin, helped to found the Kadet Party and later chaired the Second State Duma.

Until his appointment as Moscow governor, Dzhunkovsky had little contact with the zemstvos, but he was undoubtedly aware of their growing radicalism. In the chaotic days after the promulgation of the October Manifesto, he took steps to protect the zemstvos and their employees when they came under attack by workers and peasants whipped into frenzy by reactionary "Black Hundred" agitators. He ordered the police to suppress all assaults on the zemstvos and zemstvo workers. He required the land captains to make clear to the peasants that the tsar's manifesto called on the people to maintain peace and good order and to explain to them that the zemstvos existed to serve the public good. "You should especially remind the peasants that hospitals and schools and all other [zemstvo] institutions exist chiefly for [their] . . . use," he wrote, "and that attacks on them and those who work there are not only violations of the tsar's will but also senseless and crude."[7] Yet as he assumed his new post Dzhunkovsky must have known that he could expect opposition from the zemstvo and had no reason to think that its current leaders would look upon him favorably.

The new governor was not afraid of giving offense, however, and from the outset made clear his displeasure with the leftward direction that the Moscow zemstvo had taken. Using the powers granted under the terms of the decree on "maximum security," he ordered the dismissal of some eleven zemstvo employees he deemed too radical, a decision that prompted strong protest at the extraordinary zemstvo assembly in February 1906.[8] Sometimes Dzhunkovsky took steps that appear excessively legalistic, even petty. In September, he learned that Golovin and another member of the zemstvo executive board, M. V. Chelnokov, had gone to Helsinki to attend a meeting of the Kadet party. Members of zemstvo boards had the status of state officials and were required to obtain the governor's permission before leaving the province, something both men failed to do. Although previous governors had winked at this, Dzhunkovsky stuck by the letter of the law and saw to it that the two Kadets received official reprimands.[9]

Later, at the session of the provincial zemstvo assembly in December 1906, Dzhunkovsky raised a storm of opposition when he blocked an attempt by liberals to increase their power by including several of their number as "candidate members" with the right to vote, something he believed was illegal. He summoned the Standing Committee on Zemstvo and Urban Affairs into emergency session to review the matter. The committee supported the governor and ordered that the candidates not be seated. Angry delegates debated furiously whether to appeal the committee's decision to the Senate and only after long dispute decided against it.[10]

In his annual report for 1906 Dzhunkovsky brought his conflicts with the zemstvo to the attention of the tsar. He complained that the Moscow zemstvos refused to accept any intervention from governmental authority. They had adopted an insolent tone in their dealings with the administration and even declined to use the traditional forms of address. They no longer "presented" requests or "petitioned" concerning their needs; now they simply "declared" them. They freely condemned actions of officials and the laws themselves.[11] In their absorption with politics, Dzhun wrote later, zemstvo leaders displayed "an almost complete lack of intelligent activity and an indifference to the interests of the local population."[12]

By late 1907, however, the mood in the zemstvos shifted. During 1906 peasant revolts shook the countryside throughout the empire. The "red cock" crowed, and the spectacle of burning manor houses caused many nobles to repent of oppositional politics. While Moscow was spared the worst of these disturbances, Dzhunkovsky observed with some satisfaction that "a general weariness of political agitation and the insecurity of life and property it caused led moderates in the zemstvo to make a sharp turn to the side of order." Soon conservatives took charge and the institutions again began to take up nonpolitical, practical matters. Dzhun recalled that during the years of turmoil, even the marshals of the nobility had been distracted by revolutionary events and had not been able to devote themselves to their required duties. But as the storm passed, they too were able to return to useful work.[13]

Dzhunkovsky's prickly relations with Dmitrii Shipov, a venerated leader in the Moscow zemstvo, displayed clearly his attitude toward the elected institutions. In many ways the conflict between the two seems puzzling. Shipov was fourteen years older that Dzhunkovsky, but both came from families with a military tradition and were graduates of the Corps of Pages. On a broad range of important issues, Shipov's views did not differ sharply from the governor's. Dignified, honorable, and humane, Shipov, like Dzhunkovsky, was deeply religious, believed in the importance of law, and respected human dignity. He would have warmly embraced Dzhun's family motto *Deo et proximo.*

Like the governor, Shipov strongly supported the monarchy. He rejected Western-style constitutionalism and accepted the Duma with great reluctance. One of the most conservative of zemstvo activists, Shipov enjoyed respect in high government circles. After the promulgation of the October Manifesto, Prime Minister Sergei Witte tried unsuccessfully to persuade him to join his cabinet.[14] Prior to dissolving the First Duma, Stolypin attempted to convince Shipov to head a new government, but he declined.[15] Despite Shipov's moderation, however, disputes developed between him and the governor that revealed a significant difference between Shipov's "conservative liberalism" and Dzhunkovsky's "liberal conservatism."

The issue that divided them concerned the proper function of the zemstvos and their relationship to the state. On these questions Shipov's outlook showed strong traces of Slavophilism, the Russian version of romantic nationalism that proclaimed the compatibility of autocracy and personal liberty. Slavophiles revered the tsar and accepted his unlimited power. But they rejected what they saw as the repressive bureaucratic state, with institutions and laws borrowed from the West, that Peter the Great and his successors had created. Slavophiles looked back to the seventeenth century and imagined that then a "true civil order" had existed: the tsar enjoyed the power to act, while the people possessed the right to opinion and freedom of speech.[16]

While not a Slavophile in every sense, Shipov accepted their view that an unhealthy tension existed between the state and society at large. He distrusted government officials and saw elected institutions, especially the zemstvos, as true representatives of Russian society, able to bring the voice of the people to the ear of the tsar and check bureaucratic arbitrariness. Shipov believed in law and a legal order, but also that laws and bureaucratic pettiness should not hinder the public from making its needs and wishes known. He felt that existing regulations often blocked the zemstvos from performing this vital function. Shipov encouraged zemstvo leaders to expand their sphere of activity and resist official intrusion in their work.[17]

Dzhunkovsky also respected the zemstvos. He knew that they served as a valuable school for public service and had done much to improve life in the provinces. Still, he saw them primarily as useful adjuncts to the state. He did not believe that an unbridgeable gulf separated government and society, and consequently he took a "strict constructionist" position in regard to the zemstvo statutes. These institutions ought to limit their activities to local economic and social measures like building and maintaining hospitals and schools. He rejected Shipov's notion that the zemstvos should be empowered to bring the needs of the nation to the tsar or limit the authority of government officials. Given the fact that the tsar had created the State Duma, which now provided a means for the public to make its will known, the zemstvos should confine their activities to spheres sanctioned by existing laws.

Dzhunkovsky recognized Shipov's personal moderation but felt that, nevertheless, his impact on local politics had been pernicious. During the heyday of his influence, Shipov gave the hired employees of the zemstvos a free rein, allowing the Third Element's doctors, teachers and statisticians to spread radical ideas throughout the counties. Together with left-leaning delegates, they had infected the zemstvos with "the spirit of protest."[18]

Even after the zemstvos swung in a conservative direction, Shipov continued as a strong voice of opposition. At the annual meeting of the provincial zemstvo in January 1909, Shipov rose to protest Dzhunkovsky's decision to confirm several proposals that the zemstvo executive board did not submit for approval to the previous year's assembly, which had been cut short by left-wing obstructionism.[19] Shipov claimed that Dzhunkovsky's action was unprecedented and charged him with exceeding his legal authority. He called on the delegates to defend their rights against this arbitrary exercise of state power. In a similar vein Shipov unsuccessfully urged the provincial assembly to reject Dzhunkovsky's request that it require the Moscow county zemstvo to give appropriate consideration to a protest he had made concerning disorder in local schools. To do as the governor asked, Shipov claimed, would undercut the independence of county zemstvos and display "subservience" to the administration.[20]

Shipov's influence steadily declined as the Moscow zemstvos shifted rightward, much to Dzhunkovsky's satisfaction. Although he denied any vendetta against Shipov, his memoirs reveal that he took considerable pleasure when, in the fall of 1909, the grand old man of the zemstvo lost elections in two counties. The governor blocked what he felt was an irregular procedure that would have enabled Shipov, despite his electoral defeats, to serve as a delegate to the provincial zemstvo assembly. The Senate subsequently overturned his ruling, but Dzhunkovsky was not chastened. "I consider the decision of the Senate mistaken," he wrote years later, adding smugly: "Senators were also human and by their nature capable of error."[21]

As the number and power of liberal delegates dwindled, Dzhunkovsky began to exert positive leadership in zemstvo affairs. In January 1908 he opened the provincial assembly in the newly remodeled House of the Nobility with a speech that outlined what he believed to be the institutions' appropriate sphere: "Public education, medical care and sanitation, road construction—these are the cornerstones which, properly and firmly laid, can alone guarantee the solidity and beauty of the zemstvo structure." He urged the zemstvos to give greater attention to the schools of the province and to take steps to improve local infrastructure. Dzhunkovsky noted that financial constraints made major construction projects impossible, but he encouraged the zemstvos to undertake small-scale efforts to upgrade provincial roads.

The governor warned of an impending cholera epidemic. The crisis would require the building and supply of barracks for the sick, and a general improvement of medical and sanitary departments. He called on the zemstvo to heighten supervision of sanitary conditions in towns, villages, and factories. It should see that all existing health regulations were obeyed, and issue new ones that met the demands of the moment, paying special attention to the suburbs lying close to Moscow. He closed his address pledging to work in concert with the elected institutions: "[T]he administration of the province will always be prepared to support all legitimate undertakings of the zemstvo and to cooperate . . . in realizing zemstvo measures on behalf of the population. My sincerest wish will always be to go hand in hand with the zemstvo *within the limits of the law*."[22]

Dzhunkovsky followed the debates that marked his first foray into zemstvo politics carefully. Years later he recalled, with an almost malicious delight, a clash that took place between a monarchist peasant delegate, Ia. V. Ilin, and a group of the old-line liberal members, including Shipov. Ilin claimed that in the past these zemstvo leaders had ignored real peasant interests in favor of radical gestures, a charge the liberals vigorously denied but with which the governor readily concurred. Summing up the debates, Dzhun asserted that they showed clearly "how little attention the former [zemstvo] executive board, distracted by politics, paid to the practical side of zemstvo affairs. . . . The left-wing group of delegates always tried to stress the tendentious [views] of the Right . . . , but the facts spoke for themselves."[23]

The conservative trend in local politics soon created a comfortable situation for Dzhunkovsky and allowed him to deploy his personal charm and public relations skills to good effect. After the January 1908 sessions of the noble and provincial zemstvo assemblies, he gave a dinner at the governor's mansion to honor the marshals of the nobility and zemstvo delegates and to express his thanks for their hospitality during his tours of the counties. He concluded his remarks by raising a glass, drinking to the health of his guests and to "the unity of the nobility, the zemstvo, and the administration in their common work for the well-being and prosperity of Moscow province."[24] Shortly thereafter the nobles and zemstvo leaders returned the favor, hosting the governor at the elegant "Hermitage" restaurant. Again, they drank toasts to mutual cooperation, and Dzhun was touched when they presented him with a special souvenir menu decorated with watercolor paintings in the old Russian style, the work of a member of the zemstvo executive board.[25]

Dzhunkovsky developed firm friendships and solid business ties with Nikolai Fedorovich Rikhter, who in 1907 replaced Golovin as the head of the provincial zemstvo executive board, and Alexander Dmitrievich

Samarin, who became the provincial marshal of the nobility and ex officio chairman of the zemstvo assembly in 1908. Both were staunch conservatives who kept the weakened liberal faction in check and steered the zemstvo toward practical goals. The governor admired Rikhter, who directed zemstvo affairs "with a firm hand" and "boldly cast aside all those confused tendencies, alien to zemstvo work, that unfortunately arose during the 'time of liberation.'"[26] He deeply regretted Rikhter's death in November 1911, which deprived the zemstvo of this indefatigable and deeply knowledgeable leader.[27]

The governor's bond with Samarin was even stronger. Soon after taking office, Dzhun spotted the marshal's "outstanding ability and industriousness."[28] In 1906 he used his close personal tie to the emperor and his status as an aide-de-camp to secure Samarin's ahead-of-schedule advance to the rank of state councilor (*statskii sovetnik*) and the court title of chamberlain (*kamerger*).[29] The scion of a prominent Slavophile family, Samarin was more conservative than Dzhunkovsky on many political issues. In 1908 he led the assembly of the Moscow nobility in presenting an address to the tsar that seemed to call for a return to unlimited autocracy, an act that caused a national scandal.[30]

Still, the governor worked closely with the marshal in managing the affairs of the zemstvo and the nobility and could always rely on Samarin's authority and discretion in dealing with delicate, potentially disruptive service-related matters. When county marshal Pavel Sheremetev failed to carry out his duties and replied to Dzhunkovsky's admonitions in "a completely improper tone," the governor could turn to Samarin. "Take upon yourself the task of thrashing out this unfortunate incident in the comradely circles of the marshals of the nobility," he wrote. "Help me end it in a dignified way, without putting the question on an official plane which would be undesirable for me [given my] feelings of respect for the nobility." Samarin did as he was asked.[31] His impeccable "service tact" helped Dzhunkovsky keep his popularity with the Moscow gentry extremely high. Later, the two men moved to important positions in St. Petersburg and both suffered for their opposition to Rasputin. After the revolution they would share a cell in Taganka prison.

Both Dzhunkovsky's memoirs and his annual reports to the tsar show that, after 1908, conflict between the governor and the zemstvos declined noticeably. In 1909 he opened the provincial zemstvo assembly by laying out an extensive program. He stressed the need to improve fire protection for the suburban regions of Moscow and urged the zemstvos to pay more attention to the construction of hospitals and roads.[32] But Dzhunkovsky acknowledged that these projects required substantial outlays and that the zemstvos' resources were limited. At year's end he called the emperor's attention to the fact that the cost of the tasks that the institutions of self-government were being asked to assume exceeded both the monies they got from the central ministries and their own ability to raise additional revenues. Roads were crucial to economic growth and the province needed much new construction, yet local zemstvo taxes were simply not enough to cover the expense. The central government had to pitch in but budgets were tight everywhere, and neither the Ministry of Internal Affairs nor the Ministry of Transportation could come up with the necessary funds.[33]

When Dzhunkovsky opened the zemstvo assembly in January 1910, he happily greeted the new, more conservative deputies elected the year before. He spoke briefly in a supportive and confident tone: "I'm sure your efforts will be productive, [but] I can't refrain from hoping for calm and balance in your work. The previous session wasn't distinguished by that kind of . . . [tranquility]. That session lasted more than a month, detained the delegates in Moscow, had a negative effect on [zemstvo] work in the counties and the localities, [and] disrupted the proper course of zemstvo affairs in the province. Therefore, I wish for you, above all, calm and balance in your work."[34] The zemstvo responded positively to Dzhun's appeal. Guided by Rikhter and Samarin, the assembly attended to business seriously and its debates were far less bitter and stormy than those of the previous years. The session lasted twenty days and laid the basis for a number of positive developments especially the expansion of schools and libraries throughout the counties.[35]

This straightforward and businesslike turn in zemstvo activity may have led Dzhunkovsky to mellow a bit toward his frequent antagonist, Dmitrii Shipov. In his memoirs, he quotes completely the laudatory address that a large group of delegates read to Shipov at his Moscow home after the close of the assembly. In it they lavishly praised the old man's past services and expressed regret that he had not been able to attend the session. (Dzhunkovsky's ruling had not yet been overturned by the Senate.) They voiced the hope that he would soon resume his work for the zemstvo.[36] But disappointed by local and national political trends, Shipov soon left the province. He returned during World War I to write his memoirs and, after the revolution, was associated with the anti-Bolshevik "National Center." Arrested several times in 1919, he died in the Butyrka prison hospital on January 13, 1920.[37]

By 1911 Dzhunkovsky's relations with the zemstvo had grown even warmer, and he welcomed the circular that Prime Minister Stolypin sent to all governors on February 17 calling for them to turn a more friendly face to these institutions, especially in the sensitive matter of confirming their elected officers and other appointments. Excessive strictness in this area produced unnecessary conflict with local self-government and was detrimental to the larger interests of the state.[38] But while tensions between Dzhunkovsky and the Moscow zemstvos had largely disappeared in the last years of his governorship, he did encounter some foot dragging on a matter that he regarded as being of the greatest national importance—the Stolypin land reform.

At the beginning of the twentieth century, most Russian peasants still held their lands communally and wrested a living from the soil much as their ancestors had done for generations. The three-field system prevailed: one-third of the land planted with winter grains, a second with a spring crop, and a third lying fallow. Fields alternated in a triennial cycle. As in the European Middle Ages, peasant households tilled their portion of the land not in single plots but in numerous scattered strips, an arrangement designed to see that all would have a share of good and poor quality soil. To those who were familiar with the prosperous agriculture of western Europe and the United States, Russian farming seemed woefully conservative and inefficient, sustaining the peasants at little more than a subsistence level. To many peasants, however, it was familiar, and although it did not make them rich it spread risk around and provided a hedge against the terrible prospect of famine. This was the system that the Stolypin reform aimed to change, by encouraging consolidated holdings and more clearly defined private ownership.

Stolypin's program for agrarian restructuring had goals that went far beyond reshaping land tenure, however. Most broadly stated, it aimed to reshape Russians, turning peasants (the vast majority of the population) into citizens. Although the emancipation of 1861 had given peasants personal freedom, in a very real sense they had remained in bondage, with the commune or mir replacing their former masters in many significant ways. Peasants occupied a distinct and subordinate status expressed by the term *muzhik*, the diminutive of a Russian word for "man." In the eyes of the law, peasants were "little men," not fully competent, who had to be segregated, governed by special rules designed to protect them from outsiders—and themselves. The commune kept them in a world apart (the word *mir* also means "world"); it tied them to the soil (the essence of serfdom) by making its members collectively responsible for taxes and a variety of dues. In the commune, peasant households *held* land but did not really *own* it; throughout the Great Russian areas of the empire most mirs periodically repartitioned allotments to take into account the growth or decline of family size.

At the time of the emancipation, the government had supported the mir as a way to prevent the peasants' impoverishment—since communal tenure made it difficult for them to sell their holdings—and as a means to control the rural areas with only a small number of salaried officials. Populist radicals saw the commune differently but still in a favorable light. They believed that the mir with its collectivist practices and regular repartitions reflected the peasants' egalitarianism and might become the basis of a future socialist society.

By the end of the century, however, government and the public began to view the commune more critically. Increasingly, state officials and economic experts became convinced that the mir was a cause of peasant poverty, a barrier to rational agriculture. It perpetuated archaic practices and prevented the adoption of more modern farming techniques. Repartitions and joint responsibility for communal obligations stifled personal initiative and blocked the growth of a class of self-sufficient agriculturalists. The commune isolated the peasants and prevented their integration into the larger society. Among radicals, too, support for the commune had waned. While the populist SRs continued to proclaim its virtues, the Marxist Social Democrats believed that the mir was in decline, doomed by the unstoppable growth of capitalism. Stolypin's reform plan flowed from the growing anticommunal consensus. Its aim was to break the grip of the mir and let the peasants emerge into a wider world.

Stolypin's goal was a stable and prosperous countryside. The revolution of 1905 had shown that the peasants yearned for a "black repartition," by which all state, church, and private lands would become theirs. But looking to the experience of nineteenth-century France where landownership had turned the chateau-burning "Jacques" into a comfortable petit bourgeois, Stolypin and his supporters reasoned that once Russia's "Ivan" had obtained secure possession of his own property, he would learn to respect his neighbor's and become a conservative force.

Prosperity was sure to follow. Peasants wasted much time trudging from plot to plot, and the spaces marking the boundaries between the various strips were lost to farming. Consolidated private landholding would eliminate these problems and more. By reshaping the fields of Russia, it would transform the thinking of those who worked them. The fully emancipated agriculturalist could now lavish his attention and energy on what was truly his; he would invest in it, improving the land, its product, and his life. "The aim of the government," Stolypin said, "is completely definite: the government wishes to lift up peasant landholding, it wishes to see the peasant rich, satisfied, since where there is sufficiency, there, of course, is enlightenment, there also is real freedom. But for this we must give a chance to the capable, industrious peasant, that is, the salt of the Russian earth, to free himself from the vise in which he is now caught."[39] Stolypin called his program *stavka na silnykh*, a wager on the strong. It would benefit the "capable" and the "industrious," but it threatened the communal safety net. Those unable to compete might fall by the wayside, forced to become hired agricultural workers or to swell the ranks of the urban proletariat.

Dzhunkovsky embraced Stolypin's agrarian program wholeheartedly. It embodied his practical, unsentimental view of the people that began to form as early as 1892 when, during that "hungry year," he witnessed the peasantry in extremis. His experience in the Moscow Guardianship and his brief brush with *zubatovshchina* had strengthened this attitude. He came to know workers who were recent migrants from the countryside, many still tied to their communes. These people might be ignorant, but they were not stupid. If properly approached they could be made to see where their true interests lay; they would seize available opportunities when they clearly understood them.

In September 1906 Dzhunkovsky began his active involvement with the reform. In accordance with a government decree issued on March 4, he summoned a conference of marshals of the nobility and chairmen of zemstvo executive boards to create land settlement commissions that would consider questions relating to peasant land tenure.[40] The tasks they took up were fairly limited at first: they aimed to assist the peasants in purchasing land from private owners and from the Peasant Bank and help them exchange plots of land and eliminate the spaces between allotments. Most important of all, they would try to determine the correct boundaries of peasant holdings, since uncertainties about these were a major source of confusion and dispute.[41]

Despite these modest goals, the establishment of the land settlement commissions met with vocal opposition in the zemstvo. Sixteen liberal delegates in the provincial assembly, including Shipov, refused to participate in their election. Dzhunkovsky considered this antagonism to the commissions unjustified, and he ascribed sinister motives to the resisters: "Oppositional groups . . . feared any undertaking by the government that tended to improve the life of the peasant population, since such measures would paralyze the peasants' hostility towards the government that . . . [these] elements always tried to encourage."[42] In Zvenigorod county, reform opponents went even further. There, the chairman of the zemstvo executive board, Prince A. V. Golitsyn, called on the delegates not to elect any commission members at all, and the assembly followed his lead. Dzhunkovsky believed that by encouraging the delegates to shirk their duties Golitsyn had broken the law. He immediately convened the Standing Committee on Zemstvo and Urban Affairs, which found the chairman of the county executive board guilty of illegal incitement and presented the matter to the Ministry of Internal Affairs. The MVD soon removed Golitsyn from office.[43]

Even after the land settlement commissions began their work, things moved slowly. In his annual report to the emperor for 1907, Dzhunkovsky noted that peasants seemed reluctant to abandon the traditional commune and that only seven hundred households had applied to reconfigure their holdings under the terms of the law of November 9. The peasants' hesitation may have stemmed from their innate conservatism, he explained, but it also reflected the fact that the soil of Moscow province was not particularly rich and peasants had abundant opportunities to find work in the area's many factories. Still, the governor felt that interest in the reform was growing, and he told the tsar that he was attempting to inform peasants of the opportunities that the new law afforded them. At the same time, however, he declined to apply pressure to increase participation: "[It is] my deep conviction that the success of the pending land reform will not result from a forcible break-up of the existing system of land use but from giving the population all the means [they need] to make a fully conscious transition to a . . . [better] form of agriculture."[44]

In this spirit, Dzhunkovsky rallied the land captains of the province to spread the message of reform. These often demoralized officials were a crucial link to the villages, but their frequently arbitrary behavior created a barrier of distrust between them and the peasants. The governor knew that the pay the land captains received for their difficult jobs was abysmally low, causing the more competent among them to seek better-paying positions in state service or the private sector, and he regularly pressed for higher salaries in his annual reports.[45] Now he sought to inspire and guide their efforts on land settlement. At a conference in June 1908 he stressed the importance of the reform legislation but warned against using force to achieve its goals: "Departure from the commune is entirely voluntary," Dzhunkovsky told them, "and any attempt to artificially destroy the commune where it is still completely viable . . . does not correspond to the views of the government . . . [and] contradicts the basic idea of the law [itself]." Propaganda, not compulsion, was the key.[46] The governor acknowledged the difficulty of the task ahead but pledged his support. Tell him their problems, he urged, and "by our common effort we will strive to . . . [find] the correct solution." The land captains enthusiastically drew up plans for realizing the goals of the reform, and Dzhunkovsky decided to bring them together regularly to discuss practical issues as they arose.[47]

Although fully committed to the Stolypin reform, Dzhunkovsky was not an expert in the problems of agriculture or the technical aspects of rural restructuring. Fortunately, Fedor Shlippe, the head (permanent member) of the Moscow Provincial Land Settlement Commission, proved to be an extraordinarily knowledgeable and effective assistant. The two men developed a solid working relationship, and a bond of personal respect and admiration is eloquently expressed in their memoirs, written years and miles apart.[48] Dzhunkovsky described Shlippe as a specialist who understood agriculture and land settlement in both theory and practice and who possessed a "lively mind and broad vision." Shlippe knew how to choose excellent subordinates and his even-tempered, easy-going nature made it possible for him to forge an effective team whose members worked together "like a single family."[49] For his part, Shlippe saw the governor as "a wonderful person, intelligent, benevolent, unbelievably hard working, . . . very kind and polite in his treatment of others." Shlippe remembered that, although burdened by the many duties of his office, Dzhunkovsky found time to join him on a number of trips into the countryside, which "opened up a broad picture of the entire work of land settlement, [and] illuminated the psychology and hopes of the people." At the meetings of the Land Reform Commission, held weekly at the governor's house, Dzhunkovsky paid close attention to the ideas of the agricultural specialists, but, Shlippe noted, "his personal outlook was always determined by a feeling of justice and concern for the peasantry. All his views and decisions expressed his pure, good-hearted nature; [although] he could be stern and demanding."[50]

During his tours with Shlippe and his frequent inspections of the province, Governor Dzhunkovsky regularly spoke with peasants about his support for the Stolypin reform. He knew many peasants personally and the respect he enjoyed among them helped bring villages to adopt individual tenure. But sometimes a small assist from technology was needed to close the deal.

In his memoirs Dzhunkovsky recounts how in Podolsk county peasants of a large village voted to break up the commune and consolidate their strips of land into single farmsteads. But when the government surveyor arrived to begin work, he found that an agitator opposed to the reform had convinced most of the villagers to reconsider and now only fifteen out of fifty heads of household remained willing to abandon the mir. The surveyor set about his task anyway, gathering together those still wishing to adopt the new style of agriculture and starting to develop a plan. The other peasants withdrew, but they watched things from afar.

Then the surveyor proposed to take a group picture of the peasants who were adopting the reform and set up some photographic equipment. Suddenly, the peasants who had decided to remain in the commune crowded around clamoring to be included. When the surveyor told them that only those establishing individual farms were being photographed, they whispered together and then announced that they had changed their minds and that now they, too, would leave the commune. One of them explained: "We know very well why you're taking a picture of this group. You're going to show it to the governor, and the governor's going to ask: 'And where's Sidorov? Where's Ponomarev? Where's Semenov?' . . . No, we don't want to answer that; we're all setting up individual farms. Now take the picture."[51]

After a rather slow start, land reform in Moscow province gathered speed. By 1909 the number of households leaving communes had more than doubled, and Dzhunkovsky's trips into the countryside convinced him that the attitude of the peasants toward the land settlement institutions was on the whole positive.[52] The governor continued to be critical of the zemstvos—chiefly their hired Third Element, and several annual reports noted the reluctance of agronomists employed by the zemstvos to provide the help that peasants leaving the communes needed.[53] Dzhun's enthusiasm for the reform remained high, however, and in his report for 1911 he informed the emperor that the pace of change was quickening and that many newly enclosed farmsteads were prospering.[54]

Historians debate whether the Stolypin land reform ever obtained broad support among the peasants or whether it could have succeeded in the long run. But it was unquestionably popular with the nobility who believed it would satisfy the peasants' economic aspirations and exorcise the specter of a "black repartition." Stolypin's reform plans went well beyond agrarian restructuring, however. He envisioned a major overhaul of provincial administration and self-government designed to produce a more rational and effective structure for state institutions, integrate the zemstvos more completely into this network, and create a local political system that put nobles and peasants on a more equal footing.

Stolypin proposed to increase central control over the governors but also to expand their power over all provincial administrative institutions and merge the existing boards and committees into a single provincial council that would include government officials and representatives of the nobility and the zemstvos. His scheme would reshape county administration and put it under an appointed state official assisted by a county council composed of government and zemstvo personnel. Appointed "district supervisors" would replace the land captains as the state officials closest to the peasants.

The most radical aspect of the proposed reform concerned cantonal administration. It would broaden what had been exclusively a peasant institution and give it jurisdiction over all rural residents, regardless of estate status. An all-estate cantonal zemstvo and an elected "elder" would be the lowest unit of government. The reformed zemstvo structure would be better integrated into the state machine. Zemstvo representatives would regularly participate in a central deliberative body, the Council for the Affairs of the Local Economy. This would serve as a kind of "pre-Duma" that could develop legislative proposals relevant to provincial needs.[55]

These institutional reforms were not simply designed to produce a clearer and more rational governmental hierarchy. They were a natural and necessary concomitant to Stolypin's agrarian restructuring. The land reform aimed to "unbind" peasants from the commune and allow them to emerge as full-fledged property-owning citizens. For them to exercise their enlarged rights, however, restrictions and limitations based on estate status would have to be reduced or eliminated. Stolypin's institutional reforms would be a significant step in the direction of establishing a regime based on civic equality. But these proposals proved unacceptable to the nobility, whose political clout Stolypin had enhanced under his "Third of June System."

The Moscow nobility, led by Alexander Samarin and his brother Fedor, were among the most vocal critics of Stolypin's proposed local government reforms, which they believed would destroy the gentry's leading role in provincial life and submerge it in a mass of rural dwellers who were largely uneducated and disrespectful of private property and who held ideas about self-government that were primitive at best. To nobles throughout the country, Stolypin's reform proposals seemed to threaten the status quo with expanding bureaucratic control from above and mob rule from below.

Dzhunkovsky supported the "unbinding" of the peasantry, but apparently he did not see Stolypin's provincial and local government reforms as a crucial part of this larger process. Consequently, he approached these proposals cautiously and piecemeal. In 1908 he traveled to St. Petersburg to take part in the March–April and November–December sessions of the Council for the Affairs of the Local Economy where a mix of state officials, zemstvo representatives, and marshals of the nobility from around the country considered Stolypin's reforms. On the controversial question of the appointed county chief, Dzhunkovsky sided with the majority in favor of the change.[56] Experience had shown him that county administration did not always mesh well with provincial institutions and that marshals could be uncooperative or incompetent. But Dzhun's position put him at odds with the views of the Moscow gentry and his friend Alexander Samarin, who at the council session led twenty-five other delegates in asking to delay final approval of the measure. Their request was denied, but since the issue had been decided by a narrow margin, the proposed law stayed within the Ministry of Internal Affairs and never went to the Duma.[57]

In March 1909 Dzhunkovsky again attended the session of the Council for the Affairs of the Local Economy when it considered the Stolypin plan for provincial administration. Here, despite his respect for the prime minister, Dzhun joined the minority in opposing the reform. He felt that the proposed provincial council would not substantially improve the existing system and that a root-and-branch overhaul was unnecessary.[58] Dzhunkovsky's objections, however, were also probably based on other considerations. He knew that behind the provincial council project lurked the further goal of subordinating governors more thoroughly to the Ministry of Internal Affairs, and weakening their personal tie to the emperor. This was a change he almost certainly opposed, though about this his memoirs are silent.

Stolypin ultimately had to shelve the entire package of provincial and local reforms, in a series of events that marked the erosion of his power and the beginning of the end of his efforts to lead the country in new directions. By 1909 the prime minister had come under increasingly vicious attacks from the extreme Right and its influential organizations, the Union of the Russian People and The Union of the Archangel Michael. In April the tsar refused to approve a bill, sponsored by Stolypin and passed by both the Duma and the State Council, establishing a naval general staff. This was a relatively minor issue in itself, but it was seen as a test of the tsar's support for his prime minister and for the constitutional system he had created. Although Nicholas refused to let Stolypin resign in response to the veto, it was clear to all that Stolypin was increasingly vulnerable.

Reflecting on these developments years later, Dzhun felt that Stolypin had made a fatal mistake when he failed to launched a determined attack on his right-wing opponents and close their organizations for "their scandalous behavior, their open insubordination, and their blatant struggle against government authority, the state structure, and the Fundamental Laws." Dzhunkovsky believed that, as a result, the empire crossed the threshold into dangerous times. "To me it seems that from this moment Russia began to slowly slide down hill, restraining herself somehow until 1915, when nothing could hold her back [anymore], and propelled forward by the dregs of society and governed by nonentities, she flew into the abyss."[59]

Dzhunkovsky may not have had this dark premonition in 1909. Two years later, however, further troubling signs appeared. In early 1911 a massive student strike shook Moscow University. Police stormed onto the campus, arresting student activists and innocent bystanders. The Ministry of Education dismissed three professors, prompting twenty-five senior and seventy-four junior faculty members to resign. Dzhunkovsky felt that these events inflicted a "gaping wound" on the body of the university.[60] It was a clear sign of the growing political tensions that threatened Stolypin's rule.[61]

Then in March the prime minister suffered a grievous legislative defeat when the State Council blocked his effort to extend zemstvos into the western provinces of the empire. For a time it seemed that he would fall. Stolypin again offered the tsar his resignation, and Nicholas once more refused to accept it. Ultimately, Stolypin convinced—some say forced—the emperor to suspend the sessions of the Duma and State Council for a brief period so that he could push through the western zemstvo bill using Article 87. But this end-run around the legislature shook the fragile foundations of Russian constitutionalism and once more undercut the idea of a law-based state. It embarrassed Nicholas and further weakened his support for the prime minister and his system. Alexander Guchkov, the Octobrist president of the Duma, stepped down, and it soon became clear that the State Council would never pass the law should Stolypin resubmit it within the legally required sixty days. To avoid another defeat, the prime minister adjourned both houses on May 13. When late in the year they reconvened, the State Council reversed its position and finally approved the zemstvo bill that had caused such turmoil. But by then Stolypin was dead.[62]

Dmitrii Bogrov shot the prime minister at the Kiev Municipal Theater on September 1, 1911; four days later, he died. The assassin, an unstable young man from a well-to-do Jewish family, had ties to both the SR terrorists and the tsar's secret police. His murderous act deprived the empire of the gifted and dynamic leader who had come to symbolize Russia's recovery from the trauma of 1905. Stolypin's sudden removal left a gaping hole at the center of the empire's political life. Russia headed into a dangerous and uncertain future guided by far less capable hands.

Dzhunkovsky raced to Kiev in the hopes of paying his respects to a still living Stolypin, but he arrived too late. He attended the huge funeral of the statesman, who had asked to be buried where he died, and witnessed his interment in the walls of the Pechersky Monastery, one of Russia's holiest places. Stolypin's death was a profound personal loss for Dzhunkovsky.

Although his contacts with the late prime minister had been relatively infrequent, Dzhun saw him as a fearless knight, a warrior for the Russian state who had fought valiantly against the revolution and "the dark ignorant circles [and] court intrigues [that] allowed him no rest."[63] As he learned more about the circumstances of the assassination, Dzhun blamed it on the criminal negligence of junior secret police officers that pointed to much larger failings in the Department of Police itself.[64] Two years later he would get the opportunity to try to remedy what he believed were the structural and moral weaknesses of that institution.

Toward the end of 1911 another dark cloud had appeared. Dzhunkovsky had already heard whispers about a certain Grigorii Rasputin, a Siberian peasant and purported holy man (starets), whose debauched behavior and growing influence with the royal family were raising concern in some quarters of St. Petersburg society. Rasputin had come to the attention of Nicholas and Alexandra in 1905 as "a man of God . . . from Tobolsk province," and he soon became an important figure in their world. His power to alleviate the suffering of their hemophiliac son, Alexis, won him the almost fanatical devotion of Empress Alexandra, a distraught mother fearing for the life of her child. In addition, his peasant simplicity and sincere affection for the imperial couple, whom he addressed as "Batushka" and "Matushka," provided them with a sense of political comfort in the turbulent period after the first Russian revolution. Rasputin claimed to be the voice of the true Russians, the peasant masses, who, he insisted, were unwaveringly loyal to their tsar, unlike the troublesome intelligentsia and much of the country's elite. He reinforced the tsar's own prejudices against the Duma and the quasi-constitutional system that had emerged after 1905.

As of 1911 Dzhunkovsky had little concrete information about Rasputin and was probably ignorant of the heir to the throne's medical condition, which was a major source of the man's influence. He considered the rumors about Rasputin to be "simply gossip" and was indignant when his name was linked to those of the emperor and empress. But now critical voices grew louder, and Ella, with whom Dzhun remained very close, may have shared her growing disquiet about the imperial couple's "friend." As a result his own anxiety deepened, and he began to consider what steps he might take should this disreputable figure at some point make an appearance in his life.[65]

Chapter 10

National Pageantry

By 1912 Governor Dzhunkovsky was deeply involved in a series of national patriotic pageants that would culminate in the celebration of the tercentennial anniversary of the Romanov dynasty's accession in 1613. Beginning in 1909 the tsar, the court, and the government staged lavish and solemn commemorations of historic triumphs and achievements, designed to burnish the reputation of the empire's ruling house and to apply a balm to the wounds caused by the humiliating defeat by Japan and the traumatic recent revolution. The first of these celebrated the bicentennial of the battle of Poltava, the decisive engagement where Peter the Great defeated Charles XII of Sweden and won Russia her place as a great European power. Then in 1911 the country observed the fiftieth anniversary of the manifesto that had announced the end of serfdom and opened the era of the "Great Reforms."

Dzhunkovsky fully appreciated the significance of both events. His formal historical education may have been limited to the lessons provided by Rudolf Menzhinsky at the Corps of Pages, but Dzhun's understanding of Russia's past went well beyond the textbooks of his school days. His memoirs indicate that he had a serious and solid interest in history. He was familiar with the works of the great historian Nikolai Karamzin, and while still an adjutant to Sergei Alexandrovich, he had heard talks given by Vasilii Kliuchevsky, Russia's leading contemporary historian who had been a frequent guest of the governor-general.[1]

When he attended the Poltava celebrations, Dzhunkovsky grasped the historic and patriotic importance of the moment and was swept up in it. The arrival of Nicholas II accompanied by Stolypin, the presence of both the Semenovsky and Preobrazhensky Guards regiments, the emperor's meetings with representatives of the nobility and common people, and the laying of wreaths on the graves of the fallen heroes, all left a powerful impression. He remembered the tsar's words spoken at a luncheon for officers and cadets who attended the ceremonies: "Russia has recently passed through difficult times, but I believe that from now on she will enter onto the path of growth and prosperity and that for future generations it will be easier to live and to serve their motherland; but for that it is necessary that all my true subjects help their sovereign." Dzhun returned to Moscow full of treasured memories and under their spell may have believed with Stolypin that the glorious ceremonies showed that the revolution was truly past and forgotten.[2]

Two years later Dzhunkovsky assumed a large role in organizing and leading Moscow's commemoration of the decree emancipating the peasants on February 19, 1861, when, as he put it, "one stroke of the pen destroyed the old state system based on servile and unfree labor and laid the basis for an entirely new structure." The observances exalted the dynasty in the figure of Alexander II, the "tsar-liberator," and sought to put recent conflicts behind by celebrating the unity of nobles and peasants in freedom, mutual respect, and their common love for the sovereign. Religious services honoring the late emperor, wreath-laying at his memorial in the Kremlin, ceremonial gatherings, with toasts and speeches proclaiming loyalty to tsar and fatherland, marked the day. It concluded with a banquet Dzhunkovsky hosted for almost three hundred peasants—cantonal elders and judges—at one of the Guardianship's "people's houses" named in honor of the tsarevich. Guests dined on a Lenten meal of fish and cabbage soup, pierogi, sturgeon-in-aspic, broiled cod, salad, fruit compote, and tea. Afterwards, the peasants, many of whom had never seen the inside of a theater, attended a gala performance of Glinka's patriotic opera "A Life for the Tsar" at the Bolshoi.[3] The theme of the work, in which the heroic peasant Ivan Susanin gives up his life to protect the first Romanov tsar, Mikhail, from Polish assassins, was more than appropriate to the celebration and the audience.

The 1909 and 1911 celebrations were the prelude to those of 1912, when, after an interval of ten years, the tsar would come to Moscow to lead two enormous, highly emotional commemorations. The first began on May

28, when Nicholas, accompanied by the empress, their children, the dowager Maria Fedorovna, other members of the royal family, and a host of dignitaries, arrived for the dedication of the statue of Alexander III before the Cathedral of Christ the Redeemer and for the opening of the Fine Arts Museum that bore his father's name. Later, the emperor would also visit nearby Sergiev Posad to pray at the Holy Trinity Monastery, founded by St. Sergius of Radonezh. The second, even more important event was scheduled for August, when the tsar would return to the ancient capital to observe the centennial of the Fatherland War of 1812 and the battle of Borodino.

Extraordinary pomp greeted the tsar and the imperial family upon their arrival in May. A month of preparation had transformed Moscow with flags, crests, and a host of other patriotic decorations. The route that took the royals from the train station to the Kremlin was lined with soldiers on one side and enthusiastic schoolchildren on the other. Provincial Marshal Alexander Samarin, the mayor, Nikolai Guchkov, and others welcomed the sovereign with traditional gifts of bread and salt and with loyal speeches designed to expunge the stain of Moscow's bloody revolutionary days. Later, the tsar and his family offered prayers at the site of the memorial cross that had been raised on the spot of Grand Duke Sergei's assassination and together with Ella visited his tomb. At ceremonies the next day, provincial and civic leaders again passionately expressed their loyalty to crown and fatherland.

The unveiling of the statue of Alexander III on May 30 was an elaborate display of filial piety as Nicholas honored the memory of his father. When the shroud covering the monument fell away, the tsar gave the command for the assembled troops to present arms and the strains of the "Preobrazhensky March" sounded, accompanied by cannon salutes and the ringing of church bells throughout the city. Dzhunkovsky, who had been a member of the committee in charge of raising the statue, was touched by the ceremonies, which brought to mind his own devotion to the late emperor, the "tsar-peacemaker."[4] But not all witnesses were as kind. To many, the statue seemed a monstrous, impassive idol. Others were disturbed by the fact that the security imposed by City Commandant Adrianov was too tight, had led to many arrests, reduced the size of the crowds, and kept the tsar isolated from his subjects.[5]

Dzhunkovsky prepared a much different kind of reception for Nicholas when he came to Sergiev Posad and the Holy Trinity Monastery. Based on his own experience of a close relationship between the administration and the public, he sought to make possible more direct contact between the emperor and the people. A month before the scheduled arrival of the tsar and his family, the governor took steps to ensure that the behavior of the residents of Sergiev Posad would be exemplary. To this end, Dzhunkovsky issued a proclamation that informed the town's inhabitants of the impending visit and called on them to clean the streets and sidewalks and to fix up the facades of their homes. "I do not doubt for a moment," he concluded, "that the residents of [Sergiev] Posad, recognizing the holiness of their dwelling place where rest the remains of Russia's great Saint, and with love and loyalty to the throne, will do everything possible to make pleasant the most august visit of their imperial highnesses."[6]

New regulations put security in the hands of local authorities, and Dzhun was determined to maintain the tsar's safety and at the same time see that His Majesty was not separated from his people. Three days before the tsar's arrival, Dzhunkovsky plastered the town and all villages within a ten kilometer radius with announcements of the impending event that were intended to draw as large a crowd as possible. "I feared most of all," he later recalled, "that even if all the inhabitants of the Posad (about 30,000) thronged to the meeting, they might not fill the entire route and that the large town square would seem empty."[7] Ever the detail man, Dzhunkovsky blocked an attempt to have the imperial party travel from the railroad station to the monastery in automobiles instead of horse-drawn carriages. The people along the route would be simple country folk, unaccustomed to motor cars, and the governor was concerned that the unexpected appearance of such vehicles might produce an undesirable impression. He also kept a tight rein on the police and took no repressive measures even toward those inhabitants that the gendarmes viewed as "untrustworthy." He put a few suspicious individuals under surveillance but did not limit their movements in any way.

The imperial visit came off without a hitch. Crowds were large and close, and they maintained perfect order, while security measures were unobtrusive. At the time of his departure Nicholas thanked Dzhun, saying that here at last he had seen the people and not just the police. Shortly thereafter, Dzhunkovsky received a letter from Minister of Internal Affairs A. A. Makarov that relayed the emperor's praise for his handling of the royal visit and for his entire conduct in office: "Standing at the head of Moscow province for the past seven years, Your Excellency has without doubt displayed outstanding energy and efficiency in all aspects of your administration."[8]

The dedication of the Alexander III memorial was largely a dynastic event by which the emperor sought "to reclaim Moscow as the principal sacred site of the [Romanov] myth."[9] The centennial of the "Fatherland War" of 1812 would be something else, a truly national celebration recalling the epic victory in which the Russians, after great cost and suffering, overcame Europe's greatest conqueror, a triumph that affirmed the empire's might and demonstrated the bond uniting tsar and people. The commemoration had international significance as well. France, the former enemy, was to receive due regard, for the Third Republic was now Russia's close ally.

Memorialization of the war had been going on throughout the year, designed not just for the educated element but for common folk as well. Lavishly illustrated historical works appeared along with a full-length movie, "the first Russian blockbuster war film," containing vivid battle scenes.[10] The high point of the national observance would come in August with celebrations both solemn and patriotic. The first would be on the battlefield at Borodino, where, heroic in defeat, the Russian forces under General Kutuzov inflicted heavy losses on Napoleon's Grande Armée. Then Moscow, which had burned during the enemy's occupation, would be honored as a symbol of national resistance, suffering, and triumph. Events at Borodino promised to be especially complex, and since the site lay outside the ancient capital, Dzhunkovsky as provincial governor assumed much of the responsibility for both their preparation and their execution.

Some major improvements to the battlefield had started a year in advance and included building a five-kilometer road from the Borodino railway station to the main Smolensk highway, laying two kilometers of temporary track from the Borodino station to the battlefield, and the construction of a special pavilion where the imperial train would stop. Plans called for the remodeling of the Borodino station itself in the style of the time of Alexander I and refurbishing the sites of important moments in the fighting: the fortifications called the Bagration (Semenovskie) flèches, the Shevardino redoubt, and Raevsky's battery. All existing roads on the field had to be repaired, new bridges constructed, and additional roads built to connect important historic points. Dzhunkovsky supervised much of this work and also took direct charge of repairing the main Borodino monument and the grave of Prince Bagration, a hero of the battle, as well as building a new home for invalids with a small museum inside.

Dzhun's duties did not end there. He had to organize and oversee the construction of a proper parade ground at the Borodino monument, the establishment of stations to provide food for up to one hundred thousand visitors, and the building of sanitary facilities, an infirmary, and a temporary hospital. He was charged with laying out a campsite for peasant representatives who were going to come from all over the empire, with constructing temporary barracks and arranging other accommodations for visiting military and civilian delegations, as well as with providing necessary transportation. Dzhunkovsky set up a place where slideshows of scenes of the battle could be presented and oversaw the lighting and decoration on the field. Finally he was responsible for maintaining security throughout the celebration.

The good relations that Dzhunkovsky had developed with the provincial zemstvo now paid off handsomely, and he was able to call on that institution to undertake the needed roadwork, the establishment of sanitary and medical facilities, and the decoration of the field. The Moscow Guardianship set up the feeding stations, and prisoners from the city jails provided much of the manual labor. The governor was especially grateful for the diligent efforts of the combat engineers (sappers) from a battalion of grenadiers who had been assigned the task of repairing battlefield sites. Dzhunkovsky formed a special bond with these men, and he would meet some of them again during the Great War when a company from the battalion was attached to his division. As at Borodino, their service was exemplary, and the unit maintained its discipline and effectiveness even after the February revolution of 1917.

Despite the difficulties, Dzhun's enthusiasm for the Borodino project was enormous and he undertook to pay for a number of things out of his own pocket. In St. Petersburg he bought mahogany furniture in the Alexandrine style for the small museum attached to the home for invalids, and he trolled the antique stores of Moscow in search of an appropriate bust of Tsar Alexander I to put there. He found one, but the price—ten thousand rubles—was beyond his means. Later, however, a wealthy collector, L. L. Zubalov, obtained the statue and, when he learned of Dzhunkovsky's interest in the piece, donated it to the museum. Since the main Borodino monument was surrounded by peasant fields that when plowed would restrict access to the site, Dzhun purchased a small amount of land so that a road could be built leading from the museum to the memorial.[11]

The governor was also involved in negotiations for obtaining land for the location of other monuments, and he played an especially important part in securing a place for the memorial to General Kutuzov that the War History Museum wanted to build near the village of Gorki on the spot from which he had commanded the Russian forces. At first the peasants refused to sell part of their fields to the museum, claiming that the loss of cropland might cause the village economic hardship. But when Dzhunkovsky intervened on the museum's behalf, the peasants changed their minds and simply gave a plot of some 1,020 square yards to him personally. Kutuzov's monument rose on the peasants' gift to their governor.[12]

Maintaining security and good order during the celebrations was, unquestionably, Dzhunkovsky's chief concern, and here he applied the experience he had gained at the time of the tsar's visit to Sergiev Posad. Again, his aim was to ensure the imperial family's safety while still permitting the emperor to have real contact with his people. The governor was liberal in issuing tickets to the event and did not demand that visitors display proof that they were "trustworthy." For the purpose of maintaining order, Dzhunkovsky divided the field into discreet districts each to be monitored by a small number of police commanded by officers and gendarmes he had personally chosen. This arrangement allowed for surveillance that was at once tight and unobtrusive.

All these efforts demanded enormous labor not only from Dzhunkovsky but also from his personal staff and many coworkers. The governor's job was made more difficult and complex by the visit of several foreign delegations passing through Moscow on their way to the funeral of the emperor of Japan, and by the need to combat the fires that raged near the city in late July. During the first half of August, the governor went regularly to Borodino by automobile and train, but after August 18, he left Moscow altogether, putting day-to-day business in the hands of his vice-governor. He took up residence at the site of the celebration, so that he could take direct command of the final stage of the preparations.

The imperial family was due to arrive at Borodino on August 25, but a wave of government officials and the military units that one hundred years before had participated in the battle preceded them. Officials also brought to the scene a few old men who claimed, at least, to be veterans or eyewitnesses of the historic engagement. On August 23, the preparations at the field were virtually complete, the flags, arches, and other decorations in place, when near disaster struck. During the day it began to rain and that night a violent wind storm with an accompanying downpour blasted the field. By the morning of August 24, all the newly built roads had been largely washed out, banners and decorations in tatters. "I fell into complete despair," Dzhunkovsky recalled, "when . . . I rode around the battle field and saw the total destruction." In this dark mood he welcomed Prime Minister Vladimir Kokovtsev, who did his best to calm the despondent governor.[13]

Fortunately, the rain stopped, and the sappers of the grenadiers' battalion sprang into action. Working through the day and into the early hours of the next, they repaired most of the damage. Dzhunkovsky spent several sleepless nights and nervous energy alone kept him going. Anxiously, he toured the field and then reviewed security arrangements along the rail line leading to Borodino accompanied by Nina's oldest son, Vladimir, whom he had taken on as an official for special assignments. On August 25, the day dawned clear, and at ten in the morning, the governor stood at the station, prepared to greet the imperial party and visiting dignitaries.

Upon arrival Nicholas reviewed the units that had taken part in the historic engagement, met with representatives of Moscow's French community, and spoke with the elders who said they had witnessed the battle. One of them, who claimed to have seen Napoleon, described him as "a fine broad-shouldered fellow" and pointing to his waist added, "with a beard down to here"; another showed the tsar a wound he had received.[14] Dzhunkovsky guided the emperor through the museum at the home for invalids and his majesty was clearly pleased, thanking the governor several times for his efforts. The emotional high point of the day was the procession accompanying the wonder-working Virgin of Smolensk icon that a century before had blessed the Russian arms. As a chorus sang the hymn "How Glorious Is Our Lord in Zion" (*Kol' slaven*), the imperial family followed the icon from the invalid house past the site of Raevsky's battery toward the Borodino monument, stopping at the field chapel of Alexander I for a memorial service.[15]

The next day a further procession with the icon of the Smolensk Virgin brought the emperor to the Borodino monument through closely packed crowds of people, standing with bared heads in reverential silence. Later, Nicholas reviewed the assembled troops who then passed by him

Nicholas and Alexandra at Borodino Celebration. Hoover Institution Archive (HIA), Sviatopolk-Mirskii Collection, box 5, folder 15.

in a ceremonial march. After lunch, the tsar surprised Dzhunkovsky by asking him to ride at his side on a tour of the battlefield and to provide detailed information on all the monuments and historic places. Normally the commander of the Moscow military district, General Pleve, would have had that honor, and the tsar's request caused Dzhun a momentary embarrassment, fearing that he would be seen as having intrigued against his superior. But Pleve graciously raised no objection, and the governor gladly assumed the role of the emperor's personal guide.

Dzhunkovsky took the tsar past the major points on the field while Nicholas pressed him with all kinds of questions, showing interest in even the smallest details. During the tour they came upon the sapper unit that had done so much work on the monuments and roads. The men were taking their ease and not properly prepared to receive their sovereign who rode unannounced into their midst to thank them for their efforts, but their wildly enthusiastic welcome more than made up for their disarray.

The way to the monument honoring the Pavlovsk Life-Guards would bring the tsar through the village of Utitsa, but Dzhunkovsky proposed that they get there using a rough bi-way so that his majesty might experience "a real Russian rural road." The tsar agreed, and they soon were picking their way along a barely passable trail marked by huge breaks and giant potholes filled with water. At the end, a jolted Nicholas thanked Dzhun saying that, were it not for him, he would never in his life have seen such a road, about which he had only heard stories.[16] The tsar then appeared unexpectedly to the villagers in Utitsa who gathered about him in a large, ecstatic crowd.

The most emotional moment in the tour came when the tsar visited the camp where some five thousand peasant representatives were staying. Thunderous hurrahs shook the air as Nicholas rode among the people drawn up in rows to welcome him, and Dzhunkovsky was himself somewhat stunned by their response. "I have been to many celebrations," he recalled, "but the rapture with which the peasants greeted their monarch defies description." The tsar was deeply moved, even shaken, by the event, and after taking leave of his cheering subjects turned to the governor and warmly clasped his hand. The day ended with the emperor's visit to the site of the monument to the French dead, followed by a concert at his headquarters.[17] At midnight the imperial family parted with Dzhunkovsky, thanking him again for all he had done. At six o'clock the following morning Dzhun watched as the train carrying the still-sleeping royals eased out of the Borodino station. Then he jumped in an automobile and sped to Moscow, arriving about an hour before the imperial train pulled in.[18]

The next three days in the ancient capital continued the high pitch of patriotic enthusiasm. Cheering throngs lined the routes that the imperial party took, and security, while still tight, gave the tsar better access to the people than he had experienced in May. City Commandant Adrianov, who was primarily in charge of the celebrations, had learned something from his earlier mistake, but many still felt that the hand of the police lay too heavily on the entire event.[19] Dzhunkovsky's obligations in Moscow were limited to maintaining order and security at the parade that took place on Khodynka field on August 28, since that area was outside the city limits.

Although national pride, dynastic loyalty, and the unity of tsar and people were the themes of both events, the Moscow observances differed from those at Borodino by having a political tone that reflected the tsar's displeasure with the Duma. Representatives of Russia's parliament had always been scarce; only the chairmen of the Duma and State Council received invitations to Borodino. But now, while the planners of the event invited members of the State Council to Moscow, they pointedly excluded delegates from the lower house, a painful and embarrassing slight that led Mikhail Rodzianko, the Duma's president, to boycott the celebrations.[20] Speeches by leaders of the nobility, most notably Alexander Samarin, had an emphatically conservative and ultramonarchist tone. After a delegation of nobles had presented Nicholas with a banner in the ancient Russian style, bearing the image of the "Savior not Made by Hands," on one side and St. George on the other, Samarin spoke in their name pledging the continued loyalty of Russia's first estate to their "Sovereign Leader" and "Autocrat." Conservatives felt this to be the most important moment in the entire commemoration of the Fatherland War, a reaffirmation of the nobility's unbreakable tie to their ruler.[21]

For Dzhunkovsky, the celebrations closed on a clear note of triumph amid muted sounds of danger. Just before the final ceremonial banquet at the Great Kremlin Palace on August 30, the tsar called Dzhunkovsky into his chambers. He sincerely thanked him for his work in organizing the events at Borodino and for maintaining order and security at the Khodynka parade, which, he said, had made those days "happy and joyous." In memory of that service, the emperor presented Dzhunkovsky with a jeweled frame containing his photograph inscribed: "To Moscow governor Dzhunkovsky. Nicholas. 25–30 August 1912. Borodino—Moscow." He kissed Dzhun who in turn kissed his sovereign on the shoulder.

When Dzhunkovsky returned after his meeting with Nicholas, he found many people wondering what had happened, and one of his well-wishers inquired if the tsar had made him an adjutant-general. Dzhunkovsky felt that the honor would have been unprecedented—no sitting governor had ever been given such a promotion. At the same time, however, he had begun to sense something else: signs of displeasure toward him on the part of Empress Alexandra. He recalled that on the first day of her arrival at Borodino she had been extremely kind and gracious, "but then I felt a certain reserve [on her part] towards me, and I thought that its cause was the definite position I had taken in regard to Rasputin, about which the friends of the latter hastened to inform the empress." Dzhunkovsky certainly had not made his opinions known to the imperial couple directly, but some word about his concerns may have circulated. Most likely, it was his continued closeness to Ella and her clear distaste for the "holy man," that led Alexandra to cool toward him.[22]

Indeed, the apprehensions about the empress that Dzhunkovsky recounts in his memoirs may well be hindsight. The celebrations at Borodi-

Grigorii Rasputin. Hoover Institution Archive (HIA), Russian Pictorial Collection, envelope AG XX764 10 AV.

no and Moscow had been an enormous personal success for the governor, and he knew that the gratitude the emperor had expressed was both warm and genuine. All that had taken place seemed to justify Dzhun's open-handed style of governance, attentive to public opinion, marked by a light touch and loosened control, reflecting his sincere belief that the Russian people truly loved their tsar. He had little reason to worry about the loss of imperial favor. Still, the Rasputin question hung in the air. In January 1912 the issue had surfaced in the press and in the Duma; for the first time the legislature touched upon the intimate life of the tsar's family. Nothing came of this immediately, but it encouraged the birth and spread of rumors, many of them false, that over time would discredit the throne.[23]

The escalating "Rasputiniad" was but one of many developments disturbing the political life of the empire. In early April 1912 troops fired on striking workers at the Lena goldfields in Siberia leaving roughly 170 dead and 200 wounded.[24] The event provoked indignation across the entire political spectrum, indicating broad support for workers and their struggle for economic betterment.[25] The government's response displayed a tin ear for the music of public opinion. When Minister of Internal Affairs Makarov came before the Duma to answer questions about the event, he deplored the loss of life. But he claimed that the soldiers had acted in self-defense against a mob attempting to disarm them. In this case, he argued, shooting was justified, and he added: "So it was, so it will be" (*Tak bylo, tak budet i vpered'*). For many, these words came to define the heartlessness of the tsarist regime; the workers' strike movement, largely dormant since 1907, revived with a vengeance, building steadily to a peak on the eve of the World War. Public subscription raised money to send a group of lawyers to Siberia to defend the workers. One of its members, Alexander Kerensky, found the experience transformative. It deepened his radicalism and filled him with contempt for "a capitalist utopia in which the government served as the handmaiden of capital."[26]

Like most Russians, Dzhunkovsky deplored what had taken place, but it did not shake his loyalty in any way. In his memoirs he quoted in detail Makarov's response to questions posed in the Duma, yet more than a decade after the "sorrowful events" at Lena, he refused to pass a final judgment. To do so, he felt, required a thorough knowledge of local circumstances and conditions, something he did not possess. Of one thing he was sure, however, the massacre showed the folly of the government's policy of sending incompetent officials eastward, "beyond the Samara meridian."[27] Here he was probably referring to the author of the tragedy, Irkutsk assistant police chief, Captain N. V. Treshchenkov, whose checkered career had led to his Siberian posting.[28]

The infamous Beilis case was also roiling the political waters. The arrest of Mendel Beilis in August 1911 on the charge of murdering a Christian boy for ritual purposes had set off a storm of anti-Semitic diatribes in right-wing publications spreading tales of Jews drinking Christian blood. By 1912, however, the weight of evidence, much of it published in reputable newspapers, suggested that the charges were groundless and pointed instead toward a conspiracy of high-placed officials and the police as well, designed to railroad an innocent man and defame Jews in general. The result was a growing scandal with international repercussions that besmirched the good name of Russia and the tsar's government.

Unfortunately, we can only guess as to Dzhunkovsky's attitude at the time. His memoirs, which carefully cover the major events of this period, remarkably contain no discussion of the case and the public outcry it provoked. Nothing that Dzhunkovsky wrote leads us to think that he believed the legends of ritual murder or the anti-Semitic ranting of the gutter press. He firmly supported the idea of a law-based state, and the Beilis case was a clear miscarriage of justice. He was hostile to the extremists on the political Right and cited their anti-Jewish outbursts in the Duma with obvious distaste. Moreover, by the time Dzhunkovsky wrote his memoirs in the 1920s, the whole sordid saga of the Beilis case was well known and showed that the tsar was to some degree implicated. Nicholas had received the trial judge, given him a gold watch, and promised him a promotion if a "government victory," that is, a conviction, resulted.[29]

Thus, it is virtually certain that Dzhunkovsky's puzzling refusal to discuss the matter did not stem from either approval or ignorance.[30] His silence becomes more understandable when we recall that his memoirs also fail to mention Grand Duke Sergei's anti-Semitism and the expulsion of Jews from Moscow that accompanied his appointment as governor-general in 1891. Two emotions were basic to Dzhunkovsky's personality: patriotism and devotion to the emperor. He loved his country and revered the dynasty; Sergei's Judeophobia, the Beilis case, and the tsar's complicity dishonored both. Dzhunkovsky was too honest to attempt a whitewash; silence was his only refuge.

In the midst of rising labor unrest and troubling public scandals, the five-year mandate of the Third State Duma expired, requiring new elections. The results did not bode well for the prospects of the Russian parliament. Even before the assassination of Stolypin, the Center-Right coalition that supported many of his measures had broken down and now those parties fragmented. The members of the Fourth Duma divided into three roughly equal groups—Right, Center, and Left—which made it impossible to form a stable majority or to develop consistent programs. The disunity in the new Duma was evident from November 13, 1912, its first day. As State-Secretary Ivan Golubev prepared to read the tsar's manifesto opening the session, all stood when he pronounced the imperial name. Suddenly from the Right came the cry: "Long live the Sovereign Emperor—Autocrat of all Russia! Hurrah!" From the Left, burst the shout: "Long live the constitution!" and its benches gave forth another loud "Hurrah!" The Duma chose Centrist Mikhail Rodzianko as its president, but when he spoke of strengthening the constitutional order and eliminating official arbitrariness, the delegates from the Right staged a symbolic walkout.[31] A majority could not agree on a reply to the speech from the throne, and in the end none was sent, only a telegram couched in bland and loyal tones. In this spirit the parliament drifted, increasingly marginalized by the government, which, without a strong leader, lost much of its cohesion. Ministers began to pursue uncoordinated policies, more and more dependent on the favor and whims of the tsar.

For Dzhunkovsky, the elections to the new Duma would have unexpected and fateful consequences. Voters in Moscow's workers' curia chose as their representative Roman Malinovsky, a rising star in the Social Democratic movement, who had recently joined the Central Committee of Lenin's Bolshevik faction. In the Fourth Duma he would emerge as a powerful tribune of the Left, a gifted speaker, and an uncompromising radical. Unbeknownst to the public, however, he was also a paid agent of the tsar's secret police.[32] Although Dzhunkovsky and Malinovsky would not meet for six years, and then only briefly, their fortunes became curiously linked. In 1914 Dzhunkovsky brought Malinovsky's parliamentary career to an end. Four years later, in a strange twist of fate, Malinovsky would save Dzhunkovsky's life.

The recruiting of informants from the ranks of subversive groups had been a regular practice of the Russian security police since the beginnings of the revolutionary movement in the 1860s, and it had been brought to a high level of effectiveness by Sergei Zubatov in the years around the turn of the century. Following the suppression of the 1905–1907 revolt, police agents within the revolutionary parties contributed to their growing disarray. This success held its own dangers, to be sure, and at several points produced national scandals. In 1909 the public learned that the head of the SR Combat Organization, Evno Azef, who helped plan the assassinations of Viacheslav Pleve and Sergei Alexandrovich, was also an agent of the secret police. Stolypin's killer, too, had ties to the SRs and the Okhrana. The Azef and Bogrov affairs damaged the reputations of both the Socialist Revolutionaries and the security forces and reinforced the general revulsion against spying and those who practiced it. Secret informants were universally called *provokatory*, the Russian equivalent of "agents provocateurs," although for the most part they did not engage in the incitement of criminal acts. Even ardent defenders of the monarchy regarded them as a species of loathsome vermin who deserved to be exterminated.

Malinovsky had been a police agent since 1910 while simultaneously enjoying great success as a Social Democratic activist. By the end of 1911 he had come to the attention of Bolshevik leaders in Moscow, and in 1912 they sent him to the Prague Party Conference that Lenin had organized, proposing his inclusion in the Central Committee. When Lenin met Malinovsky, he was immediately taken with the energetic and forceful young man, a real worker with trade union experience, who could speak and organize. He insisted on Malinovsky's election to the Central Committee and soon hatched bigger plans: Malinovsky should be the Moscow Bolsheviks' candidate for the Fourth State Duma.

Ironically, Stepan Beletsky, the director of the Department of Police, was thinking along the same lines as Lenin, although with a different aim in view. Labor discontent was rising and the Bolsheviks' influence was growing. Having Malinovsky on their Central Committee would enable the secret police to penetrate the heart of Lenin's conspiracy. Moreover, as a Bolshevik spokesman in the Duma, Malinovsky could help prevent the reunification of Lenin's faction with the rival Mensheviks and so perpetuate the division that weakened the Social Democrats' effectiveness as a revolutionary force. There was, however, a slight problem. Malinovsky had a criminal past, which made him ineligible to serve in the parliament. This had to be covered up and any other impediments removed from his path. And what about Governor Dzhunkovsky, should he be told?

The Malinovsky episode would cast a long shadow in Dzhunkovsky's life. What he knew about the police agent and when he came to know it were questions that dogged him after the revolution. In three separate testimonies, first to the Provisional Government's Extraordinary Investigating Committee in the summer of 1917, later at Malinovsky's trial in November 1918, and finally in his memoirs, Dzhunkovsky consistently maintained that, at the time of Malinovsky's election to the Duma, he had no idea about either the man's criminal past or his status as an secret informant and that the Department of Police had deliberately concealed the facts from him. He learned of these only after he became assistant minister of internal affairs with oversight of the police, and then he took steps to deal with the problem.[33]

On the other hand, Alexander Martynov, the head of the Moscow security bureau maintained that Dzhunkovsky was fully informed from the beginning. Martynov claimed that he received a coded telegram from Beletsky, probably in August, ordering him to tell the governor about Malinovsky's role as a secret agent and to convey Beletsky's wish that nothing interfere with his election. According to Martynov, he showed the telegram to Dzhunkovsky who with a "sour and hostile smile" replied: "Tell your chief that I will do everything possible."[34] For his part, Beletsky gave contradictory accounts, at first claiming that Martynov had informed the governor and later stating that Martynov had failed to do so.[35]

Historians are divided on the issue. Jonathan Daly, the leading American specialist on the imperial security forces sides with Martynov. Anastasia Dunaeva, Dzhunkovsky's Russian biographer, and Isaak Rozental, author of the most recent study of Malinovsky, conclude that the governor was ignorant of the machinations of the secret police until after he became assistant minister.[36]

It may be that both Martynov and Dzhunkovsky were telling the truth according to their lights, and that what occurred was a classic failure to communicate across the barrier of distrust that often separated governors and representatives of the security police. With some justification, local security chiefs felt that governors were unable to maintain confidentiality and that sometimes members of their staff were untrustworthy. As a result, secret policemen were circumspect in their relations with governors, playing their cards close to their vests, revealing as little as possible. Governors understood this, and resented it.[37] Martynov was clearly one who believed that letting governors in on the secrets of security policing was risky, and Dzhunkovsky's reputation for openness and the popularity he enjoyed even in liberal circles made him doubly suspect.[38] The coded telegram from Beletsky has not been found in the archives, so it is reasonable to think that if Martynov told Dzhunkovsky anything about Malinovsky, he did so only verbally and, in all likelihood, in a guarded, oblique manner.

Dzhunkovsky already distrusted the security police. Early in his governorship he had blocked efforts by its officers to recruit informants from among the political prisoners being held in the jails under his control. He believed that because of this, in 1909, the then head of the Moscow security bureau, Colonel Mikhail fon Koten, engineered the escape of a group of inmates from the Novinsk women's prison, some of whom were convicted terrorists. The aim of the plan was to discredit both the governor and the prison inspector for failing to maintain proper control over the jails and then to demonstrate the competence of the security organs by immediately recapturing the escapees. The ruse failed because the agent who facilitated the breakout was in fact aiding the revolutionaries, most of whom easily slipped away.[39]

Given his jaundiced view of the security forces, and fully absorbed by his work on the Borodino celebrations, Dzhunkovsky might well have listened to Martynov's cryptic remarks with only one ear. Too busy to probe deeper, and desiring little or no involvement with the secret police, he let the matter slip. Whatever the case, Malinovsky was elected to the Duma in 1912 and began a brief but meteoric parliamentary career, his role as an informant for state security hidden until 1917, when revolution opened the government's files.

Even before the Fourth Duma met for the first time, Dzhunkovsky had taken a well-deserved rest. In early November 1912, he departed for Kislovodsk, a fashionable resort and spa in the North Caucasus, to relax and take the waters. His heart had been giving him trouble of late, and he was exhausted from his work on the two Moscow celebrations and the parliamentary elections. Far from the burdens of office, he was free to wander the town, climb the nearby hills, bathe in the Narzan (a strong carbonic spring), imbibe the "drink of heroes" that flowed forth from it, and listen to music in the shady park across the way. The brisk, clear Caucasian air refreshed him, and when he returned to Moscow on December 1, he felt prepared to take up the tasks that lay ahead. The year 1913 promised to be extremely busy. Celebrations of the tercentennial anniversary of the Romanov dynasty were in the offing, and Moscow was going to play a major role in these events, which would dwarf in importance even the commemoration of the Fatherland War. Dzhunkovsky was getting ready. Then in early January, as he sat at his desk looking over a stack of papers, he heard the telephone ring. A call had come through from St. Petersburg that would change the course of his life.[40]

Part Four

Security Chief, 1913–1915

Chapter 11

Celebration and Reform

Dzhunkovsky picked up the phone and heard Nikolai Maklakov, the new minister of internal affairs, boom hearty New Year's greetings and straight away ask him to become his assistant minister with responsibility for the security police. "Such a proposal, so unexpected, stunned me," Dzhun recalled, and left him momentarily speechless. But without missing a beat, Maklakov continued, talking excitedly about the many changes he had in mind for the ministry. Almost in passing, he assured Dzhun that the emperor had already approved his appointment.[1]

Dzhunkovsky's surprise was understandable. He knew Maklakov, but not well; they had met in 1912 while serving together on the Council for the Affairs of the Local Economy. Maklakov, then governor of Chernigov, had seemed energetic and capable but rather impulsive. During the Council sessions, they became friendly, although Dzhunkovsky often had to restrain his younger colleague who was prone to heated rhetoric.[2] Dzhunkovsky seems to have been unaware of the full extent of the new minister's conservative views and of his determination to roll back wherever possible the civil and political rights the public had gained since 1905.[3] Nor did he know that Nicholas's appointment of Maklakov had produced considerable consternation in government circles and that Prime Minister Kokovtsov had strongly opposed it.[4]

Why Maklakov decided to tap Dzhunkovsky to head the security police is also difficult to fathom. Pavel Kurlov, who had served as the security chief from 1909 to 1911 and who had known Maklakov from his youth, warned the new minister that Dzhunkovsky was a poor choice. He had no experience in police affairs, and his appointment might cause serious complications. Kurlov told his friend that Dzhunkovsky was prone "to seek popularity" and always displayed disdain for the police and members of the Corps of Gendarmes.[5] Maklakov went ahead anyway, for reasons that may have been practical as well as personal. The appointment of Dzhun could help Maklakov solidify his own position. The Ministry of Internal Affairs, despite its importance, was not well represented at court.[6] Maklakov knew that Dzhunkovsky had excellent connections; the tsar liked him personally and had been impressed by his successful management of security during the Borodino centennial celebrations. Selecting Dzhun was almost certain to please the sovereign and, perhaps, heighten his appreciation of the ministry.

Dzhunkovsky was not privy to these considerations, so when he recovered from the shock of Maklakov's offer, he thanked him and asked permission to come to St. Petersburg to discuss things further. Maklakov agreed, and within hours Dzhunkovsky was on a night train headed for the capital. Sitting in his wagon-lit, Dzhun felt torn. Moscow had been home for the last twenty years; there he believed he enjoyed respect, even affection, from all classes of society. Transfer to St. Petersburg would thrust him into a different world—a city full of intrigue, with a stifling bureaucratic atmosphere. But that was only part of the problem. "I was very anxious about the duties of managing the police of the entire empire that came with the job of assistant minister," he recalled. "I was tortured by the thought that I might not be equal to this difficult task."[7]

Dzhun's concerns were not exaggerated. He was not by nature a cop. He lacked an authoritarian impulse and was uncomfortable with secrecy and conspiratorial methods. He had, on two occasions, refused the post of Moscow city commandant for the very reason that it was, to his mind, an exclusively police position that just did not suit him. As governor he was open to the public and had strained relations with the security forces. He disliked Alexander Martynov, the head of the Moscow bureau, and believed that his predecessor, Mikhail fon Koten, had sought to embarrass him politically.

The job itself was dauntingly complex. Security policing in the Russian empire—as distinguished from the work of regular police forces—was in the hands of two distinct but closely linked institutions: The Separate Corps of Gendarmes and the Department of Police of the Ministry of Internal Affairs (MVD). Nicholas I had created the Corps in 1826, following the Decembrist revolt, to be a "higher" national police force with broad responsibility for security. He placed it under the Third Section of his own chancellery but, also, subordinated it to the Ministry of War. In 1880, when the successes of the terrorist "People's Will" discredited the Third Section, the government of Alexander II abolished it and established the Department of Police, which assumed the lion's share of the task of maintaining internal security. The Corps of Gendarmes remained, however, and continued to engage in security work, subordinated now to both the MVD and the Ministry of War. The minister of internal affairs became the "chief of gendarmes" and his assistant minister for police affairs was usually, but not always, the "commander." This strange institutional duality with overlapping functions, created the basis for confusion, tension, and conflict.

By 1913, in addition to the Corps's staff, headquartered in St. Petersburg, there were, subordinated to it, seventy-four provincial gendarme departments (*gubernskie zhandarmskie upravleniia* or GZhUs); twenty-nine gendarme railroad departments; gendarme divisions in St. Petersburg, Moscow, and Warsaw; a cavalry detachment in Odessa; and infantry units in Kamchatka and on Sakhalin island. The personnel of the Corps numbered about twelve thousand of whom one thousand were officers. Although security policing was an important function of the Corps, roughly 60 percent of its members served in the Gendarme Police Administration of the Railroads, which was responsible for maintaining good order on this important transportation link.

The real center of security policing was the MVD's Department of Police. It had its own director who answered to the assistant minister of internal affairs and ultimately to the minister himself. In 1913 the Department employed about fifty thousand nationwide, but its central office in St. Petersburg was staffed by just under four hundred employees. The work there was divided among several secretariats, each devoted to specific aspects of organizational management and policing. As far as security matters were concerned, the most important secretariat was the highly secret Special Section, whose widespread network of agents kept watch on parties, organizations, and individuals deemed to be subversive. The Special Section also had a Foreign Division, based in Paris, that conducted surveillance of political opponents living abroad. The Special Section and its agents (secret or not) in Russia and Europe can properly be considered the Okhrana, although that term was never employed officially. (In late imperial Russia the popular pejorative for the security police was *okhranka*, but *Okhrana* is the term most widely used today.)

In 1913 the Department of Police had under its control some twenty-seven security bureaus (*okhrannye otdeleniia* or OOs), located throughout the empire, and fourteen regional directorates. These institutions existed alongside the Corps's provincial gendarme departments but were largely independent. Although most of the operatives in the OOs were gendarme officers, they butted against those in the provincial gendarme departments who were also engaged in security police work. Chiefs of the provincial gendarme departments always outranked the directors of the security bureaus and resented the fact that the latter often received equal pay and seemed to wield greater power.[8] The entire system was complicated and cumbersome, fraught with undercurrents of jealousy. It cried out for greater unity and tighter management.

Yet as his train sped through the dark and the miles clicked by, Dzhunkovsky became more and more convinced that he should accept the proposed assignment, provided Maklakov would agree to the policies he planned to suggest, reforms that could significantly alter the image and practices of the security police and establish firmer control over its operations. Dzhun made his decision first of all out a profound sense of duty; but he also believed he could accomplish a great deal in this new and demanding position. His Moscow years had taught him much. He had seen the success of the security forces in combating the revolutionary threat. But he was also familiar with the negative side of their work, particularly the use of secret agents that had produced the Azef and Bogrov disasters and earned the security forces a mixture of contempt and fear. Dzhunkovsky believed that the secret police had largely won its war against the terrorists and other radicals bent on destroying the political and social system but had lost the battle for the hearts and minds of the public. Thus, while they had served effectively as a shield protecting tsar and state, the security forces had now become a barrier separating the sovereign from his people.

Dzhun's own experience as an administrator convinced him that this problem, too, could be overcome. While the gulf between government and society was wide, his success as governor led him to think it might be bridged. Imposing a military code of honor on the Corps of Gendarmes could restore respect for its uniform. Reducing to a minimum the employment of *provokatory* and the nefarious practice of opening private correspondence, paring back the size and intrusiveness of the police apparatus, might win broader support for the security forces and so help strengthen the tsar's authority. Surely it was worth a try, and the new minister Maklakov, "a fresh person, unspoiled by the bureaucratic atmosphere of Petersburg," who seemed "clean and honorable," might well provide the backing necessary for such a bold venture.[9]

Arriving in the capital the next morning, Dzhunkovsky stopped briefly to change clothes at the home of a friend and headed straight to Maklakov. Dzhun laid out his views on police affairs, particularly the darker side of its operations, and sketched his plans for reform. As a former governor, Maklakov may have shared Dzhunkovsky's reservations about the security police. He readily accepted Dzhun's basic ideas and, after some hesitation, agreed to make him commander of the Corps of Gendarmes as well. Dzhun considered this essential, since it would give him complete charge of the internal security apparatus and its personnel. "Then we decided another very important question," he recalled. "I would not be hindered in my actions and orders concerning the police; I would be completely independent. . . . I would take exclusively upon myself full responsibility for the affairs of the police and for security matters." Afterwards, Dzhunkovsky met with Vladimir Kokovtsov, the minister of finance who had succeeded Stolypin as prime minister. Dzhun explained his plans in detail and received Kokovtsov's full support.[10]

Although Dzhunkovsky had told almost no one about Maklakov's proposal before his departure for the capital, by the time he returned to Moscow rumors about his new assignment were flying. Then on January 18, 1913, official word appeared in the press. Dzhun began taking leave of his coworkers while the citizens of Moscow organized a series of events celebrating and honoring their departing chief—and friend. For the rest of the month he experienced what seemed a "magical dream."[11]

On January 19, while attending a performance of Ostrovsky's play "The Forest" at one of the Guardianship's people's houses, Dzhunkovsky was called on stage during an intermission. More than a hundred actors and actresses crowded around. Many were from the Malyi Theater, his favorite, and they all warmly thanked him for his work and support: "Our parting with you is sad," their address concluded. "But we're happy that we can greet you once again and thank you from our hearts for the wonderful concern you have shown for us . . . and the art we serve. May your path [ahead] be blessed!"[12]

Two days later, ninety-five members of the English Club honored him at an elegant farewell dinner, an event that had an almost family atmosphere.[13] Many times the guests toasted him, praising his long service in Moscow and wishing him future success. After dinner Dzhun's friends clustered about him, chatting amiably for a long time and finally accompanying him to the door. In the chill of the winter night, he walked across the street to the governor's mansion coatless, warmed by the sincerity of their affection.

On January 24, Dzhunkovsky opened the provincial zemstvo assembly for the last time, urging the delegates to press on with the work of providing for the material well-being of the local population, "in the spirit of the Orthodox faith and eternal state principles." He admitted he had made mistakes in the past; but they were unintended. "Permit me to hope," he concluded, "that you recognize that my actions were guided by a sense of my service obligations and a warm desire for [your] success." He shook hands with all the members of the assembly and left to the sound of their cheers.[14]

Of all the events surrounding his departure from Moscow, three touched Dzhunkovsky most deeply. On the evening of January 27, there was an enormous reception in his honor at the House of the Nobility. More than eight hundred people from all classes and walks of life attended: Mayor Guchkov, civic leaders, and representatives from all government departments, zemstvo figures, actors and actresses, and private citizens. Nina Evreinova and her son Vladimir also stood in the crowd. The hall had been decorated with tropical plants, and a lavish buffet awaited the guests. The organizing committee for the reception, headed by Alexander Samarin, the provincial marshal, met the governor, his sister, and his niece Nadezhda Shebasheva on the landing of the stairwell. To the strains of the "Preobrazhensky March," Dzhun entered the Hall of Columns, greeted by enthusiastic applause.

Champagne flowed and loud hurrahs followed a toast to the health of the tsar and the singing of the national anthem. Then Samarin gave voice to the general sentiment: "We all gather here in the common desire to express our deep respect for you, loyal servant of tsar and country, firm and just administrator. We are united by our feelings of love for you as a man of rare goodness, extraordinary responsiveness and openness. . . . In the name of all present, I have the honor to propose a toast—To the health of our beloved and respected Vladimir Fedorovich Dzhunkovsky!" Moved almost to tears, the governor raised his glass and offered a toast of his own: "I bow to you, ladies and gentlemen, for your kind attentions to me. I drink to the success of your concerted efforts for the prosperity of Holy Moscow; I drink to the health of all who have come here, to my dear Moscow friends—Hurrah!" The guests spread out in various rooms, and Dzhun went around to each thanking them and bidding farewell. He was particularly delighted by a group of peasants who gave him loud ovation, after which one of their number made a speech that he remembered as being "touching in its thoughtfulness."[15]

A few days later, the governor opened an extraordinary session of the noble assembly, called to prepare for the tercentennial celebrations of the Romanov dynasty. The nobility had always firmly supported his administration, and he used the meeting to take his leave and to express his gratitude. Gentry Marshal Samarin then asked Dzhunkovsky to become a member of the Moscow nobility by inscribing his name in its book, which the governor did as he left the assembly. The next day Samarin headed a delegation that came to the governor's mansion to apprise him formally of his induction into the Moscow *dvorianstvo* and to present him with a hinged icon with images of St. Vladimir, St. George, and Dzhun's guardian angel. The governor invited them all into his office, opened champagne, and offered a toast: "From the most junior noble of Moscow province—to the seniors."[16]

February 4, 1913, Dzhun's last day in Moscow, had a special significance. On this, the seventh anniversary of the assassination of Sergei Alexandrovich, he attended a requiem mass for the grand duke at the Chudov Monastery followed by a memorial service at his tomb. Afterwards, Ella received him and gave him her blessing. The governor then bade farewell to the officials in the provincial and county offices that were under his command and thanked them for their service. Finally, accompanied by his sister, Dzhun headed to the Nicholas Station where he would board the night train for St. Petersburg. Arriving twenty-five minutes early, he found the entire platform and the waiting rooms filled with well-wishers. At the sight of the enormous crowd, Dzhunkovsky fought to hold back his tears. He hardly had time to thank them all before the station master announced that the train was about to depart. He entered the car and promptly at half past eight the express pulled away from the ancient capital to the sound of yet one more "Hurrah!"[17]

The passionate outpouring of affection that surrounded Dzhunkovsky during his last days in Moscow surprised many. "Something very strange is going on in Moscow," proclaimed an article in *Utro Rossii* (Morning Russia), the moderately liberal daily published by the business leader Pavel Riabushinsky. How was it, the writer asked, that a governor who "even his worst enemy would not call . . . a liberal or political gradualist" enjoyed such popularity across all social and economic groups? The answer was simple, he continued: "being a truly decent man in his private life, Dzhunkovsky carried this decency over to his official life." The formula for the governor's success had three basic ingredients: "personal honesty, a lack of impulsiveness, and a respect for the law."[18]

Utro Rossii missed the point, however, when it implied that Dzhunkovsky was a singular figure whose unusual popularity showed how very little it took for a representative of authority to earn "a share of public sympathy." The governor's high standing with Muscovites was not simply a reflection of his character; he had won it by the hard work of active engagement in the life of the city and the province. Nor was he unique. In the same month that Dzhun departed Moscow, the liberal journal *Vestnik Evropy* (The Herald of Europe) reported that two other governors, P. P. Shilovsky of Kostroma and P. P. Stremoukhov of Saratov were also leaving their provinces amid similar effusions of affection and goodwill. Their formulas for success were much the same as Dzhunkovsky's, and equally simple: "They gave a certain amount of space to the natural movement of local life without crushing it by the usual repression."[19] But, we suspect, their popularity rested on more than that. During their time in office they had displayed "service tact," a commitment to legality, political skill, and public outreach. Something strange was going on, but not just in Moscow. The character of provincial rule was beginning to change as the "Stolypin generation" of officials moved to higher positions in the state.

For Dzhunkovsky, the sincerity and warmth of his sendoff had enormous significance. The space he devotes to it in his memoirs was not simply an instance of self-congratulation. Rather, it indicates the degree to which these events charged his psychic and emotional batteries. As his subsequent actions would show, Dzhun took the near universal affection that Muscovites had displayed as proof that firm conservative government could enjoy broad public support. Administrators were able to gain approval by engaging civil society and adopting consistent, honest policies infused with the spirit of the Orthodox faith and guided by a sense of justice. Dzhunkovsky believed that in St. Petersburg he might apply the lessons of Moscow to the task of reshaping the operations of state security. True, the Corps of Gendarmes and the Department of Police he would now command had much to live down, but they had honorable traditions upon which to build and a vital mission to perform. Presenting a different face to the public and cutting back to a necessary minimum the methods that had generated scandals and provoked hostility in the past could, in time, surmount the barrier of distrust that separated Russia's citizens from those who shouldered the burden of guarding their safety and the good order of the empire.

On the morning of February 5, Dzhunkovsky stepped off the train in St. Petersburg and was met by Stepan Beletsky, the director of the Department of Police and his immediate subordinates. Dzhun's brother-in-law General Dmitrii Konstantinovich Gershelman, the Corps of Gendarmes' chief of staff, was also there to greet him, and together the two kinsmen rode by car to the headquarters of the Corps, where Dzhunkovsky would live during his tenure as commander. It was a rather nondescript unimposing three-story building on the corner of Furshtatskaia Street and Voskresensky Prospect, a quiet section of town, not far from the Tauride Gardens and the Duma. Dzhun found his new apartment to be excellent, well-furnished, and large enough to have a separate room to hold his growing personal archive. The place was undergoing some small repairs, but they would be finished by the time Evdokiia and his niece arrived. Since the Gershelmans also lived in the same building, he would be able to spend some time with his other sister, Olga.[20]

The next few days saw a round of appointments with leading officials in the capital. At Tsarskoe Selo, the main residence of the emperor and his family, Nicholas received him with his usual warmth and expressed great satisfaction with his appointment. Maklakov had already informed the tsar about Dzhunkovsky's views and the changes he proposed, and Nicholas affirmed his support, wishing him strength, health, and success. Following lunch with Grand Duke Pavel Alexandrovich, Dzhun returned to St. Petersburg and his new duties.[21]

Although confident he was on the right track, Dzhunkovsky was uneasy as he began his work. Twenty years in Moscow made him feel like a stranger in his native city, and he had imbibed some of the prejudice many Muscovites felt toward the capital. Just as Americans living "outside the beltway" often look askance at the strange, alien behavior of Washington officials, insiders, and politicians, Muscovites saw St. Petersburg as an unnatural growth, a bureaucratic spiders' nest spinning webs of corruption and control that extended into the hinterlands. Dzhun's memoirs suggest that his anxiety verged on paranoia. He feared that from the outset he would have to work in a "far from benevolent atmosphere" and experience "every kind of dirty trick and intrigue" from "shady characters" and careerists sure to oppose him. In addition, he would have to fight against powerful political and social groups in the capital, to avoid falling into their "carefully spread nets." He believed that his identity and integrity would be under constant threat. Years later, he recalled his greatest concern: "I would have to exercise great effort just to remain myself."[22]

Dzhunkovsky's fears were well grounded. St. Petersburg was rife with corruption and scandal both financial and sexual, which infected much of the court and high society.[23] Not a place where the straight-laced, rather prudish Dzhun was likely to feel comfortable. Its political sands shifted rapidly, those enjoying favor one day could lose it the next. Bureaucratic inertia and court intrigue frequently blunted reform efforts, even those of the forceful and dynamic Stolypin who, despite the impetus provided by revolution and governmental crisis, had found it impossible to push through much of his agenda. Dzhun must have sensed that the time available for him to get things done would be limited, too. He was, thus, a man in a hurry, determined to implement the changes he had in mind as quickly as possible.

On his first full day in office, Dzhunkovsky sought to make clear to his subordinates and the public alike that a new spirit would now animate the Corps of Gendarmes and the security police. His Order No. 28, of February 6, 1913, set a high moral tone. The new commander reminded the gendarmes that their Corps was part of "the glorious Russian army," and that this obliged each member to see that neither his official actions nor his personal behavior brought dishonor to its banners. Officers should display the highest military qualities: "a comradely spirit, mutual trust and a noble straightforwardness towards their superiors, their subordinates and

Dzhunkovsky as Commander of Corps of Gendarmes. Personal collection.

each other." The Corps of Gendarmes, he urged, was engaged in a struggle with the enemies of the state and society. Where this criminal element threatened throne and fatherland, members of the Corps were obliged to employ all means, "acting vigilantly, confidently and, if circumstances demanded, mercilessly." But in using the wide powers granted to them, they should not overstep the bounds of necessity. "All gendarmes should reverently remember the instructions, given by the sovereign founder of the Corps to its first chief. The course of history has changed the duties laid upon the Corps since the time of its formation; but the holy commandment to do mercy, the call to dry the tears of the unfortunate, remains an unalterable motto for each of us."[24]

Within police ranks Order No. 28 doubtless met with skepticism, but the public received it well. Still, it also caused some amusement, because it recalled Nicholas I's famous "prime directive" to Count Benkendorff, the Corps's first commander: a white handkerchief for drying the people's tears. Humorists had a field day. A column in *Utro Rossii* noted that in the forests of the gendarmerie a "new bird" had sung a "new song." "We listen to his song and are astonished," the author continued, "who could have expected the warble of a nightingale from a bird with blue feathers [the distinctive color of the gendarme's uniform]?" Yet how Dzhunkovsky's melody would eventually play in the deep woods of the police was far from certain, and it was anybody's guess whether, in the end, the new commander would change the Corps, or the Corps its new commander.[25] In the St. Petersburg daily *Den'* (The Day), another wit speculated that citizens could soon expect different behavior from the gendarme who knocked on their door. To the question: "Who's there?" he would no longer gruffly reply, "Telegram," but instead answer in dulcet tones, "Handkerchief." Upon entering, he would say politely: "In accordance with the directive to the Corps of Gendarmes, I must wipe the tears from your face. Please be so kind as to hand over the keys to your writing desk."[26]

Dzhunkovsky was serious about his campaign for change and determined to win. But he already felt threatened by unwanted entanglements and dangerous intrigues. Even before he arrived in St. Petersburg, he had received overtures from Prince Vladimir Meshchersky, the influential publisher of the newspaper *Grazhdanin* (The Citizen), inviting him to visit and become part of his circle. Meshchersky had the ear of the sovereign and not a few ministers, but many deemed him odious both for his extreme conservatism and his scandalous private life. Dzhunkovsky fended off Meshchersky's advances, mustering the full degree of his legendary tact, but the episode served as a warning of things to come.

Rasputin also cast his shadow. When Dzhun made his obligatory visits to members of the royal family, all of whom expressed warm support, Empress Alexandra refused him a private audience. Dzhunkovsky believed he knew why: "I well understood that her majesty avoided me having been turned against me by circles close to Rasputin, all the more so because at the time a rumor had spread that I had hit Rasputin and thrown him out when he had come to see me. But this was false; Rasputin never visited me . . . I never met him."[27]

Dzhunkovsky quickly adopted a work schedule similar to the one he had developed as governor, but even more demanding. "Literally, there remained not a moment for myself, for my private life, and I am amazed that I could bear it all," he recalled years later when he lived quietly as a "former person." As usual he rose at seven o'clock and was in the office by eight. At nine he began his reception, open to citizens as well as officials, which lasted until eleven, followed by the report of his chief of staff. At one o'clock Dzhun had lunch, then came more reports starting at two, with the director of the Department of Police, and continuing for most of the day. At half past seven he had dinner, and at nine turned again to business, examining and signing a huge volume of papers that often took between three and four hours. But Dzhun's duties also required him to accompany the emperor, empress, or the heir to the throne when they chose to attend the theater. In this case, he would remain in his seat until their majesties left and then rush home to complete the work that still remained. Each week he reported twice to the minister, once accompanied by the director of the Department of Police, once alone. As the situation demanded, he might have to participate in any number of official commissions or appear at the Duma. And through it all came the dispatches from the provincial governors, coded or not, that concerned every possible happening. "To be sure, they never reported good things," he lamented, "and so lying down to sleep my head was always full with all kinds of troubles, which, of course, given the vastness of Mother Russia, were not few."[28]

Although he was bent on a thorough overhaul of the security service, Dzhunkovsky immediately had to confront a number of other pressing problems, including a broad reform of the regular police throughout the empire. This was a proposal, part of Stolypin's centralizing scheme, by which the roughly 120,000 regular rural and urban policemen who served in the provinces would be placed under the command of the chiefs of the various *gubernia* gendarme departments. When the measure had been discussed in the Council for the Affairs of the Local Economy, the governors strongly opposed it since it would diminish their power over the provincial constabulary while still leaving them ultimately responsible for maintaining order. The governors also feared greater subordination to St. Petersburg authorities. Fresh from their duties in Chernigov and Moscow, both Maklakov and Dzhunkovsky sided with the governors' objections and reworked the measure in accordance with their concerns.[29] In the end, however, the police reform project never became law.

Dzhun also had to come before the Duma to answer a question concerning a search that gendarmes had conducted at the apartment of one of the delegates, a violation of parliamentary immunity. In some trepidation he arrived at the huge Paladian-style Tauride Palace, where Russia's legislature met, wearing the dark blue uniform of the Corps, something that previous commanders had long avoided doing lest they "excite the Duma." But there was method in Dzhunkovsky's fashion statement. It was part of his larger campaign to change the public's image of the gendarmerie and to enhance its pride and prestige. To his considerable surprise, this gesture produced a positive impression even on the liberal and left-wing deputies.[30]

By far the most important task that stood before Dzhunkovsky was maintaining security during the ceremonies commemorating three centuries of Romanov rule, celebrations that would affirm both national and dynastic pride. They began in St. Petersburg on February 20, 1913, with a series of lavish events that continued over the next four days. The centerpiece of the celebrations in the capital was the solemn and triumphal religious service held in the Kazan Cathedral on February 21. Enormous processions brought the imperial family and a crowd of some four thousand—clergy, elite state officials, Duma members, the diplomatic corps, merchants, peasants, and non-Russians—to the huge neoclassical structure on Nevsky Prospect. There Nicholas II sat on a marble throne under a banner bearing the words "The Tsar is in the Hands of God" and read a manifesto that proclaimed the unity of tsar and people and his determination to lead them in building the national life. Concerts, receptions, theatrical performances, and balls followed over several days, reaching a climax in a splendid celebratory dinner at the Winter Palace.[31]

As the newly appointed commander of the Corps of Gendarmes, Dzhunkovsky had to tread lightly. He did not yet know enough to interfere with the security arrangements established by the St. Petersburg city commandant. But he felt that the presence of the police and military was too visible, giving the capital the appearance of an "armed camp." A rumor that terrorists had planted a bomb at the Kazan Cathedral set authorities on edge. The prospect of a demonstration by radical workers that would disrupt the ceremonies with a display of red flags and the singing of the Marseillaise terrified them.[32] But all these fears proved groundless. There were no demonstrations; indeed, Dzhunkovsky believed that they were unthinkable. Excessive security simply reflected the desire of jumpy administrators to save their own skins and did not make good sense from the point of view of state's interest.[33] He would take a different tack when the celebrations continued on a national scale in May.

Dzhunkovsky was aware of some, but not all, of the turmoil surrounding the St. Petersburg celebrations. He did not witness Rasputin's attempt to insert himself into the religious service at the Kazan Cathedral and stand in front of the place designated for the Imperial Duma, which caused Mikhail Rodzianko, the Duma president, to threaten to drag the "starets" out by his beard.[34] But Dzhun was disturbed when the extreme monarchists acquired something of a position of honor during the ceremonial dinner at the Winter Palace. In his memoirs, he almost always recalled the emperor in a positive light and never acknowledged the degree to which the sovereign he revered embraced the right-wing Union of the Russian People and other extremist organizations. In this case, Dzhun chose to believe that Nicholas had acquiesced to their presence only under duress.[35]

But even as Dzhunkovsky prepared for the work of guaranteeing the security of the Romanov royals during the tercentennial celebrations, he received signals of political difficulties ahead. On March 8 he appeared at the Duma. The legislature was discussing the stringent measures that the St. Petersburg city commandant had adopted in regard to the highly charged problem of hooliganism: the petty crimes, insults, threatening behavior, and other disruptions of public order by lower-class drunks and rowdies that were causing panic among law-abiding citizens on St. Petersburg's streets.[36] Dzhun decided to attend because the Ministry of Internal Affairs should have a representative present and because Minister N. A. Maklakov, who at the time had assumed what Dzhunkovsky called "an incongruous position" vis-à-vis the Duma, refused to go. As he listened to the speeches in the Duma, Dzhun realized that legislative opposition to the actions of the city commandant was a sign of a deeper conflict between the Duma and the minister. Many delegates—left, center, and right—made clear they believed that Nikolai Maklakov, influenced by Prince Meshchersky, was determined to reduce the importance of the Duma, even strip it of its legislative power.

Shortly after his visit to the Duma, Dzhunkovsky received a detailed written critique of Maklakov from the "Russian National Fraction," a substantial group of conservative delegates who charged the minister of internal affairs with trying to rule the country without reference to the legislature, treating it the way an authoritarian governor might deal with peasant institutions. Dzhunkovsky did not at all share Maklakov's antipathy to the Duma and realized that the hostility of the legislature toward his immediate superior might hinder the reforms he hoped to adopt. While staying clear of party politics, Dzhun cultivated good relations with Duma leaders, particularly the moderate right-wing Octobrists and their leader Alexander Guchkov, whose brother had served as mayor of Moscow. Over time Dzhun was able to gain support for his positions with regard to the Department of Police, but the tension between Maklakov and the legislature continued and must have made Dzhunkovsky more aware than ever of his own precarious situation.[37]

With this in mind Dzhun moved quickly to reform the Department of Police's established policy of using secret informants, or *provokatory*. This was a decision that put him on a collision course with the police professionals who were now his subordinates. He had no qualms about the penetration of revolutionary and subversive groups by government agents, but he believed there were two places where they should not be used: in the armed forces and among high school students.

On March 13, 1913, Dzhunkovsky banned the recruitment of police agents (*sotrudniki*) within the military. His own soldier's sense of honor may have influenced that decision, but he had solid practical concerns as well. He knew that spies in the army and navy were sometimes valuable and had recently helped scotch mutinies on several ships. But other considerations weighed against their continued use. Informants, he believed, contributed to an unhealthy relationship between the military and the security service; their presence corrupted the armed forces and undermined discipline. In Turkestan recently, secret informants guided by the local Okhrana had provoked disturbances in several army units. Dzhun was convinced that this revealed a larger problem: police agents within the military often stirred up trouble simply to advance their own reputations and careers.

Dzhunkovsky sought backing for the abolition of police agents in the army and navy from War Minister Sukhomlinov but found him unsupportive. Dzhun then turned to Grand Duke Nikolai Nikolaevich, commander of the St. Petersburg military district, with whom he and his family had long-standing friendly ties. After a breakfast meeting, the grand duke listened attentively as Dzhunkovsky laid out his reasons for wanting to eliminate police spies from the armed forces and "with a light heart" gave his approval. "I believe you implicitly," he added, "and don't doubt that, for your part, you'll do everything to help us preserve the army from criminal propaganda." With the grand duke's encouragement, Dzhun moved ahead and issued his order ending the use of police agents within the ranks of the armed forces. This did not terminate cooperation between the gendarmes and the military but ended the practice of having soldiers spy on soldiers. Gendarmes should continue their watch on military units from outside, preventing contacts between soldiers and dangerous elements. But connections between the gendarmes and the military should take place at the level of command, without inserting *sotrudniki* into the ranks. This measure did not go down well with Beletsky, but later, Dzhun found that the commanders of almost all the military districts supported it, and as a result, relations between the army and the Corps of Gendarmes improved.[38]

Shortly thereafter, Dzhunkovsky ended the recruitment of police informants among high school students, a practice he learned about soon after he took office. In March, the police had arrested two students at the Vitmer Gymnasium in St. Petersburg who were members of an underground group styling itself "The Revolutionary Union." This action provoked considerable public outrage, and in April a number of newspaper articles appeared claiming that the police were conducting "mass arrests" in high schools. Sensing a scandal in the making, Dzhunkovsky issued a statement denying any large-scale roundup of students, and he investigated further.

Going through the files, he was horrified to discover that the policy of employing students to spy on their classmates was well established. Beletsky, the director of the Department of Police, hastened to defend the practice, but Dzhunkovsky would have none of it: "Such clear-cut corruption of schoolchildren, who had not even begun to live independently, seemed monstrous to me." He forbade further recruitment but soon found that his subordinates were ignoring the decree. "I decided to resort to the most extreme measures—those guilty of disobeying my orders would be dismissed from office without any explanation."[39]

These two decisions, taken at the outset of his tenure, poisoned Dzhun's relations with the leading figures in the Department of Police. They despised him as an incompetent dilettante, a seeker after public acclaim who knew nothing about security policing and did not respect their work. Nor was their perspective entirely wrong. As an outsider, a man in a hurry, Dzhunkovsky had little interest in learning about the "culture" of the security forces. The "service tact" he so often displayed in Moscow in dealing with officials and the public alike did not mark his relations with his new subordinates.

Dzhunkovsky strongly disliked department head Stepan Beletsky. The Englishman Bernard Pares, who knew Beletsky quite well, described him as "a typical professional police official, a thorough man of the world," adding, "He was not an honest man, and could never have been regarded as such whether by himself or by others."[40] Dzhunkovsky would have concurred. What he saw as Beletsky's amorality repelled him, and he believed that the director of the Department of Police was always trying to pull the wool over his eyes and wear him down. Beletsky made excruciatingly detailed four-hour reports, burdened him with all kinds of unnecessary work, and sought to frighten him by exaggerating the dangers the country faced. Dzhun also had no confidence in Sergei Vissarionov, Beletsky's immediate subordinate and right-hand man. To be sure, he was not as bad as his boss, but his "negative character" made him objectionable. He planned to remove both men as soon as circumstances permitted, and he had acquired the necessary knowledge of police matters.[41]

Dzhunkovsky devoted the last half of March and the early part of April to preparing security for the most important part of the tercentenary celebrations. This was to take place in May, when the tsar and his family traveled through the historic towns of the upper Volga. A central moment would be the visit to Kostroma and the Ipatiev Monastery where, in 1613, the first Romanov, sixteen-year-old Mikhail Fedorovich, had received the invitation from the Assembly of the Land to take the throne. Their journey was to culminate in Moscow, with lavish ceremonies commemorating Mikhail's entry into the ancient capital and his coronation.

Dzhun toured the route Nicholas was to take, beginning in Kostroma, discussing security arrangements with provincial governors, gendarmes, and local police officials. As always, he wanted to see that the royals enjoyed full but unobtrusive protection that would ensure their safety and at the same time allow them to have real contact with the people. He modeled his plan on the security measures he had put in place at the time of the Borodino celebrations the year before, and the tsar had already given it his blessing.[42] The preparatory trip also took him to Iaroslavl, Rostov, Suzdal, Vladimir, Nizhnii Novgorod, and ultimately, Moscow. It was arduous, but Dzhun was able to form valuable impressions of local officials and to immerse himself in the history of the area, something he greatly enjoyed.[43]

Before the tercentennial celebrations took place, however, Dzhunkovsky had to arrange for Nicholas's security in Berlin during another event, set for early May, that proved to be the last meeting of the Russian, German, and British monarchs before the outbreak of the Great War. The occasion was the wedding of Kaiser Wilhelm's only daughter, Princess Victoria Louise of Prussia, to Prince Ernest Augustus of Hanover and of Great Britain and Ireland (who later reigned as the Duke of Brunswick). In addition to Nicholas, the German royal family, and Ernest's parents, the Duke and Duchess of Cumberland, both Britain's King George V and Queen Mary would attend. The love match of the two principals healed the breach between the Hohenzollerns and the House of Hanover, whose kingdom Prussia had annexed after its victory over Austria in 1866.

Dzhunkovsky left for Berlin on April 23, 1913. He came at the request of the Russian ambassador, Sergei Sverbeev, to discuss plans to protect the tsar. The safety measures that the ambassador and his staff proposed to establish at the embassy appeared sufficient. Still, Dzhun took the added precaution of renting all the rooms in the adjacent Hotel Bristol that abutted the embassy's wall. He met briefly with the head of the Berlin police and proposed to place at his disposal some of his agents working abroad who could identify Russian terrorists by sight. The offer was politely declined.

Dzhun then made a whirlwind trip to Paris where he inspected the Foreign Division of the secret police (*zagranichnaia agentura*). He found it well organized under the capable direction of Alexander Krasilnikov; but relations between Krasilnikov and Ambassador Izvolsky were tense and needed to be smoothed. The ambassador feared that Vladimir Burtsev, the revolutionary journalist and spy catcher, who was exposing the clandestine activities of the Russian police in France, would undermine relations with the empire's key ally. With some difficulty, Dzhun convinced Izvolsky to let the Foreign Division's chancellery remain within the walls of the embassy. He promised to put the operations of the Division on a legal basis by setting up a fictitious private detective agency, staffed by local agents of the Okhrana, who could then operate in accordance with French law. (By year's end the Department of Police formally abolished the Foreign Division although its watch on revolutionaries operating abroad continued using these more acceptable means.)[44] Dzhun returned to St. Petersburg on April 29. On May 1, he left for another quick inspection of the Volga towns in preparation for the tercentennial tour. He got back to the capital on May 6, just in time to leave again for Berlin, where Nicholas would arrive on May 8.

Dzhunkovsky reached the German capital a day before the tsar, and since he was there in an unofficial capacity, went about the city in civilian dress, mixing freely with the people and listening to their conversations. He sensed that Berliners were excited by the arrival of the Russian tsar and well disposed toward him. The German press convinced Dzhun that although the meeting of the three emperors was strictly a "family affair," the public attached a greater significance to it, believing that it had cleared the political and diplomatic atmosphere and held out the prospect of peace in Europe.

On his second day in Berlin, a curious and troubling incident showed him that Rasputin had become a matter of concern beyond Russia's borders. Grand Duke Ernest of Hesse, the brother of Empress Alexandra, sent word that he wanted Dzhun to come to his hotel, the Kaiserhof, the next morning. Upon arrival, he encountered not only the grand duke, but also Prince Henry of Prussia, his wife, Irene, and Victoria, Princess of Battenberg, both women sisters of the empress. He knew them all well and had met them often during his long service to Ella and Sergei. The

German royals greeted Dzhunkovsky like an old friend in what he recalled as "more than intimate circumstances." Their quarters were small, with no reception area; the room where they met was messy, with an unmade bed and toiletries strewn about. Pleasantries and small talk quickly gave way to pointed, anxious questions, chiefly from Ernest and Victoria, about their sister. First, they wanted to know about the mood of the Russian public and the army; then the conversation turned to Rasputin and his role in Alexandra's life.

Dzhunkovsky responded cautiously. He tried to play down Rasputin's significance and told his questioners that the rumors about him had been exaggerated. But he found that the empress's siblings were well informed, undoubtedly briefed by Ella.[45] His answers failed to put their minds at ease, and they urged him to try to influence their sister by telling her of all the harm Rasputin was causing the country. Dzhun protested that this was impossible, that Alexandra would not receive or speak to him. But Alexandra's brother and sisters urged him to smooth his relations with the empress. Then their questions began to focus on conditions in Russia, and Dzhun soon was able to change the subject to the plans for the upcoming tercentennial celebrations.

When the meeting was over Dzhunkovsky felt relief. He had survived a painful grilling and held his tongue in check. Years later, he recalled that the episode had not only increased his concerns about Rasputin but also aroused his suspicions about the empress's German family. "Maybe . . . , out of friendship, they just wanted to learn from me something about the actual mood in my country, maybe they questioned me purely out of sympathy, out of concern for their sister, but the tone and speed with which they put their questions made me distrustful." Dzhun never saw Alexandra's relatives again. He soon returned to Russia, and the following year the outbreak of war severed all ties with Germany.[46]

The Romanovs' tercentennial journey began on May 16 when Tsar Nicholas arrived in Vladimir. It continued the next day with his enthusiastic reception in Nizhnii Novgorod and reached an emotional peak when the imperial family arrived by boat at Kostroma. The heavily industrialized province had been a center of Bolshevik-led workers' strikes in 1905, and even the local nobility had a significant tradition of liberalism. But

Dzhunkovsky's classmate at the Corps of Pages, Governor Petr Stremoukhov, had things well in hand and the ceremonies proceeded with little disruption. An awkward incident occurred when the provincial marshal of the nobility, Mikhail Zuzin, addressed Nicholas in an oppositional tone. The tsar listened and replied curtly: "Are you finished?"[47] But Dzhun does not seem to have witnessed this (or, if he did, chose not to recall it). His memoirs recount instead a touching and amusing moment when a peasant elder, come to present the emperor with the traditional gift of bread and salt, attempted a brief speech of welcome. "Your Imperial Majesty . . . ," he began, then fell silent, tongue-tied. He tried again: "Your Imperial Majesty. . . ." Again, silence. Once more: "Your Imperial Majesty. . . ." At this point, the tsar broke through the general embarrassment and gently asked: "Do you have something else to say to me?" Relieved, the peasant shouted: "Hurrah for Your Imperial Majesty!" and handed over the bread and salt. The emperor enthusiastically replied: "Wonderful [*Vot i khorosho*]!" He grabbed the elder by the shoulders and kissed him three times.[48]

The celebrations in Kostroma left Dzhunkovsky with powerful and lasting impressions. "Those two days . . . have never been erased from my memory," he wrote after the revolution. "I was fortunate that the Lord made it possible for me to witness this incomparable upsurge of patriotic feeling among the people."[49] Only one thing marred the event: the presence of Rasputin. Dzhun had barely arrived in Kostroma when Governor Stremoukhov came to ask for his advice. Rasputin had appeared in the town and had gone to the ticket bureau, demanding a pass for all the events. Dzhunkovsky told the governor that the "starets" should not be hindered from watching the ceremonies while standing in the crowd, but tickets of admission were reserved for officials, and Rasputin was not entitled to one. If Rasputin insisted, Stremoukhov was to tell him that his request had been duly presented and refused. Despite Dzhunkovsky's prohibition, Rasputin appeared briefly at the Ipatiev Cathedral and stood near the altar, escorted there at the command of the empress by agents of court security. He did not show up at other events, however, and while Rasputin's presence disturbed some of the few who saw him, Dzhun believed that most of Kostroma's inhabitants paid no attention.[50]

Shortly after noon on May 24, the imperial party arrived in Moscow for the climax of the tercentennial. Tightly packed crowds had stood since morning along the Tverskaia, the broad avenue lined with elegant shops, apartments, and official buildings that the tsar and his family would take from the Alexander Railroad Station toward the Kremlin. Voskresensky Square, where the Tverskaia ended, held ten thousand excited schoolchildren. Just beyond, in Red Square, hundreds of thousands prepared to greet their sovereign.

After the welcoming ceremonies at the station, Nicholas mounted a palomino stallion and rode out preceded by units of his personal guard, clad in bright red Circassian coats. He was followed by high court officials and the grand dukes, also on horseback, and by an open carriage bearing the Alexandra, Alexei, and the grand duchesses. Dzhunkovsky rode on the left side of the cortege, not far from the emperor, and watched him dismount at the chapel of the Iberian Virgin to receive, together with Alexandra and the children, the blessing of Bishop Trifon.

The tsar and his family proceeded on foot into Red Square. The crowd exploded into thunderous "Hurrahs," as the imperial party made its way to the Savior's Gate with its belfry and famous clock. Moscow Metropolitan Makarii greeted and blessed them before they entered the Kremlin. In the seventeenth century, Tsar Aleksei Mikhailovich had decreed that all should pass through Savior's Gate on foot, men bareheaded, and Nicholas obeyed the law laid down by his ancestor. Inside he met a procession coming from the Uspensky Cathedral, where seventeen years before he had been crowned. The imperial party proceeded past military school cadets, stiff at attention, senators resplendent in their red uniforms, and smartly dressed army officers and civilian officials to enter the silver-domed Cathedral of the Archangel Mikhail where they prayed before the tomb of the first Romanov, Mikhail Fedorovich.

Festivities continued for the next three days, as the tsar, tsarina, the heir, and the grand duchesses paid homage to their Romanov forebears. On May 25, Nicholas performed the ceremony of bowing to the people from the Red Staircase of the Great Kremlin Palace and received delegations from the estates of the land—peasants, merchants, nobles. That evening, the tsar hosted an enormous ceremonial banquet for more than seven hundred at the Great Kremlin Palace. On May 26, the nobility of Moscow gave a grand ball in honor of the imperial party at the Great White Hall of the Noble Assembly, where the dancing lasted until one o'clock in the morning. The next afternoon the triumphal jubilee ended as Nicholas and his family rode in open carriages through cheering crowds in Red Square and along the Tverskaia. At the Alexander Railroad Station, the imperial party boarded the train for Tsarskoe Selo.[51]

The tercentennial was an Indian summer moment for the Russian monarchy that seems both fleeting and fragile given our knowledge of events to come. But the outpouring of support and affection that the imperial family experienced at the time was genuine, and few could have anticipated the world-shattering disasters just over the horizon that made those emotions so short-lived. Still, the colorful celebrations were tinged with a few dark and troubling shades. Illness and exhaustion forced Alexandra to miss many of the festivities. Her absence left a bad impression and increased the alienation of the country's elite from the imperial couple. Alexis, the hemophiliac heir to the throne, whose illness was unknown to the public, often had to be carried during the ceremonies. His visible frailty produced anxious thoughts about the future of the dynasty.

Even more serious, the tercentennial strengthened Nicholas and Alexandra's belief that a strong mystical bond united the monarchy and the people, a tie that rendered state officials and institutions largely superfluous. In this spirit the tsar had snubbed the Duma, excluding its members from most of the events. He shared with Interior Minister Maklakov the desire to reduce the Duma's role, strip away its law-making power, and turn it into a purely consultative body. Strong opposition from the other ministers would prevent this, but their influence was weakened by the success of the jubilee. The royal couple were more convinced than ever that the tsar could do virtually anything because he was supported by the "real" Russians, the peasant masses who revered him as God's anointed. Enveloped in this dreamworld, Nicholas and Alexandra drifted further from political reality and Rasputin grew increasingly important, claiming, as he did, to speak for the common man.[52]

Chapter 12

A Gendarme Manqué?

For Dzhunkovsky, the celebration of the Romanovs' tercentennial anniversary was a personal triumph: "Everyone was pleased, the governors, the citizens, the police and the higher authorities, and chief of all—the Sovereign [who] was enraptured because everywhere he had direct contact with the people, . . . [because] everything went peacefully, smoothly, with no undercurrent of intrigue." The public's affection for the tsar and the dynasty strengthened Dzhun's own belief that the danger of revolution was exaggerated, and that significant reforms of the secret police could be carried out without undermining the security of the empire. Beyond this, Dzhun felt that his own political position had been enhanced by the success of the jubilee that he had done so much to make possible. Many of those who had greeted his appointment with skepticism had now changed their minds.[1] The time had come to push ahead with his program for change.

In the next months he worked steadily to reduce the size of the Department of Police, curtail its expenditures, and he believed, improve its operations. His first step was to eliminate most of the Department's provincial security bureaus, leaving only those in Moscow, St. Petersburg, and Warsaw, and bringing secret police operations more tightly under the control of the gendarme station chiefs. Dzhun also cut back the bigger regional directorates so that only those in Siberia, the Caucasus, Turkestan, and Poland remained. He justified this move as a way to achieve greater unity in police work and because many of the bureaus had not been established by law but by administrative fiat. In his view the largely independent provincial and regional security agencies were "seedbeds of provocation," and whatever small value they had was far outweighed by the "colossal harm" they had caused.[2]

On June 26, 1913, Dzhunkovsky opened a special conference to discuss measures to combat nonpolitical crime and improve criminal investigations. In his remarks he pointed to the low level of personnel in some of the detective bureaus, caused in part by inadequate salaries. He criticized the poor quality of paperwork, insufficient control of expenditures, and a number of other practical matters. The conference focused much attention on the proper conduct of criminal investigations and the need for more specialists trained in different types of crime: fraud, theft, murder, and others. The conference adopted a number of Dzhun's suggestions concerning the behavior of police investigators. They included a prohibition of the use of violence and threats against persons who were accused or under suspicion; a ban on any provocations or measures designed to encourage others in criminal acts, such as setting up thieves' nests, gaming houses, and the like; and an injunction against secret agents passing themselves off as state officials.[3]

Toward the end of July, Dzhunkovsky sought to establish closer control over the secret sums assigned to the Department of Police. These monies, totaling over five million rubles, were "off the books," not part of the regular state budget, and were chiefly used to pay Okhrana agents and cover their various expenses. Dzhun felt uneasy about the situation. The secret sums weighed on his conscience, the more so since, in the past, expenditures had often exceeded the allotted amounts. On July 26, Dzhunkovsky reported to the tsar about these funds, providing a detailed account of their use and informing him of his plan to reduce future outlays. Some of the savings would be achieved by abolishing the provincial and regional bureaus and directorates, and he told the tsar he planned to make further reductions. Many of these involved cutting back the number of agents assigned to protect high-ranking government officials and members of the royal family. Dzhunkovsky was convinced that the dangers of terrorism had been so greatly reduced and that excessive security measures were unnecessary and possibly counterproductive.[4]

Meanwhile, another event shocked Dzhunkovsky and pushed him further on the path of reform. In mid-June, a frightened, highly agitated young woman appeared in St. Petersburg. She had a tragic story to tell, one that threatened the security of the state.

Her name was Ekaterina Shornikova, a former police informant who had helped facilitate Stolypin's coup d'état of June 3, 1907. Shornikova had been just twenty-three in 1906 when she fell into the hands of the security forces, arrested for a radical article she had written. They quickly "turned" the terrified girl, and she agreed to work for them. As their agent, she joined the St. Petersburg Social Democratic Party and soon became secretary of its military organization, created to establish contact with the soldiers and spread propaganda in the ranks. In 1907 she supplied her handlers with documents that were among the materials used to justify charges that Social Democratic representatives in the legislature were conspiring to overthrow the government. This triggered the dissolution of the Second State Duma on June 3, 1907, the arrest, trial, and imprisonment of the accused delegates, and the introduction of the new electoral law that laid the foundations of Stolypin's "Third of June System" under which Russia was now governed (see chapter 7).

Because she had been a member of the St. Petersburg Social Democrats' military organization, judicial authorities placed Shornikova on their list of wanted suspects; but the secret police, not willing to have its "provocation" exposed, refused to reveal that she was an agent. Instead, the *okhranniki* spirited her from the capital. For the next six years Shornikova hid out, chiefly in the Volga region, enduring an insecure and nightmarish existence, constantly fearful of being arrested and jailed by the government or exposed as a "traitor" to the revolutionaries and subject to vengeance at their hands. Finally, exhausted, distraught, on the verge of a nervous breakdown, Shornikova decided to come to St. Petersburg to resolve her impossible situation. She wanted her status clarified and to be given the means to leave the country, hoping to settle in South America, safe from the radicals. With her arrival in the capital on June 13, her case quickly fell into Dzhunkovsky's lap and caused a crisis at the highest levels of the government.

The fate of a single, pathetic secret police collaborator would not normally trouble the leaders of the Russian state. But Shornikova appeared, like Banquo's Ghost, a specter pointing to governmental misdeeds that could challenge the legitimacy of the political arrangements created by

Stolypin. The questions surrounding the dissolution of the Second Duma had never been completely put to rest, and the Social Democrats had sought unsuccessfully to raise them in the Third. Something had to be done about Shornikova, lest her story come out and again bring up this troubling matter.

When Shornikova arrived in the capital, Dzhun was out of town.[5] Beletsky, as director of the Department of Police, took her under his protection, supporting her during her first days in the city. Upon his return Dzhunkovsky immediately met with Shornikova and listened to her sorrowful tale. Although touched by her story, his initial response was to go by the book. On June 24, he sent a message to Beletsky, outlining what Shornikova had told him, and ordered the police to detain her in preparation for delivery to the courts.[6]

But Dzhunkovsky was not certain if Shornikova should be tried, and the next day he wrote to Minister of Justice Ivan Shcheglovitov, bringing him up to date and asking for instructions. He informed the minister that the police had established a watch on Shornikova and awaited his decision as to "whether she should be arrested now and handed over to the courts, or kept under surveillance with the view to clarifying her role in 1907 as an agent of the SPb. security bureau."[7]

Shornikova's appearance and the danger it posed alarmed Dzhunkovsky and led him directly to Prime Minister Kokovtsov's reception. There Dzhun attempted to inform him about the situation, but Kokovtsov remained uncertain as to what, precisely, was the cause of concern. Only after Dzhun brought in Beletsky to make a short report did the fog lift.[8] Kokovtsov immediately summoned Shcheglovitov home from his vacation. When he arrived, the minister of justice assured Kokovtsov that even if the documents gathered through Shornikova's "provocation" were discredited, the case against the SD deputies was thoroughly grounded and would not be overturned.[9] The affair was not quite as threatening as it first seemed, but the questions of what to do about the unfortunate Shornikova and how to keep the whole matter quiet remained.

Ultimately, it took two informal meetings of the Council of Ministers and an audience with the tsar to decide the issue. On a sweltering day in early July, most of the ministers plus Dzhunkovsky, Beletsky, and the chief procurator of St. Petersburg Supreme Court met on the porch of Kokovtsov's dacha on Elagin Island to determine what to do next.[10] Beletsky proposed an easy way out: give Shornikova a passport under an assumed name, hand her some money, and let her disappear abroad. Dzhunkovsky, Kokovtsov, and a majority of the ministers present rejected this approach, however, since it would make them party to abetting the escape of a wanted suspect, an act that could later return to haunt them. They felt that Shornikova ought to be handled in a proper and strictly legal manner. She should to be tried, exonerated, and allowed to emigrate. But everything should take place quickly, with no fanfare, while the Duma was safely out of session. Still, the ministers were reluctant to act without the sovereign's approval. Accordingly, a delegation went to brief the tsar, then sailing off the Finnish coast. He supported bringing Shornikova to trial, and the ministers, meeting for a second time, adopted that course of action.[11]

Things proceeded smoothly after that. Shornikova was formally arrested, and on July 5 gave her statement to the procurator of the St. Petersburg court. After again recounting her harrowing tale, she concluded: "In view of all this, I do not consider myself guilty since I took part in the military organization [of the Social Democrats] with no criminal intent, but solely with the aim of rendering service to the government. . . . [Later,] I knew that I was being sought by the court, but on the other hand, I had to hide out from the revolutionaries. This situation became so painful for me that I decided to give myself up to the authorities, so that they could decide whether or not I was guilty of anything."[12]

Representatives of the police verified Shornikova's testimony, and on July 9, 1913, the procurator of the St. Petersburg court concluded that Shornikova had not committed a criminal offense and that the charges against her should be dropped. On July 26, the special department of the Senate that considered crimes against the state met in closed session, with Shornikova and Dzhunkovsky the only witnesses present. It reviewed the matter once more and accepted the decision of the procurator. Shornikova was free. She received a passport, rail and steamship tickets, and a small cash grant, in all totaling a miserly eighteen hundred rubles. She went abroad, was briefly spotted in Bulgaria, then vanished.[13]

The Shornikova affair was profoundly troubling to Dzhunkovsky. It reminded him once more of the evils as well as the dangers inherent in the Okhrana's use of *provokatory* and provided a clear example of the security service running out of control. Confronting the distraught young woman and hearing her agonizing story aroused his sense of chivalry and the sympathy he always felt for those who suffered. Shornikova was a victim, pure and simple, grievously wronged. The abuse she experienced at the hands of the secret police ruined her life and set off a chain of events that ultimately threatened the stability of the country. The episode also raised painful questions about Stolypin. Had Dzhun's hero been party to the 1907 conspiracy against the Second Duma aided by the use of undercover agents? Dzhun dismissed the idea, preferring to blame Kryzhanovsky, Shcheglovitov, and Alexander Gerasimov, the Okhrana chief at the time. Still, the Shornikova affair exposed for him "a dismal page" in the history of Stolypin's ministry "since it is unworthy of a government with any self-respect to resort to provocation in whatever form."[14]

Dzhunkovsky rushed to put the unsavory event behind him and push it out of mind. But four years later, he would be forced to recall it. After the fall of the monarchy, the Provisional Government's Extraordinary Investigative Commission summoned him back from the front, where he was serving as a division commander. The Commission grilled Dzhun about his tenure as assistant minister of internal affairs and at one point raised the issue of Shornikova and her fate. Dzhunkovsky's testimony on the subject was confused and unsure as he struggled to reconstruct the events. He was clearly pained, his discomfiture so obvious that at one point the chairman of the panel questioning asked him if he would like to take a break. He refused and continued with his testimony, but his interrogators frequently had to prompt his answers.[15] In his memoirs Dzhun recalled that the members of the Commission found that he had acted properly, but he added, shamefaced: "They were surprised only by my niggardliness, that I had given Shornikova such a paltry sum."[16]

After eight months on the job Dzhunkovsky could point to a number of successes and accomplishments. But the pressure on him had been enormous. Wrestling with a new and unfamiliar position in an atmosphere that he felt was hostile, surrounded by subordinates he did not trust, managing a furious pace of work, extensive travel, the heavy responsibility for the security of the imperial family during the tercentennial, and undergoing troubling events like the Shornikova affair, all created tremendous stress. The heart condition that had been bothering Dzhun for some time worsened. At the end of the summer, his health collapsed.

On September 2, 1913, Dzhunkovsky left St. Petersburg and went to Bad-Nauheim in Germany "for treatment and necessary rest." He arrived there on September 6 completely exhausted, and his alarmed doctor began a course of treatment. But the patient's condition continued to deteriorate. The prescribed baths failed to help, and blockages developed in the veins of his right arm. On his doctor's advice Dzhun then journeyed to Wiesbaden, and by the time he got there he was gravely ill. He had lost more than forty pounds since he became assistant minister, and now he was so weak he could not walk without help. His stay in Wiesbaden would last a month, with two weeks of complete bed rest.

Dzhunkovsky's recuperative powers were enormous, however, and by mid-October he was well enough to make a brief trip to Paris where he conferred with Prime Minister Kokovstov about "misunderstandings and unpleasantness" resulting from exposure in the press of activities of the Okhrana's Foreign Department that had led to attacks on the Russian government.[17] After returning to Wiesbaden, his health continued to improve. Still, his doctors recommended that he go on to Meran, in the Tyrol, for further rest and treatment. He had to ask for an extension of his leave, which the tsar readily granted, sending Dzhun his wishes for a speedy recovery. At Meran, Dzhun steadily got better. After ten days the doctors discovered that the thromboses in his arm had dissolved and they removed the bandage they had applied. His heart now appeared to be normal, but weak. They ordered him to sleep with the windows open and to take walks on level ground, going up hills only before his mid-day meal, and after that to spend an hour lying in the sun.

Fortunately, Dzhunkovsky did not have to pass his illness alone. His sister was with him for a time in Nauheim, and later he was joined by Sergei Gadon, the hunchback brother of his close friend Vladimir. Sergei accompanied Dzhun when he transferred to Wiesbaden and his "goodness, wit, loyalty and friendship" helped sustain the sick man. While he was in Meran, Katya Balmont came over from Paris. She had remained Dzhun's close friend despite the breach between him and her husband.

Soon Dzhunkovsky's great love, Nina Evreinova, arrived. They spent two marvelous weeks together and her presence lifted his spirits enormously. They passed the time taking long walks and greatly enjoyed the cable car that took them from the valley floor into the mountains above the town. Together they marveled how, within a quarter of an hour, they could pass from a warm autumn, with flowers still in bloom, to a snow-packed winter landscape. The beauties of nature and Nina's affection were restorative, and by mid-November Dzhun felt well enough to end his leave.

He bade farewell to Meran and journeyed back to Russia. After a few days in the Crimea, Dzhun returned to St. Petersburg, and on November 24 resumed his duties.[18]

From the beginning of his tenure as assistant minister, Dzhunkovsky placed a heavy emphasis on public relations, giving this almost the same weight as he gave to institutional reform. He sought to enhance the image of the gendarmes and the security police by, among other things, regulating their behavior and improving personnel. Dzhun was determined to impress upon the Corps and the public that the gendarme's uniform was a point of pride. Many gendarme officers avoided appearing in the dark blue of the Corps, but Dzhun always wore it at official functions and issued orders requiring subordinates to do likewise.[19] He encouraged officers in the gendarmerie to respect each other. In March 1913 Dzhun had attended the funeral of one Colonel Shpeier, a high-ranking officer of the Corps who had died suddenly while serving in Perm. He was shocked to see that very few of the deceased's fellow gendarmes had come to the burial, and he sent out an order criticizing their dereliction. The failure to honor one of their own, he asserted, "showed that the feeling of comradeship among members of the Corps is not as high as it should be."[20]

Dzhunkovsky believed that the modus operandi of the security forces had to change if they were to win public confidence. One of his early steps in this direction was to inform the Corps that he would not give credence to anonymous letters and denunciations, especially from those who served in its ranks. Their "cowardice," he wrote, "shamed the military uniform"; he would destroy those letters, "holding in my heart a feeling of disgust for those who had authored [them]."[21] The personal behavior of members of the Corps was a matter of deep concern. He found displays of excessive zeal by gendarmes offensive, and dressed down those too eager to brand citizens "untrustworthy."[22]

In January 1914, a number of cases involving the abuse of travelers by members of the railroad police (where most gendarmes were employed) came to his attention. These led Dzhunkovsky to issue orders demanding that they observe polite and correct behavior toward civilians they met while on duty: "Members of the railroad police should always remember . . . [that] passengers who turn to gendarme officers are usually in

Dzhunkovsky (middle, second row) among the Gendarmes. From Anastasiia Dunaeva, *Reformy politsii v Rossii nachala XX veka i Vladimir Fedorovich Dzhunkovskii.*

a highly agitated state, and therefore the behavior of gendarmes toward them ought to be exceptionally restrained and courteous." He threatened stiff punishments for those who stepped over the line.[23]

Despite his best intentions, however, Dzhunkovsky was unable to eliminate all the practices that he knew offended the public and disturbed him personally. One of these was "perlustration," the clandestine opening of private correspondence. This was a well-established procedure that the security forces had expanded and systematized during the 1880s in response to the revolutionary and terrorist threats.[24] After 1905 perlustration appeared even more necessary, because Vladimir Burtsev's frequent exposures of *provokatory* in underground radical movements robbed the Okhrana of valuable sources of information.[25] Conducted at special "black chambers" (*chernye kabinety*) in St. Petersburg, Moscow, Odessa, and Warsaw, and also in some gendarme and police bureaus and post offices elsewhere, perlustration was supposed to be secret. But the public was well aware of it, and in July 1913 *Utro Rossii* published a detailed exposé on the subject, which caused "a minor scandal in the press."[26]

Dzhunkovsky considered perlustration to be *razvrat* (depravity) and had high hopes of ending it when he took office. But he found it was impossible to get rid of the practice; the best he could do was to regulate and regularize it. "The existence . . . [of black chambers] was unpleasant for me," he recalled, "but I had to resign myself to it and took measures only to see that the perlustration of letters was carried out in the most proper way possible, that it was pursued exclusively [to protect] the state and the dynasty, and that it was not employed to gather information for personal use or for blackmail."[27] Despite his revulsion against perlustration, Dzhun could not avoid the fruits of this poisoned tree, and files in the archive of his chancellery reveal that he examined large numbers of opened letters.[28] "It was not the most pleasant business—to read other people's mail," he wrote later, "I remember those moments with a heavy heart."[29]

Dzhunkovsky also took up another issue that was the source of considerable public discontent—the exile by administrative order of persons considered politically dangerous. Dzhun had little use for this practice. He believed it was a form of self-deception, "plugging a hole in one place and making a bigger one in another." It opened the way to all kinds of abuse and, worst of all, it had no corrective effect. "There never was a single case where someone returning from [internal] exile at the end of his term did not continue his agitational and criminal activities," he wrote. "Exile only further embittered [the offender] himself, his entire family and all his friends, increasing . . . the ranks of the discontented."[30] Those sent abroad also continued to engage in oppositional politics.

Dzhunkovsky's position gave him the chance to do something about the problem. Since the shocking acquittal of the terrorist Vera Zasulich in 1879 and the assassination of Alexander II in 1881, people accused of political offences were not handled by the regular courts but by special tribunals and administrative procedures. As assistant minister of internal affairs, Dzhun chaired a Special Conference (*Osoboe soveshchanie*) composed of police officials and procurators that handled cases of administrative exile. The Conference could quash charges against those accused or punish them by denying them the right to live in St. Petersburg, Moscow, provincial capitals, or university towns. It could sentence them to exile under police surveillance for up to five years. Conference decisions were routinely reviewed and confirmed by the minister of internal affairs, but sentences could be lightened or modified on the appeal of the prisoners or their relatives. Changes might involve the way prisoners were to travel to their place of exile (in a tightly guarded police convoy or in relative comfort at their own expense), the length and place of exile, and even the possibility of exile abroad. Such changes were technically the prerogative of the minister, but Maklakov empowered Dzhun to make these decisions on his own.

Dzhun had plans to greatly curtail or eliminate political exile, but the outbreak of war in 1914 prevented this. Still, he was able to make some significant reforms. He sped up decision-making, shortening the time a person might be held in custody. He discontinued the policy of regularly sending people to places with harmful climates like Turkestan, Narymsk, and Yakutia, reserving this for only extraordinary cases. Dzhun usually limited Siberian exile to relatively temperate Tobolsk province, and for persons suffering mild illness, to the Minusinsk region, which enjoyed even better weather. He was consistently responsive to the appeals of prisoners and their families. He claimed he never refused permission for an exile to travel to his assigned place at his own expense, and he almost always approved requests for exile abroad.[31]

By 1914 the number of persons exiled for political reasons had fallen considerably to about one thousand, and the number of politicals held at hard labor to just over two thousand.[32] Dzhunkovsky felt that part of the decline of administrative exile reflected his efforts to see that more political cases were handled by regular judicial procedures.[33] This may have been true, but it was also a sign that the security police, however much they might have complained about Dzhun's reform efforts, were still well enough armed with investigative tools to continue dealing heavy blows to revolutionary organizations. Police agents regularly penetrated radical organizations and disrupted their activities. Within Russia, the Socialist Revolutionary and Social Democratic parties were in disarray, their members fleeing arrest, heading abroad, or limiting themselves to strictly legal activities.[34]

Dzhunkovsky understood that he needed to make significant changes in personnel if his reforms were to take hold and endure. As soon as he assumed office, he began working on new regulations that would govern admission to the Corps of Gendarmes, and he introduced them on February 4, 1914. Under these rules, the recruits should be military officers with at least three years of service; they should have no debts. They could not be Poles, Catholics, married to a Catholic, or of Jewish background, even if converted. And while these ethnic and religious restrictions may seem exceptionally harsh, it is necessary to remember the context. Anti-government sentiments were particularly strong in the Polish and Jewish communities, and even a person of unimpeachable loyalty could be open to pressure from his co-nationals and co-religionists. At the time, the idea that Catholics might receive orders from the pope did not seem outlandish even in countries with much stronger traditions of religious tolerance.

The new rules required that applicants be thoroughly investigated as to their moral qualities, service background, education, and knowledge of foreign and local languages. After passing this initial screening, candidates were to be examined orally on law (civil, criminal, administrative, financial, and international), political economy, Russian history, the history of the French Revolution, current European history with an emphasis on revolutionary events, and Russian and world geography. They were then to take written exams on Russian and classical literature and historical subjects. Candidates who passed were ranked according to their test scores and admitted to the Corps as vacancies occurred. Officers who were assigned to the staff of the Corps would have five months of further study of the structure of the institution, investigative procedure, the operations of the railroad service, the history of the revolutionary movement, criminal statutes, and communications.[35] Beyond this, Dzhun envisioned creating a special political section staffed by jurists and morally upright people.[36]

Dzhunkovsky's elevated recruitment standards could not be met overnight. Just finding such paragons of virtue and knowledge would be difficult enough; inducing them to join the Corps might well be impossible. At the very least, this far-reaching reform would take many years to accomplish. In the short run, purging the leadership of the gendarmes and the police was, to Dzhunkovsky's mind, a necessary first step in improving the moral level of the security forces and burnishing their public image.

When he took over as assistant minister, Dzhunkovsky felt that he was insufficiently knowledgeable to remove the leading figures in the security police most of whom stood in the way of further reform, but by the end of 1913 he had gained more confidence. In the fall he transferred Sergei Vissarionov, the deputy director of the Department of Police, to the censorship department; in November he removed M. F. fon Koten, the head of the St. Petersburg Security Bureau. In early 1914 he retired Alexander Gerasimov, a long-standing figure in the security service who was then a special agent of the Ministry of Internal Affairs. He made a point of publicizing this "purge" so as to produce the maximum public relations impact.[37] In every case Dzhun tried to appoint in their stead men he deemed to be of irreproachable honesty, even if some of them were less competent than the people they replaced.[38] One figure he greatly distrusted was M. G. Mandarev, the director of the "black chambers." But Dzhun left him untouched: "He knew too much."[39]

The most important target of Dzhunkovsky's purge was Stepan Beletsky, the director of the Department of Police. Dzhun had immediately disliked and distrusted him but did not feel capable of dismissing him at once. Beletsky was extremely competent, hardworking, and knowledgeable. He was also well connected. But he opposed the reforms Dzhun wanted to introduce, particularly cutting back on the use of informants in the army and secondary schools. At the start of 1914 Dzhunkovsky decided to remove him and put in his place a man he believed to be impeccably honest, Valentin Anatolevich Brune de Saint Hyppolite. Maklakov agreed with Dzhun's decision and helped ease Beletsky out. Initially, the minister offered Beletsky the governorship of Vologda, but he refused being posted to an out-of-the-way province with an unpleasant climate. On January 30 Maklakov reluctantly appointed Beletsky to the Senate, a more honorific place, but one where Dzhun believed he could do less harm than in a governorship.[40] With Beletsky gone Dzhunkovsky felt that, at last, he was in full command of the empire's security forces. Now he could turn to another delicate question: what to do about Roman Malinovsky, the secret police agent who was a member of Lenin's Central Committee and the head of the six-man Bolshevik delegation in the Fourth State Duma.

From the moment the Fourth Duma opened in November 1912 Malinovsky had emerged as a leading figure on the Left. His speeches, twenty-two in the first session, thirty-eight in the second, had powerful impact, recognized even by those who strongly disagreed with him.[41] Duma President Mikhail Rodzianko called them "extremely interesting, very compelling and well-grounded."[42] Malinovsky's Duma debut ended with a ringing statement of purpose. He pledged himself and his comrades "to work to bring closer that hour when a national constituent assembly will mark the beginning of a fully democratic . . . Russia and clear the way for the proletariat to struggle for liberation from the chains of wage slavery, to battle for socialism."[43]

Malinovsky's oratory—regularly reported in the legal press—displayed in turn both rage and pathos: "Not a penny for a government whose hands are red with the blood of the Lena workers!" he thundered in a speech against an appropriation for the Ministry of Trade and Industry. Later, he touched hearts when he expressed his sorrow for sixty workers who had died in an explosion at an armaments factory: "I went myself to the scene of the explosion, I saw with my own eyes the mutilated bodies, I heard the groans of the injured, I saw the tears of the widows and orphans, I watched the sorrowing crowd, ten thousand strong, walk behind their fallen comrades, I heard the curses flung from the lips of the most peaceful, restrained, calm people, I observed the murmurs, the justified murmurs, of indignation in all the workers' apartments of St. Petersburg."[44]

Malinovsky's oratorical skill, organizing ability, and commanding presence gained him enormous authority among the workers of the capital. He may have done more to win support for the Bolsheviks than any other prewar labor leader.[45] These qualities earned him Lenin's admiration and trust. The Bolshevik leader wrote some of Malinovsky's speeches and steadily expanded his role in the party. Malinovsky became one of Lenin's favorites, a frequent traveling companion, and a chosen instrument for pursuing the important goal of deepening and making permanent the split between the Bolshevik and Menshevik factions of the Russian Social Democratic Labor Party.

As Malinovsky rose in importance among the Bolshevik leadership, his value to the secret police also grew. When Malinovsky took his seat in the Duma, Beletsky removed him from the control of the Moscow Security Bureau and became his chief handler. He scrapped his protégé's humble code name *Portnoi* (Tailor), giving him a new and more mysterious one: *Iks* (X). Beletsky treasured Malinovsky for the intelligence he provided that had led to the arrest of Bolshevik leaders Ordzhonikidze, Sverdlov, and Stalin. He strongly approved of Malinovsky's (and Lenin's) efforts to split the Social Democrats.

On carefully planned evenings, Comrade Malinovsky secretly shed his proletarian skin and, dressed in a frock coat, Mr. X met Beletsky and Vissarionov in the private rooms of some of the capital's most luxurious restaurants. There, relaxed and unhurried, with Vissarionov taking notes, Beletsky and his star agent exchanged confidences. For a while Beletsky would become the questioning student and Malinovsky the learned expert. Beletsky showed X the reports of Okhrana departments and foreign

Roman Malinovsky as Duma Member. Hoover Institution Archive (HIA), Edward E. Smith Collection, box 20, folder 15.

agents; X verified and clarified the work of Beletsky's subordinates. Malinovsky brought letters he had received from Lenin and Bolshevik leaders and told Beletsky about the plans of other Duma delegates. X let Beletsky read Lenin's drafts of the speeches he wanted his trusted spokesman to give in the Duma; Beletsky would edit them, softening some of the language. On occasion Malinovsky carried with him the entire archive of the Bolshevik Duma delegation for his handler to peruse. Money changed hands; X's pay rose. At a time when the average wage of an industrial worker in northern Russia was about 340 rubles a year, Mr. X received, in addition to Malinovsky's Duma salary, 400 rubles *a month* for his service to the Okhrana.[46] After February 1913 he earned 500 rubles monthly.

Beletsky and Mr. X shared many secrets, but Malinovsky always held something back, careful to protect his status as a Duma delegate and party leader. Beletsky understood. A powerful element of romance linked a handler and his informant. Years before Sergei Zubatov, who had perfected the spying techniques of the Okhrana, put it eloquently: Treat your informant "as a beloved woman with whom you have entered into illicit relations. Look after her like the apple of your eye. One careless move and you will dishonor her."[47]

A clandestine love affair can produce many delights. But those who lead a double life often endure constant fear of discovery and nagging feelings of remorse. While Malinovsky undoubtedly relished the secret sense of power that came from being at once a leader in a revolutionary party and a valued agent of the Okhrana, fear and guilt began to weigh heavily. By 1914 both Comrade Malinovsky and Mr. X began to show signs of emotional instability. Social Democrats in the Duma became concerned about Malinovsky's testy and erratic behavior.[48] Vissarionov fretted that Mr. X was getting out of control and that his usefulness might be coming to an end.[49]

When Dzhunkovsky first became aware of Malinovsky's double life is a matter of dispute. In his memoirs Dzhun claimed he learned of it only after he had replaced Beletsky with Brune, but this is clearly not the case.[50] During his testimony before the Extraordinary Investigative Commission in 1917 and at Malinovsky's trial a year later, Dzhun stated that he was unsure when he discovered the truth.[51] While no documentary evidence supports A. P. Martynov's charge that he had fully informed Dzhunkovsky about Malinovsky before his election to the Duma, there is good reason to believe that Vissarionov had told Dzhun as early as March 1913.[52] If this is so, then for almost a year Dzhun and Beletsky had engaged in a ritual charade. When the director of the Department of Police proudly reported to his superior the information X had divulged, the commander of the Corps of Gendarmes feigned ignorance, appearing indifferent to the secret agent's identity while harboring grave concerns about the potentially dangerous consequences of a "provocation" that might inflict damage on the security services, the Duma, and his own reputation.[53]

Even with Beletsky safely in the Senate, Dzhunkovsky did not remove Malinovsky until May. His stated reason for delay was caution: "I needed sufficient time to think things through; I wanted to do it in such a way that there would be no publicity, so there would be no scandal; for if there were a scandal, it would be huge."[54] But it is not far-fetched to think that, influenced by the Shornikova affair, Dzhun felt a degree of sympathy for the *provokator*, someone who had also been entrapped by the secret police. As a witness at Malinovsky's trial in 1918 and later in his memoirs, Dzhunkovsky painted the police agent as a victim of the Okhrana, sincerely repentant of his crimes.

If Dzhun delayed removing Malinovsky while waiting for an event that would provide suitable "cover" for both the legislature and the *provokator*, he got it on April 22, 1914, when disorder erupted in the Duma. The aged Ivan Goremykin, recently appointed prime minister, had come to present the state budget, and left-wing delegates treated him to a hostile demonstration. Some pounded on their desks while others began caterwauling. Loud shouts: "Get Down!" "Get Out!" prevented the prime minister from speaking. To restore decorum, Duma President Rodzianko eventually suspended Malinovsky and a large number of other left delegates for fifteen days. Some of them, but not Malinovsky, refused to leave and had to be removed by soldiers and the Duma's own guard. Summoned to the scene by the ministers who had come to hear Goremykin speak, Dzhunkovsky witnessed their expulsion.[55]

Dzhun seized the moment. He called in the head of the St. Petersburg security bureau, Colonel Petr Popov, and ordered him to take Malinovsky in hand and arrange the details of his removal. The policeman and the *provokator* met in Alexander Square where Popov gave Malinovsky three days in which to resign from the Duma and go abroad. Shocked, Malinovsky objected briefly, but when Popov told him that he would receive six thousand rubles, Mr. X agreed. Around three o'clock in the afternoon on May 8, Malinovsky marched into Rodzianko's office, flung his letter of resignation on the Duma president's desk and, without explanation, stormed out. Two agents of the secret police accompanied Mr. X to the border. The former pride of the Okhrana, tribune of the people, and Lenin's trusted representative, disappeared, leaving a thousand questions in his wake.[56] But he was not gone completely from Dzhunkovsky's life.

Why did Dzhunkovsky remove Malinovsky? Did he, as some on the extreme Right charged, hate the security police? Was he unprofessional? Did he harbor treasonous intent?[57] Or did he realize that Malinovsky would not change the political line of the Bolsheviks' Duma delegation and reduce its revolutionary impact of the working masses?[58] Perhaps his decision flowed from a more subtle calculation: In 1912 and 1913 Malinovsky had served well in splitting the Social Democrats, but by 1914 the Bolsheviks' strength had risen to dangerous levels thanks to a growing wave of workers' strikes. To weaken the Bolshevik threat Malinovsky, their eloquent tribune in the Duma, had to go. How better to get rid of him than by arranging a mysterious departure that would confound Lenin, discredit his leadership, and disrupt his party by fostering rumors that his favorite had in fact been a *provokator*?[59]

In his testimony before the Investigative Commission in 1917, at Malinovsky's trial, and in his memoirs, Dzhunkovsky consistently stated that he was "sickened" by the presence of a *provokator* in the Duma and wanted to avoid a scandal that could damage the institution. Later, he wondered whether Malinovsky might have become more valuable to Lenin than to the Okhrana. Simple, honorable motives often ring false in the mouths of those who vouchsafe them, and certainly Dzhun had good reason in the years following the revolution to put his deeds in the best possible light. But a number of well-informed historians accept Dzhunkovsky at his word or, at least, argue that Machiavellian machinations of the kind others have suggested "seem rather beyond his capacities or inclinations."[60] Things are not always complicated; sometimes a cigar is just a cigar.

Dzhunkovsky's ouster of Roman Malinovsky was among the last of his reforms of the security police. Soon the outbreak of war thrust new tasks into his hands. But the first year and a half of his tenure as assistant minister and commander of the Corps of Gendarmes remains the most controversial and contested period of his life. Dzhunkovsky believed the changes he introduced put the work of maintaining the safety of the empire on the right track. Others would claim that his reforms had disastrous consequences, and that by disrupting and "terrorizing" the security forces they opened the way for the revolution. As such his reforms represented monumental stupidity or, worse, outright treason. Many of these charges stem from the memoirs of secret police professionals attempting to explain why the security forces were unable to prevent the collapse of the tsarist regime. Recently their arguments have been picked up and augmented by right-wing, neo-monarchist historians and conspiracy theorists who, like the *okhranniki*, conveniently forget the fact that Dzhunkovsky's reforms were approved by Prime Minister Kokovtsev, MVD chief Maklakov, and the tsar himself.[61]

This is not to say that serious scholars do not find fault with the measures Dzhunkovsky adopted during his tenure of office.[62] But anyone familiar with the details of Dzhunkovsky's biography should dismiss the charge of treason. And while perhaps no final judgment on this matter is really possible, simple logic and the convincing evidence carefully gathered and presented by Anastasia Dunaeva strongly indicate that the measures Dzhun adopted did not, in the short run, greatly weaken the security services in their struggle with the revolutionary forces.[63] Eliminating police informants in high school classrooms had little effect. Schoolboys and schoolgirls might be radical, but they were not a significant threat to the regime and could be kept under surveillance by other means. Removing police *sotrudniki* from the ranks of the military was perhaps riskier, but the troops could be watched quite effectively from outside. Moreover, it is hard to imagine that once the Great War had begun, a relatively small number of agents could have successfully spied on the soldiers of an army vastly swollen with conscripts.[64] Dzhun's critics seem on firmer ground when they argue that getting rid of most of the provincial security bureaus and regional directorates weakened the secret police overall and demoralized its ranks. But at least one well-informed historian maintains that this reform was "not so much a dismantling of the security apparatus, as a process of reorganization" sensibly taken in response to the declining fortunes of the revolutionary movement.[65] It certainly did not prevent the guardians of order from keeping the opponents of the government on the run. As late as 1916 the major radical parties were in disarray, incapable of organizing the workers or peasants on any scale, with most of their members either abroad or being held in relatively lenient circumstances in their places of exile.[66] The revolutionaries, like everyone else, would be unprepared for the revolt that brought down the tsarist system in 1917. And this revolt occurred in the imperial capital, where a large security bureau was still present.

The fall of the monarchy was not caused or even seriously facilitated by a weakening of the security apparatus. Dzhunkovsky's reforms were beside the point. During the Great War elite disaffection caused by defeats, economic disruption, blatant mismanagement, and political disarray "hollowed out" the tsarist regime to the point that a normally manageable urban riot was sufficient to topple it. This process of dissolution was something beyond the power of the Okhrana to stop, just as seventy-five years later the Soviet Union's KGB and other security agencies, commanding vast networks of informants and enormous arbitrary authority, could not avert the collapse of a state whose seemingly unshakable power held the world in awe.[67]

Many historians believe that a revolution was about to begin, perhaps as early as the summer of 1914, had it not been for the outbreak of war and the patriotic upsurge it called forth.[68] There is much that supports this thesis. Worker discontent was rising, society was polarizing, political opposition was growing. But the country was also becoming more prosperous; the army was strong, getting stronger, and most important, still loyal. The countryside was at peace. Russia had many problems; still, in 1914 very few people outside the small group of committed radicals desired a replay of 1905.[69] Had revolution occurred in 1914, however, the changes Dzhunkovsky introduced would have had, by then, little effect one way or the other on the ability of the security forces to combat it.

Yet if Dzhunkovsky's reforms did not seriously hamper the security forces in their struggle with the revolutionaries, neither did they achieve his goal of changing the image of the secret police and gaining it greater acceptance with the educated public. To have any reasonable possibility of success, his reforms would have had to be pursued over a substantial period, and Dzhun's time in office was short. More to the point, no attempt to remake the reputation of police and intelligence agencies is likely to rapidly alter the attitude of those who, rightly or wrongly, view them with suspicion. This has certainly been true with regard to the CIA, NSA, and FBI in the United States today. In late imperial Russia, the public had more and much better reasons to fear and distrust the Okhrana.

Dzhunkovsky's reforms are perhaps best understood and evaluated in terms of his broader concept of state security, something he never elaborated in a systematic way, but which flowed from his core beliefs and practical experience. Jonathan Daly is right when he terms Dzhunkovsky a "moralist."[70] Conceptions of morality and honor formed by family tradition, religious training, and schooling at the Corps of Pages were the bedrock of his personality and determined his outlook. Equally important was his dynastic loyalty, personal devotion to the emperor, and his firm belief that the tsar truly enjoyed the love and support of his subjects. Dzhunkovsky's monarchism was, moreover, combined with an almost democratic faith in the basic good sense of people, be they peasants, workers, merchants, nobles, or members of the intelligentsia. This was not sentimental populism or political liberalism but a rather pragmatic conviction that, if approached honestly in ways that touched both their moral sense and their self-interest, most men and women would respond positively. Dzhun also believed that the government had the means to meet many of its subjects' demands; it needed only the will.

Dzhunkovsky's "ideology" was based in large part on experience and insight gained as an administrator—both as governor and security chief. His attitude toward *provokatsiia* is a case in point. Dzhun believed that spying by the police was necessary, that inserting agents into organizations dedicated to the overthrow of the monarchy was a legitimate act of self-defense. Such information-gathering was not in itself "provocation," but there could be too much of a good thing. When police agents became so deeply enmeshed in the conspiracy they were supposed to thwart that they organized and participated in illegal acts, they not only behaved immorally, they also became a danger. Dzhun saw how Azef and Bogrov, agents of the Okhrana, caused the deaths of government leaders, including Stolypin. He realized that the scandalous potential in the Shornikova and Malinovsky affairs posed threats to the political order and the institutions of the state.

Similarly, curtailing the security bureaus could be justified both on practical economic grounds and by the fact that the terrorist and revolutionary threat had declined. The outpouring of loyalty and support for the monarchy that Dzhun witnessed during the celebrations at Poltava, Borodino, and Moscow, the success of the tercentennial, gave solid support to this belief. Excessive security measures that separated the tsar from his people and methods that offended the public were dysfunctional. To be sure, Dzhunkovsky was less concerned than he might have been about the discontents felt by the elite and the educated upper classes. But a lifetime of experience going as far back as 1897, when he overcame the hostility of the doctors and nurses in the medical team sent to Thessaly, and especially his years as governor of Moscow, convinced him that it was possible to bridge the gap between government and society. An open hand, a straightforward, honest approach—in short, good public relations, pursued consistently—could work wonders. And in time of peace, did the Kadets and their ilk, however vocal and annoying, really pose a serious threat to the state?

As for the workers, whose strike movement, growing steadily since 1912, alarmed many leading officials, Dzhunkovsky was concerned, but not overly so. Because of his long involvement with the Moscow Guardianship of Public Sobriety and its brief connection to *zubatovshchina*, Dzhun had gotten to know workers better than most government figures, better, indeed, than many radicals did. He understood that their grievances were real and deeply felt, but he refused to believe that revolution was an immediate threat. Genuine reforms could take the edge off workers' discontents and achieve labor peace. As war clouds gathered in the summer of 1914, Dzhunkovsky would test these convictions against the realities of a bitter strike in the oilfields of Baku.

Chapter 13

Mission to Baku

IN THE FIRST MONTHS OF 1914, DISCONTENT AMONG INDUSTRIAL workers in Russia rose to a level not seen since 1905. Strikes exploded. Militants voiced demands that went well beyond labor's immediate economic needs and targeted the political system itself. The year promised to be worse than the one before, when almost nine hundred thousand workers had laid down their tools.[1] St. Petersburg and Moscow were epicenters of these labor tremors, but the situation in Baku, the hub of the empire's petroleum production, had grown ominous.

Set on the southern edge of the dry, largely treeless Apsheron peninsula that jutted like a palsied finger into the Caspian Sea, Baku baked in summer and shivered in winter, lashed perpetually by winds from both north and south. Oil was everywhere: in the air, the water, the dust of the streets, and in the eyes and nostrils of the people.[2] Baku was a flammable place—and not just from the black gold that gushed from its thousands of wells. The city was a mix of peoples and cultures, where Azeri Turks, Russians, Armenians, Persians, and Jews lived and labored uneasily side by side. Communal hatreds, like the oil, lay close to the surface and in 1905 had erupted in murderous fury as Azeris slaughtered Armenians with abandon.

Baku spewed forth enormous wealth. At the turn of the century the region was the source of over half the world's oil supply and 95 percent of the empire's. Since then Baku's output had fallen—from 10,745,000 tons in 1901 to 9,234,900 tons in 1913—due in part to Russia's domestic troubles, but still, no single spot on earth produced more crude. Profits continued to be high, and fortunes were still being pumped from the earth. Foreigners, most notably the Nobels and Royal Dutch Shell, dominated, controlling 60 percent of the production and, for a time, the American robber baron John D. Rockefeller cast covetous eyes on the fields; but Russian companies also played a significant role in the oil economy.[3]

Although today Baku bids fair to become a world-class tourist destination with gleaming, modernistic architecture, posh hotels, and a vibrant nightlife that proclaim it a gateway to the twenty-first century and beyond, one hundred years ago it held far fewer attractions.[4] To be sure, it had made enormous progress since the time Alexandre Dumas likened a visit there to "penetrating one of the strongest fortresses of the Middle Ages."[5] In 1914 Baku was a booming, brawling, complex, exotic city—"as if the industry of Pittsburgh and the frontier lawlessness of Dodge City had been superimposed on Baghdad."[6] A person who came there then had a limited choice of hotels, restaurants, and other amenities. Stench and dirt were probably the area's most notable feature, and the traveler intrepid enough to tour its oilfields was advised to "wear his oldest clothes and boots on account of the pools of oil."[7]

Workers in the petroleum industry were very productive and enjoyed relatively high wages, but the conditions of life and labor in Baku were as harsh as its climate.[8] Misery made class conflict a constant; and the oil patch became fertile ground for radical agitation, a place where a young man could learn the trade of revolution and hone his skills. "Three years of revolutionary work among the workers of the oil industry steeled me as a practical fighter," "Koba" Dzhugashvili would recall, after he had become Stalin. "It was there, in Baku, that I thus received my second baptism in the revolutionary struggle. There I became a journeyman in the art of revolution."[9]

In 1913 a general strike, led by the oil workers, started in late July and flared on and off until October. As many as thirty-five thousand men walked off the job. The strikes ended when management boosted wages, but discontent simmered. Workers complained of compulsory overtime, wretched living conditions, delays in being paid, and abusive overseers. They charged that the oil companies failed to carry out promises they had made at the end of the strike. Wildcat walkouts and on-the-job scraps began and grew steadily worse.[10]

By April 1914 workers in Baku readied for a new strike, so eager and determined that the Bolsheviks, directed by Stepan Shaumian, struggled to restrain them.[11] Worker representatives from various firms formed the All-Baku Strike Committee and with the Social Democrats drew up "The General Demands of the Baku Oil Workers." They called for an eight-hour workday; improved living places, sanitation, and water supply; an immediate pay raise of as much as 50 percent for low-paid workers; a guaranteed annual pay increase of 10 percent; better medical care; and the establishment of schools and libraries for the workers and their children. Workers wanted management to recognize and bargain with labor organizations and also to create institutions to mediate and resolve disputes with their employers.[12] The Strike Committee announced its demands on May 27, 1914, and spread them by leaflets throughout the city's factories and workplaces. The next day workers at the Mirzoev Oil Company struck and those at other firms quickly joined them. By June 1, more than 30,000 employees of some 227 enterprises had left their jobs.[13] In a letter to Lenin, Shaumian expressed doubts about the success of the strike, but stated that "the mood of the workers was so militant that it was impossible to stop them."[14]

Faced with the walkout, oil company bosses wavered. They rejected concessions and refused to consider another demand from the workers: that they get paid for the time they were on strike. Management threatened to dismiss those who failed to return to the job within three days. But when the deadline passed, the oilmen did not pay off the strikers, which would have marked a final break. Instead, they resolved to wait out the strike and try to bring the workers back in line by other means. They made some efforts to use scabs, but with little vigor or success. The oil companies appeared confident that things would work to their advantage. Ultimately the authorities would break the strike by force, and in the meantime, the shutdown in production would lift prices.[15] The Baku Strike Committee rallied the workers and enforced discipline by distributing proclamations listing the names and locations of "strikebreakers" and "traitors to labor's cause."[16]

Both sides dug in and the strike dragged on. Prodded by management, authorities in Baku began to take steps to end the walkout. They arrested a number of strike leaders and some of those who engaged in illegal acts including violence against workers who wanted to go back on the job. They deployed troops to maintain order and protect property. Officials also sought to prevent the development of a broader strike by blocking work stoppages in the public service sector—water supply, electricity, and transport. Starting on June 14, the oil firms finally began paying off employees and forcing them to vacate their living quarters. Expulsions often took place at night with the help of Cossacks. While a few workers offered resistance and were quickly arrested, most went peacefully. Authorities also ordered many of those no longer on the job to leave the Baku area.[17] But at the end of June, the strikers still held firm.

In St. Petersburg, the lengthening strike and the deepening international crisis triggered by the assassination of Archduke Franz-Ferdinand, heir to the Austro-Hungarian throne, fostered concern about a disruption of oil supplies. By June 25 Minister of Trade and Industry Sergei Timashev had received so many complaints from oil producers, Volga River shippers, and provincial trade committees that he appealed to Prime Minister Goremykin for help. Two days later, Goremykin wired authorities in the Caucasus demanding that they take "energetic measures" to maintain order and to see that those workers wishing to return to the job were protected.[18] But on June 28 Acting Viceroy Alexander Myshlaevsky replied, outlining what had been done to date. He stated that all legal means for ending the strike had been exhausted, and that additional, extraordinary measures threatened to incite armed clashes with the workers.[19]

Goremykin immediately called the Council of Ministers into emergency session and invited Dzhunkovsky as the chief of the empire's internal security to attend. At the start of the meeting, Minister of Agriculture Alexander Krivoshein, a powerful voice in the cabinet, proposed that they petition the emperor to dispatch a special representative to the scene armed with extraordinary authority. He suggested Dzhunkovsky and, turning to him directly, asked: "You wouldn't refuse, would you?" Dzhun demurred, protesting that he knew very little about conditions in Baku and was, therefore, not the right man for the job. Most of the other ministers seemed to accept his objections, and he left the meeting feeling relieved.[20]

His reprieve proved short-lived. On June 28 Goremykin presented Nicholas with the view of the Council of Ministers that a specially empowered official should be sent to Baku.[21] Two days later Dzhunkovsky received a personal letter from the prime minister: "Deeply esteemed Vladimir Fedorovich, I am writing you from the yacht 'Strela,' which has taken me to Peterhoff and His Majesty. On the report of the Council of Ministers concerning measures directed against the strikes in the industries of Baku, the Sovereign was pleased to write the following resolution:

'Send Major General of our Suite Dzhunkovsky, and give him the powers granted to Major General Baron [Fedor] Taube in 1907.' Informing you of this, let me add that this evening and tomorrow afternoon I shall be home, if you should wish to see me."[22]

Dzhunkovsky called on the prime minister that evening, troubled by the emperor's command. Goremykin assured Dzhun that the tsar had strongly supported the idea of sending a personal representative to Baku and had spoken of him in the most flattering terms. Dzhun then asked about the nature of his mission. Was it to be a punitive expedition? Repressive measures were decidedly not to his liking, he added, and Goremykin quickly allayed his concerns. The mission would not be punitive, the prime minister stated, but was conceived of in "much broader terms." He authorized Dzhun to bring to Baku all personnel he felt were necessary. Dzhunkovsky left the prime minister satisfied as to his mission's purpose but uneasy about what lay ahead.[23]

The next day he received a dispatch from Goremykin that listed the almost dictatorial powers he had been granted. While in Baku, he could prohibit all public and private meetings, suppress publications, close commercial operations, hand criminals over to military courts, exile people from the region, issue decrees for maintaining public order, and dispose of available military and police forces—all without prior approval of either the viceroy of the Caucasus or the ministries in St. Petersburg. While the authority given to Dzhunkovsky was extraordinary, the reference to the Taube mission of 1907 was important. Taube had gone to Baku to break a strike by sailors on the Caspian Sea merchant fleet that was threatening to disrupt oil shipments. He used his extensive mandate to end the troubles quickly, with little violence. Clearly, Dzhunkovsky was expected to do the same.[24]

During the next week, Dzhun prepared. He gathered information on the strike from the Ministry of Trade and Industry and spoke to people who knew about the situation in Baku. He chose carefully the group he would take with him: hardworking, capable, and honorable men, who were loyal and shared his views. Dzhun did not look on his commission as an obligation to end the strike by forcing the workers back on the job. He believed that his duty was, above all, to familiarize himself with conditions of work in the oilfields, look deeper into the reasons for the strike, and end it by eliminating its causes. He had no doubt that the strike was chiefly political, and that once he had investigated the matter, he could cut the ground out from under it.[25] Dzhun assembled a six-man team including Brune de Saint Hyppolite, the new director of the Department of Police, Vladimir Arandarenko, director of the Mining Department, and Petr Istomin, the vice director of the Department of Religious Affairs, whom he knew as "very talented and capable, an indispensible worker," able to take on all kinds of complicated problems.

On July 7, Dzhunkovsky and his team boarded a train for the long trip to the Caucasus. As it pulled away from the capital, he relaxed: "Sitting in the railroad car, I only then felt how much the past days in Petersburg had tired me out, . . . tied me up in knots. I was glad to be in that car surrounded by people, dear and devoted to me, untroubled by [official] papers. For the [next] two days . . . I enjoyed complete rest and was able to gather my strength for the difficult work that lay ahead."[26] On July 9, they reached Tiflis, capital of the Viceroyalty of the Caucasus. There Dzhun met with officials of the Caucasian administration and with his brother Nikolai, who was in the service of the viceroy. Kolya confirmed Dzhun's belief that the strike was really political in nature and that the economic demands of the workers were of secondary importance.[27] Dzhunkovsky remained in Tiflis one day and, early on July 10, left for Baku. He arrived late that evening.

At the station the leading figures of Baku's civil and military administration stood with managers of the oil companies ready to receive the tsar's representative in an atmosphere charged with tension and anticipation. After greeting all in turn, Dzhunkovsky got into a waiting automobile and, declining the offer of a Cossack escort, drove straight to the Hotel National where a large suite of rooms awaited him and his staff. City Commandant Colonel Martynov gave a report that brought Dzhunkovsky up to date on the situation and contained some discouraging news. At the beginning of July, workers at many firms showed signs of wanting to end the strike and return to the job. But when word of Dzhun's mission reached the city, strike leaders used the information to convince workers that he would soon pressure the oil producers to make major concessions. The backs of the workers had stiffened; the walkout continued.

Martynov left, and Dzhunkovsky crafted a plan of action. As a first step he dictated an announcement to be issued the next day to the strikers and the public at large. Printed in Russian, Armenian, and Azerbaijani, it outlined the nature of his mission. He had come as a representative of the emperor to gather firsthand information about conditions in the oilfields, restore public order, and restart production. He called on the population of Baku to help: "By remaining calm and having faith in my orders, the local inhabitants will create the conditions that will make it possible for me to achieve the desired goal."[28]

At eight the following morning, Dzhunkovsky, accompanied by his team and a single bodyguard, drove by car to the oilfields to investigate conditions. On two successive days he spent up to eleven hours on-site, and what he saw sickened and outraged him. At the Moscow Guardianship and as governor, he had come to know the difficult conditions in which many workers lived and labored. He had seen the degradation of the Khitrovo slums, but he had never encountered anything like this. The miserable barracks of the workers sat in the middle of the fields, surrounded by forests of wooden and iron pyramids that covered the wells. Filthy pools filled with oil and other waste were everywhere, sources of constant danger that might explode in flames at any time. Unmarked by barriers, they lay in wait, potential traps for the children of the workers. A pall of smoke and the stench of oil hung over the fields, and in the workers' quarters the lack of adequate sanitation produced another layer of disgusting odor. When Dzhunkovsky attempted to enter one of the barracks, the repulsive smell drove him back. According to an Armenian newspaper, he stopped his nose with a handkerchief and exclaimed: "Dreadful!" Forced to live in filth, workers lacked easy access to water for drinking and bathing. Food stores were few and offered products of the lowest quality. Dzhunkovsky came away with the feeling that labor's discontent was well grounded and justified.[29]

Dzhunkovsky saw that working conditions at the larger firms were harsh, difficult, and dangerous. But at smaller establishments, which escaped the supervision of government factory inspectors, they were horrifying. There workers, often Persian immigrants, desperately poor and brutally used, took oil by primitive means. A narrow well was dug, wide enough for only one person, that filled with oil seeping in through the ground. A completely naked Persian worker with a bucket was lowered by rope and pulley down the tight shaft into the pool below. He filled the bucket, then yanked on a cord to be hauled up. He emptied his bucket while others scraped off the black gold that covered his body. Then he would be sent down again. Dzhunkovsky watched these procedures and learned that accidents caused some of the Persians to drown in oil. To avoid problems with the police, the well owners simply left the bodies down in the shafts until they gradually dissolved in the muck. "I did not want to believe it when they told me," Dzhun recalled. "But such incidents had occurred relatively recently. It was simply a nightmare."[30]

He tried to speak to some of the workers, but their reaction was deeply discouraging to a man who had had cordial relations with laborers in Moscow. "It was difficult even to get a word out of them," Dzhun remembered. "They were stubbornly silent, displaying either complete indifference or distrust; only small groups at a few . . . [fields] were willing to talk to me, declaring that they had no objection to going back to work, but they feared violence."[31]

Later, he watched workers being evicted from their living quarters. They went without protest and, as they gathered their belongings, tried to make clear that they were leaving in accordance with the orders of the court. They would obey the law, but they would not return to the job. After two days in the fields, Dzhunkovsky saw clearly the size of the problem before him: "I understood that it would not be easy to set things right, . . . the roots of the strike had gone too deep. It had lasted a month and a half, during which neither the oil producers nor the administration had taken any realistic measures. It seemed to me that both . . . were to blame."[32]

Dzhunkovsky found the city commandant of little use in his efforts to end the strike. Martynov was undoubtedly a man of great personal courage, who had been partially crippled by a terrorist attack, but he was muddleheaded and tactless. At the beginning of the walkout, his administration failed to break up the strike committee swiftly and uncover its leaders. This was not entirely Martynov's fault, however. The presence of Baku's Social Democratic Duma delegate Matvei Skobolev—later minister of labor in the second Provisional Government—complicated things. Dzhun believed the deputy was secretly acting as a leader of the strike, protected from arrest by parliamentary immunity. He slapped a visible police tail on Skobolev and, despite bitter complaints, refused to call it off. Frustrated, the Duma member soon left town.

Dzhun became convinced that the oilmen's record of bad faith also prolonged the strike. In the past, when the workers had walked out demanding better living conditions, management had readily promised improvements. As soon as the strikes ended, however, the oilmen began to renege on their agreements. The workers were determined that this time things would be different, and Dzhunkovsky was sure that wage concessions alone could not achieve long-term labor peace. For that to happen, the workers needed to understand that strikes would not get them what they wanted, and more important, their employers had to be convinced to undertake reforms that would eliminate the real sources of discontent.[33]

After two days in Baku, Dzhunkovsky wired Prime Minister Goremykin about the situation. Nothing had changed since his arrival, he stated, and in fact the strike leaders had used his presence to intensify pressure on workers to stay off the job. At the same time Dzhun denied an impending oil shortage. Despite the strike, oil flowed to waiting tankers in an amount greater than that of the previous year. Rising prices for oil were the result of speculation, not a deficit. Dzhunkovsky told Goremykin that he planned to bring the oil producers together at a conference that would develop tactics for ending the strike.[34]

The same day Dzhunkovsky issued a new proclamation to the workers, calling on them to end their walkout but making clear that they had the right to quit their jobs. "Labor in the oilfields is not compulsory. Every worker who is dissatisfied with the terms of the contract into which he has entered is free to leave . . . [provided] he has fulfilled his legal obligations." But he also promised to shield those who wanted to go back on the job from the wrath of the strikers. "Let every worker in the Baku oilfields know that in returning to peaceful labor, he will be protected in his interests by all the power I possess, and that persons guilty of violent acts against him will be subject to the strictest punishments."[35] This second proclamation had limited impact and called forth an angry response from the strike committee.

> The arrival of Dzhunkovsky, [and] his first orders [should] again convince you that the workers can expect nothing from police authority, that in the struggle of labor with capital it will always stand on the side of the exploiters. Continue in the cause we have begun. Let us convince the Dzhunkovskys and Martynovs that the proletariat has declared a struggle against the bosses in earnest. Strengthen the strike; expose the policies of Dzhunkovsky at your meetings. Remember that we will only achieve our demands by the power of solidarity and organized struggle. Close your ranks and victory will be ours. Continue the strike. Long live the strike.[36]

Although his telegram to Goremykin and the proclamation to the workers gave the impression of calm deliberateness, Dzhunkovsky felt growing pressure as Europe stumbled toward disaster and the strike continued. On July 10/23 Austria-Hungary, backed by Germany and determined to punish Serbia for its complicity in the assassination of Franz-Ferdinand, presented that country with a harsh ultimatum. Serbia was certain to reject it, giving the Dual Monarchy pretext to attack Russia's Balkan client. Two days later Dzhun received a telegram from his chief of staff: "It has been decided to rebuff Austria. Soon mobilization will be ordered. I foresee the possibility of war. Street disorders [in St. Petersburg] have calmed down, but when mobilization is declared, I believe more serious disturbances are likely." The next day Dzhunkovsky learned of the partial mobilization against Austria. This news disturbed him deeply. "To be far from my post while Russia was living through these moments was very difficult," he recalled.[37] He had to end the strike quickly. But he remained determined not to use force.

The escalating international crisis was not the only thing weighing on Dzhunkovsky. Baku's weather made life miserable. The intense heat of the day was debilitating, and at night the awful humidity provided no relief; sleep often proved elusive. South winds off the Caspian enveloped the city in steamy moisture; Dzhun and his team worked bathed in sweat. When the wind shifted and came in from the north, it carried clouds of fine dust that reduced visibility to zero and brought traffic to a standstill. Walking on the streets required special goggles. Unstoppable, the dust forced itself into the houses despite tightly closed windows. Dzhun hoped to gain some relief from the weather by swimming, but an oil slick covered the water's surface near the beach, giving it a repellant violet cast. Work provided the only escape; the urgency of the task, the sense that there was not a minute to lose, made it possible to forget temporarily the heat, humidity, and choking dust.[38]

Dzhunkovsky believed that the conference he had scheduled with the leading oil producers for July 15, held the key to the situation. Here he could test their willingness to deal with the underlying causes of labor discontent and pressure them to improve conditions in the fields. To prepare, Dzhun gathered information on the way the oil companies responded to earlier strikes. On July 14, he summoned all the factory inspectors in the area. They gave him the names of those employers who failed to keep the agreements they had made with workers as well as those who had not broken decisively with strikers in the present crisis.

Working into the night Dzhunkovsky's staff went through the information received while he planned for the next day. He was determined to be well prepared. To see that the oilmen took the conference seriously he decided to turn the weather to his advantage, displaying an uncharacteristic touch of sadism. Although Baku sweltered, he decreed that those who attended the meeting must wear formal attire. "This was, perhaps, cruel on my part," he admitted years later, "but I considered it necessary to give the session a completely official character and to maintain a certain decorum."[39]

On the July 15, 101 frock-coated representatives of Baku's oil companies trooped to the meeting. Dzhunkovsky dominated the proceedings. He opened the conference with a lengthy speech that underlined the gravity of the situation and explained the nature of his mission. The duration of the strike and the stubborn resistance of the oil workers had alarmed managers in other industries dependent on petroleum. More important, the repeated strikes in the oilfields, going back to 1904, had made Baku one of the main centers of the workers' movement throughout Russia. The emperor had sent him to the Caucasus because "the time had come to investigate the root causes of the unceasing disturbances among the workers and to establish lasting conditions for labor peace." Dzhunkovsky told the oilmen that he was not concerned with the political currents that were swirling around the strike or with the immediate economic demands of the workers; they were not justified. He would discuss the issue in the broadest terms, avoiding formalities and technicalities. "We cannot forget, gentlemen," he continued, "that in addition to the law . . . there are also the demands of justice and the obligation of everyone to strive to eliminate those conditions that favor the development of disorders, dangerous to the state and the public welfare."

Dzhun denounced the terrible work environment that deprived workers of the elementary comforts that those in other industries enjoyed. To be sure, the problems in the industry could not be solved overnight. But to construct quarters for workers in the midst of the fields, "where the air reeks of oil and the ground is saturated with filth" was unacceptable. The lack of elementary sanitation, water supply, and adequate food stores was an abomination. These things made the oil patch a breeding ground for discontents, easily exploited by revolutionary agitators. The interests of the country and of the oil producers themselves demanded reform, and better living conditions were the key. Yet the failure of the oilmen to recognize the crying need to move the workers' dwellings away from the fields and to give them, and especially their young children, the chance to enjoy fresh air ran "like a red thread" through the whole history of the strikes in Baku.

Dzhun slammed the misguided policies of the oilmen toward the labor movement that fostered and sustained unrest. Because management acted only in response to strikes, it educated the workers in the techniques of class struggle, led them to make immoderate demands and to think that walkouts were the only way that they could better their conditions. Once the workers returned to the job, the companies often broke faith. This only deepened the atmosphere of discontent and distrust.

Toward the end of his speech, Dzhunkovsky outlined an eight-point agenda of reform. The oil producers had to forge a plan to build new workers' quarters away from the oil patch and create transportation linking them to the fields and the city of Baku. They must immediately improve sanitation and water supply, erect safety barriers designed to keep non-workers away from danger spots, increase the number of food stores serving the workers and their families, and construct "people's houses" where workers might find recreation. Dzhun concluded his reform proposals on a highly personal note: "There is, gentlemen, one other question which I do not feel I have the right to propose for consideration, but which, nonetheless, I call to your attention. . . . This is the matter of expanding the existing children's colonies [located away from the workplace], since the children of the workers suffer most of all from the terrible climate and all the circumstances of life in the fields."

Dzhunkovsky asked that the oilmen view his proposals not as an expression of the workers' demands "but as the opinion of a person sent to you by imperial command." He hoped that they would now respond willingly. "I would be happy to inform His Imperial Majesty that you have recognized the importance of the measures I have mentioned and have displayed the goodwill to develop and implement them in the near future."[40]

Dzhunkovsky's remarks did not go unanswered. A. O. Gukasov, chairman of the executive committee of the Conference of Baku Oil Producers, responded with a forceful rebuttal. One of the richest men in Russia, Gukasov spent much of his time in England, and his presence testified to the seriousness of the situation. He admitted that Dzhun's charges were basically true, but he blamed the ministers of the central government and the Baku authorities who, he claimed, had blocked needed changes. Gukasov outlined the difficulties that the oil companies faced. The cost of constructing new housing would be very high and at the moment the oil producers were strapped. The Baku fields were in poor shape and future prospects were dim: "Output from the old wells is falling; the hope of recovering its former greatness has been lost; all that is left to us is to press on to the end and be satisfied with what is." True, the workers' housing needed to be upgraded and "the economic interests of the employers ought to be subordinated to the demands of humanity." But, Gukasov concluded, it would be wrong to ignore the many practical difficulties that stood in the way of speedy improvements.

Other oil producers and their representatives made similar arguments, but Dzhunkovsky brushed aside their objections and rammed through his proposals. The empire's security chief put it bluntly: Did the oil producers agree that it was necessary to work out immediately a plan for the construction of new housing away from the oilfields? Those who did could remain seated; those opposed should stand. No one moved. In a similar manner Dzhun achieved unanimous approval for providing better transportation within the oilfields and with Baku. The oilmen all agreed to improve sanitation, water supply, and food distribution quickly and to construct new recreational facilities for the workers.

Having whipped the representatives of the oil companies into line on the matter of reform, Dzhunkovsky turned to the question of the strike and how to end it. He chastised the oil producers for not having paid off the strikers as soon as it had become clear that the work stoppage would be prolonged. Their failure to do so had nourished the strikers' hopes that, in the end, the demands they had put forth would be met. Now, he urged management to stand firm and make no further economic concessions.

The oilmen strenuously objected and tried to convince Dzhunkovsky that matters were more complicated than he had assumed. The producers and the strikers were bound by numerous ties, they argued. Many workers who had joined the walkout were longtime employees who possessed great and much-needed expertise. To pay them off once and for all was impossible; it would be difficult to find proper replacements. One of the oilmen, A. I. Mancho, even went so far as to suggest that a long strike was beneficial to everyone, since once it was over an extended period of labor peace would follow. These remarks caused Dzhun to explode: "You want this? Let the workers strike for two months; that's to your advantage, then, at least, they won't strike again for two years! Good. Tomorrow I'll leave and withdraw the troops."

Dzhunkovsky's demand that the oil producers make no economic concessions caused considerable confusion, especially after Baku's provincial governor, V. V. Alyshevsky, urged compromise in view of the threatening international situation. But Dzhun held his ground, and in the end the representatives of the oil companies agreed not to meet the economic demands of the strikers. He also extracted a firm pledge from Gukasov that the oilmen would undertake the agreed upon reforms with the greatest possible dispatch. Dzhunkovsky told them that he would issue a proclamation supporting the oil companies in their hard line against wage concessions while outlining the promised improvements in living and working conditions.[41]

Dzhunkovsky's brusque treatment of the oil companies' representatives was not a sign of the anticapitalist bias often attributed to tsarist officials, especially those from the Ministry of Internal Affairs. During his years in Moscow, he had forged excellent relations with the business community and worked to support its interests. He recognized the dangers inherent in a "zubatovite" approach to the labor question—mollifying workers with small concessions—and believed strikes that simply wrested higher wages from employers often became schools for class struggle. Working conditions were another matter, however, more fundamental and important. Improvements here could eliminate the real sources of labor's discontent, making strikes less frequent and promoting greater social and economic stability. Providing workers with decent quarters, access to basic necessities, and opportunities to escape from their places of employment to find rest and refreshment in things like people's houses, were crucial to labor peace. Dzhunkovsky believed he had seen this work in Moscow—his governorship had not been troubled by many strikes—and given the brutal circumstances prevailing in Baku, it was almost certain to help break the dangerous cycle of walkouts and wage concessions that gave ready work to the journeymen of revolution.

Dzhunkovsky left the meeting satisfied with the outcome but physically spent. "That evening after the conference, I was so tired I could do nothing. The terrible Baku heat and the strain of having to lead the session had completely exhausted me." But on July 16, his spirits soared when he learned some workers were seeking to go back to the job: "This was the first step in weakening the strike."[42] The next day, he issued a new proclamation to the workers that he hoped would end their resistance.

Dzhunkovsky began by telling the strikers not to expect immediate economic benefits. He denied rumors that the government planned to compensate workers for the pay lost during the strike, and he supported the oil producers in their refusal to go beyond the wage concessions they had made in August 1913. But, he promised, things would get better. He informed the workers about the conference on July 15 and then listed the specific reforms the oilmen had agreed to make. He called on the strikers to go back to the job, and concluded: "Further stubbornness on the part of the workers will indicate that they are under the influence of ill-intentioned people, and will greatly hinder my ability to help improve conditions of life in the fields."[43]

Dzhunkovsky believed that his proclamation of July 17 was the first of his efforts to have a noticeable impact on the workers. A number of strikers began to return to the job, and by the end of the day he wired Goremykin that the walkout showed signs of ending.[44] But by then news of impending war had reached Baku, and nationalistic demonstrations began to divert popular support from the strike. On the evening of July 17, a huge crowd, singing patriotic songs, surged through the city carrying flags and portraits of the tsar. The demonstrators stopped before the hotel where Dzhun and his team were staying and, when he appeared on the balcony, threw their hats in the air and thundered "Hurrah!" One of the leaders of the demonstration asked him to convey to the tsar their expressions of loyalty and tell him of their readiness to fight for the honor of Russia. Dzhun thanked them and urged them to maintain order at this difficult moment for the empire.[45]

Two days later Germany declared war on Russia. Throughout the country, strikes evaporated; by July 20, only eight thousand workers remained off the job in Baku. Dzhunkovsky believed that his mission was accomplished and wired the emperor asking leave to return to St. Petersburg. Within hours, the tsar approved his request. The strike was now rapidly dissolving, but the strike committee, still defiant, did not acknowledge defeat until its final proclamation on August 7: "The strike is lost. But . . . it serves us as a lesson for the future. . . . This strike shows us that every economic struggle is a political struggle. In another political situation our struggle would have had a different outcome. There would have been no Martynovs and Dzhunkovskys with their Cossacks, prisons, exiles, and bullets. . . . Therefore we need a firm political organization—strengthen it. . . . Therefore: from disorganization to organization! From defeat to victory! The strike is lost! Long live the strike!"[46]

On the morning of July 21, Dzhunkovsky prepared to leave for St. Petersburg, but events suddenly delayed his departure. At the train station in Sabunchi, about fifteen kilometers north of Baku, some of the reservists being called up for duty rioted and killed the local police chief. Dzhun immediately ordered the Baku city commandant to the scene, then telephoned General Myshlaevsky, the acting viceroy of the Caucasus, asking him to declare martial law in the city and appoint a temporary military governor-general. Myshlaevsky complied at once, and Dzhunkovsky hastened to Sabunchi to check on the situation and learn the mood of the reservists. What he saw was deeply disturbing. After the troops had been loaded and their train was about to depart, Dzhun wished them a safe journey. While many responded politely, others stared back sullenly, "with bestial faces." Later, he toured the barracks at the main assembly point for all reservists to ascertain the temper of those being called up. He found them calm for the most part, but as he left, someone threw a rock at his automobile. Dzhun paid no attention, however, believing the situation was now well in hand. After posting final orders to the local authorities and thanking those who had helped him during his mission, he left Baku at six o'clock in the evening bound for Tiflis.[47]

As the train began the thirteen-hour journey across the Transcaucasian steppe toward the mountains and the viceregal capital, Dzhunkovsky reflected on the ten days just passed. Although the strike had begun to collapse by the time he left, he knew that his actions had not in themselves ended the walkouts. While still in Baku, he received word from St. Petersburg that newspapers on the extreme right notably *Russkoe znamia* (The Russian Banner)—a mouthpiece for the Union of the Russian People—had criticized his actions as being insufficiently "energetic" and "too humane" in failing to break the strike by force.[48] Dzhun knew that these charges would only strengthen the opinion of those who opposed his reforms and saw him as a man whose alleged pandering to liberal public opinion threatened the established order. Certainly the extent of the powers granted to him and the means available made a forceful solution entirely possible, and for a moment he fretted that perhaps he had not truly fulfilled the tsar's commission. He quickly dismissed this concern, however. Repression would not have served the interests of the state. The strike had been peaceful for the most part; using force against it could have triggered a violent response. It would certainly have been a public relations disaster, with unforeseeable, dangerous consequences.[49]

Dzhunkovsky believed that his mission had identified the causes of the repeated Baku strikes and had clarified the means necessary to end them. But he realized that matters could not rest there. In the months ahead, despite wartime pressures and ably assisted by Petr Istomin, he would follow up on the promises made to the workers in July. On October 15, Dzhun learned that the Baku oilmen were meeting and that the question of improving housing was not on their agenda. The next day he forwarded copies of the protocol of the conference he had with the oilmen to Minister of Agriculture Krivoshein and Minister of Trade and Industry Timashev.[50] A week later, he sent Timashev a detailed letter outlining what he had done during his mission. He reminded the minister of the agreement the oil companies had entered into and of his proclamation to the workers telling them of management's commitments. He had grave concerns that the oilmen were dragging their feet, preparing to renege, and that their failure to act would pose a threat to the state. Leaving the Baku oil industry in its current condition, he wrote, "not only prepares the soil for future labor disorders, but also strengthens among the workers the dangerous thought that despite the obvious deprivations endured by laboring people, the government does not recognize the necessity of rendering them the help that justice demands." Dzhunkovsky ended his letter stating that he would bring this matter to the attention of the tsar in his annual report.[51]

Timashev replied on November 5, assuring Dzhun that he and the viceroy of the Caucasus recognized the importance of the agreements made regarding the housing question and that they were determined to press on. Next year, thanks to the efforts of Istomin, the oilmen worked out a plan for connecting the projected new dwellings to the workplace by streetcar lines.[52] Dzhunkovsky also monitored the construction of water lines for the benefit of the workers. When wartime transportation problems threatened to delay or prevent the delivery of the pipe needed, he intervened with the Ministry of Transportation to speed things along, something he continued to do until the time he was dismissed from his position of security chief in August 1915.[53] During his service in the front lines of the Great War,

Dzhunkovsky could not follow closely the developments in Baku, but he learned that in 1916 the Duma had passed a measure mandating the construction of the new living quarters for the workers. Looking back from the 1920s Dzhun still believed that these humane reforms "created a new basis for securing the well-being of workers in Russia" and that only the revolution prevented their implementation.[54]

Dzhunkovsky's handling of the Baku oil strike demonstrates clearly his outlook and administrative style, the approach to Russia's security problems that had set him apart from the police professionals whose work he supervised and sought to direct. Their aim was to interdict, subvert, and repress those who threatened the established order. Because of past success, they saw little reason to change. Dzhunkovsky did not deny the achievements of the security police, but he believed that the costs associated with their achievements were very high. In the context of post-1905 Russia, these methods were becoming counterproductive and needed to be scaled back. An effort to find and eliminate the root causes of popular discontent combined with a sensitivity to public opinion were what the current situation required. Dzhun believed this "liberal conservative" approach was fully compatible with a strong monarchical government, albeit one that accepted the Duma and the rule of law.

Whether Dzhunkovsky's view was correct is impossible to say. The way the Baku strike ended leaves a tantalizing question mark. Still, his ten-day mission shows him working confidently in a situation where he felt himself to be in control, applying with considerable success the lessons he had learned during his long administrative career. But the Great War and its tragic course would change everything. Unexpected and unprecedented events now captured and swept along Dzhunkovsky and his fellow countrymen, ultimately shattering their world and destroying all the certainties of the past.

Chapter 14

In War at Home

As Dzhunkovsky's train propelled him toward the capital, the Russian empire passed from peace to war. Across the country recruits gathered at military depots, waiting to be dispatched to units heading west. Everywhere there were tense and painful scenes of parting, as peasants torn from their fields and workers from their benches said farewells to family and friends, leaving for a war they little understood. Many believed, or at least hoped, that the war would be short. Almost none could foresee the horrors of battle that lay ahead or the years of chaos and disruption the great conflict would spawn.

In his railroad car Dzhun received regular reports that, overall, the mobilization was proceeding smoothly; but from his window he could see disturbing scenes of disorder and drunkenness that accompanied the call-up of troops. The government prohibited the sale of vodka during the mobilization, but recruits, facing long separation from home and the prospect of battle, demanded fortification. When troop trains stopped at stations along the way, they surged toward the liquor stores. "If they were open," Dzhun recalled, "things proceeded more or less properly . . . , [but] if a shop was closed, [the men] broke in, and disorder exceeded all bounds." Several times Dzhun tried to intervene, but with little success. The railroad gendarmes he saw were exhausted from trying to maintain order, but he was proud of the way they struggled to do their duty. At the Vladikavkaz station he marveled at one young officer who, after quieting a large trainload of drunken recruits, walked through all the cars seizing vodka bottles and smashing them against the rails.[1] Dzhun's trip was not simply a sequence of unfortunate events, however. In Moscow he witnessed a heartening surge of patriotic spirit that gripped people of all classes.

Stepping off the train at St. Petersburg's Nicholas Station early on July 27, he got more good news. Baku City Commandant Martynov had wired that the strike was now virtually over and that the authorities there had carried out the mobilization without further incident. This was "a reward for all that I had lived through," Dzhun recalled, and he was also pleased when he learned that he was to go at once to the tsar at Peterhoff. Stopping briefly at his home Dzhun quickly composed a report stating simply that he had successfully carried out his commission to end the Baku strikes. He then drove by car to his audience with the emperor.

Waiting in the tsar's reception chamber, Dzhunkovsky found it difficult to concentrate or master his emotions: "I completely forgot about the mission from which I had just returned; my mind was occupied only by thoughts about the Sovereign and of what he had gone through in declaring war. How I wished that I could find the proper words to express the depth of my feeling, to tell him how full my heart was with limitless sympathy for all that he had suffered and was suffering for Russia." Then the door swung open, and he saw the tsar. As Dzhun approached, Nicholas extended his hand. Impulsively, Dzhun seized it in both of his and kissed it, and the emperor, seeing how upset he was, kissed him in response. Calming slightly, Dzhunkovsky spoke a few words about the war, and the tsar brightened. Nicholas told him how well the mobilization had gone and of his firm belief that God would not abandon Russia in her hour of trial. Dzhun then briefly outlined what he had done in Baku, and the emperor accepted his written report without comment.

The next day Nicholas returned the report marked simply with two dots and a line indicating that he had read it. This and the fact that the emperor, who had so enthusiastically recommended him for the mission, did not even briefly thank him upon its completion, caused Dzhun to worry: "Was this just an accident? Maybe the tsar had simply forgotten and neither Maklakov nor Goremykin thought to remind him. Or perhaps it was intentional, and the groups that condemned my actions in Baku had turned the emperor against me." Dzhunkovsky remained unsure, but he did not pursue the question further.[2] The pressure of wartime duties pushed these concerns to the back of his mind.

The outbreak of hostilities thrust many new responsibilities on the MVD, the Corps of Gendarmes, and Dzhunkovsky himself. Maintaining public order was more important than ever. Mobilization and the passions it evoked showed that even patriotic feelings could cause problems. In St. Petersburg—its name changed to the less German-sounding Petrograd on August 18—patriotic demonstrations that greeted the start of the war had quickly degenerated into riots. Angry crowds stoned stores bearing what they took to be German names (sometimes they were simply foreign) while a mob sacked the recently rebuilt German embassy at the northwest corner of Mariinsky Square, destroying a valuable collection of Renaissance art belonging to Ambassador Pourtalès.[3] This pogrom was not simply the work of hooligans, even fashionable upper-class ladies took part, and Dzhun was displeased to learn that police and civic authorities stood by indulgently as the destruction proceeded and only when the crowd's fury was largely spent arrested several dozen youthful demonstrators.[4]

In Moscow and other parts of the country, mobs followed the lead of the capital and also launched attacks on German property. However understandable, this was a sign of dangers to come. Patriotism and hostility toward the national enemy provided a necessary basis for civic unity and the success of the war effort. But Russia was a multinational empire, and Germans, both Russian subjects and foreign nationals, performed important functions in government, the military, manufacturing, and commerce. Permitted to get out of hand, chauvinistic manifestations could disrupt the economy and, if they spilled over into attacks on other ethnic groups, might create destabilizing nationality conflicts. Even more ominously, patriotic demonstrations could easily become vehicles for the expression of worker and peasant anger and envy toward all those who seemed to have more than they.[5]

Of all the tasks that war imposed on Dzhunkovsky, none seemed more important than guaranteeing the security of the emperor and his family when they traveled, as they did beginning August 3, 1914. Again they visited Moscow to pray at her shrines for the victory of Russian arms. Their presence produced scenes of popular excitement that recalled those of 1912 and 1913 but far exceeded them in their patriotic fervor. Nicholas's entourage was smaller than before—many of the grand dukes were serving in the army—but this time he was accompanied by the ambassadors of

Russia's two allies, Britain's Sir George Buchanan and France's Maurice Paléologue. The high point of the visit was the solemn service at the Uspensky Sobor where thunderous cheers greeted the imperial family and the allied envoys as they emerged from the cathedral onto the square.[6]

Always sensitive to public opinion and convinced that the tsar enjoyed the love of his subjects, Dzhun tried to make security as unobtrusive as possible. He removed the military from the work of guarding the royal family on rail journeys, entrusting this solely to gendarmes. In Moscow, too, security arrangements were kept to a minimum: "The people themselves provided protection and maintained order," he recalled.[7]

Dzhun was clearly caught up in the spirit of the moment, as the detailed account of the Moscow visit in his memoirs reveals. But looking back years later, he could also see the fateful impact of these enthusiasms. Toward the end of the ceremonies, Nicholas and his family went to the Holy Trinity Monastery to pray at the tomb of St. Sergius of Radonezh. There the tsar met a deputation of peasants from Dmitrov county and one of their number, Liamin, the elder of Rogachev canton, made a patriotic speech that praised the decision to ban vodka sales during the mobilization and asked that they be forbidden altogether. Nicholas was already weighing forceful measures to combat alcoholism.[8] As Dzhun later learned from Alexander Samarin, Liamin's entreaty tipped the scales. On August 22, the emperor imposed wartime prohibition despite the vigorous objections of his ministers.[9] Once again, popular demonstrations of support had strengthened the tsar's belief in his mystical bond with the people and he felt free to ignore the advice of leading government officials. This time, the consequences would be disastrous. Revenues from vodka sales were the largest item in the Russian budget, and the tsar's decision produced an annual loss of between four hundred and nine hundred million rubles, roughly 28 percent of the state's income. "Never since the dawn of human history," one informed observer lamented, "has a single country, in time of war, renounced the principal source of its revenue."[10] Even in peacetime, such a move was likely to have unfortunate results, as Mikhail Gorbachev's ill-fated sobriety campaign seventy years later would demonstrate. Russia's "great experiment" during World War I soon generated serious problems: economic dislocation, corruption, demoralization, evasion, and social conflict—a growing gap between tipsy haves and thirsty have-nots.[11]

After he had accompanied the imperial family back to Tsarskoe Selo, Dzhunkovsky returned immediately to Moscow. He then went on to

Baranovichi, headquarters (*Stavka*) of the Russian supreme commander, Grand Duke Nikolai Nikolaevich, arriving on August 9. Like most Russians, Dzhunkovsky had welcomed the appointment of Nikolai Nikolaevich to lead Russia's armies. "He was very popular," he recalled, "and his name was surrounded by many legends, all in his favor; they made him out to be a knight, a fighter for justice. And he was so in fact."[12] But Dzhun had little basis upon which to assess the grand duke's capacity for wartime leadership, which, events would show, was less than solid. This weakness was compounded by the tsar's insistence that General Nikolai Ianushkevich, a man with almost no command experience, serve as chief of staff.[13]

At Stavka, Dzhunkovsky spoke with the grand duke and Ianushkevich on matters related to spying, counterespionage, the treatment of enemy aliens, and the situation in the Baltic provinces, with their large and powerful German populations. Dzhun informed them that he intended to visit that region, assess the situation, and report back. The next day he traveled to Belostok where he met with General Zhilinsky, the commander of the northwestern front, who was preparing to launch the Russian drive into East Prussia. Dzhunkovsky recalled him being worried about immediate prospects and already troubled by the shortage of artillery shells. After a day at Zhilinsky's headquarters, he returned to the capital.[14]

Once in St. Petersburg, Dzhunkovsky focused on three related internal threats to the empire: spying, enemy aliens, and Russian subjects whose ethnic identity now made them suspect, most notably the Germans. Dzhun's involvement with counterespionage was limited. Since 1911, the struggle against enemy spies had been primarily the responsibility of the military, concentrated in the Chief Administration of the General Staff (GUGSh). Dzhun was kept informed by regular reports from Colonel Erandakov, who served as his liaison to counterintelligence. Dzhunkovsky had a rather low opinion of the colonel and of counterintelligence operations in general, however. Although early in his tenure as security chief he had ordered the full cooperation of the Corps with the struggle against foreign espionage, Dzhun felt that the efforts of GUGSh to expose and capture enemy agents had been ineffective. Here Dzhun's vision may have been clouded by his moral sensibilities. He found Erandakov's reports gossipy and too willing to accept unsubstantiated charges. Before the war Dzhun was disturbed by the measures GUGSh used to gain access to information from foreign diplomats. Much of this intelligence was gathered by "women of various circles, [who] to attain their goals were not fastidi-

Grand Duke Nikolai Nikolaevich. Hoover Institution Archive (HIA), Russian Pictorial Collection, envelope A(1).

ous as to their methods." Now, he felt, similar slipshod and questionable techniques were being employed.[15]

Dzhunkovsky's negative assessment of counterespionage may have been reinforced by the wave of denunciations that inundated the Corps of Gendarmes in the months that followed the outbreak of the war, reflecting the spy mania then beginning to grip the country. Dzhun put little stock in these charges. He believed that, in the main, those who made them were trying to use the passions and fears generated by the national emergency for personal gain or to settle scores with old enemies and rivals. He issued a lengthy circular to the Corps urging caution in handling these denunciations so as to prevent malicious individuals from exploiting the situation. Gendarmes should examine all charges carefully and make arrests only after they had thoroughly investigated both the facts and the motives of the accusers.

Although he sought to avoid overreaction to charges of spying and treason, Dzhunkovsky issued a circular to the provincial governors ordering them to take decisive measures to scotch rumors and other activities that could lead to disorders in the countryside. He feared that such disturbances, even in isolated areas, would become known to soldiers in the army and produce "feelings of confusion and alarm." Despite the patriotic upsurge throughout the country, he cautioned, "forces hostile [to the state] continue to act, waiting to take advantage of propitious moments." Normally a stickler about observing the letter of the law, he felt that the emergency required some corner-cutting. He told governors to move swiftly and resolutely without troubling too much about legal niceties. "Your Excellencies should remember that the penal code exonerates those who exceed their authority if such action is taken in response to extraordinary circumstances. Now such circumstances obtain throughout all Russia." Governors who overstepped legal limits to defend the lives and property of peaceful citizens or to suppress breaches of the peace could count on the firm support of the Ministry of Internal Affairs.[16]

The coming of war immediately raised the question of how to treat resident aliens who were citizens of enemy countries. Standard European practice involved interning these people and restricting their economic activity. In his manifesto issued at the start of the conflict, Tsar Nicholas had proclaimed national unity. Russians would put aside all internal differences and rising "like a single person . . . boldly strike the enemy." At the same time, the government declared that it would refrain from actions directed against enemy aliens on Russian soil. On July 26, 1914, the Ministry of Internal Affairs sent out a circular stating that Austrian and German subjects who were peacefully employed could remain under the full protection of the laws or be free to leave the country.[17] This protection did not extend to enemy alien men of military age (18–45), however. They were declared prisoners of war, arrested, and sent to an assigned place under strict surveillance; those who were actually in the armed services of an enemy power, presumably reservists, were immediately turned over to military authorities. Russian policy made exceptions for men who were sick or otherwise unable to serve. It also exempted those born in Alsace-Lorraine, Italian subjects of Austria-Hungary, and former residents of Austrian Galicia, provided they obtained the appropriate certification from the French and Italian consulates and Czech and Russo-Galician societies. In the case of Austrian and German subjects leaving the country, Dzhunkovsky imposed strict limits on the amount of Russian or foreign currency and other valuables they could take with them.[18]

But even as Russia proclaimed national unity and, in that spirit, took steps against enemy aliens, it began to raise the expectations of its own subject nationalities. On August 1, Supreme Commander Grand Duke Nikolai Nikolaevich issued a call to the Poles: "The hour has come when the cherished dream of your fathers and grandfathers can be realized," he announced. Under the scepter of the Russian tsar, the tragic partitions of the eighteenth century would be undone. Russian troops were coming as liberators and Poland, "free in its faith, language, and self-government," would soon be reborn and reunited. "The dawn of a new life for you is breaking," the proclamation continued. "Let the sign of the cross glow in that dawn—the symbol of the suffering and resurrection of a people." A few days later, the grand duke issued a similar appeal to the East Slavs (Ukrainians/Ruthenians) of Galicia promising that Russian arms would free them from Austrian rule and give them a place in the "bosom of mother Russia."[19] Although designed to help pave the way for the advance of Russian armies into enemy territory, these proclamations would have dangerous and unintended consequences, stimulating the hopes of Poles, Ukrainians, and other ethnic groups for separate nationhood.

The early course of the Great War would have a significant impact on Dzhunkovsky's duties.[20] The original Russian war plan, which envisioned a holding action against the Germans in the north and a full-scale offensive against the Austrians in the south, had been modified at the insistence of the French who demanded a major thrust into East Prussia to relieve the pressure from the anticipated German drive in the west. As a result Russia undertook an advance on both fronts and achieved an inconclusive mixture of triumph and disaster. Her armies swept into Galicia, administered severe defeats on the Austro-Hungarian forces, captured Lemberg (Lvov, Lwów, Lviv), the provincial capital, and invested the fortress of Przemysl. Determined to make this "ancient Russian land" a permanent part of the empire, Russian officials quickly established a governor-generalship in the newly acquired territory.

Russian victories in the south were overshadowed, however, by a terrible setback in the north. After a successful initial advance into East Prussia, the Russian armies stumbled. At the battle of Tannenberg in late August, German forces commanded by Generals Ludendorff and Hindenburg surrounded and destroyed the Russian Second Army under General Samsonov, inflicting seventy thousand casualties and taking one hundred thousand prisoners. In the following engagement at Masurian Lakes, the Germans drove the Russians almost completely from East Prussia with further enormous losses. Although the Germans' advance stalled, their victories threatened Russia's position on the Baltic coast and made the question of how to treat the large German population there a matter of grave concern.

In early September, Dzhunkovsky undertook a fact-finding tour through the provinces of Estland, Livland, and Kurland to assess the mood of the population, the loyalty of the Baltic Germans, and the ability of the local administrations to deal with the situation there. Accompanied by P. V. Istomin, he visited Revel (Tallin), Riga, and Mitau (Mitava, Jelgava) collecting information for a report to Minister Maklakov. Russian defeats in East Prussia made the inspection necessary, but equally important were alarming newspaper reports painting the Baltic as a nest of disloyalty and espionage with its local Germans engaging in a conspiracy against the state.[21] The Baltic was a sensitive area where ethnic tensions, class conflict, and revolutionary activity simmered. The Germans comprised a privileged elite, proud of their distinct culture, cut off from the Estonian, Latvian, and Lithuanian populations who made up the peasantry and the urban plebs. During the revolution of 1905–1907 the Germans, who had vigorously and sometimes brutally defended the existing order against lower-class insurgency, were viewed with favor in St. Petersburg. But now the war cast the "barons" in a different light, and non-Germans eagerly sought to tar them with the brush of treason.

Dzhunkovsky's inspection convinced him that most of the rumors about treasonous activities by Baltic Germans were false.[22] But it was equally clear that their enthusiasm for the war was far less than that of the Estonians and Latvians. He found that many German cultural and educational societies in the area—closed with the outbreak of war—had strong ties to the *Kaiserreich* and some had spread anti-Russian propaganda in school texts. Dzhun was particularly disturbed by a textbook on Russian history that claimed the terrorist movement had been a response to the oppression of the people by an arbitrary tsar and his corrupt officials. It referred to Sergei Alexandrovich as the "hated uncle" of the emperor and criticized the "incompetence" of the autocracy.[23]

Dzhunkovsky also took the measure of local institutions and provincial governors. He found the administration of Governor Izmail Korostovets in Estland to be solid and well able to uphold the interests of the Russian state; Korostovets should be kept in place. The situation in Livland was different. There Dzhun encountered the largest number of accusations of German disloyalty and espionage. In the main these were unfounded, but their frequency strongly suggested that Governor Nikolai Zvegintsev did not enjoy the trust and respect of the local population. Both he and the vice governor were insufficiently competent and decidedly too sympathetic to the German elite. Dzhunkovsky recommended that both be removed from office. Kurland's governor, Sergei Nabokov, on the other hand, was a fine administrator, but he too seemed to be under the influence of the German nobility. Dzhun proposed Nabokov's transfer to one of the central Russian provinces.[24]

Dzhunkovsky ended his report with several specific recommendations: restrict the formation of German cultural organizations, limit colonization of the Baltic provinces by Germans coming from other parts of Russia, and forbid foreign subjects from renting or purchasing land outside the ports and major towns. The government should require the use of Russian in administrative, judicial, and private institutions. Dzhun felt that zemstvos should be introduced into the region but warned of "the need to reckon with rapid growth of socialist currents among the Latvians and Estonians." Overall, he counseled caution and a balanced approach.[25] Soon after Dzhunkovsky's return to Petrograd, authorities dispatched N. P. Kharlamov, a high-ranking official in the Ministry of Internal Affairs, to the area for a more detailed inspection. His report confirmed most of Dzhun's conclusions.[26]

Dzhunkovsky also had to deal with the potential of espionage by members of German organizations in other parts of the country, especially the Russian branch of the German Navy League (*Deutscher Flottenverein*) that spread Pan-German ideas abroad. At the end of August, local authorities raided the offices of the organization and searched the homes of its members throughout the country. Arrests and exiles followed. Upon investigation Dzhun found that many of those listed as League members were not active or had enrolled pro forma. He stopped further exiles and ordered the return of those who had already been sent from their homes. Actions against the leaders of the League and those engaged in wrongdoing should be taken through regular judicial channels.[27]

The concerns about German espionage were part of a broader and growing indignation against what many Russians saw as "German dominance" (*nemetskoe zasil'e*) in the country. These feelings were especially strong in the lower classes, reflecting a general hostility toward wealth and privilege. The mix of xenophobia and class conflict appeared in the first days of the war, and it burst out again in mid-October. On October 9, 1914, news that Antwerp had fallen triggered a big demonstration in Moscow. Crowds gathered at the Serbian and French consulates to show their support for Russia's allies. But with nightfall, the patriotic manifestations degenerated into an anti-German pogrom, and the police, not wanting to appear to side with the national enemy, refused to intervene. Crowds broke windows in German-owned establishments throughout the city, and several large firms suffered severe damage. To his credit City Commandant Adrianov quickly posted a declaration that condemned the riot in strong terms and ended: "It causes particular indignation when the crowd covers its criminal acts with patriotic songs. The national hymn is a prayer, and to combine a prayer with outrages is blasphemy."[28] But after investigating the riots Dzhun found Adrianov's efforts to be insufficient. He especially blamed "agitators" who deliberately incited crowds to attack any business with a German or German-sounding name. The chief culprit was a nationalistic society called "For Russia," formed in early August. Dzhun's report to Maklakov led the minister to issue a stern warning to the city commandant. The riots undermined governmental authority and threatened the country in parlous times, Maklakov declared. Should such events recur, "responsibility for them will fall entirely on the local administration."[29] But even the strongest ministerial directive could not stem the tide of popular discontent that increasingly threatened the foundations of the state.

As Russia plunged deeper into war, the emperor began regular trips to Stavka and regions near the fronts where he inspected operations and visited hospitals caring for the wounded. Dzhunkovsky usually attended the tsar on these occasions—which often happened on short notice—overseeing security measures, drawing up the lists of persons and officials who would be presented to the sovereign, trying to see that Nicholas's inspections gave him a true picture of local circumstances and the conditions of the wounded. These duties required him to race ahead of the tsar's party, and for this he needed regular access to an automobile. At his own expense he had a special railway car (*vagon-garazh*) built, very like the one used by the emperor himself. It enabled Dzhun to transport his personal automobile and unload it quickly, which greatly facilitated his efforts.

Beginning in late September 1914, Tsar Nicholas was traveling much of the time. Between September 20 and 26 he visited staff headquarters at Baranovichi and then went to Rovno, Osovets, and Vilna. From October 21 to November 3, he toured the Northern and Southwestern Fronts and the towns of Minsk, Rovno, Lublin, Kholm, Ivangorod, Lukov, Sedlets, Grodno, and Dvinsk. From mid-November to late December, Nicholas traveled through central Russia visiting Smolensk, Tula, Orel, Kursk, and Kharkov. He then went to the Caucasian front where, since October, the empire had been engaged in a struggle with the Turks.

The tsar's travels were designed to create support for the war and to show him actively exercising leadership in the national struggle. By and large they were remarkably effective.[30] Troops everywhere greeted their tsar with extraordinary enthusiasm, and Dzhunkovsky was particularly moved by the reception Nicholas received at Sarakamysh in the southern reaches of Russian Armenia, not far from the frontline trenches. Afterward, the emperor returned to headquarters via Voronezh, Tambov, Riazan, and Moscow. His journey was marked by outpourings of patriotic feeling that appeared to Dzhunkovsky entirely sincere and heartfelt. Looking back on those days, he reflected sadly: "if at that time someone had said that in two years there would be a revolution and the Romanov dynasty would be overthrown, no one would have believed it."[31] Dzhun felt that the people's loyalty and devotion to the tsar displayed at this time were misunderstood and squandered, not least by Nicholas himself, when in the following year he decided to take personal command of the Russian armies and "cast the internal affairs of Russia to the whims of fate."[32] But at the time, the patriotic demonstrations appear to have deceived Dzhun as well, concealing a growing crisis that would erupt in 1915.

At the onset of winter the situation of Russia's armies still appeared favorable. They had made solid gains against Austro-Hungarian forces and, despite the defeats in East Prussia in August–September and the loss of Łodz in early December, had prevented the Germans from taking Warsaw. But field position would not determine the outcome of the next campaigns. The Russians were now desperately short of rifles, bullets, artillery shells, boots—indeed all the supplies needed for a protracted struggle with a much better-equipped enemy. Beyond this Russia's losses had been enormous—a million and a half dead, wounded, or taken prisoner—and her officer corps was seriously depleted.

The increasingly dire circumstances at the front inspired efforts by public-spirited and patriotic citizens to alleviate the situation. In the first weeks of the war zemstvo representatives from across the country formed the All-Russian Union of Zemstvos for the Relief of Sick and Wounded Soldiers, and this was soon joined by the All-Russian Union of Municipalities. The work of these two groups, usually referred to as Zemgor, was directed chiefly by Georgii Lvov, a nationally respected zemstvo leader and Duma member. From the start, however, they met with suspicion and opposition from the government, particularly Minister of Internal Affairs Maklakov. But the pressure of events was building. In the new year defeat and scandal would steadily discredit the authority of the tsar's ministers and of the tsar himself. An aroused public began to demand ever greater concessions from a regime that was clearly failing.

If Dzhunkovsky's memoirs are a reliable guide, the growing public activism did not immediately trouble him. But he did begin to observe other dangerous signs. In early November he had taken a brief side trip to newly conquered Galicia in order to assess the situation there. What he saw was disturbing. The administrators put in place after the Russian armies swept in were poorly informed about the complexities of the region and its mixed ethnic and religious character. Operating on the assumption that Galicia would be forever a part of the tsar's empire, they ran roughshod over the Ukrainian (Russin) inhabitants of the region, forcing them to abandon their Uniate practices and embrace Orthodoxy. They also failed to appreciate the position of the Jews who enjoyed rights under Austrian rule that their co-religionists in Russia did not. While critical of Russian policy in Galicia, Dzhunkovsky did not see malevolence but, rather, a tragedy of good intentions. "We thrust there people with hearts full of love," Dzhun recalled, "wanting only to save our blood-brothers, forgetting . . . the obligation of any conqueror: . . . 'make your actions . . . correspond to the character of the country and its people.' We should have studied carefully the political and economic situation in Galicia, guided not so much by impulses of the heart as by cool *raison d'état* and experience." The task of ruling Galicia demanded skilled and well-prepared administrators who were familiar with the local conditions and the people. Instead the Russian administration resembled "a good-hearted nanny," eager to soothe a beloved child who had been injured but with no real idea how.[33]

In February 1915 Dzhunkovsky received an extensive and highly intelligent report with a detailed discussion of Ukrainian and Polish political groups in Galicia, which, he thought, might have provided the basis for a more effective administration of the area.[34] In early April, he accompanied the tsar on tour there. Dzhun felt that the trip was ill advised, but at the time the situation seemed secure.[35] A month later, however, a massive Austrian and German offensive began that ultimately drove the Russians from the area. They would not regain the western regions of what is now Ukraine until 1939, when Hitler and Stalin destroyed the second Polish republic and divided its lands between them.

Even before the Austro-German breakthrough in the south, however, the Russians suffered a defeat in the north, with repercussions that would push

Romanov rule toward the brink. In late 1914 the Germans shifted four army corps from the western front to the east and secretly prepared for a massive new attack on enemy positions, targeting the sliver of East Prussia still held by the Russians. Their aim was to repeat the kind of two-pronged assault that had proved so successful at Tannenberg and Masurian Lakes. On January 18, 1915, German artillery opened the battle with a barrage of eighteen thousand shells, delivering for the first time in the conflict a new weapon: gas designed to irritate the eyes and lungs of the enemy.[36] A few days later, after a delay caused by a horrific snowstorm, the Germans launched their main attack. The Russian Tenth Army, caught by surprise, was hurled back. After hard fighting and the stubborn resistance offered by the III Siberian Corps, the Germans seized the strategic rail head at Lyck, then encircled and destroyed the XX Army Corps at the Augustowo Forest, capturing 110,000 prisoners and 300 guns. A sudden thaw bogged the Germans down, and they could not immediately exploit their stunning victory, but the shock of the unexpected defeat caused many Russians for the first time to question seriously the successful outcome of the war.[37] "*Kto vinovat* [Who is to blame]?" This perennial Russian question now floated in the air; soon charges of treason would take wing.

In mid-December a young lieutenant, Iakov Kolakovsky, had appeared at the Russian embassy in Stockholm and told the military attaché there a remarkable story. Captured by the Germans early in the war, he suffered terrible conditions as a POW. Seeking to gain his freedom Kolakovsky volunteered to spy for the enemy. He agreed to carry out missions behind Russian lines, including the assassination of Grand Duke Nikolai Nikolaevich, all the while planning to deceive his captors and return to Russian service once he had been released. Kolakovsky stated that he had been told to contact a German agent currently working in Russia, a certain Colonel Sergei Miasoedov now attached to the staff of the Tenth Army. Miasoedov had a checkered past; a former gendarme with a reputation for corruption, he once fought a duel with the Octobrist Party leader Alexander Guchkov. But he also had many important contacts, including Minister of War General Vladimir Sukhomlinov. Although Kolakovsky's tale at first appeared fantastic, the documents he carried were genuine and corroborated his account. Miasoedov was investigated and quickly arrested. On the basis of dubious evidence—none of which indicated that he had spied during wartime—he was tried in a drumhead proceeding and hanged in the early hours of March 19, 1915.[38]

The reasons behind the railroading of Miasoedov are still matters for discussion and dispute.[39] Certainly the "discovery" that a Russian spying for the Germans had penetrated the ranks of the Tenth Army could help explain the recent disaster in the Augustowo Forest and whitewash the failings of Stavka. But the episode quickly morphed into something larger and much more dangerous. The public was shocked. How many more traitors and enemy agents were operating to undercut Russia's war effort? Where were they hiding? Who were their confederates? Political figures, some impeccably loyal, others hostile to the regime, soon cast broader aspersions. A trail of accusations led toward War Minister Sukhomlinov, and a spy mania, incipient since the war began, steadily intensified, fed by jingoism, anti-Semitism, and fears of "German dominance."[40] Ultimately government ministers, the court, the royal family, and even the tsar himself would come under suspicion. Treason, it seemed, might hide anywhere.

The Miasoedov scandal was one of many that soon tore at the vitals of the imperial regime and helped cause its demise. But its impact would extend far beyond the fall of the monarchy and the subsequent triumph of the Soviets. In the years ahead suspicions of vast conspiracies and widespread disloyalty infected the country's political culture. They would be enhanced and extended by Marxist ideas of class conflict and the bitter experience of civil strife—a war against the counter-revolutionary "Whites," and later, the struggle to subdue and collectivize a recalcitrant peasantry. The fear of an implacable "foe within" could not be put to rest and ultimately came to justify a mass terror that engulfed millions, Dzhunkovsky among them.

Dzhunkovsky always remained firmly convinced of Miasoedov's guilt perhaps because he was peripherally involved in the case.[41] On January 8, 1915, he had ordered the head of the Petrograd Security Department (OO), Colonel P. K. Popov to interrogate Lt. Kolakovsky, and on February 6 passed along Popov's report to the investigators on the General Staff.[42] This document seems to have had little impact on the military's decision regarding Miasoedov, however, and the comprehensive study of the case by William Fuller does not even mention it. Despite his belief that Miasoedov had, indeed, engaged in espionage, Dzhun was not swept up in the frenzy to uncover "foes within." In April 1915 the army pressured the Department of Police into establishing security zones around the country and deporting all enemy subjects from these areas.[43] But Dzhun refused to join in the spy scare or to fan fears of "German dominance." Wherever possible, he continued to operate in what could be called a "liberal conservative" style, struggling to maintain the security of the empire while respecting the limits imposed by law even for those who were clearly enemies of the existing order. In November 1914, the Bolshevik deputies in the Duma were arrested for their opposition to the war. He strenuously opposed their being brought before military courts that could have imposed the death penalty. When Justice Minister Shcheglovitov objected, Dzhunkovsky used his close connections to Grand Duke Nikolai Nikolaevich to keep the matter in civilian hands. As a result the Bolsheviks, tried and convicted in February 1915, were only sentenced to exile in Eastern Siberia and lived to play their part in the revolution that began two years later.[44]

Dzhunkovsky's actions produced outrage in extreme conservative quarters. According to Nikolai Tikhmenev, his "right circles" considered Dzhunkovsky a representative of the "'Kadet-leaning' administration." He was a "renegade" about whom they were "especially indignant."[45] Now long-standing suspicions of his political loyalty were strengthened and linked to charges of "Germanophilia." But because he still enjoyed the confidence of the tsar and Interior Minister Maklakov, his position as security chief appeared safe. Yet, within a few months, dramatic changes on the battlefield together with new scandals and conflicts on the home front swept him from office in disgrace.

Chapter 15

Riot, Rasputin, Ruin

Russia's armies faced many difficulties in the first months of 1915, particularly in the area of procurement and supply, but the situation was not entirely dark. They had blunted German advances in the north and had good reason to anticipate further success against the Austrians. Then in April, the Central Powers launched massive offensives that overwhelmed Russian positions south and north forcing a long and painful retreat that would not end until mid-September. In addition, an increasingly dangerous situation started to unfold on the home front. Dzhunkovsky soon found himself confronting two closely linked problems that threatened to destabilize the country and discredit the dynasty: scandals associated with the figure of Grigorii Rasputin and escalating popular anger directed at alleged "German dominance."

Dzhun had not met Rasputin, but the imperial favorite had long troubled him. Now, rumors of Rasputin's debauchery and baleful influence, including opposition to the war with Germany, circulated widely, creating a serious public relations problem—and a dilemma. Dzhunkovsky knew that both Stolypin and Kokovtsov had warned the tsar that Rasputin was undercutting the prestige of the dynasty, but to no avail. Dzhun also knew that his own disapproval of the man was an open secret and had already seriously damaged his relations with the empress. In 1914 Dzhun placed Rasputin under surveillance, gathering information on his contacts and activities, and his watch intensified after an attempt on Rasputin's life in June.[1] Still, he realized that for the tsar and his wife Rasputin was a "family matter," something normally untouchable. But troubling events in 1915 heighted Dzhunkovsky's concerns to the point that he would risk intruding into the charmed circle of Nicholas and Alexandra.

One of the first signs of a building crisis appeared in Moscow. On May 5 the tsar appointed Prince Felix Felixovich Iusupov Count Sumarokov Elston its military governor (*glavnonachal'stvuiushchii*) and subordinated City Commandant Adrianov to him. Adrianov had been under a cloud since the October 1914 riots, and many felt the need for stronger authority in the ancient capital. But Dzhunkovsky, who knew and liked Iusupov personally (they had served together as adjutants to Sergei Alexandrovich), believed he was a disastrous choice, with neither the administrative experience nor sufficient intelligence to handle the complex tasks of ruling Moscow.[2] Iusupov, perhaps the richest man in Russia, displayed an intense hostility to anything that smacked of "German dominance," something that weighed in favor of his selection. But soon Iusupov's strident and often illegal measures against enemy aliens began to trigger many complaints.[3]

At the same time, another issue connected with Moscow demanded Dzhunkovsky's attention. In early May, having accompanied the tsar on his travels for much of April, he returned to Petrograd to face a stack of police reports and a spate of rumors concerning the activities of Rasputin. Among the various accounts, one stood out as especially disturbing: a scandalous incident supposed to have taken place at Moscow's Yar restaurant on the night of March 26/27. A police report sent by A. P. Martynov on April 1, indicated that Rasputin had visited the Yar on the night in question but nothing more. Concerned, Dzhun fired off a telegram to Adrianov ordering him to provide a detailed account, but to his surprise and displeasure, instead of writing, the city commandant came personally to Petrograd (on either May 15 or 16) and reported orally on Rasputin's "disgraceful, indecent behavior . . . in very unsavory company."[4] Dzhun suspected that Adrianov was too fearful of Rasputin's influence to put anything on paper; still he asked the city commandant to go back to Moscow and submit a written statement. A week passed, but no report came. On May 26, Dzhun wrote Adrianov again, reminding him of his oral report and asking for detailed information "in view of the recently increasing rumors [*tolkov*]" about Rasputin's "highly immoral behavior" in the ancient capital.[5] Once more, nothing. Finally, he dispatched a subordinate to Moscow to insist on the commandant's report. On May 31 it arrived.[6]

Adrianov wrote nothing himself, stating simply: "I have the honor to forward to Your Excellency the original report of the superintendent [*pristav*] of the second department of the Sushchevsky district, Lt. Colonel Semenov."[7] Dzhunkovsky found its contents so disturbing that, years later, he would not permit the full text to appear in his memoirs. Partly because of that, some historians have charged that the "report" was a fake concocted by Dzhunkovsky. But Anastasia Dunaeva uncovered the original document in Dzhunkovsky's archive. It read:

> On the night of March 26/27 of this year, Rasputin arrived at the Yar restaurant in the company of Soedov, Reshetnikova and some other young woman and summoned to the restaurant Kugulsky [a well-known reporter for the Moscow newspapers]. Rasputin arrived already drunk. The entire company repaired to a separate room, invited a Russian chorus and ordered supper. Rasputin commanded the chorus to sing, ordering [them] to dance obscene [*tsinichnye*] dances, while he himself danced the Russian. [He] had the singers sit down with him and spoke with them suggestively, inviting them to his apartment. Rasputin permitted himself to mention disrespectfully the name of the empress saying: "I can imagine how angry she would be with me if she could see me now." Then pointing to his shirt, boasted to the singers saying that the empress herself had sewn the shirt for him. Rasputin behaved most indecently [*kraine tsinichno*] from the beginning; as soon as the singers arrived he . . . [here Dzhunkovsky crossed out and pasted over two lines in the original text] saying that he always got to know women this way. Everything was paid for by the young woman who accompanied Rasputin, whom he ordered to pay the singers as well. Rasputin gave several of the singers notes he himself had written. In the notes were various phrases, for example: "Love unselfishly," etc. The entire company stayed in the room for several hours and left. Rasputin announced to everyone who he was.[8]

What was in the passage that Dzhun so carefully covered up? We cannot be sure of the exact wording of the offensive text, but another, somewhat later report preserved in the archives of the Moscow Okhrana, makes clear its gist: "[Rasputin] exposed his sexual organs and in that condition continued to converse with the singers."[9] Was Semenov's report true? It was not on official paper; it had no number and date. For Dzhunkovsky to find out would require a detailed and extensive investigation. This could take time, and knowing how sensitive the Rasputin question was, he ordinarily would have been cautious. Indeed, on the day the Semenov report came in, he wrote Martynov asking him for details about the alleged Yar incident.[10] But by that time another unexpected event was forcing Dzhun's hand. Days before Semenov's report arrived, Moscow had exploded in a vicious anti-German pogrom.

By mid-May the ancient capital was on edge. Food shortages, rising prices, distressing news from the front, rumors of spies, an outbreak of cholera, and concerns about "German dominance" charged the atmosphere. Military Governor Iusupov contributed to the tension by making public speeches denouncing German influence, visiting factories and asking workers to give him names of suspect Germans and citizens of countries at war with Russia. He deported enemy aliens from Moscow and handed out lists of those exiled to the press. In the process he ran roughshod over limits set by the Council of Ministers and the High Command.[11] At the same time, gossip about Rasputin's scandalous behavior and alleged disloyalty raised a cloud of distrust over the royal family that extended to its most visible member in Moscow, Grand Duchess Elizaveta Fedorovna. Despite Ella's devotion to Russian Orthodoxy, her charitable good works and service to the poor and the wounded, to many she was a "German princess" whose support for the national struggle was in doubt.[12]

Indeed, it was an incident at the headquarters of a committee the Grand Duchess had founded to aid the families of soldiers that triggered the May riots. On the afternoon of May 26, about a hundred women, mostly wives and widows of men in the ranks, gathered to receive material to be sewn into undergarments for the troops. This was something the women regularly did to earn a bit of extra money. But that day they were told there was no work to be had because the army's Quartermaster Department had assigned the job to a firm that had once belonged to Germans. The firm was actually in Russian hands, but the disappointed women did not know this. They began to shout that Germans were taking the bread from their mouths and threatened to storm the building. The police arrived and prevented violence by urging the women to go to Prince Iusupov, who received them and promised to investigate.

The same day fifteen hundred workers at the Giubner printing factory went on strike demanding that all the plant's Alsatian employees be fired.[13]

In the evening they gathered at the factory waving national flags and shouting anti-German slogans. They then marched on a nearby munitions plant where recent explosions had been ascribed to German sabotage. Rumors also circulated that the current incidence of cholera was caused by Germans poisoning the water supply. Police prevented the workers from breaking into the munitions factory, and they soon disbursed. But the disturbances had only just begun.

On the morning of May 27, crowds marched under Russian flags and started to attack what they believed were German firms. Order in the city quickly dissolved, and for two days mobs stormed through Moscow in search of enemy aliens. They invaded factories, stores, and homes, killed at least eight people, and injured forty others. Stolen vodka, cognac, and other spirits fueled the rioters. "That was some party!" one of their number wrote later. "Like never before, almost all Moscow was drunk."[14] In the end, three hundred firms burned along with dozens of apartments and houses. The value of destroyed property exceeded seventy million rubles, and while subjects of countries at war with Russia were the chief objects of popular rage, rioters also victimized Russian citizens of foreign descent. Signs of the class struggle were clearly evident, too, as workers directed their anger at foremen and managers as well as business owners. Behind the facade of anti-Germanism lurked the antagonism of poor against rich.[15]

Although mayhem and looting were the chief preoccupation of the rioters, the crowds frequently shouted political and anti-dynastic slogans. On Red Square people hurled insults at the royal family, demanded that Rasputin be hanged, the empress sent to a convent, and Grand Duke Nikolai Nikolaevich crowned as Nicholas III. Crying "Away with the German woman!" a mob converged on the Convent of Mary and Martha, the residence of Grand Duchess Elizaveta Fedorovna, accusing her of harboring a German spy and of hiding her brother, Grand Duke Ernest of Hesse, on the premises.[16] A police official who had lived through the events of 1905 commented: "Neither then, nor at any other time in my life did I see such bitterness or rage in the crowds . . . ; they were literally mad . . . hearing nothing and understanding nothing."[17]

Confronted by mass violence Moscow authorities seemed at best paralyzed and at worst complicit. City Commandant Adrianov was reluctant to employ firearms against the rioters even as the city descended into chaos.[18] Prince Iusupov expressed sympathy for the demonstrators and blamed the breakdown of order on government officials who were "soft" on Germans. Speaking to the Moscow duma in the midst of the disturbances, he announced: "One can say that every German has two protectors, one in Petrograd, one in Moscow. We've been too good to them. I'm on the side of our workers. Their patience is exhausted. . . . I've seen the people who have come out into the streets. They go about with joyful faces."[19]

Neither Adrianov nor Iusupov informed authorities in Petrograd about the escalating riots. On May 27 Dzhunkovsky learned through informal channels that something was amiss in the ancient capital but, when he telephoned Iusupov, was told that nothing serious had taken place. Next day, however, Dzhun received details on the pogrom from the provincial governor, Count Nikolai Muravyov. He went immediately to Maklakov and brought him up to date. The minister ordered Dzhunkovsky to Moscow and informed the emperor.[20]

When Dzhunkovsky arrived, the riots were still going on, painting a tableau of senseless destruction. At Kuznetsky Most (Smiths' Bridge), a fashionable shopping area, he was horrified when he saw the wreckage of the Tsimmerman musical instrument store and warehouse: "Half the street was blocked by broken pianos that had been thrown out of an upper storey window onto the bridge," he recalled sadly. But the worst was over. Iusupov and the Moscow mayor, Mikhail Chelnokov, had issued proclamations calling for an end to the disturbances. On May 29 Iusupov summoned troops, and in three places they fired shots into the crowds. The violence abated, and Dzhunkovsky went to work, rapidly gathering information about the pogrom and its causes.[21] Before leaving Moscow that evening, he dined with Iusupov and his wife. He told his host that he blamed the police for failing to intervene early and for letting things get out of control. He planned to recommend Adrianov's removal and the dispatch of a special investigator from the Ministry of Internal Affairs to make a more thorough inquiry. "Iusupov obviously did not like this," Dzhun recalled, "but I said that I could not do otherwise."[22] Once a friend, Iusupov now became a dangerous enemy.

Dzhunkovsky's inspection in Moscow also strengthened his belief that Rasputin had become a serious danger to the state and the monarchy. "The insolent behavior of Rasputin that had recently taken place in Moscow cast a shadow on the imperial family," he wrote later, "it began to be seen as an open, clear-cut demonstration by a pro-German party, feeling that it had powerful support. All the events of the past days had created very great hostility toward Germans and, unfortunately, a strong anti-dynastic mood."[23]

Back in the capital, Dzhun got more bad news. The executive committee of the All-Russian Union of Municipalities and the city duma announced that they would conduct their own investigations into the Moscow riots. Dzhunkovsky was alarmed: their interference in this administrative matter was, to his mind, "completely impermissible." But just then the emperor wrote to Maklakov: "Has Dzhunkovsky returned from Moscow? When he gets back, send him to me at once. N." The minister replied that Dzhunkovsky was in Petrograd, and Nicholas ordered him to appear at Tsarskoe Selo on June 1 at ten o'clock in the evening.[24] By then Dzhun had received the Semenov report. He believed that he had to act.

Dzhunkovsky states that he spent the entire first day of June preparing for his meeting with the emperor. His report on the causes and course of the Moscow riots was done, and his recommendations were clear: Sack Adrianov and send Senator I. S. Krashenninikov to make a thorough and dispassionate investigation. Maklakov had already signed the document and given Dzhun permission to present it personally to Nicholas. Dzhun's chief concern that day was another report: a detailed account of the information he had gathered on Rasputin and the scandals he had caused.

Dzhunkovsky linked these reports because he saw two forces threatening the government and the monarchy. The Moscow riot revealed the danger of mass violence from below. In May it had been leaderless, unconscious, and purely destructive; but unfortunate events in the future might trigger and focus such disturbances. Should the troops support them or even remain passive, they could play into the hands of the enemies of the state.[25] Rasputin posed a threat of a different order. He was discrediting the imperial family in the eyes of both the masses and the elite. Together these dangers made an explosive concoction.

Dzhunkovsky understood the risks that making a report about Rasputin entailed. From personal experience he knew that any intrusion into Romanov family matters was sure to be resented, and he must have realized that he did not have overwhelming evidence to back up his charges. The Semenov report in particular was thin and not yet fully substantiated; the other reports he recently requested from Moscow had not arrived.[26] Still Dzhun went ahead, believing that recent events—defeats at the front, the Moscow riots, and the growing assertiveness of nongovernmental bodies like the Union of Municipalities—made his intervention right and necessary: "[T]he association of the imperial family with a man such [as Rasputin] was shaking the throne and threatening the dynasty . . . ; I would not be fulfilling my duty as a loyal subject if I hid even one of the facts my report contained."[27] He also may have hoped that in this time of national crisis Nicholas would follow the example of his father, Alexander III, who had always shown "that monarchy was the idea of subordinating [personal] interests and desires to a higher truth."[28]

By six o'clock in the afternoon, Dzhunkovsky had finished his report. He ordered his secretary to type a single copy and then destroyed the handwritten draft. "I did not want to let anyone in on this, or leave a single trace in the official record." The only people who knew about his plan to inform the tsar were his loyal subordinates Brune de Saint-Hyppolite, director of the Department of Police, and Vladimir Nikolsky, the Corps of Gendarmes chief of staff. He also personally told Maklakov about the contents of the report, since he could not act without the permission of his superior. Dzhun said that he would present his findings to the emperor not as the assistant minister of internal affairs, but as a private person, a member of the tsar's Suite. "Maklakov approved of my intentions," he recalled. "[He] kissed me and, deeply moved, sent me on my way." Dzhun also alerted Evdokiia: "It was easy to imagine unpleasant consequences from the report, and I wanted to have her moral support."[29]

That evening Dzhunkovsky left for Tsarskoe Selo and around ten o'clock was standing in the tsar's reception hall at the Alexander Palace. Precisely on the hour, the door to the sovereign's office opened. Dzhun entered, and Nicholas stepped forward, extending his hand. After asking how long Dzhun had been in Moscow and when he had returned, the tsar sat down at his desk and indicated a chair on the right. Dzhun sat and began a detailed account of the events in Moscow and their causes, outlining his recommendations for change and further investigation. When he finished, Nicholas approved the report and gave the order for its implementation. At this point Dzhunkovsky summoned his courage to present the information he had gathered about Rasputin. "Without taking my report from my briefcase," he recalled, "I asked the sovereign's kind permission to tell him that which had long troubled me as a loyal subject and allowed me no peace. The tsar's face changed slightly and took on a more serious expression; he looked at me intently and said: 'Please, speak.'"

Nervously and a bit disjointedly, Dzhunkovsky began. Then, calming down, he described in some detail how Rasputin had behaved while he was away from Tsarskoe Selo. Since no copy of his report exists, we cannot know precisely what Dzhun told Nicholas. He undoubtedly mentioned the incident at the Yar. But given the prudishness he displayed in his memoirs, he may not have given the tsar a "full frontal" account of that event, sparing the emperor's sensibilities and, to a degree, Rasputin's reputation. We can be certain that he did not claim that Rasputin was corrupting members of the royal family or influencing government policy in a negative way. Dzhunkovsky never saw him as that kind of "dark force." Rather, the "starets" was a public relations disaster, whose ties to the royal family gave rise to totally unfounded but dangerous rumors, a gift to the monarchy's enemies that kept on giving.

As Dzhun talked, seeking to explain "all the harm that Rasputin was causing the dynasty and Russia," Nicholas listened intently; only his pale face revealed his emotions. Then at the end the tsar asked in a quiet voice: "Have you laid it all out, do you have a written report?" Dzhunkovsky answered that he did, and Nicholas said: "Give it to me." Dzhun reached into his briefcase and handed over the document. Nicholas took it, placed it in a drawer of his writing desk, and locked it with a key.

For several moments, neither man spoke. Then Dzhunkovsky broke the silence, telling the tsar that his report was a personal statement, not the official position of the Ministry, that there were no copies, and that he had destroyed the draft. Nicholas responded simply: "Thank you," and Dzhunkovsky felt relief. "These words made me happy and confident," he recalled. "Many before me, even members of the imperial family, had often begun to speak about Rasputin, but I was the first to whom the Sovereign . . . did not say: 'I ask you not to interfere in my personal family affairs.'"

This sign of the tsar's approval emboldened Dzhun further. He told Nicholas that he believed Rasputin was being used by the enemies of the state to destroy Russia and the dynasty. He asked permission to keep the "starets" under strict surveillance, taking note of all whom he visited and other contacts, especially those asking him to pass on requests for the sovereign to review. Nicholas replied: "I ask you to do this, but everything that you note, you will tell me personally; all this will be between us."

The conversation then turned to other topics and lasted until half an hour past midnight, when the tsar thanked Dzhunkovsky for his loyalty and dismissed him. Dzhun lingered in the reception hall for a few minutes, speaking to the duty officer. Suddenly, the door of the tsar's study opened and Nicholas appeared. He shook Dzhunkovsky's hand once more and said casually: "I want to walk a bit. It's a marvelous night." With that, he disappeared into the garden.[30]

Since Dzhunkovsky's is the only account we have of his fateful meeting with Nicholas, the reader may wish to view its details with a measure of skepticism. But there is no doubt that the meeting took place.[31] In recent years, however, the long-accepted story of the Yar incident that triggered Dzhunkovsky's report has been called into question. A number of revisionist historians claim that nothing untoward took place at the restaurant and that Dzhunkovsky and his subordinates concocted the evidence. The latest contribution to the revisionist library is by Douglas Smith, a very reputable scholar. According to his book on Rasputin, Dzhunkovsky was dissatisfied with Martynov's report of April 1, which had not mentioned anything scandalous, and wired the Moscow Okhrana chief on May 31 urgently demanding details. Smith then states: "Martynov knew just what his superior was asking of him." Aware of Dzhunkovsky's "hatred" of Rasputin, and having been told what was expected of him when Dzhunkovsky "visited" Moscow in late May, he put together the story of Rasputin's misbehavior, sending along the Semenov document. And despite the fact that Adrianov had told Dzhun that Rasputin had not committed "the slightest impropriety," Dzhunkovsky now had the information he wanted and "[l]ate one June evening at one of his regular audiences with the tsar, summarized the Yar incident."[32] Summarizing his own findings, Smith concludes that Dzhunkovsky lied.[33]

Had Smith availed himself of the work of Anastasia Dunaeva and become better acquainted with the facts of Dzhunkovsky's biography, he might have curbed his revisionist enthusiasm on the Yar incident. As it is, he gets the time line wrong, is forced into some dubious speculation, and ignores the context of the events. Dzhunkovsky did not just urgently wire Martynov out of the blue on May 31. The record shows that he had been trying to get information about the Yar events for the better part of a month. There is no documentary proof that he compelled Adrianov or Martynov to fabricate evidence against Rasputin, and it is sheer speculation to state that they somehow divined his wishes. The three men were not on particularly friendly terms, and it is improbable that they would have joined to become co-conspirators in an act of falsification designed to deceive the emperor. It was Adrianov, not Martynov, who first sent on the Semenov report, contradicting his later claim that he had told Dzhunkovsky Rasputin had done nothing improper (see below). In his message of June 5, Martynov repeated the Semenov account that had been dispatched six days before. Finally, in discussing the Yar incident, Smith does not make clear that Dzhunkovsky reported to Nicholas in the immediate aftermath of the May riots in Moscow, an ominous sign of a future mass revolt. Dzhun had not just "visited" the ancient capital in late May, he had come there, with disturbances still raging, to examine and report about a very serious and dangerous event. It is unlikely that he took time from this important work to enlist Martynov and Adrianov in a scheme to bring down Rasputin.

We may never know exactly what transpired at the Yar on the night of March 26/27 and conspiracy theories will continue to spin. But what can be said at this point is that the available documentary evidence does not support the claims and speculations of the revisionists. The Semenov report exists, and although it may or may not have been truthful, it is clear that Dzhunkovsky took it to be so and was shocked by its contents. If Dzhunkovsky was guilty of anything it was that he made his report to Nicholas at a time when the evidence he had on the Yar episode at least was rather thin, although it would be further substantiated in the weeks that followed. It is equally clear that Dzhunkovsky acted not out of "hatred" for Rasputin, a man he had never met, but in a state of genuine alarm aroused by the Moscow riots and escalating rumors about the "starets." As for the tsar, it appears that he accepted the validity of Dzhun's report at the time and, according to some accounts, called in Rasputin, verbally chastised him, and ordered him to leave for his home in Siberia.[34] (Like so much about the Yar incident, this story, too, is disputed.)[35] Rasputin did return to Siberia in mid-June and remained there for almost two months under continued police surveillance. Dzhunkovsky's effort to protect the monarchy would soon backfire, however, causing further damage to the dynasty and shattering his own career.

While Dzhunkovsky sought to deal with the May riots and the danger posed by Rasputin, Russia's Western Front began to crumble. The armies of the Central Powers now pressed eastward relentlessly. "Hurricane fire" from German and Austrian artillery blasted the Russians' positions, while their guns, short of ammunition, could answer only feebly or not at all. The soldiers of the tsar, often without weapons or bullets, fell back, demoralized. Many surrendered, casualties mounted astronomically, and as the Russian armies retreated, a vast stream of civilian refugees accompanied them. Large numbers went voluntarily, fearing the consequences of falling behind enemy lines, but Russian military policy forced many more from their homes. Poles, Lithuanians, and Germans who lived in the areas being abandoned suffered grievously, and Russian generals, including Ianushkevich, the army chief of staff, singled out the Jews for special punishment, branding them as potential or actual traitors and spies. In many places Russian soldiers carried out pogroms, robbing, raping, and murdering these innocents. The military authorities took prominent Jews hostage to guarantee the good behavior of their co-religionists. The horrors being inflicted upon the Jews and the plight of their refugees were so shocking that they became an international scandal and deeply troubled the Council of Ministers, hardly a locus of pro-Jewish sentiment. In early August the Council abolished the Pale of Settlement—the region of western Russia in which most Jews had been confined since the time of Catherine the Great. Until war's end at least, Jews would be permitted to live in any town or city of the empire.[36]

As the battlefield shook with the thunder of German guns, setbacks at the front produced a political earthquake in Petrograd. From the beginning of the war, the Russian government had attempted to manage the conflict with little reference to the Duma and the public, a policy strongly supported by the most conservative ministers, Maklakov, Shcheglovitov, Sukhomlinov, and Sabler. Now the defeats made this policy impossible. Private citizens and nonofficial bodies began to assert themselves, demanding a greater role in the defense of the nation. On May 21, pressured by Nikolai Nikolaevich and Duma president Rodzianko, the tsar created a Special Conference for Increasing the Supply of the Army to deal with the munitions crisis. Chaired by the minister of war, the Conference included Rodzianko, four members of the Duma, and four leading industrialists. It was subordinated directly to the emperor and outside the control of the Council of Ministers. Maklakov and Shcheglovitov strongly opposed it, but this was just the beginning of a major government shake-up.[37]

On May 24, Pavel Riabushinksy's business-oriented newspaper, *Utro Rossii*, called for a "government of national defense" that would include "public elements." Two days later, the IX Congress of Trade and Industry demanded the reconvening of the Duma as a first step to changing the composition of the current government, a program soon endorsed by the Unions of the Zemstvos and Municipalities.[38] The Congress also proposed creating a series of War-Industries Committees to speed the work of supplying the army. Leading industrialists quickly took up the idea and by July had formed a national organization that united the efforts of local committees in support of the war and the Duma. The dominant figure in this new social and political force was Alexander Guchkov, the former leader of the Octobrists.[39]

Within the Council of Ministers, Alexander Krivoshein led a group demanding that members unpopular with the public be forced to step down. On the evening of May 26, Krivoshein and four colleagues visited Prime Minister Goremykin and threatened to resign unless Interior Minister Maklakov, War Minister Sukhomlinov, Justice Minister Shcheglovitov, and Holy Synod Procurator Sabler were dismissed. Maklakov was first on their hit list. On May 30, Goremykin reported to Nicholas on the situation, and the next day Duma president Rodzianko spoke to the tsar urging changes almost identical to those proposed by the Krivoshein group. Nicholas, who had long prized the minister of internal affairs for his staunch support of monarchical power, gave way. On June 5 he dismissed Maklakov while warmly praising his loyalty and service. Over the next months other "odious" ministers would also fall.[40]

Absorbed by the May riots in Moscow and Rasputin, Dzhunkovsky appears to have been largely oblivious to the political currents and maneuverings that were swirling around him. Thus, Maklakov's dismissal came as an unexpected and painful shock. Dzhun learned about the tsar's decision only the day before the order was officially announced when Maklakov called him in and told him the news. Although he believed that his chief had made serious mistakes and had come under harmful influences, he saw Maklakov as a friend, a man of principle, who loved his sovereign and his country "with every fiber of his being." Maklakov was far more conservative than Dzhunkovsky, especially in regard to the Duma, but he had given his assistant minister a completely free hand in dealing with security matters. Dzhun worried that Maklakov's successor, Prince Nikolai Shcherbatov, might be more intrusive.[41]

At the time Dzhunkovsky did not know he was being considered as a replacement for Maklakov and was on the "short lists" of both the Krivoshein group and the tsar himself.[42] Later, he learned from Goremykin that Nicholas had told his prime minister: "I have two candidates—Prince Shcherbatov and Dzhunkovsky. Ask Shcherbatov if he agrees to be minister of internal affairs. If yes, send out the order for his appointment. If Shcherbatov refuses, draw up an order [appointing] Dzhunkovsky without asking him." In his memoirs, Dzhun reflected on what he saw as good fortune: Shcherbatov's willingness to take over the MVD had saved him from what would have been a "nightmarish . . . assignment."[43]

Dzhunkovsky had reservations about his new chief, however, who he felt was "insincere and crafty." He worried that he might not have the same independence he enjoyed under Maklakov. He asked Shcherbatov if he had his own candidate for the position of assistant minister, and if so he would immediately resign. But Shcherbatov urged him to stay and assured him of a continued free hand. Dzhun told the new minister to be straightforward and let him know at once if they differed on any important matter. It soon turned out that Shcherbatov displayed little interest in the work of the ministry and left Dzhun to his own devices. Still, he always sensed that Shcherbatov was not fully trustworthy.[44]

Events in June convinced Dzhunkovsky that he enjoyed the full confidence of both his sovereign and Grand Duke Nikolai Nikolaevich. On June 9 he left for Stavka a day in advance of the tsar's visit there. The war news was grave; Lvov had just fallen. "All Russia was agitated and shaken," he recalled. Nikolai Nikolaevich gave Dzhun a warm welcome, and they discussed the situation on the home front at length. The grand duke told him that he planned to ask the tsar to remove Minister of War Sukhomlinov and replace him with General Aleksei Polivanov. Sukhomlinov had not supplied the army with the equipment it needed and was under a cloud because of the Miasoedov affair. Dzhun learned that the grand duke also intended to propose a broader shake-up of the Council of Ministers with the dismissal of Shcheglovitov and Sabler.

As soon as Nicholas arrived at Stavka, Dzhun saw the grand duke enter the tsar's railroad car and speak to him for some time. When he left the tsar, the supreme commander passed close to Dzhunkovsky, standing with other members of the Suite. "All done," he whispered, and Dzhun knew immediately that the emperor had agreed to sack Sukhomlinov. Later, after lunch, Nikolai Nikolaevich confided to Dzhun the details of his conversation with the tsar, a clear indication of the grand duke's high regard.

Dzhunkovsky recalled that the tsar, too, showed his favor. In the early afternoon Nicholas invited him for a long walk in the woods where they spoke candidly about domestic politics. First, the emperor asked Dzhunkovsky how Maklakov had taken his dismissal. Dzhun replied that, although saddened, the minister had accepted the decision without complaint. "I expected no less from him," the tsar responded, "I was sorry to part with him, but it had to be." Nicholas spoke about the dismissal of Sukhomlinov and asked Dzhun's opinion of that move and of the new war minister, Polivanov. Dzhunkovsky supported the decision but did not blame Sukhomlinov for all the shortcomings and failures of the army. Dzhun said that Sukhomlinov's chief weakness was his inability to manage people. As for Polivanov, Dzhun believed he was energetic, competent, and enjoyed the confidence of the Duma and the public. The tsar then asked him for his views on Justice Minister Shcheglovitov. "Everyone tells me that I need to remove him . . . , but when I ask why, nobody can give me a straight answer," the emperor complained. "Even Nikolai Nikolaevich tells me that Shcheglovitov has to go, but when I inquired what information he had on the subject, he said to me: Ask Dzhunkovsky, he'll tell you."

Dzhun was taken aback, flattered by the tsar's interest in his opinions, but unsure how to begin. Finally, he started by telling the emperor about the conflict he and the grand duke had had with Shcheglovitov over the question of whether to try the Bolshevik deputies in military or civilian courts. The minister of justice wanted to hand them over to the military, while he and the supreme commander wanted to keep the matter in civilian hands. Dzhun recalls telling Nicholas: "I found it to be unworthy of a government with any self-respect to use [the excuse] of wartime to rid itself of deputies it hated." Then he added: "Shcheglovitov's chief failing . . . was that as minister of justice he did not fulfill his main responsibility: he did not stand on guard for the [sanctity of the] law but bent it and interpreted it in accordance with circumstances and the needs of the moment." Shcheglovitov made contradictory applications of Senate rulings and in some cases even undermined the dignity of the Senate itself. The tsar listened with what appeared to be satisfaction and then remarked: "Well, at last I've heard a real judgment on Shcheglovitov, with facts; up 'til now I heard only unsubstantiated complaints."[45]

On June 12 Polivanov appeared at Stavka with Krivoshein close behind. The next day, Goremykin and the other ministers arrived, minus Shcheglovitov and Sabler.[46] Prince Iusupov, slated to report on recent events in Moscow, joined them. He was bristling with indignation and ill will toward Dzhunkovsky, blaming him for "protecting" Germans, a policy that outraged the common people of the city and led to the pogrom. He criticized the decision to send Senator Krasheninnikov to investigate the causes of the riots.[47] Dzhun was not invited to the special session that day where the tsar and his ministers heard Iusupov's assessment of the disturbances, an hour-long diatribe that left "a strange, unclear impression."[48] Still, at Iusupov's suggestion, the ministers adopted new and tougher rules regarding enemy aliens and foreigners in general, restricting access to citizenship, and authorizing deportations of all enemy subjects regardless of age or sex.[49]

On June 14, the Council of Ministers met at Stavka under the chairmanship of the tsar, and Nicholas announced his willingness to bring the Duma and nongovernmental agencies into the work of winning the war. With Grand Duke Nikolai Nikolaevich and his chief of staff present, the Council considered ways to coordinate the activities of unofficial organizations and state institutions to improve supply for the army. At the end of the session, the tsar made public a rescript to Prime Minister Goremykin. It acknowledged the serious defeats that the country had suffered but asserted that, with God's help, Russian arms would triumph. "The enemy will be broken," Nicholas pledged. "Until then there can be no peace." The emperor called on the nation to unite its forces to secure victory: "With firm faith in the inexhaustible power of Russia, I expect from all government and public institutions, from Russian industry, and from all true sons of the Motherland without regard to belief or station, a firm, collective effort to meet the needs of our glorious army. From now on all the thoughts of a united, invincible Russia will be focused on this single national task." The tsar ordered Goremykin to summon the Duma back into session no later than August "so as to hear the voice of the Russian land."[50] A new kind of politics was beginning to emerge. In the midst of war, the forces of an incipient democracy and a decaying autocracy would now engage in a tragic final struggle.

Dzhunkovsky left Stavka before the session of the Council of Ministers. He visited the headquarters of the Northwestern Front, and returned on June 16. Learning that the tsar intended stay until the end of the month, Dzhun then went back to Petrograd to attend to business there. On June 22 he came again to Stavka where he remained until the twenty-seventh. Once more in the capital, he witnessed a series of political changes. On July 4 the tsar made Alexander Samarin procurator of the Holy Synod, and two days later Alexander Khvostov took over as minister of justice, replacing Shcheglovitov. Both appointments delighted Dzhun. Samarin, was a close personal friend, deeply religious, a loyal son of the church; they shared concerns about Rasputin. Dzhun knew Khvostov was a solid jurist who would uphold the law.[51]

But other aspects of the new politics had already disturbed him. On June 11, some nine hundred delegates assembled in Moscow for a conference to discuss the problem of rising prices. But they quickly put forward a much broader agenda. "The mood of the participants . . . was unquestionably patriotic," Dzhunkovsky recalled, "but at the same time it was hostile to the existing 'irresponsible government.'"[52] Pointing to the growing strike movement and the government's repressive measures,[53] one of the workers in attendance ominously proclaimed: "There are two wars going on now: one with a foreign enemy, the other with a domestic one. In a time of terrible suffering for our country the government can find nothing better to do than to wage a merciless, stubborn war against the workers." The conference ended with a call for unity in the national struggle, equal rights for all citizens, freedom for workers' organizations, and a government composed of people enjoying the trust of the nation. Dzhunkovsky followed the work of the conference closely and understood its importance. But he was not pleased: "The conference left a painful impression and made me ponder things seriously; it presaged nothing good."[54]

On July 19, the State Duma reconvened. The session began in the spirit of patriotism and national unity, as Prime Minister Goremykin's opening speech seemed to herald a new mood. The government, he stated, would now act "only in complete agreement with the opinions of the legislative institutions," words that elicited shouts of "Bravo." He called on all Russian citizens, regardless of race, language, or faith to unite. In Russia there was only one party, he proclaimed, "the party of war to the end." There was only one program: "Victory."[55]

Goremykin hoped that his words would unify parliament and the administration. But it soon was clear that a majority in the Duma favored a reconstitution of the government and the creation of a "Cabinet enjoying public confidence [*Kabinet obshchestvennogo doveriia*]." The first signs of what would become the "Progressive bloc" appeared. When it finally emerged in August, the bloc extended across the political spectrum, excluding only the extremes of Right and Left, backed by 235 of the 422 Duma deputies and significant elements in the State Council. It enjoyed the support of important civic institutions and public organizations and the growing network of War Industries Committees. While its program called for broad political and social reforms, the bloc was open to compromise with the government and found some backing within the Council of Ministers on the part of Krivoshein, Polivanov, Sazonov, and Shcherbatov. But it met stiff resistance from Nicholas, Alexandra, Goremykin, and forces on the Right.[56]

Despite a developing conflict between the government and the "progressives," there were some hopeful signs of cooperation. At the start of the session the Duma called for an investigation of the munitions shortages that had contributed to the disastrous defeats the army was suffering. The target was former War Minister Sukhomlinov, accused of criminal negligence in handling the task of supplying the war effort, mismanagement that some felt verged on treason. The Council of Ministers supported the Duma, and on July 29 Nicholas created "The Supreme Commission for the Complete Investigation of the Circumstances that Caused the Late and Insufficient Supplies of Munitions." Its membership included government officials and deputies from the Duma and State Council. With this began a long and ultimately inconclusive process that continued after the February revolution and ended in the first months of Soviet power. Sukhomlinov would be arrested, imprisoned, released, rearrested, condemned, and finally, amnestied.[57] But the immediate result of the investigation of the former minister of war was to undercut the prestige of the tsar and his government.

In July the government took an even more significant step. It proposed legislation that would create four Special Conferences: Defense, Fuel, Food Supply, and Transportation. Each headed by the appropriate minister, the conferences would include Duma deputies and representatives of public institutions: Zemgor and the War Industries Committees. Designated "state institutions of the highest order," they would have extensive powers in the areas assigned to them.[58] Within the space of a month this measure was discussed, amended, and passed by both houses. The emperor signed it on August 17, and on August 22, he opened the Conferences with a ceremony at the Winter Palace in the presence of Empress Alexandra, Tsarevich Aleksei, and the highest dignitaries of the state. Unfortunately, the positive symbolism of the event hid the tsar's determination to bring the Duma session to an end.[59]

Dzhunkovsky witnessed the political turmoil of June and July with concern. Yet he felt secure in his own position and was convinced that Nicholas had accepted his warnings about the "starets." The departure of Rasputin for his home in Siberia in mid-June seemed a clear sign of that, as did the solicitude the emperor displayed during the Stavka meeting. In July Dzhun left Petrograd to spend a week with the Evreinovs in Kursk apparently unaware that he had become a target of conservative forces, most notably Empress Alexandra. Shortly after his June 1 meeting with the emperor, news about his report on Rasputin had leaked. Dzhunkovsky was now increasingly vulnerable, and his enemies began working hard to bring him down.

Exactly when and how the word got out, what was divulged and by whom, remains unclear to this day. Although Dzhun maintained that his report had been for the tsar's eyes alone, some historians believe he broke his promise to Nicholas and was himself responsible for the leak.[60] But he need not have done this for the news to spread. Dzhunkovsky's antipathy to Rasputin was common knowledge, and a number of people were aware he was making a report to the tsar. Once others learned of this it was easy for them to surmise its contents, and rumors—not all of them reliable—would take wing. Alexander Samarin spoke about the report at the time he visited Stavka between June 19 and 21. There he told Dmitrii Sheremetev and Vladimir Orlov that he had learned from unnamed "informants" (*sobesedniki*) that after Dzhunkovsky's report on the activities of Rasputin the emperor gave it to Anna Vyrubova, a close confidante of the empress and an ardent Rasputin supporter, with the words: "take this, read it, just look at your idol!"[61] While this confrontation may not have taken place, the claim that it had indicates that others knew of Dzhun's report before Samarin and were speculating about its impact.

None of this should be surprising. Petrograd floated on rumor, gossip, and political intrigue; secrets seldom kept for long; good stories were readily embellished. Tales about Rasputin—allegations of corruption, lechery, pro-German sentiments, his supposed influence on the royal family—were swirling. Word of Rasputin's participation in a scandalous incident of some kind at the Yar restaurant had been tossed around almost as soon as it occurred and figured in the May riots in Moscow.

In the charged atmosphere of the crisis summer of 1915, word that Dzhunkovsky, a man with a reputation for honesty, had spoken to the tsar about Rasputin—even if the precise details of what he said were unknown—raised hopes in some quarters, fears in others. For those who desired Nicholas to cooperate with the Duma and the public, news of Dzhun's report was a positive sign that indicated a growing momentum for change. For those determined to maintain the sovereign's full prerogatives, an attack on Rasputin, no matter how loyal its motivation, was a act of subversion that had to be punished.

When Empress Alexandra either read the report or learned of its contents, she quickly went on the offensive. In a letter to Nicholas on June 22, she fiercely denounced her "enemy Dzhunk":

> Ah, dear, he is not an honest man, he has shown that vile, filthy paper (against our Friend) to Dmitri who repeated it to Paul and he to Alia. Such a sin & as tho' you had said to him, that you have had enough of these dirty stories & wish him to be severely punished. You see how he turns your words and orders around—the slanderers were to be punished & not he—& that at Headquarters one wants him to be got rid of (this I believe)—ah it is so vile—always liars, enemies—I long knew Dzh. hates Gr. & that the "Preobrazhensky" clique therefore dislikes me as through me & Ania he [Rasputin] comes to the house. In winter Dzh. showed this paper to Voeik. asking him to give it over to you & he refused doing anything so disgusting. . . . I am sorry to say these things, but they are bitter truth, & now Samarin added to the lot—no good can come of it.

The empress continued in the same slightly incoherent vein: "If we let our Friend be persecuted, we & our country shall suffer for it. . . . [S]uch a horror! Speak, please to Voeikov about it, I wish him to know Dzhunk.'s behaviour & false using of yr. words." Alexandra demanded her husband come down hard on her foe. "Ah my Love, when at last will you thump your hand upon the table and scream at Dzh. & others when they act wrongly?—one does not fear you—& one must—they must be frightened of you, otherwise all sit upon us." Nicholas should pull Dzhunkovsky up short: "If Dzh. is with you, call him, tell him you know (no names) he has shown that paper in town & that you order him to tear it up & not to dare speak of Gr. as he does & that he acts as a traitor & not as a devoted subject, who ought to stand up for the Friends of his Sovereign, as one does in every other country. Oh my Boy, make one tremble before you—to love you is not enough, one must be affraid [*sic*] of hurting, displeasing you!"[62]

It is by no means clear to what Alexandra was referring when she wrote about a "vile, filthy paper" that Dzhunkovsky had shown "in town," a paper that he had supposedly tried to get Voeikov, the court commandant, to pass on to Nicholas sometime "in winter." Was it the report he made in June? The timing of the report makes this unlikely. The Semenov document is, however, a much stronger candidate. It does not appear in the police archives but exists among Dzhunkovsky's own papers. He could have shown this to a few trusted individuals—Grand Dukes Pavel Alexandrovich and Dmitrii Pavlovich (but not Voeikov)[63]—without, in his own mind, violating his pledge to the emperor to keep the June 1 report strictly confidential. But Dzhunkovsky got the Semenov report only at the end of May, not "in winter."

Of course, it is entirely possible that the "paper" Alexandra wrote about did not exist as such. The empress certainly knew that rumors and writings about Rasputin had long circulated; many were "vile" and "filthy." When word that Dzhunkovsky had made a report about Rasputin to the tsar spread "in town," Alexandra may have conflated the two facts and assumed Dzhun was the author of the "paper" she referred to. The disjointed, almost hysterical tone of the empress's letter reveals a woman in a high state of agitation, even confusion, something understandable given the crisis atmosphere of the moment. With the war going badly, and loyal conservative ministers falling left and right, Alexandra feared for her husband and children. The prospect that Rasputin might be forced to remain in Siberia and so deprive her beloved son of the protection of their "Friend" was simply too terrible to contemplate. She had to fight, using all the means at her disposal.

We cannot say for certain how Nicholas reacted to Alexandra's diatribe, an outburst that may have caught him by surprise.[64] But we have good evidence that he always believed in Dzhunkovsky's personal honesty,

Empress Alexandra, ca. 1915. Hoover Institution Archive (HIA), Russian Pictorial Collection, envelope AI.

loyalty, and sound intelligence. Their extensive conversation at the time of the June Stavka meeting—after Dzhun had made his report on Rasputin—was a strong indication to that effect. Moreover, Dzhunkovsky was at Army Headquarters when the tsar would have received the empress's letter. But Nicholas did not call Dzhun in and voice his displeasure as she had demanded. Even more significant is the fact that although Alexandra's letters—the one of June 22 and many written afterward—continued to denounce Dzhunkovsky, the tsar never responded with a bad word about his wife's "enemy."

Alexandra pressed her attack on Dzhunkovsky, joined and encouraged by others. One of these was the shadowy "political adventurist" Prince Mikhail Andronnikov, a lover of intrigue, a collector of information, a spreader of rumors. Reputed to have a dissolute lifestyle and questionable finances, the prince was on the extreme right politically, a member of the Union of the Russian People. Over the years he had gained access to many important government officials, including Witte and Kokovtsov, but did not acquire their respect. Kokovtsov called him "a very bad lot" (*bol'shaia drian'*).[65] Andronnikov sought to ingratiate himself with Dzhunkovsky as well and in 1915 sent him an expensive, gold Easter egg. Dzhun felt that accepting such a lavish gift from "a well-known scoundrel" was entirely inappropriate and returned it to the sender, an act that produced hard feelings.[66]

Andronnikov had met Rasputin in 1914 and become part of his circle. He befriended Anna Vyrubova and through her opened a conduit to the empress. He had a strong personal dislike of the new Interior Minister Shcherbatov and had a replacement in mind: Aleksei Khvostov, the uncle of the minister of justice, a former governor, and currently a leading figure on the far Right in the State Duma. Andronnikov also proposed an appropriate successor for Dzhunkovsky: Stepan Beletsky. Long hostile to Dzhunkovsky's reforms, still smarting from his dismissal in 1914, the erstwhile director of the Department of Police was happy to join the ranks of his former chief's opponents.[67]

Alexandra undertook her own investigation of the Yar incident, commissioning a trusted adjutant, Nikolai Sablin, to go to Moscow and look into the matter. According to Dzhunkovsky, toward the end of July Sablin approached him, claiming that the empress had shown him the confidential report he had made to Nicholas. Sablin asked for the names of people who could verify it, assuring him that his aim was to "open the empress's eyes" about Rasputin, something he could do because he enjoyed her confidence. Naively, Dzhun complied. Sablin then interviewed Adrianov who had originally passed on the scandalous Semenov report in May. Now Adrianov had a score to settle. On June 4 Nicholas had removed him from his post as city commandant in response to Dzhun's report on the Moscow riots. Angry and eager to curry favor with Rasputin, Adrianov told Sablin that while the "starets" had been drunk at the Yar, the rest of the story was an "idle fantasy" concocted by Dzhunkovsky. Alexandra now had the "proof" she needed to press the case for his dismissal.[68]

By the beginning of August Dzhunkovsky was under attack from other quarters as well. Prince Iusupov and his wife, deeply offended by Dzhun's implied criticism of the prince's handling of the May riots, blamed him for Senator Krasheninnikov's inspection of Moscow.[69] They now joined with others in a campaign to show that the empire's security chief was "soft" on Germans and insufficiently firm against their "dominance." Dzhunkovsky knew that hostile rumors about him were circulating among right-wing deputies in the Duma, but he had not attempted to respond. Then he learned that on August 3, Aleksei Khvostov was scheduled to make a major speech on the subject of "German dominance," criticizing government policy in general and Dzhunkovsky's actions in particular.

Dzhun prepared his defense, believing that he would have the Council of Ministers behind him. But signals changed rapidly. First, Shcherbatov assured him that the entire cabinet would go to the Duma and respond to Khvostov's challenge. Then the minister informed him that the Council members had decided not to attend, and that he should not go either. Finally on August 3, minutes before the Duma was scheduled to begin that day's session, Shcherbatov called to tell Dzhunkovsky that he must appear at the Duma and, if necessary, reply to Khvostov's criticism. Hastily, he pulled his materials together and headed to the Tauride Palace. When he entered the box reserved for government representatives, he found that save for his private secretary and Brune he was alone.[70]

Khvostov began denouncing German influence in the economy—landownership, industry, and banking—then launched an attack on the intelligence agencies of the state. From the very first days of the war they failed to prevent outbreaks of violence of the kind that had occurred most recently in Moscow and had been ineffective in handling enemy aliens and people of German and Austrian extraction. Khvostov specifically blamed Dzhunkovsky who, he claimed, at the start of the war encouraged detained foreign subjects to apply immediately for Russian citizenship. Hundreds did so and many were quickly accepted. "And don't think that they just accepted old ladies, pensioners, and nannies," Khvostov continued. "Most of them were the owners of commercial companies or the employees of various banks." These Germans got protection from people in high places, especially Dzhunkovsky. In a gibe that drew general applause from the right and even from some in the center and left, Khvostov thundered: "And now, when every prominent person has one or two Germans on behalf of whom he petitions, Assistant Minister Dzhunkovsky petitions for ten."[71]

The protection that Germans enjoy, Khvostov continued, makes Russian workers seethe, while recent Russian military setbacks embolden the Germans. Russian defeats led many German and Austrian subjects who earlier petitioned for Russian citizenship to withdraw their applications, a claim that provoked shouts of "Shame!" in the chamber. The softness of officials like Dzhunkovsky, he continued, explained the wrath that the people expressed in the Moscow disturbances. Khvostov concluded on a populist note: "At the present moment we need a government that can deal with a German dominance within the country that insults us all; one that with regard to inflation will finally put the interests of the population higher than those of the banking circles; one that will cease to be guilty in the eyes of the people; only then can it command and the people follow."

After a brief recess Dzhunkovsky rose to answer Khvostov. He cited in detail ministerial orders and the decisions of the Council of Ministers that governed the treatment of enemy aliens during the war. He stoutly defended the MVD's response to the Moscow riots, noting the failure of local authorities to inform officials in the capital of the developing crisis with the proper dispatch, and calling attention to the dismissal of Adrianov in its wake. He reminded the deputies that the riots were still being extensively investigated by means of a Senatorial inspection. Dzhunkovsky dismissed accusations that he was in some way pro-German. All who knew him, even in the slightest, whether as governor of Moscow or in his present position must realize that the charge of Germanophilia was unfounded. "I believe," he continued, "that these attacks stem from the fact that it is my custom on the days I hold receptions to receive all who come to me. On these reception days I also receive subjects from enemy countries, accept their petitions, which I review attentively and examine thoroughly. I believe that this approach is the only one worthy of Russia, and I will continue this way in the future." Dzhun denied that he was exempting able-bodied enemy aliens residing in Moscow from deportation to other areas after Prince Iusupov had issued orders to that effect. When he ended his speech by citing the six cases of what he felt were justified exceptions, deputies responded: "Correct, of course, correct."

Dzhunkovsky returned from the Duma exhausted by his ordeal, fearing a similar attack when he appeared the next day before the State Council. To his surprise, he met a friendly reception, with especially strong support from the distinguished jurist Anatolii Koni.[72] For the moment Dzhun may have felt he was out of the woods. Beginning August 5, he traveled on business to Moscow, Stavka, Vilna, and Riga, returning to the capital on August 14. But his days in office had already been numbered. In late July the emperor quietly sounded out Shcherbatov about replacing Dzhun with Stepan Beletsky.[73] News of his impending fall reached distant Siberia by August 9. That morning, recovering from a drunken binge at his home in the village of Pokrovskoe, Rasputin announced to the police agents keeping watch on him: "Dzhunkovsky will be dismissed from service, and he maybe will think that they fired him because of me, but I don't know who he is [*ia ne znaiu kto takoi*]."[74]

For Dzhun, however, the blow came with shocking suddenness. On August 15, the day after he got back to Petrograd, Shcherbatov called him to his dacha on Aptekersky Island. There, appearing somewhat embarrassed, he handed his assistant minister a brief, handwritten command just received from the tsar: "I insist on the immediate removal of Dzhunkovsky from office; he is to remain in the Suite. Nicholas."[75]

Part Five

Dzhunkovsky's War, 1915–1918

Chapter 16

Finding Peace in War

IN STUNNED DISBELIEF DZHUNKOVSKY READ, THEN REREAD the brief message Shcherbatov handed him. He knew that his position was becoming precarious, "but," he recalled, "I never expected this finale." The cruel brevity of the order shocked him. The words: "I insist on the removal" seemed strange. "It became clear to me," he wrote years later, "that the tsar had been influenced . . . , obviously the note had been dictated to him by the empress. It could not have been otherwise."[1]

He said nothing of this to Shcherbatov but asked only to be freed from the duties of assistant minister while continuing to serve as commander of the Corps of Gendarmes until publication of the official decree relieving him. He then offered the minister his final report which, among other things, warned about the radical Duma deputy Alexander Kerensky whose activities were "harmful and dangerous for the dynasty and for Russia itself." The current situation justified taking serious measures, including arrest, to block Kerensky's revolutionary efforts.[2] But he recommended that, before acting, the ministers of justice and war should examine carefully the possible repercussions. Shcherbatov accepted the report and expressed his sympathies, adding that he believed he would not long remain as the head of the MVD.[3]

As Dzhunkovsky drove home he felt a growing sense of relief. He could set down the heavy burdens of office, escape the political intrigues of the capital he felt ill equipped to fight, and perhaps go on active duty in the army.[4] But the hurt caused by his abrupt dismissal was not easily put aside. Shortly after the event—before it had become public knowledge—Petr Stremoukhov, his classmate at the Corps of Pages, was dining at the Petrograd English Club when Dzhun came in, briefly whispered something to Alexander Bulygin, the former minister of internal affairs, and then sat down at a distant table. Later, Stremoukhov saw the two men animatedly talking in an obscure corner of the club. After their conversation ended and Dzhunkovsky started to leave, Stremoukhov approached and asked what was going on. "They sacked me," Dzhun replied abruptly. "Why? What's it all about?" Stremoukhov stammered. "Ask Alexander Grigorievich, I'm in a hurry," he responded and dashed away.[5]

Dzhunkovsky's sorrow and confusion were both evident in the anguished letter he wrote to the emperor the day after his dismissal, the shattering end of his government career:

> Your Imperial Highness. With profound pain I read yesterday your harsh judgment. . . . To be removed from office, without the opportunity to resign is, of course, hard to bear, made all the more so because Russia is experiencing such a difficult time. But harder still, is that I have no idea what I have done wrong so that I cannot say a word in my defense; that I do not know what act on my part suddenly destroyed the trust of Your Majesty that I always enjoyed during my many years of service, something of which I was so proud and which lightened the difficult moments I had to live through in the course of my duties.
>
> It is hard for me to write; forgive me if I write disjointedly. I leave and surrender both my offices with the sense that I have fulfilled my duties. My conscience is clear; I have never pursued personal interests, but have always striven to do all that I could for the benefit of Your Majesty and of our great country. This is why not knowing what I did wrong is so hard to bear. Your Imperial Majesty wrote to Prince Shcherbatov of removing me from office but retaining me in Your Suite. . . . I know . . . that you do this solely out of the goodness of your heart; it cannot be pleasant to Your Majesty to have in Your Suite someone in whom you have lost confidence, and for me it is very hard to remain in the Suite knowing that I no longer have your trust. How will I feel among my comrades in the Suite? It will be torture. Do not increase, Your Majesty, my emotional pain; I know that in my long years of service I have been of some use, otherwise Your Majesty would not have honored me so much, especially in these last years.

> Permit me to retire, even though it is in time of war. Please, Your Majesty, believe me it will be better and easier for You and me. When I have recovered to a degree from what has happened, and my health improves, let me return to service in the front lines of our army in the field—grant me this great kindness.
>
> Your Majesty, please forgive my frank letter. Believe me, Sovereign, that although I leave the service in accordance with Your august will, Your Majesty will always have in me the same loyal subject as before.

Dzhunkovsky's letter was less than perfectly candid. He sensed that his report on Rasputin was at the heart of the matter, but he was unwilling to provoke Nicholas further by raising the issue. At Dzhun's request, Shcherbatov delivered his letter to the tsar who responded with a laconic resolution: "Retain in the Suite; active service in the army granted."[6]

Dzhunkovsky's belief that Nicholas dismissed him in response to Alexandra's angry and fearful defense of the imperial family's "friend" was undoubtedly correct. But the tsar also made his decision under the pressure of the military and political crisis of 1915. Since late May, defeats, panic at Stavka, the restiveness of his own ministers, and the growing assertiveness of the public backed him into a corner. First he responded by making unpleasant concessions, dismissing trusted conservatives Maklakov, Shcheglovitov, Sukhomlinov, and Sabler, summoning the Duma, and permitting broader participation of voluntary organizations in the war effort. Yet these failed to stabilize the situation and seemed to energize the opposition. Appalled, the empress and political conservatives demanded that the tsar push back, lest his autocratic powers be further diminished and the empire endangered.

By the end of July Nicholas had decided on a fateful step: to dismiss Nikolai Nikolaevich and take personal command of the Russian armies, now in full retreat. This decision—roundly criticized by contemporaries, Dzhunkovsky included—has been seen as an act of folly that set the monarchy on the glide-path to oblivion. But Dominic Lieven, one of Nicholas's most perceptive biographers, considers the tsar's move both "courageous" and "correct." The grand duke and Ianushkevich, his chief of staff, had proved poor commanders. The war effort suffered from a lack of coordination between the military and civilian authorities. The tsar's assumption of supreme command could possibly eliminate this. And, of course, Nicholas had no intention of directing military operations himself; the competent General M. V. Alekseev would serve as the new chief of staff. To make all this work, however, Nicholas needed to be able to leave in Petrograd a cabinet united in his support, able to work with the Duma and the various nongovernmental organizations. Instead, he had to face near total opposition in government and political circles.[7]

When War Minister Polivanov informed the Council of Ministers of the tsar's intention at the session of August 6, the news produced universal consternation. Arkadii Iakhontov, the Council's secretary, described the scene: "The revelation . . . evoked the greatest excitement. . . . Everyone spoke at once, and there was such a cross fire of conversation that it was impossible to catch individual statements. One could see that the majority was shaken by the news they had heard—the latest stunning blow in the midst of the military misfortunes and internal complications which were being suffered."[8] In the weeks that followed, the ministers, joined by Duma leaders, made repeated efforts to get the tsar to change his mind. But Nicholas's resolve remained firm. In September he prorogued the Duma, and his distrust of the ministers who had opposed him grew. Within the space of a year, he replaced almost all of them. The result undercut the original purpose of the tsar's decision, however "courageous" and "correct" it may have been. While at Stavka Nicholas did little to improve coordination of civil and military authorities. Instead, he became isolated from the regular processes of government, increasingly reliant on his wife and a small conservative clique.

These political developments cast a somewhat different light on the emperor's decision to remove Dzhunkovsky from office while keeping him in the Suite. For Nicholas, Dzhun's hostility to Rasputin or even the charge—never proved—that he had betrayed his trust by leaking his report may not have been the chief issue. Rather, it was the tsar's unwillingness to go to Stavka leaving behind ministers who opposed him and a security chief the empress disliked and feared. Dzhun was also unpopular with conservatives and had been attacked by Aleksei Khvostov, the right-wing Duma member already being considered as Shcherbatov's replacement. The harsh order firing Dzhun was intended to satisfy Alexandra's wrath, but retention in the Suite signified Nicholas's continuing regard and gave a measure of protection to the man he had just cast down. Even in disgrace, a *svitii general* could not be treated lightly. Of course, the tsar might have been applying the maxim ascribed to the fictional Vito Corleone: "Keep your friends close, your enemies closer."[9] But Nicholas would be ill cast as a Mafia don and, as future events will show, he never saw Dzhunkovsky as an "enemy."

Following his sudden dismissal, Dzhunkovsky struggled to get his bearings. His sister quickly found a new apartment on Kamenoostrovsky Prospect and he began transferring his papers and belongings there. He wanted to remain in service and go on duty with the army in the field, but this would mean loss of the eight-thousand-ruble pension he was entitled to as a retired commander of the Corps of Gendarmes. His friends did not desert him, however. War Minister Polivanov and Finance Minister Petr Bark petitioned the emperor who, in another sign of favor, issued a special order guaranteeing that Dzhun could receive that pension no matter when and from what position he might later retire.[10]

Dzhunkovsky's firing spawned various responses, rumors, and expectations. Condolences from family and friends poured in. Alexander Protopopov, the Octobrist vice-president of the Duma came by and left a card saying that he expressed the sympathies of more than two hundred members of the parliament. They had all wished to come personally but feared that this might be considered a "demonstration."[11] At the Council of Ministers meeting on August 18, Dzhunkovsky's removal was seen as one more sign of governmental disarray. "The dismissal of General Dzhunkovsky is a fact," the Council's secretary Iakhontov wrote. "The impression it made on the public is a great one, because of the rumor which has spread that this dismissal was the consequence of an attempt to struggle with the 'influences.'" Others drew different conclusions. For Minister of Agriculture Krivoshein, Dzhunkovsky's departure was "an enormous scandal"; but he incorrectly assumed that it was voluntary and faulted Dzhun for leaving his post in wartime to make a political protest. "If the statesmen who possess [public] sympathy are going to run away," he lamented, "then with whom is the government . . . going to be left?"[12]

Alexander Guchkov, the leading figure in the War Industries Committees, saw a chance to gain an ally in the struggle against the government's current direction. One of the founders of the Octobrist Party who had guided it in the first three Dumas, Guchkov had broken with his party and moved away from his strong support of the monarchy and the existing political system. Even before the war he had lost faith in the permanence of the autocracy and in the ability of the Duma to carry out needed reforms. Now Russian defeats, munitions shortages, growing labor unrest, the influence of Rasputin, the intransigence of Nicholas, Alexandra, and the conservative clique, all pushed Guchkov in a more radical direction. He had begun to contemplate measures to remove the emperor and the existing government, replacing them with men able to save the state and lead Russia to victory.[13] In that spirit, he addressed Dzhun in an impassioned appeal, dated August 17:

> Dear Vladimir Fedorovich,
>
> I am with you with all my heart. I know what you are living through. But do not lament, be joyful. You have been freed from prison. You see that "they" are doomed; no one can save them. Petr Arkadevich tried to save them. You know how they repaid him. I have tried to save them; but I failed. You tried to do it, but you have failed. But it is Russia that needs to be saved. And she will not dismiss you. She needs people such as you. Serve her.[14]

The prospect of joining the political opposition held no attraction for Dzhunkovsky. He could not turn against the tsar. On August 19 he replied to Guchkov, thanking him for his sympathy and concern but firmly rejecting his proposal: "You know me well; you know my ideals and my service. No matter what becomes of me, no matter what happens, whatever misfortunes may befall me, I cannot betray those ideals and the pledge with which I began my service to the Monarch and to Russia."[15] That same day Dzhun left Petrograd on a brief trip to Kursk to tell Nina and her family what had happened and of his intention to go to the front. He returned to the capital on August 23 and continued winding up his affairs.[16]

In early September Dzhunkovsky journeyed to Stavka to speak with General Alekseev about an assignment at the front. Alekseev counseled him to avoid service in the Guards in favor of regular army units, especially the Siberian divisions, where he would find the opportunity to study military operations more quickly and with greater seriousness. Service there would be colorless but more practical and in line with Dzhunkovsky's character. It would take him far from the spotlight and political intrigues to a post that would not arouse envy.[17]

Alekseev's advice confirmed Dzhunkovsky's determination to avoid anything that smacked of a protest against his dismissal. In the army's ranks he could find both the opportunity to serve his country and—almost as important—obscurity. But others kept pushing him toward the limelight. In late September he traveled to Moscow to participate in the noble assembly where his name was put in nomination as a candidate for the State Council. Although moved by his fellow nobles' expression of respect and sympathy, Dzhun feared that his election might be seen as a demonstration against the tsar that could cast the Moscow *dvorianstvo* into disfavor. He sought to decline, telling the assembly that his impending departure for the front made service in the State Council impossible. Their kindness touched him deeply, Dzhun continued, and would always inspire him: "On the field of battle I will strive to be worthy of the high honor the Moscow nobility has bestowed upon me." But as he spoke, shouts of "*Prosim, prosim* [Please, please]" erupted from the delegates. He agreed to let his candidacy stand and applause rocked the hall. By a vote of 172 to 24 Dzhunkovsky was chosen an elector (*vyborshchik*) from the Moscow nobility. A month later, on October 23 he took part in the national conference of electors from the *dvorianstvo*, which would choose delegates to the Council. Here he might have been elected to a nine-year term that would have run until 1924. But determined to put politics behind him, he withdrew his name from consideration.[18]

Following the events in Moscow, Dzhun traveled to Kislovodsk in the Caucasus to take the waters and enjoy much needed rest before his departure to the front. He visited his brother, Nikolai, whose ill health was of great concern. As it turned out, the brothers were seeing each other for the last time. Kolya died just before Christmas in 1916 while Dzhunkovsky was still on active duty. Dzhun also went to the headquarters of Grand Duke Nikolai Nikolaevich, now in charge of the struggle against the Turks. The grand duke encouraged him to serve under his command as Ataman of the Terek Cossack forces. But Dzhun declined, determined to fight in the main theater against the Germans and undoubtedly concerned that close association with the grand duke might be seen in Petrograd as a gesture directed against the tsar.[19]

Dzhunkovsky's fears were well founded. His enemies were following his actions closely, ascribing sinister motives to them. Alexandra inveighed against him in letters to her husband, warning him to make sure that appointments to high positions did not "go Dzhunk.———."[20] Learning of Dzhunkovsky's intention to visit the Caucasus, she saw the danger of a plot together with Nikolai Nikolaevich: "birds of a feather flock together," she fretted, "what new sin are they preparing?"[21] The empress continually pointed to her "enemy Dzhunk." as the source of scurrilous reports about "our Friend";[22] he was "utterly false,"[23] a "dangerous man pretending to be a martyr."[24] She was indignant about the possibility that Dzhunkovsky might receive an appointment to one of the Guards regiments: "too much honour after his vile behaviour—it spoils the effect of the punishment."[25] The tsar passed over her attacks with a silence that speaks volumes.

Dzhunkovsky's foes in the Union of the Russian People and the Union of the Archangel Michael also rejoiced at the dismissal of a man they considered a renegade, "Kadet-leaning" (*kadetstvuiushchii*) administrator. But they feared he might make a political comeback, and they rushed to blacken his name. In the autumn of 1915 the right-wing journalist Nikolai Tikhmenev published a small book, *General Dzhunkovsky in Retirement.* It portrayed Dzhun as a duplicitous figure who rose as the result of conservative connections but after 1905 had turned his coat, seeking acclaim and popularity by adopting liberal poses. Dzhunkovsky came by his double-dealing naturally, Tikhmenev claimed; it was a family tradition. Pointing to the career of Dzhun's long-dead uncle Stepan Stepanovich and the strange spiritual odyssey that took him from Orthodoxy to Roman Catholicism to Anglicanism and back to Orthodoxy, Tikhmenev implied that the Dzhunkovskys carried a traitorous gene. Vladimir Fedorovich's first breach of faith occurred in 1905, when he released political prisoners from the Moscow jails, and continued during the years that followed.

Tikhmenev drew up a long list of Dzhunkovsky's failings in the present war. He had ignored the dangers of "German power," was soft on enemy aliens, and insufficiently vigilant in the struggle against espionage. He weakened the secret police, had been slow to pick up on the Miasoedov affair, and failed to head off the Moscow riots. He hindered Prince Iusupov's efforts to harness popular discontent and was caught flat-footed when the pogrom broke out. Tikhmenev charged that, after his dismissal, Dzhunkovsky sought to enhance his popularity by speaking at a closed session of the Moscow nobility falsely claiming to be a fighter for truth brought down by intrigues. But, Tikhmenev concluded, Dzhunkovsky had only himself to blame. His negative qualities and mistakes made him a "luxury" that Russia could no longer afford. Ironically, the one "sin" of Dzhunkovsky that Tikhmenev failed to mention was his opposition to

Rasputin. At the time, the name of the "starets" could not be broached in the press.[26]

Dzhun was well aware of the rumors and charges swirling around him, and he followed with growing concern the swift change of ministers that occurred in September—the removal of Shcherbatov and Samarin, the appointment of Aleksei Khvostov to head the MVD, and worst of all, Beletsky's triumphant assumption of the post Dzhun had recently held. A sense that things were running out of control alarmed him. He read Vasilii Maklakov's famous article "A Tragic Situation," which depicted the country as a car careening along a dangerous road driven by an incompetent, possibly mad, chauffeur, the passengers frozen with fear, unwilling to risk seizing control of the vehicle. In his memoirs Dzhun reproduced the document without comment. But were any words necessary?[27]

As the domestic conflict escalated Dzhunkovsky prepared for the front. He acquired a fine saddle horse, a pair of excellent pack animals, and a two-wheeled carriage. He would transport these, and his personal belongings, in a suite of three railway cars: one for him and his effects, the second for the horses, feed, and baggage, the third a flatcar for the equipage. With these bare necessities gathered, Dzhunkovsky left Petrograd on October 31; only a small group of family and friends saw him off. Parting was hard, but Dzhunkovsky felt at peace: "My heart was calm, even joyful, in the knowledge that I was going where the fate of Russia would be decided; that to me had fallen the happiness of sharing the work of battle with all those defending the Motherland."[28] Now he could escape the politics and the intrigue and cast himself on the winds of war, let go and let God.

The army that Dzhunkovsky left Petrograd to join had just passed through the deep shadows of the "Great Retreat." The enemy had conquered Poland with its factories and mines, erased the Russian's hard-won gains in Galicia, seized fortresses holding vast quantities of vital supplies and equipment, killed or captured thousands of soldiers. The morale of the troops sagged dangerously and near panic seized Stavka and the capital. In early August Minister of War Polivanov had pronounced to the Council of Ministers in hysterical tones: "The army is no longer retreating—it is simply running away."[29] To some it seemed likely that the enemy would take Kiev, "the mother of Russian cities."

By the end of September, however, it was clear that summer's despair, gloom, and panic were overblown. Russia's armies had accomplished their retreat in remarkably good order, winning admiration from their German foe for their "brilliant conduct." Fears that Kiev might fall proved groundless. Although the Germans had advanced into Lithuania and White Russia, the front stabilized and the Russians undertook a few brief counterattacks.[30] Russian forces had pulled back a long way, but when seen in historical perspective their withdrawal was not disastrous. In 1812 Napoleon beat the Russians just outside Moscow and occupied the city; and as bad as the defeats of 1915 were, they pale beside those that would be inflicted by the Germans in 1941. The "Great Retreat" shortened the front considerably, making defense easier, and by year's end the Russians began to overcome the shortage of rifles, cartridges, and artillery shells that had bedeviled them since the start of the conflict. In 1916 the morale of the troops rose and Stavka could contemplate a new offensive.

Dzhunkovsky's memoirs do not suggest that he fully grasped Russia's strategic position. He was simply eager to join the fight and to leave the poisonous atmosphere of the capital behind. His goal was Minsk and the headquarters of General Evert, now the commander of the newly formed Western Front.[31] Still, he carried with him something of the Petrograd penumbra, and along his route leading local officials came out to greet him. At Vitebsk he met Governor Artsimovich and the head of the provincial gendarmes, and at the Orsha station he found Mogilev governor Alexander Pilts and Vladimir Nikolsky, his former chief of staff at the Corps of Gendarmes, standing on the platform. At Minsk the next morning, Governor Aleksei Girs escorted him to his meeting with General Evert.[32]

Dzhun got a friendly reception at Evert's HQ. News of his fall had reached the front: "They had all heard rumors about the reason for my disgrace, and this enhanced my reputation in their eyes."[33] The elderly General Evert could not say offhand where there were free brigades, but he urged him to find a command as soon as possible. Dzhun, who had never led men on the battlefield, was taken aback. He confessed that he lacked the necessary experience, but Evert cavalierly brushed this objection aside. "He told me that all [these concerns] were small beer, that I had lived a lot and could always orient myself . . . and quickly get accustomed to the situation." Dzhun fumbled about trying to find a place where he might serve and at last was convinced to take a post in the 8th Siberian Rifle Division of the Tenth Army's III Siberian Corps. Its commander was a "serious fighting general" who knew his division thoroughly. Under his guidance Dzhun could learn a great deal. Better still from Dzhunkovsky's perspective, a position as a brigade commander there would not open up for at least a month, time enough, he hoped, to get the hang of things.[34]

Dzhunkovsky then presented himself at the headquarters of the Tenth Army where he met its CO, the stern, experienced General Evgenii Radkevich, who months before had led the III Siberian Corps during its heroic defense of Lyck and the fighting escape from German encirclement at the Augustowo Forest during the winter battles in Masuria.[35] If Radkevich had misgivings about the untried Dzhunkovsky, still smelling of the capital, he did not voice them. He issued orders assigning Dzhun to the 8th Siberian Rifle Division and gave him a detailed, secret map that displayed the disposition of all the Corps's units. Dzhunkovsky returned to his railroad car, slept soundly, and awoke the next morning in Molodechno. There he had his cars attached to a troop train and around midday arrived at the railhead in Prudy, about three miles from the HQ of the III Siberian Corps.

Eager to get to his new post, Dzhunkovsky saddled up and headed out—into misadventure. He was unfamiliar with his mount, having ridden her only once at the Moscow Manège; the horse knew only city streets and shied at every puddle, bush, rock, and fence. Her jitters made progress difficult. Although before leaving he consulted the map he had been given, Dzhun got lost and wound up in a swamp. To reorient himself, he reached into his pocket for the linen packet that held the map; it was gone! A wave of panic swept over him. In enemy hands the map could bring disaster. How had this happened? He had no idea.

Dzhun dismounted and began to lead his horse back the way he had come, looking to every side along the road. Nothing. How, he wondered, could he present himself to the commanders of the Corps and the division? He had lost the secret map! But to conceal this fact would be an even worse crime. For two hours he searched fruitlessly as dusk began to gather. Finally, all hope abandoned, he decided to return to Prudy.

Dzhun rode slowly, lost in the darkest thoughts. Then, suddenly, as he approached a small village, he saw it—the missing packet lying in the road. He rushed to pick it up—the map was intact! Joy, relief, and a silent

Te Deum, thanking God for his mercy. Exhausted, Dzhun finally reached his sleeping car. It was already night. Headquarters would have to wait until morning.[36]

He awoke to a violent snowstorm but, rejecting further delay, pressed ahead through the blizzard to Corps headquarters. There he dined with its commander, General Trofimov, and proceeded to 8th Division HQ at Kaskevichi accompanied by a convoy of two Cossacks. The division's CO was not present, but his assistant, General Romanov, received Dzhunkovsky and helped him get settled. Romanov warned him that headquarters lay only a few miles from the front lines, well within the range of the German guns that frequently shelled Russian positions. But Dzhun slumbered undisturbed.[37]

Dzhun hastened to orient himself and learn about his unit. On November 7, three days after his arrival at division headquarters, General Romanov gave him a partial tour of the division's positions and they inspected several regiments standing in reserve. Dzhunkovsky took in everything eagerly; it was all new and unfamiliar. Immediately he focused on the condition of the men, struck by their ragged uniforms, a stark contrast to the sharply dressed Guards regiments he had seen in the rear. He questioned Romanov about this and received a disheartened response: "What's to be done when the quartermaster still hasn't given out overcoats." Dzhun met regimental officers with feelings of respect that bordered on awe. "Most of them were Siberians," he remembered, "many had fought in every kind of battle, many had been wounded and had returned to the ranks." These veterans gazed on Dzhunkovsky, his uniform bearing the distinctive insignia of the Imperial Suite, like seasoned cowpokes inspecting a dude from the east, and he immediately sensed their amused contempt. "They looked at me quizzically, . . . [O]bviously they all were thinking: 'Why has he come here, to our dismal circumstances? What will he do here? He's probably not even going to come and look at our trenches.'" Dzhunkovsky had governed one of the empire's most important provinces and had managed the state's internal security institutions; he had exercised great power and knew how to command men. Yet he was genuinely intimidated by these "modest grey heroes." At the same time, however, he was determined to immerse himself in their world, to become part of "this drab but selflessly courageous mass." The next day Dzhun attended religious services at the front and was deeply moved: "The men prayed so well." Again he was shocked by the tattered, catch-as-catch-can dress of the troops, some of their boots wrapped in rags; but the men's spirit impressed him even more. "They looked to be hearty and in good mood," he recalled, "and to my greeting . . . they replied as one man. Their loud: *'Zdravia zhelaem!'* [We wish you good health] . . . echoed through the forest."[38]

Dzhunkovsky rushed to learn all he could about the division, so that after a week he felt he was no longer a complete greenhorn and was ready to present himself to his commanding officer, General Aleksei Efimovich Redko, who returned to the division on November 14. The gruff, combat-hardened Redko was clearly displeased with his new officer. "He looked at me like an empty place," Dzhunkovsky recalled, "and without a word extended his hand." Dzhun was braced for this. "I knew that in his eyes a general of the Suite and, what is more, a [former] assistant minister from Petrograd, was a good-for-nothing big-shot, someone who would not want to get his hands dirty, the kind of person that a man of [Redko's] character could not stand." But Dzhun refused to be put off and spoke to his CO as soon as possible. He told Redko about his past and explained how he had come to the front. He made it clear that he had no intention of just sitting idle and asked that Redko assign him any task, no matter how seemingly menial or undignified, the harder the better. Dzhunkovsky recalled that as Redko listened his expression began to change and when, at length, he spoke, his tone had warmed. "So this means you want to work? I thought that you'd come to the front to get a few medals and do nothing. If this is so, then I'll put you in harness straight away; but you probably don't know anything. Do you even know how the division is positioned?" Dzhunkovsky replied that he did, and Redko gave him a thorough exam, pleasantly surprised by the extent of his new subordinate's quickly acquired knowledge. Redko then sent him to inspect the trenches occupied by the 32nd Regiment and to study the disposition of the reserves. Dzhun spent an arduous morning and early afternoon on his tour and returned to give his CO a full report. Redko was impressed by Dzhun's observations, especially his attention to the weaknesses of the regiment's position and accepted his proposals for strengthening it. Redko put aside his reservations, and a bond between the two men began to form. Dzhunkovsky's regard for his chief increased by the day. Redko was "a soldier, head to toe, brave, tireless, hearty." Although severe, almost rude, possessed of an explosive temper, and very demanding, he truly cared about his troops and was determined to see that they got what they needed. Redko valued honesty and expected this quality in his subordinates, but he made an exception when dealing with the Quartermaster Corps. He said that any officer who failed to inflate his supply requests would leave his troops ill clad and hungry. Dzhunkovsky especially liked the fact that Redko was not a "telephone commander" but always in the field near the front, visiting the trenches at least twice a week, living full-time with his division.[39] In this rough-cut Siberian, he sensed he had found a man who could teach him the craft of war.

As Dzhun adjusted to life at the front, his confidence grew. He was pleased when, briefly under fire for the first time, he did not "bow to the bullets," although he admitted tensing up considerably. Later, while inspecting the trenches of a regiment stationed about three hundred paces from the enemy, he displayed foolhardy bravado. As he passed between platoons on an exposed stretch of ground, bullets whizzed by, but he recalled an almost "sporting exhilaration." "I deliberately slowed my steps and even stopped, addressing superfluous questions to the company commander and officers. It was needless braggadocio; I wanted to show off my sang-froid." But when he reached the relative safety of the covered trenches, Dzhun said a silent prayer of thanks for having escaped unharmed.[40]

Increasingly important duties came his way. In late November Redko assigned Dzhunkovsky the task of inspecting the provisioning and feeding of the division. He attended to the matter with characteristic attention to detail and produced a substantial report. As he had done during his days at the Moscow Guardianship, Dzhun made sure to sample what the men got to eat. Of one company mess, he complained that the food lacked sufficient fat and was tasteless, something certain to have ill effects on the health of the soldiers. He blamed the quartermaster for shortchanging the troops, and his report provided a comprehensive list of the necessary food that the regiments had ordered but failed to get. Redko also called on Dzhun to oversee the training of regimental noncoms. This was a particularly arduous duty that took him all over the territory of the division, working extremely long hours. But he gained an enormous fund of knowledge about the men, their abilities and conditions.

Dzhunkovsky watched as the division received a detachment of reinforcements from Siberia. They were a marked contrast to the troops recently sent up from other parts of the empire. Those had often been unlettered and poorly trained, conscripted factory workers who were hostile and had a negative influence in the ranks. The Siberians, on the other hand, were literate, lively, sharp, and ready for action. Dzhun accompanied Redko as he talked to them, impressed by the way the general's simple, direct language established an instant rapport and left a lasting impression. In all, Dzhunkovsky's first weeks at the front gave him a crash course in soldiering, and he proved a quick study. His modest demeanor, "people skills" honed in the Guardianship and as governor, combined with his visible competence, won him the respect of his fellow officers and the CO. By early December, when General Redko left his post for a few days, Dzhunkovsky could take command, convinced that he was fully up to speed on the affairs of the division. Later in the month, he assumed command again, this time for five weeks, when Redko temporarily replaced General Trofimov as CO of the III Siberian Corps.[41]

Dzhunkovsky began his first extended period at the head of the division feeling that he enjoyed the support of the officers and men. The front was quiet, no major attacks were expected, and Dzhun focused on strengthening the division's fortifications. But almost at once, supply difficulties surfaced. First, the division failed to receive its expected shipments of bread from Minsk, the troops were reduced to eating hardtack, and complaints flew. Dzhun relentlessly pressured the quartermaster: "I sent out dispatches, each one more threatening that the last, laying it on thick." Then there was a problem with meat, which began to arrive frozen and unflayed. Much time was needed to thaw it and remove the hide; the process produced waste that sickened some of the men. An angry howl arose from the regiments.

Dzhun summoned his supply officer and ordered him to send a dispatch to the Corps's quartermaster stating that the division would not accept meat from which the skin had not been cleaned. The man blanched and begged off; if he signed such a dispatch, he was sure his superior would eat him alive. Dzhun sent the message himself and then forbade the head of the division commissary to accept any meat with the hide still on it. If necessary, the division would buy its own or feed the men with canned goods. When the Corps's quartermaster sent one more shipment of unskinned carcasses, the division refused it; thereafter the meat arrived properly flayed.[42]

During his five-week stint as chief of the 8th Division, Dzhunkovsky got his first battlefield assignment, one that taught him a lesson in military politics as well. On December 20 he received orders to undertake a reconnaissance in force of the enemy's lines two days hence to determine the disposition of his troops and capture as many prisoners as possible. After consulting with field commanders, Dzhun devised a plan for a small, irregular operation to begin at midnight and employ 150 men camouflaged with white capes. The Germans would be diverted by artillery and infantry actions, enabling a surprise assault that, he believed, would net many prisoners. Corps HQ vetoed this idea, however, opting for a larger operation requiring no less than two battalions, starting at eight o'clock in the evening. Dzhunkovsky thought that this much more conventional attack, launched at a time when the enemy was certain to be on alert, was likely to have poor results. He raised his objections with Corps Command, but they were dismissed. He carried out the maneuver as ordered, and while the losses were smaller than he anticipated (six killed and forty wounded), he felt that the intelligence gathered was disappointing.

Later Dzhunkovsky found out why his modest plan had been rejected. The tsar was touring the front, and Tenth Army Command wanted to show that although things were quiet, Russian forces were not asleep. Larger operations would make a bigger and better impression on the sovereign. This news caused Dzhun to worry: the efforts of the 8th Division enjoyed only limited success; had his leadership been insufficiently energetic? To his surprise, however, he learned that the performance of other divisions conducting similar missions had been worse and that General Evert had commented favorably on his accomplishments.

Still, the whole business left a bad taste in Dzhunkovsky's mouth. Undertaking military operations simply to please the emperor revealed a pernicious consequence of Nicholas's decision to take command of the armies. "A reluctance to contradict, [even] when circumstances demanded it," he wrote years later, "fear of speaking the truth and the desire to present everything in a rosy light . . . [now] became a distinctive feature not only of courtiers but also of generals in the field."[43]

After two months at the front Dzhunkovsky had found his piece of the war and a measure of personal peace as well. He was now accepted as a full-fledged member of the III Siberian Corps. On the last day of 1915, a delegation from Moscow met him, still temporarily commanding the 8th Division. S. V. Puchkov, a member of the group, described the encounter in an article published in the newspaper *Russkoe slovo*. Dzhun was delighted that "dear Muscovites" had come to visit his division's position. He saw it as a good omen. Later, during a dinner in honor of the visitors at which General Redko was present, Puchkov offered a toast to Dzhunkovsky as "one of our own, a much loved Muscovite." But Redko immediately objected: "Dzhunkovsky," he said, "was now a Siberian, he had been reborn in the Siberian regiments, and they 'would never give him up.'"[44]

Dzhunkovsky obviously took pride in his Siberian "adoption." Immersion in their gray ranks also helped him to get past the humiliation of the tsar's abrupt dismissal; he hoped that the intrigues of the capital lay behind him. But in early February, Konstantin Androsov, who had worked under him during his governorship, wrote proposing to send a special medical detachment named in honor of Grand Duchess Elizaveta Fedorovna to the 8th Division. The prospect put Dzhun on edge. He wanted to work "in the shadows," and a medical unit bearing an august name was certain to lift him from the obscurity he sought. He also smelled something fishy, and on February 8 Evdokiia raised an alarm. She had heard about the plan and learned from the grand duchess herself that "this detachment would be neither R[ed] Cr[oss] nor military *but du gouvernement.*" She urged caution: "Androsov [should] tell you precisely and accurately how he arranged this and from whom he got the money. I warn you, you need to be careful with him."[45]

Dzhunkovsky took her advice and soon found out that the proposed unit would be financed by the Ministry of Internal Affairs, something that would connect him with his enemies Khvostov and Beletsky. He also feared the project might link Elizaveta Fedorovna with these unsavory characters who, he believed, were ruining Russia: "Her name should always be pure." Freeing himself from this entanglement was not easy, however. In the face of increasingly firm refusals, Androsov continued to press the issue, and finally Dzhun broke off the correspondence. The medical unit was formed but sent to another front.[46]

Events soon pushed aside these trivial concerns. In January 1916 Dzhunkovsky heard rumors of an impending offensive; his division might be attacking in the Vilna region. One thousand new troops strengthened its ranks, and he and the men received training in handling and defending against poison gas. In mid-February, the III Siberian Corps transferred from the Tenth to the Second Army. With the 8th on the march, Dzhunkovsky sent many of his personal effects back to Petrograd. On February

26 Dzhun learned that his brigade would be attached to the Corps's commander and stationed at the village of Liubki about fifteen miles from the division's advanced positions. "This news was not very pleasing," he recalled, "I had dreamed of being on the front lines, but instead found myself held in reserve." His disappointment did not last long. He and his men would soon see the harsh face of war at the battle of Naroch Lake.[47]

Chapter 17

In Dubious Battles

NAROCH LAKE AND AFTER

THE "NAROCH OPERATION" IS SELDOM REMEMBERED TODAY. It is just a name on the long list of bloody, futile engagements of the Great War. But this battle, which thrust Dzhunkovsky into combat, proved to be an important moment in the conflict. It sprang, somewhat unexpectedly, from the mix of tactical and strategic concerns that faced Russia and her allies at the beginning of the contest's second winter.

The year 1915 had been a bitterly disappointing year for the Entente. Repeated costly attacks failed to dislodge the German armies dug deep into northern France. Italy's entry into the war produced few benefits, while in the Balkans, Austro-German and Bulgarian forces devastated Serbia, occupied the country, and drove the remnants of its army into Montenegro and Albania. Winston Churchill's brainchild, an effort to force the Straits, led to the disaster at Gallipoli, and Russia's "Great Retreat" rounded out an entirely gloomy picture. Austro-German advances in the east ceased as Russian resistance stiffened, and the Kaisers' generals could see no advantage in further penetrating the vastness of the country. But the Germans started burrowing, and what had been a war of movement threatened to become a static stalemate with the soggy plains of Belorussia a new version of Flanders fields.

At the inter-allied conference at Chantilly in December 1915, the French commander in chief, General Joseph Joffre, summed up the situation. The enemy's goals were clear: "To husband his resources . . . to be in a condition to continue the struggle indefinitely . . . and to pursue the realization of the German imperial idea contained in the phrase 'Drang nach Osten' . . . to acquire so strong a position in the East that, whatever the issue of the struggle, he could not be forced to surrender it." Thwarting these plans required coordinated action: "Great Britain, France, Italy and Russia will deliver simultaneous attacks with their maximum forces on their respective fronts as soon as they are ready to do so and circumstances seem favorable." Joffre and his British allies were planning a summer offensive in the area of the Somme preceded by a Russian assault strong enough to draw substantial German forces from the west, making possible the long-sought breakthrough in northern France. But until then, Joffre wrote, "those powers which still have reserves of man power (Great Britain, Italy and Russia)" must wear down the Austro-German forces by vigorous attacks.[1]

Russia's representative at Chantilly, General Zhilinsky, proposed that in the event of enemy attacks on any one of the Allies, the others should launch separate offensives in response. At the time Joffre responded sourly, implying that Russia was asking France to come to her aid every time the Germans advanced. But on February 8/21, 1916, the Germans opened what would be a yearlong assault on Verdun, and on February 19/March 3, Joffre wrote urgently to General Alekseev, Tsar Nicholas's chief of staff: "On the basis of the decisions taken at Chantilly, I ask that the Russian armies immediately begin to prepare for an offensive."[2]

Russian forces were ready for a fight. In the months after the "Great Retreat," the sober, workaholic Alekseev, together with the energetic War Minister Polivanov and various public organizations, had accomplished something of a miracle. By the beginning of 1916, new recruits coming up to the line were better equipped and trained than ever before. The Russians had overcome the munitions shortages that had plagued them hitherto. Artillery units were increasingly well supplied, and with weapons and ammunition in hand, the troops' spirits rose.[3]

Nor did Russia's generals lack strategic vision. In December 1915 Alekseev had proposed a bold strike designed to knock Austria out of the war. Russian armies would drive through the Carpathians to link up in central Hungary with Allied forces pressing north from Salonika. This combined offensive would cut Germany off from her Turkish ally and leave her alone to face an Anglo-French advance on their western front. Although in the opinion of at least one well-informed historian this plan might have been successful, it was "condemned to oblivion by the parochial strategies of . . .

[Russia's] allies" who were convinced that victory could only be won in the west.[4]

On a less grand scale General Evert, commander of Russia's Western Front, foresaw the likelihood of a German attack against the French early in the year. On January 3/26, 1916, he wrote to Alekseev proposing a winter offensive. Intelligence reports showed German troop movements, which suggested that an assault on Franco-British positions was in the offing. "We are obliged to begin an attack immediately . . . with all our energy and speed," Evert argued, and January and February provided a window of opportunity.[5] Weather conditions were good, the ground still frozen, and Russian troops, able to move without getting bogged down by spring thaws, could strike the Germans before they began their new campaign in the west.[6] Evert's proposal made considerable sense, but Stavka dithered, and the window closed. Not until Joffre sent his appeal did Alekseev, despite some serious reservations, commit to an attack in March.

He envisioned a broad assault along Russia's Northern and Western Fronts. The main armies of the Northern Front were to drive toward Ponevezh (Panevėžys) while forces from the Western Front, chiefly the Second Army, would fight their way in the direction of Sventsiany (Ŝvenčiónys) and Vilkomir (today Ukmerge). Flanking forces on the Northern Front would advance toward Bausk (Bauska) and on the Western Front toward Vilna (Vilnius).[7] But as the offensive developed, the thrusts from the Northern Front failed to materialize fully, as did the drive toward Vilna. The main burden of the fighting fell to the Western Front's Second Army whose commander, General Smirnov, took sick on the eve of battle and was replaced by General Ragoza, a man unfamiliar with the forces he was asked to lead.

Still, Russian prospects appeared reasonably good. A substantial part of the German army had shifted to France, giving Second Army a decided superiority over the enemy: 350,000 men and 982 light and heavy guns against their opponent's 75,000 men and 440 guns.[8] Russian troops were ready and in no way ill disposed toward those in command. "Despite extremely difficult conditions," the Soviet historian N. E. Podorozhnyi wrote, "the soldiers courageously bore the deprivations of life at the front, maintaining the appropriate level of military discipline and were ready to go into battle at any moment."[9] Bernard Pares, who visited the Russian front lines at about this time, found the soldiers' talk "full of a glorious spirit of courage" and contrasted their mood to that of the home front, which by then had become "one long grumble."[10]

Terrain and weather were major obstacles to success, however. The Second Army would be attacking over the boggy ground north and south of Lake Naroch, and by March the spring thaws made movement difficult. If past (and future) Russian armies got help from "General Winter," in early 1916 "Marshal Muck" would aid the Germans. More serious still were the weaknesses in the Russian high command. Having acquired for the first time a sufficiency of artillery shells, Russian generals did not know how to exploit it properly. They had little experience in trench warfare, and Russian positions were poorly constructed. Nor had they maintained secrecy; the Germans knew that an attack was coming and were ready.[11]

For purposes of the offensive, Second Army divided into three groups: one on the right, commanded by General Mikhail Pleshkov; a center group, led by General Otto Sirelius, and on the left, units directed by General Petr Baluev that included V Army Corps and III Siberian Corps with the regiments commanded by Dzhunkovsky. The battle began on March 5/18 and continued for the next two weeks, ending on the morning of March 18/31. The result was a disaster, caused chiefly by incompetence in the Russians' higher echelons. The advantages in manpower and artillery were squandered; soldiers had to push forward through freezing swamps, stand in trenches filled with water, and sleep in the open during bitterly cold nights. Rain was constant, turning the battlefield into a morass that swallowed up men, machines, and animals. At the end, nothing was gained. Pleshkov's group in the north actually lost ground, while at the center Sirelius's forces made no progress. The Baluev group was the only bright spot—if it could be called that. After fierce fighting, it managed to gain only a few yards. The Russians suffered 78,000 casualties, many the victims of frostbite; German losses were less than half their foe's.[12]

For Dzhun the battle of Naroch Lake began with him commanding the 31st and 32nd Siberian Regiments—designated "the brigade [*otriad*] of General of the Suite Dzhunkovsky"—stationed for the moment at the village of Liubki. He arrived in late afternoon on March 2 and billeted in a small, filthy peasant hut. Immediately, he faced a merciless enemy; a horde of voracious bedbugs infested the place. Dzhun forthwith formed his batman and orderly into an effective swat team, and by nightfall they had overcome the beasts. The next day he inspected his command. The troops made a splendid impression by their lively, happy appearance: "They were all literally bursting to go into action and expressed the hope that they would soon get moving."[13]

On March 4 word that the offensive would start the next day electrified Dzhunkovsky: "It is difficult to describe the feeling that enveloped me," he remembered. A sense of "pride, joy, the grandeur of the moment, its seriousness" swept over him. He gathered the leaders of the units under his command and read them the orders; they all crossed themselves and went to their posts. Soldiers in the ranks also seemed ready: "The riflemen received the news with delight and enthusiasm," Dzhun recalled, "and I thought that if they had sent us forward then, the attack would have been so bold that no German force could have withstood it."[14] But the III Siberian Corps was held in reserve and several frustrating days passed before Dzhunkovsky and his troops saw action. By then, the initiative the Russians seized at the start of the battle had been lost, and the advances made by V Army Corps stalled. The Germans closed the gaps in their lines and dug in deeper.

Dzhunkovsky's waiting ended on March 8 when he received orders to take charge of units of the 29th and 32nd Regiments, now on the front line, with the 30th and 31st in reserve. His command post lay just to the west of the village of Stakhovtsy in the remains of a field hospital. He reached it late in the evening, after picking his way for about five miles through a swamp on a road so poor that he had to dismount and go much of distance on foot. Dzhun billeted in a low, narrow, windowless hole in the ground, roughly ten feet square, roofed by three large logs and about fifteen hundred sandbags. Well within the range of German guns, the dugout might withstand one, possibly two, direct hits in succession; one more, and nothing would be left. For the next nine days he shared these cramped, dangerous quarters with five others—his own orderly; Colonel Kostiaev, the commander of the 32nd; the colonel's adjutant; and two enlisted men in charge of the field telephones.

It might have been possible to lie down and sleep in this place, but Dzhun chose not to. Instead he sat in a chair, a cloak spread on top of his greatcoat, nodding off when the hour and circumstances permitted, often leaving the dugout to inspect the front lines and visit his units' battery and observation posts. He met troops coming and going from the advanced positions, bucking them up, and offering support and comfort to the wounded being taken to a nearby first aid station. Enemy bombardment was almost constant, and from their positions about a mile distant, Germans raked the Russian lines with machine-gun fire and lobbed shells containing formalin gas, irritating eyes and producing nausea.

Not far from Dzhunkovsky's dugout, a road led back to the village of Stakhovtsy through a depression troops had named "the valley of death." German guns blasted this spot with hundreds of shells almost every time they opened up, punishing anyone bold enough to attempt a crossing. Often the Germans began by shelling Stakhovtsy, then gradually moving back toward Dzhun's command post and the Russian trenches. As he felt the explosions come ever nearer the dugout, he was torn: Should he sit tight or get out? Once an eight-inch shell landed some fifteen feet away; tensely he waited for a direct hit to follow, but the next one burst on the other side. During his nine-day stay at the front, Dzhun's dugout would be struck three separate times, but fortunately these single blasts were not immediately followed by second or third strikes.[15]

On March 10 Dzhunkovsky's units were ordered to seize an area known as "the long woods" (*dlinnyi les*) then held by the Germans. At 3:15 a.m. the next day he sent troops of the 29th and 32nd Regiments forward into a fierce fight, and they did not gain control of the position until nine o'clock in the morning of March 11. Losses were heavy; as many as eight hundred of Dzhun's men fell. The retreating the enemy continued his fire and because the woods gave little cover, the Russians could not dig solid trenches. On the evening of March 11 Dzhun was called to 8th Division headquarters where he was told to prepare for an assault on a small elevated German salient known as "Ferdinand's Nose" (*Ferdinandov nos*). From this point, so named because it supposedly resembled the nose of the Bulgarian tsar Ferdinand, the Germans raked the flanks of the units in the "long woods" and other spots along the Russian lines.[16]

Waiting through the day of March 12, Dzhunkovsky weighed the chances. They did not look good. The "nose" was heavily fortified, and attacks by other units had already been beaten back. Weather conditions were awful: heavy rain fell hard upon snow, the men had no chance to dry off, ice formed on their greatcoats, and they were numbed with cold. Still Dzhun's troops surprised him with their spirit: "Nowhere did I hear any complaint, they were all filled with a sense of duty and bore the harsh conditions with calm and patience." While making his way among his units in the worst of the storm, with bullets crackling about, Dzhun met a lone rifleman, drenched to the skin, who when he saw his commander, snapped to attention and saluted smartly.[17]

At 3:30 a.m. on March 13, Dzhunkovsky ordered the 32nd Regiment to attack. An advance team pressed ahead to cut the German barbed wire; the rest followed, company by company, separated by roughly fifty feet. The 32nd's right flank was supported by about a company and a half from the 7th Division's 26th Regiment. By 4 a.m. the advanced party had reached the German wire and cut three openings from three to six feet wide. But the Germans opened up with artillery and unleashed a hail of bullets from small arms and machine guns. As losses mounted, Dzhun's men dragged up one of their own machine guns and tried to suppress the enemy's fire. Suddenly, the situation of 32nd became more precarious. The men from the 26th began to waver; some of them fell back, others surrendered to the Germans. A lieutenant from Dzhun's unit turned his machine gun on the deserters, but only got off two bursts before he fell, shot in the back.

With 20 percent of the 32nd's lead battalions killed or wounded and several companies reduced to thirty men, Dzhunkovsky turned to Division Command for artillery support. Some of his troops were pinned down in front of the wire, he reported, but others had reached the enemy's breastworks. The attack could press forward if he got help from the 26th Regiment. Without that, his men might be ripped apart by enemy crossfire. Dzhun told Division Command they were digging in, waiting for artillery strikes. None came.

At noon Dzhunkovsky established communications with the commander of the 26th Regiment who reported that his troops were stymied and that enemy positions had not been breached. Still, Dzhun was unwilling to give up. "Units of my 32nd Regiment and those of the 30th[18] supporting us from the left . . . were spoiling for a fight. Despite the losses, their spirit was high. I decided that with nightfall we would advance beginning at 8 p.m., hoping that by a surprise assault we could take 'Ferdinand's Nose' even without the aid of the 26th." But then orders came down from Division: break off the attack; pull the troops back.

"Retreat was very difficult," Dzhun recalled, "the riflemen had suffered heavy losses; many of the wounded had to be left on the field." But by 11 p.m. his dejected soldiers had returned to their former position, and he now worried about what the Germans might try next. His concern increased when Division Command insisted on withdrawing the 31st Regiment, serving on his flank, into reserve despite the battering the 32nd had just received. Of Dzhunkovsky's detachment only remnants of the 32nd and the 30th Regiments were left, men exhausted by battle, who had not eaten hot food in almost twenty-four hours. He watched the 31st disappear into the darkness, then returned to his dugout, overwhelmed by a sense of failure.[19]

After drinking some tea and exchanging a few words with Colonel Kostiaev, Dzhunkovsky slumped into his chair, bone weary. Silence descended on the battlefield, and in the dugout, the two officers took this to mean that the Germans were resting from the fight as well. Reconnaissance squads reported that the enemy was strengthening his own position and repairing wire. Occasionally the Germans sent out teams to capture unrescued Russian wounded, but they had been driven off. Dzhun drifted into sleep.

At about 3:30 a.m., he awakened to the sound of artillery rounds exploding. At first, he took it to be the desultory shelling the Germans regularly visited on the Russian positions, but quickly realized it was something else. This was "hurricane fire," the heavy bombardment that signaled the start of an attack.

Dzhun roused Kostiaev and they rushed out of the dugout. It was still night, rain was falling, but German flares had made the area as bright as day. Almost immediately Colonel Iziumov, commander of the 30th Regiment, phoned: his men were taking cover, losses were heavy, he expected a German attack in the area of the "long woods" and needed two more battalions. Dzhun called Division Command for reinforcements. Then the phones went dead, wires cut by enemy artillery.

Dzhunkovsky sent out a detachment of signalmen to restore connections; they failed and most were killed. He then resorted to runners to carry dispatches, but many of them died as well. Dzhun remembered standing near the dugout when one of the runners arrived with a message. Dzhun read it, jotted a quick response, and then without turning his head, held the envelope out to the runner. There was no hand to receive it. Swinging around, he saw the man lying on the ground. An enemy bullet had killed him instantly. Deafened by the roar of the guns, Dzhun had not heard him fall.[20]

Dispatches continued to arrive, often desperate appeals. At 5:30 a.m., Lt. Colonel Zinevich of the 30th Regiment wrote: "Germans have cut the 32nd off from the 30th. Eighth Company of the 30th falling back. Sent 1st battalion to assist. All communications disrupted. Total confusion. *Need very quick and energetic support.*" Shortly thereafter, he wrote again: "30th Regiment in chaos. . . . Again I ask for *energetic support*, otherwise the whole position we took with so many casualties will be in German hands. . . . *It seems* they have also cut us off from the right. For God's sake, *help, help, help.*"[21]

As the battle raged, seemingly out of control, Dzhunkovsky was momentarily gripped by a sense of helplessness: "It is a terrible situation," he wrote years later, "when you feel that you cannot even give orders, when you need to put everything into the hands of God and wait." But just then he was forced to act and command. Colonel Iziumov of the 30th rushed up, pale and distraught, crying: "I don't have my regiment, everything's lost, everything's destroyed!" Dzhun tried to buck him up by dressing him down. If Iziumov's regiment had been destroyed, he ought to have died with it, Dzhun snapped. He should go out and search for his men. And if he could not pull them together, Dzhun warned, he would face a court marshal. Iziumov steadied for a minute, but then rocket fire revealed a few Germans not more than three hundred yards away signaling to their comrades of the success of the attack. Iziumov panicked again and proposed that they run, but a withering look made the colonel get a hold of himself once more. Still, the situation was critical; Dzhun knew he could be captured and that the advancing Germans might attack his units from the rear.

Dzhunkovsky ordered the 30th and 32nd to counterattack. He told Iziumov and Kostiaev to head for their regiments, and when they got there send runners to inform him. But he also knew that reinforcements were desperately needed, and for that, he had to reestablish communications with Division HQ. At about 7 a.m., he gathered a small group of field-phone operators and removed the apparatus from the dugout. Together they set out for the nearest battery from where he hoped to regain a telephone connection and direct the fight. To reach it, he and his men would have to pass through the "valley of death."

The danger was high, but Dzhunkovsky's low mood made him heedless. "It seemed to me that all was lost, and that I was obviously to blame. Because of inexperience and ignorance, I had probably failed to foresee something I ought to have done—but what it was I did not know." As Dzhun headed toward the battery, shells burst nearby, shrapnel flew, great clods of earth rained down. The brave signalmen who were with him often hit the dirt. Dzhun simply trudged on, his mind full of thoughts about his troops. Had they succeeded in launching a counterattack? The prospect that he might remain unhurt while his men were being overrun filled him with shame. Suddenly, up ahead, he saw a gray horse standing alone in the field. As he looked, a shell fragment ripped off one of its legs and a portion its hindquarters; yet somehow, the wounded beast continued to stand, shaking and making strange snorting noises. A wave of pity swept over him, but Dzhun slogged on. Twenty minutes after leaving the dugout, he reached his goal.

The battery was in ruins, five of its six guns knocked out. Only the commander of the unit and a couple of gunners remained. They, too, had lost telephone connections but continued to fire on enemy positions with their one remaining field piece. Dzhunkovsky realized he would have to go farther to the rear to get in touch with Division HQ and pressed on to another intact telephone station about six hundred yards distant. There he finally established contact with General Redko who gave permission for him to throw several reserve battalions into the fight. Meanwhile, the men of the 30th and 32nd had followed Dzhun's orders. They rallied, turned on the enemy troops, and forced them back into the woods. There entrenched German reserves checked the advance with heavy rifle and machine-gun fire. But strengthened by their own reinforcements, the Russians pressed ahead and by noon had recovered much of the lost ground.

At 3 p.m. Dzhunkovsky returned to his dugout command post, again crossing the "valley of death." Once more, German shells dropped around him, but this time his mood was entirely different: "I did not walk downcast, but full of spirit; the position had been saved; my riflemen had fought like lions." Twenty years later the Soviet historian of the "Naroch Operation" wrote a bare-bones account of what had taken place: "The battle for the long woods was extremely bitter. During the fighting, rain suddenly poured down. Everything was mixed up in a single ball of inconceivable filth. Despite it all, the stubbornness of the Siberians carried the day." One of the junior officers who had survived the engagement described for Dzhun how a German and a Russian unit had clashed, the men throwing themselves on each other in wild rage, stabbing with bayonets, bashing with clubs and fists, even biting their foes.

Hard fighting continued the next day, as Dzhunkovsky's units recaptured all their former positions. But the losses had been heavy. Eight days of combat produced almost nine thousand casualties, close to half of his command. On March 16, the 30th and 32nd Regiments were pulled off line for rest and reinforcement. For the first time in more than a week Dzhun changed his clothes and slept in a bed. As the larger battle wound down, General Baluev ordered other regiments forward in another futile attack on "Ferdinand's Nose." The "Naroch Operation" was over. Dzhunkovsky had no illusions; the Russians had lost. But he was fiercely proud of his Siberians.[22]

The importance of Naroch Lake lies not in its futility, casualties, and defeat. World War I saw many failed "operations" that hurled thousands of young men at entrenched enemies in search of a breakthrough and ultimate victory. Rather, its significance lay in the fact that it diverted the Russians from what might have been a much more effective strategy. An operation in the north able to tie down a substantial portion of German forces could be combined with a massive blow against the Austrians designed to knock them out of the war. If successful, victory might be won on the plains of central Hungary instead of in the fields of northern France. Had the offensive in the Naroch area been undertaken in the late spring or early summer and linked with what would become known as the Brusilov offensive in the south, it could have dramatically altered the war.

As it was, Russia's military timetable had been adjusted to meet the demands of her western ally, and Russian boys needlessly died for France. The Naroch Lake battle may have produced a slight hiatus in the German campaign against Verdun, but it caused no troops to be withdrawn and in no way determined the outcome of the German effort to bleed France white. Instead, the failure at Naroch made General Evert, the commander of the Russian Western Front, extremely cautious, unwilling or unable to support the Brusilov offensive when it began.[23] The defeat at Naroch Lake condemned a large portion of the Russian army to inactivity, something that proved to be a very dangerous thing. Napoleon was right when he said that an army marches on its stomach, but it also marches on its hopes. An idle army, like an idle brain, is the Devil's playground, and when Satan makes an appearance in the trenches, there can be Hell to pay.

In the aftermath of Naroch Lake, Dzhunkovsky soon found himself again in battle, this time for the honor of his regiments and the III Siberian Corps. "Victory finds a hundred fathers," the maxim goes, "but defeat is an orphan," and an effort is usually made to determine the paternity of the unwanted child.[24] Soon after the fighting ended, various Russian commanders sought to shift the burden of responsibility for the loss onto the backs of others. Military politics quickly entered the picture. Within the Baluev group it would be impossible to fault V Army Corps, since that was Baluev's own unit; the III Siberian must be to blame. But that Corps's 7th Division could not be held responsible, since General Trofimov had once been its commander. Fingers pointed at the 8th Division and the units that had been under Dzhun's command.[25]

Not prepared to be the goat or to have the courage of his men slighted, Dzhunkovsky counterattacked. He ordered his subcommanders to present their own accounts of the battle and, based on the information they supplied, prepared a detailed report for General Redko. Reproduced in his memoirs, this document takes up seven pages. It gives a blow-by-blow account of the events of March 13 and 14—the failed attack on "Ferdinand's Nose," and the German breakthrough in the "long woods" that followed, devoting special attention to the latter.[26]

Concluding his report, Dzhunkovsky summed up the tasks assigned to his units during the Naroch Lake engagement: occupy the "long woods"; take "Ferdinand's Nose"; recover the positions lost after the sudden German advance on March 14. The first task, Dzhun maintained, had been fulfilled brilliantly, and the second, the assault on "Ferdinand's Nose," would have been successful had it not been called off at the last minute. The third assignment, recovering the lost positions in the "long woods," had also been carried out successfully. As for the German breakthrough, Dzhun ascribed it to several factors: the Germans, who had previously held the area, knew the terrain with "mathematical precision"; the terrible weather favored the attackers; "hurricane fire" from German guns disrupted communications; Russian trenches in the woods had been constructed only as temporary shelter, not designed to be a bulwark against attack; the

30th and 32nd Regiments received insufficient support from other Russian units. In conclusion, Dzhunkovsky asserted that troops in the units he commanded "do not deserve even the slightest criticism, but, on the contrary, fought with a courage and selflessness that upheld the military glory of the Siberian riflemen. They religiously fulfilled their duty to Tsar and Country."[27]

Dzhunkovsky did some finger-pointing of his own. When General Evert, the commander of the Western Front, asked all unit chiefs to give their opinions on the causes of the failure at Naroch Lake, Dzhunkovsky assigned greatest blame to the artillery, which was poorly coordinated with the infantry and failed to pave the way for the attacks on enemy positions. Russian guns did not have enough ammunition to generate the kind of "hurricane fire" that the Germans did and could not break up the enemy's barbed wire defenses before Russian troops reached them. The problem was made worse because frontline commanders did not have the authority to call down artillery strikes even from those batteries nominally under their control.

There were other problems as well. The assaults on German positions were not sufficiently massive to take full advantage of initial successes, one wave did not follow another closely, and reserves were not properly employed. In making attacks, headquarters often used units from various regiments and it was difficult to coordinate their actions. Troops were wasted by being jerked around from place to place, often at night. The men were kept out in the open, in swampy ground during heavy rain; many suffered frostbite. Finally, commanders of fighting units were constantly harassed by unnecessary communications from the rear that distracted them from the work at hand.[28]

Demands for information and analysis of the causes of the defeat continued to rain down. Dzhunkovsky was pleased to learn that he, personally, was not considered to be at fault for the failure, but he bristled when rumors circulated that men under his command had performed poorly and were guilty of cowardice. In the weeks that followed the battle, he stridently defended his troops to all who would listen, and his tenacity amazed many of the officers at Corps Headquarters. They advised him to get used to the buck-passing that was standard operating procedure in the military, but Dzhun would have none of it.[29] In early April, he continued his fight while representing the III Siberian Corps at a commission of inquiry summoned by General Baluev.

Dzhunkovsky believed that Baluev had created the commission not to analyze objectively the reasons for the defeat of the "Naroch operation" but to pin the blame for the failure on the III Siberian Corps and so protect the reputation of V Army Corps, his own command. Baluev was a thick-set man with a loud voice and an ugly birthmark spread across his face.[30] He sought to dominate the proceedings, abruptly dismissing any questions other commission members might raise, trying to cow them into silence. But Dzhunkovsky had come ready for a fight, determined not to back down. On the second day of the conference he engaged Baluev in yet another battle over "Ferdinand's Nose."

When Baluev criticized the III Siberian Corps for failing to take that position, Dzhunkovsky sprang to its defense. He directly challenged Baluev, pointing out that the 10th Division of the general's own V Corps had also unsuccessfully attacked the "Nose." Why was that not a subject for investigation and criticism? Baluev angrily denied that the 10th had ever undertaken such an attack, and when Dzhun continued to press his challenge, the general tried to end the discussion. "I say that the 10th Division did not attack, and that is enough!" he shouted. But Dzhun refused to let it go, and in the end General Walter (Val'ter), V Corps's chief of staff (a Russian of English descent), intervened to support him.[31]

Dzhunkovsky felt he had made his point, and by the end of the conference his relations with Baluev smoothed. The two men dined together, and Dzhun apologized for any offense he might have given. Baluev did the same, and they parted on good terms.[32] In time, Baluev became Dzhun's supporter. Following the February Revolution, Baluev, by then commander of the Western Front, would be instrumental in seeing that Dzhunkovsky was made head of the III Siberian Corps. He stood up to War Minister Alexander Kerensky—even threatening to resign—in order to push the appointment through.[33]

Dzhunkovsky remembered getting something of a hero's welcome when he returned to the headquarters of the 8th Division. Even the normally somber Redko could scarcely conceal his delight. "I felt like I was among my own family; it was wonderfully pleasant." Dzhun believed that he had won his spurs both by his conduct in the battle of Naroch Lake and by his stout defense of III Siberian Corps at Baluev's conference. His fellow officers—even those with much greater experience—began to treat him as an equal and listen to his ideas with respect. He soon learned that among the soldiers his nine days on the front line, in the heat of battle, had become the stuff of legends: "Various tales spread around that during the [German] breakthrough I had personally led first one then another company in the counterattack. There were riflemen who told these cock-and-bull stories, claiming to be eye-witnesses, and could not be convinced otherwise." Dzhunkovsky found all this rather amusing, even a bit embarrassing, and he refused to ascribe these yarns to any great achievements on his part. They simply showed how easy it was to gain the affection of soldiers in wartime. All you had to do was to carry out your duties conscientiously and take good care of the men under your command, to see to their needs, and to look on them as human beings, not cannon fodder. "Nothing more was needed for troops to follow such a commander wherever he led, and to endure with him every hardship."[34]

The battle of Naroch Lake was the last significant engagement of the Russian armies on their Western Front. Throughout 1916 Dzhunkovsky continued to serve in the advanced positions for much of the time, but he saw little action.[35] The prevailing calm permitted him to display his administrative skills to good effect, and General Redko was soon pushing for his promotion to division commander. In mid-May, Redko called Dzhun in and read the evaluation he had written about him:

> With great life experience and an understanding of people, he has established himself very well in the division, where he enjoys general affection and respect. He loves the military life and is whole heartedly devoted to it. He seeks out work and unfailingly carries out all orders. He is cool under fire and correctly assesses the circumstances. Has excellent self-control and can convey this to those around him. While living through the difficult, crucial days of battle as the commander of fighting units in the Naroch Lake engagement, he displayed his best qualities: the ability to give sensible orders and to direct the units under his command. He kept his head even in the most difficult moments of the battle.
>
> After seven months of wartime work, he has gained the necessary knowledge and experience. I therefore consider him worthy of promotion to the duties of division commander.[36]

Dzhun was embarrassed by Redko's effusive praise but thanked him, adding that, if even half of what he said were true, he was more than pleased and would do his best to live up to his commander's high opinion.

Dzhunkovsky's good reputation soon extended far beyond the trenches. Toward the end of May, he received a letter from his sister who told him that one of their relatives had been asked to sound him out about two possible new assignments: command of the 2nd Guards Infantry Division or command of a brigade that was being sent to France. He told Evdokiia that neither posting had any attraction, but he asked her to say he had not responded to her questions. "I would not have been happy to transfer to the Guards and leave my Siberians," he wrote later. "Besides, I could not stand these secret overtures. I also refused to take a brigade to France, I wanted to stay in Russia."[37]

Dzhunkovsky was also determined to remain in the shadows and avoid any contact with Petrograd's poisonous swamp of intrigue and back-stabbing. Although immersed in the gray world of the trenches, he had kept in touch. Letters from his sister and friends assured him that he continued to be highly regarded in many quarters. But these, as well as visits by Evdokiia and Nina during the spring and summer, also told him of growing troubles around the country and in the capital.[38] The battle lines on the Northern and Western Fronts were stable, and Brusilov's successful summer offensive in the south showed that Russia's armies still had plenty of fight left in them, but by late 1916, serious economic difficulties had emerged and the political life of the empire was descending into chaos.

The economies of all the nations that entered the Great War suffered dislocations. But, like Tolstoy's unhappy families, each was dislocated in its own way. For Russia a deep and painful economic rift between town and country produced a food supply crisis with revolutionary potential. Its cause was not an absolute shortage of grain but, rather, a perfect storm of troubles: the shift of industry away from the production of consumer goods, a surging inflation, and a sharp rise in urban populations as the factory workforce grew and refugees arrived from the war zone. With little to buy and an increasingly worthless ruble to buy with, peasants had fewer incentives to bring grain to market, and the country's rail network proved less and less able to transport what food there was to where it was needed. Yet in late 1916 the army was still being fed and the cities were not starving. A competent and properly focused government might have been able to deal with the situation. But by the year's end, Russia's political life was in disarray.[39]

The year 1916 had begun on a hopeful note. In February, the emperor called the Duma back into session and took the unprecedented step of appearing in the chamber and making a short speech. But this gesture of goodwill was undercut by the fact that, in January, Nicholas had replaced the aged prime minister Goremykin with Boris Shtiurmer (Stürmer). The tsar may have picked him for his reputation as a master of political compromise, but by the time of his appointment, Shtiurmer was widely considered a shallow, dishonest reactionary with little ability.[40] Rumored to be a creature of Rasputin and the empress, his German name heightened suspicions.

Despite public disapproval, Nicholas invested Shtiurmer with great authority, appointing him in turn minister of internal affairs (March–July) and foreign minister (from July), making him for a time virtual dictator, before finally discharging him in November. Simultaneously, the tsar dismissed the competent Minister of War Polivanov, respected Minister of Foreign Affairs Sazonov, and highly regarded Minister of Internal Affairs Alexander Khvostov, formerly minister of justice. Rightly or not, many ascribed this "ministerial leapfrog" to the machinations of Rasputin and Alexandra. Then came the tsar's last bad choice. In September he appointed Alexander Protopopov, vice president of the Duma, his minister of internal affairs. But the new minister soon displayed both ignorance and incompetence.[41] Protopopov enjoyed the strong support of Rasputin and Alexandra, but he was utterly incapable of coming to grips with the country's food supply problems. Rumored to be mad, suffering from advanced syphilis, Protopopov, a man in over his head, symbolized a monarchy that had lost its mind.[42]

Confronted with the spectacle of governmental mismanagement, the Duma was powerless. Vasilii Maklakov's image of paralyzed passengers in a car driven by an insane chauffer seemed increasingly apt. Disdained by Nicholas, Alexandra, Rasputin, and the conservative court clique, its "Progressive bloc" in disarray, the legislature could do little more than voice alarms about the dire situation. This it did very well, becoming the sounding board for accumulated public fears, resentment, and disillusionment. In a fiery speech delivered on November 1, Kadet leader Pavel Miliukov presented a long list of government mistakes, each followed by the question: "Is this stupidity, or is this treason?" a haunting refrain that spread nationwide. Miliukov may have believed the answer was "stupidity," but many thought otherwise, blaming "dark forces"—the "German" empress and her dissolute "friend"—bent on selling the country to the enemy.[43] Hostility to the government was now embraced even by extreme rightists, and a longtime defender of autocracy, the protofascist Vladimir Purishkevich, joined the ranks of those who denounced the regime, ready to go beyond mere words.

As frustration and panic gripped Petrograd, a plan to murder Rasputin took shape. Led by Purishkevich, young Felix Iusupov (heir to the largest fortune in Russia), and Grand Duke Dmitrii Pavlovich (the favorite nephew of the emperor), the conspirators finally accomplished their goal on the night of December 16/17, 1916. Details of the plot and its grisly consummation need not detain us.[44] The importance of the event lies in this: it marked the complete desertion of the dynasty by its last real supporters. Nothing stood between the Romanovs and revolution.

While the political storm clouds gathered in Petrograd, Dzhunkovsky plunged deeper into life at the front. At the beginning of August, he was ordered to take temporary command of the 7th Siberian Rifle Division. The unit's chief, General V. N. Bratanov, had become ill, and at the time Dzhun believed this assignment might be permanent. He quickly immersed himself in the problems of command, strengthening the division's positions and paying particular attention to the condition of hospitals and the well-being of the troops. When he took over the division he feared he would find a cold reception, but he quickly won the cooperation and support of the officers and men. Dzhun proved to be a rather demanding CO, quick to note deficiencies but ready to praise improvements when they were effected. He regularly inspected the trenches of the front lines and was usually pleased by what he found but, on occasion, encountered "astounding examples of good-natured breaches of discipline . . . on the part of ill-trained old timers coming to the war directly from the plow."[45] By the end of September he felt himself to be fully in charge and comfortable with the situation, but on October 4 he learned that Bratanov was returning to his unit. Dzhun parted from the 7th with regret but was heartened by the affectionate send-off he received.[46] His reception upon his return to the 8th was equally warm.[47]

Dzhunkovsky's stay with the 8th Division would be brief, however. Units on the Western Front were being reconfigured; new divisions were in the process of formation. It soon became clear that Dzhun would be assigned command of one of them, probably the 131th Infantry Division. Because of this, he took a short leave in late October, visiting the capital and Moscow as well. It is hard to believe that Dzhun got no sense of the dangers enveloping the monarchy, but his memoirs give no indication of this. At the time he may have been deliberately oblivious, resolutely following the course he had set after his dismissal and avoiding all politics. Later, perhaps, he found the subject too painful to recall. In any case, a new challenge soon absorbed his energies. On November 13, he received orders to take command of the 131st.[48]

Dzhunkovsky bid farewell to the 8th, writing brief, affectionate notes to the regimental commanders, recalling their service together in the Naroch Lake engagement.[49] Then he began putting together his new command, eventually renamed the 15th Siberian Rifle Division and formed chiefly from battalions taken from the 7th and 8th Divisions of the III Siberian Corps.[50] Organized as the 57th, 58th, 59th, and 60th Regiments, it would go on frontline duty on January 17, 1917, part of the Grenadier Corps of the Second Army.[51]

The month of December 1916 was difficult, even traumatic. On December 17, Dzhunkovsky received a telegram from Nikolai Nikolaevich informing him that his brother lay gravely ill and was unlikely to recover. The next day he got a coded dispatch from Vladimir Nikolsky, his former chief of staff at the Corps of Gendarmes. It read simply: "Grishka was killed today." Almost immediately, another telegram arrived from the grand duke: "Do you want to assume the office of governor-general of the [conquered] Turkish territories? Value your work; count on your excellent service."[52]

The three messages stunned Dzhunkovsky. He was well aware of his brother's ill health, but he had not expected him to decline so rapidly. Rasputin's murder was another matter. The death of the man responsible for his fall from grace caused him no joy, only grave concern. When he informed his staff what had happened, they were surprised that he did not share in their elation. "It's the beginning of the end!" he recalled telling them. The problem, he tried to explain, was not the personality of

Rasputin, but the fact that such a figure could appear; his death did not guarantee that another like him would not soon emerge. The murder, he added, further compromised the throne: "The killers have played into the hands of revolution." When the details of the assassination became clear a few days later, Dzhun could only feel disgust for the "heroes" who had accomplished this supposedly "great deed."

The offer of a governor-generalship posed a different problem. Dzhunkovsky had the highest regard for Nikolai Nikolaevich and was honored by his proposal. But he had not finished putting together his new division. The advice he sought was mixed. General Evert simply assumed he would take the post, but others counseled against. Finally, after considerable soul-searching, Dzhun turned the offer down. He wrote the grand duke: "Having received permission last year to go to the front . . . I firmly resolved to remain on active duty in the army until the end of the war. Were I to change [my mind], I would always blame myself. For an entire month now, I have been in command of a new division which is [still] in the process of formation. I have put my whole heart into this work and do not feel I have the right to leave without having completed it and tested the results in battle." Nikolai Nikolaevich soon wired back, accepting Dzhun's response: "Fully understand your decision. Am deeply touched by your feelings."[53]

The reasons for the grand duke's sudden and unexpected proposal are unclear, but they almost certainly reflect the political intrigues of the moment. He made his offer to Dzhun in the immediate aftermath of Rasputin's murder, a clear sign of the unstable situation in the capital, the precarious position of the emperor and empress, and the prospect of revolution. Conspiracies were swirling, and at their center was Georgii Lvov, the leader of Zemgor. In December he hatched a scheme to overthrow Nicholas and make Nikolai Nikolaevich tsar. The grand duke would reject the idea when it was presented to him in early January, but it is hard to believe that prior to that he had no sense of what was in the air. With political sands shifting and dangerous days ahead, the grand duke may well have seen Dzhunkovsky, whom he trusted and respected, as the ideal man to "have his back" in uncertain times.[54]

Absorbed in his work at the front, Dzhunkovsky probably had no inkling of the plans for a coup against the tsar, something he surely would have opposed. His rejection of the grand duke's offer signified his continued desire for obscurity and freedom from the chains of Petrograd politics.

But in February 1917, he was made an offer he could not refuse. A letter from his sister informed him that he was going to be chosen to head the 1st Guards Infantry Division. Grand Duke Pavel Alexandrovich, who until late 1916 led the I Guards Corps, had told Evdokiia that, although there were many candidates for the post of 1st Division chief, he believed Dzhunkovsky was the only person truly suited in all regards, "experienced, knowledgeable, loyal." Paul had taken the matter directly to the emperor, and when he indicated to Nicholas that he had but one choice in mind, the tsar interrupted: "I know of whom you want to speak—Dzhunkovsky." Pavel Alexandrovich admitted that this was so, and Nicholas responded simply: "Of course; I am very, very happy."[55]

Why the tsar accepted the advice of the father of one of Rasputin's murderers to appoint to an honorific post a man he had cast down for trying to warn him about the "starets," is a minor mystery that defies easy answers. Was Nicholas reaching out to the anti-Rasputin faction, now that the cause of so much animus had been removed from the scene? Was it one more example of the illogic that frequently characterized his decisions? Or was it simply a sign of the moral and physical exhaustion noted by former Prime Minister Kokovtsov when they met for the last time?[56]

If Dzhunkovsky was puzzled about the tsar's decision, he does not mention it in his memoirs. They record only that the thought of leaving his newly formed unit was painful and that he feared a command in the Guards would make him far less independent. But the prospect of leading the division that contained his beloved Preobrazhensky Regiment gladdened him. How could he reject such an honor? Beyond this, there were the words of the tsar himself. For Dzhun they were "proof that, in his heart, the Sovereign continued to have trust in me, despite the fact that in 1915 he had so abruptly removed me from office."[57]

Dzhunkovsky awaited transfer orders, but they never came. In the last days of February, demonstrations and food riots began on the streets of Petrograd, efforts to suppress them failed, garrisons mutinied, and a paralyzed government lost control of the capital. Warned of the danger and the need to act, a befuddled tsar, isolated at Stavka, dithered until it was too late. On March 2, 1917, pressured by Army and Duma leaders, Nicholas II abdicated in favor of his brother Michael, who in turn refused the crown. The Romanov dynasty—which four years before had celebrated its tercentennial amid pomp, pageantry, and thunderous cheers—was no more.

Dzhunkovsky and the men of his division knew nothing of these events. "On 2 March," he wrote in his memoirs, "we were far from the thought that in Petrograd there had been a revolution, that the tsar had abdicated, that the monarchy had ceased to exist. There were no rumors, no signs. The front was quiet. My division stood steadfast at its position, loyally and unwaveringly carrying out its duty to tsar and country, bearing with complete selflessness all adversities and deprivations."[58]

Chapter 18

Red Flags at the Front

DZHUNKOVSKY FIRST FELT TREMORS OF THE PETROGRAD earthquake on March 3, 1917, when he received a puzzling order from General Parsky, commander of the Grenadier Corps: "To avoid false rumors in the army, explain to all officers and men (1) that no withdrawal of troops from the front . . . will be permitted (2) that confirmation of the new ministers is expected shortly . . . (3) that the attention of the army and all soldiers from general to private must be focused on the enemy. . . . Everyone needs to remember that the motherland expects us all to defend her from her wicked foe."[1] Obviously, something had happened—but what? Then another message arrived, signed by General Iurii Danilov, the chief of staff for General Ruzsky, the commander of the Northern Front. It announced the abdication of Tsar Nicholas.

Dzhun and the officers of his command read it, dumfounded. "This dispatch blasted us like a thunderbolt," he recalled, "none of us could utter a word." When Dzhun recovered his powers of speech, he advised his regimental commanders to disregard Danilov's message and wait for clarification from their own headquarters. The dispatch, he said, might be an enemy provocation, designed to spread confusion in the front lines. Dzhunkovsky's comrades agreed with him and dispersed, but he remained deeply troubled. "I could not sleep all night," he remembered, "thoughts, each one more alarming than the last, raced through my mind; I had to be ready for anything."[2]

It soon became clear that Danilov's dispatch was not a hoax, and on March 5, Dzhunkovsky performed the heart-wrenching task of making public the texts of Tsar Nicholas's and his brother Michael's abdications and the list of the new ministers of the Provisional Government. Always a stickler for proper forms, Dzhun faced an emotional dilemma when he came to sign the order. Normally, he would have written: "Major General of His Majesty's Suite Dzhunkovsky," but since Russia no longer had a tsar this would not do. Still, he could not bring himself to sign simply: "Major General." That, he felt, would mean "I was renouncing the title that I had borne so proudly." Therefore he signed: "Major General of the Suite." "Perhaps this was illogical," he admitted, "but at that time it was too painful to immediately cast away the words 'of the Suite,' to seemingly trample upon the ideals by which I had lived."[3]

For Dzhunkovsky, to issue an order was not enough. He went to all the units under his command to read the abdication manifesto and offer the troops some words of his own. The tsar's decision to renounce the throne for himself and his son was an act of sacrifice motivated solely for the good of the country, he told the men, and "it is our duty to hold a fond memory of him in our hearts." He gave the command: *Na molitvu* (Let us pray), and when heads were bowed he added: "Cross yourselves and pray that the Lord will help our former leader bear with courage the suffering that God has laid upon him and that the sacrifice he has offered makes possible the happiness of our Mother Russia."[4]

In the weeks ahead Dzhunkovsky continued to tour his units answering the questions of soldiers and officers, trying to stamp out the rumors that were rife and to prevent them from influencing the troops. He wanted the men to learn what was happening from their leaders, not scuttlebutt, and he ordered company commanders and all officers to talk constantly with the soldiers, to read them the newspapers and to explain what they said. But the social and political impact of events unfolding in Petrograd and throughout the country soon reached the trenches and vastly complicated the tasks of leadership for Dzhunkovsky and all officers serving at the front.[5]

The fall of the Russian monarchy—long the nightmare of some, the fervent dream of others—shook all sleepers awake. For both those who feared and those who hoped, the February Revolution came with shocking swiftness. Unplanned and unexpected, it abruptly shattered the autocratic system; fragments of its power lay in the streets. Soon two groups reached for the shards.[6] The eager fingers of moderate politicians, both from within the Duma and outside it, grasped the institutions of the state to form a caretaker, Provisional Government. The rough hands of the workers and soldiers, whose muscle had toppled the old regime, sought to grip available instruments of force and build a new authority, the Petrograd Soviet of Workers' and Soldiers' Deputies.

This development produced the phenomenon of "dual power"—*dvoevlastie*, the Revolution's hallmark and its curse—that would prevail between February and October 1917. It reflected the vast gulf that separated privileged Russia, the slim stratum of the propertied and the educated, from toiling Russia, the great, gray mass of workers, peasants, and soldiers in the ranks. The Provisional Government was composed at first of Duma leaders of the moderate left and center. Headed by Prince Georgii Lvov, the longtime zemstvo activist and leader of Zemgor, it was dominated by the Kadet Pavel Miliukov, serving as foreign minister, and the former Octobrist Alexander Guchkov, minister of war and navy. Its membership was decidedly "bourgeois" and contained only one avowed socialist, Alexander Kerensky, the minister of justice. The Petrograd Soviet, on the other hand, elected by committees of factory hands, the employees of smaller enterprises, and common soldiers, was led by radical *intelligenty*, Menshevik Social Democrats and Socialist Revolutionaries, who dominated its Executive Committee (Ispolkom). But these "leaders" sat uneasily atop the Soviet's turbulent main body. Composed of peasants in uniform and workers, many recently ripped from the countryside, it resembled in the words of one historian "an unruly village assembly."[7] In the heady days of February and March, the Provisional Government and the Soviet proclaimed common goals: establishing full freedom and civic equality for all Russians and pursuing the war to a victorious end. Soon, however, the enormous differences between the constituencies of the two "powers" steadily pulled them apart.

Remembering the experience of 1905, both the Provisional Government and the Soviet feared counterrevolution and took steps to prevent it. But the measures they adopted had fateful consequences. Determined to guarantee Russians' civil rights, the Provisional Government dismissed the provincial governors and eliminated or "reorganized" almost all of the old regime's police institutions—actions that, over time, weakened the new leaders' ability to control events in the country's vast hinterlands.[8] For its part, the Petrograd Soviet sought to make sure that the military forces in the capital could not be turned toward repression. To protect the workers and to secure the support of the soldiers, on the first day of March it issued "Order No. 1" to the garrison of the Petrograd district, unquestionably the most important document of the Revolution's early days.

Order No. 1 called on all army and naval units of the capital, from the company level up, to elect immediately committees composed of soldiers and sailors of the lower ranks. Every company was also to select one representative to the Petrograd Soviet. The order established a new relationship between officers and enlisted men. Arms were now to be placed under the control of soldiers' committees, and "in no case should they be turned over to officers, even at their demand." While on duty, soldiers were required to observe "the strictest military discipline," but off duty they were to enjoy the rights of all citizens. Troops no longer had to stand at attention or salute officers when not in ranks or address them using titles such as "Your Excellency" or "Your Honor"; a simple "Mister" would suffice. When speaking to their men, officers were to employ the polite *Vy* (you) form instead of the familiar *ty* (thou), and soldiers were required to report their commanders' breach of this new etiquette or any other rudeness to their committees. The order subordinated the army and navy forces in Petrograd to the Soviet and the soldiers' committees and stated that directives from the Military Committee of the State Duma were to be obeyed only if they did not conflict with the orders and resolutions of the Soviet.[9]

Order No. 1 freed enlisted men from the many onerous restrictions and humiliations that up until then had attended their service in the Imperial Russian armed forces. They could not be banned from parks, restaurants, and streetcars, or forbidden to smoke in public; they no longer had to endure the regular abuse and harsh punishments arbitrarily inflicted by their officers. At a stroke, the Soviet gained the loyalty of the troops of the capital. It was *their* institution, protecting them and expressing their deep-seated desire for equality and dignity.

Order No. 1 also reflected the relative strengths of the Provisional Government and the Soviet. Theoretically, the Provisional Government spoke for Russia and assumed full administrative responsibility, while the Soviet supervised its activities, watching out for the interests of the workers and soldiers. Reality was different, however. Order No. 1 showed that, from the outset, the Soviet's Ispolkom was able to administer and legislate on its own with little or no reference to the government. Leading members of the Provisional Government quickly recognized that they had relatively limited authority. As early as March 9, 1917, Alexander Guchkov would confess that government orders "are executed only in so far as this is permitted by the Soviet of Workers' and Soldiers' Deputies, which holds in its hands the most important elements of actual power, such as troops, railroads, postal and telegraph service. It is possible to say that the Provisional Government exists only while this is permitted by the Soviet."[10] This disparity, growing with time, would have a profound impact on Russia's armies, almost seven million strong, spread along a vast front that stretched from the Baltic to the Black Sea, across the mountains of eastern Turkey into northern Persia, and stationed in garrisons behind the lines.

Order No. 1 had been directed solely at the army and naval units of the capital, but it made its appearance in the trenches almost immediately following the news of the tsar's abdication. How and by whom the order was transmitted remains something of a mystery.[11] But as to its reception, there is little doubt. For soldiers in the ranks, the order was an act of liberation, joyfully celebrated. For officers, it was a satanic force, depicted in countless memoirs—Dzhunkovsky's included—as "an almost mystical, intangible evil, nowhere, yet everywhere sapping the foundations of the Army."[12] The Provisional Government's efforts to clarify the limits and applicability of the order were largely unsuccessful, and on March 5, Minister of War Guchkov issued his Order No. 114 that affirmed the soldiers' human and civil rights stated in Order No. 1 and made them law throughout the Russian armed forces.[13] Dzhunkovsky saw this as a major step toward the destruction of military discipline; he published it to the division "with an aching heart."[14]

Although he had been deeply wounded by his abrupt dismissal from office in 1915 and, in years to come would suffer imprisonment and endure the many dangers and indignities of life as a "former person," the year 1917 may well have been the most emotionally painful period of Dzhunkovsky's life. The monarchy he had served with such devotion was suddenly gone, and now he would have to watch the army, where he had been reborn and given a new sense of purpose, embark on a long slide toward dissolution. For the next nine months he struggled against the steadily escalating disaster, employing the administrative and management skills he had acquired over the course of his life, trying to maintain the discipline and fighting potential of the units he directed for as long as possible. It was a mournful and ultimately doomed effort, but when it was finished, Dzhun could look back on what he had done with a measure of pride: order in his commands did not collapse, and he kept the affection and respect of his men while remaining true to his basic principles.

Dzhunkovsky was able to deal with the difficult and increasingly dangerous situation that confronted him because he had real knowledge of the *narod*, derived from his experiences in the Moscow Guardianship, as governor, and as security chief. At "people's houses," in the oilfields of Baku, and on factory floors, Dzhun had become familiar with the conditions and aspirations of workers. During his regular inspections of Moscow province, he had met with hundreds of peasants, talked with them about their needs, answered their questions, and patiently explained the details of the complex Stolypin land reform. He had known ordinary Russians in their varied moods: as respectful petitioners at gubernatorial receptions, as knowledge-hungry clients in the Guardianship's reading rooms and lecture halls, as angry strikers and mutinous villagers. He had seen them in the midst of revolution; he had led them in battle. Dzhun respected their steadfast courage, but he did not idealize them. He knew that the men who now wore the greatcoat could be confused and deluded. Still, they were rational human beings and would respond as such when treated firmly and fairly.

Dzhunkovsky approached the task of leading these men through the difficult months ahead guided by the Christian spirit expressed in his family's motto *Deo et proximo* and the personal values that English speakers encounter in Kipling's poem "If." His natural tact, honed and strengthened during his years of service, would also be crucial in this effort. He had learned well the fine art of giving orders while not giving offence, of creating relations based on mutual respect if not equality or complete agreement, of gaining support without pandering. But the circumstances he now faced were more challenging than he had ever met before; the ground beneath his feet was dangerously unstable, and the power of the state he sought to represent and defend shrank by the day.

Shortly after news of the monarchy's fall reached the front, a relatively minor event would put his skills and his principles to a test. While touring the positions of his division, Dzhunkovsky encountered a detachment of sappers marching under a red flag. The sight no doubt offended him, but he kept a tight grip on his feelings. He stopped the men and asked them why they were flying the red banner. They replied that it was a sign of freedom. Dzhun begged to differ. The color red symbolized blood, not freedom, he stated; the red flag was the emblem of bloody revolution, but

Russia's revolution had been bloodless. He quickly added that he had no intention of forbidding their display; they could go ahead if it pleased them. He had just stopped by to let them know his view of red flags in general and to say that many things permitted in the rear were out of place at the front lines where all thoughts should be focused on victory over the enemy. With this he left. By the time he returned, the red flag was gone.[15]

Dzhunkovsky's tactful handling of a sticky situation—a gracious acceptance of the soldiers' right of political expression combined with a fatherly admonition about their duty—would be a regular feature of his management style. In the early, good-humored days of the revolution it would be quite effective. Dzhun believed that initially the troops were far more interested in food than in politics. But, very quickly, larger and more troubling issues emerged. On March 9, an instance of fraternization with the enemy took place in his division, and though the practice was not repeated it was a harbinger of things to come.[16]

As Dzhunkovsky wrestled with the problems of command in the early days of the revolution, he also sought to come to terms in his own mind with questions of personal loyalty and honor. Much of this focused on his membership in the Imperial Suite. From the moment he issued the proclamation of the tsar's abdication, he understood that his status as a *svitii general* was illogical, even absurd. But to cast off the title and the insignia could be taken as a sign that he had turned his coat, something that was offensive and painful especially since his critics on the political right had frequently charged him with breach of faith and playing at liberalism. Yet Dzhun also understood that continuing to wear the trappings of the Suite could be seen by the men in ranks as a sign that he opposed the revolution and would undermine his position in their eyes. He sought to resolve this problem by immediately putting in for promotion to lieutenant-general, something he was in line for since he had served eight years in his present rank and which would automatically require him to remove the Suite's insignia. Dzhun received his promotion in April, but by then the Provisional Government had resolved his dilemma; on March 21, 1917, it abolished the Suite altogether.[17]

Equally troubling for Dzhunkovsky was the requirement that he and his men take an oath to the Provisional Government. Again he felt the painful tug of war between old loyalties and new obligations. Rumors were circulating among the soldiers that because of his status in the Suite he would refuse the oath, but on March 11 he appeared on horseback, publicly swore allegiance to the new regime, and ordered his troops to do likewise. Dzhun tried to put the best possible face on things, but it was agonizing. "Giving the order weighed heavily on my spirit," he remembered, "for by that oath it was as if I renounced everything that I had revered since childhood. But for the good of the country it was necessary; I had to give an example of loyalty to the Provisional Government although I could not feel much sympathy for it in my heart. . . . I had to get control of myself so as not to give an outward sign of the conflict that was taking place in my soul, for if I did, I would then be unable to maintain the stability of my division and prevent it from breaking down."[18]

Dzhunkovsky's attitude toward the Provisional Government was common to many officers who had been loyal to the monarchy. He accepted it as a fait accompli without any enthusiasm, at least at first. But—while he never would have admitted it—his feelings may have been more complex than most. His long, intimate service to the dynasty had given him the chance to see many of its key members at very close range; he was aware of their strengths and weaknesses. In 1915 the tsar had cruelly cast him out of office, and while he accepted this harsh blow stoically and in the spirit of Christian humility, Dzhunkovsky was not a saint, and it is hard to believe he felt no resentment. His memoirs contain a number of points where he alludes to mistakes made by the tsar and to failings of members of the dynasty: Nicholas's decision to take command of the armies and cast the internal affairs of the country to the whims of fate; the hysterical tendencies of Alexandra that in time would have guaranteed the appearance of a second Rasputin. Beyond these there are the resounding silences in the memoirs where Dzhun fails to mention even more important problems about which he was very familiar: the tsar's failure to back Stolypin sufficiently; his partiality to the organizations on the extreme right; his hostility toward the Duma; his anti-Semitism. Perhaps even more important was the contrast—implicit but never voiced—between the autocrat "in the fullest sense of the word," Alexander III, who placed duty above the personal, and his son, who for the sake of domestic happiness, yielded in matters of state to the fears and demands of his unbalanced wife.

All this is not to say that Dzhunkovsky had wished for or welcomed the fall of Nicholas II. Far from it. His grief over the tsar's abdication was real. Still, his own observations and his painful personal experience must have given him a better sense than many had of the degree to which the monarchy became its own worst enemy and Nicholas the architect of his own destruction. Without consciously recognizing it, Dzhun had already begun to make a subtle shift in loyalty from tsar and dynasty to nation and people. Service at the front, immersion in the "gray heroic mass" of the soldiery had hastened this process and made it easier for him to continue his adjustment to the demands of a radically altered situation.

Dzhunkovsky's support if not enthusiasm for the Provisional Government solidified further when, in March, Nikolai Shchepkin, a prominent Kadet politician from Moscow, appeared at the front as representative of the new regime. Dzhun remembered well his harsh words and provocative actions in support of antigovernment elements during the revolution of 1905, but now he was favorably impressed. Shchepkin spoke clearly and eloquently in support of the war and of the Provisional Government's determination to pursue it to a victorious conclusion. Dzhunkovsky put past antipathies behind him and, to the cheers of the soldiers, embraced Shchepkin on the platform pledging his support and that of his men for the new government in the common cause of Russia's triumph.[19]

As he moved toward accepting and supporting the Provisional Government, Dzhun had to face a much more concrete problem—how to deal with the soldiers' organizations, assemblies, and committees that sprang up immediately after the February Revolution and Order No. 1. They reflected the underlying tension between officers and men, but many army leaders adopted them as a means of restoring working relations with their troops and checking the spread of conflict and disorganization.[20] After some hesitation and resistance, the Army Supreme Commander Alekseev sent a telegram (No. 2137) encouraging officers to participate in order to "take events in hand" and to avoid needless conflicts.[21] Dzhunkovsky received the order on March 12 and immediately began to put it into effect, hoping to prevent further decline in his division's fighting spirit.[22]

The soldiers' organizations presented a serious challenge; they were without precedent in the army where the strictest discipline and command hierarchy had always prevailed. In spite of the intentions of Alekseev to "meet the threat of 'organization from below' with 'organization from above,'" they brought to the front a strong element of the dual power that had developed in the rear.[23] In his memoirs Dzhunkovsky noted that many officers found it impossible to adjust, with tragic consequences: "While fine fighting commanders, honorable and selfless . . . , their character was such that they could not come to terms with the demands of the moment, could not understand what was happening. These commanders immediately lost all influence over their units; the units began to break down completely, and their commanders became unsuited for further service at the front."[24]

For Dzhunkovsky, however, adapting to the new situation, while not pleasant, was easier than for many others. To begin with, his style of command had already built up a reservoir of goodwill on the part of the soldiers. This became clear at the time of the first meeting of his division's assembly on March 22, 1917, which gathered to work out resolutions to be carried to Petrograd by elected delegates. Dzhunkovsky did not attend the session and awaited its outcome with considerable trepidation. But in the end, the results were gratifying. The assembly adopted resolutions that called for the continuation of the war to victory and rejected the idea of a separate peace. The assembly hailed the Petrograd Soviet but asked it to dispel rumors of any rift with the Provisional Government. In addition, the assembly expressed its thanks to Dzhunkovsky for his defense of the interests of soldiers and officers and his concern for the well-being of the riflemen, a resolution greeted with a loud "hurrah."[25]

Dzhun understood that such support could be fleeting, however, and he worked hard to establish solid working relations with the soldiers' organizations once their existence was formalized and legitimized in mid-April.[26] He approached the task armed with the experience of his governorship, which had taught him how to cooperate with, guide, and sometimes oppose the work of elected institutions, zemstvos, city dumas, even peasant assemblies. Tact and powers of persuasion would always be important, but so would be the establishment of a useful institutional structure and regular procedures.

On April 22, the division committee held its organizational meeting. Dzhun was uneasy. "[It was] the first time I had to open such an assembly which did not share my views on military matters, and therefore the role I had to play was incredibly difficult," he remembered. He called the meeting to order, but once the business was under way, he left. Still, he did not let things slip. Although the meeting went smoothly, he felt he needed to find a way to direct the committee's work. He set up a special political section, which published all regulations concerning the committees in the division (company, regimental, divisional) as well as news of the political life in the various units. It made public the protocols of assembly meetings together with Dzhunkovsky's resolutions, for or against the decisions, as well as his views on pending political matters. He appointed Staff-Captain Piadishev, a highly intelligent, capable, and well-respected officer, as his division point man. As a result, Dzhun avoided serious conflicts with the committees. "All the protocols of the sessions were presented to me," he wrote, "and decisions went into effect only after my confirmation. This process which I was able to set up helped to preserve good order in the division."[27]

Sensible procedures were important and valuable, but personal intervention was often the only way to head off serious problems. In the first weeks after the revolution, Dzhun learned a painful but valuable lesson when the officers and men of the 57th Regiment demanded the removal of their commander, Colonel Stukalov. They presented their request in a fully correct form and there was no disruption of discipline. Still, it was a bad sign, and Dzhunkovsky felt that he was partly responsible because he had not acted soon enough. He knew that Stukalov was tactless, rude, and poorly educated, ill suited to command a regiment in these difficult circumstances. Dzhun had planned to step in and give Stukalov an honorable way out, but the whirlwind events in early March had made that impossible. Now, faced with the request from officers, men, and even the regimental chaplain, Dzhunkovsky let Stukalov put in sick and immediately transferred him to the rear. At the same time, Dzhun took steps to discourage other such incidents. When he replaced Stukalov, he chose someone from another regiment, so as not to reward any of the officers who had expressed opposition to their superior.[28]

Serious difficulties could occur almost without warning, requiring Dzhunkovsky to display not only sangfroid but also a talent for quick thinking and improvisation. On April 18 (May 1 by the Western calendar), Stavka sent out a command calling for the army to observe International Workers' Day. Dzhun complied, but the order he issued also reminded his troops that their chief duty was to defend the country and its newly gained freedom. In honor of the event, he canceled regular exercises and work details, but otherwise the day passed quietly with no celebrations in his units. In some of the neighboring divisions, however, May Day was greeted much more enthusiastically, with music, speeches, and red flags. As a result, the men of the 60th Regiment became extremely upset and rumors began to circulate that there had been an officers' plot to suppress the news of the workers' holiday.

Dzhunkovsky quickly went to the unhappy regiment where he encountered a man who demanded to present the concerns of the soldiers. "Sizing him up," he recalled, "I knew at once that before me stood a typical Jew," a man whose life's work was stirring up trouble. But he let him have his say. The speaker announced that the men of the 60th were embarrassed because they had not celebrated May Day, that soldiers of other units were laughing at them calling them backward. He blamed the officers for not having told the men in advance about the holiday. Dzhun responded coolly: "You . . . are engaging in cheap agitation," he told the man bluntly. It displayed ignorance and could only mislead the troops. This kind of complaint was possible before the revolution, he continued, but now that officers and enlisted men stood on equal footing, it was unfounded and unworthy. Somewhat deflated and subdued, the agitator replied simply: "All the same, we are hurt that we have missed the holiday."[29]

Turning to the men, Dzhunkovsky quickly suggested a solution: Why not observe the first of May by the Russian calendar, a real May Day, not some date in April? This, he told them, would give everyone ten days to prepare, adding "[then] you will celebrate in the Russian way, not by aping foreigners." The troops accepted their general's proposal, and the holiday went off without a hitch. It was a bit of the old and the new, marked by both prayer and banners celebrating the revolution and calling for a democratic republic. Dzhun was particularly gratified that there were no slogans demanding an end to the war or a separate peace. The festivities also gave him another chance to speak to the men reminding them of their duty. May Day, he stated, honored those who worked, and those who celebrated should reflect on whether they were properly fulfilling their obligations. "The title of free citizen." he concluded, "lays on each of us great responsibility before God, conscience, and country."[30]

After three months of revolution, Dzhunkovsky could survey the circumstances in his division with a measure of satisfaction if not confidence. The situation was far from being completely in hand; troops were committed to the war, but only in a defensive sense. Willingness to risk life and limb was very low, goldbricking was a growing problem, and there had been one instance, quickly terminated, of a unit refusing to go into the frontline trenches. Officers were struggling to carry out their duties, but many felt that they were sitting on the rim of a volcano, aware that the smallest mistake on their part or a rhetorical spark struck by an agitator could destroy the trust of their men and undo all their efforts. Still, discipline was holding and Dzhun was pleased that Toshiro Obata, a representative of the Japanese military mission who visited the division and toured its front lines, had been greatly impressed by the good order that prevailed in the ranks and by the fact that, despite many declarations guaranteeing soldiers' "rights," they continued to salute smartly. When in late April, Dzhunkovsky read the order of General Gurko, Supreme Commander of the Western Front,

Dzhunkovsky at the Western Front. From Anastasiia Dunaeva, *Reformy politsii v Rossii nachala XX veka i Vladimir Fedorovich Dzhunkovskii.*

denouncing the extensive fraternization taking place between Russian and German troops, he was surprised and felt a twinge of pride mixed with alarm. There had been only one instance of this kind in his division; it had occurred very early and had not been repeated. Obviously the situation was different elsewhere, and much more serious: "I knew that in many units fraternization had happened, but I did not think that our army could sink to such a level of shame."[31] Soon political currents swirling from the rear would accelerate the kind of breakdown Gurko's order had described.

In the three months following "Glorious February," both the Provisional Government and the Petrograd Soviet struggled as unremitting pressure from the lower classes made it difficult for the men who claimed to lead the country to catch their breath. Workers pushed ahead of the Soviet, forcing changes that both threatened the output of needed munitions and further dislocated the economy. First in Petrograd and Moscow and later throughout urban Russia, they demanded and got their long-standing goal of an eight-hour day. Then they struck repeatedly and in growing numbers for higher wages. They formed factory committees to represent their interests, and workers' militias soon appeared to defend the gains of the revolution against what they saw as the forces of reaction. Dubbed "Red Guards," they provided muscle to back up the claims of the proletariat.

Meanwhile, in the depths of the countryside, the peasants began to hear the notes of revolution. Slowly and hesitantly at first and then with growing confidence and determination, they moved against the estates of the gentry to realize their ancient dream of a "black repartition." The Provisional Government tried to slow and regularize the process, promising a final resolution of the issue by the projected Constituent Assembly. Increasingly, however, the peasants refused to wait, and the prospect that the redivision of the land might take place without them began to exercise a powerful magnetic pull on their sons in uniform.

The war loomed over everything. The conflict that had brought on the revolution now became its greatest problem. Initially, government and Soviet leaders unanimously proclaimed the goal of victory. But what would "victory" mean? How would it be gained? What would it cost in terms of blood and treasure? These issues became more pressing and contentious as the country's economic crisis deepened and the war weariness of both soldiers and civilians grew stronger and more vocal.

As with Order No. 1, the Petrograd Soviet stole the march on the Provisional Government, and on March 14 issued an "Appeal to the Peoples of All the World." It announced that Russian democracy would "oppose the policy of conquest of its ruling classes by every means," and it summoned the peoples of Europe to "common, decisive action in favor of peace." At the same time the appeal stated that: "We will firmly defend our liberty against all reactionary forces both from within and from without. The Russian revolution will not retreat before the bayonets of conquerors, and will not permit itself to be crushed by foreign military forces."[32]

The Soviet's declaration expressed the opposition of its socialist leaders to what they saw as the "imperialist" character of the war and reflected, albeit dimly, the much greater ambivalence of their worker-soldier constituents. It immediately posed a problem for the Provisional Government, which sought to represent the interests of the Russian state and to reassure the nation's allies of its determination to continue the struggle. Foreign Minister Miliukov was reluctant to abandon the war aims inherited from the old regime, which included acquisition of the Straits and Constantinople; but the Soviet's leaders pushed for a peace without annexations or indemnities.

Eventually, the two sides reached a compromise, and on March 27, the

Provisional Government issued a statement of its war aims in a proclamation to the Russian people. It vowed to defend the nation's liberty and its "own inheritance" but declared that the Russian people did not intend to "increase its world power at the expense of other nations." At the same time the declaration also asserted that the Provisional Government would fully observe "all obligations assumed toward our allies" and would not permit Russia "to emerge from this great struggle humiliated and sapped of its vital forces."[33]

Miliukov quickly sought to "clarify" the government's declaration so as to prevent Russia from losing the fruits of an allied victory. On April 1/14, he dispatched a note to Russia's embassies in Rome, Paris, and London denying that she was giving up her claims to the Straits and Constantinople.[34] Later, Miliukov instructed his diplomats to stress that the Provisional Government was confident of victory and certain that "the leading democracies will find a way to establish those guarantees and sanctions which are required to prevent new bloody encounters in the future."[35]

Miliukov's notes soon became public, and their thinly veiled demand for annexations produced a political storm. Soldiers and workers poured into Petrograd's streets in protest. The Provisional Government immediately issued its own "clarification" that reaffirmed its non-annexationist goals.[36] But demonstrations continued and for the first time since February blood was shed. The April crisis ended when Miliukov and Guchkov stepped down and on May 2, the Soviet Ispolkom reversed its position forbidding participation of its members in the cabinet. By May 5, a coalition emerged. Menshevik Social Democrats and Socialist Revolutionaries took a number of ministerial portfolios, for the first time saddling themselves with governmental responsibilities. Alexander Kerensky assumed the post of minister of war.

As the first major crisis of the Provisional Government unfolded, a train arrived at Petrograd's Finland Station in the evening of April 3, and Vladimir Lenin, the leader of the SD Bolshevik faction, stepped onto the stage of the Russian revolution after a decade of foreign exile. For the past three years he had watched Europe's tragedy from the vantage point of neutral Switzerland, convinced that the conflict presaged the imminent collapse of capitalist imperialism and the onset of a worldwide proletarian revolution.[37] Lenin's apocalyptic vision of capitalism's "end of days," to be followed by an international socialist millennium, set him apart from almost all other Russian political leaders. It freed him from any concerns about the Russian state, its unity, national interests, or the victorious conclusion to the war.

Lenin immediately presented a shorthand version of his program in the

"April Theses." It was brutally simple: No support for the Provisional Government, no support for the war; smash the existing state by eliminating the police, army, and bureaucracy; replace it with a commune state, based on the Soviets, that would give power to the proletariat and the poorest peasantry. Toward these ends, Lenin demanded extensive propaganda among the workers to expose the falseness of the Provisional Government and among the soldiers in the field to turn them against the war and to encourage fraternization with opposing troops.[38]

Lenin's radicalism shocked many, including some members of his own Bolshevik faction that up until then had taken a mildly "defensist" position.[39] To non-Bolsheviks, his words seemed to be the ravings of someone who had completely lost his grip on political reality. Events would prove Lenin wrong about the impending collapse of global capitalism and the coming of the proletarian utopia but would prove him right about the tactics his party should adopt in the Russian revolution. In this he received unwitting help from the Provisional Government itself.

The new coalition that emerged in May planned to reinvigorate the army and, together with Russia's allies, launch an offensive that would break the enemy and gain the desired peace. On May 5, Prime Minister Prince Lvov spoke for his government: "In order to pass on an honorable name to future generations, in order to hold her head high within the ranks of the great democracies, it is essential that revolutionary Russia should raise the might of her army to an adequate level. . . . The country must express its imperative will and send its army into combat."[40] A week later Alexander Kerensky, the new minister of war, departed Petrograd for an extended tour of the front designed to rally the armed forces. His order of the day set the tone of his campaign: "Warriors! Officers, soldiers and sailors. . . . It is impossible to expel the enemy by standing still. On the points of your bayonets you will bring peace, right, truth and justice. . . . Let the freest army in the world demonstrate that freedom is strength, not weakness. . . . Forward to liberty, land and freedom. . . . And do not forget, warriors of the revolution, that your names will be accursed if you do not accomplish the feat of defending the free honor and dignity of Russia. . . . I am summoning you to this feat; is it possible that you will not heed my voice?"[41]

The months ahead would answer Kerensky's question and determine the fate of the revolution.

Chapter 19

The End of a World

IN THE LAST DAYS OF MAY 1917, AS MINISTER OF WAR KERENSKY toured the fronts whipping up enthusiasm for the planned offensive, the Provisional Government's Extraordinary Investigating Commission (*Chrezvychainaia sledstvennaia komissiia*) summoned Dzhunkovsky to Petrograd. The Commission, established immediately after the February revolution, had been charged with gathering information about the illegal activities of high-ranking officials of the tsarist regime.[1] A distinguished lawyer, Nikolai Muravyov, was chairman, armed with the powers of an assistant minister of justice. The Commission's membership included a number of liberal and socialist political figures: Duma member Fedor Rodichev, Academician Sergei Oldenburg, N. D. Sokolov from the Soviet Ispolkom, and P. E. Shchegolev, editor of the historical journal *Byloe* (The Past). The poet Alexander Blok served as the chief editor of the Commission's stenographic record.[2] Many of the leading figures of the old order had already appeared before it; now it required Dzhun's testimony.

For Dzhunkovsky the Commission's summons was "more than unpleasant," but he was less upset than his division staff. "They all believed that I would never return and upon arrival in Petrograd I would be arrested and join the ministers already incarcerated in the [Peter and Paul] fortress."[3] He discounted the prospect of arrest but was deeply concerned about what might happen to the division in his absence. Discipline in his units was shaky, and army command had become unstable following the

April crisis, the reconstitution of the Provisional Government, and Kerensky's assumption of the post of minister of war.

In preparation for the new offensive, Kerensky had issued Order No. 8, a declaration of soldiers' rights.[4] It contained little that was new but provoked strong objections from some military leaders. General Gurko, commander of the Western Front, attempted to resign, and Kerensky reduced him to the rank of division chief.[5] On May 21 Kerensky dismissed General Alekseev as supreme commander and replaced him with Aleksei Brusilov who had led the successful offensive on the Southwestern Front in the summer of 1916. Although Brusilov was at the peak of his fame, Dzhun had no respect for him. In his memoirs he called Brusilov "a lackey from head to toe," who had accelerated the army's collapse.[6] But as a relatively obscure frontline commander, Dzhunkovsky was powerless to change things, and on May 30, he left for the capital accompanied by the best wishes of his staff and the division soldiers' committee.[7]

"It was strange and frightening to arrive in the city of Peter—the first time since the revolution," Dzhunkovsky recalled. "Everything appeared to be in place, the same houses, streetcars, cabbies, but somehow it all seemed to bear the imprint of sloppiness, disorder. The streets and sidewalks were unrecognizable for their dirt and trash, there were many signs of destruction." He made his way to his apartment on Kamenoostrovsky Prospect, where he reunited with his sister, happy to feel at home once more. Almost immediately, however, he headed for the offices of the Investigating Commission, located in an unused portion of the Winter Palace. Commission chairman Muravyov greeted Dzhunkovsky warmly and told him that he would be questioned about the Department of Police and Rasputin. Dzhun then met two other Commission members, Rodichev and Senator S. V. Ivanov. After speaking with them, he realized he had not been summoned as someone accused of a crime but simply as an informant. They agreed that he should testify four days hence, and he left the palace with a feeling of relief.[8]

Dzhun used his free time to visit friends in the capital. Although he expected the worst, he found them in surprisingly good spirits. Even Maria Leonardovna Maklakova, whose husband, his former chief, was imprisoned in the Peter and Paul Fortress, seemed to be holding up well. "I was very sorry for her," Dzhun remembered, "although she, like a true Christian, bore the cross that had been laid upon her without complaint."

The four days passed swiftly, and on June 2, 1917, Dzhun made his first appearance before the Commission.[9]

Initially, Alexander Blok was not impressed by the lieutenant-general who sat in the witness chair. "Uninteresting person. Hair close-cropped. Speaks carefully, calmly, quietly, intelligently. High forehead. Very youthful face, tanned." But his opinion changed as Dzhunkovsky started to testify. "No, a significant person. Honorable. A direct gaze [with] grey-blue eyes. The characteristic marks of a soldier. . . . Beautiful Russian speech."[10] Dzhunkovsky must have appeared ill at ease, however, because soon after the questioning began, Commission Chairman Muravyov interrupted to remind him that he was not accused of any crime. The Commission, he explained, was simply exercising the power it had been granted to demand "explanations" concerning the actions of higher government officials.[11] Although Dzhun already knew this and Muravyov's words may have reassured him further, his answers continued to show signs of stress and discomfort.

The Commission's earliest questions concerned the Department of Police, especially its secret agents and "provocation." Dzhun spoke at length about his efforts to reform the Corps of Gendarmes and the Department, removing secret agents from the army and high schools. He had opposed provocation and tried to end it, but he was quick to add that his efforts were limited by the nature of his office: "I did not get involved in all small, strictly practical [matters], feeling that this was not the duty of the assistant minister. He should only issue guidelines and other organs should put them into effect."[12]

The Commission asked Dzhun to clarify his views: What did "provocation" mean? He responded that while the insertion of *sotrudniki* into revolutionary groups was legitimate espionage, participation of a police agent in the incitement or commission of a crime constituted "provocation." Asked how he felt about a person, paid by the state, remaining in a subversive organization whose purposes violated criminal statutes, Dzhunkovsky appeared embarrassed. He admitted that he was disturbed by this problem but never really dealt with it. He had decided that his chief task was to "clean up the atmosphere" in the Department of Police by getting rid of its leading figures Beletsky and Vissarionov, men he did not trust and who opposed his reforms.[13] Dzhunkovsky spoke about his struggle with Beletsky, and of replacing him with the honorable Brune de Saint-Hyppolite. He also told of his success in reducing departmental expenditures, gave details about the secret funds held by the Department, and outlined his attempt to establish better accounting and control of them.[14]

Commission chairman Muravyov then switched to a new subject. "What," he asked, "were the most important matters in the life of the Department of Police during your tenure? . . . [D]idn't one of these concern the case of [Roman] Malinovsky who was a member of the State Duma?"[15]

The question was clearly painful. Blok noted that when Dzhunkovsky spoke about Malinovsky, the veins on his face stood out visibly, and the record shows that his testimony was often unsure, even evasive.[16]

"When did . . . [Malinovsky] become known to you?" Muravyov began.

"It's difficult for me to say exactly," Dzhun replied. "In any case, I don't think it was in my first year. It seems that I learned about this in 1914."

"You reacted to this then, in 1914?" Muravyov asked.

"I reacted at once."

Dzhunkovsky told the Commission that Beletsky had regularly reported to him about information received from a source called "X." But, "I didn't dig deeper, didn't even ask [for details], because it sickened me," Dzhun claimed. "Later," he continued, "it seems Beletsky told me that . . . ['X'] was Malinovsky. Then I wasn't just frightened, but horrified: a representative of the Soc[ial] Dem[ocrats], making inflammatory speeches in the Duma."

Questioning turned to Malinovsky's election in 1912. Dzhunkovsky claimed that as Moscow governor he knew nothing of the plans of the Department of Police to get its secret agent elected, but he recalled being disturbed when he learned that Malinovsky would be one of province's representatives in the Duma. "As far as I remember," he added, "when the elections were over and Malinovsky went to the Duma, there were rumors that the *okhrannoe otdelenie* was pleased."

Dzhun claimed that he had heard these rumors before he became assistant minister, but after he arrived in the capital he had forgotten about Malinovsky and had no idea that he was police *sotrudnik*.[17] Muravyov then asked Dzhunkovsky if he had known that Malinovsky had already been arrested three times for theft and was ineligible to sit in the Duma. Dzhun replied that he learned about it later but was not sure when. Was it at the same time as he found out that Malinovsky was a police agent? Muravyov inquired. Once more, Dzhun's memory failed: "I don't remember."

Muravyov continued to probe: When and how had Dzhun learned that Malinovsky was an Okhrana agent? Did Beletsky inform him in a report? Dzhunkovsky reflected: perhaps it was not Beletsky who told him after all, but Brune. Questioned further, he also admitted that he had *not* acted immediately upon discovering that Malinovsky was a police *sotrudnik.* He had thought things over carefully and moved slowly so as to avoid scandal and to "preserve decorum." Dzhun maintained that he became aware that Beletsky and Vissarionov vetted Malinovsky's parliamentary speeches only late in the game. Asked why he had not brought criminal charges against the two men, he gave his stock answer: "I simply did not want a scandal."

Dzhunkovsky denied that he had discussed removing Malinovsky with Duma president Rodzianko before acting. He had spoken to Rodzianko about Malinovsky only after the agent had left the country and then simply to confirm information the Duma leader already had.

"And didn't you ask Rodzianko how he knew this?" Senator Ivanov inquired.

"I don't remember," Dzhun replied. "Several people in the Duma suspected as much. . . . The hurried departure, the hurried flight of Malinovsky prompted conversations."[18]

Dzhunkovsky's testimony continued with many answers indicating uncertainty: "I can't affirm that." "Maybe I'm mistaken." "No, I don't remember." "As far as I recall. . . ." Clearly, it was all very troubling. The same held true when the questioning turned to the matter of Ekaterina Shornikova, the young woman entrapped by the Okhrana who had played a role in the dissolution of the Second Duma and Stolypin's coup of 1907. He remembered the whole sad business with considerable difficulty and had to be prompted regularly; at times he seemed almost distraught.[19]

Dzhunkovsky's first day before the Commission was not a brilliant performance, but it does not appear that he sought to deceive. While undoubtedly self-protective, especially in regard to Malinovsky, his testimony, with all its gaps and uncertainties, also reflects the fact that he was coming from another world. He had been almost two years at the front, immersed in the problems of command and, most recently, the task of holding his units together in the face of growing difficulties. By June 1917, his work as the empire's security chief must have seemed a distant, painful memory. The job had involved him with matters he considered questionable if not dishonorable and forced him to compromise some of his basic principles.

That he would repress memories of those things is fully understandable. It is understandable, too, that the Commission recalled him on June 6 to give supplemental testimony.[20] Then on the day following, Dzhun testified again. This time he felt on firmer ground.

The Commission asked about his general impressions of government policies and the problems he had faced as assistant minister, and about the Ministry of Internal Affairs and the Council of Ministers. What did he know about the replacement of Kokovtsov by Goremykin, the relation of the two prime ministers to the Duma, and Goremykin's actions in regard to the press? Commission members may have anticipated a flood of insider revelations, but if so Dzhun sorely disappointed them. He had attended only a couple of Council sessions, could not explain why Kokovtsov had been dropped and Goremykin chosen in his stead, and was unable to say anything about Goremykin's relations with the Duma or his policy toward the press.[21] Frustrated, Chairman Muravyov changed the subject.

"What do you know about unaccountable, outside influences on the ministers of your time?"

"Do you have in mind, strictly speaking, Rasputin's influence?" Dzhun replied coyly.

"Yes," Muravyov answered, "and the influence of people surrounding Rasputin."

Dzhunkovsky told of his growing concerns about Rasputin, his decision to place him under close surveillance, the incident at the Yar, and the report to the emperor that led to his dismissal.[22] Asked to explain the tsar's decision, Dzhun ascribed it to the influence of his wife. "Until my report had been given to the empress," he stated, "[the emperor] treated me very well. I accompanied him on trips and relations with him were even kinder than before, but then when, as I learned, my report had been passed to Alexandra Fedorovna, I saw and felt that something had happened."[23]

Later Muravyov asked Dzhun whether he knew why and when the tsar gave the report to his wife. Dzhunkovsky said that he believed that Nicholas showed the report to the empress in late June, but he did not speculate about the emperor's motives. Nor did he ascribe his fall exclusively to the actions of the empress; others, too, were very displeased with his work, especially Beletsky. Shcherbatov, he said, had warned him that the former director of the Department of Police was spreading "all kinds of things" about him in the State Council, but he had done nothing in response.

When questioning returned to the subject of the empress and the reasons for her hostility to him, Dzhun answered: "I think that the empress was so blinded . . . by the influence of Rasputin, that she didn't know what to do. Besides, she firmly believed that without Rasputin the heir would die. That was her *idée fixe*." Asked to explain further Rasputin's influence on Alexandra, he answered: "I ascribe it to psychosis."

"Caused by what?"

"Caused by hysteria."

Muravyov then inquired what form the connection between Rasputin, "an ignorant, depraved person," and the imperial family had taken, but Dzhunkovsky refused to speculate: "I don't know. There are many rumors, but I have no facts upon which to base a judgment."[24] He also had little to say about Rasputin's influence on government appointments, the dissolution of the Duma, or his attitude toward the war. Dzhun stated that he had had no contact with the "starets," and believed himself to be one of the few government officials who had never received so much as a note from the man.[25]

Toward the end of the session, the Commission questioned Dzhunkovsky about the opening of private correspondence by agents of the Ministry of Internal Affairs and the Department of Police. Dzhun was obviously uncomfortable; the practice was illegal and he disapproved of it but admitted that he had done little to eliminate it and had himself read and passed on "perlustrated" letters. Muravyov was at times aggressive, and his interrogation made Dzhun squirm with embarrassment:

"Vladimir Fedorovich, you knew about the perlustration of letters of members of the State Duma. Didn't you take any measures to reestablish a legal order?"

"True, I took no measures." Dzhun responded. "This was a custom that had existed for more than a hundred years. I knew, I had clear proof, that they read my own letters—and I could do nothing about it."

"You don't remember that you did anything to establish a legal order . . . during Maklakov's tenure?"

"Measures to eliminate perlustration altogether? No, I didn't take any."

"Why?"

"Because although the practice was, perhaps, illegal, in all countries it was done just as we did."[26]

Muravyov continued, confronting Dzhunkovsky with specific examples of illegally opened letters. Dzhun rather lamely justified most of these on national security grounds, necessary wartime counterespionage.[27]

Dzhunkovsky's ordeal concluded with embarrassing questions about a police spy who had penetrated several antigovernment groups and had attended a meeting of Lenin's followers in Galicia during late September 1913. At that time, the agent had advocated terror and expropriations. By Dzhun's own definition this was clearly an illegal act of provocation and when confronted with a signed document proving that he had authorized payment for the agent's trip to the meeting, he squirmed again. Perhaps he had signed off without reading it, he mused shamefacedly, and in the end admitted: "It would have been better not to have paid. I don't remember why I did it."[28] At this point, the members of the Commission had no further questions, and Dzhunkovsky stepped down.

His testimony finished, Dzhunkovsky visited Alexander Kerensky who had invited him to come by his office in the Admiralty. In 1915 Dzhun had seen Kerensky as a dangerous radical, and although now the war minister appeared better dressed than in his Duma days, nothing else about him left a positive impression. Kerensky asked Dzhunkovsky a few questions about the situation at the front, then launched into a monologue about the planned offensive, its certain success, and his intention to continue rallying the troops. Dzhun felt Kerensky's words lacked conviction. He seemed exhausted, without spark, burned out. "[E]verything he said about the army revealed only how little he understood. . . . I left him with the very unpleasant feeling that Russia was lost." Dzhun felt that he had somehow dirtied himself by meeting the war minister: "It seemed to me that I had done something bad, that I had betrayed someone."[29]

Meanwhile, disturbing news filtered back from his division: breakdown of discipline; the arrest of a regimental commander by his troops, growing influence of radical agitators coming from the rear. Dzhun secured the Investigating Commission's permission to leave, and on June 16, began his journey back to the front. But parting with his family was not easy, and he feared for their safety: "I left my loved ones [in Petrograd] with great sadness and considerable anxiety, the atmosphere was very unpleasant."[30]

Dzhunkovsky's returned to duty via Kursk, where he passed several days with Nina and other friends. En route, he experienced the country's growing railroad crisis. The train to Kursk was eight hours late, and his subsequent trip from Kursk to Minsk was hellish. Dzhun spent the first part of that journey standing up in a cramped corridor. At stations along the way he was shocked by the large mobs of soldiers milling about the platforms. "It seemed like some kind of migration," he recalled. Dzhun's arrived at the Bakhmach railhead to learn that the train for Minsk had already left. He hired a cab, transferred to another station, and waited until next morning to start the last leg of his trip.[31]

At Minsk he met General Anton Denikin, the new commander of the Western Front, and was pleased with his "honorable, direct view of things. . . . [Denikin] had no illusions," Dzhun recalled, "but he considered it his duty, for as long as he was able, to firmly and unwaveringly defend the motherland to the last."[32] Dzhun's perception was correct. Denikin was pessimistic, and on June 11 had sent a very negative assessment to General Brusilov. With regard to the Second Army, where Dzhunkovsky served, he concluded: "[Its] morale . . . is worse than that of the other armies and, apparently, considerably worse than the army commander imagines." His observations prompted Brusilov to comment: "Is it worth while to prepare a blow there with such morale?"[33]

On June 19, Dzhun reached his division's headquarters where the staff gave him a welcome that both touched and disturbed him. They pinned too many hopes on his return, and there were problems everywhere. His newly assigned chief of staff was a hopeless alcoholic and had to be removed. Reports of the regimental commanders contained nothing encouraging. The men were poorly housed, reserves were falling apart, the "revolution was deepening," and as "soldiers' rights" steadily expanded, duties were forgotten. In addition to arresting its commander, Colonel Ellerts, the 58th Regiment had voiced no confidence in all its officers. Troops of the division were unwilling to go on the attack—the very word was hateful—and they were not inspired by what Dzhun called the "hysterical" orders of Kerensky.[34]

By the time of Dzhunkovsky's return, the much anticipated offensive had already begun on the Southwestern Front. It quickly ended in disaster. German and Austrian troops counterattacked, drove the Russians back, and soon recovered all the ground they had lost in the Brusilov offensive the year before. This failure triggered riots in the capital that threatened to topple the Provisional Government and put tremendous pressure on moderate leaders in the Soviet. During the "July days" in Petrograd, the Bolsheviks rallied workers, and many believed they had attempted a coup. Then information emerged purporting to show that Lenin's party had received "German gold." Authorities cracked down; some of the Bolshevik leaders landed in jail, while Lenin shaved his beard, donned a wig, and fled to a hideout in Finland. The party barely survived. In the aftermath of the disturbances, the Provisional Government tried to strengthen discipline in the army. It tightened military censorship, reintroduced the death penalty at the front, and established firmer control over military commissars.[35] These measures enjoyed short-lived success, but could not stop the disintegration already under way.

Despite the difficult circumstances, Dzhunkovsky was able to maintain control of the 15th Siberian Rifles using a mixture of exhortation and traditional discipline. But he had to take strong measures to thwart attempts to subvert his authority. In late July, he received an order from Minsk to convene a conference (*s"ezd*) of the troops in his division. It came from the soldiers' committee of the Western Front and was supported by the front command. Convinced that a division conference would have a disastrous impact on discipline, Dzhun rushed to Western Front HQ. There he laid out his objections to the Provisional Government's commissar K. M. Grodsky and with great difficulty won his case. "Finally, [Grodsky] agreed with me," he recalled, "and under my dictation wrote an urgent dispatch that categorically countermanded the order concerning the conference and forbade all talk about its convocation." Dzhun was not always so successful, however. In August, he was ordered to send ninety soldiers for training as propagandists (agitators) with a view to strengthening support for the government. Dzhun feared that in the rear these men would quickly be corrupted by Bolshevik ideas and strongly warned against the proposal. But aside from dispatching a note criticizing the plan, he could do little.[36]

Dzhunkovsky's style of command helped him maintain discipline. He regularly visited his division's positions, walked along the front lines alone, talked to the men, and tried to obtain a clear picture of their conditions and needs. The front was quiet for the most part, but danger could erupt unexpectedly, and when it did, Dzhun sped to the scene. In early August, German guns, silent for some time, bombarded the artillery of the division, inflicting serious damage on one of its batteries and disrupting communications. Dzhunkovsky jumped into his car and headed toward the position being attacked to get a firsthand look.

He approached under enemy fire, astounded by what he saw. "The battery had stood in a deep wood, very well concealed," he remembered. "[But now] you would think that the forest had been hit by a hurricane; huge trees lay piled on one another and since the entire road was blocked, I had to leave the car and go on foot for half a kilometer." Reaching the battery, Dzhun found one of the guns wrecked and a fire raging. A number of shells containing poison gas had been hit and were pouring forth their contents. The gas sickened several of the artillerymen struggling to put out the flames, one of them seriously. Despite hellish conditions the men of the unit continued to fight the fire, and Dzhun marveled at their heroism. He went around the entire position, encouraging the men and thanking them for their selfless attention to duty. He then led the gassed soldiers to his car and took them to a first aid station.[37]

Direct, personal leadership paid many dividends, and Dzhun could take considerable satisfaction when he had the opportunity to compare his units to others in the Second Army. Troops in a neighboring division had become little more than robbers and hooligans. "I feared them much more than the Germans," he recalled. In mid-August, Dzhun visited the 29th Regiment of the 8th Division, a unit he had once commanded, on the occasion of its regimental holiday. He got a warm reception, but one he felt was too well lubricated by vodka and wine. During the celebration Dzhun witnessed an angry exchange of words between officers and men, seated at the same table. "I looked and listened to this, and my heart became heavy." The disrespect of the enlisted men for their superiors, the growing threat of violence against the officers, was pushing the army toward collapse.[38]

About the same time, a delegation from the British military mission headed by Colonel Benet inspected Dzhunkovsky's division. He showed them everything and, at the end of their stay, organized a dinner at which a string orchestra from the 60th Regiment played. The musicians had mastered the British national anthem, and when Dzhunkovsky raised a toast to George V, they struck up "God Save the King." As he recalled: "My guests, restrained Englishmen, had tears in their eyes." The British delegation left, pleased and perhaps surprised by the good order that prevailed in the trenches and among the reserves of the 15th Siberian Rifles. Upon his return to Petrograd Colonel Benet visited Evdokiia and, through her, conveyed to Dzhun his positive impressions. Later he sent Dzhunkovsky a letter that concluded: "Finally, I must thank you above all for the toast you proposed at dinner. It was the first time in more than a year that

I have had the pleasure of hearing a Russian officer propose the health of my King."[39]

Dzhunkovsky was far from sanguine, however. At the end of August he sent a report to General P. D. Shreider, the commander of the IX Army Corps, that painted a dark picture. The division was holding the line well enough, but the enlisted men distrusted their officers while the officers were indifferent to their subordinates. Neither had a strong sense of duty. Troops were being radicalized: "There are many adherents of Lenin among the soldiers," he wrote. "Their preaching is met with sympathy and their propaganda is conducted forcefully. . . . Many forbidden newspapers are being distributed." Soldiers' committees at the company level were worthless; regimental committees worked better but were too eager to criticize their officers. In general the men were uninterested in the war, caring only about food and the prospects for peace. Recent events—the Germans had just taken Riga—caused soldiers to suspect army command and called forth "a hatred for the 'burzhui' i.e. the officers."[40]

Although Dzhunkovsky was popular with his troops, in late August he received an anonymous letter containing a death threat. He responded with characteristic aplomb. After a highly visible tour of the front lines, he issued an order that mentioned the letter and contemptuously dismissed all attempts to frighten him: "My hour will not strike when the scoundrel who has written this letter wants it," he announced, "but when it pleases the Lord God; if it [should come] by a German bullet or one from a Russian traitor, it is all the same to me. . . . As long as I have sufficient strength to carry out the task I have assumed to defend the Motherland, no threat, [now] or in the future, will force me to deviate from my duties." Dzhun was gratified when the soldiers' committee of the 59th Regiment passed a resolution in his support and denounced the anonymous author of the letter.[41] Still, the situation at the front grew increasingly unstable, while events taking place in Petrograd and Moscow were unleashing forces that would accelerate the army's demise.

In addition to its attempts to impose greater discipline in the army following the failed June offensive and the "July days," the Provisional Government tried to suppress "anarchy" in the capital and throughout the country. It issued laws strengthening the penal code, giving authorities the power to close all meetings and assemblies, and granting them broad powers of arrest, detention, and deportation.[42] The cabinet reshuffled, and Kerensky attained near dictatorial status. He assumed the office of Premier while remaining war minister assisted by Boris Savinkov, the former terrorist. Still, Kerensky realized that his authority was weakening and, in order to mobilize broader public support, convened a State Conference in Moscow in mid-August.[43] The Conference failed to generate the desired sense of national unity and purpose, however. Instead, it revealed serious political divisions, and Kerensky, who had hoped to use the event to solidify and enhance his standing as national leader, appeared distracted and exhausted. Called to save the Russian state, the Conference ended leaving the impression that things were spiraling out of control. Many felt that a firmer hand was needed, maybe a man on horseback.

Eyes turned toward Lavr Kornilov, the colorful and charismatic general Kerensky had appointed supreme commander after he suddenly dismissed Brusilov in mid-July. Kornilov, a man of plebian antecedents, was devoted to the revolution but disturbed by the disintegration of the army and the growing disorder in the rear. He insisted on a free hand in restoring discipline at the front and in reserve positions behind the lines. He also broached the idea of subjecting workers in defense industries and transport to military discipline. Kornilov's demands initially angered Kerensky, but the general assured him that he was loyal and only wanted to tame the dangerous powers of the Soviet in Petrograd and the soldiers' committees at the front. These were Kerensky's goals as well, and at the Moscow State Conference he called Kornilov "the first soldier of the Provisional Government."[44] But by the end of the Conference, Kerensky's star was fading, and the new supreme commander had become the focus of conservatives hoping to check "anarchy" and restore order.

In the weeks that followed the Moscow Conference, Riga fell to the Germans and Russia buzzed with rumors of a Bolshevik coup or a right-wing putsch. Kerensky and Kornilov, both believing they were called to save the State and the Revolution, struggled to find common ground, each wary of the other's intentions. For a time it appeared they had reached a compromise. They agreed to create a new cabinet and restrict the Soviet's power; Kornilov would bring troops into Petrograd to secure the city and suppress an expected Bolshevik bid for power. But the deal, negotiated by Savinkov, quickly fell apart. Garbled messages convinced Kerensky that Kornilov aimed to overthrow him, so he dismissed Kornilov as supreme commander. Kornilov, believing that Kerensky had betrayed him, ordered troops toward the capital. In response, Kerensky rallied left forces, including the Bolsheviks, and by August 27, the "Kornilov revolt" had evaporated. The Provisional Government arrested the general and his closest associates and soon released the Bolshevik leaders who had been in jail since July.

Kerensky had won a pyrrhic victory. In defeating Kornilov, he alienated conservative and moderate elements without gaining stronger backing from the left. Mensheviks and SRs steadily turned against him, while the Bolsheviks' support in the capital and at the front grew apace. The Provisional Government now became little more than a hollow shell, and for the next two months the country drifted leftward. Political initiative passed to Lenin, still hiding out in Finland.[45]

Dzhunkovsky learned of the Kornilov revolt only after the event. What he thought about it at the time is unclear, but given the opportunity, he would probably have supported the general's efforts to restore order. He believed Kornilov to be "unquestionably honorable, a man of iron will," vastly superior to Kerensky and Savinkov but sadly lacking in political judgment. Writing years later, he assessed the conflict at the heart of the episode: "The minister of war [*sic*] was the famous Savinkov, the chairman of the Council of Ministers—Kerensky. The latter two sought not to save the Motherland, but to realize their political ideas. With regard to Kornilov, he wagered everything to save the country. Naturally the two [sides] could not come to terms, since they pursued different goals."[46] In the last days of August, however, circumstances at the front gave Dzhun scant opportunity for political ruminations of any sort, and soon he confronted a new and unexpected challenge.

On September 15, Dzhunkovsky was offered command of the III Siberian Corps, strongly supported by the soldiers' committee. The proposal took him by surprise and he was of two minds about the assignment. "The III Siberian Corps was home to me," he recalled, "I had begun my wartime service there, but [now] the Corps was terribly undisciplined." By mid-July its troops had forced the removal of the Corps's commander, Dzhun's former CO General Redko, as well as his chief of staff, the chief of staff of one of the divisions, four regimental commanders, and one brigade commander. Since the departure of General Redko, the Corps had had no permanent CO; the post was currently occupied by General Kondratovich, but he had never been confirmed in the position.[47] Obviously, leading the III Siberian would be difficult, but despite serious misgivings, Dzhun agreed to accept. Four days later, he learned that Army Command had proposed his appointment to the War Ministry.

As Dzhun prepared to part with the 15th Siberian Division, both officers and men offered touching expressions of affection and support. The troops of the 60th Regiment took up a collection to create a stipend in his name at an orphanage, and at a dinner in his honor one of the soldiers raised a toast: "We will never forget our division commander whom we could always meet, day or night, simply walking along the trenches, alone and unarmed, with only his little crooked stick." But things did not go quite as planned. Dzhunkovsky soon learned that Kerensky had not signed off on his appointment. Papers flew and pressure mounted on Dzhun's behalf, while he again had mixed emotions. Kerensky's hesitation offended his vanity, but he also felt relief: "It meant that the Lord God had granted me an honorable exit from all the mess that was taking place at the front." He left for Petrograd to wait things out, certain that if his promotion did not come through he would be put in the reserves.[48]

Dzhunkovsky spent the last days of September in the capital. "I passed the time in Petrograd calmly and happily," he recalled, "I enjoyed a cozy life in homey surroundings." Best of all, he was free from the heavy burden of command. Disquieting news from the front increased his reluctance to return. An ugly incident took place in the 60th Regiment where a soldier threw a hand grenade into an aid station wounding many doctors and other medical personnel, and he heard that the commander of the 5th Infantry Division had committed suicide. But on October 2, Dzhun received word that Kerensky had finally approved his appointment, and he accepted it with quiet resignation. He left for the front two days later, heading into the unknown, troubled to leave his family and friends behind in dangerous circumstances.[49] German forces had occupied islands in the Gulf of Riga, posing a direct threat to the capital; rumors circulated that the Provisional Government might evacuate. And unbeknownst to Dzhun, since mid-September, Lenin had been sending out increasingly strident demands trying to force a reluctant Bolshevik Central Committee to act. The time was ripe, he believed, for the seizure of power.

Dzhunkovsky reached his new command on October 6 and spent the first day trying to get a picture of the Corps, now composed of the 7th and 8th Siberian and the 7th Turkestan Divisions. The soldiers' committee impressed him favorably; its members were polite and correct and appeared easy to work with. He was less pleased with the division commanders, only one of whom seemed to be competent. By the end of the day he realized he faced a colossal task: "The Corps was on the edge of complete collapse; clearly it had been without a head. Division commanders had received no directives or support from their immediate superior and they themselves showed no initiative." The 17th Siberian Division, once a part of the Corps, had been disbanded and its regiments reassigned causing hard feelings that increased Bolshevik influence. The mood of the 7th Turkestan Division was also threatening.[50]

Soon after his arrival Dzhunkovsky attended a meeting of the Corps's assembly. He believed it was his duty, but he feared a possible confrontation with hostile agitators. He found the delegates seated as in a miniature duma, with Kadets to the right, SRs and Mensheviks in the center, and Bolsheviks and Left SRs on the left. As he waited for a chance to speak Dzhun fretted that he might be introduced as "Comrade Dzhunkovsky," something that would have been "terribly unpleasant." To his relief, however, the chairman simply announced: "The Corps commander would like to say a word." He greeted the delegates, wished them success, warned that the enemy might soon attack using poison gas, and urged them to keep the Corps at the appropriate level of combat readiness. When Dzhun finished, the right applauded while the left sat silent. He departed the meeting disappointed but thankful that he had not been booed off the stage. Later, he learned that his speech had not proved a complete bust. It produced a generally good impression although the left delegates criticized him for predicting a German attack: "They were convinced that I had wanted to frighten them, and had made it all up in order to raise morale." Dzhun took grim satisfaction when, three days later, the enemy launched an assault that was beaten back only with considerable difficulty.[51]

Signs of collapsing discipline in the Corps now appeared everywhere. On October 15, at a stormy meeting of the 25th Turkestan Regiment, soldiers beat up one of the battalion commanders and the next day a soldier of the same unit verbally abused a doctor serving at an aid station for not sending him to a hospital in the rear. Troops of the 25th Siberian Regiment forced out their commander, one of the best in the Corps. The morale of the officers was extremely low, many of the soldiers' committees lacked authority and were unable to check "excesses" by the troops, although these incidents were quite rare. The men proved reluctant to carry out military exercises, and some units went for days without fulfilling a single assignment. Efforts to strengthen the Corps's positions were largely unsuccessful, and troops of the 7th Siberian and 7th Turkestan Divisions plundered several nearby Jewish stores.[52]

On October 21, Dzhunkovsky carried out an inspection of the 27th Siberian Regiment and several of its battalions showed up without the proper equipment and weapons. The officers were clearly frightened, and when Dzhun met with the troops in an effort to defuse the situation the men were reluctant to speak at first. Then, he recalled, they began asking questions, "one more absurd than the other," about the "generals' treason" and the "sale" of Riga to the Germans. Dzhun tried to answer calmly, but when he pointed out the errors in their charges, the soldiers lapsed into a hostile silence. At this point he announced that since all their questions had been exhausted, he would head on to inspect another unit. The soldiers who had surrounded him gave way, and he extracted himself from their midst "not without pleasure." At some distance from the crowd, Dzhunkovsky looked back. He saw an agitator standing on a table speaking and gesticulating. From far away, he could not catch all that was being said, but two words came through clearly and repeatedly: *vlast' sovetov*—Soviet power.[53] In Petrograd four days later, the Bolsheviks overthrew the Provisional Government.

By the time the Bolsheviks seized control of the capital, their influence among the troops on the Western Front was already high, and after the coup they steadily took over the soldiers' committees in all three armies. Bolshevik success was particularly swift in the Second Army—with the exception of the III Siberian where, on October 25, the Corps committee passed a resolution that condemned the Bolsheviks' action as "undemocratic" and called for the formation of an "all-socialist government."[54] The mood of the Corps was the calmest of all the Second Army units, although tensions between officers and men were high. Discipline along the Western Front declined sharply in the days after Lenin's victory, but in the III Siberian Corps order was well maintained. Dzhunkovsky did not take personal credit for this but ascribed it to the fact that he had excellent relations with the Corps soldiers' committee, which was dominated by SRs who resisted Bolshevik efforts to take control. "The committee's relations with me were more than correct," he recalled, "it did not undertake anything . . . without asking for my consent. Thanks to this, order in the Corps was not disrupted . . . our positions were defended, there was no fraternization with the Germans, nighttime reconnaissance continued; as for the artillery . . . one could not ask for anything more."[55]

The III Siberian Corps continued to be comparatively stable into the first days of November. Still, the situation of the officers worsened, several were removed from command by the troops. Discipline declined, and the soldiers performed their military duties reluctantly, but the Corps saw no acute disturbances. Dzhunkovsky did his best to keep up the morale of the officers and regularly toured both the trenches and the rear positions.[56] Soon, however, severe shortages of both food and warm clothing threatened his men.

Faced with a possible catastrophe Dzhunkovsky summoned a conference of all division commanders, supply officers, and the presidiums of the Corps's soldiers' committees on November 8. As the meeting convened, a commissar from the new regime appeared. He was a Bolshevik, an extremely modest fellow, who had served in the rear and knew nothing about the front or economic matters. Dzhunkovsky made every effort to defer to the man, asking his approval for various decisions. But this only confused the commissar who stayed for three days and then disappeared. The conference proved unable to solve the clothing shortage; the supplies of warm gear had been plundered first in Moscow and then along the way to the front. The question of food proved more manageable and thanks to the efforts of the Corps's supply officer, provisions were found and the prospect of starvation averted.[57]

Soon Dzhun felt authority slipping from his grasp. On November 9–10 troops still followed his orders to conduct reconnaissance, shooting back when their patrols came under fire. But stress caused his own health to fail. Heart problems flared up, and after he suffered a series of cardiac episodes, doctors at the Corps advised him to take a seven-week medical leave in the Caucasus. Dzhun was reluctant to abandon the III Siberian, feeling that he could still help hold things together, and he decided to postpone his departure until after the election for the Constituent Assembly, scheduled for November 22. But by November 14 there was little for him to do. The Corps committee was now in Bolshevik hands, and while his relations with the new leadership continued good, he gave up his regular inspections of the front lines and spent most of the time in his quarters, resting, reading, and playing solitaire. Then on November 18, a member of the Corps committee urged Dzhun to take his leave as soon as possible. "The atmosphere," he said, "was not good; it felt somehow threatening." Dzhun got the same advice from his chief of staff. Clearly it was time to go.[58]

At 1 p.m. the next day, Dzhun's staff gathered for a final meal in the canteen. It was a sad occasion; all sensed they were parting for the last time. "After dinner," Dzhun recalled, "we took a group picture; I said goodbye to them, and my heart was heavy. It was hard to leave all these good, devoted comrades, abandoning them, as it were, to the whims of fate. What did the future hold for each of us?" But as Dzhunkovsky drove away, sounds of gunfire lifted his spirits: "It was my loyal artillerymen, firmly defending their position and, it seemed, telling me in parting that I need not worry about them, they were doing their duty to the last."[59]

Dzhun may have expected an untroubled return to Petrograd, but upon reaching the railhead at Orsha, he quickly sensed danger. He saw General Buivid, the commander of his old unit the 15th Siberian Division, under arrest, and learned of the savage murder of General Dukhonin, the last chief of staff of the old army, who had resisted Bolshevik demands concerning an armistice with the Germans. As Dzhun stood on the platform trying to make sense of the situation, the station master rushed up and pointed to a salon car belonging to the head of the Libavo-Romensk railroad line, who was leaving for the capital. "Go to him in that car," he urged in worried tones. "Don't stay in the station, you are attracting too much attention . . . go quickly." Dzhun told the man that two other generals were traveling with him and he replied: "Go, all of you, and be quick about it; don't stay here." Dzhunkovsky and his companions obeyed and got a friendly welcome from the salon car's owner (whose name Dzhun could not remember). He offered them tea, but before they finished, a train loaded with soldiers and sailors stopped briefly on tracks nearby. The men were drunk, and their brash, surly behavior left no doubt about what might happen should the generals fall into their hands.[60]

No sooner had the disorderly troop train pulled away from the station than a young man wearing a smart khaki uniform entered the salon car, an adjutant to Ensign Nikolai Krylenko, the Bolsheviks' newly appointed "Supreme Commander." He examined the documents of Dzhunkovsky and his two companions and then gave orders that upon arrival in Petrograd they should be taken immediately to the Military Revolutionary Committee at Smolny, the former girls' school, now the nerve center of the Bolshevik regime. Two arrested generals were added to the company, and soon the train left Orsha behind.[61]

Arriving at Smolny, Dzhun met Evdokiia, to whom he had sent a note informing her of his situation, and as they spoke his spirits rose. He fully expected to be brought before Vladimir Antonov-Ovseenko, the head of the Military Revolutionary Committee, and then released, since he had not been formally arrested. But the commissar was busy, and Dzhun learned that he and his companions were to be taken to the Peter and Paul Fortress. At the time, he believed it was all a mix-up that would quickly get straightened out. But signs of trouble were soon evident, and Dzhunkovsky got a taste of things to come. Awaiting transport, he began chatting with a junior officer, observing that until recently an act depriving someone of liberty would cause indignation since it infringed upon his personal inviolability. "Inviolability?" the young man responded dismissively, "that's a bourgeois prejudice." Dzhunkovsky recalled, "I looked at him astonished, but I did not continue the conversation, since after those words it was superfluous." Dzhun's astonishment might have been all the greater had he known what Commissar Antonov-Ovseenko—clearly a man free from bourgeois prejudice—had written on the order of incarceration: "To the fortress. Shoot."[62]

At 5 a.m. a car arrived to take Dzhun and his companions to prison. But as they were about to depart, Krylenko's young adjutant appeared. Appalled by the situation, he tried to get Antonov-Ovseenko on the phone but was not put through. He sought to convince the guard that Dzhunkovsky and the two other generals were not under arrest; he had brought them to Smolny simply to verify their identities and register them. His efforts were to no avail, however, and later that day Dzhun and the two generals found themselves in the Alekseevsky ravelin, the grim prison of the Fortress that had held so many opponents of the tsarist regime. Closed in 1884 it had reopened under new management. Dzhun and his companions sat in a cell graced by five beds with straw mattresses. Looking around, they saw writing on the wall, autographs of earlier guests, including Vladimir Gurko, former commander of the Western Front, with the dates of their arrival and departure. In a rather jovial mood, unaware of Antonov-Ovseenko's order, they hastened to inscribe their names and the date: November 22, 1917.

Conditions were not exactly cheery, but Dzhunkovsky's former service as security chief paid off. One of the prison guards recognized him and took pains to supply Dzhun and his cell mates with bread, tea, and other food. Evdokiia and Dzhun's niece soon appeared, and from them he learned that his situation was under sympathetic review at the Military Revolutionary Committee. The danger of summary execution passed, and by the end of the day, he was free. With no reason to return to an army rapidly falling apart, he put in for retirement on grounds of ill health.[63] In early December Dzhun entered the Military Clinical Hospital in Petrograd where doctors examined him for twelve days. They found serious heart problems: chronic inflammation and arterial sclerosis. On the basis of their report he was honorably discharged and soon granted a pension of just over forty-five hundred rubles per month.[64]

Dzhunkovsky's war was over, but the ties of service and affection that bound him to the men he had led were not completely severed. Shortly after his retirement, Dzhun sent for the personal things he had left at the front in the care of the soldiers' committee. He did not expect much; the army was rapidly disintegrating, the slogan "loot the looters," that is, the *burzhui*, had become the order of the day. To Dzhun's great surprise, however, he received everything, "down to the last thread," including an unfinished bottle of Madera wine and an opened box of cookies. "Such consideration and kindness to me from the committee and members of my staff moved me deeply," he recalled. "I was touched to the point of tears."[65]

Part Six

In the Shadows, 1918–1938

Chapter 20

Pensioner, Prisoner, Witness for the Prosecution

RETIRED FROM THE ARMY, SETTLED IN THE APARTMENT he shared with his sister Evdokiia, Dzhunkovsky seems to have had no immediate plans or ambitions. Since 1915 he had sought obscurity, and now recovering from the strains of war at the age of fifty-two, he appeared content with a private life. The prospects of a pension offered the hope that he might support himself and his sister on a modest scale, but the political turmoil that began with the fall of the monarchy and accelerated after the Bolshevik seizure of power had called up a storm of social change. Dzhunkovsky, who had already witnessed the disintegration of order at the front, could have had few illusions that his private life would be tranquil.

Soon his thoughts turned elsewhere. Nina Evreinova was on her family estate at Borshchen, a situation that may have caused Dzhunkovsky some anxiety. Although the Evreinovs appear to have been on good terms with the surrounding peasants, the life of any noble landowner in the post-1917 countryside was likely to be getting dangerous. Motivated perhaps by this concern, his uncertain health, as well as by a desire to enjoy a better climate and the warmth of their friendship, Dzhun traveled south at the end of January 1918 and spent February and part of March with Nina in Kursk province.[1] But by mid-month he had returned to Petrograd to face the vast changes that the revolution had made in the city of his birth.[2]

"It is the end of a world . . . ," the French diplomat Louis de Robien mused as he watched Petrograd enter the year 1918. "[A]s I crossed the Troitsky Bridge I gazed at the Imperial city in the rays of the setting sun: it is already dead and its magnificence will soon be only a memory."[3] The brilliant European capital of 1914 was gone. But gone, too, was the vibrant birthplace of the revolution it had become three years later. On his return to "Piter," the Russian writer Viktor Shklovsky found the city strangely silent: "Like after an explosion, when it's all over, when everything is blown up. Like a man whose insides have been torn out by an explosion, but he keeps on talking."[4]

Poverty and hunger were everywhere. Provisioning the capital proved almost impossible as the economic links between town and country, strained by years of war, snapped under the weight of revolution. Lines snaked outside shops; basic necessities often could not be had. Major factories shut down, throwing thousands out of work. The large Petrograd garrison, underfed, underemployed, but well armed, enveloped the streets like a vast gray shroud, and the winter darkness deepened with the loss of almost all outdoor illumination.

"We have no order." The words that marked the beginning of Russian history now seemed entirely contemporary.[5] Anarchy lay just below the surface of life and often jutted above it. Since the "alcoholic lunacy" that swept Petrograd following the Bolshevik coup, the new authorities had only a shaky grip on the city they claimed to rule.[6] What passed for government could not deliver even the most elementary of services. Snowdrifts swallowed sidewalks; the frozen carcasses of horses lay in nearly impassible streets, usable parts swiftly scavenged by the starving. Penury, misery, and idleness—the mothers of vice—gave birth to a staggering crime wave. In a city that before the war had a population of just over two million, officials recorded 135 murders and 15,600 burglaries in a single month, and many others must have gone unreported. Stickups, even in broad daylight, were commonplace, with victims relieved of all valuables, some even stripped of their clothes.[7]

Normal civil relations became almost impossible. People watched passersby with suspicion and fear. In the atmosphere of class warfare conjured by revolution and socialist propaganda, demands for social justice mixed easily with criminality and simple vengeance. "The most malicious, partly criminal element congregated around the Soviets," the liberal political figure Adriana Tyrkova indignantly recalled. "They formed the new governing class, unfettered by law, tradition, public opinion. . . . They could arrest, rob, assault, murder as much as they liked with perfect impunity."[8]

Those of the former privileged classes were now the most vulnerable, especially the old, suddenly thrust into a new and terrifying world. With banks closed, assets frozen, and life savings swept away, they had few means of survival. The sight of miserable *burzhui*, selling whatever they could on the street, provoked only derision from the triumphant lower orders. "Red Guards" invaded, searched, and plundered homes; authorities forcibly lodged workers in the apartments of the once comfortable. In the name of the revolution, newly formed housing committees tyrannized erstwhile elites. They could mobilize anyone under the age of fifty for compulsory labor and make them clean streets and sidewalks, watched by vigilant representatives of "Soviet power." Protests or complaints were useless and might provoke violent reprisals.[9]

Neither Dzhunkovsky's memoirs nor the materials in his archive tell us much about how he and his sister survived the early months of 1918. They sold many of their belongings, including Dzhun's library, and eventually moved into two rooms. They did, however, preserve his personal archive and found a place where these papers could be stored.[10] The pension that the general duly received from April until his arrest in September undoubtedly made their situation better than that of many others left over from the old order. Still, finding food and fuel was extraordinarily difficult, and much of the burden may have fallen on the shoulders of the doughty Evdokiia. Always devoted, resourceful, and gravely concerned for her brother's health, Dodo probably became the chief hunter-gatherer. Dzhunkovsky's medical problems were not the only reason for him to stay off the streets. Despite his status as an honorably retired general enjoying a measure of governmental largesse, Dzhun had to be careful not to call attention to himself while also fulfilling official requirements concerning the registration of officers from the tsar's army. Events made a low profile increasingly necessary. The Bolsheviks' decision to move the capital to Moscow diminished government authority in Petrograd and made the lives of the "formers" there increasingly precarious. More important, the humiliating peace of Brest-Litovsk, which the Soviets signed with Imperial Germany in March 1918, shocked Russians of all political colorations. It nearly split the Bolshevik party itself and provoked growing opposition. By the summer Lenin's 1914 slogan—"turn the imperialist war into a civil war"—was about to become reality.

The Bolshevik coup in Petrograd and the "triumphal march" of Soviet power into the provinces prompted the abrupt and panicked flight of many who had lost position and property in the growing tumult. Soon they gathered on the outskirts of what they would contemptuously call "Sovdepiia," often under foreign protection. In Kiev and elsewhere they ate, drank, gambled, grumbled, and denounced the Communist usurpers from what seemed a safe distance, hoping for the return of a world they refused to see had been lost forever. Armies of resistance, staffed mostly by officers loyal to the old regime, began to form, first on the Don and later in Siberia and other outlying regions. The struggle that ensued between "White" and "Red" would convulse Russia for almost three years. Savage and cruel, it cost millions of lives and left the country exhausted, impoverished, and filled with "grudge and mortal hatred."[11]

Despite an increasingly ominous situation, not all members of the old elite would fight or flee. Many sat tight hoping for the quick return of "order" and better times. Some sincerely tried to find a place in the new system. Others simply could not contemplate leaving their native land.[12] Dzhunkovsky was one of those who chose not to fight Soviet power or abandon Russia, but he never clearly stated his reasons. The ill health that justified his retirement from the army was certainly important. Yet future events showed Dzhun to be remarkably resilient, able to endure harsh conditions and poor food in Soviet prisons and long hours of hard work after his release. Those who saw him then remarked on his enormous energy and vitality. In his seventy-second year, it would take a bullet to stop him.

Evdokiia, Nina Evreinova, and others dear to him living in the areas under Bolshevik control unquestionably stood hostage to Dzhunkovsky's good behavior, but his experience in the Great War may have been equally important in explaining his decision not to fight. He had seen the horrors of combat and its attendant suffering. Years in the trenches gave him a strong regard and affection for all who had put on the greatcoat in defense of the motherland. Now bleeding Russia needed peace, order, and stability. He had no desire to draw his sword in a country that had already endured so much.

Dzhun rejected emigration; love of country was his pole star. Although he commanded good French, passable English and German, he did not feel at home in foreign cultures. Bolshevik rule might threaten Russian *statehood*, but the historic community of Russia and her people remained to be served, even in these dark times. Dzhunkovsky revealed his feelings in a conversation with Iurii Bakhrushin, when he quoted approvingly the words of his friend Sergei Sheremetev: "I will curse those of my children who leave Russia and go abroad. We must suffer together with her all the sorrows and misfortunes that fall upon her and our people. I see Russia mighty and glorious."[13]

Neither the execution of Tsar Nicholas, announced on July 20, 1918, nor the news that came later of the slaughter of the tsarina, "the most august children," and saintly Ella, bludgeoned and thrown down a mineshaft while still alive, could make Dzhunkovsky abandon his country.[14] These events shocked and horrified him, almost beyond words. His memoirs, which devote so much attention to the imperial family and members of the dynasty, never give the details of their fates. Instead they exclaim silently: "Always think of it, never speak of it." Faced with this tragedy Dzhunkovsky was sustained by his strong Russian Orthodox faith. God's will was unknowable, but even terrible events had a purpose. History, chronicles, and the lives of saints showed that the Almighty had more than once dispatched "merciless heathens" to punish the country for its sins, and that from earliest days Russia's land had been cleansed and made holy by the blood of princely martyrs. Through their deaths they expiated the sins of the nation and then, robed in purple, interceded for their people before the heavenly throne.[15] How much more necessary that expiation and intercession now, when the ignorant multitude, misled by godless rulers, desecrated churches, unearthed sacred relics, and mocked the divine law!

The murder of the Romanovs soon became but a symbol of the larger terror engulfing Russia. As civil strife loomed on the frontiers of "Sovdepiia," the Bolsheviks faced more and more opponents within their own sphere of control. Peasants rose in opposition to government grain requisitions, their protests swiftly and brutally suppressed. In the cities, attacks on Soviet officials led to mass reprisals. Early June saw an uprising of the Left Socialist Revolutionaries in Moscow and a revolt in Iaroslavl instigated by Boris Savinkov, the former terrorist and assistant minister of war in the Kerensky government. At the end of August the Bolshevik leader Moisei Uritsky fell victim to an assassin in Petrograd. In Moscow Fanya Kaplan, a young SR, shot and seriously wounded Vladimir Lenin.

In response the Bolsheviks strengthened their chief instrument of repression, the All-Russian Extraordinary Commission for Combating Counter-Revolution, Speculation, Sabotage, and Misconduct in Office, known by its initials Ve-Che-Ka. Founded in late 1917, it steadily increased its power to deal with the enemies of the proletarian dictatorship. By 1918 the Vecheka had already become something of a state within a state, answerable only to the Council of People's Commissars (*Sovnarkom*), and unrestrained by traditional legal norms. At its head stood Felix Edmundovich Dzerzhinsky, a Pole who had spent the better part of his adult life in tsarist prisons and exile. Ascetic, incorruptible, and indefatigable, utterly devoted to the goal of building a socialist society, Dzerzhinsky embodied both the best and the worst of Russia's radical tradition. Like Chernyshevsky's Rakhmetov or the nihilist supermen of Nechaev and Bakunin's "Catechism," he had "no other thought, no other passion" but the revolution. Yet, unlike many of his colleagues in the Vecheka, Dzerzhinsky was not personally cruel, and he could see good in some of those whose background made them "alien" to the new order. There was something tragic about "Iron Felix," who had once considered the priesthood and now felt that the necessary struggle against the "class enemy" tainted his own soul.[16]

The Red Terror had been building since the Bolshevik coup, but it came out full blown after the assassination of Uritsky and the attempt on Lenin's life. On September 5, 1918, the Council of People's Commissars proclaimed it, stating that "in the present situation it is absolutely essential to safeguard the rear by means of terror; . . . that it is essential to protect the Soviet Republic against its class enemies by isolating these in concentration camps; that all persons involved in white guard organizations, plots and insurrections are to be shot; and that it is necessary to publish the names of all those shot, giving the grounds for their execution."[17] With the decree on Red Terror—"an open license to kill"—no non-proletarian could feel safe.[18] Former officials of the old regime were particularly vulnerable, and even workers who questioned government measures trembled. The prisons of Moscow and Petrograd filled rapidly, conditions worsened, and shootings occurred nightly. In the provinces, an even more desperate situation prevailed. Local Chekas, operating with almost no central control, took the decree to mean that all things were permissible. Arbitrary arrests, frightful tortures, and summary executions became their order of the day.[19]

At just this moment Dzhunkovsky set out on another journey south, headed to Kursk, Putivl, and Poltava. His aim was innocent and the trip carefully planned; but with it began a nightmare for Dzhun and Evdokiia that lasted more than three years. During that time Dzhunkovsky suffered imprisonment in some of the country's worst jails and endured conditions that put his health in grave danger. He would stand before Soviet tribunals as both a witness and a defendant, and hear a state prosecutor call for his death. Dzhunkovsky always believed that his life was in the Lord's hands; but if, indeed, he survived his ordeal by the grace of God, it is clear that the Almighty worked his will through the agency of Dzhun's devoted sister, his many loyal friends, and one unexpected benefactor.

In a letter he addressed to Felix Dzerzhinsky after his arrest, Dzhunkovsky explained that he left Petrograd because he wanted to visit relatives and gain a respite from the privations of life in the former capital, particularly the shortage of food and its high cost. He further stated that, had he been able to settle in the south, he intended to return for his sister and nieces. Dzhunkovsky stoutly denied any intention to abandon his country and go over to Ukraine. "I am above all a Russian, and not a Ukrainian separatist," he asserted. True, he had roots in the Poltava region and even held a Ukrainian passport, "but I never made application to renounce Russian citizenship and have no desire to gain the advantages of being a Ukrainian subject." Nor had he been concerned for his safety: "I lived through the entire period of Red Terror following the murder of com. Uritsky and was not at that time arrested or subjected to search."[20]

Other sources confirm Dzhunkovsky's claim that he never feared for his person. According to his sister, her brother made no attempt to hide his identity or conceal his travel plans from Soviet authorities and systematically gathered the documentation necessary to legitimize his trip. The journey required an enormous amount of official paper—striking proof that, within a year after the birth of Soviet power, revolutionary suspiciousness had fertilized established bureaucratic roots to produce a luxuriant thicket of red tape. In all, Dzhunkovsky obtained seven separate documents: a certificate from his place of residence concerning his medical condition, verified by the Medical Department of the Petrograd Region; an attestation from the Criminal Investigations Section to the effect that he had not been convicted of a crime; an affidavit from the regional Commissariat for Military Affairs confirming his discharge from the army; an authorization from the Housing Committee giving him the right to return to Petrograd, which also had been approved by the Soviet of Workers' and Peasants Deputies of the Petrogradskaia Storona District; a personal identification issued by the Commissariat of the Petrograd Region of the Northern Commune; another I.D. from the Commissariat of Nationalities of the Union of Communes of the Northern Region; and, finally, written permission to travel on a hospital train from the Department of Hospital Trains for Refugees.[21]

Armed with these documents Dzhunkovsky left Petrograd on September 12, 1918. But his trip would end at Orsha, where less than a year before he had been detained. "At Orsha a commission looking over my documents found them to be in order," he told Dzerzhinsky, "but then an agent of the Extraordinary Commission appeared and asked me if I were a relative of the former assistant minister. When he received the answer that I was the very same, he ordered me to gather my things and come to Extraordinary Investigating Commission where I was detained."[22]

The precise reasons for Dzhunkovsky's arrest are far from certain, although surname, former service, and his Ukrainian destination were probably sufficient.[23] On September 18, the newspaper *Izvestiia VTsIK* charged that Dzhun was connected to the counterrevolutionary Union for the Salvation of the Motherland and Freedom, an organization founded by Savinkov, and also claimed that he was heading south to join White forces led by General Krasnov. The account added that Dzhunkovsky was "slated to command one of the armies fighting against Soviet power. Huge sums have been assigned for his liberation."[24] These accusations were absurd, especially the alleged link with Savinkov, whom Dzhunkovsky despised both for having organized the murder of Grand Duke Sergei Alexandrovich in 1905 and for his activities in the Provisional Government. But unconcerned or ignorant of realities, the local Cheka jailed him in Smolensk.

We have little direct information about what Dzhunkovsky had to endure in the days that followed. In his letter to Dzerzhinsky he spoke of "terrible conditions." His sister imagined dank cells, inadequate food, and constant danger.[25] She was probably not far off the mark. Provincial prisons in these years were invariably described as hellholes, places of hunger, cold, and overcrowding, with unsanitary conditions that made them breeding grounds for every conceivable disease. Doctors were few, resources limited, and care could be provided at the most primitive level. Local Chekas were guilty of the wildest abuse of their charges. By 1919 Smolensk prisons had acquired a reputation for being some of the most dangerous and unpleasant, and it is unlikely that things were much better earlier.[26] While held by the Cheka, Dzhunkovsky was interrogated twice and in one session was accused of counterrevolutionary activity for opposing Rasputin "who helped the Bolsheviks." Later, he told friends that early in his incarceration he endured several mock executions. Since in Moscow jails his conditions were relatively mild, it seems likely that he was referring to the time spent in Smolensk.[27]

Evdokiia learned of her brother's arrest on the evening of September 17, 1918, when the late edition of *Petrogradskaia Pravda* printed the bulletin.[28] The news stunned her; she had no idea what to do next. Then, bewildered but determined, she embarked on what would soon become a well-worn path trod by millions desperately seeking to learn about, aid, or if possible, free loved ones held in the iron grip of Soviet power, a trail of tears over half a century long. She knew nothing of Smolensk and wisely decided she could be of no help there. Given the already slow pace of the growing Soviet bureaucracy, going through channels would likely do no good. Better start at the top. Evdokiia had been active in education, and Dzhun had many connections in the theatrical world; perhaps People's Commissar of Enlightenment Anatolii Lunacharsky might help. But when Evdokiia contacted him, Lunacharsky simply penned a brief note asking Commissar of Justice Dmitrii Kursky to receive her.[29]

To Evdokiia, an appeal to Vladimir Dmitrievich Bonch-Bruevich, secretary of the Council of People's Commissars, seemed even more promising. A close friend of Lenin, he was a revolutionary and a scholar, active in the struggle against autocracy since 1896. As a Social Democrat, he had been an effective party propagandist; as a historian and anthropologist, he was a noted expert on the Russian sectarians. Bonch-Bruevich was reputed to be a humane person. Maybe he could be convinced to intercede with his comrades.

Evdokiia revealed her fear and confusion at this time in a letter she sent to a friend asking for help in gaining Bonch-Bruevich's ear: "Visit Vl. B-B, I pray, beg him to take protective measures. The situation is desperate.

Vladimir D. Bonch-Bruevich. Photography Collection of the Miriam and Ira D. Wallach Division of Art, Prints and Photographs, New York Public Library, Astor, Lenox and Tilden Foundations.

I am not talking about conditions of confinement in a damp cellar without food, . . . [prisoners] are subjected to insults, beatings, etc. At any minute they can expect execution. . . . I pray you to take all measures to save [Vladimir's] life. Where should I turn, whom should I ask? I have a letter to the wife and sister of Lenin. Should I go? I will be home at 6. Please come."[30]

By September 23, however, Dodo had pulled herself together sufficiently to address a long, carefully worded petition to Bonch-Bruevich in his official capacity. She gave the secretary of Sovnarkom details about her brother's trip and the documentation he had gathered in preparation. She outlined Vadya's career, recalled how the tsar had summarily dismissed him from his post as assistant minister of internal affairs, and told of his service at the front and medical discharge. "Since his retirement, living in Petrograd," she continued, "[my brother] has not joined any party organizations or unions. [Although] of Ukrainian background, [he] has not given up Russian citizenship . . . and [undertook] his trip to Kursk . . . solely to recover his health." Finally she wrote of her brother's honorable nature: "According to all who have had dealings with my brother, the distinguishing feature of [his] . . . character and of his service was: attention to duty, justice and humanity. He always followed his conscience and never went against it." She assured Bonch-Bruevich that there were no grounds for Dzhunkovsky's arrest and that the circumstances in Smolensk prison gravely endangered his health.[31] The next day Evdokiia sent Sovnarkom a copy of the original certificate that described her brother's medical condition and asked that he be transferred to Moscow if he could not be liberated immediately.[32]

Bonch-Bruevich quickly passed Evdokiia's petition and the supplementary material on to the appropriate officials in the Commissariat of Justice—People's Commissar Kursky and Mechislav Kozlovsky, the head of its Investigative Department. In cover letters Bonch-Bruevich wrote that Dzhunkovsky had "completely fulfilled all formalities in Petrograd" and, at the time of his arrest, had in hand "all the necessary papers from the Soviet authorities of the Petrograd Commune."[33] That same day Evdokiia addressed another letter to Kursky asking for her brother's release or transfer to the capital.[34] She decided to move to Moscow, and by October 5 was living there in the heart of the Arbat district.[35]

Dzhun's devoted sister did not simply appeal to Soviet officials. Through a friend she sought help from Boris Avilov, a Social Democratic journalist who had worked on the newspaper *Novaia zhizn'*. She approached T. Kristensen, an attaché at the Norwegian embassy. The results were not encouraging. Avilov told Evdokiia that her brother's arrest was clearly a political decision and cautioned that "at the present moment petitions for his release have little chance of success." Avilov stated that his own strained relations with the Soviet authorities would make him a poor intermediary and suggested she apply to Maxim Gorky. But in conclusion he added: “I am fully prepared to certify that in 1914, by order of V.F. Dzhunkovsky, I was released from prison and spared exile, and that V.F. regularly set aside or sharply reduced harsh punishments imposed by administrative means on persons engaged in political activities.”[36]

Dodo’s appeal to Mr. Kristensen was somewhat more successful. The attaché wrote to Bonch-Bruevich testifying to Dzhunkovsky’s good character and nonpolitical status: “I personally know Dzhunkovsky to be an entirely upright person and am completely convinced that at the present he is occupied exclusively with personal matters.” He requested that Bonch-Bruevich investigate the causes of Vladimir’s arrest and, if they were not justified, take action to gain his release.[37] But when Kristensen’s letter reached the People’s Commissariat of Justice, it had no effect. On October 7, the Norwegian received a curt reply: “In answer to your request concerning the release of V. F. Dzhunkovsky, the Investigations Department of the P.C.J. states that the former assistant minister of internal affairs cannot be freed.”[38]

Dodo refused to give up. Once established in Moscow, she wrote letter after letter calling for her brother’s release. Each time she added more detail about Vadya’s worthy deeds: his struggle against Rasputin, and his intervention on behalf of condemned prisoners and revolutionaries. She pressed for his transfer to a Moscow prison, for reasons of health and his longstanding connection to the capital.[39] Evdokiia sought to mobilize others, and she found ready support from a group of artisans whom her brother had helped during his governorship. In 1911 they had approached Dzhunkovsky seeking to rent a portion of state land to establish a settlement where they could practice their craft of furniture making. But because they were petty traders (*meshchane*), they were not permitted to obtain land that the law reserved for peasants. State officials had blocked all their efforts, and the governor was their last resort. Dzhun took up their cause, going directly to the minister of agriculture, then to the tsar himself, and in May 1912, an imperial order gave the craftsmen the land they sought. Deeply grateful, they named their settlement “Vladimiro-Dzhunkovsky.” Now they wrote to the Vecheka, and in a lengthy petition told of their difficulties in setting up their community and of the crucial aid the former governor had provided. “We cannot forget our founder,” they concluded. “And remembering the gratitude that is printed on our hearts and on all generations of [our] children . . . we cannot be at peace until we have made his past known.”[40]

Finally Evdokiia turned to Lenin himself. On October 19, she sent a letter detailing again the story of Dzhunkovsky's arrest, his precarious health, and the hardships he endured in Smolensk. She told of his service as assistant minister of internal affairs and commander of the Corps of Gendarmes, but she insisted that his conduct in office had always been honorable. "My brother accepted these positions as the result of his service obligations," she wrote, "but he always fought against those methods which he believed were impermissible: arbitrary abuse of authority, illegal provocation, harmful influences, . . . and always held to a straight path." Dodo repeated the story of Vadya's wartime service, his retirement, and subsequent obedience to Soviet authorities. Her brother had no ties to any counterrevolutionary organizations or with the White armies. He should be released or at least transferred to Moscow.[41]

Evdokiia's passionate entreaties to Soviet officials fill a substantial file in the archive of the Commissariat of Justice, but they produced no results. The first months of Red Terror were a time of vengeance, not mercy, and a person's class background was sufficient to determine his fate. A former head of the tsar's state security could expect no kindness. That Dodo's brother avoided summary execution in Smolensk during those bloody days can only be ascribed to good fortune, the notorious inconsistencies of Cheka administration, and the arbitrariness of terror itself. Ultimately Dzhunkovsky's salvation came not from the hard work of those who loved him but from an entirely unlikely source: Roman Malinovsky, the Bolshevik leader and police spy he had forced from the Duma four years earlier.

Malinovsky's surrender of his parliamentary mandate and departure from Russia in May 1914 caused the Bolsheviks consternation and embarrassment. Even before his resignation from the Duma, rumors had circulated that Malinovsky was an Okhrana agent; but there was no firm evidence, and Lenin refused to countenance the allegations. Fresh charges now arose, coming from Lenin's opponents in the Social Democratic movement—the Mensheviks and the so-called liquidators, who wanted to dismantle the underground party in favor of more open methods of struggle. Treasuring Malinovsky as a real proletarian and unwilling to give his enemies satisfaction, Lenin continued to defend his protégé who, upon leaving Russia, came immediately to Bolshevik headquarters at Poronin in Austrian Poland. Malinovsky told Lenin he had quit the Duma because he feared that criminal activities in his past were about to come to light.

Lenin accepted Malinovsky's explanation but immediately set up an investigative commission to look into charges of an Okhrana connection. As in the past the evidence uncovered was inconclusive, and even Vladimir Burtsev, the ace revolutionary spy catcher, believed that Malinovsky was not a *provokator*. While the commission affirmed Malinovsky's honesty, the Bolshevik leadership condemned him for deserting his post and excluded him from party ranks. But Lenin held out the prospect of his rehabilitation.

With the outbreak of war Malinovsky was drafted and soon fell into German hands. For a time it appeared that he had been killed, and Lenin and Grigorii Zinoviev wrote his obituary. When news came that Malinovsky was alive in the Alten Grabov prison camp, the two published a small note in a party newspaper: "They say that people who have been [mistakenly] declared dead live long lives. We hope this for R. V. Malinovsky." Lenin, Krupskaya, and Zinoviev sent letters and packages of food and warm clothing to the POW. For his part Malinovsky became an active propagandist for socialism among his fellow prisoners, giving speeches and regular lectures, believing, perhaps, that his past betrayal of the cause lay safely hidden.

The February Revolution opened the files of the Okhrana and proved conclusively that Malinovsky had been a police agent since 1910. When news of his treachery reached the German prison camp in May 1917, he admitted his guilt before his fellow socialists and declared his intention to return to Russia at the first possible moment. In August 1917, Malinovsky wrote to the Provisional Government's minister of justice, A. S. Zarudnyi, requesting to be brought home from Germany so that he could stand trial.[42] But he would have to wait for over a year, getting back to Petrograd on October 20, 1918.[43] Malinovsky sought to turn himself in to Soviet authorities, but it took three tries before he could present himself to S. M. Gessen, the Petrograd Party secretary, ask to stand trial before Soviet justice, and finally be taken into custody.[44] The Vecheka shipped him off to Moscow and deposited him in its Lubyanka prison for interrogation. On November 5, 1918, he appeared as a defendant before the Supreme Revolutionary Tribunal of the All-Russian Central Executive Committee (VTsIK).

Malinovsky's trial was the main reason the Vecheka decided to move Dzhunkovsky from Smolensk to Moscow on November 4. Thanks to Evdokiia's barrage of letters and requests, Party leaders knew his whereabouts. As a witness the former governor and head of tsarist security was now worth more alive than dead. Dzhunkovsky's transfer may have also owed something to efforts of David Riazanov, the eccentric Bolshevik who had opposed the dissolution of the Constituent Assembly and the reintroduction of the death penalty, and who often intervened on behalf of prisoners in Vecheka hands.[45] Still, judicial considerations—or what passed for them—were undoubtedly paramount.

Although Malinovsky's trial would be brief, the verdict and the sentence predetermined, the emerging system of Soviet justice sometimes paid obeisance to traditional forms. In this case the testimony of witnesses seemed useful, if not obligatory, and "public accuser" Nikolai Krylenko (the term "prosecutor" would not be used until 1922) submitted a substantial list of those who might be summoned. But while many were called, few would, or could, appear. At least one key figure—Stepan Beletsky, Malinovsky's former handler—had (inconveniently) been shot. Others, including Alexander Martynov and Mikhail Rodzianko, were either in hiding or beyond Soviet reach.[46] In the end, Krylenko produced only three witnesses to make the case against Malinovsky: Valerian Pletnev, a Menshevik and working-class activist of long standing; Sergei Vissarionov, erstwhile assistant head of the Department of Police; and Vladimir Dzhunkovsky.

Legal niceties received short shrift. Malinovsky protested that he had been given almost no time to read the indictment, having obtained it at five in the afternoon the day before. His defense attorney, Matvei Otsep, complained that he had been handed the case late and only learned of the trial date on 4 November. He could not become familiar with the details of the case and had met with the defendant just once. Malinovsky and his lawyer requested a four-day delay in the proceedings, but Krylenko opposed these requests, and the chairman of the tribunal, Otto Karklin, agreed with the "public accuser."[47]

Defense motions denied, the trial proceeded at a brisk pace. Karklin read the lengthy indictment: Malinovsky willingly, consciously, and for reasons of personal gain became an agent of the Okhrana; he betrayed party comrades and secrets to the police and had sown confusion in the ranks of the working class. After accepting a final reward of six thousand rubles, Malinovsky deserted his post in the Duma without explanation, an act that dealt a severe blow to the workers' movement and permitted the enemies of the revolution to slander the proletariat and its leaders.[48]

The charges against Malinovsky were not based on legal statutes but reflected the concept of "revolutionary justice." Russian revolutionaries had long seen themselves as the true representatives of the people and believed they could judge and punish officials and agents of the government, including the tsar. This idea inspired the terrorists who for decades had targeted those whose actions, however legal, they deemed harmful. The concept of a "higher law," before which those opposing the revolution might be called to account, found acceptance not only among the Populist *narodniki* and their Socialist Revolutionary successors but also in large segments of the educated Russian public. The Social Democrats rejected terror on tactical but not moral grounds, while they resorted to blackmail, seduction for economic gain, and highway robbery. The more moderate Kadets, although refusing to employ terror, could never bring themselves to condemn it outright; thus they tacitly accepted it as "revolutionary justice."[49]

With the October revolution, the concept of a "higher law" that criminalized legal acts and decriminalized illegal ones easily joined Marxist notions of the class struggle. Under the Bolsheviks' "proletarian dictatorship" this higher law became a central pillar of a new judicial system and the revolutionary tribunals, established in December 1917, embodied it. Indeed, their creators never saw them as courts in the traditional sense. Armed with the death penalty after June 1918 and guided by the "dictates of revolutionary conscience," the tribunals were, instead, "special organizations for the fight against counter revolution" wherein "the principle of suppression prevailed over that of justice."[50]

In the case of police spies, the Bolsheviks had already established this form of jurisprudence, and despised *provokatory* were routinely shot.[51] Malinovsky could have had no illusions about his fate, although he may have hoped for leniency. Neither he nor Otsep, his appointed defender, challenged the legitimacy of the proceedings, and after Karklin finished reading the indictment, the court asked Malinovsky if he had committed the acts alleged. He assented, objecting only to minor points, and with that the trial began.

The court required those testifying to begin with a statement about what they knew of the accused and the charges against him. Valerian Pletnev, the first called, told of his early suspicions that Malinovsky might be a police agent. But when no hard evidence surfaced, he had pushed these doubts aside. Krylenko posed a few short questions about whether Malinovsky was a Marxist and what kind of Party worker he had been. Pletnev answered that Malinovsky was indeed a Marxist and seemed to have been an outstanding Party worker.[52]

Dzhunkovsky's testimony came next and, while brief, it excited great interest. No eyewitness has left a description of his appearance or demeanor, but two months spent in Smolensk jails and his current accommodations at the Lubyanka could not have been refreshing. Yet Dzhun spoke clearly and with assurance, although on some points he seemed uncertain. This was his second appearance before a postrevolutionary tribunal, but his current position was much more precarious than it had been in mid-1917. He knew that no former tsarist official could expect sympathy in a Soviet court, the questions asked could be tougher, and soon he might face the kind of "justice" now being meted out to Malinovsky.

Still, Dzhun determined to tell the truth as he recalled it. His initial statement reiterated in capsule form what he had said a year and a half before. When he learned of Malinovsky's dual status as Duma leader and police spy, he resolved to end it. "I valued the title of Duma member too highly and could not allow a Duma delegate to be [at the same time] a person in the service of the Department of Police" he explained (*Delo*, 189); then he told how he tried to protect the Duma from Malinovsky. As long as Beletsky headed the Department of Police he had not acted, but once he had pushed Beletsky out, he gave orders to remove Malinovsky without publicity and to send him abroad at once so there would be no scandal or gossip about the incident. Dzhunkovsky stated that he had ordered Malinovsky to be given six thousand rubles upon leaving the country.

Under Krylenko's questioning Dzhun again denied that he knew about Malinovsky's status as an Okhrana agent at the time of his election to the Duma in 1912. He stated that he had learned of Malinovsky's double role only after becoming assistant minister of internal affairs and commander of the Corps of Gendarmes, although he was unsure how he had obtained that knowledge (190–91).

Krylenko quizzed Dzhunkovsky about Malinovsky's departure from the Duma, and why he had not made public the fact that Malinovsky was a *provokator*. "I was sickened by that fact," he answered, "it would have caused a very big scandal" (191–92).

Krylenko concluded by asking again about the money Malinovsky had received at the time of his departure: "Do you verify the fact of a grant of six thousand rubles . . . ?"

"Absolutely," Dzhunkovsky replied (192).

Defense counsel Otsep then took up the questioning: "Did you know when Malinovsky left?"

"I was informed afterwards that he had left, and somewhat later was told that he had gone abroad."

"How did . . . [Malinovsky] behave at the time? What was said about this?"

"I don't know, I didn't ask" (192).

Suddenly, Malinovsky himself broke in and addressed Dzhunkovsky, the only time he questioned any witness and, as far as we know, the only moment these two men, so fatefully linked, actually conversed.[53] His question was something of a non sequitur: "Why," he asked, "did your orders concerning my leaving the Duma coincide with the suspension [of the Social Democratic delegates] for fifteen days?"

"That they coincided was entirely accidental," Dzhunkovsky replied (192).

At this point one of the judges intervened to cut off any further exchange and open a new line of questioning: "[W]eren't you interested in what sort of a person Malinovsky really was?" he asked Dzhunkovsky. "Certainly there were people who reported to you on that subject. Wasn't there discussion as to whether he was a convinced monarchist or whether he acted simply for material gain?"

This question seems to have caught Dzhunkovsky by surprise. "I never heard that he was a convinced monarchist," he answered, adding: "I imagined him this way . . . that he really belonged to the Social-Democratic party and was, as an intelligent person . . . a leader."

Dzhunkovsky then injected a note of sympathy for the defendant: "I also imagined that the Department of Police had somehow ensnared [him] as it was with many people entangled by the police. I don't know how to say this, but I think you understand me. But as to his being a monarchist, that I never heard."

"Did you ever summon Malinovsky? Did he come to you?" the judge then asked.

"No, I have no recollection" (192–93).

Dzhunkovsky's observations about entrapment reflected his long-held belief that many so-called *provokatory* were victims of a nefarious police practice. Brief as these comments were, they changed the course of the discussion. Defense counsel Otsep pounced and asked Dzhunkovsky to give further information about Okhrana methods.

"Please tell us, how, precisely, this entrapment by the Department of Police took place," he began.

Dzhun answered tentatively: "At first [the Department] gave [an agent] small assignments and then such tasks as would compromise the party and then the trap was sprung, and the person fell into the net. I can't give you details; I was never interested in them" (193).

Otsep pressed for more: "How did the Okhrana lure its victims? Didn't you hear from someone why it was that a person, perhaps stable, perhaps unstable, but all the same sensible, would surrender to this. Give us a general picture."

"Sketching such a picture would be difficult," Dzhunkovsky began. "Do you want to know how it was with Malinovsky as well as with other people?"

"My interests are nearer to [Malinovsky's] life. How did the struggle for him proceed?" (193).

"With regard to Malinovsky, it's hard to say, because I don't know his material circumstances. But, with some agents it was like this—a terribly poor person with no means to live on and a starving family is offered money. Of course, the first time he takes it against his will and carries out some small task; the second time he takes a more serious assignment; again he takes the money and becomes accustomed to it" (193).

"And in addition," Otsep asked, "wouldn't you say that the victim . . . [might be] ensnared by threats of exposure?"

"This, of course, obviously happened. I can't give [specific] facts, but I can tell you straight that such cases took place."

"In addition to threats, were there any other psychological means known to you by which party workers were drawn into the ranks of police spies?" (193–94).

Dzhun did not get a chance to reply. Otsep's attempt to make Malinovsky appear a victim and Dzhunkovsky's sympathetic responses angered the court. Chairman Karklin abruptly broke in and admonished the defense.

"Ask questions that concretely concern the issue at hand. Don't ask questions that aren't relevant to the case" (194).

Undeterred, Otsep pressed on. "I'm interested not only in facts, but also in those motives that explain Malinovsky's behavior," he told the tribunal. Then, turning again to the witness, he continued: "I want to know, was there anything that could be called psychological torture?"

"I never heard of any."

"And physical?"

"I also heard nothing" (194).

Determined to discredit the defense's line of argument, Krylenko now posed a final question to Dzhunkovsky.

"May we establish that you had no direct knowledge of Malinovsky and no direct knowledge of the circumstances of his participation in police spying?"

"Yes," Dzhunkovsky responded, "only in general terms."

At this point Krylenko seemed satisfied, and with no further questions, Dzhunkovsky stepped down (194).

Dzhunkovsky's testimony and Otsep's quick response to it upset the momentum of the proceedings, and when the court called its final witness, Sergei Vissarionov, Krylenko sought to regain his balance. He was bothered by something Vissarionov said in his opening statement—that by 1913 Malinovsky had become a dangerous property, whose "double role" was such "a burden" that he no longer merited "the government's confidence" (195). Not wanting to leave the impression that Malinovsky had been of little value to tsarist authorities, Krylenko returned to that question, but Vissarionov repeated that the *provokator* was emotionally troubled and that this caused problems for the police (199).

Vissarionov's testimony emboldened Otsep: "Which of . . . [Malinovsky's] two roles was most characteristic of him, [police] informant . . . or member . . . of a faction in the State Duma?"

Vissarionov replied that Malinovsky was most comfortable as a Duma leader because he "preserved in the depths of his soul his loyalty to the . . . [Social Democratic Party]" (202).

Krylenko jumped in once more and bluntly challenged Vissarionov: "Which was of greater value," he demanded, "[Malinovsky's] activity as a Social Democrat or the information he gave the Okhrana?" (202).

"From my point of view his activity as a Social Democrat prevailed," Vissarionov replied (203).

"That's your opinion as a man standing on guard for the established order," Krylenko snapped (203).

When the three witnesses finished, the Tribunal asked Malinovsky several questions about other police agents and other specific events. Then, after a short break, the trial wound up with statements by Malinovsky, Krylenko, and Otsep. In a scenario that would become familiar in later Soviet show trials, the accused confessed, the state attorney thundered, and the defense lawyer offered mild statements designed to mitigate the sentence. In these early days, however, the script had not been worked out beforehand and each of the three major figures freely and spontaneously presented his position.

Malinovsky acknowledged his crimes and did not ask for mercy: "I cannot imagine that I could live among you now. . . . To me your verdict is clear; I accept it calmly, because I deserve no other" (221–22). Krylenko agreed. The Okhrana agent had delivered a "severe blow" to the revolutionary cause: "I believe that he can receive only one verdict—death by shooting!" (231). All Otsep could do was to plead for leniency. A death sentence would violate the ideals of justice and humanity that were fundamental to socialism. "As a defense attorney and also as a man," he concluded, "I ask from you humane treatment for my client" (235).

Looking back on the trial years later, Dzhunkovsky recalled sympathetically Malinovsky's "sincere repentance."[54] But the contrition of the accused and his lawyer's plea had no impact on the tribunal. The court retired and quickly returned. The verdict was guilty, the sentence was death—to be carried out within twenty-four hours (237). Newspapers published accounts of the proceedings and the outcome, but the event received scant public attention. The first anniversary of the October Revolution was at hand. Amid the hoopla of the celebration, the trial and execution of Bolshevism's greatest traitor passed almost without notice.[55]

With Malinovsky buried, his story, while not forgotten, was relegated to a footnote in the history of triumphant Bolshevism, with Lenin's long embrace and strong defense of the *provokator* carefully shielded from public view. The testimony concerning Malinovsky that Lenin and his comrades gave to the Provisional Government's Investigative Commission was not published in its seven-volume stenographic record, *The Fall of the Tsarist Regime*, and did not appear until the waning days of Soviet power.

The same was true of the other key documents, including the transcript of the trial.[56] But although the whole episode was treated with great circumspection, it was common knowledge among the Bolshevik elite—and for one member of that select group, the Malinovsky saga may have had a special significance.

Joseph Stalin was arrested in 1913 on the basis of information supplied by Malinovsky, a man he called friend.[57] So, to him, the life and fate of this police agent was likely to have been of more than passing interest and may have formed the germ of an idea that would grow with time. Malinovsky had succeeded in his nefarious work thanks in large part to Lenin's enthusiastic support. The implication of this was clear: despite his revolutionary genius, Bolshevism's founder was a bad judge of character. Such an observation might seem particularly meaningful to the man haunted by Lenin's "Testament," written a few years later, that deemed him "too rude" and unworthy of the high post of Party General Secretary.[58] If Lenin had been unable to see Malinovsky for the traitor he was, perhaps he had surrounded himself with others who had been spies, wreckers, and diversionists from the very beginning. Such is the idea, never voiced, that would run like a red thread through the bizarre and ghoulish protocols of the Great Purge Trials at the end of the 1930s. These proceedings placed in the dock all those mentioned favorably in the "Testament" and offered a tacit but forceful riposte to Lenin's judgment. At these "docudramas" staged by Stalin, the shade of Malinovsky hovered in the wings.

One contemporary and several historians have claimed that Lenin attended Malinovsky's trial while still recovering from the wounds he suffered in August. Some have him taking notes and even nodding sympathetically during Malinovsky's speech. It seems unlikely that Lenin would have felt any sympathy for the defendant, however.[59] Lenin almost certainly learned of Dzhunkovsky's testimony, if he did not hear it in person, but what he thought about it is anybody's guess. It is hard to believe, however, that he viewed with favor the tsarist official whose refusal to expose Malinovsky's role as a police spy in 1914 kept the Bolsheviks in the dark and led to considerable embarrassment three years later. In June 1917 Lenin had angrily demanded that Dzhunkovsky be brought to trial.[60] What did he want to do now that the former head of state security was in his power?

Had Lenin given serious consideration to the matter, he might have realized that Dzhunkovsky's decision to keep Malinovsky's status as a spy under wraps spared the Bolshevik Party as well as the Duma and the secret police a devastating scandal. Revelation of the fact that a *provokator* sat on his Central Committee would surely have weakened Lenin's position in the struggle with his Social Democratic rivals. Lenin seldom revised his judgments, but it is worth noting that the fates of the two secret police figures who appeared in the Malinovsky proceedings proved strikingly different. Vissarionov, who had been in custody since shortly after the February Revolution, was shot before the end of 1918. Dzhunkovsky, on the other hand, was released from jail after three years. He outlived Lenin and most of those who had carried out the Bolshevik coup d'état.

Although gratitude on Lenin's part is highly doubtful, support from another quarter may have helped Dzhunkovsky escape Vissarionov's fate. Shortly after the Malinovsky trial, Sovnarkom received a remarkable petition from leading figures of the Moscow stage:

> The former governor of Moscow, Vladimir Fedorovich Dzhunkovsky, is currently under arrest. We the undersigned artists have decided to turn to the Council of People's Commissars with the fervent request for his release. Leaving aside the fact that while governor he always attended to the needs of the artists with care and responsiveness, many of us can confirm that he also, on numerous occasions, acted on our requests to lighten the conditions of political prisoners and exiles without delay, deciding [things] in a matter of hours, even minutes. Thus in 1905, at the request of A. I. Iuzhin, he freed more than 100 Georgians being sent via Moscow to Perm and other northern provinces . . . and gave them the means to return to their homes. When the artist of the Moscow Malyi Theater, S. A. Golovin, petitioned on behalf of his brother who was imprisoned in Moscow for political reasons and was being tormented by the prison administration, Vladimir Fedorovich Dzhunkovsky, in the course of one hour, investigated, improved [the prisoner's] conditions and issued a severe reprimand to the warden of the jail.

The petition mentioned Dzhunkovsky's "honorable role" in opposing Rasputin and called the former governor "a man of extraordinary responsiveness, highest humanity, and exceptional nobility." The signatories included such luminaries as Maria Ermolova, Olga Knipper-Chekhova, Alexander Iuzhin, Vladimir Nemirovich-Danchenko, and as many as one

Felix Dzerzhinsky. Hoover Institution Archive (HIA), Robert H. B. Lockhart Collection, box 9, folder 6.

hundred others from the Malyi, Bolshoi, and Moscow Art Theaters and the Opera Theater of the Moscow Soviet.[61]

Writing to the Bolshevik leadership in defense of a man who had once headed the tsar's internal security apparatus required a good measure of civil courage, especially in the white heat of Red Terror. Relations between the Soviet government and the various performing groups were far from smooth at the time, and some of those who signed the document were, at that very moment, negotiating with Lunacharsky and the Commissariat of Enlightenment concerning the future status of their theaters.[62] Their petition is striking testimony to the high affection in which the Moscow theatrical community held Dzhunkovsky and, perhaps, a further sign of Dodo's relentless campaigning on Vadya's behalf, prodding and mobilizing all those he had helped over the years. The appeal also reminds us that in the first years of Bolshevik rule the battered remnants of Russian civil society still believed they could influence the behavior of the new regime.

Lenin read the petition and did not reject it out of hand. Let someone else make the call. "Comrade Dzerzhinsky, your conclusions. 4/XII. Lenin," he scrawled on the top of the document. Later, another pen gave it the appropriate bureaucratic treatment: "No.15885. 18/XII."[63]

The conclusions "Iron Felix" reached upon reading the artists' request are also unknown, but Dzhunkovsky survived. Despite his fearsome reputation the Vecheka chief was not entirely insensitive to this kind of appeal and from time to time liked to play the role of protector of worthy "formers."[64] The petition showed that Dzhunkovsky enjoyed considerable respect and affection; he had been a useful witness at the Malinovsky trial. Perhaps he could be useful again. As a new institution the Vecheka was facing a host of administrative problems. Recent assassinations and the nearly successful attempt on Lenin's life showed there was much to learn about protecting high government officials. Local Chekas were often out of control; what was the best way to subordinate them to the center? Dzhunkovsky knew a lot. Potentially he was a valuable *spets* (specialist); worth keeping around—for a while.

Chapter 21

Before the Bar of Soviet Justice

IMMEDIATELY FOLLOWING THE MALINOVSKY TRIAL, DZHUNKOVSKY remained a guest of the Vecheka at Lubyanka in what were, almost certainly, deplorable circumstances. A report sent to Dzerzhinsky toward the end of 1918 described "extremely terrible conditions. . . . [Many prisoners] sleep on the floor with no mattresses, and all receive inadequate food—poor, un-nourishing soup and 1/8 of a pound of bread per day." Things were substantially better at Moscow's Butyrka prison, the report continued.[1] Fortunately for Dzhunkovsky, he was transferred to those familiar premises in early December.[2]

A move to Butyrka was a step up in the hierarchy of Soviet jails, but only a relative improvement. A tough prison before the revolution, Butyrka had earned an even more frightening reputation under Soviet management. Following the attack on Lenin, those held there described a "soul racking" experience amid "a bacchanalia of Red madness and terror."[3] Cells bulged with new arrivals, as facilities designed to hold eleven hundred prisoners strained to swallow over three thousand.[4] Soon, however, things started to settle down. Inmates became more secure and life more regular. In the winter of 1918–1919, Butyrka began to receive, from concentration camps and various provincial prisons, leading representatives of the old regime who, like Dzhun, had survived the first wave of mass executions in September and October. Many presented a sorrowful picture, cringing before authority, reduced to an animal lust for food, and eagerly repentant of their past deeds.[5]

Conditions in Soviet places of confinement differed sharply, not only between prisons but also within them.[6] Curiously, distinctions of class and rank often continued to be observed. In Butyrka groups of former high officials occasionally received what can be called, with some stretch of the imagination, privileged treatment. In early 1919 those who been provincial governors enjoyed a special status. Cell No. 11 on corridor 14 was referred to as the "gubernatorial room," where some sixteen former *nachal'nik gubernii* were held. While other cells were crammed with prisoners, the number in the *gubernatorskaia* never changed. Most of the governors kept their dignity. They had to do menial tasks—carry out the slops and keep the premises neat—but they did them with style. For men who had once maintained the good order and well-being of entire provinces, these duties posed no problems, and their quarters were remarkably clean and tidy. The governors also enjoyed considerable freedom within Butyrka's walls.[7]

According to Vasilii Klementiev, his Butyrka contemporary, Dzhunkovsky stood out even among the privileged former governors. "[A] relatively young man with a dark complexion and an athletic build," Dzhunkovsky enjoyed greater freedom than the rest, including the right to move throughout the entire prison, albeit under supervision. Many guards, it seemed, believed that Dzhun was slated for early release and so treated him with deference. Klementiev felt that Dzhunkovsky had the air of a person who himself thought he might not have to serve long in jail.[8]

Dzhunkovsky enjoyed a favored status in part because he was well-known to the prison staff, many of whom remembered him fondly from earlier days. Some administrators may have been aware that the former governor was a prisoner of special interest to the Vecheka, something noted on the jacket of his prison file,[9] and that he was, on a number of occasions, taken from Butyrka for further interrogation. Dzhunkovsky's relatively mild treatment at this time could also have been both an incentive and a reward for his cooperation.

Although we have no official documents concerning the interrogations that Dzhunkovsky underwent, they seem to have gone in two directions. According to the memoirs of Sergei Golitsyn, Dzhun stated that Dzerzhinsky himself had asked how the prerevolutionary Okhrana had maintained the tsar's security. Dzhunkovsky apparently had no qualms about answering that kind of question, a purely technical matter that did not compromise or implicate anyone, and at the request of the Cheka chief he prepared a lengthy report on the subject. Golitsyn also asserted that Dzhunkovsky made further reports on a number of technical matters.[10]

Still, it is difficult to believe that by this time the Vecheka had adopted Dzhunkovsky as a "specialist." There is no doubt that in late 1918 and early 1919 Dzerzhinsky and his colleagues had realized that the expertise of those who had worked for the Okhrana was useful and should be employed. Vecheka agents also sought to gather relevant published documents and archival materials. But men who had held top positions in the tsar's police remained highly suspect.[11] Dzerzhinsky saw no reason to allow Dzhunkovsky's release. On February 29, 1919, he wrote Ivan Ksenofontov, his deputy chairman: "In view of the fact that Dzhunkovsky's friends are carrying on a whole campaign with the aim of obtaining his freedom, I ask that you on no account set him at liberty without my knowledge."[12]

Dzerzhinsky's concerns may explain why Dzhunkovsky's interrogation was not limited to a "debriefing" on technical and administrative questions. In time, it took a second direction: an examination of his service career and, in particular, his actions in defense of the government against the revolution. On March 22, 1919, the head of Butyrka prison received orders to present Dzhunkovsky to the Investigative Commission of the Moscow Revolutionary Tribunal, meeting two days hence.[13] After the questioning, the Commission determined that it had sufficient grounds to put him on trial for crimes against the proletariat and the revolution.

As in the case of Roman Malinovsky, the indictment that brought Dzhunkovsky before the Moscow Revolutionary Tribunal did not accuse him of breaking any legal statute, tsarist or Soviet. The essence of his alleged offence was that he had violated the "higher law" of revolution by taking actions that sought to block the efforts of workers and peasants to overthrow the autocracy and advance their economic interests. Where Dzhunkovsky's trial differed from Malinovsky's was its much more public character and erratic course. The Malinovsky proceedings were open, but we are unsure how many people watched them.[14] They took place within the Kremlin's walls, however, and admission was probably controlled. The prosecution called no important Bolsheviks to testify, and the whole case was, by any standard, a "rush to judgment," designed to punish the police spy while sparing Party leaders every conceivable embarrassment.

In sharp contrast, Soviet authorities made Dzhunkovsky's trial readily accessible, apparently with an "educational" goal. By trying instead of simply shooting him, they may have sought to show that "revolutionary justice" was justice all the same. Revolutionary tribunals had broad discretion to determine the character of trials, whether they would be public or closed, whether there would be witnesses, and whether the accused would have defenders.[15] In this case, it had been decided to give Dzhunkovsky a public trial with witnesses and a full-fledged defense. How better to expose the "crimes" of the old regime and its officials and let those who had suffered at the hands of the tsar's minions come forward and confront their former oppressors?[16] But from the beginning, things took an unexpected turn.

A brief announcement in *Izvestiia* informed the public of Dzhunkovsky's impending trial before the Moscow Revolutionary Tribunal. It called on all who wished to give testimony either for or against him to appear before an investigator at a preliminary hearing. The publication of this notice caused a considerable stir among those who knew Dzhunkovsky in his days of power. Was the announcement some kind of trap? Many potential witnesses felt that they, too, might soon sit in the dock before the tribunal. Dare they go? But in the end, they set aside their fears and appeared before the investigator in large numbers.[17]

Ekaterina Kuskova, a leading Menshevik, had several pieces of testimony to offer on Dzhunkovsky's behalf. But when she arrived at the investigator's office, she found it overflowing with people wanting to voice their support for the former governor. Kuskova thought that the room resembled "a kind of club," a gathering of Moscow's cultural elite, one of those "artistic circles from the past where any evening you could meet 'everybody.'" And that was not all; a pair of prominent communists appeared. They, too, wanted to stand in Dzhunkovsky's corner.[18]

Dzhunkovsky's two-day trial opened on May 5, 1919, at the former Merchants' Club on Malaya Dmitrovka Street. The accused arrived under guard, but on the steps leading into the hall, a large crowd of friends and supporters pushed through the police cordon to embrace and kiss him. The former governor's appearance startled those who had known him from earlier days. The artist Margarita Voloshina-Sabashnikova recalled that "a great beard, which he had not had before, and his eyes, which had become still larger and brighter, transfigured his face so that it resembled that of an icon. He radiated complete calm." Kuskova, too, remembered "huge, beautiful eyes in an emaciated face" and Dzhunkovsky's strong, erect carriage. When the prisoner entered the court room, another crowd enveloped him; this time it was the craftsmen of Vladimiro-Dzhunkovsky. He embraced them as they thrust into his hands packages containing milk, bread, and eggs.[19]

A huge bust of Karl Marx, stylized to resemble a sphinx, dominated the hall and fixed its stony, inscrutable gaze on the proceedings. Below and to the right was the rostrum for the "accuser"; to the left, a table and chair for the defendant. A barrier separated the audience from the court, and the three-man tribunal sat center stage at a long table covered with a red cloth. Two members of the panel, Comrades Savinov and Potatkov, were ordinary workers, but the presiding judge was a figure intimately associated with the brutal excesses of Red Terror: Iakov Khristoforvich Peters.

A former Latvian worker and strike leader, Peters (birth name Jekabs Peterss) had been arrested during the revolution of 1905 and tortured by the tsarist police.[20] After his release in 1908 Peters made his way to England where he remained until 1917. During his British sojourn Peters was implicated in the infamous Houndsditch murders and is believed by some to have fired the shots that killed three London policemen. But when he stood trial, a British court acquitted him.[21] Returning to Russia after the February Revolution, Peters participated in the October seizure of power and had been at Dzerzhinsky's right hand in the early days of the Vecheka, forging the institution and developing its methods of operation.[22] When he assumed the chairmanship of the Moscow *Revtribunal*, Peters enhanced its frightening image. "Rivers of blood flowed," Sergei Kobiakov, a defense attorney at the time recalled. "There began a bacchanalia of death. Peters brought to the Moscow Tribunal the ways of the Cheka. Every day several people were condemned to death. They shot people for all manner of crimes."[23]

Voloshina-Sabashnikova was not sure that Peters deserved his cruel reputation. To her he looked a bit like a blond Beethoven, but he cut a pathetic figure, a victim of the very system he was helping to create. "His face was endlessly sad and weary. Sorrow and weariness . . . were heard in his voice. He spoke in broken Russian and [obviously] felt completely out of place."[24] Kuskova was less kind, but she, too, depicted Peters as being ill at ease in his judicial role: "Peters could not sit still for a second. He crossed and uncrossed his legs . . . he greatly resembled an ape."[25] As for Peters's alleged cruelty and bloodthirstiness, Voloshina's assessment has the ring of truth. The proceedings would soon demonstrate that the dreaded commissar did not always impose a death sentence.

Iakov Peters. Hoover Institution Archive (HIA), Robert H. B. Lockhart Collection, box 9, folder 12.

In contrast to the clearly discomfited Peters, Dzhunkovsky presented a picture of tranquility that struck all who saw the trial. "The accused stayed calm and carefully listened to the witnesses and from time to time made entries in a notebook," reported the correspondent of *Vechernie izvestiia* (The Evening News).[26] Voloshina-Sabashnikova remembered Dzhunkovsky standing with military bearing before the tribunal "like a completely spiritually free, independent person might stand before his legal superior." Initially surprised by this demeanor, Voloshina soon came to see it as an expression of Dzhun's deep Orthodox faith. "For this religious man," she wrote, "the words of the Apostle Paul 'there is no power but of God,' had not lost their meaning." At the trial Dzhunkovsky answered all questions precisely, openly, and in accordance with his conscience. Voloshina found herself envying "the wholeness of the Orthodox-Monarchist worldview of this man who knew no doubts."[27]

Unlike the Malinovsky case, no official transcript of the proceedings against Dzhunkovsky's has been published, and it is entirely possible that none exists.[28] This is certainly unfortunate, for Dzhunkovsky's trial was radically different from most of those that took place during the Red Terror. "It is unlikely that any court heard such testimony or such Homeric laughter from all those present," Kuskova remembered. "Often the accused himself laughed. They called in the witnesses; each of them, to the accompaniment of Peters's derisive gesticulations, presented some kind of evidence in favor of the defendant."[29] Newspaper accounts are incomplete, dry, and matter-of-fact. Still, they give us a rough outline of events, while the memoirs of Voloshina-Sabashnikova and Kuskova add color and spice to the uninspired journalism of the time.

The trial's first day—May 5—was devoted to the testimony of witnesses and questioning of the accused. The former governor's supporters, many well-known figures from the arts and politics, quickly dominated the stage. Dzhunkovsky may have been surprised to see Konstantin Balmont among them, considering the break in their relations that had occurred in 1905. By 1919, however, the poet had long lost his enthusiasm for revolution and had developed a profound aversion to Bolshevism. He would leave Russia forever in 1920.[30] The newspapers did not report Balmont's testimony, but it was undoubtedly in accord with the letter he sent to the tribunal's investigative commission. There the poet asserted that, during years of repression after 1905, Dzhunkovsky had improved the conditions of many political prisoners, saving them from prison, exile, and worse.

Balmont claimed that, during the first revolution, he had watched as Dzhun rescued an accused citizen from the wrath of a Black Hundred mob.[31] Alexander Sumbatov-Iuzhin, the actor and playwrite; Fedor Golovin, the Kadet president of the Second State Duma; and Nikolai Muravyov, the prominent defense counsel who had chaired the Provisional Government's Extraordinary Investigative Commission and now headed the Committee of the Political Red Cross, also spoke for the defense. Like Balmont, they affirmed Dzhunkovsky's good character, sensitivity, humanity, and responsiveness to the concerns of the public.[32]

Golovin testified that during the revolution of 1905 he, then chair of the Moscow zemstvo's executive board, had turned to Dzhunkovsky on a number of important matters and always found a sympathetic ear. Kuskova recalled that Muravyov offered a speech, "brilliant in both form and content," that elicited the rapt attention of the audience and judges alike. He stated that, as a defense attorney in political cases, he often appealed to the governor in the interests of his clients. Even when Dzhunkovsky was unable to do anything for them, he displayed an obvious concern about their fate. Muravyov continued that in other aspects of his own public life also he always found Moscow's governor favorably disposed to the initiatives of liberal society.[33]

Dzhunkovsky's supporters were not exclusively representatives of the intelligentsia. A waiter who had worked at one of Moscow's "people's houses" told of the former governor's concern for the quality of the food that would be served to its working-class patrons. He refused to be intimidated despite Peters's efforts, and his comic manner provoked considerable laughter in the courtroom. A soldier who had been at the front with Dzhunkovsky called him "a shining hero."[34] Even more striking, two former convicts, P. P. Iagodzinsky and V. M. Kozitsky, also offered testimony on the former governor's behalf. They recalled his humane treatment of prisoners after he had subdued the riot at Butyrka prison in 1911 that left several guards dead.[35]

The two Bolshevik witnesses appeared. The first stated that when political prisoners who had been exiled to Iakutiia complained about their conditions, the former assistant minister of internal affairs had taken steps to improve their treatment. Not to be outdone, the second communist, a woman, made the wildly exaggerated claim that Dzhunkovsky had toured Siberia and bettered the circumstances of all the convicts there. According to Kuskova, this enthusiastic overstatement—Dzhunkovsky had never made such a tour—prompted a gentle admonition from the defendant: "Madam, believe me, I am extremely grateful for your willingness to testify on my behalf . . . , but . . . there's a mistake here." She must be referring to someone else, he added. Flustered, the overzealous Bolshevik admitted her error, much to the amusement of the audience.[36]

Perhaps the most unusual testimony in Dzhunkovsky's favor came from the old man who spoke for the denizens of Vladimiro-Dzhunkovsky. He explained to Peters how they had turned to the governor in desperation after other officials had blocked their efforts to obtain land. "He received us without any anger, like a father," the old man recalled. "He listened attentively, understood our request, sent someone out to verify everything, and promised to pass our petition on to the tsar. Soon a document signed by the tsar arrived according to which we were given the land we requested." Peters interrogated the artisans' spokesman as to their number and the amount of land they had obtained. Then he asked if there had been any revolutionary disturbances in Vladimiro-Dzhunkovsky and received a sincere, but quite unexpected, answer: "God forbid! Never, never, has there been anything like that! Once in a while . . . some of our boys drink a bit too much, play the accordion, and sing; but as for uprisings, we've had nothing like that, thank God!"[37]

Confronting a torrent of pro-Dzhunkovsky testimony, the prosecution could produce only a single witness to make its case, one Polushin, then a member of the Moscow Soviet of Workers' Deputies. He told the tribunal that during Dzhunkovsky's mission to Baku in July 1914, there had been arrests and shootings, but he failed to point to any concrete facts. Inadequate though it was, Polushin's story led Peters to interrogate the defendant about Baku and other aspects of his service career. In regard to Baku, Dzhunkovsky gave a strong defense of his actions, insisting that he had told his superiors at the outset that his intention was not to employ repressive measures against the workers but, instead, to find out the causes of the disturbances and deal with them. He informed the court about his conference with the oil field owners and managers and of the demands he had made for them to improve conditions. "Dzhunkovsky said that the first thing necessary was to move the workers' living quarters away from the work place and to connect them by streetcar lines and to establish water supply," *Izvestiia*'s correspondent reported.[38]

Peters pushed further, demanding that Dzhunkovsky tell him the number of workers he had executed during his tenure as governor. He replied that while he had ordered arrests, they "frequently served to prevent worse measures." But, he continued, "I never signed a single death sentence, that was not [something] within the sphere of my duties."[39] Peters next asked about Dzhunkovsky's service as head of the security forces. Had he undertaken this duty willingly?

"Yes."

"Why?"

"Because it seemed important to me to clean up and better organize the police."

Dzhunkovsky then spoke of his struggle against "provocation" and told of the steps he had taken to force Roman Malinovsky from the Duma.[40]

In further testimony Dzhunkovsky mentioned his efforts to remove Rasputin, his report to the emperor, and its consequences.

"Why were you against [Rasputin]?" Peters inquired.

"Because his role undercut the prestige of my monarch."

"Does that mean that you wanted to support the tsar's power?"

"Well, of course," Dzhunkovsky replied, "I would have been a low, base person if I had served [the tsar] and not wanted to help."

Dzhunkovsky then argued that police institutions were something necessary in all societies and specifically defended his management of prisons while governor of Moscow: "I tried wherever possible to maintain order and humane conditions," he stated. "You can compare the old rules, pieces of which you can find scattered on the floor of the Butyrka, with the new ones. The former were much more lenient."[41]

The first day of the trial was a disaster for the prosecution. The testimony of the witnesses overwhelmingly favored Dzhunkovsky, and even Peters's pointed interrogation failed to uncover any crimes committed by the defendant or shake his claim of innocence. The second day, May 6, was devoted to the arguments of counsel, however, and here the state's "accuser" (according to the papers, his name was either Kuperman or Guberman) hoped to recoup. The prosecution introduced documents, which, among other things, showed that Dzhunkovsky had petitioned the governor-general of Moscow to close teahouses where peasants were gathering to discuss and protest government policies.[42] Dzhunkovsky's "accuser" also presented evidence regarding his dispatch of soldiers from the Semenovsky regiment to break up a strike at the Liamin factory in Dmitrov county at the end of 1905, an act that resulted in arrests but no shootings.[43]

In its summation the prosecution charged that Dzhunkovsky was an administrator who repressed the workers and covered up his misdeeds with charitable acts. "[Z]ealous service in the work of suppressing and stifling the worker-peasant movement" alone explained his rise to high rank.[44] Recalling charges made at the time of his arrest in 1918, the people's attorney further claimed that Dzhunkovsky's planned travel to Ukraine was proof of a desire to "go over to the Hetmanate and [continue] his policies there." The "accuser" denounced Dzhunkovsky's clear monarchist sympathies as a threat to the Soviet regime. He demanded that the prisoner receive "the highest measure of punishment—to be shot."[45]

Dzhunkovsky's defense counsel, Alexander Brusilovsky, did not directly challenge the legitimacy of the trial but obliquely touched on that question when he asserted that it was not proper to punish a person for failing to resign from government positions during the years of reaction following 1905. He also pointed out that while the prosecution had been unable to produce any evidence implicating Dzhunkovsky in the shooting of workers and peasants, ample testimony showed him to have been attentive to their demands. Brusilovsky reminded the tribunal that the defendant had also displayed concern for the circumstances of arrested revolutionaries and had often sought to ameliorate their situations.[46]

Throughout the arguments of counsel, Dzhunkovsky sat impassively, continuing to display an air of complete calm, and occasionally jot down notes. Now, at the trial's end, he spoke its final words, brief and to the point: "I came before the Revolutionary Tribunal with a clear conscience and with a clear conscience I leave it. I am prepared to accept any sentence, no matter how severe it may be."[47]

The tribunal retired to deliberate. Once more Dzhunkovsky's friends and supporters surrounded him, pushing past the courtroom barrier while the guards did nothing to stop them. After about an hour the judges returned and, to a hushed courtroom, delivered a verdict and sentence that demonstrated both the weakness of the prosecution's case and the determination of Soviet authorities to keep Dzhunkovsky in custody. They found the defendant guilty of helping suppress the revolutionary movement in 1905, and, in particular, of breaking up the Liamin factory strike, albeit without using armed force against the workers. Furthermore, "as a servant of the former autocratic system in Russia . . . [Dzhunkovsky] occupied high administrative posts and . . . by his actions and orders resisted the growth of the revolutionary movement among the workers." The tribunal's decision noted that

Dzhunkovsky had not been responsible for shooting workers or peasants and that "in his personal life he had shown gentleness and humaneness." Still, by his service, he had, "despite his own goodwill," carried out policies aimed at smothering "the people's awakening." Finally, "Dzhunkovsky is a convinced monarchist and, in the conditions of civil war, dangerous to Soviet power." The tribunal rejected the prosecution's call for the death penalty, however, and instead sentenced the accused to "imprisonment in a concentration camp until the end of the Civil War without the possibility of amnesty."[48] The audience, which had apparently expected the worst, greeted the verdict with what the *Izvestiia* reporter described as "a thunder of applause."[49] A deflated Peters, looking exhausted and glum, snorted: "This is not a theater."[50] Guards now led Dzhunkovsky away, and Kuskova overheard one say gently: "Let's go home, Vladimir Fedorovich . . . [Time for] tea; they've been tormenting you here. They've been tormenting you."[51]

The ovation that followed the tribunal's verdict expressed the joy, relief, and surprise of Dzhun's supporters. In the face of the prosecution's demand for the death penalty, the court had come about as close to exonerating the defendant as was possible in the atmosphere of Red Terror. The sentence—incarceration in a concentration camp until the end of the war—also appeared remarkably mild. There can be little doubt that the tribunal's decision represented an appreciation of the facts of the case, but it may have reflected, in addition, the desire of leading figures in the Vecheka to preserve for future use a person whose knowledge and administrative expertise might prove extremely valuable.

The tribunal's verdict can also be seen as a concession to public opinion, a sign of Bolshevik insecurity at a time when the outcome of the Civil War was far from clear. In early May, White forces under General Iudenich lunged toward Petrograd, and two days after the end of the Dzhunkovsky proceedings, Peters rushed to the former capital to take part in its defense. Yet if, by their decision, Soviet leaders sought a measure of societal approval, they need not have bothered. The dramatic two-day trial of Moscow's popular former governor, well covered in the press, seems to have left almost no lasting impression on the public's consciousness. Only two brief published memoirs recall its remarkable character, course, and outcome; even Muravyov, who had spoken so eloquently in Dzhunkovsky's defense, failed to note it in his recollections.[52] Instead, the whirlwind of events of 1919, the absorbing difficulties, terrors, and privations of the times, quickly expunged the case from memory.

But in the eyes of those who presided over the developing Soviet justice system, Dzhunkovsky's trial and its results may have taught an important and enduring lesson. If in future such proceedings were to have their desired pedagogic effect, better preparation was necessary. Authorities had to control the witnesses and the courtroom crowds and give high priority to that "medieval principle of jurisprudence," the confession of the accused.[53] Indeed, Dzhunkovsky's trial shines as a model of judicial rectitude when compared with those that came later. Within three years the trial of the SRs (June–August 1922) would display a complete disregard for normal legal procedures. Demonstrators organized by the Communist Party were permitted into the courtroom to hurl accusations at the defendants and howl down the chief lawyer for the defense, Nikolai Muravyov. His bitter riposte, "Woe to a people prepared to throw stones at those who defend the law made by the people themselves," was prophecy.[54]

Despite the seemingly lenient sentence, Dzhunkovsky's fate remained insecure and uncertain. A concentration camp regime might be harsh, especially dangerous to a person in ill health. Moreover, in these places of confinement, people could, and did, disappear. The Vecheka had the power to transfer prisoners where it wished, and in camps outside Moscow it was easy for executions to take place with little or no public knowledge.[55]

As it turned out, however, Dzhunkovsky never went to a camp, although that remained a possibility for some time. After the trial he returned to Butyrka, but on June 11 authorities transferred him to Taganka prison, where his conditions appear to have significantly improved. In late 1919 some prisoners, at least, enjoyed considerable freedom to move about and visit others. They were able to make their cells reasonably homey, whitewashing the walls and even hanging photographs for decoration.[56] Conveniences of various kinds were also allowed, and for a time Dzhunkovsky had the luxury of an electric samovar.[57] Prisoners could receive packages (Dzhun got three a week) and on weekends they were also permitted visits from friends and family.[58]

For several months Dzhunkovsky had the good fortune to share his cell with his old friend Alexander Samarin, who had been provincial marshal of the Moscow nobility and later chief procurator of the Holy Synod. The two had always been on the best of terms, but common experience now made their ties even closer. All prisoners had to work, and the authorities assigned many of those who had good educations to the "Department of Juvenile Offenders" where they would teach some of the *besprizornye*, orphaned or abandoned youths rendered homeless and wild by the disruptions and privations of revolution and civil war. Samarin accepted the post of secretary of the "pedagogical council," but he refused to take part in the actual teaching, stating that it was impossible to educate children without giving them instruction in "God's law," something that Bolshevik ideology did not permit. Whether Dzhunkovsky enjoyed a similar opportunity is uncertain, but his position would probably have been the same as Samarin's. In any case, the two assumed another task, caring for the rabbits that the prison raised to feed the convicts. Both men eagerly applied themselves to the work, which regularly took them outside their prison cell to a plot of land near the Moscow River.[59]

As in Butyrka, Dzhunkovsky received special treatment and respect from the prison personnel who had served at Taganka before the revolution. Sergei Trubetskoi, who was held there between 1920 and 1922, found it extremely amusing that the "old guard" greeted the current head of the prison in a lax and careless manner, sometimes not even bothering to get up when he passed by. Yet these same men snapped to attention and gave their smartest salute whenever Dzhunkovsky appeared, trudging along wearing his filthy work apron. Samarin and other political detainees also enjoyed a certain degree of deference from these guards, but clearly, in their eyes, Dzhunkovsky stood in a class by himself.[60]

During this time Dzhunkovsky was also questioned by the Vecheka. When the interrogations took place or what their nature was remains unclear. But conversations seem to have been relatively friendly and left no hard feelings on Dzhunkovsky's part. Years later, when he was negotiating the sale of his memoirs to the State Literary Museum, he claimed that while he was being held in the Taganka prison "representatives of the Cheka" had encouraged him to set down his recollections. Their suggestion, he remembered, "was put so nicely" that when he left jail he was "drawn to paper" and began to write.[61] As we will see, Dzhunkovsky had probably planned to write his memoirs even before the revolution and to that end had gathered a large archive of personal and service-related documents. When he told this tale, he may have been trying to assure the museum's director, Vladimir Bonch-Bruevich, that his work had received an advanced blessing from the Soviet "organs," if not a *nihil obstat.* Still, this scrap of information also suggests that, while imprisoned, the former head of the tsar's security services had been asked to supply advice based on his past experiences. His excellent memory and recall may have amazed his interlocutors and prompted the suggestion they put "so nicely."

Although Taganka's terms of confinement were relatively mild, the prison regime took a toll on Dzhunkovsky's health. By May 1920 he was again showing signs of an aggravated heart condition, hardening of the arteries and chest pains.[62] At this point Evdokiia petitioned the Moscow Revolutionary Tribunal to allow her brother's transfer to the Alexandrinskaia Hospital, an institution where she had once served as chairman under the auspices of the Russian Red Cross.[63] The Tribunal approved the request, but before Vadya could be moved, Dodo herself suffered a health crisis involving heart problems and renal complications. On June 4, 1920, Dzhunkovsky requested the Penal Department of the People's Commissariat of Justice for a furlough of two days to visit her. "My sister is quite old, 63 years, and she has given herself over entirely to caring for me," he wrote. "That I am a cause of my sister's illness, of course makes me suffer greatly." Dzhunkovsky pledged that, if given leave, he would not deviate from the straight path between prison and her home. "[T]he the Penal Department has nothing to fear," he added, "I have never deceived anyone."[64] Although authorities permitted Vladimir his leave, only for one day and under guard, it appears that he did not exercise the privilege. On June 12, he entered the hospital for treatment.[65]

Upon his arrival doctors found Dzhunkovsky to be suffering from an enlarged heart, hardened arteries, a severe rash over much of his body, and recurring boils. They also noted chest pains, eye pain when standing, and disturbed sleep.[66] In August the Alexandrinskaia Hospital closed for repairs, but physicians regarded Dzhunkovsky's condition to be still serious enough to warrant transfer to the Surgical Hospital in Gagarin Lane, not far from his sister's home.[67]

Dzhunkovsky's hospitalization resulted in a rapid recovery, and for several months in late 1920 and early 1921 he enjoyed improved health and considerable freedom. He had a private room at the hospital, gave lessons to the children of the hospital's manager, walked about the city unguarded, and was able regularly to attend mass and visit his sister.[68] In the meanwhile, on November 7, 1920, the Revolutionary Tribunal had altered his sentence. Instead of being held in a concentration camp until the end of the Civil War, he was now to serve five years compulsory labor and imprisonment. The official document construed this as an "amnesty," but by late 1920 the Civil War was almost over and the new sentence meant that Dzhun could now be kept in jail until September 1923.[69]

The liberty that Dzhunkovsky enjoyed during his hospitalization ended in February 1921. Agents of the Vecheka were not sleeping. They noted not only his relative freedom but also the fact that he "attended midnight services, visited well-known counterrevolutionary clerics, . . . and often got together with prominent figures like Count Tatishchev, Prince Muratov, Sabashnikov, M. V., Prince Shcherbatov, N. S., . . . generals and people who previously had held important positions." The Chekisty also reported that he had conducted correspondence "entirely shielded from supervision using primarily hand delivery." In their eyes he was a dangerous figure who "maintained contacts with counterrevolutionary elements, striving with all their might to undermine the authority of the government." Police agents worried that the former governor "enjoyed considerable respect and could thus give directions to any manner of counterrevolutionary machinations."[70] Authorities took note; they searched the homes of Dzhunkovsky, Samarin, and Shcherbatov and, despite the fact that they found no incriminating evidence, returned Dzhunkovsky to the Taganka prison in early February 1921.[71] Subsequent investigations determined that permitting him to continue in a state of relative freedom might cause "harm to the Republic," and on February 18, the presidium of the Vecheka ordered that Dzhunkovsky serve out the prison term ordered by the Revolutionary Tribunal. While at Taganka, Dzhun resumed his work with the rabbits and also served as political "elder" (*starosta*), responsible for drawing up lists of political prisoners and for receiving food packages from the Red Cross. He was able to move about the prison unsupervised and was permitted visits from his sister and other relatives.

On March 23, 1921, the Vecheka transferred him to the internal prison of its Special Section, where he was held for twelve days without explanation or interrogation. On April 4, the police removed him to Butyrka.[72] At that time his prison dossier contained a note stating that, in addition to serving a five-year sentence, Dzhunkovsky was also to be considered a "material witness" for the Vecheka.[73] Dzhunkovsky found his "witness" status difficult. Although he was given a single cell on account of his illness and was permitted to work in the prison library, he was denied the right to have visitors.[74] Dzhun continued to be a model prisoner, however, and by the summer of 1921, there were signs of changing times. The Civil War was now over, and at its Tenth Congress in March, the Communist Party had dramatically altered course. It scrapped the oppressive and unproductive practices known as "War Communism"—the nationalization of all industry, the abolition of private trade, the introduction of comprehensive planning, the forcible requisition of the peasants' grain—and adopted the so-called New Economic Policy that permitted a limited return to capitalism and the market. Social tensions, too, seemed to ease. With victory assured, Communist leaders saw "formers" as less of a threat and scaled back the terror. Many people who had opposed the Bolsheviks started to reconcile to the new order. The "Changing Landmarks" movement would soon appear, gaining adherents first among émigrés but then in Russia as well. According to its tenets, the Bolshevik regime had abandoned many of its economic and internationalist follies and was becoming a true national government, defending Russia's historic interests. The former foes of the revolution should now "go to Canossa" and accept and serve the Soviet state.[75]

In this context Soviet authorities seemed uncertain what to do with the former governor and security chief; rumors about him circulated. "The crazed cats are racing about the burning house before leaping out the windows," the historian Iurii Got'e wrote in his diary on June 15, 1921. "The Bolsheviks have reexamined the Dzhunkovsky affair and have decided that he is so proper that he can be released to freedom, but . . . bearing in mind the complications with Japan (!?) he must continue to sit in Butyrka. Such is their logic."[76] On July 2, the Soviet's Central Executive Committee (VTsIK) adopted a resolution concerning his liberation, but shortly thereafter, when officials at the prison asked the Cheka if the former governor might be let go, they were told that, for the moment, it was not possible. Dzhunkovsky remained under arrest, but on August 31 he was transferred for a time to the Moscow Prison Hospital where he continued to be uncertain as to his status. "It seems strange," he wrote on September 25, "I have never been accused of doing anything against Soviet power; I have always been more than loyal to it, and deserve no reproach."[77] Then, on November 25, the VTsIK finally decreed his release, and Iosif Unshlikht, in his capacity as head of the Moscow Cheka, signed the appropriate order the next day. On November 28, 1921, Dzhun emerged into the light of freedom.[78]

The end of Dzhunkovsky's incarceration came as a surprise to his family, friends, and perhaps even to the prisoner himself. At Butyrka his release generated something of an impromptu celebration as jail personnel from the highest to the lowest ranks accompanied him to the gate. This large entourage amazed the driver of the sleigh in which he sped away.

"Who are you that all those people give you such a send off?" he asked.

"I am Dzhunkovsky," Vladimir replied.

"Are you a relative of our governor?"

"I am he, himself."

"What!?" The surprised *izvozchik* reined in the horses and turned around. "Let me have a look at you," he demanded. "My God! How you've changed! So thin! With that beard, I'd never have known you." Then, driving off, he exclaimed delightedly: "Today I'm going to every teahouse and tell all the cabbies—our governor is free!"[79]

Chapter 22

That the Descendants of the Orthodox Might Know

THE MOMENT DZHUNKOVSKY, FRESH FROM BUTYRKA'S CELLS, stepped across the threshold of his sister's apartment in Moscow's Arbat district, he began to vanish. From late 1921 to early 1938 we can seldom say with assurance what he did on any given day or construct a completely accurate chronology of his life. He simply appears from time to time, often at dates uncertain, a face in the crowd, an elderly gentleman waiting for a streetcar, a passing figure, pointed out by father to son. The pictures we possess show him thin and frail at the time of his release, dressed in a peasant shirt and wearing the full beard he adopted while in prison. Later photographs and drawings suggest recovered health and a more vigorous mien. Dzhunkovsky turned sixty in 1925, but those who saw him about that time stated that he retained his military bearing and appeared well dressed. Few available sources give us details of extended meetings or conversations, but sometimes we encounter his words—in a note sent to an old friend, an expression of thanks or a murmur of condolence, a "report" to a government official, the response to an interrogator, a tale told in a prison cell. In time the former governor became little more than a word, uttered with respect, opprobrium, or derision. Finally, "Dzhunkovsky" was simply a name on a list.

Reentry into society is always difficult for any released prisoner. For Dzhun it posed some special problems. Although he would have traded his captivity for freedom in a minute, incarceration had, to a certain degree, given him refuge from the hardships of Russian life during the Civil

Dzhunkovsky in 1922. From Anastasiia Dunaeva, *Reformy politsii v Rossii nachala XX veka i Vladimir Fedorovich Dzhunkovskii.*

War. Ironically, being locked up protected him from many of the harsh indignities that workers, soldiers, and peasants spontaneously inflicted on the despised remnants of the privileged and educated classes. In jail Dzhunkovsky enjoyed the respect of his captors and, we must assume, the personal sense of honor that comes with being an innocent victim. Prison spared him the humiliation of having to sell treasured possessions at the Sukhareva or other Moscow flea markets in order to acquire the means of existence. It guaranteed him something to eat, however meager and unpalatable, while those on the outside enjoyed the liberty to scrounge and steal their food and fuel. Memoirs and descriptions from the times indicate that the burden of searching for life's necessities fell heavily on women. How Dodo managed to support herself and, at the same time, send parcels to her imprisoned brother we may never know. But her weakened health—and Vadya's guilt—was the price paid for this achievement.

Now Dzhunkovsky, who had lost his pension as the result of his arrest and conviction, would shoulder responsibility for providing for himself and his sister in a world radically transformed. The Moscow over which he had once presided was gone. Buildings and major landmarks remained, but revolution, civil war, and a host of dislocations had transformed the social circumstances, altering the flow and form of urban life. The near collapse of public services made daily existence harsh and unpleasant for everyone. Joblessness sent large numbers of workers back to their native villages in search of food; emigration and enlistment in the White cause ripped gaping holes in the fabric of educated society. Gangs of homeless children roamed the streets, engaged in every kind of criminal activity. Although once again the capital of an empire, Moscow in 1921 was a poorer, colder, and darker place than when it had been the second metropolis of the tsar's realm.

As Dzhunkovsky left prison the New Economic Policy (NEP) had begun to take hold, but the privations of "War Communism"—extreme scarcity, exacerbated by a surging inflation—were still prominent features of life.[1] Opportunities for employment were slim. Dzhun had abilities that could be useful in a number of situations but finding any kind of work would be difficult given the position he and so many others occupied in the new society emerging from the revolution.

Dzhunkovsky was now a member of a social estate that had no precedent in tsarist times. The broad descriptive term for those in this group was *lishentsy*—"the deprived"—people who, by virtue of their birth, occupation, or socioeconomic status in prerevolutionary Russia, were denied electoral rights under Soviet law. But the debilities that attached to this situation went far beyond the loss of the vote. "The deprived" constituted a caste occupying a position roughly comparable to that of the Jews in prewar Nazi Germany. Although *lishentsy* were technically citizens, officials of the new regime often treated them as resident aliens, people who had no place and no rights in the country and who should properly stand on the lowest rung of society. Not only were they outcasts, they were enemies, people whose social origins and "class consciousness" made them foes of the new order being built by, and for, those who had previously been the "wretched of the earth."[2]

The 1918 constitution of the Russian Soviet Federative Socialist Republic disenfranchised persons using hired labor—kulaks, urban entrepreneurs, and artisans—as well as those living off unearned income. It denied suffrage to private traders and middlemen, monks and priests of all religious denominations, employees and agents of the tsarist police and security service, members of the former royal family, the mentally ill, and those sentenced for crimes.[3] Like many Soviet social categories, the *lishenets* status was both vague and elastic. Subsequent regulations, laws, and constitutions expanded the list of those who might be stripped of civil rights. Ultimately, almost anyone who lacked bona fide proletarian credentials, or who could not demonstrate that he or she was a poor or middle peasant, might be ascribed to the new pariah estate.[4]

All *lishentsy* faced grave difficulties. Former nobles, even those who had possessed little or no land or property before the revolution, were particularly vulnerable. By virtue of their demeanor and manner of speech, members of the old social elite were easy to recognize and were suspicious in the eyes of those committed to the new order. Neighbors might lodge complaints with local authorities or the secret police, triggering searches, confiscations, arrests, and forced relocations. Throughout the 1920s periodic calls to "cleanse" the institutions of the proletarian society of the dangerous remnants of the "exploiting classes" often cost the jobs of these "former people" (*byvshie liudi*) and others cast into the ranks of "the deprived," forcing them into frantic searches for new ways to earn a living. In the "workers' state" unemployment, even if involuntary, might cause one to be deemed a parasite, not entitled to ration cards, medical care, or pensions.[5]

In these circumstances, Dzhunkovsky seems, at first glance, to have been a man marked for trouble. His noble birth, his previous service as head of the tsar's gendarmes and governor of Moscow, and his conviction by a revolutionary tribunal and subsequent imprisonment guaranteed loss of the franchise. No one better fit the definition of the "class enemy," and as such he would have great difficulty getting a job and could expect constant surveillance and frequent harassment. Liable to be arrested at any moment, the first year following his release would not be easy.

Dzhunkovsky regularly attended religious services, to some Soviet officials a sign of disloyalty. During the early months of 1922 the Bolsheviks adopted measures designed to impoverish and diminish the authority of the Orthodox Church. In February authorities ordered the seizure of all valuable church property, including articles used for liturgical purposes. Ostensibly this was to acquire gold and silver that could be used to aid the victims of the terrible famine that gripped the country, although there is no evidence that any of the precious metal thus obtained was ever employed to that end.[6] Church leaders had long expressed their willingness to donate valuables in their possession to aid the starving, but they protested vigorously when the government demanded consecrated liturgical items. On February 28, 1922, Patriarch Tikhon denounced this measure as an act of sacrilege prompting unorganized spontaneous demonstrations and, in some places, physical resistance.[7] Communist leaders saw a conspiracy of the "Black Hundred clergy," and Lenin sent an angry secret letter to the Politburo on March 19, 1922, urging his comrades to "give battle . . . [to the enemy] in the most decisive and merciless manner and crush its resistance with such brutality that it will not forget it for decades to come."[8]

In the midst of this ferocious anticlerical campaign, the State Political Administration (GPU)—since February the Vecheka's successor organization—summoned Dzhunkovsky to Lubyanka on April 24, 1922, and interrogated him about his beliefs and activities. He had never hidden his Orthodox Christian faith, and now he candidly described himself as a monarchist but denied any counterrevolutionary involvement. When asked if he had engaged in "agitation" during public demonstrations in March opposing the government's confiscations, he replied: "I can say positively that I have conducted no such agitation, and did not appear in the crowd." Dzhunkovsky's answers appear to have satisfied his interrogators, who quickly released him. Still the secret police continued to keep watch, and on August 16, 1922, its agents once more carried out a search of Dzhun's home. They found him lying ill with a broken leg, and although they uncovered nothing incriminating, suspicions lingered. Then in January 1923, V. Ia. Sheshkin, an agent of the GPU's *sekretnyi otdel*, wrote a report stating that although it was clear that Dzhunkovsky continued to have contact with dangerous elements, searches and surveillance had failed to turn up any evidence of counterrevolutionary activities. In accord with that finding, on January 31, 1923, the GPU's Collegium closed the case on the former head of the tsar's internal security and sent his file to the archives.[9]

From this point until the late 1930s, Dzhunkovsky passed virtually unscathed through times when believers, "former people," and members of the old intelligentsia were objects of intense hostility and were subject to interrogations, arrest, exile, and even execution. The hardships that resulted from being one of the "deprived" caused many to petition Soviet authorities for the restoration of their civil rights.[10] But Dzhunkovsky seems to have been untroubled in his *lishenets* status. Luck and exemplary behavior cannot fully explain why the deeply religious, convicted counterrevolutionary Dzhunkovsky escaped the fate that befell so many of his fellow "formers." One reasonable solution to this puzzle could be that he enjoyed consistent "protection"—provided, perhaps, by Viacheslav Rudolfovich Menzhinsky who from September 1923 served as Dzerzhinsky's second-in-command at the GPU (rechristened OGPU in November) and, in 1926, became his successor as chief.[11]

The phenomenon of early Soviet protection (*pokrovitel'stvo*) has been as yet little studied, and we are unsure as to its full extent and precise nature. Still, it is clear that during the 1920s a number of the communist oligarchs sought to shield certain members of opposition parties, "former people," nonconforming cultural figures, and specialists of various stripes from the waves of repression that occurred with regularity throughout the decade. The motives for these elite figures' protection were diverse; they might be the result of personal friendship, an awareness of a person's past services and achievements, or basic human sympathy. Frequently *pokrovitel'stvo* reflected the patron's sense that the individuals they were shielding possessed talent, skills, or knowledge that made them useful to the new order. Elite protection did not always mean smooth sailing, however. Workers and lower echelon Party members often continued to view those being shown favor with suspicion and sought to thwart the efforts of the higher-ups.[12]

That Menzhinsky was the one who provided Dzhunkovsky long-term protection is unproved, but it is not implausible; for it would seem that only a patron who enjoyed a high place and an extended tenure of office could have enabled Dzhun to avoid the surrounding dangers for as long as he did. Menzhinsky meets those criteria, and since he was a backer of Stalin and his policies, his patronage would have been especially valuable. But what might have led him to support the former governor and chief of the tsar's internal security?

One reason was that Dzhunkovsky accepted the revolution and submitted to the new order. To be sure, he was a monarchist, a Russian patriot, and a believing Christian who showed no sympathy for communism; but he had stayed at the front after the Bolshevik takeover, obeyed all Soviet rules and regulations during his days in Petrograd, cooperated in the Malinovsky proceedings, acknowledged the legitimacy of his own trial in 1919, and was a model prisoner in the years that followed. A number of people who had made similar submissions to Soviet power were not treated as kindly, however. What else might explain Dzhunkovsky's favored status?

While documentation is lacking, many reputable historians believe that Dzhunkovsky established some kind of ties with the "organs" as early as 1919 and that he served Dzerzhinsky in an advisory capacity.[13] Another source asserts that Vladimir Fedorovich entered Soviet service in 1924.[14] Beyond this, it has long been rumored that Dzhunkovsky participated in the Cheka/OGPU's "active measures" directed against the White emigration, specifically the famous "Operation Trust," an early success of Soviet counterintelligence. Created at the end of the Civil War, the Trust was an elaborate deception designed to persuade the enemies of the Soviet regime abroad (particularly the monarchists) that a vast counterrevolutionary organization existed in Russia and that it was only a matter of time before it would overthrow Bolshevism and restore the tsars. Secret police operatives convinced gullible Whites not to unleash violent attacks on Soviet Russia, claiming that such actions would undermine the conspiracy (which had to depend on internal forces) and delay its success. The Trust and related scams spread all kinds of false information that was picked up by foreign intelligence services. It disrupted the nefarious schemes of the British agent Sidney Reilly and the counterrevolutionary terrorist Boris Savinkov, both of whom were captured by the OGPU's counterintelligence arm, the KRO (*Kontrrazvedivatel'nyi otdel*).[15]

Operation Trust ended in the mid-1920s and for years remained a closely guarded secret in the Soviet Union.[16] In the late 1950s, however, its successes began to be publicized, the subject of novels and even television shows. These early works presented Dzerzhinsky, Artur Artuzov, and Menzhinsky as the Trust's inventors and guiding spirits, but stories about Dzhunkovsky having played some part in this adventure were circulating in the 1980s and early 1990s. Then at the start of the new century a number of books and articles appeared claiming that Dzhunkovsky was the real "father" of the Trust, and the tale quickly became a staple of popular history.[17]

Not a shred of documentary evidence supports the claims concerning Dzhunkovsky and the Trust, however. In 2003 Boris Gudz', a lone survivor from the early days of the KRO and a close friend of Artuzov, flatly denied that the former head of the tsar's internal security was involved with the Trust (although he believed that Dzhunkovsky and Dzerzhinsky were acquainted).[18] Serious Western and émigré scholars who have extensively investigated the Trust do not mention Dzhunkovsky.[19] Currently, A. A. Zdanovich, a Russian historian with access to the archives of the Trust, has stated that he has found nothing to indicate Dzhunkovsky's participation.[20] Even a deliberate effort to give the benefit of every doubt to the stories about his role could only produce the Scottish verdict: "Not proven."[21]

That a convicted counterrevolutionary monarchist would be called on to join in developing such a sensitive operation as the Trust seems unlikely.[22] But it is virtually impossible to *prove* a negative. Rumors and legends usually have "legs," however thin and wobbly. In one of the interrogations conducted during his imprisonment, Dzhunkovsky might have discussed *zubatovshchina*. The Trust had "zubatovite" features, most notably the goal of deflecting émigré opponents of the Soviet regime from committing harmful acts by using phony organizations, much as the Okhrana had sought to lure workers from the revolutionary path by means of police controlled "unions." Dzhun's observations about Zubatov could have been remembered, giving rise to the legend of his "fatherhood" of the Chekists' first counterintelligence success. Stories of Dzhun's active participation in the Trust could be an effort by "court historians" of the post-Soviet security services to create a broader and more honorable pedigree for today's "organs." They might also be echoes of the hostility toward Dzhunkovsky that extreme right-wing journalists, politicians, and Okhrana professionals had expressed beginning with the first Russian revolution and continuing well after his fall from power in 1915.[23]

Leaving aside the question of the Trust, however, certain facts of Dzhunkovsky's life during the 1920s and 1930s raise questions that are most easily answered by positing some kind of fairly long-term connection to the "organs" or, at the very least, the protection of someone in their ranks. Why, for example, was his case file abruptly closed at the beginning of 1923 despite his open display of religious belief and his continued contacts with potentially dangerous elements? During the 1920s Dzhunkovsky was able to travel freely and frequently to Petrograd/Leningrad to use his large personal archive, held at the Academy of Sciences, as he composed his memoirs. How do we interpret this?

Recent research reminds us that with the end of the Civil War, the Soviet security apparatus was not dismantled but, rather, strengthened and made a regular part of the governmental system. The Cheka/Vecheka —an "extraordinary," virtually autonomous institution—was abolished and its successor, the GPU/OGPU, nominally subordinated to the People's Commissariat of Internal Affairs (NKVD). Despite this "normalization," however, the power of the secret police and its surveillance of suspect elements actually increased, and every regional OGPU headquarters had a list of "enemies" including former tsarist civil servants.[24] Yet Dzhunkovsky was able to go about his business in peace. All of this strongly suggests "protection," whether earned or not.

Then, as we shall see, at the turn of the decade representatives of the OGPU began to ask Dzhunkovsky for advice concerning a number of important matters, sensitive issues of immediate relevance to current domestic and foreign concerns.[25] Would the "organs" have consulted a man with Dzhunkovsky's past had they not previously vetted him and determined that he was reliable and worthy of confidence? In the late 1920s and early 1930s Soviet leaders and the public ramped up hostility toward "former people" and members of the old intelligentsia. During these perilous times, Dzhunkovsky's name surfaced in connection with the communist regime's struggle to gain greater control over the Academy of Sciences. Wrongdoing on his part was imputed, and he was linked with people accused of engaging in an anti-Soviet plot; yet the former head of the tsar's internal security apparatus escaped serious consequences and continued to be a valued consultant.[26] It is hard to believe that this was due entirely to chance.

No direct evidence proves that Menzhinsky was Dzhunkovsky's protector, but chronology is suggestive. The end to Dzhun's time of troubles and the beginning of a period of relative tranquility and security roughly coincides with the appointment of Menzhinsky as Dzerzhinsky's second in the OGPU. The organs' most intense utilization of Dzhunkovsky's expertise occurred after 1926, when Menzhinsky stood at their helm, a position that would have enabled him to keep Dzhun out of serious difficulty during the conflict over the Academy of Sciences. What Menzhinsky's motives were can only be conjectured. But Dzhunkovsky's contacts with Dzerzhinsky (something that is widely accepted) and, perhaps, his usefulness as an informant might have formed a basis for trust. The knowledge and expertise that Dzhunkovsky possessed made him a valuable resource, well worth preserving.

The fact that Dzhunkovsky had studied history with Menzhinsky's father at the Corps of Pages may have fostered a more personal tie. Menzhinsky seems to have revered his father, naming not one but two of his sons after him. Dzhunkovsky harbored respect, even affection for his old teacher, although in his student days he and other pages regarded Menzhinsky père as something of a pedant.[27]

If a shared memory formed one element of a bond, common personal characteristics might have provided the basis for another. Neither Dzhunkovsky nor Menzhinsky exactly fits our image of a secret service chief. Exquisite manners, a sense of decorum, and of course, tact were personality traits the two shared. Both had strong cultural interests and even similar artistic associations. In his younger days Menzhinsky was drawn to the circle centered on the "decadent" writer Mikhail Kuzmin; for ten years Dzhunkovsky had been close to the symbolist poet Konstantin Balmont. Each man harbored literary ambitions. Menzhinsky dabbled in poetry and had published a novel.[28] Dzhunkovsky never seems to have sought admission to the world of belles lettres, but he gathered a large array of personal materials and documents from his career, a clear indication that he contemplated putting down his recollections well before he began to work on them in the 1920s. Years later Dzhunkovsky told Vladimir Bonch-Bruevich that "representatives of the Cheka" had encouraged him to write.[29] Was Menzhinsky one of those "representatives?"

Thus, while the patronage of Menzhinsky can only be surmised, it seems almost certain that Dzhunkovsky enjoyed some kind of protection from about 1923 onward. But even if he earned it by assistance to the Soviet organs, such service did not constitute regular employment. To support himself and his sister even at a modest level, the former governor needed additional work. Given his status and record, however, this had to be found at the margins of the Soviet economy.

Only a few sources tell us about the way Dzhunkovsky's earned his bread in these years. One claims that he taught physical education in the schools.[30] Given his age and health, this is unlikely, but he certainly would have relished such work. Dzhunkovsky was an exponent of the principle *mens sana in corpore sano*, an avid gymnast, cyclist, and swimmer. As governor he criticized the Moscow zemstvos for failing to support athletics in their schools.[31] Other occupations have also been proposed. A newspaper article published in the late 1920s announced gleefully that Moscow's former governor now worked as a watchman (*storozh*) at the Church of St. John the Baptist on Chernigovsky lane.[32] Dzhunkovsky's deep religious faith and devotion to the church makes this entirely plausible. Finally—and here we have good documentation—Dzhun gave language lessons, French, and perhaps English as well. This was a task he took very seriously, working with students up to nine hours a day, much to the consternation of his friends.[33]

All these jobs had two things in common—they were humble and unremarkable. The obscurity Dzhunkovsky had sought since 1915 now enveloped him even more completely, and a rumor circulated that he had become a monk.[34] Following his release Dzhunkovsky was seldom visible and seems to have had restricted contacts with other *byvshie*, including some with whom he had associated in better times. Still, had he wanted it, an active social life would have been readily at hand.

Since the fall of communism, some excellent work has been done on the "former people," providing splendid pictures of their private worlds and folkways.[35] They show that as "formers" struggled—on occasion quite successfully—to find a niche in the new order, they also continued to maintain family and friendship ties that served as the basis of support networks sustaining them through difficult days. In the broad sea of Soviet Russia, *byvshie* created small islands on which they preserved some vestiges of the old order—a close-knit social life with weddings, baptisms, funerals, get-togethers, and celebrations of all kinds, even, mirabile dictu, balls.[36] At one such event—modest in the extreme—Dzhunkovsky's close friend Vladimir Gadon carried out the traditional and demanding duties of director just as the two of them had done long ago during their service as adjutants to Grand Duke Sergei Alexandrovich.

As far as we can determine, however, Dzhunkovsky seldom—if ever—participated in the social life of the "formers." Instead, he maintained a small circle of friends; the Bakhrushins, the Sabashnikovs, Sumbatov-Iuzhin, Gadon, and Anatolii Koni were among them. Two female relatives from his mother's side of the family, Evgeniia Makarenko and Nadezhda Shebasheva, provided support for him and his sister in the late 1920s and early 1930s. (They called themselves "nieces" and referred to Dzhunkovsky as their "uncle," but by Anglo-Saxon genealogical reckoning they were first cousins once removed.) Vladimir Fedorovich probably kept some contact with his brother's son, Nikolai Nikolaevich Dzhunkovsky, who after graduating from the Petrograd Polytechnic Institute departed for still independent Georgia where his wife, Elena Georgievna Dadiani, a "Radiant Princess" (*Svetleishaia kniazha*) from a Mingrelian noble clan, had family. He would be arrested at the end of the 1920s but was released and went on to a distinguished engineering career.[37] And although no correspondence has survived, Uncle Vladimir was not forgotten. Years later his grand-nephew, Georgii Nikolaevich Dzhunkovsky, told a friend of his family tie to the former head of the tsar's security service, and apparently with some pride.[38]

Dzhunkovsky spoke of his isolation in the years following his release from prison, an isolation both physical and spiritual. Particularly painful was Nina Evreinova's decision to emigrate and join her children now living in western Europe. Nina was his great love and, next to his sister, probably the most important person in his life. It is not difficult to imagine the impact this loss would have. But Dzhunkovsky knew well that Nina had always put her children first, and he must also have realized that, with a daughter and three sons to help her, life in the West was likely to be better than in Russia. Thus, shortly after Dzhunkovsky's return from prison, they traveled to Petrograd to dispose of the things that Nina had in her apartment there. She would leave Russia forever in 1922.[39]

For some time the two corresponded. How frequently we cannot say. One postcard that Dzhunkovsky sent to Nina in 1923 has survived, and it gives us a window on his mood—both one of sorrow and Christian affirmation. "One cannot follow our Crucified Lord without a cross," he wrote,

> What is that cross? It is the various inconveniences, burdens and humiliations that are laid upon us, within and without, on the path of an honorable fulfillment in life of the Lord's commandments in the spirit of his injunctions and demands. That cross is bound to a Christian so that where there is a cross there is [also] a Christian, and where there is no cross there [cannot be] a Christian. The general desire for life's pleasures is not for the true Christian. His task is to cleanse and correct himself. . . . He must go against the world around him; and how can this be done without burdens and constraints? Be joyful when you feel the cross upon yourself, for this is a sign that you are following the Lord on the path to salvation in paradise. Endure but for a little while! The end will come.[40]

And do we not also find in Dzhunkovsky's choice of text, with its emphasis on the cross, suffering, self-denial, cleansing, and correction, a faint echo of his guilt for the passion he and Nina had shared so long before?

The sadness caused by the departure of such a close friend must have strengthened Dzhun's desire to withdraw from society. There were other reasons as well. His status as a former governor, erstwhile head of the Corps of Gendarmes, and convicted counterrevolutionary made him a dangerous acquaintance, and consideration for the safety of others may have induced him to keep his circle small and not to seek unnecessary ties. In one of the few places in his memoirs where he mentions events after 1918, Dzhunkovsky states that, when he got out of jail, the craftsmen of Vladimiro-Dzhunkovsky asked him to spend the summer with them at a dacha they had prepared. "I was, of course, deeply touched by such concern," he recalled, yet in the end he refused their offer, "fearing to bring upon myself and the inhabitants of the village the attentions of the authorities." He was certain that they would suspect "agitation" and "counterrevolution" in even so innocent an association.[41]

Dzhunkovsky's caution reflected the concerns of a man just released from prison. But it seems that in years to come that caution continued, suggesting that he had an acute understanding of his peculiar situation. He may have sensed that he enjoyed some kind of protection but knew that it would not necessarily extend to those with whom he came in contact. He also realized that he might be questioned about people he knew. Moreover, as a seasoned administrator, Dzhunkovsky was well aware of the gulf that separated the upper and lower echelons of the state machine, whether tsarist or Soviet. Experience taught him that in police matters the right hand did not always know what the left hand was doing, and he could be almost certain that some local officials were likely to be ignorant of or indifferent to any patronage he might enjoy. And although he could be subject to harassment, those who befriended him were liable to suffer something worse.

Whatever his reasons may have been, Dzhunkovsky's quest for invisibility was successful. He now faded into rumor, speculation, and misconception, although the "unsleeping eye" of the secret police undoubtedly kept watch. He spent most of his days close to home, caring for his sister and giving lessons. But these occupations could not satisfy his restless energy. On the wall of the small apartment he shared with Dodo, Dzhun hung a portrait that the Grand Duchess Elizaveta Fedorovna had painted of him years before. Beneath this treasured relic from a vanished world, he turned to a task that would occupy him for the better part of a decade—writing memoirs that told the story of his life and sketched the picture of an age.[42] Soon Dzhunkovsky's researches into times past would guide his present, causing him to strengthen old ties and develop new connections. Then, as page piled upon page, his recollections took on a life of their own, paralleling and even prefiguring that of their author. Ultimately, the memoir and the materials upon which it was based would exercise significant influence on important events in which the writer himself played no part.

Dzhunkovsky's reminiscences do not begin with an explanation as to why he wrote. They simply start by recounting his ancestry and then proceed straightforwardly to the events of his life. In their final form the memoirs sprawled to thirteen volumes in typescript, which, with the handwritten drafts and copies that accompany them, must take up a considerable block of space on the shelves of the State Archive of the Russian Federation. The published portions of the work, covering the years from 1905 to 1917, comprise three stout, closely printed tomes, with a heft sufficient to stop a door in all but the fiercest gale.

Although unstated Dzhunkovsky's motives for writing are not difficult to surmise. All those who produce memoirs seek a measure of immortality, and Dzhun was no exception. Still, the nature of the work suggests that he had other purposes. Although it tells the story of his life, the memoir is far from an autobiography. Dzhunkovsky does not concentrate on his own development, and as we have seen, he is silent on important personal matters. Of course, the author holds center stage as an actor; but he is equally a camera's eye, focusing on the people and events that flowed around him. As such Dzhunkovsky's recollections stand on the border of memory and history, with the latter dimension almost as important as the former.

In every memoir the author seeks to retrieve and hold events and persons steadily slipping away with the passage of time. Yet many Russians who wrote after the revolution were tormented by a special sense that their past was being separated from the present by a huge and rapidly growing gulf, a rift that would soon be so wide as to render the world that existed before 1917 incomprehensible. The social and political changes that had transpired during Soviet rule were not the only barriers to an understanding of the bygone years. Official propaganda was distorting to an appalling degree what had taken place not long before, and these obvious falsifications cried out for a response. When Dzhunkovsky's contemporary Prince Sergei Dmitrievich Urusov learned of the misconceptions Soviet schools were imparting to his grandchildren, he was shocked. (Among the things they were being told was that the emancipation of the serfs had not taken place until after the fall of tsarism.) Well before the revolution, Urusov had published an account of his governorship in Bessarabia, and afterward he resolved to write no more about his life. Now he changed his mind. Urusov pressed ahead with his memoirs in the hope that he could salvage some portion of the truth for the next generation.[43]

For his part Dzhunkovsky seems to have long contemplated putting his recollections on paper. But an incident that reflected on his own achievements may well have generated a sense of urgency. During the 1912 Borodino centennial he had been instrumental in building, on a portion of the battlefield, a new home for invalids that contained a small museum. When he left Moscow a year later to assume his duties in the capital, the citizens of the Mozhaisk region requested and received imperial permission to hang Dzhunkovsky's portrait in the museum, accompanied by an inscription thanking the former governor "for his constant attention and great concern for the population and the needs of the county." The half-length portrait graced the museum's walls through years of war, revolution, and civil conflict. Then in December 1921 a communist writer, Alexander Zharov, visited the site, saw the picture, and wrote in the visitors' book: "Why . . . the portrait of Dzhunkovsky? It has neither historical nor any other kind of value. I recommend that you make it an exhibit in the cesspool, consign it to the flames, or give it to people who bow and scrape in the old way." The museum director took fright; the governor's portrait vanished.[44] Public memory of what Dzhunkovsky had done was purged—in a manner curiously prefiguring the fate soon to befall so many Soviet leaders, their faces expunged from official photographs, their accomplishments erased from history.[45]

This event, itself insignificant, must have reminded Dzhunkovsky how quickly the past could be distorted or simply swept away, and like Urusov he determined to combat falsification with fact. His memoir would not be simply an attempt to save his own name and deeds from oblivion, however. Dzhun sought to depict the world in which he worked, the many people he had known and the things that they, as well as he, had accomplished. He did not write in a mournful tone, freighted with regret for what had been lost. Instead, the memoir is a steady and dispassionate record of men and events as he saw them, pedestrian in the true sense of the word, devoid of extensive introspection, lachrymose self-justification, conceptual leaps, or flights of fancy. Indeed, it seems that Dzhunkovsky, the ardent lover of the theater, cast himself as a latter-day Pimen, the monk-chronicler in Pushkin's *Boris Godunov*, writing his final tale:

> So that the descendants of the Orthodox might know
> The bygone fortunes of their native land,
> Their great tsars remember
> For their labors, for their glory, for their good—
> And for their sins, for their dark deeds,
> To our Redeemer humbly pray.[46]

Dzhunkovsky strove for accuracy to a degree bordering on pedantry. He stuffed the text with quotations, at length or in full, from documents he had written or received, as well as the words spoken by contemporaries, even if he had not heard them firsthand. Yet the memoir left many things unsaid, maddening silences that conceal painful aspects of his personal life or moments that reflected badly on his country. His account of the Great War displays little hatred of the Germans nor does it dwell on the horrors of combat. Rather it emphasizes the stoic bravery of ordinary soldiers. On occasion, the author tempers historical truth by presenting many of the men and women he knew in a positive way. Dzhunkovsky found it hard to judge people harshly, and his personality sketches sometimes display an endearing naiveté, particularly in regard to the imperial family, whose members, especially the tsar, are almost always portrayed in a warm light. Recalling his life, Dzhunkovsky seemed unwilling to countenance fully the subtle shift in his loyalty from tsar and dynasty to nation and people that had occurred since 1915. He longed for what he saw as the pure idealism of his youth, and now in old age, as the past unrolled before him, he lived anew.

The monarchist spirit that Dzhunkovsky openly proclaimed in 1922 permeates the work, but it is not a call for restoration. Rather, without apology or extenuation, the memoirs show that under the ancien régime life was not unrelievedly dark and that the tsar's government was neither deliberately cruel nor consistently repressive. At the same time, however, Dzhun tried to avoid giving his work a slant that could be considered counterrevolutionary. Radical parties, their leaders, and their deeds are treated obliquely, en passant. Even when recounting the horrific assassination of Grand Duke Sergei Alexandrovich, Dzhunkovsky's sorrow is restrained and the anger he must have felt at the time neither displayed nor recalled. He pulled his punches because he did not write his memoirs for private consumption or "for the drawer" in the expectation that some future historian might find them useful. Dzhunkovsky intended his work for the candid world, and the connections he enjoyed with the Sabashnikov family and their still-functioning publishing enterprise gave him good reason to hope that his words would see the light of day.

Yet for all their prosaic qualities, Dzhunkovsky's memoirs are not devoid of message. His belief in the importance of religious faith and moral principles in a man's life, and of law in the life of a society, shine through the text. He was a man of the state, but he sought to show that although a ruler or administrator should be firm his firmness ought to be guided and tempered by fairness and a sense of justice. The individual—his or her rights, dignity, "soul"—must always be kept in view. Dzhun's memoirs express another faith as well, a belief in the power of simple facts, honestly presented, to ultimately triumph over lies.

The reader who has come thus far does not require a discussion of what Dzhunkovsky's memoir contains. The first three-quarters of this book heavily—shamelessly—depends upon it. But how did Dzhun compose and construct his magnum opus? Unsurprisingly, the answer is not entirely clear. Here, as in so many other areas of Dzhunkovsky's life after 1918, we have to weave reasoned supposition together with the relatively few available facts.

Dzhunkovsky's memoir appears to be based on two bodies of source material. The first of these is his substantial personal archive: family records, service papers, and public documents of various kinds, wartime field journals, letters received from almost four hundred correspondents, newspaper clippings, memorabilia, and photograph albums. The size and completeness of the materials are clear proof of Vladimir's pack-rat nature, as well as his self-awareness and the determination, reached relatively early in life, to tell his own story. Dzhunkovsky would use these sources extensively in his memoirs, sometimes copying into the text, verbatim, documents that were the size of small books. Today this collection resides in the State Archive of the Russian Federation (*fond* 826) and contains the bulk of his personal and official papers (over one thousand items). A second *fond* (270) holds a much smaller body of materials relating to his work as head of the tsar's security services, but this was probably not put together by him.

According to his own account Dzhunkovsky began collecting materials about his life while still a student at the Corps of Pages. By the time he left Moscow to take up his post as assistant minister of internal affairs and commander of the Corps of Gendarmes in 1913, his archive was large enough to require a special room for its storage. When he was dismissed from his posts in August 1915, Dzhun took all the materials he considered to be of a personal nature and moved them to his new home at 54 Kamenoostrovsky Prospect. At the time of his departure for the front at the end of 1915, he was concerned about the fate of his papers should he be killed during the war. On the advice of Senator Anatolii Koni, he turned to Boris Modzalevsky, a scholar and bibliographer working at Pushkin House (*Pushkinskii dom*), which was a repository for important unpublished materials controlled by the Academy of Sciences. Modzalevsky examined the papers, deemed them to be suitable for preservation at Pushkin House, and Dzhun agreed to have them transferred there when he returned from the front or in the event of his death.

After his retirement from the army in 1918, however, Dzhunkovsky could not immediately turn over his papers, now augmented by materials from his wartime service, because of unsettled conditions at Pushkin

House. Dzhun's subsequent arrest further delayed the transfer. When his sister moved to Moscow, she left her brother's archive in Petrograd in the care of an old family retainer, stored in rented rooms first on Kamenoostrovsky Prospect and later on Tavricheskaia Street. After his release from prison, Dzhunkovsky traveled to Petrograd and finally deposited the materials in Pushkin House where they remained until 1929.[47]

The other main source for the memoirs is assumed to be an extensive diary that Dzhunkovsky kept throughout his life. We can find no trace of this document, however, and can only posit its existence because of the length and character of the memoirs themselves.[48] The structure of the work, its chronological, chronicle-like listing of event after event, linked together with longer accounts of what he and others did, interspersed with liberal quotations from relevant materials, give us good reason to think that a diary of some kind formed the essential matrix binding together the memoir as a whole. But the fate of the putative diary remains a mystery. Some have suggested that it was lost when Dzhunkovsky's materials were removed from Pushkin House at the end of the 1920s.[49] This is one possibility, but given that Dzhunkovsky spent most of his time in Moscow while he was composing his memoirs, it is very likely that he had his diary close at hand at the time. The memoir may well be, in essence, a sanitized version of the diary, purged of intimate and painful matters (like his romance with Nina), and augmented by documents copied from his archive in Petrograd/Leningrad. Thus, it is also possible that, after the diary had served his purposes, Dzhun destroyed it to prevent it from falling into the wrong hands—those of the secret police or snooping historians.[50] Of course, there is an outside chance that no diary ever existed. Dzhunkovsky was famous for his excellent memory; but that he had the total recall necessary for the writing of a memoir of the length and detail that he eventually produced seems questionable. In any case a diary, missing from his personal archive, is not found in the small cache of papers he donated to Bakhrushin's Theater Museum during the 1920s, nor was it among the materials seized at the time of his arrest in 1937.[51]

Dzhunkovsky probably began composing his memoir in 1922, shortly after his release from prison, but he did not write in a straight chronological line. He started with his years as governor and commander of the Corps of Gendarmes. By 1924 he had carried the story down to his departure for the front in 1915, and perhaps as far as his return from the war in 1918. In 1925 he turned to his early days. He had almost finished the manuscript by 1929, began typing it in 1930–1931, and by August 1933 it was virtually complete.[52] The work was arduous and time-consuming, requiring extensive travel to Petrograd/Leningrad. For although Dzhunkovsky may have had his diary in Moscow most of the documents he would refer to and quote lay in the former capital.

The distant location of his archive undoubtedly slowed and complicated Dzhunkovsky's writing. Sergei Fedorovich Platonov, the distinguished historian who directed Pushkin House, and others who had worked there also, all testified to the fact that Dzhunkovsky regularly visited Petrograd/Leningrad to consult his archive during the 1920s, although the dates and lengths of his stays in the old capital were unspecified. These witnesses further stated that Dzhunkovsky's papers were housed in a garage and that he had virtually unrestricted access to them, bringing boxes of materials at will to a reading room for his use.[53] It is also entirely likely that Dzhun was able to take documents back with him to Moscow, returning them when he was finished.[54]

Sometime toward the end of the decade, although the manuscript still may not have been complete, Dzhun put his memoir into the hands of Mikhail Sabashnikov for publication in the series *Zapisi proshlogo* (Notes of the Past).[55] Correspondence attending his subsequent sale of the memoirs to Vladimir Bonch-Bruevich in 1934 suggests that Dzhunkovsky was still engaged in last minute work on the document, an impression strengthened by the fact that one small segment—a section that contains the account of his travel to famine-stricken Saratov in 1892—remained untyped (see below).

Speculations concerning the composition of Dzhunkovsky's memoir are, in the end, not all that important—we have what we have. Yet they serve as a useful reminder of his diligence, energy, and workaholic nature. Beyond this they lead us to a small window on another aspect of Dzhunkovsky's life in the 1920s: his deepening friendship with former senator Anatolii Fedorovich Koni, the great liberal jurist of late imperial Russia who, like Vladimir, had been cast up on the beach of "Sovdepiia."

Dzhunkovsky probably made Koni's acquaintance during the 1890s through his connections with the Bakhrushins, Sabashnikovs, and Evreinovs. But given the difference in their ages—Anatolii Fedorovich was twenty years Vladimir's senior—it is unlikely that they became close until after Dzhun moved to St. Petersburg in 1913. His memoirs contain few mentions of Koni early on. Later, however, the elder statesman gave moral support when Dzhunkovsky was under fire from the right wing in the Duma and State Council concerning the question of "German power" in the wake of the Moscow riots of 1915, something, Dzhun wrote, "that touched me very much."[56] Koni was among those officials who strongly sympathized with Dzhun after his dismissal from office and regarded his opposition to Rasputin as a great national service.[57]

Following the revolution the two men found themselves holding similar views. Like Dzhunkovsky, Koni was a devout Orthodox Christian who rather quickly accepted the fall of the monarchy and the October coup. According to Anatolii Lunacharsky, Koni saw even heavy-handed Bolshevik rule as a preferable alternative to the prospect of anarchy and national collapse. "If the revolution does not create a dictatorship," Lunacharsky quotes him as saying at the end of 1917, "then we will, in all likelihood, enter a Time of Troubles, the end and limits of which we cannot see, and from which only God knows what will come, perhaps the destruction of Russia."[58] These considerations led the former senator to make himself available to the new regime, teaching and giving public lectures under its auspices. Koni's willingness to serve was not shaken even when he was subjected to searches and humiliations by representatives of Soviet power during the Red Terror.[59] In 1919, when both age and health could have justified retirement, Koni continued his educational efforts, appearing before Red Army soldiers, much to the disgust of some who remained unreconciled to the new order.[60]

While his own circumstances were very different, Dzhunkovsky's attitudes and actions were similar in essence to Koni's. He accepted a pension from the Bolshevik authorities after his retirement from the army and followed their regulations to the letter. He showed no interest in emigration or supporting the White cause. Dzhun's behavior and statements during his imprisonment and trial made it clear that he recognized the legitimacy of Soviet power, and his subsequent willingness to consult with the "organs" strongly suggests that, like Koni, he saw the Bolsheviks as a force for order and stability at a time when Russia desperately needed both. Dzhunkovsky, it appears, responded positively to Koni's favorite motto, advanced by the senator's hero, Dr. Fedor Gaaz: "Hurry to do good."[61] In the eyes of both men, part of that "good" was to help their country through its difficult trials and, where possible, to transmit the positive values of prerevolutionary legality and administrative practice to the new society and government arising from the revolution. This they could accomplish by teaching, consulting, and preserving the truth about the past for the generations to come.

Dzhunkovsky's trips to Petrograd/Leningrad as he worked on his memoirs enabled him to renew and deepen his friendship with Koni. In the mid-1920s, a correspondence between the two men ensued—albeit spare and limited—that provides some insight into their thinking as Russia settled into the NEP. Most of the letters we have came from Koni, but he clearly wrote as to a person who, he was convinced, shared his views. Neither man seemed sanguine about the state of things. In a new year's message sent at the end of 1925, Koni wrote of "our unfortunate country."[62] Later, he bemoaned the prevailing moral climate "when the human soul is considered a priestly invention, and man himself the product of apes developed in a materialistic culture." Yet the former senator had no nostalgia for times past. "Have you read the fourth volume of the protocols of the [Provisional Government's] Investigative Commission?" he asked his younger confidant. "It is impossible to read the testimonies of Protopopov and Beletsky without horror and revulsion. [To think] that our domestic policy was in the hands of such people!"[63]

Both Koni and his longtime companion, Elena Ponomareva, wrote Dzhunkovsky expressing concern for his health and the fear that he was working too much. "I am so disturbed by the news that you are busy nine hours a day with your teaching duties," Ponomareva cautioned, "and I decided to write to ask that you take timely measures against overwork."[64] In 1926 Koni received a pension from the Soviet government at the request of the Academy of Sciences, a grant that significantly reduced his need to travel and lecture. In a letter sent in August he expressed his sadness that, despite great services to the country, Dzhun had not been given one as well.[65]

For his part Dzhunkovsky did not complain to Koni about his financial situation, lamenting, instead, the physical distance that separated him from his friend. "How I wish I could see you face to face," he wrote. "Often, often I turn to you in thought, especially in those difficult moments that one frequently has to live through." By the middle 1920s, Dzhunkovsky, too, was feeling more and more out of tune with rapidly altering circumstances. "People with whom you can talk and be understood have become fewer and fewer," he told Koni, "and not because they have left; but it is a rare person who has not changed and started to look at things with different eyes."[66]

To Dzhunkovsky, Koni was a beacon in an increasingly gloomy scene; and this feeling of being alone deepened further when the great jurist died in September 1927. For a time Dzhunkovsky continued to correspond with Ponomareva, who sent him Koni's portrait at the end of the year.[67] After Koni had been laid to rest in the Tikhvin cemetery at the Alexander-Nevsky Lavra, Vladimir sent a cross for his grave.[68] But soon, even that symbolic tie to his old friend—and to the world before the revolution—would be lost. In the 1930s Soviet authorities exhumed Koni's remains and reinterred them, together with those of other literary figures, in the Volkov cemetery.[69]

Chapter 23

Overtaken by the Night

As his personal world shrank, Dzhunkovsky put the final touches on his memoirs. With a view to publication, he read portions of the work to Mikhail Sabashnikov and other friends, amazing them with his tremendous recall of prerevolutionary times.[1] But soon current events intruded, pushing him in new, unexpected directions and frustrating hopes for presenting his recollections to the public.

In 1928 the Soviet Union launched the first Five Year Plan, abandoning the moderate policies and mixed economy of the NEP in favor of rapid, state-driven industrialization and the forced collectivization of agriculture that would cost millions of lives. The civil peace, artistic tolerance, and intellectual pluralism that had marked the 1920s so far ended in a "cultural revolution." Joseph Stalin consolidated his dictatorship, and the government adopted the posture of civil war. Soviet leaders sought to awaken the proletariat, strengthen its fighting spirit, and rearm it for the struggle against the "class enemy." Foes of the working class were everywhere, they declared, especially in the ranks of engineers, technicians, scientists, and cultural figures from the prerevolutionary era, not to mention "former people" and other human detritus of the tsarist regime. According to official propaganda, the dangers posed by domestic holdovers and capitalists abroad had been clearly demonstrated by the so-called Shakhty affair.

In 1927 the OGPU claimed to have discovered that "bourgeois specialists" and foreign experts were engaged in sabotage ("wrecking") at the coal mines of Shakhty, a town in the North Caucasus. The charges were based upon dubious evidence, but Stalin seized them with both hands. More than fifty engineers and technical personnel, including a number of German nationals, were arrested and brought to trial in May 1928. Most were convicted and sentenced to terms in prison; five were shot. The sensational court proceedings electrified the nation and generated hostility and suspicion toward all "formers," whatever their skills. Stalin now began to put forth his theory of the intensification of the class struggle as the construction of socialism advanced. "It is not true that we no longer have class enemies," he warned. "They not only exist, they are growing and trying to take action against the Soviet Government. . . . This was shown by the Shakhty affair . . . a joint attack on the Soviet regime launched by international capital and the bourgeoisie in our own country."[2]

Given the tenor and temper of the times, it seems both surprising and strange that in 1928 the OGPU summoned Dzhunkovsky for a consultation.[3] As far as we know, he had not been called in by the "organs" since his hostile interrogation in 1922. He fit the profile of the "class enemy" about as closely as anyone could, yet the representatives of the secret police now treated him with respect. It is clear that they regarded what he had to say as both trustworthy and important.

He was met by Alexandra Andreeva, an established figure in the "organs'" secret departments.[4] She had known about Dzhunkovsky since the early 1920s and had signed off on the report about him submitted by Sheshkin in 1923.[5] Now she questioned him specifically about how the arrival of foreigners had been managed before the revolution. The significance of this topic seems clear enough, for Soviet leaders faced a difficult problem. Anxious to demonstrate the achievements of communism to visitors from abroad and aware that the industrialization drive would require them to employ the skills of Western engineers and technicians, they also saw these travelers and hired specialists as potential spies and wreckers. But they had to be handled with care. The Shakhty affair had provoked the hostility of Germany and other key trading partners.[6]

Thus, the issue of how foreign guests and imported technical personnel should be treated and, of course, watched and controlled was a matter of considerable concern.[7] As Moscow governor, Dzhunkovsky had received many distinguished visitors from abroad, and while head of the tsar's internal security he had dealt with the problem of enemy aliens during the Great War, experiences that now must have appeared highly relevant.

At the time of his conversation with Andreeva, another high-level OGPU agent sat in. Dzhun never learned his name, but always attentive to the details of military dress, he remembered that the officer's uniform bore a number of medals and four rhomboids, indicating a rank held by the head of a department (*otdel*).[8]

The identity of this figure is uncertain, but a likely candidate is Karl Pauker, since 1923 the head of the OGPU's Operations Department with general responsibility for the security of party and state leaders. He was a protégé of Menzhinsky and had once served as his batman. Menzhinsky put Pauker in charge of Stalin's personal bodyguard, and he became very close to the Soviet leader. A jovial Jew with a gift for storytelling, Pauker was the "clown prince" of Stalin's entourage, a great favorite with his children.[9] If, as many believe, Menzhinsky provided Dzhunkovsky with a measure of "protection," Pauker's presence at the interview is understandable. But it also underlines the seriousness with which Dzhunkovsky's advice was taken. The fact that Dzhun would be called for even more important consultations several years later indicates that the OGPU was satisfied with his performance in 1928.

It is also worth noting that the information sought from Dzhunkovsky in this first interview was not unique to him. Other *lishentsy* such as S. D. Urusov, a former governor and assistant minister earlier exonerated in a Soviet legal proceeding and now working in state enterprises, could have answered the OGPU's questions almost as well. So the reason a convicted counterrevolutionary was chosen as a consultant remains unclear. But it is logical to think that Dzhunkovsky's selection was part of an ongoing pattern of protection that had kept him out of trouble since his release from prison. With all prerevolutionary holdovers now suspect, how better to protect the former head of the tsar's internal security than by giving him a chance to demonstrate his loyalty and usefulness to the regime?

Dzhunkovsky's thoughts and feelings at the time of this and later interviews are unknown. After his arrest in late 1937 his nieces, Evgeniia Makarenko and Nadezhda Shebasheva, wrote to Stalin that their uncle felt no animosity toward the Soviet regime and was willing to render assistance whenever he could. But they were obviously trying to cast their kinsman in the best possible light.[10] In all likelihood Dzhunkovsky felt considerable anxiety when he received his "invitation" from the OGPU, yet the little information we have suggests that he was fully prepared to cooperate. He had always been an unswerving patriot; here was an opportunity to "do good" for his "unfortunate country" by giving its leaders the benefit of his knowledge and administrative experience. Dzhunkovsky had enthusiastically supported Stolypin's call for "a great Russia" and as a soldier witnessed his country's defeat in the First World War. Did he respond positively to the nationalistic aspects of the Five Year Plan? On more than one occasion in his memoirs, he lamented the decline of postrevolutionary Russia's standing vis-à-vis Europe.[11] Did the Soviet government's determination to overcome the nation's backwardness—later expressed in Stalin's cri de coeur, "We are fifty or a hundred years behind the advanced countries. We must make good this distance in ten"—touch him in some way?[12]

Whatever the case may be, other related developments soon had a significant impact on Dzhunkovsky's life. As the assault on the old intelligentsia and the holdovers, personal and institutional, from the tsarist order gathered steam, Russia's rulers engineered important "reforms" at the Academy of Sciences. In the process "Dzhunkovsky," a name almost forgotten by the public, would make a sudden and surprising reappearance.

In the decade following 1917, the Academy of Sciences retained its independence and defiantly stayed in the old imperial capital, Peter the Great's "window cut through to Europe." Soviet authorities tolerated its autonomy with some misgivings because of the institution's value and the international prestige of its members. But the Five Year Plan required mobilization of the country's intellectual as well as material resources. The Academy should now turn its research in the natural sciences to the practical tasks of economic reconstruction and direct the humanities toward justifying the changes that were to come.[13]

The goal of a more pliant and useful Academy necessitated significant changes to its structure and personnel, accomplished in a series of well-orchestrated stages. In May 1927 a press campaign charged that Academy libraries and institutes harbored suspect "former people."[14] Then came the imposition of a new charter for the institution that weakened the position of the humanities, substantially increased the number of academicians, and opened up the procedure for nominating new members to a variety of social organizations and institutions.[15] Toward the end of 1928 elections held amid strong party pressure and public criticism produced forty-one new academicians, most favored by the government.[16] A purge of the Academy's institutions and staff followed in 1929, conducted in the hostile spirit of the Shakhty show trial. In July 1929, a commission headed by Iurii Figatner interrogated Academy employees. The commission issued a report damning the institution as "an asylum for alien elements hostile to Soviet power" and charging that Pushkin House and other bodies under the Academy's aegis conducted inconsequential research. By the end of August, authorities had fired close to 15 percent of Academy employees.[17] This was just the beginning. A new phase was about to start in which Dzhunkovsky's name and archive became weapons in the hands of the Academy's enemies.

In a report to Stalin, the OGPU claimed that on October 12, 1929, it first learned that several libraries under the control of the Academy of Sciences were concealing important political documents from the Soviet government: the originals of the abdication of Nicholas II and his brother's refusal to accept the throne; the archives of the Kadet, Menshevik, Octobrist, and SR central committees; the diaries of Grand Duke Konstantin Romanov; and the papers of Vladimir Dzhunkovsky. This discovery focused intense suspicion on Sergei Oldenburg, the Academy's permanent secretary, and Sergei Platonov, the distinguished historian who had directed the Academy's libraries.[18]

The "shock" expressed about the "hidden archives" was largely feigned. Government authorities had long known that libraries of the Academy of Sciences contained many papers of great political and historical interest. Lenin had visited these repositories and expressed satisfaction with the way they preserved the documents in their care. Academy officials informed a government commission of their holdings in 1926, when they successfully resisted efforts by the leading Communist historian, Mikhail Pokrovsky, to transfer these materials to state archives under his control.[19] All this mattered little now. The Council of People's Commissars created a new investigative commission composed of Figatner, Iakov Peters, and Iakov Agranov, the latter two long active in the work of the "organs."

On October 24, 1929, this threatening trio descended on Leningrad to interrogate Academy personnel about its archives, paying considerable attention to the papers of Dzhunkovsky.[20] The documents he had deposited were extremely useful in advancing the idea that subversive, anti-Soviet activities were afoot within the Academy's subordinate institutions. That the former head of the tsar's gendarmes had not only given his papers to

Pushkin House but also had been allowed to use them regularly became a theme to which Agranov, Figatner, and Peters eagerly returned as they grilled their hapless suspects. Of equal interest was the more sinister question as to whether Dzhunkovsky had removed compromising materials from his archive, and Dzhun's persona, as well as his papers, became an important issue.

"When Pushkin House considered the question of permitting [Dzhunkovsky] to work there, didn't you know very well that he was the former head of the gendarmes?" thundered Agranov at the clearly discomfited and soon-to-be-arrested senior curator N. V. Izmailov. "And look, in the land of the Soviets, in the city of Leningrad, you permitted such an odious figure, an enemy of the revolution, an enemy of the working class, a man who was always an enemy! You permitted him to work on his own archive!"[21]

"Can you guarantee that not a single paper has been removed from the archive?" Figatner chided Izmailov in the same accusatory tone.[22]

"In '19, Dzhunkovsky was put on trial and sentenced to a concentration camp until the end of the Civil War," Peters, Dzhun's former judge, informed Platonov as he questioned the historian's motives for giving Dzhun access to his papers. "[A]nd that sentence remains in effect. He was sentenced as head of the Corps of Gendarmes; he hid from the state a number of documents which in no way can be seen as his personal papers. The documents of the chief of gendarmes are not the papers of Dzhunkovsky. Therefore these materials should be in our [state] archives so that they could be properly used."[23]

These and other accusations rained down as the three inquisitors sought to prove that incompetent management and poor judgment at the Academy had led to the misappropriation of materials in its collections. All objections to these charges were brushed aside, and on October 28, 1929, Figatner sent a report to Grigorii ("Sergo") Ordzhonikidze, Stalin's close associate. It detailed the failure of the Academy's leaders and staff to handle properly the precious documents in their keeping, particularly Dzhunkovsky's papers.

"Comrade Sergo," Figatner wrote, "I consider it necessary to call to your attention [the fact] that the archive of Dzhunkovsky was stored in a garage without any security and that Dzhunkovsky . . . was permitted several times to work with his archive. The last time he was permitted [to come] was this year, and for about a week he went daily to Pushkin House where they brought him boxes in accordance with his requests. What [things] he took from these boxes and what was done [with them]—no one knows."[24] The implication was clear: with the connivance of Academy personnel, Dzhunkovsky had removed valuable, perhaps incriminating documents.

An intensified purge of Academy personnel ensued, and soon expulsions combined with arrests. Oldenburg stepped down as permanent secretary, and Platonov relinquished all his Academy posts. By mid-December, just over 130 members of the Academy's regular staff had been fired, along with 520 contract employees.[25] A large number of important academicians, chiefly in the humanities, became suspects, and in early 1930 Platonov was in police hands under interrogation. Other arrests followed. The Academy, disgraced and submissive, could offer little resistance.

Meanwhile the "secreted" documents, including the papers of Dzhunkovsky, were quietly taken into custody and transferred to state archives and the Lenin Institute.[26] The archival scandal now folded into the "academic case," as four academicians—Platonov, Evgenii Tarle, Nikolai Likhachev, and Matvei Liubavsky—as well as over 100 staff members, faced political charges. They were accused of organizing or participating in "The All-National Union of Struggle for the Revival of a Free Russia," with the aim of overthrowing the Soviet government and restoring the monarchy. In the new regime that was to arise from this coup, Platonov would be prime minister and Tarle minister of foreign affairs.

The "plot" was a ludicrous OGPU fabrication—the idea of an anti-Soviet seizure of power led by aging historians and literary scholars a particularly delightful absurdity—and it is testimony to the common sense of its inventors that they never gave this "case" the dignity of a public show trial. A three-man OGPU tribunal (troika) sentenced the accused to prison terms of from three to ten years or extended periods of internal exile, the "leaders" of the conspiracy treated less severely than their supposed followers.[27] But, strangely, the man whose name could have lent solid substance to the diaphanous, undocumented charges, a logical candidate for minister of internal affairs or head of the police in a new monarchist regime, was not included. The "odious figure," the "enemy of the revolution," the "enemy of the working class"—Vladimir Fedorovich Dzhunkovsky—remained at liberty in Moscow.

❖

Free, but not completely untouched. In late October 1929 the police twice searched Dzhunkovsky's flat and confiscated a few personal items. Surprised and uncertain what was going on, Dzhun's confusion receded on November 6, when he read a newspaper article about the discovery of important political documents at the Academy of Sciences that mentioned both his name and his archive. Shortly thereafter the OGPU called him in to explain how his papers had ended up in Pushkin House. On November 9, in the wake of that interrogation, Dzhun submitted a "report" (*dokladnaia zapiska)* outlining the history of his archive to Abel Enukidze, then secretary of the Presidium of the Central Executive Committee of the USSR and the chairman of the government commission working on the "reform" of the Academy. The report is notable as much for its tone as for its contents. Despite the somewhat alarming circumstances attending its creation, its style was neither timid nor ingratiating; Dzhunkovsky simply gave a straightforward account of how his papers came into the possession of Pushkin House. He did not mention his memoirs or the research he had conducted in order to compose them.[28] Dzhunkovsky's less-than-complete report appears to have satisfied the authorities, however. Although his archive had figured prominently in the initial accusations against Platonov et al., and the Party's inquisitors implied that he had taken documents from his files, Dzhunkovsky continued in the good graces of the authorities. The protection of Menzhinsky or another highly placed persona is almost palpable.

It appears that the OGPU had made Dzhunkovsky an unwitting instrument of the state's purposes. The secret police were deeply involved in the struggle for control of the Academy; its leading figures undoubtedly knew of Dzhunkovsky's memoirs and of his frequent trips to use his archive at Pushkin House. Agranov and Peters understood the value of those documents as a cudgel with which to beat down opposition in the institution's ranks. Peters, certainly, and in all likelihood Agranov knew about the former head of the tsar's internal security and may not have considered him such an "odious" figure. Dzhunkovsky himself may have sensed that something was under way as the storm gathered. At the time of his arrest Platonov stated that Dzhunkovsky once came by his apartment to thank him for permission to work at Pushkin House.[29] Could this have been in June 1929, the last time Dzhun had access to his papers?

Unfortunately, these suspicions and questions must remain unanswered. But Dzhunkovsky does not seem to have suffered from his oblique connection to the Academy imbroglio. Still, the tumult of the first Five

Sketch of Dzhunkovsky in 1929 by M. M. Osorgin. Personal collection.

Year Plan era caused him to move, willingly or not, beyond the limits of Moscow. By 1933 he and his sister were living just north of the city in the small town of Perlovka, at the home of his niece Evgeniia Makarenko.

Wherever he may have lived, Dzhunkovsky continued to consult for the OGPU. In 1932 Andreeva and the same high-ranking figure who had spoken with him in 1928 again sought his expertise. This time, however, Andreeva did not conduct the interview. Instead, Dzhunkovsky was taken to a different office where he met with another agent, one Mikhail Sergeevich. Dzhunkovsky never learned his interlocutor's last name, but he was probably M. S. Gorb, then a highly placed official in the OGPU's Foreign Section (INO). The two men conversed for four hours about the internal passport system, something that had been abolished with the revolution, but which the Soviet regime now deemed necessary in order to cope with the massive population shifts caused by collectivization and industrialization and to gain better control of dangerous social elements. Apparently, Dzhunkovsky supplemented his oral presentation with a detailed written report.[30]

Exactly how this information was used in developing the passport legislation is uncertain, for few materials about that process survive.[31] But several historians believe that Dzhun's contribution was important.[32] The small number of available documents suggest a point where his knowledge may have been profitably employed. On November 15, 1932, the Politburo created a commission headed by the OGPU's assistant chairman, Vsevolod Balitsky, that included Iakov Agranov. Its purpose was "the development of concrete measures, of both a legislative and organizational-practical character," regarding a passport system. They had twenty days to do the job.[33]

Balitsky and his comrades finished their work with time to spare and reported their success to Stalin. Balitsky wrote that "having familiarized itself with the passport system and registration of the population in prerevolutionary Russia and abroad, and also having studied local practice," the commission had developed project decrees for both a new unified passport law and population registration, as well as instructions governing the entering and leaving of the cities of Moscow, Leningrad, and Kharkov.[34]

Accomplishing this task so quickly required good knowledge of tsarist law, administrative operations, and foreign legislation. Balitsky had some legal training,[35] but it would seem that few, if any, of his co-commissioners had comparable experience. Dzhunkovsky, on the other hand, with his service as head of the imperial state security and long tenure as a provincial governor, enjoyed great familiarity with earlier passport regulations and their local application; he probably knew something about foreign procedures as well. The information he supplied to Mikhail Sergeevich Gorb, readily available to Balitsky and Agranov, may have helped speed the work of drawing up the final legislation.

Ironically, the reintroduction of internal passports, which Dzhunkovsky's consultations presumably assisted, best explains his move beyond the city limits. Between January and April 1933 the police began issuing passports in Moscow, Leningrad, and a number of designated areas. At the same time they denied these documents to "dangerous" elements—escaped kulaks, former convicts, *lishentsy*, and those not engaged in socially useful labor—forcing some ninety-eight thousand Moscow residents to leave the city. Dzhunkovsky fit the profile of those being refused passports, so he may have moved to avoid fines or possible arrest. Still, he remained in the Moscow region, something that suggests he enjoyed a special status. The OGPU permitted its local operational departments to leave in place individuals who were important to ongoing investigations.[36] The "organs" continued to see Dzhunkovsky as a useful informant and ultimately gave him a passport.

Sometime thereafter the OGPU called Dzhunkovsky in for another interview. During the interrogation following his arrest in 1937, Dzhun stated: "In 1933 I was summoned to the OGPU to Mikhail Sergeevich for questions about the structure of the Ministry of Internal Affairs where I gave detailed information about the structure of the Ministry of Internal Affairs and the question of protecting the emperor while he travelled on the railroads. I was not summoned to the OGPU-NKVD again."[37] But Dzhun may have been mistaken about the date and, perhaps, even the person with whom he spoke. Recently, Anastasia Dunaeva obtained from the archives of the Russian Federal Security Service (FSB) a document entitled: "Conversations of Comrade K. V. Pauker with Citizen Dzhunkovsky," dated March 20, 1934. This appears to be the record of the third interview Dzhun spoke about in 1937. Mikhail Sergeevich may have been present, or, more likely, Dzhunkovsky confused Pauker and Gorb.

Pauker's questions initially focused on technical matters concerning the functioning of the Okhrana and the Corps of Gendarmes: how it chose and disciplined its personnel, and how it maintained the security of high officials and the tsar. From the outset Pauker was at pains to reassure Dzhun about the purpose of their meeting: "I am not interrogating you, but simply carrying on a conversation," he stated. "I know about your liberalism and that you speak with complete candor." Then Pauker added, with less than perfect tact: "You are an old man, and you don't have long to live. We won't bother you, but we need this information for history." And indeed, Pauker seemed to have had a strong interest in purely historical questions, including information as to whether Dzhun's former chief, N. A. Maklakov, was a hard worker, how much time Dzhun himself spent on the job, and what his salary had been. Pauker also wanted to know about the 1915 Moscow riots and about Dzhun's report to the tsar concerning Rasputin.[38]

Pauker's inquiries on technical matters such as the organization of the tsarist MVD and gendarmes undoubtedly had considerable practical significance in view of impending changes in the Soviet police apparatus that, within the year, resulted in the abolition of the OGPU and the subordination of the institutions of state security to a reconfigured NKVD.[39] The same can be said about the information Dzhun provided about maintaining the safety of Nicholas II when he journeyed on the railroads. To the man in charge of Stalin's personal security, this was of high importance and, according to one source, Pauker adopted Dzhunkovsky's ideas virtually without change.[40] The purely historical questions were probably not the products of Pauker's idle curiosity, however, but may have been important in their own right, reflecting concerns about Dzhunkovsky's memoirs that had been raised in the higher ranks of the Soviet security service.

The end of the NEP had radically changed Dzhunkovsky's prospects for publishing his recollections. The memoirs were almost complete, and the Sabashnikov press planned to include them in its respected series, *Zapisi proshlogo*. By late 1928 or early the following year, the bulk of the manuscript was probably in the hands of the publisher. But in 1929, the nationalization of private businesses forced the Sabashnikov house to close, and in December 1930 Mikhail Sabashnikov was briefly arrested. For some time he was able to keep his enterprise limping along as a "cooperative" under the designation *Sever* (The North) and continued printing memoirs until 1934.[41] Dzhunkovsky's would not be among them, however. Perhaps because of their size or the renewed notoriety of their author, Sabashnikov and his associates decided not to bring out Dzhun's recollections and returned the text to him. A list of manuscripts in the portfolio of the cooperative dated December 1, 1933, does not include Dzhunkovsky's *Vospominaniia*; nor is it found in a similar document compiled a year later.[42] He was left to seek a new outlet for his work. The memoirs now began a journey through many hands and various institutions, not reaching their intended audience until sixty years after the author's death.

Although Dzhunkovsky wrote his memoirs to preserve something of the lost world of late imperial Russia, he must also have hoped that their publication might augment his income. Now, with that prospect unlikely, he decided to sell the manuscript to a museum or archive. In the spring of 1933 Dzhunkovsky turned to Vladimir Dmitrievich Bonch-Bruevich, Lenin's longtime colleague, the former executive secretary of Sovnarkom, and the man to whom Evdokiia had repeatedly appealed in the months following her brother's arrest in 1918.

In the early 1920s Bonch-Bruevich abandoned political activity and turned to academic and scholarly pursuits. In 1933 he founded The Central Museum of Belles Lettres, Criticism and Political Journalism, soon to be renamed The State Literary Museum (GLM), and sought to gather a variety of artifacts, manuscripts, and other materials of literary and historical interest.[43] Moreover, like a number of "Old Bolsheviks," Bonch-Bruevich was appalled by the difficulties being encountered by "former people" in the Five Year Plan era. Buying the memorabilia of these unfortunates and encouraging them to write and sell their reminiscences was a way for him to help people in need and expand his museum's collections.[44]

We do not know exactly when Dzhunkovsky offered his memoirs to Bonch-Bruevich, but the two men made contact early in 1933. Their first dealings concerned the sale to the museum of a portrait of one of Alexander Pushkin's daughters, then in the possession of Vladimir's kinswoman Evgeniia Makarenko. In a letter dated May 9, 1933, Dzhunkovsky informed Bonch-Bruevich that questions about the painting's ownership had been resolved, and he attached a document proving that his niece's husband had legally purchased the work. Dzhun explained that Makarenko was selling the portrait to finance a trip that she and he were making to visit her sick husband, exiled in Ust'-Sysol'sk (present-day Syktyvkar). The money obtained would enable them "to support . . . [her husband] and, if not too late, save his life." He asked Bonch-Bruevich to pay for the painting as soon as possible.[45] The museum director complied, and on May 15 Dzhunkovsky signed a receipt acknowledging that the museum had given five hundred rubles for the portrait.[46] Presumably, he and Makarenko left on their journey soon thereafter.

Later, probably early June, Dzhunkovsky approached Bonch-Bruevich about selling his memoirs, appearing personally at one of Vladimir Dmitrievich's receptions at the museum.[47] He followed up quickly, providing a detailed outline of the memoir and a description of its contents.[48] Finally, on August 2, 1933, Dzhun sent Bonch-Bruevich a letter with a formal proposal for the sale of the manuscript, stating its price, a schedule of payments, and the conditions governing its use. He requested the enormous sum of eighty thousand rubles: twenty thousand rubles up front, with the remaining sixty thousand to be paid in monthly installments of five thousand rubles. He insisted that the memoir not be published until twenty years after the last events described, that is, not before January 1938. Portions of the memoir might appear prior to that date, but only with his approval.

Dzhunkovsky told Bonch-Bruevich that most of the text had been typed, with a smaller portion still in handwritten form. He proposed to turn over the first three volumes at the time a contract was signed and deliver the rest in installments over the next six months. Dzhunkovsky ended on a confident note, asserting the memoir's value: "In conclusion, I must add that the . . . manuscript represents my diligent and painstaking work of many years, based on materials I gathered over the course of my entire conscious life, and I therefore permit myself to hope that you will find my proposal acceptable."[49]

Apparently taken aback by the size of the sum demanded, Bonch-Bruevich did not reply for almost half a year. On December 1, 1933, an anxious Dzhunkovsky wrote once more: "Your silence leads me to conclude that my memoirs are not of interest to your museum, and that my proposal regarding their acquisition cannot be realized. If this is so," he continued, "do not refuse to confirm my assumptions, so that I can consider myself at liberty. . . . [I]t is very difficult to be kept in the dark—it is already six months to the day since I came to you and entrusted to you the fate of my memoirs, that colossal and conscientious work into which I have poured my entire soul."[50]

Bonch-Bruevich's silence did not imply lack of interest; he never doubted the value of the memoirs. But paying the large sum that Dzhun asked for was out of the question. With the demands of industrialization and collectivization straining the state's resources and the government selling priceless national art treasures abroad in order to gain desperately needed hard currency, he knew that the purchase of the memoirs of a former governor and gendarme chief was certain to generate suspicions that could spell danger for the museum and himself. Aware of the risks, Bonch-Bruevich proceeded cautiously. In December he entered into direct negotiations with Dzhunkovsky to reach mutually acceptable terms. At the same time, he kept People's Commissar of Enlightenment Andrei Bubnov, to whom he normally reported about his archival purchases, in the dark. He would seek his approval obliquely, after the fact, reminding Bubnov of an earlier agreement permitting the museum to purchase "valuable, interesting material from the pens of members of the imperial family and their entourages . . . and also materials belonging to former ministers of the tsarist government."[51]

In all likelihood, the two principals conducted their negotiations face-to-face, for the archives hold no correspondence on this point. In the end Bonch-Bruevich convinced Dzhunkovsky to halve the price he originally proposed, and in early January 1934 the author agreed to accept the still quite substantial sum of forty thousand rubles. The barrier to an earlier agreement may have been a misunderstanding. A letter Bonch-Bruevich sent after the deal had been struck suggests that the reason for Dzhunkovsky's enormous initial demand was his belief that a large tax would be due at the time of sale and he had, therefore, raised the price accordingly. Bonch-Bruevich evidently had persuaded the author that his concern was unfounded and now wrote to reassure him further. "I personally inquired at the very center of our tax institutions and received . . . the response that on all purchases [made by the museum] no taxes will be imposed." This kind of taxation made no sense, he continued: "It would be extraordinarily strange for the state to pay out money with one hand and take it back with the other."[52]

At the time of the sale Bonch-Bruevich urged Dzhunkovsky to surrender his manuscript quickly. The museum was now making many purchases, he cautioned, and if Vladimir Fedorovich were late, there might be extensive delays in paying him the promised sums.[53] But Dzhunkovsky seems to have had some problems putting the final touches on his work. In a letter dated March 2, 1934, Bonch-Bruevich complained that the author had delivered neither the final volume of the memoir nor the handwritten early drafts he had promised.[54] It would not be until early April that the rest of the memoir passed into the museum's possession.[55] When he chided Dzhunkovsky for being tardy, however, Bonch-Bruevich was engaging in a bit of deception, concealing from the author the disturbing fact that portions of his life's story were no longer in the archives of the museum. Almost a month earlier, the secret police had "arrested" the volumes of the memoirs that covered the years of his governorship and service as head of internal security and were keeping them in custody.

This strange turn of events seems to have been triggered by the way that Bonch-Bruevich was building his museum's collections: buying materials rapidly and paying substantial sums. He also hired suspicious "former people" and members of the old intelligentsia.[56] Given the spirit of the times, which demanded strict accounting and extraordinary vigilance toward those regarded as "class enemies," both these activities came under scrutiny. Then in late 1933 or early 1934, a member of the museum's staff, Igor Ilinsky, was arrested, charged with disloyalty. Bonch-Bruevich vigorously defended his employee, writing to Karl Pauker to vouch for Ilinsky's devotion to the cause of socialism.[57] He soon learned, however, that Ilinsky's case was not in Pauker's hands. Mikhail Sergeevich Gorb, now the assistant head of the OGPU's Secret Political Section (SPO), who had consulted earlier with Dzhunkovsky about passports, was in charge of the investigation.

Bonch-Bruevich went to Gorb to speak in Ilinsky's defense. But it quickly transpired that the OGPU agent had additional interests. Gorb asked that the museum hand over two archival collections it had recently purchased: the diaries of the writer Mikhail Kuzmin and the memoirs of Dzhunkovsky. Bonch-Bruevich complied and on February 1, 1934, received a curt acknowledgment:

> The archive of M.A. Kuzmin, *opis'* No. 500, 7942 sheets in all, and also the archive of Dzhunkovsky, No. 1233, four folders [*papki*] have been received by me from the Lit. Museum from com. Bonch-Bruevich received.
> Asst. Ch[ief] SPO OGPU
> M. GORB
> 1/II-1934[58]

Shortly thereafter, Gorb wrote to Bonch-Bruevich asking for information on the way the museum solicited and purchased materials for its collection. The director replied in a detailed letter on February 4. He stressed the relatively low cost of the acquired documents and provided a list of many of the works obtained. By this time, however, it was becoming clear that Gorb had no intention of returning the two archives he had just taken. The OGPU had decided to hold them in its own files.[59]

Bonch-Bruevich immediately wrote Genrikh Yagoda, the acting head of the OGPU's Collegium, seeking to regain the confiscated archives. In a letter dated February 10, 1934, he began by reasserting his belief in Ilinsky's loyalty but then quickly switched to other matters. He informed Yagoda of the value of the papers at issue, explained why they had been purchased, recounted the negotiations leading to their acquisition, and assured him that the collections had been obtained for a good price. He guaranteed that the materials of both Kuzmin and Dzhunkovsky were and would remain under strict control. The length of the letter and Bonch-Bruevich's effort to cover all the bases strongly suggests that he was unsure why the documents had been seized.[60]

To this day, the motives of the secret police in this matter remain obscure. Both Dzhunkovsky and Kuzmin were, in the eyes of some, questionable, even "odious" characters; both, we believe, had ties to Viacheslav Menzhinsky, now in his last months of life. Did his imminent death strip the two of the protection they had hitherto enjoyed? Kuzmin was well known to be a homosexual. Did the OGPU seek information about that demimonde? Gorb was already acquainted with Dzhunkovsky. Did he believe that his memoirs would reveal undiscovered agents of the Okhrana? Perhaps. Yet on one point, we can be certain: the confiscated collections were taken as evidence to be used in one of a series of inspections of Bonch-Bruevich's museum and its activities.

Between the time of the State Literary Museum's creation in 1933 and the outbreak of the Soviet-German war in 1941, at least ten investigative bodies, established under various auspices, examined its work.[61] In 1934 it was the Central Committee's Cultural-Propaganda Department that weighed in with a criticism of the museum's collection practices, using the Kuzmin and Dzhunkovsky materials as cases in point. In May it informed the Politburo that the papers of Kuzmin "possessed no museum or literary value" because of their frequent homosexual themes. The memoirs of Dzhunkovsky were not worth the forty thousand rubles paid for them. They had "no relation to literature and no value to the museum, since they consisted exclusively of a description of the general's life."[62]

These charges forced Bonch-Bruevich to wage a two-front campaign: first for the honor and perhaps the very survival of his museum; second for the return of the confiscated archives of Kuzmin and Dzhunkovsky.

In a letter to Bubnov he dismissed negative evaluations of the seized materials and praised Dzhunkovsky's memoirs effusively. "The entire memoir," Bonch-Bruevich declared, "is filled and interspersed with documents and primary materials which have never been published anywhere, and which, for the most part, are unknown." Only a small portion of the work focused on the author himself, certainly the right of any memoirist. Dzhunkovsky, writing "in his old fashioned way," was entirely sincere. "When these memoirs are published," Bonch-Bruevich concluded, "the editors can eliminate all [unnecessary] ballast and provide the required introduction, notes and commentary. . . . [Then] these recollections will be an epoch in the memoir literature of our time concerning tsarist Russia."[63]

Bonch-Bruevich successfully defended his museum, but repeated efforts failed to recover the confiscated archives. In addition to Bubnov, Vladimir Dmitrievich wrote to Yagoda, Gorb, Agranov, and perhaps others. His requests met with silence, however, and by year's end it appears that he temporarily abandoned his attempt to regain the lost documents.[64] He was wise to do so. On December 1, 1934, the assassination of Sergei Kirov, head of the Party's Leningrad organization, set the nation on a path toward growing terror. Stalin's purges soon inflicted heavy damage on the ranks of the "Old Bolsheviks," especially those who had been close associates of Lenin. In these nightmare years it would have been risky for Bonch-Bruevich, Lenin's longtime comrade in arms, to trouble the secret police about the diaries of a homosexual writer or the memoirs of a tsarist governor, general, and gendarme.

The saga of the archives did not end here, however. In late June 1939, with the worst of the terror past, the tenacious Bonch-Bruevich renewed his efforts to retrieve the confiscated materials. This time he wrote to Lavrentii Beria, the powerful new commissar of internal affairs, reminding him how Gorb had seized the Kuzmin archive and four volumes of Dzhunkovsky's memoirs.[65] He told of his unsuccessful attempts to recover the papers, and how, when letters failed, he resorted to the telephone. "I called everyone possible," he lamented. "They always promised that these materials would be returned right away, but up to now they have not been returned." Bonch-Bruevich implored Beria to resolve this problem once and for all, as soon as possible; but the mills of the god ground slowly. The lost materials would not come back to the GLM until March 1940.[66] They did not stay there long.

In 1941 authorities transferred the manuscript collections of the State Literary Museum to the newly created Central State Archive of Literature and Art (TsGALI).[67] In 1948 Dzhunkovsky's memoirs passed to the state's historical archives, which were then undergoing almost constant reorganization and redesignation. There they joined his personal and official papers that had been confiscated from Pushkin House in 1929.[68] All these materials were kept under tight control; scholars began to use them only after Stalin's death.[69] In the 1960s the Institute of History of the Academy of Sciences proposed to publish Dzhunkovsky's memoirs, but the Scientific Department (*nauchnyi otdel*) of the Central Committee of the CPSU quashed this initiative.[70] Portions of his recollections started appearing in print following the collapse of the Soviet regime. A two-volume edition of the memoirs covering the years 1905 to 1915 came out in 1997, and in 2015 a third volume, recounting Dzhunkovsky's war experiences, followed.

Dzhunkovsky was probably unaware of the wrangling taking place over his memoirs. His great work done, he no doubt believed that, in time, "the descendants of the Orthodox" would be able to see the vanished world of late imperial Russia. Forty thousand rubles could guarantee a comfortable life ahead. Five hundred rubles a month was a very good salary in those days, and Dzhunkovsky, never a big spender, had learned frugality during the 1920s.[71] The sum that the memoirs had earned could support him and those he loved for many years. He continued to enjoy protection. By 1935 Dzhun and his sister had returned to Moscow to live with Nadezhda Shebasheva at her home on Begovaya Ulitsa on the outskirts of the city. At some point, we cannot be certain when, a local department of the regular police (*militsiia*) seized his passport and ordered him to leave Moscow within ten days. The former head of the tsar's Corps of Gendarmes had only to protest and the confiscated document was immediately returned to him at his residence.[72] In November 1935 Dzhun's life was darkened by the death of Evdokiia, whom he buried in the Vagankov cemetery, but he continued to live in pleasant circumstances: a two-room apartment in a small dwelling covered with ivy and surrounded by a garden. The front yard was filled with flowers—lilacs, gladioli, and phlox—which the old man loved to gather and give as gifts to friends who came to visit. It seemed a tranquil finale to a life of service and stress.[73]

Tragically, one more awful adventure lay ahead. In 1937 Stalin's purge, until then targeting the remnants of opposition groups within the Communist Party and their suspected sympathizers, began to envelop larger segments of the population. The terror was about to become "great." A paranoid logic, implicit since the beginning of the five-year plans, now became explicit and drove events ineluctably toward a hideous conclusion.

"We must destroy and cast aside the rotten theory that with every advance we make the class struggle here of necessity would die down," Stalin informed the plenum of the Central Committee on March 3, 1937. "On the contrary," he continued, "the further forward we advance . . . the greater will be the fury of the remnants of the broken exploiting classes, the sooner will they resort to sharper forms of struggle, . . . the more will they clutch at the most desperate means of struggle, as the last resort of doomed people." Inevitably, they would league with the "class enemy" in the capitalist states encircling the USSR and continue their vicious assaults. "We must remember all this," Stalin concluded ominously, "and be on our guard."[74]

By early summer 1937 Soviet leaders were ready to act on the dictator's warnings. The assault on Party cadres intensified, and on July 2 the Politburo decreed a "mass operation" directed at "anti-Soviet elements." On July 31, 1937, it approved the NKVD's Operational Order No. 00447—drawn up by Stalin and Nikolai Ezhov, then head of the secret police—that designed guidelines for the purge.[75] It mandated a roundup of the usual suspects: former kulaks, members of anti-Bolshevik political parties, gendarmes, officials of the old regime, and a wide variety of people with criminal records. Authorities were to divide the "repressed" into two categories: the first—those deemed most dangerous—were to be shot; the second—those who posed a lesser threat—would be sent to labor camps for terms of from eight to ten years, all sentences to be determined by a troika, a three-man secret police tribunal. The decree set regional quotas for each category. In the Moscow area, five thousand were to be shot and thirty thousand sent to camps.

With pedantic legalism, Order No. 00447 dictated an accelerated and simplified investigative procedure. When making an arrest, police were to conduct a thorough search of the premises in order to uncover and seize weapons, counterrevolutionary literature, items of value, and correspondence. Arresting officers then had to set up a case file containing the warrant, a report on the search with a list of items confiscated, an outline of basic information on the person arrested, the protocol of his or her interrogation, and the conclusions reached by the investigators. These materials would be forwarded to a troika for a final decision. The entire operation was set to begin August 5, 1937, and conclude four months later.[76]

Agents of the NKVD arrested Dzhunkovsky at his home on December 3, 1937. Their arrival probably came as no surprise; many "formers" were falling into police hands. At the end of August, Dzhun's old friend Vladimir Gadon had disappeared, and a month later Andrei Ustinov, once his vice-governor, was seized. Even more recently, the police had arrested his confessor and spiritual advisor, Father Sergei Uspensky.[77] Dzhunkovsky must have realized that the bell would soon toll for him as well; but always certain that his fate was in God's hands, he could await the knock on the door with Christian fortitude.

Many of those swept up in the mass operation triggered by Order 00447 were processed, imprisoned, or executed quickly, with minimal examination of their "cases."[78] Dzhunkovsky received a more extensive treatment. The search of his house uncovered nothing incriminating, just six books, a few picture postcards, and some letters, all destroyed as unnecessary to the investigation. On December 5, two days after his arrest, Dzhunkovsky was interrogated by one Comrade Mukomel about the awards he had received from the tsar's government and asked whether he had served and defended "the tsarist monarchical system." "Yes," he replied without equivocation. "Did you carry on an active struggle against the revolutionary movement?" Mukomel continued. "Yes," Dzhunkovsky admitted. "I carried on an active struggle with the revolutionary movement in the execution of my governmental duties, first as governor of Moscow and then as ass[istant] minister of in[ternal affairs]." He denied that he had any continuing associations with members of the tsar's service save for two people. One was a former gendarme, the other was Andrei Ustinov who, Dzhunkovsky continued, was already in the hands of the NKVD. "I am not a member of a counterrevolutionary organization, and have not conducted counterrevolutionary activities. I deny any guilt in that regard," he stated firmly.[79]

The next day Mukomel questioned two "witnesses"—Abdul Khasianov and Sergei Zhogov—who worked as janitors (*dvorniki*) at the building where Dzhunkovsky and his nieces lived. They said that the former governor made disparaging remarks about the Soviet system and its leading figures, including Stalin, and pined for the return of the old order. According to Zhogov, Dzhunkovsky had complained: "Now there are no leaders, only bonzes who live on the people's money." Khasianov noted that the old man "was not employed and did not participate in public life."[80]

Except for the facts of Dzhunkovsky's lack of gainful employment and reclusiveness, the testimony of Khasianov and Zhogov was almost certainly a fabrication. Even before the revolution, janitors had always been agents of the police; it is highly unlikely that the careful former governor and security chief would express dangerous political opinions within their earshot, let alone directly. Given what we know about the way in which the NKVD carried out its "investigations," the two witnesses might have been coerced or simply asked to sign off on "testimony" already drawn up beforehand.[81] (What do janitors know of bonzes?)

At this point Comrade Mukomel may have felt that he could close the file on Dzhunkovsky's case and pass it on for final consideration. But on December 14, Dzhun's nieces, Nadezhda Shebasheva and Evgeniia Makarenko, sent a letter to Stalin appealing to him on behalf of their uncle. They informed the dictator that since his early release from prison in 1921 Dzhunkovsky had lived in Moscow and had not been troubled by the authorities. "In all these years," they continued "he not only did not act against Soviet power but, on the contrary, rendered help wherever possible. More than once he was called to the OGPU for consultations, the last time in regard to the introduction of the passport system, concerning which he made a detailed written report [*konsul'tatsii*]." They also cited the fact that their uncle's passport had been seized and then returned by the police as proof that he was not considered dangerous. Finally, Shebasheva and Makarenko appealed to Stalin's sympathies. Their uncle was advanced in years and very sick; he would not live long and should be released. "Knowing your sensitive concern for older people," they concluded, "we hope you will find it possible to grant our request."[82]

It is doubtful that the best friend of the elderly read this letter, but the NKVD deemed it of sufficient interest to warrant investigation. Consequently, Mukomel resumed his interrogation of Dzhunkovsky on December 28. This time he asked the prisoner specifically when and why he had been summoned by the "organs." Dzhunkovsky was not entirely forthcoming. He told his questioner about his consultations with the OGPU in 1928, 1932, and 1933 (1934?) in some detail, but he omitted any mention of his interrogations in 1922 and 1929. Mukomel did not press the issue further, however, and returned to a matter he had raised before, again asking Dzhunkovsky about his contacts with former gendarme officers. Once more Vladimir Fedorovich stated that he knew only one erstwhile member of the gendarmerie, the man he had mentioned earlier, whom he had last seen three years ago, and who was at that time an employee of the Moscow zoo.[83]

Comrade Mukomel was still not satisfied, and at their final meeting on January 9, 1938, accused Dzhunkovsky of delaying the investigation and of failing to give open and truthful answers. The old man stood his ground: "I fully confirm my previous testimony, and have nothing new to add," he stated firmly. But the NKVD's interrogator pushed once more on the question of police spies, summoning the shade of the long-dead Roman Malinovsky. Dzhunkovsky affirmed that he had been a witness at the *provokator*'s trial but had not been asked then about his knowledge of secret agents. "About that, I knew nothing in 1918 and know nothing at this time, since those questions were handled by the Special Section of the Department of Police and familiarity with them was not in the sphere of my duties as an official responsible for oversight [*kak organ vysshego nadzora*]."[84]

Dzhunkovsky's interrogation ended, and Mukomel forwarded the materials relating to his case for judicial consideration. On February 21, 1938, a troika examined the "evidence," reached a decision, and issued its summary verdict:

> Heard [the case of]:
> Dzhunkovsky, Vladimir Fedorovich, born 1865 in Leningrad, non-party. Nobleman, son of a general in the tsarist army. In 1919 sentenced to five years for counterrevolutionary activity. At the time of arrest, unemployed.
> Accused of carrying on counterrevolutionary activity.
> Decision:
> Dzhunkovsky, Vladimir Fedorovich
> To be shot.[85]

At some point after his arrest Dzhunkovsky again spent time within the familiar walls of Butyrka prison. In cell No. 79, he found himself sitting beside the distinguished literary critic and intellectual historian Razumnik Vasil'evich Ivanov, best known by his pseudonym, Ivanov-Razumnik. Despite the gloomy circumstances Dzhun was in fine form. "He was a charming old man," Ivanov-Razumnik recalled, "brisk and cheerful despite his seventy years whose attitude to his own situation in prison was simply one of irony. In the three days we were together he told me so many interesting things about bygone times that I could have filled a whole book with them."[86] Then he disappeared.

On the night of February 25/26, black "ravens" flew south to Butovo. In Butyrka No. 79, Ivanov-Razumnik wondered where his charming and informative cellmate had gone.

Conclusion

We have no record of Dzhunkovsky's final hours, but everything we know about his life tells us that he endured them with dignity and courage. He had faced death many times, sustained by his Orthodox Christian beliefs. Suffering was redemptive. "Be joyful when you feel the cross upon yourself," he had written, "for this is a sign that you are following the Lord on the path to salvation in paradise."[1] On the killing ground at Butovo, the words of the Apostle Paul, martyred by the tyrant Nero, may have been in his thoughts, providing not simply comfort but perhaps a sense of triumph: "For now I am ready to be offered and the time of my departure is at hand. I have fought a good fight, I have finished my course, I have kept the faith."[2]

Nor would such thoughts have been unjustified. Although no person can be fully consistent in life, Dzhunkovsky had kept remarkably true to his faith and the ideals of his youth and had struggled to apply them in the performance of his public duty. He was a monarchist, a patriot, a devoted servant of the state, but these secular values were informed and tempered by a commitment to God and neighbor. Deeply religious, but not demonstrably pious, he manifested his faith in the treatment of others. With regard to workers, peasants, and common soldiers this took the form of patriarchal concern for their welfare; in the case of the more privileged and educated, he displayed it in his respect for the law and proper procedures and in the willingness to extend an open hand even to those with whom he might strongly disagree.

This approach served Dzhunkovsky well both as governor of Moscow and as a field commander in the Great War. It was far less effective in his efforts to manage and reform the security apparatus, especially the Okhrana, with its long-established administrative culture rooted in secrecy and conspiracy. He was offended by what he perceived as its amorality and cynicism but was also alarmed by the dangers he believed its methods posed to the state. For their part, the men he sought to supervise and direct regarded his reform efforts with contempt, an unwarranted intrusion by a well-connected incompetent.

Although Dzhunkovsky's brief tenure as security chief and his efforts at police reform continue to attract the attention of historians and generate controversy, they are not—from a biographical perspective—the most important moments in his long life. Still, they open a window on a larger development taking place in late imperial Russia. The charge that his reform attempts were products of "pre-modern fantasies" of honor and dignity is only partially correct.[3] To be sure, Dzhunkovsky was a gentleman of the old school, pained by the prospect of reading other people's mail. But his actions also reflected a change in the style of administration in Russia that was becoming increasingly evident in the decades before the outbreak of the First World War.

The "Great Reforms" of the 1860s, however limited and inadequate they might have seemed, had by the end of the nineteenth century significantly altered relations between Russia's government and the society over which it presided. Russia had become a much more pluralistic country: state power was fragmented, elected institutions and a national parliament were increasingly important, the "free" professions and nongovernmental institutions proliferated. In these circumstances, those who attempted to rule had to become, to some degree at least, "politicalized," that is to say, capable of seeing problems in more than administrative terms, willing and able to use the techniques that we associate with politics today: public relations and outreach, compromise, palaver, pressing the flesh.

The "politicalization" of Russian administration was clearly visible in the behavior of provincial governors during the last years of the empire. Of all the higher officials of the state, they had to confront most directly the increasingly messy pluralism of Russian life. Whether they liked it or not (and many did not), success often depended on their ability to combine more traditional authoritarian and patriarchal techniques with skills resembling those of a modern local elected leader.[4] Governors who were determined to rule in a blatantly heavy-handed manner would discover that the forces of local society could, in the end, frustrate their efforts.[5]

It was this "politicalized," approach derived from his civic and gubernatorial experience that lay at the heart of Dzhunkovsky's reform effort with regard to the Department of Police and the Corps of Gendarmes. Although guided by moral concerns and striving for economy and efficiency, he did not seek to change the inner workings of these institutions fundamentally. He was chiefly concerned to alter the image of the security services and the way they interfaced with the public. *Provokatory* in the ranks of the military and among schoolchildren, excessive "perlustration" of correspondence, and the exile of subversives without trial and in harsh conditions were practices that aroused indignation and fostered opposition. He believed they could be significantly modified or eliminated without doing serious damage to the ability of the tsarist "organs" to perform their core functions and to combat effectively the enemies of the state.

Dzhunkovsky's conflict with the *okhranniki* was to some degree ironic, illustrating the complexity of modernizing developments in late imperial Russia. The secret police were one of the most professionalized and modern elements of the state machine. The Okhrana's training methods and its techniques of surveillance, information gathering, and analysis put it well ahead of its European counterparts. Its Soviet successor would build upon these achievements. Yet for all its "modernity," the Okhrana was out of sync with Russian social and political trends, especially those in the years after 1905, which were steadily making politics more important and public opinion more powerful. Dzhunkovsky, on the other hand, although "old-fashioned" in his notions about honor and decency was better attuned to the music of the times, with an instinctive sense of the importance of image and public relations.

Dzhunkovsky's career had brought him into the upper ranks of those who have been called the "serving intelligentsia," elite government officials who, while sharing most of the cultural and moral values of the intelligentsia at large, devoted themselves to strengthening the state.[6] This sociopolitical element began to emerge in the late eighteenth century and crystallized during the reigns of Alexander I and Nicholas I. It fostered the growth of a legal consciousness within the administration and acquired the information and expertise that made possible the reforms in the era of Alexander II.[7] For much of the nineteenth century these "serving *intelligenty*" worked within the governmental apparatus. But by the beginning of the twentieth century, the pluralism that the reforms of the 1860s fostered and that the revolution of 1905 extended made it possible and necessary for the serving intelligentsia to cast off the bureaucratic cover, emerge from the chancellery closet, and participate more openly and directly in public life. This development made differences within both the government and the larger society more visible, accelerating the growth of "politicalization" in which the two sides participated. On the eve of the Great War, the boundaries between state and society had become increasingly blurred. Government officials, business leaders, members of the free professions and voluntary associations mixed and mingled, forming a complex variety of previously unthinkable, even paradoxical, social connections and political alliances.[8]

In his own life and work Dzhunkovsky embodied many of the complexities and contradictions of the time, easily moving across the lines that a generation earlier had constituted rigid divisions between individuals and social groups. Although he was a devoted monarchist, he supported the Duma, established ties with a number of its leading figures, ignoring the hostility to the parliament that was shared by both his revered sovereign, Nicholas II, and his friend and superior, N. A. Maklakov. A man of service nobility antecedents, Dzhunkovsky relished his induction into the landed gentry of Moscow province while remaining sympathetic to peasant needs and concerns. He was comfortable with the business elite, a promoter of industrial and commercial development, yet he was solicitous of workers' welfare and prepared to jawbone employers vigorously on their behalf. A political conservative, Dzhunkovsky rejected the extremists on the Right, supported the civic initiatives of liberal society, and eagerly embraced modernity. Although he held firm principles, there was a certain protean quality to his public life.

While unique in many ways, Dzhunkovsky's path paralleled those of a number of others in the "Stolypin generation" of the serving intelligentsia. This was a cohort—a product of the "Great Reforms"—whose members in the second decade of the twentieth century stood at the cusp of power but were, for the most part, still too junior to wield it. Where their roads might have led, and whether their "politicalized" approaches to Russia's needs would have significantly helped the country overcome the conflicts and divisions that plagued it, is impossible to say. The Great War and the revolution it spawned cut off that possibility as Russia spiraled downward into tumult, tyranny, and terror. This storm swept the elite of the serving intelligentsia away, killing some, driving others into exile. Only a relative few, like Dzhunkovsky, remained alive on Soviet shores.

But the wreck of imperial Russia did not extinguish the desire of these men to serve their "unfortunate country." In Dzhunkovsky's case, his consultations for the OGPU, no doubt undertaken in part as a response to force majeure, constituted one instance. Much more important, however, was the memoir into which he "poured . . . [his] entire soul." For almost sixty years this work lay in the archives, accessible only to a few scholars. The imbroglio attending its purchase and the refusal to publish it in the 1960s implies that it was considered suspect, even dangerous, in part because it drew a picture of the tsarist regime that did not correspond to the one found in official historiography. But more troubling, perhaps, were the ideals it espoused: that government existed for the people, not people for the government; that firm authority could be based on the rule of law, respectful of individual rights and receptive to public opinion. During Soviet times these notions were more than a little subversive, but since the collapse of the communist system they have acquired greater relevance. The publication of Dzhunkovsky's memoirs, still ongoing in Russia, strongly suggests that his voice resonates with the generation emerging from under the rubble of Stalinism. Of equal importance may be Dzhunkovsky's own story: the journey of a decent man through turbulent and indecent times.

Notes

Prologue

1. On the executions at Butovo, see *Butovskii poligon*; Schlögel, *Moscow, 1937*, 472–504.

Chapter 1. Youth and the Corps of Pages

1. The best survey of the great reform era, its achievements and shortcomings, is Lincoln, *The Great Reforms*. Other English-language works of great value are Field, *The End of Serfdom*; Emmons and Vucinich, *The Zemstvo in Russia*; Wortman, *Legal Consciousness*.

2. The first lines of the Russian law code (*Svod zakonov Rossiiskoi imperii*) proclaimed: "The All-Russian emperor is a monarch autocratic and unlimited. To obey his supreme power, not only out of fear but for conscience sake, God himself ordains." This is derived from St. Paul's injunction in Romans 13.5: "Wherefore ye must needs be subject [to the powers that be], not only for wrath but also for conscience sake."

3. From the proclamation "To the Young Generation," by N. Shelgunov and M. Mikhailov, quoted in Venturi, *Roots of Revolution*, 248.

4. Pamphlet entitled "Young Russia," quoted in Venturi, *Roots of Revolution*, 295–96.

5. Chernyshevsky, *What Is to Be Done?* 271–93.

6. This document can be found in Dmytryshyn, *Imperial Russia*, 303–8.

7. A useful, if not entirely complete, genealogy of the Dzhunkovsky clan is "Rodoslovnye: Dzhunkovskie," at http://www.MTU-NET.ru/sherbach/rodoslov/djun.html/. Dzhunkovsky gives a detailed account of his family's history in the first volume of his memoirs, "Vospominaniia, 1865–1884," Gosudarstvennyi Arkhiv Rossiiskoi Federatsii (GARF), f. 826 (V. F. Dzhunkovskii), op. 1, d. 38, *ll.* 1–6. (These memoirs will hereafter be cited by year dates and *list* numbers; initial citations to the different volumes will give the archival *delo* number.)

8. On Russian interest in Mongol ancestry, see Figes, *Natasha's Dance*, 361–63.

9. "Rodoslovnye: Dzhunkovskie"; Dzhunkovskii, 1865–1884, *ll.* 1–6.

10. Samborsky, it would seem, had an eagle eye for talent. It was he who first noticed the bright young son of a village priest in Vladimir, Mikhail Mikhailovich Speransky. See Raeff, *Michael Speransky*, 2.

11. On Stepan Semenovich, see V. L. Telitsyn, "Dzhunkovskii, Stepan Semenovich"; "Rodoslovnye: Dzhunkovskie"; Dzhunkovskii, 1865–1884, *ll.* 6–7; Priklonskii, *Biografiia tainogo sovetnika S.S. Dzhunkovskogo*. Also of great value is the recent article by Anastasiia Dunaeva, "Mezhdunarodnye kul'turnye," 176–81. On Samborsky, see Isabel de Madariaga, *Russia*, 568.

12. On Stepan Stepanovich, see "Rodoslovnye: Dzhunkovskie"; Dzhunkovskii, 1865–1884, *ll.* 5–6; also "Dzhunkovskii, Stepan Stepanovich," at http:// www.rulex.ru/01050395.htm/.

13. Tikhmenev, *General Dzhunkovskii*.

14. Dzhunkovskii, 1865–1884, *l.* 8.

15. Dzhunkovskii, 1865–1884, *l.* 49. Unless otherwise noted all translations from the original Russian are mine.

16. Maria Karlovna was the granddaughter of the French Russian sculptor Jacques-Dominique Rashett. Her grandmother was Danish, which probably accounts for her Lutheran faith. See Dunaeva, "Mezhdunarodnye kul'turnye sviazi," 179–80.

17. Dzhunkovskii, 1865–1884, *l.* 7

18. Dzhunkovskii, 1865–1884, *l.* 10.

19. Dzhunkovskii, 1865–1884, *l.* 12.

20. Dzhunkovskii, 1865–1884, *ll.* 8–9.

21. Dzhunkovskii, 1865–1884, *ll.* 9–10; "Zachislit' za VChK," 88.

22. Dzhunkovskii, 1865–1884, *ll.* 13–19 (quotation *l.* 17).

23. For the Corps of Pages in the early years of the reign of Alexander II, see Kropotkin, *Memoirs of a Revolutionist*, 70–153. For later periods, see Gerua, *Vospominaniia*, 1:49–53; Konstantin V. Semchevskii, "Vospominaniia," part 2:2, Bakhmeteff Archive, Columbia University (BAR); Grabbe, *Windows on the River Neva*, 89–101.

24. Dzhunkovskii, 1865–1884, *ll.* 21–24.

25. Semchevskii, "Vospominaniia" (BAR), 2:14. See also Gerua, *Vospominaniia*, 1:49–53; Grabbe, *Windows on the River Neva*, 89–101.

26. Petr P. Stremoukhov, "Vse v proshlom: Vospominaniia, 1865–1935," GARF, f. R-6546 (P. P. Stremoukhov), op. 1, d. 2 (1865–1904), *ll.* 34–35.

27. Gerua, *Vospominaniia*, 1:54.

28. Gerua, *Vospominaniia*, 1:26–27; Dzhunkovskii, 1865–1884, *l.* 150.

29. Kropotkin describes earlier forms of hazing, prevalent in the late 1850s, in *Memoirs of a Revolutionist*, 75–82. In his memoirs from a later period, Semchevskii states that while hazing continued, it was not terribly harsh, less severe than at the U.S. Military Academy. "Vospominaniia" (BAR), 2:8–11.

30. Stremoukhov, "Vse v proshlom," in GARF, f. R-6546, op. 1, d.2, *l.* 40.

31. Dzhunkovskii, 1865–1884, *l.* 23.

32. Dzhunkovskii, 1865–1884, *ll.* 74–75.

33. Dzhunkovskii, 1865–1884, *ll.* 30–31.

34. Dzhunkovskii, 1865–1884, *ll.* 72–73.

35. Dzhunkovskii, 1865–1884, *l.* 48.

36. Dzhunkovskii, 1865–1884, *ll.* 48–51.

37. Dzhunkovskii, 1865–1884, *l.* 41. It is indicative of Dzhunkovsky's lack of understanding of and interest in the revolutionary movement that in his memoirs he ascribes Zasulich's escape from punishment to "the brilliant defense of her by the famous A. F. Koni." In fact, Koni was not the lawyer for the defense but the trial's presiding judge, whose conduct of the trial favored the defense. When the jury found Zasulich "not guilty," the government and conservative circles blamed Koni for the result. This was the impression that Dzhunkovsky must have gathered from his parents and then carried forward. By the time he wrote his memoirs, he had become a close friend of Koni, but this association had not corrected his youthful impression. A good summary of the Zasulich trial is found in Kucherov, *Courts, Lawyers and Trials*, 214–25. For Koni's own account, see his "Vospominaniia o dele Very Zasulich," in Koni, *Sobranie sochinenii*, 2:24–256.

38. Dzhunkovskii, 1865–1884, *l.* 53.

39. Dzhunkovskii, 1865–1884, *l.* 55.

40. Dzhunkovskii, 1865–1884, *l.* 64.

41. V. F. Dzhunkovskii, *Vospominaniia*, 1:667. (Dzhunkovsky's memoirs covering the years 1905–1915 were published in two volumes in 1997; a third volume was published in 2015, which covers the war years 1915–1917.)

42. Dzhunkovskii, "Vospominaniia, 1893–1897," GARF, f. 826, op. 1, d. 43, *l.* 88 (hereafter cited as Dzhunkovskii, 1893–1897, with *list* number).

43. Dzhunkovskii, 1865–1884, *l.* 46. On Savina and her career, see McReynolds, *Russia at Play*, 113–31.

44. Dzhunkovskii, 1865–1884, *l.* 43.

45. Dzhunkovskii, 1865–1884, *ll.* 76, 79–86.

46. Dzhunkovskii, 1865–1884, *l.* 122.

47. Dzhunkovskii, 1865–1884, *ll.* 131–32. The wedding ceremonies are described in Mager, *Elizabeth, Grand Duchess of Russia*, 93–96.

48. Dzhunkovskii, 1865–1884, *l.* 131.

Chapter 2. Guardsman and Courtier

1. Dzhunkovskii, "Vospominaniia, 1884–1891," GARF, f. 826, op. 1, d. 41, *l.* 12 (hereafter cited as "Dzhunkovskii, 1884–1891," with *list* number).

2. On the prerevolutionary officer corps, see John Bushnell, "The Tsarist Officer Corps, 1881–1914: Customs, Duties, Inefficiency," *American Historical Review* 86 (October 1981): 753–80.

3. Dzhunkovskii, 1884–1891, *l.* 27. For a good description of a *dirizher* at work, see Leo Tolstoy, *Anna Karenina*, trans. M. and L. Maude (New York: W. W. Norton, 1970), 71–72. On the skills required, see Lidiia Vasil'chikova, *Izcheznuvshaia Rossiia*, 158.

4. Dzhunkovskii, 1884–1891, *ll.* 27, 90, 150. On the wet nurse, *l.* 112.

5. Dzhunkovskii, 1884–1891, *ll.* 38, 47–48, 73–74.

6. Dzhunkovskii, 1884–1891, *ll.* 21, 183.

7. Lieven, *Nicholas II*, 37.

8. Dzhunkovskii, 1884–1891, *l.* 163.

9. Dzhunkovskii, 1884–1891, *l.* 169.

10. The terms "the elder" (*starshii*) and "the younger" (*mladshii*) are used to distinguish the brother of Alexander II from his son, also Nikolai Nikolaevich, who served as Russian supreme commander at the beginning of the Great War until Nicholas II personally assumed that role in mid-1915.

11. Dzhunkovskii, 1884–1891, *l.* 81.

12. Dzhunkovskii, 1884–1891, *ll.* 81–82.

13. Wortman, *Scenarios of Power*, 2:293; Verner, *Crisis of Russian Autocracy*, 117–18, 136–39, 147–48.

14. Louis Greenberg, *The Jews in Russia: The Struggle for Emancipation*, 2 vols. (New Haven: Yale University Press, 1944, 1951), 2:41–47.

15. Bogdanovich, *Tri poslednikh samoderzhtsa*, 80.

16. Alexander, Grand Duke of Russia, *Once a Grand Duke*, 140.

17. Queen Marie of Roumania, *The Story of My Life*, 7.

18. This poem has been reproduced in many places, see "Kniaz'-muchenik," *Blagovest: Pravoslavnaia gazeta*, March 7, 2005, at http://www.cofe.ru/blagovest/article.asp?heading=32&article=8569/.

19. Marie, Grand Duchess of Russia, *Education*, 19–22.

20. Bokhanov, "Sergei Aleksandrovich," 345–46.

21. Mager, *Elizabeth*, 73–74, 99, 103. Christopher Warwick explores this problem and makes the same point in his more recent study of Elizaveta Fedorovna, *Ella*, 130–35.

22. Bokhanov, "Sergei Aleksandrovich," 336–38.

23. Dzhunkovskii, 1884–1891, *l.* 13.

24. Dzhunkovskii, 1884–1891, *l.* 19.

25. Dzhunkovskii, 1884–1891, *ll.* 41–42.

26. Dzhunkovskii, 1884–1891, *l.* 46.

27. Dzhunkovskii, 1884–1891, *l.* 46.

28. Dzhunkovskii, 1884–1891, *ll.* 107–8.

29. Dzhunkovskii, 1884–1891, *l.* 149.

30. Dzhunkovskii, 1884–1891, *l.* 162.

31. Dzhunkovskii, 1884–1891, *l.* 202.

32. For a far-ranging study of late nineteenth-century El Niños and their consequences, see Mike Davis, *Late Victorian Holocausts: El Niño Famines and the Making of the Third World* (New York: Verso, 2001).

33. For a general treatment of the relief campaign, see Robbins, *Famine in Russia*. A useful assessment of the demographic impact of the famine is provided by Wheatcroft, "The 1891–92 Famine in Russia."

34. Dzhunkovskii, "Vospominaniia, 1891–1892," GARF, f. 826, op. 1, d. 40, *l.* 8 (hereafter cited as "Dzhunkovskii, 1891–1892," with *list* number).

35. Dzhunkovskii, 1891–1892, *l.* 30.

36. Dzhunkovskii, 1891–1892, *ll.* 30–31.

37. Dzhunkovskii, 1891–1892, *l.* 32.

38. Dzhunkovskii, 1891–1892, *ll.* 31–32.

39. Dzhunkovskii, 1891–1892, *l.* 35. After the revolution, the peasants of Khvalinsk remembered their generosity and would come to the aid of the Medems' son Alexander, defending him from the Cheka. Albert Rhys Williams, *The Russian Land* (New York: New Republic, 1927), 167–85.

40. Dzhunkovskii, 1891–1892, *l.* 36.

41. Dzhunkovskii, 1891–1892, *l.* 37.

42. Dzhunkovskii, 1891–1892, *ll.* 41–42. The copy of the report is inserted in the memoirs, *ll.* 43–52.

43. Dzhunkovskii, 1891–1892, *l.* 53.

44. Service, *Lenin*, 86–88.

45. On Guchkov in 1891–1892, see Robbins, *Famine in Russia*, 160–61.

46. Dzhunkovskii, 1891–1892, *ll.* 7–8.

47. Dzhunkovskii, 1891–1892, *l.* 16.

48. Dzhunkovskii, 1891–1892, *l.* 67.

49. Dzhunkovskii, 1893–1897, *ll.* 17–18, 26–27.

50. Castiglione, *The Book of the Courtier*, 210.

51. Dzhunkovskii, "Vospominaniia, 1898–1904," GARF, f. 826, op. 1, d. 45, *l.* 5 (hereafter cited as "Dzhunkovskii, 1898–1904" with *list* number), *ll.* 450–51.

52. Warwick, *Ella*, 312.

53. Alexander, Grand Duke of Russia, *Once a Grand Duke*, 140. Nor did these qualities dim with age. In 1914, now fifty and dressed in the habit of a nun, Ella was, in the eyes of the French ambassador Maurice Paléologue, "as elegant and seductive as in the old days before her widowhood, when she still had inspired profane passions." Quoted in Lincoln, *Passage*, 48.

54. Marie, Grand Duchess of Russia, *Education*, 20–21.

55. Dzhunkovskii, 1893–1897, *l.* 142; Dzhunkovskii, 1898–1904, *l.* 7.

56. Razgon, *True Stories*, 111–13.

57. Dzhunkovskii, 1893–1897, *l.* 97.

Chapter 3. Love, Labor, Loss

1. Sabashnikov, *Zapiski*, 41; Andreeva-Bal'mont, *Vospominaniia*, 146; Voloshina-Sabashnikova, *Zelenaia zmeia*, 92.

2. Andreeva-Bal'mont, *Vospominaniia*, 206.

3. Sabashnikov, *Zapiski*, 33, 48–49.

4. Sabashnikov, *Zapiski*, 81–88.

5. Andreeva-Bal'mont, *Vospominaniia*, 143–44.

6. Andreeva-Bal'mont, *Vospominaniia*, 140.

7. Sabashnikov, *Zapiski*, 57, 64–67; Andreeva-Bal'mont, *Vospominaniia*, 180–81.

8. Andreeva-Bal'mont, *Vospominaniia*, 189–90.

9. On *Severnyi vestnik*, see Belov, *Knigoizdateli Sabashnikovy*, 18–19; *Russkaia periodicheskaia pechat' (1702–1894)*, ed. A. G. Dement'ev et al. (Moscow: Gosudarstvennoe izdatel'stvo politicheskoi literatury, 1959), 667–68.

10. Andreeva-Bal'mont, *Vospominaniia*, 190.

11. Andreeva-Bal'mont, *Vospominaniia*, 193.

12. Andreeva-Bal'mont, *Vospominaniia*, 198.

13. Sabashnikov, *Zapiski*, 210.

14. Sabashnikov, *Zapiski*, 181–83.

15. "Kantseliariia ego imperatorskogo velichestva po priniatiiu proshenii na 'vysochaishee' imia prinosimikh." For a brief description of this institution and its function, see *Gosudarstvennost' Rossii*, 2:198–99.

16. The question of divorce in Russia is treated extensively in Engel, *Ties that Bound*; on the Baranovskys, 93–94. 172–73, 247. See also William G. Wagner's *Marriage, Property and Law*, esp. 88–100.

17. Sabashnikov, *Zapiski*, 133–37.

18. Andreeva-Bal'mont, *Vospominaniia*, 240–47, 248–86.

19. Voloshina-Sabashnikova, *Zelenaia zmeia*, 92.

20. Dzhunkovskii, 1891–1892, *ll.* 101–2. In his memoirs, Benois mentions his friendship with Sergei Gadon but makes no note of meeting Dzhunkovsky. Aleksandr Benua, *Moi vospominaniia v piati knigakh*, 2nd ed., 2 vols. (Moscow: Nauka, 1990), 1:463–64.

21. Dzhunkovskii, 1893–1897, *ll.* 45–46.

22. Andreeva-Bal'mont, *Vospominaniia*, 226–27, gives a good description of Nina's religious/political outlook in her memoirs. By now Vladimir's religiosity and conservatism should be adequately documented.

23. In his memoirs Dzhunkovsky refers to Nina as his "great friend" (*bol'shoi drug*), a term that in Russian implies a special closeness but has no precise English equivalent. Dzhunkovskii, *Vospominaniia*, 2:245.

24. We have no direct evidence of Nina's involvement in the Andreeva-Balmont romance; in her memoirs Katya does not mention that her friend played any role. But given the closeness of the two women, it is impossible to imagine that Nina was not privy to what was going on. We do know that immediately after their marriage, Katya and Balmont would stay with Nina in Biarritz, France. Andreeva-Bal'mont, *Vospominaniia*, 317–18.

25. Kupriianovskii and Molchanova, *Poet Konstantin Bal'mont*, 65; Andreeva-Bal'mont, *Vospominaniia*, 311–13.

26. Andreeva-Bal'mont, *Vospominaniia*, 313.

27. See the two letters Balmont sent to Dzhunkovsky dated September 28 and November 3/15, 1896. "Pis'ma K. D. Bal'monta k V. F. Dzhunkovskomu," in *Konstantin Bal'mont, Marina Tsvetaeva i khudozhestvennye iskaniia XX veka*, 63–64 (hereafter cited as "Bal'mont-Dzhunkovskomu").

28. At least this is the impression that Evdokiia would try to convey in her letters to her brother.

29. On Dzhunkovsky's distraction, see Evdokiia's letter of June 9, 1896 (all Evdokiia's letters are in GARF, f. 826, op. 1 and will henceforth be cited by only delo and *list* numbers), d. 534, *l.* 87.

30. Wortman, *Scenarios*, 2:345.

31. Wortman, *Scenarios*, 2:348–51.

32. The nature and structure of Dzhunkovsky's memoirs strongly suggest that a diary of some sort formed a basis for the work. A more extensive discussion of the composition of Dzhunkovsky's memoirs can be found in the penultimate chapter of this book.

33. Dzhunkovskii, "Koronatsionnye torzhestva," 20. This is an excerpt from portions of Dzhunkovsky's memoirs not included in the volumes published in 1997.

34. This was not an entirely unwarranted assumption. At the coronation of Alexander III in 1883, the behavior of the people at a similar event had, in fact, been remarkably calm, something that became a matter of national pride.

35. Krasnov, *Khodynka*, 46.

36. Dzhunkovskii, "Koronatsionnye torzhestva," 22.

37. Dzhunkovskii, "Koronationnye torzhestva," 22.

38. Dzhunkovskii, "Koronatsionnye torzhestva," 23. The emperor's decision to attend the ball owed much to Sergei and the other grand dukes. They urged Nicholas to avoid anything that might be considered "sentimental" and might imply weakness. Wortman, *Scenarios*, 2:361–62.

39. Dzhunkovskii, 1893–1897, *l.* 235.

40. Marie, Grand Duchess of Russia, *Education*, 32. Maria Pavlovna may have employed this pseudonym because she was writing her memoirs while in exile during the 1920s. Evdokiia was, as far as Maria knew, still alive in Russia. The use of a false name could have been designed to protect the former governess from any danger that might result from her previous association with the Romanov family. Maria Pavlovna's concern may have been exaggerated, but Evdokiia was, indeed, still living in Moscow. She died in 1935.

41. Marie, Grand Duchess of Russia, *Education*, 32.

42. Marie, Grand Duchess of Russia, *Education*, 40.

43. Marie, Grand Duchess of Russia, *Education*, 43.

44. Marie, Grand Duchess of Russia, *Education*, 43.

45. Marie, Grand Duchess of Russia, *Education*, 42–43.

46. Marie, Grand Duchess of Russia, *Education*, 43.

47. Maria Pavlovna would later realize that Evdokiia's advice on major life decisions was often better than that given by her aunt and guardian, Elizaveta Fedorovna. In her memoirs, she recounts how Evdokiia urged her to be accepting of her father's second (morganatic) wife (Marie, Grand Duchess of Russia, *Education*, 47–48) and cautioned her to take her time in considering what proved to be an ill-fated marriage to Prince William of Sweden (94–96). Evdokiia was the only Russian to attend the christening of Maria's first-born (127–28); and in late 1917, after the fall of the monarchy and on the eve of the Bolshevik coup, Evdokiia was present to help Maria at the time of her second wedding (331).

48. Evdokiia to Dzhun, June 9, 1896, in GARF, f. 826, op. 1, d. 534, *ll.* 84–87.

49. Evdokiia to Dzhun, June 10, 1896, GARF, f. 826, op. 1, d. 534, *l.* 88.

50. Evdokiia to Dzhun, June 13, 1896, GARF, f. 826, op. 1, d. 534, *l.* 92. It seems that none of Dzhunkovsky's letters to his sister survived. But Evdokiia's letters to her brother refer to his correspondence and give insight into what he wrote and felt at the time.

51. Evdokiia to Dzhun, June 13, 1896, GARF, f. 826, op. 1, d. 534, *l.* 93.

52. Evdokiia to Dzhun, June 10, 1896, GARF, f. 826, op. 1, d. 534, *l.* 88.

53. Evdokiia to Dzhun, June 19, 1896, GARF, f. 826, op. 1, d. 534, *l.* 98.

54. Evdokiia to Dzhun, June 10, 1896, GARF, f. 826, op. 1, d. 534, *l.* 88.

55. Evdokiia to Dzhun, August 7, 8, 1896, GARF, f. 826, op. 1, d. 534, *ll.* 115–20.

56. Evdokiia to Dzhun, August 7, 1896, GARF, f. 826, op. 1, d. 534, *l.* 115.

57. Kupriianovskii and Molchanova, *Poet Konstantin Bal'mont*, 65–69; Dzhunkovskii, 1893–1897, *l.* 248. Dzhunkovsky implies that the deception Balmont employed was not all that unusual and that other couples who had used a similar device would usually then petition the emperor for forgiveness in breaking the law.

58. Balmont to Dzhun, September 28, 1896, "Bal'mont-Dzhunkovskomu," 63–64.

59. Balmont to Dzhun, November 3/15, 1896, "Bal'mont-Dzhunkovskomu," 64.

60. Evdokiia to Dzhun, November 18, 1896, GARF, f. 826, op. 1, d. 534, *l.* 152.

61. Dzhunkovskii, 1893–1897, *l.* 249.

62. Evdokiia to Dzhun, November 20, 1896, GARF, f. 826, op. 1, d. 534, *l.* 153.

63. Balmont to Dzhun, December 21, 1896, "Bal'mont-Dzhunkovskomu," 65.

64. Evdokiia to Dzhun, January 10, 1897, GARF, f. 826, op. 1, d. 535, *l.* 8.

65. Evdokiia to Dzhun, January 18, see also January 22, 1897, GARF, f. 826, op. 1, d. 535, *ll.* 15, 21.

66. A short summary of the events leading up to the war and its aftermath is provided by L. S. Stavrianos, *The Balkans since 1453* (New York: NYU Press, 1961), 470–71. Although a small-scale episode, the Greco-Turkish war attracted the attention of the world and some of the time's leading journalists. One of those to visit the scene of the conflict and write about it was Stephen Crane, the famous author of *The Red Badge of Courage*. His reportage from the Greek side is collected in *War Dispatches of Stephen Crane*. For an account of events from the Turkish side, see Steevens, *Conquering Turk*.

67. Dzhunkovskii, 1893–1897, *l.* 261.

68. A splendid account of the rise and radicalization of the Russian doctors is Frieden, *Russian Physicians*.

69. Dzhunkovskii, 1893–1897, *ll.* 263–64.

70. Dzhunkovskii, 1893–1897, *l.* 280.

71. Dzhunkovskii, 1893–1897, *ll.* 327–31.

72. Dzhunkovskii, 1893–1897, *l.* 333.

73. Dzhunkovskii, 1893–1897, *l.* 337.

74. Evdokiia to Dzhun, April 25, 1897, GARF, f. 826, op. 1, d. 535, *ll.* 39–40.

75. Evdokiia to Dzhun, September 7, 1897, GARF, f. 826, op. 1, d. 535, *l.* 116.

76. Evdokiia to Dzhun, September 7, 1897, GARF, f. 826, op. 1, d. 535, *ll.* 118–19.

77. Evdokiia to Dzhun, September 13, 1897, GARF, f. 826, op. 1, d. 535, *l.* 128.

78. Evdokiia to Dzhun, September 13, 1897, GARF, f. 826, op. 1, d. 535, *l.* 129.

79. Evdokiia to Dzhun, December 27, 28, 1897, GARF, f. 826, op. 1, d. 535, *ll.* 157, 161. Also Evdokiia to Dzhun, January 3, 1898, GARF, f. 826, op. 1, d. 536, *l.* 1.

80. Evdokiia to Dzhun, December 30, 1897, GARF, f. 826, op. 1, d. 535, *l.* 163.

81. Evdokiia to Dzhun, January 20, 1898, GARF, f. 826, op. 1, d. 536, *l.* 9.

82. Evdokiia to Dzhun, January 29, February 3, 1898, GARF, f. 826, op. 1, d. 536, *ll.* 21–22, 25–26.

83. Kupriianovskii and Molchanova, *Poet Konstantin Bal'mont*, 78.

84. Evdokiia to Dzhun, February 19, March 31, 1898, GARF, f. 826, op. 1, d. 536, *ll.* 36–37, 43.

85. Nikolai Fedorovich to Dzhun, April 12, 1898, GARF, f. 826, op. 1, d. 527, "Pis'ma Dzhunkovskogo N.F. Dzhunkovskomu, V. F.," *ll.* 33–36.

86. Dzhunkovskii, 1898–1904, *l.* 5. In the memoirs Dzhunkovsky gives no hint of a romantic purpose.

87. Evdokiia to Dzhun, April 23, 1898, GARF, f. 826, op. 1, d. 536, *ll.* 55–56.

88. Evdokiia to Dzhun, May 1, 1898, GARF, f. 826, op. 1, d. 536, *l.* 58.

89. Evdokiia to Dzhun, May 6, 1898, GARF, f. 826, op. 1, d. 536, *ll.* 61–62.

90. Evdokiia to Dzhun, May 20, 1898, GARF, f. 826, op. 1, d. 536, *ll.* 65–66.

91. Evdokiia to Dzhun, June 8, GARF, f. 826, op. 1, d. 536, *ll.* 69–70.

92. Balmont to Dzhun, June 13/25, 22, 1898, GARF, f. 826, op. 1, d. 463, "Pis'ma Bal'monta, K. D. Dzhunkovskomu, V. F.," *ll.* 9, 10.

93. See his friend E. P. Zaime to Dzhun, August 16, 1898: "From my heart I hope you have a chance to fulfill your desires. Thank God, I have everything, a wife and daughter." GARF, f. 826, op. 1, d. 564, "Pis'ma Zaime, E. P. Dzhunkovskomu, V. F.," *l.* 46.

94. Evdokiia to Dzhun, July, August 15/16, 19, 28, September 7, 1898, GARF, f. 826, op. 1, d. 536, *ll.* 97–98, 99–100, 101–4, 105.

95. Evdokiia to Dzhun, January 13, 1897, May 6, 13, 1898, GARF, f. 826, op. 1, d. 535, *ll.* 11–12, and d. 536, *ll.* 61–62, 64.

96. Dzhunkovskii, 1898–1904, *ll.* 64, 83, 140.

97. Nemirovich-Danchenko, *My Life in the Russian Theater*, 123–30; Vladimir A. Teliakovskii, *Vospominaniia, 1898–1917* (Petrograd: Vremia, 1924), 81–85, 120–22.

98. Dzhunkovskii, 1898–1904, *ll.* 121, 126 (quotation).

Chapter 4. Green Snake, Red Flag

1. This brief description of Moscow at the start of the twentieth century draws heavily on Joseph Bradley's magisterial *Muzhik and Muscovite* and on his summary essay "Moscow: From Big Village to Metropolis," in Hamm, *The City in Late Imperial Russia*, 9–42. Also of great value are Robert E. Johnson's *Peasant and Proletarian: The Working Class of Moscow in the Late Nineteenth Century* (New Brunswick, NJ: Rutgers University Press, 1979), and Lincoln, *In War's Dark Shadow*, esp. 69–102. On the merchant class, two works are extremely useful: Alfred J. Reiber, *Merchants and Entrepreneurs in Imperial Russia* (Chapel Hill: University of North Carolina Press, 1982), and Jo Ann Ruckman, *The Moscow Business Elite: A Social and Cultural Portrait of Two Generations, 1840–1905* (DeKalb: Northern Illinois University Press, 1984). For a highly valuable Russian account, see Rozental', *Moskva na pereput'e.*

2. A solid overall treatment of alcohol abuse and the efforts to combat it (especially the vodka monopoly and its consequences) in the last years of the old regime is Herlihy, *Alcoholic Empire*. Other useful works include McKee, "Taming the Green Serpent"; Pechenuk, "Temperance and Revenue Raising."

3. McKee, "Taming the Green Serpent," 161–80.

4. Herlihy, *Alcoholic Empire*, 16. By 1904 there were 772 committees and over 50,000 members. McKee, "Taming the Green Serpent," 181.

5. The "people's house" is a little-studied institution. For an illuminating discussion see Lindenmeyr, "Building Civil Society."

6. Herlihy, *Alcoholic Empire*, 14–16, and on Moscow as a showcase, 24; McKee, "Taming the Green Serpent," 181–94.

7. See Brooks, *When Russia Learned to Read*, 295–352, for a discussion of the response of the educated elite to what they viewed as the dangers of popular culture (on the guardianships, 313–14, 347, 350). See also Swift, *Popular Theater*, 39–87.

8. The national liquor monopoly was established in 1896 but was introduced in various places at different times.

9. Dzhunkovskii, 1898–1904, *ll.* 98–101, 126–28.

10. GARF, f. 826, op. 1, d. 479, "Pis'ma Bil'derling, A.A. Dzunkovskomu, V.F."

11. Dzhunkovskii, 1898–1904, *l.* 132.

12. Dzhunkovskii, 1898–1904, *ll.* 132–33; Herlihy, *Alcoholic Empire*, 23.

13. Dzhunkovskii, 1898–1904, *ll.* 137–38.

14. Dzhunkovskii, 1898–1904, *l.* 210.

15. Dzhunkovskii, 1898–1904, *l.* 132.

16. Dzhunkovskii, 1898–1904, *l.* 201.

17. Sellers, "The Russian Temperance Committees," 871–72.

18. Sellers, "The Russian Temperance Committees," 873.

19. Sellers, "The Russian Temperance Committees," 873.

20. Sellers, "The Russian Temperance Committees," 873–74.

21. Sellers, "The Russian Temperance Committees," 874.

22. A good discussion of traditional Russian views on the labor question is found in Schneiderman, *Sergei Zubatov*, 19–23.

23. On early Russian factory legislation, see Rimlinger, "Autocracy."

24. On interministerial disputes concerning labor policy, see Schneiderman, *Sergei Zubatov*, 28–48.

25. Schneiderman's *Sergei Zubatov* concentrates on his attempts to influence the working class. A more recent study emphasizes his reforms of security police operations and utilizes archival material opened after the end of the Soviet regime; Daly, *Autocracy under Siege*, 73–153.

26. Schneiderman, *Sergei Zubatov*, 99–172; Bonnell, *Roots of Rebellion*, 80–86; Daly, *Autocracy under Siege*, 126.

27. Lenin's most famous work, *What Is to Be Done?*, was written in part as a response to the impact of *zubatovshchina*. Schneiderman, *Sergei Zubatov*, 304–5.

28. Daly, *Autocracy under Siege*, 130–42; Schneiderman, *Sergei Zubatov*, 350–61.

29. Dzhunkovskii, 1898–1904, *ll.* 235–36.

30. *Otchet moskovskogo stolichnogo popechitel'stva o narodnoi trezvosti za 1904*, xxxviii–xxxix.

31. Herlihy, *Alcoholic Empire*, 28–29.

32. Swift, *Popular Theater*, 171–72.

33. Dzhunkovskii, 1898–1904, *l.* 445.

34. Dzhunkovskii, 1898–1904, *l.* 265.

35. Dzhunkovskii, 1898–1904, *ll.* 266–69 (Grand duke's letter quoted on *l.* 269; original italics).

36. Dzhunkovskii, 1898–1904, *ll.* 270–71. Dzhunkovsky's letter was dated November 12, 1902.

37. Dzhunkovskii, 1898–1904, *l*.272.

38. Sergei Sabashnikov to Dzhun, December 2, 1902, in GARF, f. 826, op. 1, d. 725, "Pis'ma Sabashnikova, S. Dzhunkovskomu, V. F.," *l.* 6.

39. Balmont to Dzhun, August 27, 1903, GARF, f. 826, op. 1, d. 463, "Pis'ma Bal'monta, K.D. Dzhunkovskomu, V. F.," *l.* 26 (original italics). See also Evdokiia to Dzhunkovsky, August 9, 1903, GARF, f. 826, op. 1, d. 538, "Pis'ma Dzhunkovskoi, E.F. Dzhunkovskomu, V.F, 1 I 1901–13 IX 1907," *ll.* 100–101.

40. Liubimova and Golovkova, "Butovo—Russkaia golgofa," at http://www.martyr.ru/content/view/8/18/.

41. Evdokiia to Dzhun, April 4, 1904, GARF, f. 826, op. 1, d. 538, *l.* 108.

42. Balmont to Dzhun, July 12, 1904, GARF, f. 826, op. 1, d. 463, *l.* 32.

43. *Poeziia bol'shevistskikh izdaniiakh, 1901–1917*, ed. I. S. Eventov (Leningrad: Sovetskii pisatel', 1967).

44. *Russkaia literatura* 3 (1963): 162. Balmont read his poem a month after the minister of education, N. P. Bogolepov, was attacked and fatally wounded.

45. Balmont to Dzhun, December 7, 1901, GARF, f. 826, op. 1, d. 463, *ll.* 20–21.

46. Balmont to Dzhun, December 27/28, 1901, GARF, f. 826, op. 1, d. 463, *l.* 22.

47. Balmont to Dzhun, February 13, 16, 1902, GARF, f. 826, op. 1, d. 463, *ll.* 23, 24.

48. Belyi, *Nachalo veka*, 220–21.

49. Bal'mont, "Skvoz' stroi," 211–12.

50. Dzhunkovskii, 1898–1904, *ll.* 303–4.

51. See Balmont to Dzhun, August 28, 1905, asking Dzhun to say a few words to the Moscow city commandant (*gradonachal'nik)* on behalf of a certain S. A. Sokolev. GARF, f. 826, op. 1, d. 463, *l.* 33. (This is the last dated letter in the file.)

52. These poems would be gathered in the collection *Pesni mstitelia* published in 1907.

53. In his memoirs, Dzhunkovsky describes meeting Katya Balmont in 1911 and 1913. He refers to her affectionately as a very close friend (*bol'shaia priiatel'nitsa*) but does not mention his connection to her husband. Both times he describes her as *zhena poeta* (wife of the poet). Dzhunkovskii, *Vospominaniia*, 1:569, 2:245.

54. Ascher, *1905*, 1:71–72.

55. Dzhunkovskii, 1898–1904, *l.* 408.

56. Dzhunkovskii, 1898–1904, *l.* 409.

57. Dzhunkovskii, 1898–1904, *ll.* 416–17, 424, 450–51.

58. The S.R. proclamation is quoted in Savinkov, *Memoirs of a Terrorist*, 85–86.

59. Dzhunkovskii, 1898–1904, *ll.* 452–53.

60. Verner, *Russian Autocracy*, 117–24.

61. Dzhunkovskii, 1898–1904, *l.* 455.

62. Dzhunkovskii 1898–1904, *l.* 457. Dzhunkovsky's letter was dated December 27, 1904.

Chapter 5. Storm Signals

1. Dzhunkovskii, *Vospominaniia*, 1:29; *XX vek: Khronika, 1900–1910 gg.*, 225, citing story in newspaper *Russkie vedomosti*, January 4, 1905.

2. Dzhunkovskii, *Vospominaniia*, 1:28.

3. *XX vek: Khronika, 1901–1910 gg.*, 226–27 citing stories in *Russkie vedomosti*, January 6, 9, and 13, 1905.

4. Dmytryshyn, *Imperial Russia*, 380.

5. The most complete English language account of "Bloody Sunday" and the developments that led up to it is Sablinsky, *Road to Bloody Sunday*. See also Ascher, *1905*, 1:74–101. Lincoln provides a dramatic depiction of the events, in *War's Dark Shadow*, 288–91. See also the report of Vladimir Gadon concerning the shootings on Palace Square in *Revoliutsiia 1905–1907 gg. v Rossii: Dokumenty i materialy. Nachalo pervoi russkoi revoliutsii, ianvar'-mart 1905 goda*, 58–61.

6. Dzhunkovskii, *Vospominaniia*, 1:33–34.

7. Ascher, *1905*, 1:97–108.

8. On the powers and duties of the city commandant, see *Svod zakonov Rossiiskoi imperii*, vol. 2 (St. Petersburg: Kodifikatsionnyi otdel pri gosudarstvennom sovete, 1892), arts. 861–87.

9. Dzhunkovskii, *Vospominaniia*, 1:29.

10. Dzhunkovskii, *Vospominaniia*, 1:37–38.

11. Dzhunkovskii, *Vospominaniia*, 1:38.

12. Savinkov, "Vospominaniia terrorista," in *Izbrannoe* (Leningrad, 1990), 98, 107.

13. Dzhunkovskii, *Vospominaniia*, 1:41–42.

14. Dzhunkovskii, *Vospominaniia*, 1:43.

15. Letter quoted in Savinkov, "Vospominaniia terrorista," 99–100.

16. Dzhunkovskii, *Vospominaniia*, 1:43.

17. Dzhunkovskii, *Vospominaniia*, 1:50.

18. Dzhunkovskii, *Vospominaniia*, 1:52; Shevelev, *Chinovnyi mir Rossii*, 411–14; Iu. S. Vorob'eva and I. V. Karpeev, "Figel'-ad"iutant," in *Gosudarstvennost' Rossii*, vol. 5, pt. 2, 441–42.

19. Shevelev, *Chinovnyi mir Rossii*, 413; Dzhunkovskii, *Vospominaniia*, 1:54.

20. Dzhunkovskii, *Vospominaniia*, 1:50–51.

21. Dzhunkovskii, *Vospominaniia*, 1:56–57.

22. Ascher, *1905*, 1:97–98, 103–5, 112–13, 119–22.

23. Dzhunkovskii, *Vospominaniia*, 1:48–49, 62; Savinkov, "Vospominaniia terrorista," 103.

24. Dzhunkovskii, *Vospominaniia*, 1:62 (original italics).

25. Dzhunkovskii, *Vospominaniia*, 1:62–63.

26. Dzhunkovskii, *Vospominaniia*, 1:63.

27. Dzhunkovskii, *Vospominaniia*, 1:63–64.

28. Toward the end of the nineteenth century the Ministry of Internal Affairs had sought to "professionalize" the office of vice-governor. Its efforts were embodied in the law of April 19, 1904. See *Polnoe sobranie zakonov Rossiiskoi imperii* (St. Petersburg: Tipografiia II otdeleniia sobstvennoi ego Imperatorskogo Velichestva kantseliarii, n.d.), 3rd series, no. 24388; Robbins, *The Tsar's Viceroys*, 28–29.

29. Dzhunkovskii, *Vospominaniia*, 1:65–66; for a more complete discussion of provincial institutions, their strengths and weaknesses, see Robbins, *The Tsar's Viceroys*, 91–123.

30. Dzhunkovskii, *Vospominaniia*, 1:65–66.

31. The manifesto of August 6 can be found in *Konstitutsionnye proekty v Rossii XVIII–nachalo XX v.* (Moscow: Institut rossiiskoi istorii RAN, 2000), 716–28; Ascher, *1905*, 1:180.

32. Dzhunkovskii, *Vospominaniia*, 1:69.

33. Ascher, *1905*, 1:196–97; Dzhunkovskii, *Vospominaniia*, 1:70–71. For a detailed discussion of the universities during 1905, see Kassow, *Students, Professors*, 237–85.

34. Dzhunkovskii, *Vospominaniia*, 1:71–72; on the September strike movement, see Engelstein, *Moscow, 1905*, 73–91.

35. Engelstein, *Moscow, 1905*, 95–96.

36. Ascher, *1905*, 1:119–20.

37. Dzhunkovskii, *Vospominaniia*, 1:73.

38. Engelstein, *Moscow, 1905*, 124, 134.

39. Ascher, *1905*, 1:215.

40. V. F. Malinin, "Zabastovka," 9.

41. Malinin, "Zabastovka," 9–10; Dzhunkovskii, *Vospominaniia*, 1:78, 80. For the most part, Malinin's memoir of the waterworks strike diverges only slightly from the story as told by Dzhunkovsky and the basic facts are seldom at issue. Interestingly, Malinin does not mention Dzhunkovsky's name. He did so because he did not want to cause trouble for a man who, as far as he knew, was still alive in Soviet Russia. Malinin, "Zabastovka," 13–14.

42. Malinin, "Zabastovka," 11–12; Dzhunkovskii, *Vospominaniia*, 1:73.

43. Malinin, "Zabastovka," 11.

44. Dzhunkovskii, *Vospominaniia*, 1:79.

45. On this point the memoirs of Dzhunkovsky and Malinin disagree. Malinin claims that he was the one who discovered the Bromley engineer; Dzhunkovsky maintains that he did it. Malinin, "Zabastovka," 14–15; Dzhunkovskii, *Vospominaniia*, 1:79. Both agree on his usefulness and his desire to work under cover. Neither memoir mentions his name, perhaps out of concern for the engineer's safety.

46. Malinin, "Zabastovka," 16–17; Dzhunkovskii, *Vospominaniia*, 1:79–80.

47. Dzhunkovskii, *Vospominaniia*, 1:80–81.

48. Dzhunkovskii, *Vospominaniia*, 1:81–82; Malinin, "Zabastovka," 19–21.

Chapter 6. Moscow Explodes

1. The story of the events leading up to the October Manifesto has been told by many authors. See, among others, Verner, *Crisis of Russian Autocracy*, 218–45; Lincoln, *War's Dark Shadow*, 301–3; Ascher, *1905*, 1:222–29. On Grand Duke Nikolai Nikolaevich's refusal to be dictator, see Robinson,

Grand Duke Nikolai Nikolaevich, 67–70. The English translation of the text of the Manifesto is in Mehlinger and Thompson, *Count Witte*, 331–32.

2. Document reproduced in full in Mehlinger and Thompson, *Count Witte*, 335.

3. Ascher provides an excellent summary and analysis of the complex events. *1905*, 1:275–303.

4. Dzhunkovskii, *Vospominaniia*, 1:87.

5. Dzhunkovskii, *Vospominaniia*, 1:88–90; Engelstein, *Moscow, 1905*, 138–39.

6. *XX vek: Khronika moskovskoi zhizni, 1901–1910 gg.*, 266. Engelstein, *Moscow, 1905*, 138–39.

7. Dzhunkovskii, *Vospominaniia*, 1:88.

8. Ascher, *1905*, 1:247.

9. Rozental', *Moskva na pereput'e*, 59–60.

10. Dzhunkovskii, *Vospominaniia*, 1:97.

11. Dzhunkovskii, *Vospominaniia*, 1:97–99.

12. Dzhunkovskii, *Vospominaniia*, 1:105. Dzhunkovsky received the title "acting governor" (*ispravliaiushchii dolzhnosti gubernatora*) because his current rank was only that of colonel. A governor's rank was normally equal to that of a major general.

13. Ascher, *1905*, 1:299–301.

14. Dzhunkovskii, *Vospominaniia*, 1:106.

15. *Moskovskii arkhiv*, 460.

16. Dzhunkovskii, *Vospominaniia*, 1:109.

17. Ascher, *1905*, 1:313.

18. Ascher, *1905*, 1:314–15; Engelstein, *Moscow, 1905*, 202–4.

19. Dzhunkovskii, *Vospominaniia*, 1:113–16; Engelstein, *Moscow, 1905*, 202–6. In his memoirs Dzhunkovsky gives the date of the events described as December 9, but clearly they took place on the tenth.

20. Dubasov's diary for these days is published, see "'Dostoinstvo vlasti trebuet ne mstit,' a razobrat' vinovnost' kazhdogo': F. V Dubasov o dekabr'skom vooruzhennom vostanii 1905 g. v Moskve," *Istoricheskii arkhiv*, no. 5–6 (1998): 87.

21. Ascher, *1905*, 1:318–19.

22. Ascher, *1905*, 1:331; Dzhunkovskii, *Vospominaniia*, 1:128; Reichman, *Railway Men*, 212.

23. Ascher, *1905*, 1:320–22.

24. Dzhunkovskii, *Vospominaniia*, 1:110.

25. Dzhunkovskii, *Vospominaniia*, 1:110.

26. Dzhunkovskii, *Vospominaniia*, 1:116.

27. N. N. Kisel-Zagorianskii, memoirs, Kisel-Zagorianskii Papers (BAR), 111.

28. Dzhunkovskii, *Vospominaniia*, 1:121; *XX vek: Khronika, 1901–1910*, 283, citing accounts in *Russkoe slovo*, December 19, 1905.

29. Dzhunkovskii, *Vospominaniia*, 1:122; see also Dzhunkovsky's report to the minister of internal affairs P. N. Durnovo, dated January 27, 1906, in *Revoliutsiia 1905–1907 gg. v Rossii: Dokumenty i materialy. Vysshii pod"em revoliutsii*, 1:757–61.

30. Dzhunkovskii, *Vospominaniia*, 1:130.

31. Factory directors to Dzhunkovsky, December 20, 1905, in *Revoliutsiia 1905–1907 gg. v Rossii: Dokumenty i materialy. Vysshii pod"em revoliutsii*, 1:802.

32. Dzhunkovskii, *Vospominaniia*, 1:130.

33. Dzhunkovskii, *Vospominaniia*, 1:131–32.

34. Dzhunkovskii, *Vospominaniia*, 1:133–34.

35. Dzhunkovskii, *Vospominaniia*, 1:135; Mager, *Elizabeth*, 223; Warwick, *Ella*, 232–33.

36. Dzhunkovskii, *Vospominaniia*, 1:136.

37. *Moskovskii arkhiv*, 2:471.

Chapter 7. Learning the Ropes

1. Dzhunkovskii, *Vospominaniia*, 1:138.

2. An English translation of the Fundamental Laws is found in Dmytryshyn, *Imperial Russia*, 386–93.

3. Ascher, *Stolypin*, 141–42.

4. The best overall coverage of this period is to be found in the second volume of Ascher's *1905* and in his *Stolypin*, 97–207. A useful short summary of the problems facing Stolypin is Waldron, *Between Two Revolutions*. On political terrorism the best account is Geifman, *Thou Shalt Kill*. (The Stolypin land reform will be discussed in more detail below.)

5. For a more complete discussion of the governorship, its history and functioning, see Robbins, *The Tsar's Viceroys*.

6. Dzhunkovskii, *Vospominaniia*, 1:139 (my italics).

7. Dzhunkovskii, *Vospominaniia*, 1:155–56.

8. Dzhunkovskii, *Vospominaniia*, 1:231.

9. GARF, f. 826, op. 1, d. 114, "Zapiski . . . ob osmotre . . . goroda Klina," *l.* 2.

10. Dzhunkovskii, *Vospominaniia*, 1:165–68. The schedule planned for the tour can be found in GARF, f. 826, op. 1, d. 118, "Zametki Dzhunkovskogo i dr. materialy o poezdki po Moskovskoi gub. 1906 g.," *l.* 6.

11. Schneer, "The Markovo Republic," 104, 112, 114, 117.

12. Ryzhov's telegram is reproduced in Smirnov, *"Markovskaia respublika,"* 79.

13. Dzhunkovskii, *Vospominaniia*, 1:171–72; GARF, f. 826, op. 1, d. 117, "Dokladnaia zapiska Dzhunkovskogo Ministru vnutrennikh del o rezul'tatakh osmotra im goroda Podol'ska, Klinskogo, Volokolamskogo, Mozhaiskogo i Vereiskogo uezdov, 1906," *ll.* 4–5.

14. Smirnov, "*Markovskaia respublika*," 58.

15. Dzhunkovskii, *Vospominaniia*, 1: 172.

16. Dzhunkovskii, *Vospominaniia*, 1:171–73; Schneer, "The Markovo Republic," 118.

17. Dzhunkovskii, *Vospominaniia*, 1:173–74.

18. Dzhunkovskii, *Vospominaniia*, 1:174. The account of the peasants' actions in Smirnov, "*Markovskaia respublika*," contains no reference to these plans.

19. Dzhunkovskii, *Vospominaniia*, 1:65–66, 149.

20. Dzhunkovskii, *Vospominaniia*, 1:429–30.

21. F. V. Shlippe, Memoirs, 2:190 (Shlippe Collection, BAR).

22. "Kak zhil v Moskve i rabotal V. F. Dzhunkovskii," 3; Dzhunkovskii, *Vospominaniia*, 1:430.

23. Dzhunkovskii, *Vospominaniia*, 1:430–31. Dzhunkovsky's workday corresponds closely to those of other governors. See, Robbins, *The Tsar's Viceroys*, 47–53.

24. Dzhunkovskii, *Vospominaniia*, 1:501–2.

25. Dzhunkovskii, *Vospominaniia*, 1:437–38.

26. Dzhunkovskii, 1893–1897, *ll.* 254–55; Dzhunkovskii, 1898–1904, *ll.* 51–53. Mikhalkov's fate was a matter of concern for many years, and his death in 1915 pained Dzhun grievously. Dzhunkovskii, *Vospominaniia*, 3:85. See also Dunaeva, *Reformy politsii*, 51–52.

27. Dzhunkovskii, *Vospominaniia*, 1:433–35.

28. See for example, Dzhunkovskii, *Vospominaniia*, 1:186.

29. Dzhunkovskii, *Vospominaniia*, 1:436–37.

30. Dzhunkovskii, *Vospominaniia*, 1:240, 376.

31. Dzhunkovskii, *Vospominaniia*, 1:143–44; see also Thurston, *Liberal City*, 72.

32. Daly, *Watchful State*, 42.

33. Dzhunkovskii, *Vospominaniia*, 1:181–82.

34. Dzhunkovskii, *Vospominaniia*, 1:183.

Chapter 8. A Governor con Brio

1. Dzhunkovskii, *Vospominaniia*, 1:215–17, 236.

2. Dzhunkovskii, *Vospominaniia*, 1:693–94.

3. Dzhunkovskii, *Vospominaniia*, 1:298–300; *XX vek: Khronika. 1901–1910*, 421–22, citing stories in the newspaper *Moskovskie vedomosti*, April 11, 12, 1908.

4. Dzhunkovskii, *Vospominaniia*, 1:300–307. See also *Otchet Moskovskogo gubernskogo komiteta po okazaniiu pomoshchi postradvshim ot nadvodneniia v 1908 godu* (Moscow, 1909).

5. Zakharovo to Dzhun, June 15, 1908, and Lokhino to Dzhun, n.d., in GARF, f. 826, op. 1, d. 139, "Pis'ma krest'ian . . . Dzhunkovskomu s vyrazheniem blagodarnosti," *ll.* 1, 3.

6. See his annual report for 1910, in GARF, f. 826, op. 1, d. 107, "Otchety moskoskogo gubernatora," *ll.* 88–89.

7. Dzhunkovskii, *Vospominaniia*, 1:154. Dzhunkovsky recalls the strike beginning on April 19, 1906, but newspaper reports show that it began earlier. *XX vek: Khronika, 1901–1910*, 306, citing *Russkie vedomosti*, April 12, 13, 1906.

8. Dzhunkovskii, *Vospominaniia*, 1:217–18.

9. Dzhunkovskii, *Vospominaniia*, 1:361–62, 385–86.

10. Dzhunkovskii, *Vospominaniia*, 1:535–37.

11. In his annual report to the emperor for 1911 Dzhunkovsky's account of these events and their consequences says almost nothing of his own actions, citing instead the heroism and sacrifice of the prison guards. GARF, f. 826, op. 1, d. 107, *ll.* 119–29. See also F. V. Shlippe's account based on a recalled conversation he had with Dzhunkovsky at the time. Shlippe memoirs (BAR), 110; *XX vek: Khronika 1911–1920*, 9, citing the newspaper *Golos Moskvy*, January 22, 1911.

12. For a discussion of accommodation and conflict between Moscow's elected officials and the central authorities, see Thurston, *Liberal City*. Although Thurston's paradigm sets liberal Moscow against the autocratic state, his account shows that serious state-city conflict occurred rather late. Significant, too, is the fact that Dzhunkovsky's name does not appear in Thurston's book, underlining his noninvolvement in city political struggles.

13. Dzhunkovskii, *Vospominaniia*, 1:383–84.

14. Rozental', *Moskva na pereput'e*, 50.

15. The observation was Woody Allen's.

16. Dzhunkovskii, *Vospominaniia*, 1:223–25.

17. Dzhunkovskii, *Vospominaniia*, 1:391–94; *XX vek: Khronika 1901–1910*, 469–70, citing *Golos Moskvy*, April 28, 1909.

18. Dzhunkovskii, *Vospominaniia*, 1:472.

19. *100-letie Moskovskoi prakticheskoi akademii kommercheskikh nauk* (Moscow: Tipografiia t-vo I.D. Sytina, 1910).

20. Dzhunkovskii, *Vospominaniia*, 1:526; *XX vek: Khronika 1901–1910*, 551, citing *Russkie vedomosti*, December 17, 1910.

21. Dzhunkovskii, *Vospominaniia*, 3:124–224.

22. Dzhunkovskii, *Vospominaniia*, 1:455.

23. Dzhunkovskii, *Vospominaniia*, 1:490.

24. Dzhunkovskii, *Vospominaniia*, 1:483–84.

25. Rosssiiskii gosudarstvennyi arkhiv sotsial'no-politicheskoi istorii (RGASPI), f. 2 (V.I. Lenin) op. 1, d. 24038, "V upravlenie delami Sovet narodnykh komiissarov," *ll.* 1–2.

26. In all likelihood the Georgians were released along with the other "politicals" freed after the promulgation of the October Manifesto, but Dzhunkovsky does not mention any request on the part of Sumbatov-Iuzhin.

27. Bulatsel', *Bor'ba za pravdu*, 173.

28. Dzhunkovskii, *Vospominaniia*, 1:177–78; Daly, *Watchful State*, 39–40.

29. Dzhunkovskii, *Vospominaniia*, 1:325, 464–65, 468–69.

30. Dzhunkovskii, *Vospominaniia*, 1:606.

31. Ascher, *Stolypin*, 376.

32. GARF, f. 826, op. 1, d. 107, *ll.* 85–86.

33. Dzhunkovskii, *Vospominaniia*, 1:609.

34. Dzhunkovskii, *Vospominaniia*, 2:94.

35. Dzhunkovskii, *Vospominaniia*, 1:313.

36. Dzhunkovskii, *Vospominaniia*, 1:343.

Chapter 9. Provincial Politics

1. See his comments on Konstantin Pobedonostsev, the chief ideologist of the reign of Alexander III and tutor of Nicholas II, in Dzhunkovskii, *Vospominaniia*, 1:209.

2. Dzhunkovskii, *Vospominaniia*, 2:243.

3. Dzhunkovskii, *Vospominaniia*, 1:132, 202–3. In the course of the elections Dzhunkovsky did try to make clear the government's concerns and program.

4. Dzhunkovskii, *Vospominaniia*, 1:242–43, 229–30.

5. In 1906 there were only three peasant delegates in the Moscow provincial zemstvo assembly. The same held true for 1912; see Vazhenin and Galkin, *Moskovskoe zemstvo*, 16. The nobility was dominant in other provincial zemstvos as well: see for example, Catherine Evtuhov, *Portrait of a Russian Province: Economy, Society, and Civilization in Nineteenth-Century Nizhnii Novgorod* (Pittsburgh: University of Pittsburgh Press, 2011), 147.

6. An excellent discussion of zemstvo appeals to the Senate is Thomas Fallows, "The Zemstvo and the Bureaucracy, 1890–1904," in Emmons and Vucinich, *The Zemstvo in Russia*, 184–93. For an earlier period, see Iartsev, *Senat i zemstvo*. For a general overview of governor-zemstvo relations, see Robbins, *The Tsar's Viceroys*, 155–66. For a short, useful survey of the zemstvos, see Walkin, *Pre-revolutionary Russia*, 153–80.

7. Dzhunkovskii, *Vospominaniia*, 1:94.

8. Vazhenin and Galkin, *Moskovskoe zemstvo*, 26.

9. Dzhunkovskii, *Vospominaniia*, 1:183–84.

10. Dzhunkovskii, *Vospominaniia*, 1:191–92.

11. GARF, f. 826, op. 1, d. 107, "Otchety Moskovskogo gubernatora," *ll.* 7–8.

12. Dzhunkovskii, *Vospominaniia*, 1:194.

13. Dzhunkovskii, *Vospominaniia*, 1:194–95. For a discussion of the rightward shift in zemstvo politics after the revolution of 1905, see Roberta T. Manning, "Zemstvo and Revolution: The Onset of Gentry Reaction, 1905–1907," in Haimson, *Rural Russia*, 30–66.

14. Mehlinger and Thompson, *Count Witte*, 76–77.

15. Ascher, *Stolypin*, 112–13.

16. For a clear statement of the Slavophile position, see Konstantin Aksakov, "On the Internal State of Russia," in *Russian Intellectual History: An Anthology*, ed. Marc Raeff (Amherst, NY: Humanity Books, 1999), 230–51.

17. A useful summary and analysis of Shipov's political views can be found in Schapiro, *Rationalism and Nationalism*, 143–69. George Fischer gives an interpretation of Shipov that stresses his ties to Slavophilism, in *Russian Liberalism: From Gentry to Intelligentsia* (Cambridge, MA: Harvard University Press, 1958), 23–26, 177–89. See also Yaney, *The Systematization of Russian Government*, 365–66.

18. Dzhunkovskii, *Vospominaniia*, 1:265 (citing his annual report for 1907). On the radical activities of the Third Element in the period of the first Russian revolution, see Manning, *Crisis of the Old Order*, 193–94.

19. He believed he was empowered to do so by Article 95 of the zemstvo statute.

20. Dzhunkovskii, *Vospominaniia*, 1:358, 360–61.

21. Dzhunkovskii, *Vospominaniia*, 1:420–21. Shipov believed that in this matter Dzhunkovsky was pressured by "the reactionary element" headed by Alexander Samarin; see Shipov, *Vospominaniia*, 535.

22. Dzhunkovskii, *Vospominaniia*, 1:267–69 (my italics).

23. Dzhunkovskii, *Vospominaniia*, 1:271.

24. Dzhunkovskii, *Vospominaniia*, 1:283.

25. Dzhunkovskii, *Vospominaniia*, 1:287.

26. Dzhunkovskii, *Vospominaniia*, 1:461.

27. Dzhunkovskii, *Vospominaniia*, 1:616.

28. Dzhunkovskii, *Vospominaniia*, 1:194.

29. Dzhunkovskii, *Vospominaniia*, 1:187. Samarin was two years short of the time in rank normally required for these promotions.

30. Wcislo, *Reforming Rural Russia*, 257; Dzhunkovsky quotes the address without comment, in Dzhunkovskii, *Vospominaniia*, 1:279.

31. Dzhunkovskii, *Vospominaniia*, 1:211–12.

32. Dzhunkovskii, *Vospominaniia*, 1:355–57.

33. Annual report for 1909, GARF, f. 826, op. 1, d. 107, *ll.* 68–70.

34. Dzhunkovskii, *Vospominaniia*, 1:456.

35. Dzhunkovskii, *Vospominaniia*, 1:461. Statistics on the expenditures of the Moscow zemstvo are provided in Vazhenin and Galkin, *Moskovskoe zemstvo*, 164–65. For an excellent survey of developments in zemstvo politics nationwide that puts events in Moscow province in a larger context, see Ruth D. MacNaughton and Roberta T. Manning, "The Crisis of the Third of June System and Political Trends in the Zemstvos, 1907–1914," in Haimson, *The Politics of Rural Russia*, 184–218.

36. Dzhunkovskii, *Vospominaniia*, 1:462–63.

37. S. V. Shelokhaev, introduction to the 2007 edition of Shipov's memoirs; Shipov, *Vospominaniia*, 17–24.

38. Dzhunkovskii, *Vospominaniia*, 1:551–53. The memoirs reproduce the entire circular No. 5/1341.

39. Speech made on May 10, 1907, quoted in Ascher, *Stolypin*, 157.

40. On the decree, see Yaney, *The Urge to Mobilize*, 257–59.

41. Dzhunkovskii, *Vospominaniia*, 1:184.

42. Dzhunkovskii, *Vospominaniia*, 1:213.

43. Dzhunkovskii, *Vospominaniia*, 1:214; Annual report for 1907, GARF, f. 826, op. 1, d. 107, *l.* 22.

44. GARF, f. 826, op. 1, d. 107, *l.* 20.

45. Reports for 1906, 1907, and 1908, GARF, f. 826, op. 1, d. 107, *ll.* 10–11, 20, 36–38.

46. Dzhunkovskii, *Vospominaniia*, 1:322.

47. Dzhunkovskii, *Vospominaniia*, 1:323–24.

48. Dzhunkovsky composed his recollections in Russia during the 1920s; Shlippe wrote in exile in the 1940s.

49. Dzhunkovskii, *Vospominaniia*, 1:432.

50. Shlippe, Memoirs, 88, 109–10 (BAR).

51. Dzhunkovskii, *Vospominaniia*, 1:618.

52. Dzhunkovskii, *Vospominaniia*, 1:395–96.

53. Annual reports for 1909 and 1911, GARF, f. 826, op. 1, d. 107, *ll.* 70, 110.

54. Report for 1911, GARF, f. 826, op. 1, d. 107, *l.* 109.

55. On Stolypin's proposed provincial and local government reforms, see Ascher, *Stolypin*, 219–27; Waldron, *Between Two Revolutions*, 82–86; Wcislo, *Reforming Rural Russia*, 210–27; Weissman, *Reform in Tsarist Russia*, 124–47.

56. Dzhunkovskii, *Vospominaniia*, 1:340.

57. Wcislo, *Reforming Rural Russia*, 274.

58. Dzhunkovskii, *Vospominaniia*, 1:380–81.

59. Dzhunkovskii, *Vospominaniia*, 1:390.

60. Dzhunkovskii, *Vospominaniia*, 1:550–51.

61. Kassow, *Students, Professors*, 353–66.

62. Ascher, *Stolypin*, 327–62.

63. Dzhunkovskii, *Vospominaniia*, 1:602–3.

64. Dzhunkovskii, *Vospominaniia*, 1:607.

65. Dzhunkovskii, *Vospominaniia*, 1:618–19. Dzhunkovsky makes no mention of the grand duchess at this point. But she began to express her concerns about Rasputin to Nicholas and Alexandra about this time. Warwick, *Ella*, 264–67; Mager, *Elizabeth*, 249–60.

Chapter 10. National Pageantry

1. Dzhunkovskii, *Vospominaniia*, 1:565–66, 589.

2. Dzhunkovskii, *Vospominaniia*, 1:403. See also Wortman, *Scenarios*, 2:424.

3. Dzhunkovskii, *Vospominaniia*, 1:553. See also *XX vek, Khronika 1911–1920*, 15, citing *Golos Moskvy*, February 20, 1911, and *Russkoe slovo*, February 20, 1911.

4. Dzhunkovskii, *Vospominaniia*, 1:660–67.

5. Wortman, *Scenarios*, 2:431; Bogdanovich, *Tri poslednikh samoderzhtsa*, 509–10; Rozental', *Moskva na pereput'e*, 139.

6. Dzhunkovskii, *Vospominaniia*, 1:650–51.

7. Dzhunkovskii, *Vospominaniia*, 1:674.

8. Dzhunkovskii, *Vospominaniia*, 1:679.

9. Wortman, *Scenarios*, 2:501.

10. Dmitrii Gutnov, "Moskovskii gubernator V. F. Dzhunkovskii i organizatsiia iubileinykh borodinskikh torzhestv 1912 g.," at http://gutnov.ucoz.ru/publ/. A clip from the movie about the battle of Borodino can be viewed at this site.

11. Dzhunkovskii, *Vospominaniia*, 2:6–9.

12. Dzhunkovskii, *Vospominaniia*, 2:11.

13. Dzhunkovskii, *Vospominaniia*, 2:17–19.

14. Dzhunkovskii, *Vospominaniia*, 2:19, 24–25.

15. Dzhunkovskii, *Vospominaniia*, 2:27–28.

16. Dzhunkovskii, *Vospominaniia*, 2:34–35.

17. The monument Nicholas visited was only a temporary structure, because the one originally sent was lost at sea. The permanent monument *Aux morts de la grande Armée* was finally put in place in 1913.

18. Dzhunkovskii, *Vospominaniia*, 2:35–37.

19. Dzhunkovsky believed that Adrianov had learned his lesson, but others felt that the celebrations had a forced character. Dzhunkovskii, *Vospominaniia*, 2:41; Rozental', *Moskva na pereput'e*, 140–41.

20. Wortman, *Scenarios*, 2:436–38.

21. Wortman, *Scenarios*, 435. Dzhunkovsky cites the speech without comment. Dzhunkovskii, *Vospominaniia*, 2:42.

22. Dzhunkovskii, *Vospominaniia*, 2:63.

23. Dzhunkovskii, *Vospominaniia*, 1:628–29; Kokovtsov, *Iz moego proshlogo*, 2:17–38; Pares, *Fall of the Russian Monarchy*, 147; Smith, *Rasputin*, 254–58.

24. The numbers of killed and wounded in the Lena massacre are still unresolved. For the best discussion available, see Melancon, *The Lena Goldfields Massacre*, 101–10.

25. For a thorough discussion of the public's reaction and its significance, see Melancon, "Unexpected Consensus."

26. Abraham, *Alexander Kerensky*, 55.

27. Dzhunkovskii, *Vospominaniia*, 1:644.

28. Melancon calls Treshchenkov the "evil genius" of the event, the man responsible for the shootings. *The Lena Goldfields Massacre*, 91.

29. Figes, *People's Tragedy*, 243–44. For a useful discussion of the Beilis case and the role of the secret police, see Ruud and Stepanov, *Fontanka 16*, 247–73.

30. Ruud and Stepanov show he was aware of the case, *Fontanka 16*, 273.

31. Smirnov, *Gosudarstvennaia Duma*, 443.

32. A useful English-language biography of Malinovsky is Elwood, *Roman Malinovsky* (for his early years, see 11–25). The most complete study is Rozental', *Provokator Roman Malinovskii*.

33. *Padenie*, 5:82–83; *Delo provokatora Malinovskogo*, 189–92; Dzhunkovskii, *Vospominaniia*, 2:78–79.

34. Martynov, *Moia sluzhba*, 232–33. See also his testimony in *Delo provokatora Malinovskogo*, 130.

35. Beletsky in *Padenie*, 3:280; Beletsky in *Delo provokatora Malinovskogo*, 106–7.

36. Daly, *Watchful State*, 151; Dunaeva, *Reformy politsii*, 229–33; Rozental', *Provokator Roman Malinovskii*, 145.

37. Robbins, *Tsar's Viceroys*, 193–96.

38. Martynov, *Moia sluzhba*, 232.

39. Dzhunkovskii, *Vospominaniia*, 1:403–5.

40. Dzhunkovskii, *Vospominaniia*, 2:84, 96. On Kislovodsk, see Baedeker, *Russia with Teheran*, 461–62.

Chapter 11. Celebration and Reform

1. Dzhunkovskii, *Vospominaniia*, 2:96–97.

2. Dzhunkovskii, *Vospominaniia*, 1:633.

3. Daly, *Watchful State*, 136–37; Lieven, *Nicholas II*, 182–83.

4. Kurlov, *Gibel' imperatorskoi Rossii*, 156–59; Kokovtsov, *Iz moego proshlogo*, 2:74–75.

5. Kurlov, *Gibel' imperatorskoi Rossii*, 158.

6. Daly, *Watchful State*, 6.

7. Dzhunkovskii, *Vospominaniia*, 2:97.

8. This brief and, I fear, unsatisfactory outline of the system of security policing in late imperial Russia is derived from Daly's magisterial two-volume study *Autocracy under Siege* and *The Watchful State*; Iain Lauchlan's *Russian Hide-and-Seek*; and relevant articles in *Gosudarstvennost' Rossii*. A useful example of the resentment felt by regular gendarmes toward their counterparts in the Department of Police can be found in the article by D. A. Pravnikov, "Korpus zhandarmov i okhrannye otdeleniia," published by V. V. Khutarev-Garnishevskii, in "Zhandarmeriia i okhranka v pravlenie Nikolaia II," *Istoricheskii arkhiv*, no. 4 (2009): 83–96.

9. Dzhunkovskii, *Vospominaniia*, 2:96–97.

10. Dzhunkovskii, *Vospominaniia*, 2:97–99.

11. Dzhunkovskii, *Vospominaniia*, 2:105.

12. Gosudarstvennyi tsentral'nyi teatral'nyi muzei imeni A.A. Bakhrushina (GTsTM), f. 91 (V. F. Dzhunkovskii), d. 59, "Adres V. F. Dzhunkovskomu ot artistov Malogo teatra," *l.* 1; Dzhunkovskii, *Vospominaniia*, 2:101.

13. Dzhunkovskii, *Vospominaniia*, 2:101–3; *XX vek: Khronika 1911–1920*, 127, citing stories in *Golos Moskvy* and *Moskovskie vedomosti*, January 22–23, 1913.

14. Dzhunkovskii, *Vospominaniia*, 2:103–4.

15. Dzhunkovskii, *Vospominaniia*, 2:106–7.

16. Dzhunkovskii, *Vospominaniia*, 2:109–10.

17. Dzhunkovskii *Vospominaniia*, 2:112. Dzhunkovsky's last days in Moscow were covered by *Golos Moskvy* on January 26, 29, 31, February 5, 1913, see *XX vek: Khronika 1911–1920*, 127–29.

18. "Gubernator i obshchestvo," *Utro Rossii*, February 1, 1913, quoted in both Avrekh, *Tsarizm i IV Duma*, 283, and Daly, *Watchful State*, 137.

19. *Vestnik Evropy* 48 (February 1913): 376–77.

20. Dzhunkovskii, *Vospominaniia*, 2:116, 122.

21. Dzhunkovskii, *Vospominaniia*, 2:122–23.

22. Dzhunkovskii, *Vospominaniia*, 2:117.

23. To get a sense of this, the reader can thumb through the pages of Alexandra Bogdonovich's gossipy diary, *Tri poslednikh samoderzhtsa*, or consult the splendid work by William C. Fuller Jr., *The Foe Within*.

24. Quoted in Dzhunkovskii, *Vospominaniia*, 2:123–24.

25. Dzhunkovsky quotes the feuilleton by I. Lopatin in his memoirs. Dzhunkovskii, *Vospominaniia*, 2:125.

26. *Den'*, March 3, 1913.

27. Dzhunkovskii, *Vospominaniia*, 2:117–22, 126.

28. Dzhunkovskii, *Vospominaniia*, 2:134.

29. Dzhunkovskii, *Vospominaniia*, 2:135–36.

30. Dzhunkovskii, *Vospominaniia*, 2:138.

31. Wortman, *Scenarios*, 2:459–66.

32. Wortman, *Scenarios*, 2:459–60.

33. Dzhunkovskii, *Vospominaniia*, 2:148.

34. M. V. Rodzianko, *The Reign of Rasputin: An Empire's Collapse*, repr. (Gulf Breeze, FL: Academic International Press, 1973), 75–77.

35. Dzhunkovskii, *Vospominaniia*, 2:155–56.

36. The question of hooliganism and its social significance is thoroughly examined and analyzed by Joan Neuberger, *Hooliganism: Crime, Culture and Power in St. Petersburg, 1900–1914* (Berkeley: University of California Press, 1993).

37. Dzhunkovskii, *Vospominaniia*, 2:159–62.

38. Dzhunkovskii, *Vospominaniia*, 2:178–81; Dunaeva, *Reformy politsi*, 159–61. On the tension between the secret police and the army, see Fuller, *Civil-Military Conflict*, 212–18.

39. Dzhunkovskii, *Vospominaniia*, 2:177–78; Daly, *Watchful State*, 139–40.

40. Pares, *Fall of the Russian Monarchy*, 281.

41. Dzhunkovskii, *Vospominaniia*, 2:163; Daly, *Watchful State*, 143.

42. Dzhunkovskii, *Vospominaniia*, 2:163.

43. Dzhunkovskii, *Vospominaniia*, 2:163–76.

44. Peregudova, *Politicheskii*, 154–66.

45. Mager, *Elizabeth*, 257–58.

46. Dzhunkovskii, *Vospominaniia*, 2:187–91.

47. Wortman, *Scenarios*, 2:475.

48. Dzhunkovskii, *Vospominaniia*, 2:200.

49. Dzhunkovskii, *Vospominaniia*, 2:201. Governor Stremoukhov recalled the events in Kostroma in almost the same spirit as "among the brightest days of my life." "The Administrative Structure of Imperial Russia: A Governor's Perspective," *Studies in Russian History* 53, no. 3 (Winter 2014–2015): 19.

50. Dzhunkovskii, *Vospominaniia*, 2:202.

51. Dzhunkovskii, *Vospominaniia*, 2:207–15; Wortman, *Scenarios*, 2:477–79.

52. Wortman, *Scenarios*, 2:477–80; Massie, *Nicholas and Alexandra*, 239.

Chapter 12. A Gendarme Manqué?

1. Dzhunkovskii, *Vospominaniia*, 2:215.

2. Dzhunkovskii, *Vospominaniia*, 2:217–18; Daly, *Watchful State*, 140–41.

3. Dzhunkovskii, *Vospominaniia*, 2:222–23.

4. Dzhunkovskii, *Vospominaniia*, 2:230–33; Ruud and Stepanov, *Fontanka 16*, 288–89.

5. According to his memoirs, Dzhunkovsky left St. Petersburg on June 11, 1913, passing through Moscow on his way to Kursk to visit the Evreinovs. He returned to the capital on June 24. Dzhunkovskii, *Vospominaniia*, 2:221–22. A letter from his sister dated June 16, 1913, indicates that he was in Kursk at the time. GARF, f. 826, op. 1, d. 539, "Pis'ma Dzhunkovskoi, E. F. Dzhunkovskomu V.F. 29 fev. 1913–30 dek. 1915," *l.* 16.

6. Dzhunkovsky to Beletsky, June 24, 1913, no. 824, GARF, f. 270 (Kantseliariia . . . V. F. Dzhunkovskogo), op. 1, d. 48, "O Ekaterine Nikolaevne Iudkevich, po pervomu braku Shornikovoi," *l.* 3.

7. Dzhunkovsky to Shcheglovitov, June 25, 1913, no. 838, GARF, f. 270, op. 1, d. 48, *ll.* 6–7.

8. Kokovtsov, *Iz moego proshlogo*, 2:158.

9. Kokovtsov, *Iz moego proshlogo*, 2:158–60.

10. Many of the dates relating to the Shornikova affair are uncertain. The only precise dates I found were those in Dzhunkovsky's memoir and documents in the archive of his chancellery, GARF, f. 270.

11. Kokovtsov, *Iz moego proshlogo*, 2:160–61; Levin, "The Shornikova Affair," 14.

12. Statement of Shornikova, July 5, 1913, GARF, f. 270, op. 1, d. 48, *l.* 12.

13. The procurator's conclusions of July 9, 1913, and the Senate's decision are found in GARF, f. 270, op. 1, d. 48, *ll.* 18–19; Levin, "The Shornikova Affair," 15; Daly, *Watchful State*, 149.

14. Dzhunkovskii, *Vospominaniia*, 1:229.

15. *Padenie*, 5:88.

16. Dzhunkovskii, *Vospominaniia*, 1:229; Dzhunkovskii, *Vospominaniia*, 3:541–42.

17. At the time of his visit to Paris, Dzhunkovsky asked the Foreign Department not to send agents to accompany him. Document no. 1561, addressed to S. P. Beletsky, dated October 7/20, 1913, Hoover Institution Archives, Okhrana Collection, XXVd, reel 335.

18. Dzhunkovskii, *Vospominaniia*, 2:242–47.

19. Dzhunkovskii, *Vospominaniia*, 2:219.

20. Dzhunkovskii, *Vospominaniia*, 2:159.

21. Dzhunkovskii, *Vospominaniia*, 2:157.

22. In his memoirs P. P. Stremoukhov recounts an incident where Dzhun took to task an officer who went overboard on security matters during the tercentennial. "Vse v proshlom," GARF, f. R-6546 (P. P. Stremoukhov), op. 1, d. 3, "Moia gubernatorskaia deiatel'nost,'" *ll.* 274–75.

23. Dzhunkovskii, *Vospominaniia*, 2:262.

24. Daly, *Watchful State*, 4.

25. On the activities of Burtsev, the "Sherlock Holmes of the Revolution," see Robert Henderson, *Vladimir Burtsev and the Struggle for a Free Russia: A Revolutionary in the Times of Tsarism and Bolshevism* (London: Bloomsbury, 2017), esp. 135–63.

26. Daly, *Watchful State*, 142. The most thorough recent study of perlustration is Izmozhik, *"Chernye kabinety."*

27. Dzhunkovskii, *Vospominaniia*, 2:274.

28. GARF, f. 270, op. 1, dd. 12, 13, "Rassledovaniia sobytii politicheskogo, khoziaistvennogo i bytogo kharaktera vyiavlennykh iz perliustrirovannykh pisem."

29. Dzhunkovskii, *Vospominaniia*, 2:274. After the February revolution Dzhunkovsky was questioned vigorously about "perlustration" by the Provisional Government's Investigative Commission.

30. Dzhunkovskii, *Vospominaniia*, 2:290.

31. Dzhunkovskii, *Vospominaniia*, 2:290–91. When Dzhunkovsky was arrested in 1918 and during his trial a year later, numerous people came forward to give testimony on his behalf, citing many cases where he had secured the release of political prisoners and lightened their sentences.

32. Daly, *Watchful State*, 147.

33. Dzhunkovskii, *Vospominaniia*, 2:291.

34. Daly, *Watchful State*, 147–48.

35. GARF, f. 826, op. 1, d. 54, "Vospominaniia za 1914," *ll.* 57–67. (This material does not appear in the published version of the memoirs.)

36. Daly, *Watchful State*, 147.

37. Lauchlan, *Russian Hide-and-Seek*, 102.

38. Daly, *Watchful State*, 143.

39. Dzhunkovskii, *Vospominaniia*, 2:275.

40. Dzhunkovskii, *Vospominaniia*, 2:283–84; Daly, *Watchful State*, 143–44.

41. Elwood, *Roman Malinovsky*, 29.

42. Rodzianko in *Padenie*, 7:167; Rozental', *Provokator Roman Malinovskii*, 97.

43. Cited in Rozental', *Provokator Roman Malinovskii*, 94.

44. Cited, in Rozental', *Provokator Roman Malinovskii*, 97, 99.

45. Bonnell, *Roots of Rebellion*, 420.

46. *Rossiia 1913 god*, 311.

47. The Beletsky-Malinovsky "trysts" are marvelously described in Rozental', *Provokator Roman Malinovskii*, 101–3; the quotation from Zubatov is found in Daly, *Autocracy under Siege*, 86–87.

48. Elwood, *Roman Malinovsky*, 40.

49. *Delo provokatora Malinovskogo*, 199–201.

50. Dzhunkovskii, *Vospominaniia*, 2:79.

51. *Padenie*, 5:83; *Delo provokatora Malinovskogo*, 191.

52. Rozental', *Provokator Roman Malinovskii*, 145.

53. Dzhunkovskii, *Vospominaniia*, 2:79. In his memoirs Dzhunkovsky claims that "it never entered . . . [his] head" that X was Malinovsky.

54. *Padenie*, 5:83.

55. Dzhunkovskii, *Vospominaniia*, 2:307–8; Elwood, *Roman Malinovsky*, 44.

56. Dzhunkovskii, *Vospominaniia*, 2:79; Rozental', *Provokator Roman Malinovskii*, 147; Elwood, *Roman Malinovsky*, 45–46; Dunaeva, *Reformy politsii*, 233–35.

57. Charges discussed in Daly, *Watchful State*, 147.

58. A. P. Koznov, "Bor'ba bol'shevikov s podryvnymi aktsiami tsarskoi okhranki v 1910–1914 gg.," *Voprosy istorii KPSS* (September 1988): 71–72.

59. Elwood, "The Malinovskii Affair," 6–7.

60. Daly, *Watchful State*, 152. See also I. M. Dubinskii-Mukhadze, *Ordzhonikidze* (Moscow: Molodaia gvardiia, 1963), 97; Rozental', *Provokator Roman Malinovskii.*

61. Most notably in the works of "revisionist" historians who are concerned with the Rasputin story: see for example Platonov, *Ternovyi venets Rossii*, 197–98, 211; Platonov, *Zhizn' za tsaria*, 203. Works like these charge that Dzhunkovsky was a mason secretly conspiring against the tsarist regime.

62. Vladimir V. Khutarev-Garnishevskii argues that position strongly. See "Otdel'nyi korpus zhandarmov," 17–19, 24–25, and his article "Osinoe gnezdo provokatsii."

63. For her exhaustive discussion, see Dunaeva, *Reformy politsii*, 156–89, leading to her general conclusion: "despite the changes in the composition of the internal and external *agentura* that took place under Dzhunkovsky, and the changes in the methods of work with secret agents which he promoted, the direction of the activities of the organs of political investigation remained on the same basis as before" (89).

64. Lauchlan, *Russian Hide-and-Seek*, 336.

65. Lauchlan, *Russian Hide-and-Seek*, 102.

66. Daly, *Watchful State*, 163–64.

67. This observation is strengthened by considering the fate of the security organs protecting other authoritarian regimes. The Shah's Savak and Mubarak's Amn al-Dawala, more ruthless and armed with weapons and instruments of surveillance far more powerful than those commanded by the Okhrana, also failed to protect their masters.

68. This is an argument advanced forcefully by Haimson, "Social Stability in Urban Russia"; Haimson, "Revisited."

69. For a recent analysis of Russia on the eve of the Great War, see Dowler, *Russia in 1913*, especially his conclusions, 272–79.

70. Daly titles his chapter on Dzhunkovsky's time as head of internal security "A Moralist Running the Police Apparatus" (*Watchful State*, 136).

Chapter 13. Mission to Baku

1. *Rossiia 1913 god*, 404–5.

2. Jackson, *From Constantinople*, 25–26.

3. Mir Yusif Mir-Babyev, "Baku Baron Days: Foreign Investment in Azerbaijan's Oil," *Azerbaijan International* (Summer 2004): 82–85; *Rossiia 1913 god*, 43; on the Nobels, see Tolf, *The Russian Rockefellers*.

4. "Who Is Winning the Architecture Arms Race?" *New York Times Magazine* (October 12, 2013): 37–41.

5. Quoted in Tolf, *The Russian Rockefellers*, 40.

6. Audrey Altstadt-Mirhadi, "Baku: Transformation of a Muslim Town," in Hamm, *The City in Late Imperial Russia*, 284.

7. Baedeker, *Russia with Teheran*, 458.

8. For wages, see *Rossiia 1913 god*, 47, 313.

9. Joseph Stalin, "Reply to the Greetings of the Workers of the Chief Railway Workshops in Tiflis, June 8, 1926," *Works*, 8:183.

10. Martynov, "Otchet," 246. Martynov was Baku city commandant.

11. Shaumian to Lenin, May 30, 1914 in S. G. Shaumian, *Izbrannye*, 1:465. When Shaumian arrived in Baku in April he had expressed a low opinion of the oil workers (Shaumian to Lenin, April 17, 1914, in Shaumian, *Izbrannye*, 1:413), but now he found himself "pleasantly disappointed."

12. "Obshchie trebovaniia bakinskikh neftepromyshlennykh rabochikh," May 27, 1914, in *Rabochee dvizhenie v Azerbaidzhane*, 2:90–93.

13. Arutiunov, *Rabochee dvizhenie v Rossii*, 356.

14. Shaumian to Lenin, May 30, 1914, in Shaumian, *Izbrannye*, 1:460.

15. Arutiunov, *Rabochee dvizhenie v Rossii*, 356–57.

16. See the proclamations published in Popov, *Iz istorii*, 126–28. The compilers of Shaumian's writings ascribe all the proclamations of the strike committee to him. Shaumian, *Izbrannye*, 1:269–81.

17. Martynov, "Otchet," 250–55; A. Z. Myshlaevsky, telegram to I. L. Goremykin, June 28, 1914, in *Rabochee dvizhenie v Azerbaidzhane*, 2:229.

18. Goremykin telegram, June 27, 1914, in *Rabochee dvizhenie v Azerbaidzhane*, 2:223.

19. Myshlaevsky telegram, June 28, 1914, in *Rabochee dvizhenie v Azerbaidzhane*, 2:229.

20. Dzhunkovskii, *Vospominaniia*, 2:337.

21. Goremykin's report to Nicholas II, June 28, 1914, in *Rabochee dvizhenie v Azerbaidzhane*, 2:230–31.

22. Dzhunkovskii, *Vospominaniia*, 2:337. In the pages that follow, many documents will be cited from Dzhunkovsky's memoirs. They have been compared with other documentary collections and with originals in the archives. Dzhunkovsky's citations are accurate, and his memoirs are used for the greater convenience of the reader.

23. Dzhunkovskii, *Vospominaniia*, 2:337.

24. Dzhunkovsky reproduces the document in full, in Dzhunkovskii, *Vospominaniia*, 2:337–38.

25. Dzhunkovskii, *Vospominaniia*, 2:342.

26. Dzhunkovskii, *Vospominaniia*, 2:344.

27. Dzhunkovskii, *Vospominaniia*, 2:344–45.

28. Dzhunkovskii, *Vospominaniia*, 2:345–46 (proclamation, 346).

29. Jackson, *From Constantinople*, 26; Tolf, *The Russian Rockefellers*, 72–73; Dzhunkovskii, *Vospominaniia*, 2:347, 354–56; translation of an article that appeared in the Armenian newspaper *Akhali azri*, no. 6, July 18, 1914, found in Dzhunkovsky's archive at GARF, f. 826, op. 1, d. 320, "Stat'i (gazetnye vyrezki i vypiski iz gazet) o zabastovke na bakinskikh neftianykh promyslakh," *l.* 64.

30. Dzhunkovskii, *Vospominaniia*, 2:347.

31. Dzhunkovskii, *Vospominaniia*, 2:347.

32. Dzhunkovskii, *Vospominaniia*, 2:349.

33. Dzhunkovskii, *Vospominaniia*, 2:349–50.

34. Dzhunkovskii telegram, July 13, 1914, reproduced in Dzhunkovskii, *Vospominaniia*, 2:351.

35. Proclamation reproduced in Dzhunkovskii, *Vospominaniia*, 2:350.

36. Proclamation found in Popov, *Iz istorii*, 131–32.

37. Dzhunkovskii, *Vospominaniia*, 2:351–52.

38. Dzhunkovskii, *Vospominaniia*, 2:378–79.

39. Dzhunkovskii, *Vospominaniia*, 2:353.

40. Dzhunkovskii, *Vospominaniia*, 2:353–58. The quotations from Dzhunkovsky's speech and the responses of the oilmen that follow are taken from his memoirs. But they have been compared with the protocol of the session held in his archive at GARF, f. 826, op. 1, d. 314, "Protokol zasedaniia v g. Baku pod predsedatel'stvom Dzhunkovskogo po voprosu o prichinakh zabastovki na bakinskikh promyslakh i o merakh k ee prekrashcheniiu." This is a rare printed document that, to my knowledge, has been cited by only one source: Popov, *Iz istorii*. Popov found a copy of the protocol in the Baku archives.

41. Dzhunkovskii, *Vospominaniia*, 2:358–69.

42. Dzhunkovskii, *Vospominaniia*, 2:369.

43. Proclamation reproduced in Dzhunkovskii, *Vospominaniia*, 2:370–71.

44. Dzhunkovskii, *Vospominaniia*, 2:371; Dzhunkovskii, telegram to Goremykin, July 17, 1914, *Rabochee dvizhenie v Azerbaidzhane*, 2:373.

45. Dzhunkovskii, *Vospominaniia*, 2:371–72.

46. Proclamation in Popov, *Iz istorii*, 134.

47. Dzhunkovskii, *Vospominaniia*, 2:377–78.

48. Dzhunkovskii clipped and preserved various newspaper articles relating to the strike. On July 15 and 16, *Russkoe znamia* published articles demanding that Dzhunkovskii take strong measures against the strikers. GARF, f. 826, op. 1, d. 320, *ll.* 175, 204.

49. Dzhunkovskii, *Vospominaniia*, 2:379.

50. Cover letters to Krivoshein and Timashev, GARF, f. 826, op. 1, d. 310, "Pis'ma Goremykina i dr. lits Dzhunkovskomu . . . o zadachakh ego komandirovki v Baku . . . ," *ll.* 11, 12. Krivoshein's reply, October 20, is in GARF, f. 826, op. 1, d. 310, *l.* 13.

51. Dzhunkovsky to Timashev, October 22, 1914, at GARF, f. 826, op. 1, d. 307, "Perepiska Dzhunkovskogo . . . o zhilishchnykh usloviiakh rabochikh Bakinskikh neftianykh promyslov," *ll.* 6–9.

52. Dzhunkovskii, *Vospominaniia*, 2:380.

53. Baku mayor Bych to Dzhunkovsky, March 6, 1915, Dzhunkovsky to Minister of Transportation Sergei Rukhlov, March 10, 1915, Dzhunkovsky to Mayor Bych, March 12, 1914, Bych telegram to Dzhunkovsky, June 17, 1915, Dzhunkovsky to Ivan Borisov, director of the railroad department, June 19, 1915, all in GARF, f. 826, op. 1, d. 306, "Perepiska Dzhunkovskogo . . . o postroike v g. Baku vodoprovoda . . . ," *ll.* 1–7, 13–18.

54. Dzhunkovskii, *Vospominaniia*, 2:380.

Chapter 14. In War at Home

1. Dzhunkovskii, *Vospominaniia*, 2:381. The scenes Dzhunkovsky witnessed were played out all over the empire. See Colleen M. Moore, "'The Wine Is the State's and We Are the State's': Local Struggles over Prohibition during the Mobilization of 1914" (Paper presented at the 43rd Annual Convention of the Association for Slavic, East European, and Eurasian Studies, November 20, 2011, in Washington, DC).

2. Dzhunkovskii, *Vospominaniia*, 2:381–82.

3. Lincoln, *Passage*, 43.

4. Dzhunkovskii, *Vospominaniia*, 2:383.

5. This complex problem is examined by Lohr, *Nationalizing the Russian Empire* (for the initial riots and government reaction, 13–14).

6. Lincoln, *Passage*, 48–49.

7. Dzhunkovskii, *Vospominaniia*, 2:385.

8. Herlihy, *Alcoholic Empire*, 138.

9. Dzhunkovskii, *Vospominaniia*, 2:393.

10. A. Shingarev, as quoted in Florinsky, *End of the Russian Empire*, 44; Herlihy, *Alcoholic Empire*, 145.

11. Florinsky, *End of the Russian Empire*, 44.

12. Dzhunkovskii, *Vospominaniia*, 2:383.

13. Lincoln, *Passage*, 51–52.

14. Dzhunkovskii, *Vospominaniia*, 2:393–97.

15. Dzhunkovskii, *Vospominaniia*, 2:271, 399.

16. Dzhunkovskii, *Vospominaniia*, 2:402–3.

17. Lohr, *Nationalizing*, 10.

18. Dzhunkovskii, *Vospominaniia*, 2:398–99.

19. Proclamations quoted in Dzhunkovskii, *Vospominaniia*, 2:384.

20. In this chapter and in those that follow, general accounts of the course of the war at the front and behind the lines are based on various respected secondary accounts. These include Stone, *The Eastern Front*; Lincoln, *Passage*; Gatrell, *Russia's First World War*; Florinsky, *End of the Russian Empire*.

21. Andreeva, "Pribaltiiskie," 461–72.

22. Dzhunkovskii, *Vospominaniia*, 2:414.

23. Dzhunkovskii, *Vospominaniia*, 2:410.

24. Dzhunkovskii, *Vospominaniia*, 2:412–16; N. P. Kharlamov, "Zapiski biurokrata: Vospominaniia," in OR RGB, f. 261 (Izdatel'stvo M. i S. Sabashnikovykh), k. 20, d. 6, "Bor'ba s nemetskim zasil'em vo vremia russko-germanskoi voiny v 1914–1916 gg.," *ll.* 7–8.

25. Dzhunkovskii, *Vospominaniia*, 2:416–17; Lohr, *Nationalizing*, 15.

26. Kharlamov, "Zapiski," in OR RGB, f. 261, k. 20, d. 6, *l.* 7.

27. Dzhunkovskii, *Vospominaniia*, 2:418–20.

28. Lohr, *Nationalizing*, 16–17.

29. Maklakov's letter quoted in Dzhunkovskii, *Vospominaniia*, 2:432. See also Lohr, *Nationalizing*, 16–17.

30. See Wortman, *Scenarios*, 2:512–14.

31. Dzhunkovskii, *Vospominaniia*, 2:423–72; also GARF, f. 826, op. 1, d. 278.

32. Dzhunkovskii, *Vospominaniia*, 2:472.

33. Dzhunkovskii, *Vospominaniia*, 2:447–49.

34. Dzhunkovskii regarded this report as so valuable he copied the entire document into his memoirs. Dzhunkovskii, *Vospominaniia*, 2:501–15.

35. Dzhunkovskii, *Vospominaniia*, 2:535–41.

36. Lincoln, *Passage*, 118; Stone, *The Eastern Front*, 112; Root, *Battles East*, 121–22. The gas employed was Xylyl bromide, a nonlethal irritating agent. It had relatively little impact on the outcome of the battle since it promptly blew back on the Germans.

37. Lincoln, *Passage*, 119. For a more detailed account of the battle, see Stone, *The Russian Army*, 126–37.

38. Fuller, *The Foe Within*, esp. 1–2, 132–36. Fuller's superb book is the most thorough account of the Miasoedov affair and its consequences.

39. Fuller, *The Foe Within*, 159–72.

40. Fuller provides an excellent analysis of the spy mania, *The Foe Within*, 172–83.

41. Dzhunkovskii, *Vospominaniia*, 2:530.

42. Dunaeva, *Reformy politsii*, 238–41.

43. Lohr, *Nationalizing*, 125.

44. Dzhunkovskii, *Vospominaniia*, 2:523–25; Daly, *Watchful State*, 164; Lincoln, *Passage*, 108–9.

45. Tikhmenev's testimony before the Extraordinary Investigating Commission, in "Perepiska pravykh," 10:137.

Chapter 15. Riot, Rasputin, Ruin

1. In his memoirs Dzhunkovsky claimed that he undertook this surveillance in June 1914 at the behest of Interior Minister Maklakov, following an attempt on Rasputin's life. Dzhunkovskii, *Vospominaniia*, 2:330. Anastasia Dunaeva believes he began keeping a watch on Rasputin earlier (*Reformy politsii*, 245–46).

2. Dzhunkovskii, *Vospominaniia*, 2:551.

3. Dzhunkovskii, *Vospominaniia*, 2:556.

4. Dzhunkovskii, *Vospominaniia*, 2:553.

5. Quoted in Dunaeva, *Reformy politsii*, 257.

6. Dzhunkovsky states that he received the document on May 27 (*Vospominaniia*, 2:553), but Dunaeva shows that he got it on May 31 (*Reformy politsii*, 256–57).

7. Quoted in Dunaeva, *Reformy politsii*, 257.

8. The text of the report is quoted as presented in the published version of Dzhunkovsky's memoirs (*Vospominaniia*, 2:553–54). It contains the ellipsis to which the editors added this footnote: "An additional line and a half is struck out (2:554)." Dunaeva discovered the original Semenov report in the handwritten manuscript of the memoirs, in GARF, f. 826, op. 1, d. 52, *l.* 336. To the side of the deleted passage Dzhunkovsky wrote: "Leave out two lines" (*Ostavit' mesto dve stroki*). Dunaeva, *Reformy politsii*, 257–58. A photographic copy of the Semenov report is presented at the end of her

book. It shows clearly how Dzhunkovsky pasted over the words he found offensive. In presenting this important evidence, Dunaeva does not adequately explain how and why the Semenov document ended up in Dzhunkovsky's papers and not in the archive attached to Adrianov's letter of May 31, 1915, and why he covered up the "naughty bits." Was it simply his desire not to "shock posterity" (267)? Perhaps Dzhun took the report as a kind of insurance policy, a concrete proof he could present if his evidence were challenged. One other point might be made about the words *tsinichno* and *tsinichnye* that appear in the documents. These words are usually translated as "cynically" and "cynical" which makes no sense in the context. But according to *Slovar' inostrannykh slov*, 17th ed. (Moscow, 1988), 557, the synonyms are *nepristoinyi* (obscene) or *besstydnyi* (shameless).

9. Dunaeva, *Reformy politsii*, 258, citing a report from A. P. Martynov dated June 5, 1915, held in the *fond* of the Moscow *okhrannoe otdelenie*. GARF, f. 63, op. 47, d. 484, *l.* 50. Prudish Dzhunkovsky did not use this document in his memoirs but included a still later report from Martynov that left out the "piquant details."

10. Dunaeva, *Reformy politsii*, 258.

11. Lohr, *Nationalizing*, 31; Dzhunkovskii, *Vospominaniia*, 2:556.

12. Dzhunkovskii, *Vospominaniia*, 2:563; Lohr, *Nationalizing*, 42; Mager, *Elizabeth*, 281–82; Warwick, *Ella*, 279; Lincoln, *Passage*, 138.

13. The French government had requested that all persons in Russia who came from Alsace-Lorraine to be treated as French subjects.

14. Quoted in Lohr, *Nationalizing*, 44–45.

15. Lohr, *Nationalizing*, 31–54. See also Kir'ianov, "Maiskie besporiadki."

16. Massie, *Nicholas and Alexandra*, 314–15.

17. Quoted in Kharlamov, "Zapiski," OR RGB, f. 261, k. 20, d. 6, *l.* 63.

18. Lohr, *Nationalizing*, 40.

19. Quoted in Dzhunkovskii, *Vospominaniia*, 2:561.

20. Dzhunkovskii, *Vospominaniia*, 2:560.

21. Dzhunkovskii, *Vospominaniia*, 2:561; Lohr, *Nationalizing*, 35.

22. Dzhunkovskii, *Vospominaniia*, 2:567.

23. Dzhunkovskii, *Vospominaniia*, 2:563.

24. Dzhunkovskii, *Vospominaniia*, 2:568.

25. Dzhunkovsky's analysis of the meaning of the May riots is found in *Vospominaniia*, 2:566.

26. In his memoirs Dzhunkovsky cites a report he received from A. P. Martynov that confirmed many of the details concerning Rasputin and the Yar. Dzhunkovskii, *Vospominaniia*, 2:554–55. But Dunaeva has shown that while Dzhunkovsky ordered further reports from Moscow on May 31, none of them had arrived by June 1, and the one he cites was dated July 28, 1915. Dunaeva, *Reformy politsii*, 258–59.

27. Dzhunkovskii, *Vospominaniia*, 2:569.

28. Dzhunkovskii, *Vospominaniia*, 1:667.

29. Dzhunkovskii, *Vospominaniia*, 2:569.

30. Dzhunkovskii, *Vospominaniia*, 2:570–71.

31. *Dnevniki imperatora Nikolaia II* (Moscow, 1991), 531.

32. Smith, *Rasputin*, 375–77.

33. Smith, *Rasputin*, 380.

34. S. P. Beletsky claimed that he got this story from Rasputin himself. Beletskii, "Vospominaniia," 12:9.

35. Smith, *Rasputin*, 379–80.

36. Gatrell, *Russia's First World War*, 30–31; Lincoln, *Passage*, 140–43, 156–57. Gatrell gives a comprehensive treatment of the refugee question in his book *A Whole Empire Walking: Refugees in Russia during World War I* (Bloomington: Indiana University Press, 1999). See pages 17–20 for the impact of Russian defeats. On the reaction of the Council of Ministers, see *Prologue to Revolution*, 56–104.

37. Anan'ich, Ganelin, et al., *Krizis samoderzhaviia*, 551–52; Minister of War Sukhomlinov in-

formed the Council of Ministers of the creation of the Conference on May 19. The tsar confirmed its appointment on May 21. *Sovet ministrov*, 166, 393.

38. Anan'ich, Ganelin, et al., *Krizis samoderzhaviia*, 552–53; Lincoln. *Passage*, 191–92.

39. Pares, *Fall of the Russian Monarchy*, 262–63; Lincoln, *Passage*, 191–92.

40. *Sovet ministrov*, 176–77; Anan'ich, Ganelin, et al., *Krizis samoderzhaviia*, 553–54; Lincoln, *Passage*, 192–93; Kulikov, *Biurokraticheskaia elita*, 49–51.

41. Dzhunkovskii, *Vospominaniia*, 2:572–73

42. Anan'ich, Ganelin, et al., *Krizis samoderzhaviia*, 553; Kulikov, *Biurokraticheskaia elita*, 50.

43. Dzhunkovskii, *Vospominaniia*, 2:574.

44. Dzhunkovskii, *Vospominaniia*, 2:573–74.

45. Dzhunkovskii, *Vospominaniia*, 2:579–81.

46. Pares, *Fall of the Russian Monarchy*, 246; Dzhunkovskii, *Vospominaniia*, 2:581. Sabler was removed on July 4, Shcheglovitov on July 6.

47. Spiridovich, *Velikaia voina*, 159; Dzhunkovskii, *Vospominaniia*, 2:581.

48. Spiridovich, *Velikaia voina*, 159.

49. Lohr, *Nationalizing*, 48–49.

50. Rescript reproduced in Dzhunkovskii, *Vospominaniia*, 2:582; see also Pares, *Fall of the Russian Monarchy*, 247.

51. Dzhunkovskii, *Vospominaniia*, 2:586.

52. Dzhunkovskii, *Vospominaniia*, 2:597.

53. Lincoln, *Passage*, 189.

54. Dzhunkovskii, *Vospominaniia*, 2:599–600, 606.

55. Smirnov, *Gosudarstvennaia Duma*, 504, 505.

56. Smirnov, *Gosudarstvennaia Duma*, 508–13; Pares, *Fall of the Russian Monarchy*, 258–59.

57. Pares, *Fall of the Russian Monarchy*, 260; *Prologue to Revolution*, 29–32; Dzhunkovskii, *Vospominaniia*, 2:614.

58. Paul P. Gronsky and Nicholas J. Astrov, *The War and the Russian Government* (New York: Howard Fertig, 1973), 33–42.

59. Smirnov, *Gosudarstvennaia Duma*, 514.

60. For example, Kulikov, *Biurokraticheskaia elita*, 51; Smith, *Rasputin*, 378. See also Dunaeva, *Reformy politsii*, esp. 257–61, for a thorough discussion of this matter.

61. "Vstrecha v stavke," 179.

62. Alexandra to Nicholas, letter June 22, 1815, in Fuhrmann, *Correspondence*, 160–61.

63. Voeikov's memoir, *S tsarem i bez tsaria*, has little to say about Dzhunkovsky and does not mention any attempt by him to pass on a "vile, filthy paper." On the other hand Spiridovich claims that immediately after the Yar incident Adrianov rushed to St. Petersburg and reported on Rasputin's misbehavior to Maklakov and Dzhunkovsky. They then advised him to go to Tsarskoe Selo and bring this information directly to the tsar. According to Spiridovich, both he and Voeikov told Adrianov that an audience with the sovereign was not called for—the scandalous behavior of a drunken peasant in a restaurant was not something worthy of the tsar's attention. Instead, Adrianov should go back to Maklakov and Dzhunkovsky and have them bring the matter to the tsar, which according to Spiridovich, Maklakov did. All this was supposed to have taken place in late March and early April. Spiridovich, *Velikaia voina*, 111–12. Spiridovich seems to have mixed up dates and events. No other source claims that Maklakov reported to the tsar about Rasputin's misdeeds, although Nicholas's diaries indicate that he had received Maklakov on March 31. *Dnevniki imperatora Nikolaia II*, 521. Clearly, the whole Yar business is surrounded by confusion and "misremembrance."

64. In a letter sent to Alexandra on June 19, Nicholas wrote that he was sending "a tiny photo that Dzhunk. made here the last time" (Fuhrmann, *Correspondence*, 157). This suggests that he did not know the full extent of his wife's hostility to Dzhunkovsky at that time.

65. S. Iu. Vitte, *Vospominaniia*, 3 vols. (Moscow: Izdatel'stvo sotsial'no-politicheskoi literatury, 1960), 3:384–86; Fuhrmann, *Untold Story*, 158.

66. Dzhunkovskii, *Vospominaniia*, 2:532–33.

67. Dunaeva, *Reformy politsii*, 261–62; Fuhrmann, *Untold Story*, 158–61.

68. Dzhunkovskii, *Vospominaniia*, 3:18–19; Dunaeva, *Reformy politsii*, 363; Pares, *Fall of the Russian Monarchy*, 264. Sablin told his story to Pares.

69. In his memoirs Dzhunkovsky states that Iusupov was removed as Moscow's *glavnonachal'stvuiushchii* on July 20, 1915, remaining as commander of the Moscow military district (Dzhunkovskii, *Vospominaniia*, 2:609). This does not appear to be the case. He continued to wield power there until September 3 (*Sovet ministrov*, 274, 558).

70. Dzhunkovskii, *Vospominaniia*, 2:615–16.

71. This and the following summary are from Dzhunkovsky's memoirs citing the Duma's stenographic records (2:616–26).

72. Dzhunkovskii, *Vospominaniia*, 2:627.

73. Pares, *Fall of the Russian Monarchy*, 264.

74. Police report dated August 9, 1915, reproduced in Dunaeva, *Reformy politsii*, 254; also cited in Dzhunkovskii, *Vospominaniia*, 2:631.

75. Dzhunkovskii, *Vospominaniia*, 2:633.

Chapter 16. Finding Peace in War

1. Dzhunkovskii, *Vospominaniia*, 2:633.

2. On Kerensky's activities, see Abraham, *Alexander Kerensky*, 90–91.

3. Dzhunkovskii, *Vospominaniia*, 2:633–34.

4. Dzhunkovskii, *Vospominaniia*, 2:634.

5. Stremoukhov, "Vse v proshlom," GARF, f. R-9579, op. 1, d. 4, *l.* 5.

6. Dzhunkovskii, *Vospominaniia*, 2:635–36; the original letter can be found in the personal papers of Nicholas II, GARF, f. 601, op. 1, d. 1246, *ll.* 1–3.

7. Lieven, *Nicholas II*, 213–14.

8. *Prologue to Revolution*, 76–77.

9. Also attributed, incorrectly it seems, to both the Chinese general Sun Tzu and the Italian statesman Machiavelli.

10. V. F. Dzhunkovskii, *Vospominaniia*, 3:20–21.

11. Dzhunkovskii, *Vospominaniia*, 2:637.

12. *Prologue to Revolution*, 129–30.

13. A useful summary of Guchkov's development and views is Gleason, *Alexander Guchkov*, 53–70.

14. Dzhunkovskii, *Vospominaniia*, 2:637.

15. Dzhunkovskii, *Vospominaniia*, 2:637.

16. Dzhunkovskii, *Vospominaniia*, 3:16.

17. Dzhunkovskii, *Vospominaniia*, 3:26.

18. *Moskovskie vedomosti*, September 23, 1915; Dzhunkovskii, *Vospominaniia*, 3:33–34, 40.

19. Dzhunkovskii, *Vospominaniia*, 3:36–38.

20. Alexandra to Nicholas, August 29, 1915, in Fuhrmann, *Correspondence*, 192.

21. Alexandra to Nicholas, September 10, 1915, in Fuhrmann, *Correspondence*, 224.

22. Alexandra to Nicholas, September 20, October 8, 1915, in Fuhrmann, *Correspondence*, 253–54, 268–69.

23. Alexandra to Nicholas, September 17, 1915, in Fuhrmann, *Correspondence*, 248.

24. Alexandra to Nicholas, November 1, 1915, in Fuhrmann, *Correspondence*, 282.

25. Alexandra to Nicholas, October 6, 1915, in Fuhrmann, *Correspondence*, 264.

26. Tikhmenev, *General Dzhunkovskii*, 3–16, 21–23; "Perepiska," 10:137.

27. Dzhunkovskii, *Vospominaniia*, 3:27–28, 35–36. The article appeared in the liberal daily *Russkie vedomosti*, September 27, 1915.

28. Dzhunkovskii, *Vospominaniia*, 3:41–42.

29. *Prologue to Revolution*, 76.

30. Stone, *Eastern Front*, 165–93.

31. As a consequence of the "Great Retreat," the Russians divided the Northwestern Front into a separate Northern Front, standing between the Germans and Riga and Petrograd, and a new Western Front in White Russia, initially composed of the First, Second, Third, Fourth. and Tenth Armies. Stone, *Eastern Front*, 186–87; Zalesskii, *Pervaia mirovaia voina*, 451–52.

32. Dzhunkovskii, *Vospominaniia*, 3:42–43.

33. Dzhunkovskii, *Vospominaniia*, 3:44.

34. Dzhunkovskii, *Vospominaniia*, 3:43–44.

35. Zalesskii, *Pervaia mirovaia voina*, 184–85, 207; Lincoln, *Passage*, 119; Stone, *Eastern Front*, 115–19.

36. Dzhunkovskii, *Vospominaniia*, 3:45–46.

37. Dzhunkovskii, *Vospominaniia*, 3:47–48.

38. Dzhunkovskii, *Vospominaniia*, 3:49.

39. Dzhunkovskii, *Vospominaniia*, 3:52–55.

40. Dzhunkovskii, *Vospominaniia*, 3:55, 58.

41. Dzhunkovskii, *Vospominaniia*, 3:58–60, 62, 68.

42. Dzhunkovskii, *Vospominaniia*, 3:68–69.

43. Dzhunkovskii, *Vospominaniia*, 3:75–79.

44. *Russkoe slovo*, January 8, 1916. Dzhunkovsky inserted the entire text into his memoirs, 3:90–92.

45. GARF, f. 826, op. 1, d. 540, "Pis'ma 3 ianv.—4 dek. 1916," *l.* 28 (italics in original).

46. Dzhunkovskii, *Vospominaniia*, 3:117–24.

47. Dzhunkovskii, *Vospominaniia*, 3:102, 105–6, 109, 116.

Chapter 17. In Dubious Battles

1. "French Memorandum to the 2nd Inter-Allied Conference at Chantilly, December 6, 1915," at http://www.firstworldwar.com/source/chantillymemo.htm/. See also Podorozhnyi, *Narochskaia operatsiia*, 6–7.

2. Quoted in Podorozhnyi, *Narochskaia operatsiia*, 8; Lincoln, *Passage*, 184–85.

3. Lincoln, *Passage*, 183.

4. Lincoln, *Passage*, 183–84.

5. Quoted in Podorozhnyi, *Narochskaia operatsiia*, 9.

6. Podorozhnyi, *Narochskaia operatsiia*, 10.

7. Podorozhnyi, *Narochskaia operatsiia*, 15.

8. Stone, *Eastern Front*, 228.

9. Podorozhnyi, *Narochskaia operatsiia*, 34.

10. Pares, *Fall of the Russian Monarchy*, 334.

11. Stone, *Eastern Front*, 224, 227–29.

12. Podorozhnyi, *Narochskaia operatsiia*, provides the only full-scale account and analysis of the battle; Stone, *Eastern Front*, 229–31, gives a good summary account; see also Lincoln, *Passage*, 185–86; Root, *Battles East*, 184–90. Other major sources include Zaionchkovskii, *Mirovaia voina*, 2:26–28; Knox, *With the Russian Army*, 2:404–11. Russian casualties are often estimated at 100,000. Podorozhnyi's lower figure of 78,000 (*Narochskaia operatsiia*, 150–52) is accepted by Stone, *Russian Army*, 236.

13. Dzhunkovskii, *Vospominaniia*, 3:225.

14. Dzhunkovskii, *Vospominaniia*, 3:227–28.

15. Dzhunkovskii, *Vospominaniia*, 3:231–35.

16. Dzhunkovskii, *Vospominaniia*, 3:235–42; Report of General Redko, April 1, 1916, no. 527, Rossiiskii gosudarstvennyi voenno-istoricheskii arkhiv [hereafter RGVIA], f. 2520 (8-ia Sibirskaia strelkovaia diviziia) op. 1., d. 86, "Prikazy, rasporiazheniia i perepiska so shtabami 3 Sibirskogo armeiskogo korpusa," *l.* 488. Specific orders to Dzhunkovsky for March 9, 12, 1916, can be found in RGVIA, f. 2520, op. 1, d. 21, "Operativnye prikazy po divizii," *ll.* 8, 12.

17. Dzhunkovskii, *Vospominaniia*, 3:244.

18. There is a point of confusion here: In his detailed report on the battle sent to General Redko on March 17, 1916, and included in his memoirs, Dzhunkovsky refers to the 31st Regiment, not the 30th (Dzhunkovskii, *Vospominaniia*, 3:247).

19. Dzhunkovskii, *Vospominaniia*, 3:247–48; Podorozhnyi, *Narochskaia operatsiia*, 143.

20. Dzhunkovskii, *Vospominaniia*, 3:248–49.

21. Dispatches of Zinevich, nos. 182 and 183, March 14, 1916, GARF, f. 826, op. 1, d. 359, "Doneseniia . . . Dzhunkovskomu, V.F. s opisaniem boev," *ll.* 24, 26. Italics in originals.

22. Dzhunkovskii, *Vospominaniia*, 3:249–51; RGVIA, f. 2520, op. 1, d. 132, "Zhurnal voennykh deistvii divizii, 28 fev.–31 okt. 1916," *ll.* 51–58; Podorozhnyi, *Narochskaia operatsiia*, 145.

23. Stone, *Russian Army*, 247–50.

24. The maxim is credited to Count Galeazzo Ciano.

25. Dzhunkovskii, *Vospominaniia*, 3:251.

26. The report is dated March 17, 1916. Dzhunkovskii, *Vospominaniia*, 3:251–59.

27. Dzhunkovskii, *Vospominaniia*, 3:258–59.

28. This report, dated March 20, 1916, is reproduced in Dzhunkovskii, *Vospominaniia*, 3:259–61.

29. Dzhunkovskii, *Vospominaniia*, 3:262–66.

30. Knox, *With the Russian Army*, 2:410.

31. Dzhunkovskii, *Vospominaniia*, 3:270–74; V Corps's Journal of Military Operations supports Dzhunkovskii, *Vospominaniia*, and Walter on this point. RGVIA, f. 2189 (5 armeiskii korpus), op. 1, d. 369, "Zhurnal voennikh deistvii, 1 mart–30 apr., 1916," *l.* 31. General Walter, according to General Knox, spoke English like an Englishman. Knox, *With the Russian Army*, 2:410.

32. Dzhunkovskii, *Vospominaniia*, 3:274.

33. Dzhunkovskii, *Vospominaniia*, 3:274.

34. Dzhunkovskii, *Vospominaniia*, 3:275, 284–85.

35. RGVIA, f. 409 (Posluzhnye spiski ofitserov), op. 1, dd. 147–521, "Ob uvol'nenii ot sluzhby General-Leitenanta Dzhunkovskogo," *ll.* 37–38.

36. Dzhunkovskii, *Vospominaniia*, 3:287. The original document, dated May 12, 1916, can be found in GARF, f. 826, op. 1, d. 6.

37. Dzhunkovskii, *Vospominaniia*, 3:290.

38. Dzhunkovskii, *Vospominaniia*, 3:285–87, 323; also N. A. Maklakov's letter dated July 28, 1916, quoted on 302–5; Evdokiia's letter dated December 29, 1915, GARF, f. 826, op. 1, d. 539, *l.* 140; Evdokiia's letters dated January 13, February 6, March 8, 1916, GARF, f. 826, op. 1, d. 540, *ll.* 12, 25, 52.

39. Florinsky, *End of the Russian Empire*, 117–22; Gatrell, *Russia's First World War*, 134, 145–46.

40. Kulikov, *Biurokraticheskaia elita*, 165–78; Pares, *Fall of the Russian Monarchy*, 307.

41. Finance Minister Petr Bark, quoted in Lieven, *Nicholas II*, 225.

42. Lieven, *Nicholas II*, 224; Lincoln, *Passage*, 299–300.

43. Paul Miliukov, *Political Memoirs, 1905–1917*, ed. Arthur P. Mendel, trans. Carl Goldberg (Ann Arbor: University of Michigan Press, 1967), 377.

44. For good summary of those details, see Lincoln, *Passage*, 306–8; Smith, *Rasputin*, 590–96.

45. Dzhunkovskii, *Vospominaniia*, 3:345.

46. Dzhunkovskii, *Vospominaniia*, 3:351.

47. Dzhunkovskii, *Vospominaniia*, 3:357.

48. Dzhunkovskii, *Vospominaniia*, 3:358–59.

49. Dzhunkovskii, *Vospominaniia*, 3:361–66.

50. Dzhunkovskii, *Vospominaniia*, 3:368–69.

51. Dzhunkovskii, *Vospominaniia*, 3:409; Zalesskii, *Pervaia mirovaia voina*, 510.

52. Dzhunkovskii, *Vospominaniia*, 3:394 (death of Rasputin); 395 (offer of governor-generalship); 400 (illness and death of his brother). Original documents on the offer of the governor-generalship and Dzhunkovsky's refusal are found in GARF, f. 826, op. 1, d. 373; telegrams on his brother's condition, in d. 877.

53. Dzhunkovskii, *Vospominaniia*, 3:396.

54. A solid and carefully reasoned investigation of the conspiracies against the tsar and the role of Prince Lvov is given in Lyandres, "Conspiracy and Ambition," esp. 112–21. See also Robinson, *Grand Duke Nikolai Nikolaevich*, 290–91.

55. Letter dated February 13, 1917, GARF, f. 826, op. 1, d. 541, "Pis'ma 13 ianv.–16 nov. 1917," *l.* 13.

56. Kokovtsov, *Iz moego proshlogo*, 2:339; Massie, *Nicholas and Alexandra*, 382–84.

57. Dzhunkovskii, *Vospominaniia*, 3:433–34.

58. Dzhunkovskii, *Vospominaniia*, 3:446.

Chapter 18. Red Flags at the Front

1. Order quoted in Dzhunkovskii, *Vospominaniia*, 3:446.

2. Dzhunkovskii, *Vospominaniia*, 3:447.

3. Dzhunkovskii, *Vospominaniia*, 3:453.

4. Dzhunkovskii, *Vospominaniia*, 3:454.

5. In retelling the events of the Russian revolution as they affected Dzhunkovsky, I have given generally accepted facts. The literature on the Russian revolution is voluminous, and it would be impossible to list all the sources for the story presented below. The secondary works I found particularly useful were Chamberlin, *The Russian Revolution*; Pipes, *Russian Revolution*; Figes, *People's Tragedy*; and Lincoln, *Passage*.

6. The materials recently discovered and presented by Lyandres, in *Fall of Tsarism* strongly suggest that plans for a coup against the tsar were well advanced before the disturbances that rocked the capital beginning on February 9, 1917, and escalating through the month. But events upstaged the conspirators and swept them along.

7. Pipes, *Russian Revolution*, 1:295.

8. Circular of the Minister of the Interior, March 5, 1917, in *Russian Provisional Government*, 1:243.

9. The full text of Order No. 1 can be found in *Russian Provisional Government*, 2:848–89. At the time Order No. 1 was issued, the fate of the monarchy had not been decided and the Provisional Government had not yet been formed, only a temporary committee of the State Duma existed. When the Provisional Government emerged, the requirement that the committee's orders be obeyed only when they did not conflict with those of the Soviet would apply to it as well.

10. Letter from Guchkov to General Alekseev in Chamberlin, *The Russian Revolution*, 1:435. For an insightful discussion of Provisional Government-Soviet relations. See also Pipes, *Russian Revolution*, 296.

11. Wildman, *Russian Imperial Army*, 1:228.

12. Wildman, *Russian Imperial Army*, 1:230. See also Dzhunkovskii, *Vospominaniia*, 3:466.

13. *Russian Provisional Government*, 2:853.

14. Dzhunkovskii, *Vospominaniia*, 3:459.

15. Dzhunkovskii, *Vospominaniia*, 3:456.

16. Dzhunkovskii, *Vospominaniia*, 3:464.

17. Dzhunkovskii, *Vospominaniia*, 3:453.

18. Dzhunkovskii, *Vospominaniia*, 3:465.

19. Dzhunkovskii, *Vospominaniia*, 3:471–73; on past conflicts with Shchepkin, see Dzhunkovskii, *Vospominaniia*, esp. 1:71, 73, 76, 78.

20. Wildman undertakes a thorough discussion in *Russian Imperial Army*, 1:246–47. See also Chamberlin, *The Russian Revolution*, 1:228–30.

21. Wildman, *Russian Imperial Army*, 1:261–62.

22. Dzhunkovskii, *Vospominaniia*, 3:468–69.

23. Wildman, *Russian Imperial Army*, 1:262–63.

24. Dzhunkovskii, *Vospominaniia*, 3:478–79.

25. Dzhunkovskii, *Vospominaniia*, 3:477.

26. Order of War Minister Guchkov, April 16, 1917, in *Russian Provisional Government*, 2:876–77.

27. Dzhunkovskii, *Vospominaniia*, 3:500. Compare Dzhunkovsky's account of his relations with the soldiers' assemblies to Wildman: "Little is known of the Second Army which was rather

small and hidden away in the Pinsk marshes, but there are some indications that as late as May, the committees there were not functioning well and were poorly informed of events." Wildman, *Russian Imperial Army*, 1:276.

28. Dzhunkovskii, *Vospominaniia*, 3:486.

29. Dzhunkovskii, *Vospominaniia*, 3:497.

30. Dzhunkovskii, *Vospominaniia*, 3:499.

31. Dzhunkovskii, *Vospominaniia*, 3:519, 527. Gurko's order of April 23, 1917, is found in *Russian Provisional Government*, 2:903.

32. *Russian Provisional Government*, 2:1077–78.

33. *Russian Provisional Government*, 2:1045–46.

34. *Russian Provisional Government*, 2:1058.

35. *Russian Provisional Government*, 2:1098.

36. Explanatory Note, dated April 22, *Russian Provisional Government*, 2:1100.

37. The theoretical underpinnings of this conviction can be found in two of Lenin's most famous works, *Imperialism, the Highest Stage of Capitalism* and *The State and Revolution*.

38. Lenin's "April Theses," in Chamberlin, *The Russian Revolution*, 1:441–43.

39. See the editorial by Joseph Stalin in *Pravda*, March 15, cited in *Russian Provisional Government*, 2:868. In a recent article, Lars Lih argues that the Bolshevik party was far more in tune with Lenin's radicalism than has previously been thought. Lars T. Lih, "Letter from Afar, Corrections Up Close: The Bolshevik Consensus of March 1917," *Kritika: Explorations in Russian and Eurasian History* 16, no. 4 (Fall 2015): 799–834.

40. *Russian Provisional Government*, 2:1102.

41. *Russian Provisional Government*, 2:935–36.

Chapter 19. The End of a World

1. Original enactment, March 4, 1917. Final form of the decree establishing the Commission is dated March 11, 1917. *Russian Provisional Government*, 1:193–94.

2. The stenographic record was published later in seven volumes under the title *Padenie tsarskogo rezhima* (from 1924 to 1927). The record was not complete and, among other things, did not include the testimonies of Bolsheviks Lenin, Zinoviev, Bukharin, and Krupskaya concerning Roman Malinovsky. These can be found in *Delo provokatora Malinovskogo*.

3. Dzhunkovskii, *Vospominaniia*, 3:535.

4. *Russian Provisional Government*, 2:880–83.

5. *Russian Provisional Government*, 2:886–87; Wildman, *Russian Imperial Army*, 2:23.

6. Dzhunkovskii, *Vospominaniia*, 3:536–38.

7. Dzhunkovskii, *Vospominaniia*, 3:535.

8. Dzhunkovskii, *Vospominaniia*, 3:538–39.

9. Dzhunkovskii, *Vospominaniia*, 3:539.

10. Blok, *Zapisnye knizhki*, 354.

11. *Padenie*, 5:72.

12. *Padenie*, 5:72.

13. *Padenie*, 5:72–74.

14. *Padenie*, 5:75–82.

15. *Padenie*, 5:82.

16. Blok, *Zapisnye knizhki*, 354.

17. *Padenie*, 5:82–83.

18. *Padenie*, 5:83–86.

19. *Padenie*, 5:87–99.

20. This interrogation was not published in *Padenie* but can be found in GARF, f. 1467 (Chrezvychainaia sledstvennaia komissia), op. 1, d. 1E, "Sledstvennoe proizvodstvo po delu R. V. Malinovskii." See also Dunaeva, *Reformy politsii*, 230–34.

21. *Padenie*, 5:100–101.
22. *Padenie*, 5:101–3.
23. *Padenie*, 5:103.
24. *Padenie*, 5:105–6.
25. *Padenie*, 5:106–7.
26. *Padenie*, 5:117.
27. *Padenie*, 5:118–20.
28. *Padenie*, 5:121–22.
29. Dzhunkovskii, *Vospominaniia*, 3:542–43.
30. Dzhunkovskii, *Vospominaniia*, 3:543.
31. Dzhunkovskii, *Vospominaniia*, 3:543–44.
32. Dzhunkovskii, *Vospominaniia*, 3:544.
33. Denikin's report and Brusilov's comment, June 11, 1917, in *Russian Provisional Government*, 2:940–41.
34. Dzhunkovskii, *Vospominaniia*, 3:546, 548, 550; Report of General Orlov and Colonel Novikov, "Spisok nachal'stvuiushchikh lits Zapadnogo fronta otstranennykh ot sluzhby v sviazi s nedoveriem soldat," dated July 15, 1917, in *Revoliutsionnoe dvizhenie v russkoi armii*, 218.
35. *Russian Provisional Government*, 2:978–79, 982–84, 986–87.
36. Dzhunkovskii, *Vospominaniia*, 3:585; see also 3:582–84, 605–6.
37. Dzhunkovskii, *Vospominaniia*, 3:599–600.
38. Dzhunkovskii, *Vospominaniia*, 3:601, 603–4.
39. Dzhunkovskii, *Vospominaniia*, 3:595–96. Dunaeva quotes a letter from Evdokiia, dated August 30, that conveyed Benet's impressions. Dunaeva, *Reformy politsii*, 282.
40. Quoted in Dzhunkovskii, *Vospominaniia*, 3:611–12.
41. Dzhunkovskii, *Vospominaniia*, 3:606–7.
42. *Russian Provisional Government*, 3:1436–41.
43. *Russian Provisional Government*, 3:1451.
44. *Russian Provisional Government*, 3:1474.
45. Pipes, *Russian Revolution*, 439–67; Lincoln, *Passage*, 412–25.
46. Dzhunkovskii, *Vospominaniia*, 3:613.
47. Dzhunkovskii, *Vospominaniia*, 3:620; "Spisok nachal'stvuiushchikh lits . . . otstranennykh ot sluzhby," in *Revoliutsionnoe dvizhenie v russkoi armii*, 217–18; Zalesskii, *Pervaia mirovaia voina*, 478.
48. Dzhunkovskii, *Vospominaniia*, 3:624–25.
49. Dzhunkovskii, *Vospominaniia*, 3:625–27.
50. Dzhunkovskii, *Vospominaniia*, 3:627–29; "Svodka svedenii o nastroennii i sobytiiakh v chastakh Zapadnogo fronta s 14 po 21 oktabria," in *Revoliutsionnoe dvizhenie v russkoi armii*, 530–31.
51. Dzhunkovskii, *Vospominaniia*, 3:631–33.
52. "Svodka svedenii," *Revoliutsionnoe dvizhenie v russkoi armii*, 530–32.
53. "Svodka svedenii," *Revoliutsionnoe dvizhenie v russkoi armii*, 532; Dzhunkovskii, *Vospominaniia*, 3:639–41.
54. Wildman, *Russian Imperial Army*, 2:329, 339; "Svodka svedenii o nastroenii voisk i sobytiiakh v chastakh armii Zapadnogo fronta s 21 po 30 oktabria 1917 g.," in *Oktiabr'skaia revoliutsiia i armiia*, 47.
55. Dzhunkovskii, *Vospominaniia*, 3:642–43. On the problems faced by the Bolsheviks in taking over the Corps's soldiers' committee, see N. G. Petrov, *Bol'sheviki na zapadnom fronte*, 64, 68–69.
56. Report of the acting chief of staff of the Second Army, M. N. Suvorov, to P-K. F. Val'ter, chief of staff for the Western Front, November 9, 1917, in *Oktiabr'skaia revoliutsiia i armiia*, 92–93; Dzhunkovskii, *Vospominaniia*, 3:644.
57. Dzhunkovskii, *Vospominaniia*, 3:644.
58. Dzhunkovskii, *Vospominaniia*, 3:645–48.
59. Dzhunkovskii, *Vospominaniia*, 3:649.
60. Dzhunkovskii, *Vospominaniia*, 3:650–51.
61. Dzhunkovskii, *Vospominaniia*, 3:651–52.

62. Dzhunkovskii, *Vospominaniia*, 3:652–53.

63. Dzhunkovskii, *Vospominaniia*, 3:653–56.

64. The full medical report on Dzhunkovsky can be found in RGVIA, f. 409, op. 1, dd. 147–521. "Ob uvol'nenii ot sluzhby General-Leitenanta Dzhunkovskogo," *l.* 16; Dzhun quoted the relevant sections in his memoirs 3:656–57; on pension, 658.

65. Dzhunkovskii, *Vospominaniia*, 3:659.

Chapter 20. Pensioner, Prisoner, Witness for the Prosecution

1. Dzhunkovskii, *Vospominaniia*, 3:658; Evdokiia, postcard, January 22, 1918, GARF, f. 826, op. 1, d. 541, *l.* 120.

2. An excellent overall description of Petrograd in early 1918 is provided by Lincoln, *Red Victory*, 51–61.

3. Robien, *Diary of a Diplomat*, 190.

4. Shklovsky, *A Sentimental Journey*, 133.

5. Invitation to the Varangians, in the year 862, *The Russian Primary Chronicle: Laurentian Text*, trans. and ed. Samuel Hazard Cross and Olgerd P. Sherbowitz-Wetzor (Cambridge, MA: Harvard University Press, 1953), 59.

6. V. A. Antonov-Ovseenko, in his memoirs, cited in Isaac Deutscher, *The Prophet Armed: Leon Trotsky, 1879–1921* (Oxford: Oxford University Press, 1954), 323.

7. Tyrkova-Williams, *From Liberty to Brest-Litovsk*, 445.

8. Tyrkova-Williams, *From Liberty to Brest-Litovsk*, 453.

9. Robien, *Diary of a Diplomat*, 200.

10. Dunaeva, *Reformy politsii*, 285–86; "Dokladnaia zapiska," 415–16.

11. Mikhail Bulgakov, *The White Guard*, trans. Michael Glenny (New York: McGraw Hill, 1971), 9. On the flight of the "formers" and the first stage of the Civil War, see Figes, *People's Tragedy*, 555–88. "Grudge and mortal hatred," a famous phrase from Giles Fletcher's *Of the Russe Commonwealth* describing Russia in the wake of the terror launched by Ivan the Terrible.

12. A valuable discussion of the nobility's efforts to engage the revolution can be found in the recent study by Rendle, *Defenders of the Motherland*. See pages 199–241 for the nobility's varied responses to the Bolshevik Revolution.

13. Bakhrushin, *Vospominaniia*, 248.

14. The murder of Nicholas II and his family is covered in almost all accounts of the Russian Revolution. On the death of Elizaveta Fedorovna, see Mager, *Elizabeth*, 330–31, 343–49.

15. The first Russian saints, Princes Boris and Gleb, were killed during an internecine feud following the death of Prince Vladimir, the Christianizer of Russia. Their deaths were viewed as a blood offering, expiation for the sins of pre-Christian Russia, where human sacrifice had been practiced. The Saint-Princes were also seen as acting as intercessors for their newly Christian people. The manner of their deaths—nonresisting to evil—exemplified the kenotic ideal of Russian Christianity.

16. The best study of Dzerzhinsky may be the history of the institution he created. See Leggett, *The Cheka*. For a biographical sketch see pp. 22–27, on his feelings of guilt and remorse, see p. 252.

17. Quoted in Leggett, *The Cheka*, 110.

18. Leggett, *The Cheka*, 110.

19. The Red Terror is well surveyed in Lincoln, *Red Victory*, 31–62, and Figes, *People's Tragedy*, 627–49. On provincial Chekas and their abuses, see Melgounov, *Red Terror*, 145–226.

20. The letter is undated, but it was clearly written after November 4, 1918. It is contained in a police file held in GARF, f. R-10035 (Upravlenie komiteta gosudarstvennoi bezopasnosti [UKGB] po g. Moskve i moskovskoi oblasti), d. P-53985. There is no indication that it actually reached its intended recipient. It is cited in Dunaeva, *Reformy politsii*, 286–87. Dzhunkovsky's sister made a similar contention; see the "Proshenie" of E. F. Dzhunkovskaya to V. D. Bonch-Bruevich, September 23, 1918, GARF, f. A-353 (Ministerstvo Iustitsii RSFSR), op. 2, d. 494, "Perepiska po delu b. tov. ministra vnutrennikh del V. F. Dzhunkovskogo," *l.* 2.

21. "Proshenie" of E. F. Dzhunkovskaya, September 23, 1918, GARF, f. A-353, op. 2, d. 494, *l.* 2.

22. Dzhunkovsky's letter to Dzerzhinsky cited in Dunaeva, *Reformy politsii*, 286.

23. D. L. Golinkov suggests that mistaken identity may have been a factor. *Krushenie antisovetskogo*, 2:253–54.

24. *Izvestiia VTsIK*, September 18, 1918, 5.

25. Dzhunkovsky's letter to Dzerzhinsky cited in Dunaeva, *Reformy politsii*, 286; Evdokiia to Iuliia Petrovna (family name not given), undated, GARF, f. A 353, op. 2, d. 494, *l.* 10.

26. On provincial prisons, see Melgounov, *Red Terror*, 143–226. On Smolensk, see Georgii M. Sadovskii, section of memoirs entitled "V smolenskoi katorzhnoi tiur'me," 32–48 (BAR), also a doctor's report on conditions in Smolensk prison in GARF, f. A-353, op. 2, d. 653, "Svedeniia o lichnom sostave karatel'nogo otdela i mest zakliucheniia smolenskoi gubernii," *l.* 55. In his letter to Dzerzhinsky, Dzhunkovsky stated that he was held by the Cheka in its facilities and only transferred to the Smolensk prison in early November. Dunaeva, *Reformy politsii*, 286. But conditions of prisoners in the hands of the Cheka may have been even worse than those prevailing in the Smolensk prison.

27. Dzhunkovsky to Dzerzhinsky in Dunaeva, *Reformy politsii*, 287. Voloshina-Sabashnikova, *Zelenaia zmeia*, 290–91.

28. "Proshenie," September 23, 1918, GARF, f. A-353, op. 2, d. 494, *l.* 2.

29. Lunacharsky to Kursky, September 20, 1918, GARF, f. A-353, op. 2, d. 494, *l.* 19.

30. Evdokiia to Iuliia Petrovna, undated, GARF, f. A-353, op. 2, d. 494, *l.* 10.

31. "Proshenie," September 23, 1918, GARF, f. A-353, op. 2, d. 494, *l.* 2.

32. Evdokiia to Bonch-Bruevich and copy of medical certificate, GARF, f. A-353, op. 2, d. 494, *ll.* 3–4.

33. Bonch-Bruevich to Kursky and Kozlovsky, September 25, 1918, GARF, f. A-353, op. 2, d. 494, *ll.* 1, 5.

34. Evdokiia to Kursky, September 25, 1918, GARF, f. A-353, op. 2, d. 494, *l.* 20.

35. Evdokiia to Bonch-Bruevich, GARF, f. A-353, op. 2, d. 494, *l.* 18.

36. B. V. Avilov to Evdokiia, September 30, 1918, GARF, f. A-353, op. 2, d. 494, *l.* 17.

37. T. Kristensen to Bonch-Bruevich, September 30, 1918, GARF, f. A-353, op. 2, d. 494, *l.* 13.

38. People's Commissariat of Justice, reply to Kristensen, GARF, f. A-353, op. 2, d. 494, *l.* 14.

39. "Pamiatnaia zapiska," October 2, 1918; Evdokiia to Bonch-Bruevich, October 5, 1918; outline of Dzhunkovsky's service record, October 8, 1918; "Proshenie," October 15, 1918, GARF, f. A-353, op. 2, d. 494, *ll.* 21, 18, 30, 37.

40. The document addressed to the Vecheka is without date, but it was probably written shortly after October 13, 1918. It was signed by M. Bogdanov, chairman of the Committee of the Poor of the village (*poselok*) of Vladimiro-Dzhunkovskii. GARF, f. A-353, op. 2, d. 494, *l.* 38. Dzhunkovsky recounts the story of the founding of the settlement in his memoirs. Dzhunkovskii, *Vospominaniia*, 2:95–96.

41. RGASPI, f. 5 (Sekretariat Lenina), op. 1, d. 2838, "Pis'ma grazhdan g. Moskvy i moskovskoi gubernii . . . V. I. Leninu," *l.* 14.

42. A notice of Malinovsky's letter to Zarudnyi appeared in the Kadet newspaper *Rech'* on August 8, 1917. In it he stated that "any sentence handed down in my absence, whatever it may be, I cannot recognize as just."

43. The most complete account of the entire Malinovsky affair is Rozental', *Provokator Roman Malinovskii* (see 148–221 for the period after Malinovsky's departure from Russia). The older work by Ralph Carter Elwood retains its usefulness as an English language source. See Elwood, *Roman Malinovsky* (47–67 for Malinovsky's life after 1914). In 1998 Elwood updated some of his findings concerning Malinovsky's departure from the Duma and subsequent events in an article. Elwood, "The Malinovskii Affair."

44. The story of Malinovsky's attempt to turn himself in comes from his own account, given at his trial. *Delo provokatora Malinovskogo*, 221.

45. During his interrogation in connection with the infamous "Academic Case," the historian

S. F. Platonov stated that Riazanov had been instrumental in getting Dzhunkovsky moved to Moscow. See "Nachalo 'dela' Akademii nauk," 105. On Riazanov see also Leggett, *The Cheka*, 317, 424; Melgounov, *Red Terror*, 31–32.

46. Krylenko's proposed witness list is found in *Delo provokatora Malinovskogo*, 179.

47. *Delo provokatora Malinovskogo*, 180–81.

48. The full list of charges against Malinovsky is printed in *Delo provokatora Malinovskogo*, 154–78. It is not certain from the official court record how much of this was read at the trial.

49. A thorough discussion of the attitudes of various political factions to the use of terror is found in Geifman, *Thou Shalt Kill*.

50. Kucherov, *Soviet Administration of Justice*, 55. For a more recent survey of the nature and functioning of the revolutionary tribunals, see Pavlov, "Tribunal'nyi etap."

51. On the fate of police officials and *sotrudniki* after the revolution, see Daly, *Watchful State*, 215–21.

52. *Delo provokatora Malinovskogo*, 183–89. (The following account of the trial is taken from this work, and further references will be given parenthetically in the text).

53. In their book *Sledovatel' verkhovnogo tribunala* (Tallin: Eesti Raamat, 1971), 164–65, D. M. Rudne and S. I. Tsybov describe a scene where Viktor Kingisepp, the tribunal's chief investigator, brought Dzhunkovsky and Malinovsky together during his pretrial interrogation of the *provokator*. But this confrontation may be entirely fictitious. Dzhunkovsky does not mention it in his memoirs, nor does Rozental' in his detailed study of Malinovsky.

54. Dzhunkovskii, *Vospominaniia*, 2:81.

55. Rozental', *Provokator Roman Malinovskii*, 207.

56. See the introduction to *Delo provokatora Malinovskogo*, 3–6.

57. Stalin to Malinovsky, April 10, 1914, in *Bol'shevistskoe rukovodstvo: Perepiska, 1912–1927* (Moscow: Rospen, 1996), 18–19; Service, *Stalin*, 108.

58. In his recent biography of Stalin, Stephen Kotkin questions whether Lenin actually dictated this famous document, but he does not doubt that Stalin accepted it as genuine and was deeply troubled by it. Kotkin, *Paradoxes of Power*, 472–529.

59. Only one eyewitness places Lenin at the scene; Ol'ga Anikst, "Vospominaniia o Lenine," 93. Her account seems honest, however. Rozental' makes no judgment on Anikst's testimony (*Provokator Roman Malinovskii*, 206–7) but, correctly, rejects Bertram Wolfe's contention (in *Three Who Made a Revolution*, 555) that Lenin may have had and even displayed sympathy for Malinovsky.

60. "Prosecute Rodzianko and Junkovsky for Concealing an Agent Provocateur," *Collected Works*, English translation of 4th ed. (Moscow: Progress Publishers, 1964), 25:102.

61. RGASPI, f. 2 (V. I. Lenin), op. 1, d. 24038, "V upravlenie delami Sovet narodnikh komissarov," *ll.* 1–2. See also I. S. Rozental', "Stranitsy," 91.

62. Fitzpatrick, *Commissariat of Enlightenment*, 139–42.

63. RGASPI, f. 2, op. 1, d. 24038, *l.* 1.

64. Meshcherskaya, *A Russian Princess Remembers*, 14–15.

Chapter 21. Before the Bar of Soviet Justice

1. Report addressed to G. I. Petrovsky, December 10, 1918, RGASPI, f. 76 (F. E. Dzerzhinskii), op. 3, d. 39, "Doklad M. I. Latsis," *l.* 3.

2. "Zachislit' za VChK," 81. This is a collection of documents that constitute Dzhunkovsky's prison record at the Taganka prison. In the introduction to the documents A. N. Semkin states that Dzhunkovsky was transferred from Lubyanka prison to Butyrka on December 6, 1918, but was subsequently interrogated at the Lubyanka and returned to Butyrka on December 18.

3. Melgounov, *Red Terror*, 5–6.

4. Melgounov, *Red Terror*, 5–6.

5. *Che-Ka*, 129–32.

6. *Che-Ka*, 85–86.

7. Klement'ev, *V bol'shevitskoi Moskve*, 318–19.

8. Klement'ev, *V bol'shevitskoi Moskve*, 319.

9. "Zachislit' za VChK," 81.

10. Golitsyn, *Zapiski*, 573. It is possible that Golitsyn is in error about the content of Dzhunkovsky's "reports" to Dzerzhinsky. He may be confusing them with others made to the secret police at a much later date (see chapter 22 below).

11. The question of the ties between the Vecheka and the Okhrana is a source of considerable controversy. In Soviet times "Chekisty" were wont to deny any meaningful connection. Since the collapse of communism, historians are much more willing to recognize that while few high-level Okhrana personnel served the Vecheka and its successors, the experience of the tsarist "organs" was recognized as important and valuable. See Got'e, *Time of Troubles*, 202; Rozental', *Provokator Roman Malinovskii*, 217–22; Plekhanov, *VChK-OGPU*, 275; Makarevich, *Vostok-zapad*, 64–65.

12. Letter quoted in *Butovskii poligon*, 8:128. Ksenofontov was deputy chairman of the Vecheka from March/April 1919 until April 15, 1921. Sometime during this period he also served as a member of the VTsIK Supreme Tribunal for Appeals. See Leggett, *The Cheka*, 452.

13. "Zachislit' za VChK," 84.

14. Some claim that Malinovsky's trial was open and well attended; see Vaksberg, *Stalin's Prosecutor*, 34. But the paucity of eyewitness accounts raises questions as to the size of the crowd.

15. Pavlov, "Tribunal'nyi etap," 13.

16. The use of court trials for propagandistic purposes was something that preceded the revolution. In the 1870s the tsar's government produced show trials of revolutionaries, but these often backfired, creating sympathy for the defendants. Fictionalized "trials" with pedagogic intent were also staged under the old regime. After 1917, however, the Soviet regime made extensive use of this device to educate workers, soldiers, and peasants and to spread revolutionary ideas. See Wood, *Performing Justice*, 16–36. Unfortunately, Wood does little to link agitation trials with the actual tribunal proceedings in the formative years of Soviet justice. Much better in this regard is Cassiday, *Enemy on Trial*, 28–50.

17. Kuskova, "Peters i Dzhunkovskii," 2. Kuskova wrote this piece on the occasion of learning of the arrest of Peters during the party purge of the late 1930s. She may be incorrect as to the date of the announcement of Dzhunkovsky's impending trial, which she puts in the fall of 1918.

18. Kuskova, "Peters i Dzhunkovskii." Kuskova does not name the two communists.

19. Voloshina-Sabashnikova, *Zelenaia zmeia*, 287–88; Kuskova, "Peters i Dzhunkovskii."

20. According to R. H. Bruce Lockhart: "[Peters] had been in prison in Tsarist days. He showed me his nails as proof of the torture he had undergone." See *Memoirs*, 328.

21. In *The Siege of Sidney Street* (London: St. Martin's Press, 1974), Donald Rumbelow strongly asserts Peters's guilt. A more recent study by Phil Ruff finds Rumbelow's claims to be little more than fiction. See Pauls Bankovskis and Phil Ruff, "Peter the Painter [Janis Zhaklis] and the Siege of Sidney Street," *KSL: Bulletin of the Kate Sharpley Library*, nos. 50–51 (July 2007), online at http://www.katesharpleylibrary.net/rjdgpg/.

22. For a short biographical sketch see Leggett, *The Cheka*, 266–68.

23. Kobiakov, "Krasnyi sud," 266–67.

24. Voloshina-Sabashnikova cast Peters in a sympathetic light. "[A]n unconscious tool of a diabolical power, he was forced to sign one death sentence after another; he could not stop although he was exhausted by it" (*Zelenaia zmeia*, 288). Lockhart drew a similar picture: "There was nothing in his character to indicate the inhuman monster he is commonly supposed to be. He told me that he suffered physical pain every time he signed a death sentence. I believe it was true" (*Memoirs*, 328).

25. Kuskova, "Peters i Dzhunkovskii."

26. *Vechernie izvestiia*, May 6, 1919, 3.

27. Voloshina-Sabashnikova, *Zelenaia zmeia*, 288.

28. As a rule revolutionary tribunals did not make stenographic records because they lacked trained personnel and the money to pay them. Titov, *Razvitie systemy*, 10.

29. Kuskova, "Peters i Dzhunkovskii."

30. Kupriianovskii and Molchanova, *Poet Konstantin Bal'mont*, 343–44. This biography discusses Balmont's disenchantment with the Revolution and opposition to Bolshevism but does not mention his participation in the trial of Dzhunkovsky.

31. Dunaeva, *Reformy politsii*, 289.

32. *Izvestiia VTsIK*, May 7, 1919, 4; *Vechernie izvestiia*, May 6, 1919, 3.

33. *Vechernie izvestiia*, May 6, 1919, 3; Kuskova, "Peters i Dzhunkovskii."

34. Voloshina-Sabashnikova, *Zelenaia zmeia*, 289–90; Kuskova, "Peters i Dzhunkovskii."

35. Dzhunkovskii, *Vospominaniia*, 1:536.

36. Kuskova, "Peters i Dzhunkovskii."

37. Voloshina-Sabashnikova, *Zelenaia zmeia*, 289. The testimony of the representative of the craftsmen of Vladimiro-Dzhunkovsky was not reported in the press, but Voloshina-Sabashnikova's account corresponds closely to the earlier statement the denizens of the village sent to the Cheka.

38. *Izvestiia VTsIK*, May 7, 1919, 4.

39. *Izvestiia VTsIK*, May 7, 1919, 4.

40. *Izvestiia VTsIk*, May 7, 1919, 4; Voloshina-Sabashnikova, *Zelenaia zmeia*, 289.

41. Voloshina-Sabashnikova, *Zelenaia zmeia*, 288–89.

42. *Izvestiia VTsIK*, May 7, 1919, 4.

43. This incident was not mentioned in the press reports but is specifically noted in the Tribunal's sentence. "Zachislit' za VChK," 85.

44. *Vechenie izvestiia*, May 7, 1919, 4.

45. *Izvestiia VTsIK*, May 7, 1919, 4.

46. *Izvestiia VTsIK*, May 7, 1919, 4; *Vechernie izvestiia*, May 7, 1919, 4.

47. Voloshina-Sabashnikova, *Zelenaia zmeia*, 290.

48. "Zachislit' za VChK," 85.

49. *Izvestiia VTsIK*, May 7, 1919, 4.

50. Voloshina-Sabashnikova, *Zelenaia zmeia*, 290.

51. Kuskova, "Peters i Dzhunkovskii."

52. Ugrimova and Volkov, *"Stoi v zavete svoem."*

53. "The confession of the accused is a medieval principle of jurisprudence," Nikolai Bukharin famously remarked as he stood before the bar of Soviet "justice" in 1938. See Robert C. Tucker and Stephen F. Cohen, eds., *The Great Purge Trial* (New York: Grosset and Dunlap, 1965), 667.

54. Jansen, "The Bar," 214–15; Murav'ev, "Avtobiograficheskaia zametka—Chast' 2," in Ugrimova and Volkov, *"Stoi v zavete svoem,"* 109–11.

55. Jacobson, *Origins of the Gulag*, 40–43; Leggett, *The Cheka*, 145.

56. Lazarev, "Samarin," 348.

57. "Zachislit' za VChK," 91.

58. "Zachislit' za VChK," 92; Lazarev, "Samarin," 347–48.

59. Trubetskoi, *Minuvshee*, 254–55; Lazarev, "Samarin," 347–48.

60. Trubetskoi, *Minuvshee*, 255.

61. Dzhunkovsky told this story to Bonch-Bruevich in 1934. Bonch-Bruevich passed this information on to Genrikh Yagoda in a letter dated February 10, 1934, Otdelenie rukopisei Rossiiskoi gosudarstvennoi biblioteki (OR RGB), f. 369 (V.D. Bonch-Bruevich), k. 187, d. 17, "Pis'ma v OGPU . . . 1933, 1934, b.d.," *l.* 40.

62. "Zachislit' za VChK," 88.

63. "Zachislit' za VChK," 91.

64. "Zachislit' za VChK," 92.

65. "Zachislit' za VChK," 93, 95.

66. "Zachislit' za VChK," 95.

67. Dzhunkovskii, *Vospominaniia*, 1:22. The authors of the introduction cite documents held in GARF, f. R-10035, d. P-53985.

68. Dzhunkovskii, *Vospominaniia*, 1:22.

69. "Zachislit' za VChK," 96.

70. Police file on Dzhunkovsky (GARF, f. R-10035, d. P-53985), cited by Dunaeva, *Reformy politsii*, 294. See also Dzhunkovskii, *Vospominaniia*, 1:22–23.

71. "Zachislit' za VChK," 97; Dunaeva, *Reformy politsii*, 294.

72. Dzhunkovskii, *Vospominaniia*, 1:23; Dunaeva, *Reformy politsii*, 294, citing a letter from Dzhunkovsky to Trofim Petrovich Samsonov, May 21, 1921, in GARF, f. R-10035, d. P-53985, *l.* 94.

73. "Zachislit' za VChK," 97. The term used here, *sledstvennyi zakliuchennyi*, has no exact equivalent in Anglo-Saxon jurisprudence. A more precise translation might be "a person subjected to evidentiary imprisonment."

74. Dunaeva, *Reformy politsii*, 295.

75. On this see Hardeman, *Coming to Terms*. The text of the collection of essays entitled *Smena vek* can be found in *V poiskakh puti: Russkaia intelligentsiia i sud'by Rossii* (Moscow: Russkaia kniga, 1992), 207–371.

76. Got'e, *Time of Troubles*, 415. Got'e is apparently referring to the fact that a decision taken by the Moscow Revolutionary Tribunal on June 3, 1921, to permit Dzhunkovsky's early release on grounds of health had been "temporarily suspended" with the proviso "until the complete suppression of bands in the Far East." Cited by Dunaeva, *Reformy politsii*, 295.

77. Cited by Dunaeva, *Reformy politsii*, 295.

78. Dunaeva, *Reformy politsii*, 295; Dzhunkovskii, *Vospominaniia*, 1:23; Voloshina-Sabashnikova, *Zelenaia zmeia*, 290.

79. As told by Dzhunkovsky, shortly after his release. Voloshina-Sabashnikova, *Zelenaia zmeia*, 290.

Chapter 22. That the Descendants of the Orthodox Might Know

1. Russia's transition from civil war to the NEP is well described in Figes, *People's Tragedy*, 720–807. For fascinating information on prices and inflation, see Okunev, *Dnevnik moskvicha*.

2. Sheila Fitzpatrick has noted that, despite the Bolsheviks' Marxist obsession with "class," social categories developed in postrevolutionary Russia strongly resembled the "estates" (*sosloviia*) of the old regime. This was especially true for the *lishentsy*, since theirs was a strictly legal category, not defined by the relationship of its members to the means of production. See Fitzpatrick, *Tear Off the Masks!* 71–88.

3. Article 65, in Shevliakov, *Otechestvennye konstitutsii*, 22–23; Fitzpatrick, *Everyday Stalinism*, 117.

4. Smirnova, "Sotsial'nyi portret 'byvshikh'," 87–126.

5. A fascinating account of the problems faced by a family of "formers" and their friends is to be found in Golitsyn, *Zapiski*.

6. Peris, *Storming the Heavens*, 26–27.

7. "Poslanie Patriarkha Tikhona o pomoshchi golodaiiushchim i iz"iatii tserkovnykh tsennostei," in *Sledstvennoe*, 114–15.

8. Pipes, *The Unknown Lenin*, 152.

9. Dunaeva, *Reformy politsii*, 296, citing GARF, f. R-10035 (Upravlenie komiteta gosudarstvennoi bezopasnosti SSSR [UKGB] po Moskve i Moskovskoi oblasti), d. P-53985, *ll.* 146, 202–3.

10. According to Golfo Alexopolous, the key to a successful plea for the restoration of civil rights was for the petitioner to assert a "Soviet self," demonstrate loyalty, and perform useful labor. See her article, "Ritual Lament," 119–20. In time, Dzhunkovsky might have been able to make such a claim but apparently did not try to do so.

11. A useful recent account of Menzhinsky is provided in Rayfield, *Stalin and His Hangmen*, 105–46. Rayfield's book is well informed but somewhat cavalier as regards documentation. He states that Menzhinsky provided Dzhunkovsky with protection, but he cites no source (478n36).

12. For a useful discussion of a specific example of Soviet *pokrovitel'stvo*, see Weiner, "Dzerzhinskii."

13. Among these historians are Zhirnov, "Protsedura," 2; Anan'ich and Ganelin, eds., *Nikolai*

Vtoroi, 537; Rozental', "Stranitsy," 101; Litvin, *Krasnyi*, 52; Galvazin, *Okhrannye struktury*, 190; Daly, *Watchful State*, 218.

14. Martynov, *Moia sluzhba*, 332. This claim is found in a note to the Martynov text. It identifies Dzhunkovsky, mentions his memoirs, and states that they were slated for publication in the USSR. An examination of the manuscript held at the Hoover Institution shows that the note was not written by Martynov but was probably the work of the editor of the volume, Richard Wraga. Where Wraga got this information is uncertain. Wraga was a former intelligence officer attached to the Polish general staff in the interwar period. He may have heard rumors concerning Dzhunkovsky at that time.

15. The literature on the Trust and related operations is quite large, but no comprehensive scholarly work has yet been written because serious researchers have not had untrammeled access to relevant documents in the archive of the former KGB. Much of the work published by Soviet/Russian authors has come in a semi-novelistic form with few if any source references. The "classic" work from the Soviet period is Nikulin, *Mertvaia zyb'*. An English translation is available: *The Swell of the Sea*. Other works of value include Andrew and Gordievsky, *KGB*; Andrew and Mitrokhin, *The Sword and the Shield*; Bailey, *The Conspirators*; Blackstock, *The Secret Road to World War Two*; Brook-Shepherd, *The Iron Maze*; Costello and Tsarev, *Deadly Illusions*; Fleishman, *V tiskakh provokatsii*; Grant, "Deception on a Grand Scale," 65–72; *Lubianka 2*; *Ocherki istorii rossiiskoi vneshnei razvedki*; Spence, *Boris Savinkov*; Spence, "Russia's '*Operatsiia Trest*,'" 21–22; Spence, *Trust No One*; Voitsekhovskii, *Trest*.

16. By the time of its termination in around 1926, the Trust was viewed as a mixture of both successes and failures. See Artur Artuzov, "Dokladnaia zapiska nachal'nika KRO OGPU o tseliakh legendy 'Trest,'" dated April 18, 1927, in Zdanovich, *Organy gosudarstvennoi*, 630–33. Also relevant to the history of the Trust is the document found in RGASPI, f. 76 (Dzerzhinskii), op. 3, d. 356, "Dokladnaia zapiska pomoshchnika nachal'nika KRO OGPU Styrne nachal'niku KRO OGPU A. Kh.Artuzovu o kontrrazvedivatel'nikh operatsii 'Iaroslavets' i 'Trest,'" discussed in Spence, "Russia's 'Operatsiia Trest.'"

17. The most complete presentation of the story (legend) of Dzhunkovsky's alleged participation in the Trust can be found in three works of popular history: Gladkov, *Nagrada za vernost'—kazen'*; Antonov and Karpov, *Tainye informatory Kremlia*; Makarevich, *Vostok-zapad*. Western works that also assert Dzhunkovsky's role in the Trust are Rayfield, *Stalin and His Hangmen*, and most recently Haslam, *Near and Distant Neighbors*.

18. Dolgopolov, "Ot Savinkova do Ramzaia," 170–71.

19. See the works of Natalie Grant, "Deception on a Grand Scale"; Grant, "The Trust"; Spence, "Russia's *'Operatsiia Trest'*"; Voitsekhovskii, *Trest*; Wraga, "Cloak and Dagger Politics"; Wraga, "Trest"; Wraga, "Eshche o 'Treste.'" The private papers of Grant and Wraga at the Hoover Institution, which hold considerable other information on the Trust, contain no mention of Dzhunkovsky. The same is true in the case of a CIA internal study "The Trust."

20. Dunaeva, *Reformy politsii*, 297.

21. Robbins, "Was Vladimir Dzhunkovskii the Father of 'The Trust'?"

22. A point vigorously and persuasively argued by Dunaeva in *Reformy politsii* and various other works.

23. Teodor Gladkov, who produced the most detailed account of Dzhunkovsky's alleged participation in the Trust (*Nagrada za vernost'—kazn'*), would certainly qualify as a "court historian" of the KGB/FSB, writing extensively about the "organs." Historians of a conservative stamp often view Dzhunkovsky as being secretly disloyal or criminally naive. In their works they usually include assertions of Dzhunkovsky's participation in the Trust. For a random example, see the article "Diletant v golubom mundire, ili 'tretii put' generala Dzhunkovskogo," that appeared in *Krasnaia zvezda* (April 25, 2007). Citing no sources it states that Dzhunkovsky "accepted active participation in developing the plans for the famous operation 'Trust.'"

24. Finkel, "An Intensification of Vigilance"; Schlögel, *Moscow, 1937*, 501.

25. In December 1937, Dzhunkovsky was arrested. At an interrogation that took place on December 28, he specifically mentioned these consultations with the organs. Dunaeva, *Reformy politsii*,

303, citing the record of the interrogation in GARF, f. R-10035, d. P-74952, *l.* 15. These consultations will be discussed in more detail below.

26. Dzhunkovsky's connection to the infamous "Academic Case" (*Akademicheskoe delo*) will be discussed in some detail below.

27. Dzhunkovskii, 1865–1884, *l.* 26; Gerua, *Vospomianiia*, 1:49–53.

28. On Menzhinsky's connection with Kuzmin and his circle, see Rayfield, *Stalin and His Hangmen*, 109; on his novel and other writings, 112–14.

29. V. D. Bonch-Bruevich to G. G. Yagoda, February 10, 1934, Odelenie rukopisei Rossiiskoi gosudarstvennoi biblioteki (OR RGB), f. 369 (V. D. Bonch-Bruevich), k. 187, d. 17, "Pis'ma v OGPU . . . 1933, 1934, b.d.," *l.* 40.

30. S. F. Platonov stated this during his interrogation by Iakov Peters, "Nachalo 'dela' Akademii nauk," 105.

31. Annual report for 1910, GARF, f. 826, op. 1, d. 107, "Otchety Moskovskogo gubernatora," *l.* 92.

32. "Gubernator pristroilsia," *Bezbozhnik*, February 3, 1929, 3.

33. E. Ponomareva to Dzhunkovsky, January 14, 1926; Koni to Dzhunkovsky, March 21, 1926, Gosudarstvennyi tsentral'nyi teatral'nyi muzei (GTsTM), f. 91 (V. F. Dzhunkovskii), dd. 12–27, "Pis'ma Koni Dzhunkovskomu." According to testimony he gave to the OGPU in April 1922, he was already giving language lessons. Dunaeva, *Reformy politsii*, 296.

34. Liubimova and Golovkova, "Butovo—Russkaia golgofa."

35. Most notably by Tat'iana Smirnova, in *"Byvshie liudi"*; Smith, *Former People.*

36. Smith's *Former People* gives a splendid overview concentrating on the Sheremetev and Golitsyn families. See also Golitsyn, *Zapiski*, 146; Smirnova, "Sotsial'nyi portret 'byvshikh,'" 112–22; Meshcherskaya, *Russian Princess*; Serge Schmemann, *Echoes of a Native Land: Two Centuries of a Russian Village* (New York: Alfred Knopf, 1997); Okunev, *Dnevnik moskvicha*; Got'e, *Time of Troubles.* The papers of S. D. Urusov and his family (OR RGB, f. 550) are a rich source as well.

37. In the late 1920s Nikolai Nikolaevich was arrested in Tbilisi on the orders of Lavrentii Beria. Elena Georgievna suffered a collapse and was hospitalized; their son, Georgii, ended up in a gang of thieves. Elena Georgievna recovered and moved to Leningrad in order to get her son away from the criminal milieu. Ia. S. Lapovok, "50 let v efire," at http://www.cqham.ru/ua1fa_bio.htm/. Nikolai Nikolaevich became a doctor of technical science, a professor at the Moscow Engineering and Construction Institute (Moskovskii inzhenerno-stroitel'nyi institut) and was granted the title "Honored Worker in the Field of Science and Technology" (*Zasluzhennyi deiatel' nauki i tekhniki*). He married a second time to A. D. Dement'eva. N. N. Dzhunkovsky died in 1966 and is buried in Novodevichi cemetery. "Rodoslovnye: Dzhunkovskie."

38. Lapovok, "50 let v efire." G. N. Dzhunkovsky was also a successful engineer in a number of fields including artillery and rocketry as well radio technology. Lapovok states that Dzhunkovsky won a Stalin prize in 1949, but when asked to join the Communist Party he declined. He explained his decision to his friend saying, "They refused to accept me in the Komsomol because of my [noble] class background . . . and I was offended." He died in 1977.

39. Sabashnikov, *Zapiski*, 432, 565; Liubimova and Golovkova, "Butovo—Russkaia golgofa."

40. Quoted in Dunaeva, *Reformy politsii*, 298. She points out that the text is taken from the teachings of St. Feofan Zatvornik.

41. Dzhunkovskii, *Vospominaniia*, 2:96.

42. Dzhunkovskii, 1898–1904, *l.* 7.

43. Urusov hoped that his grandchildren would read his memoir—but only at a later date, "when it would not harm their educational careers." Urusov, *Zapiski*, 35–36.

44. Dzhunkovskii, *Vospominaniia*, 2:10.

45. David King, *The Commissar Vanishes: The Falsification of Photographs and Art in Stalin's Russia* (New York: Henry Holt, 1997).

46. A. S. Pushkin, *Izbrannye sochineniia v dvukh tomakh* (Moscow: Khudozhestvennaia literatura, 1980), 2:179–80.

47. "Dokladnaia zapiska," 415–16. Documents listed in the catalog of S. F. Platonov in the manuscript division of the Russian National Library indicate that the papers of Dzhunkovsky were in the possession of Pushkin House no later than March 1924. *Arkhiv akademika S. F. Platonova*, 119, 213.

48. Logic dictates that a diary existed, but Dzhunkovsky never mentioned it in his memoirs or elsewhere. The only reference to it that I have found is in a letter Evdokiia Fedorovna sent to her brother on March 1, 1916, in which she wrote: "Of course I will continue your diary—with pleasure." GARF, f. 826, op. 1, d. 540, "Pis'ma, 3 I 1916—4 XII 1916," *l.* 45.

49. This is what Drs. Panina and Peregudova assert in their introduction to Dzhunkovsky's memoirs. Dzhunkovskii, *Vospominaniia*, 1:23–24.

50. That Dzhunkovsky was concerned about such things is strongly suggested by the fact that, when he finally sold his memoirs to the State Literary Museum in the early 1930s, he stipulated that no portion of the document could be published until twenty years after the events described.

51. *Putevoditel' po rukopisnym fondam Gosudarstvennogo tsentral'nogo teatral'nogo muzeia imeni A. A. Bakhrushina* (Moscow: Gosudarstvennyi tsentral"nyi muzei im. A. A. Bakhrushina, 2002), 78–79; Liubimova and Golovkova, "Butovo—Russkaia golgofa."

52. This chronology was developed by Dunaeva on the basis of internal evidence in the manuscript (*Reformy politsii*, 13–14). On the basis of my own reading of the memoirs, I find this entirely plausible.

53. "Nachalo 'dela' Akademii nauk," 94–98, 104, 106.

54. This is the view of Dunaeva (*Reformy politsii*, 15), but witnesses to his work in Leningrad do not mention this.

55. Dzhunkovskii, *Vospominaniia*, 1:24.

56. Dzhunkovskii, *Vospominaniia*, 2:627. In his "Dokladnaia zapiska" of 1929, Dzhunkovsky stated that as of 1915 he was "very close" to Koni ("Dokladnaia zakiska V. F. Dzhunkovskogo," 416).

57. Koni to Dzhunkovsky, August 12, 1926, in Koni, *Sobranie sochinenii*, 8:338.

58. Smoliarchuk, *Anatolii Fedorovich Koni*, 196, citing an article by Lunacharsky entitled "Tri vstrechi," that appeared in *Ogonek* 40 (1927); Vysotskii, *Koni*, 388–89.

59. Vysotskii, *Koni*, 403–7.

60. Gippius, *Dnevniki*, 2:207–8.

61. E. Ponomareva to Dzhunkovsky, October 29, 1927, GTsTM, f. 91, dd. 30–36, "Pis'ma Ponomarevy Dzhunkovskomu."

62. Koni to Dzhunkovsky, December 29, 1925, GTsTM, f. 91, dd. 12–27, "Pis'ma Koni Dzhunkovskomu."

63. Koni to Dzhunkovsky, March 21, 1926, GTsTM, f. 91, dd. 12–27.

64. Ponomareva to Dzhunkovsky, January 14, 1926, GTsTM, f. 91, dd. 12–27.

65. Koni to Dzhunkovsky, August 12, 1926, in Koni, *Sobranie sochinenii*, 8:339.

66. Dzhunkovsky to Koni cited in Rozental', "Stranitsy," 102.

67. Ponomareva to Dzhunkovsky, December 8, 1927, GTsTM, f. 91, dd. 30–36.

68. Ponomareva to Dzhunkovsky, October 5, 1927, GTsTM, f. 91, dd. 30–36.

69. Vysotskii, *Koni*, 426.

Chapter 23. Overtaken by the Night

1. Sabashnikov, *Zapiski*, 496.

2. On the Shakhty affair and trial, see Kotkin, *Paradoxes of Power*, 687–700; Tucker, *Stalin in Power*, 76–80. Stalin, "Speech Delivered at the Eighth Congress of the All-Union Leninist Young Communist League," May 16, 1928, in *Works* 11:73.

3. Dunaeva, *Reformy politsii*, 303.

4. Aleksandra Azar'evna Andreeva (1887–1951) was one of the relatively few high-ranking women in the formative period of the Soviet security police and the only one to attain the rank of major. She had been employed there since 1921 and served as the assistant (*pomoshchnik*) to the deputy chief (*zamestitel' nachal'nika*) of the secret department of the Vecheka/OGPU. In 1939 she would

be sentenced to fifteen years in a corrective labor camp where she died. For details on the career of Andreeva, see Berezhkov and Pekhereva, *Zhenshchiny-chekisty*, 142–52.

5. Dunaeva, *Reformy politsii*, 303.

6. On this, see Kotkin, *Stalin*, 1:691–93, and the documents and analysis presented in the article "Zameshannykh nemtsev arestovat'."

7. On this point, see Kendall E. Bailes, *Technology and Society under Lenin and Stalin: Origins of the Soviet Technical Intelligentsia* (Princeton, NJ: Princeton University Press, 1978), 85–86.

8. Dunaeva, *Reformy politsii*, 303.

9. On Pauker, see Simon Seabag Montefiore, *Stalin: The Court of the Red Tsar* (New York: Alfred Knopf, 1994), 66–67, and at http://www.hrono.ru/biograf/bio_p/pauker_kv.php/.

10. Nadezhda Shebasheva and Evgeniia Makarenko (*zaiavlenie*) to Stalin, December 14, 1937, GARF, f. R-10035, d. P-74953, *l.* 28. Document supplied by Anastasia Dunaeva.

11. See Dzhunkovskii, 1865–1884, *ll.* 31–32, and Dzhunkovskii, 1892–1897, *l.* 292.

12. Stalin, "The Tasks of Business Executives," dated February 4, 1931, in *Works* 13:41.

13. The standard English-language treatment of the Sovietization of the Academy of Sciences is Graham, *Soviet Academy of Sciences*. A more recent interpretation is Tolz, "Formation."

14. Levin, "Expedient Catastrophe," 265–68.

15. Graham, *Soviet Academy of Sciences*, 85–89.

16. Graham, *Soviet Academy of Sciences*, 89–119; Tolz, "Formation," 54–57.

17. Levin, "Expedient Catastrophe," 270–71; Graham, *Soviet Academy of Sciences*, 122–24.

18. Report of G. G. Yagoda and E. G. Evdokhimov to Stalin on January 9, 1930, in "'Ostalos' eshche nemalo khlama v liudskom sostave.' Kak nachinalos' 'delo Akademii nauk,'" *Istochnik* 4 (1997): 114. On the press campaign, see Levin, "Expedient Catastrophe," 273–75; Graham, *Soviet Academy of Sciences*, 126–28.

19. Tolz, "Formation," 59; "Nachalo 'dela' Akademii nauk," 81, 107n10; "'Ostalos' eshche nemalo khlama,'" *Istochnik* 3 (1997): 124.

20. The record of the interrogation is published in "Nachalo 'dela' Akademii nauk."

21. "Nachalo 'dela' Akademii nauk," 99.

22. "Nachalo 'dela' Akademii nauk," 99.

23. "Nachalo 'dela' Akademii nauk," 105.

24. Figatner report to Ordzhonikidze, October 28, 1929, "Dokladnaia zapiska Iu. Figatnera o rabote komissii RKI v AN SSSR," in "Ostalos' eshche nemalo khlama," *Istochnik* 3 (1997): 111–12.

25. Dokladnaia zapiska Iu. P. Figatnera v TsKK VKP(b), December 11, 1929, in "Ostalos' eshche nemalo khlama," *Istochnik* 4 (1997): 110.

26. As ordered by the Politburo on November 5, 1929, "Ostalos' eshche nemalo khlama," *Istochnik* 4 (1997): 103; Tolz, "Formation," 59.

27. Tolz, "Formation," 60–61; Leonov, *Akademicheskoe delo*, 1:v.

28. See "Dokladnaia zapiska," 415.

29. Anketa i sobstvennoruchnye pokazaniia S. F. Platonova, January 13, 1930, in Leonov, *Akademicheskoe delo*, . . . 1:22.

30. At the time of his interrogation on December 28, 1937, Dzhunkovsky spoke of his four-hour conversation with Mikhail Sergeevich concerning the internal passports. In their letter to Stalin on December 14, 1937, Nadezhda Sebasheva and Evgeniia Makarenko told of the written report. GARF, f. R-10035, d. P-74952, *ll.* 15, 28. Documents supplied by Anastasia Dunaeva. See also her book *Reformy politsii*, 303.

31. This according to David Shearer, an American historian who has carefully studied the development of the passport legislation. Email to the author, February 4, 2003.

32. Zhirnov, "Protsedura," 2; Liubimova and Golovkova, "Butovo—Russkaia golgofa."

33. Vypiska iz protokola zasedanii Politbiuro TsK VKP(b), November 15, 1932, in "'Izmeneniia pasportnoi," 104.

34. "Zapiska V. A. Balitskogo v TsK VKP(b), November 23, 1932," *Istochnik* 6 (1997): 104–5.

35. N. V. Petrov and K. V. Skorkin, *Kto rukovodil NKVD 1934–1941: Spravochnik* (Moscow: Zven'ia, 1999), 99.

36. Shearer, *Policing*, 196–97.

37. Dunaeva, *Reformy politsii*, 303.

38. Dunaeva, *Reformy politsii*, 304–6.

39. The OGPU would be abolished by a decree issued on July 10, 1934. Its basic functions were then assigned to the Main Administration of State Security (GUGB), which was subordinated to the NKVD. At the time, these measures were seen as a "liberalization" and a means of checking the kinds of abuses that had recently occurred under the OGPU. See Hingley, *Russian Secret Police*, 156–57.

40. Makarevich, *Vostok-zapad*, 74.

41. On the Sabashnikov publishing house and the series *Zapisi proshlogo*, see Belov, *Knigoizdateli Sabashnikovy*, 156–68.

42. Dzhunkovskii, *Vospominaniia*, 1:24; OR RGB, f. 261 (Izdatel'stvo M. i S. Sabashnikovykh), k. 10, d. 3, "Kooperativnoe izdatel'stvo 'Sever': Spisok rukopisei nakhodiashchikhsia v portfele izdatel'stva," and OR RGB, f. 261, k. 1, d. 10, "Zaiavlenie v pravlenie izdatel'stva 'Sovetskii pisatel'' o neobkhodimosti prodolzhenii serii 'Zapisi proshlogo.'"

43. Shumikhin, "Stenogramma," 290–91; Shumikhin, "Pis'ma narkomam," 69.

44. Bolsheviks who opposed the drive against "formers" are discussed in Fitzpatrick, *Everyday Stalinism*, 118–22. On Bonch-Bruevich specifically, see Shumikhin, "Pis'ma narkomam," 71–72. Examples of Bonch-Bruevich purchasing materials from formers can be found in his letters to Bubnov, OR RGB, f. 369, k. 181, d. 1, "Pis'ma Bubnovu, ianv.-iiun' 1933," and d. 3, "Pis'ma Bubnovu, ianv.- iiun' 1934."

45. OR RGB, f. 369, k. 265, d. 12, "Dzhunkovskii, V. F.: Pis'ma k Bonch-Bruevichu," *l.* 3.

46. OR RGB, f. 369, k. 448, d. 79, "Raspiska v poluchenii deneg za materialy peredannye v . . . muzei E. S. Makarenko," *l.* 1.

47. Bonch-Bruevich to Yagoda, February 10, 1934, OR RGB, f. 369, k. 187, d. 17, "Pis'ma v OGPU, 1933, 1934, b.d.," *l.* 40.

48. OR RGB f. 369, k. 384, d. 3, "Vospominaniia o dekabr'skom . . . vostanii" *ll.* 1–33. The material here has been misplaced; it should be in *delo* 2, which bears the proper title "Dzhunkovskii, Vladimir Fedorovich: Zapiski—oglavleniia vospominanii." *Delo* 2 currently holds the material on 1905.

49. OR RGB, f. 369, k. 265, d. 12, *ll.* 1–2.

50. Letter quoted in Shumikhin, "Stenogramma," 316.

51. Letters sent from Bonch-Bruevich to Bubnov during 1933 indicate that Vladimir Dmitrievich regularly informed the Narkom about proposed purchases. In these letters there is no mention of Dzhunkovsky or negotiations for his memoirs. OR RGB, f. 369, k. 181, dd. 1, 2, "Pis'ma Bubnovu, 1933." Bonch-Bruevich asked Bubnov to reconfirm the right to purchase materials from former tsarist elite in a letter dated January 16, 1934. OR RGB, f. 369, k. 181, d. 3, "Pis'ma Bubnovu, 1934 ianv–apr," *l.* 9.

52. Letter dated January 10, 1934, OR RGB, f. 369, k. 143, d. 51, "Pis'ma k Dzhunkovskomu," *l.* 1. (Something as "extraordinarily strange" as taxing Social Security benefits can occur only under capitalism.)

53. Bonch-Bruevich to Dzhunkovsky, January 10, 1934, OR RGB, f. 369, k. 143, d. 51, "Pis'ma k Dzhunkovskomu," *l.* 1.

54. Bonch-Bruevich to Dzhunkovsky, March 2, 1934, OR RGB, f. 369, k. 143, d. 51, "Pis'ma k Dzhunkovskomu," *l.* 2.

55. In the file on Dzhunkovsky's *fond* (826) in GARF, there is an inventory of materials received by the museum from Dzhunkovsky that refers to an earlier *opis'* of the GLM dated April 8, 1934. This may be the date Vladimir Fedorovich completed his delivery. "*Opis'* no. 1319," GARF, *Delo* (*fonda*) 826, *ll.* 33–34.

56. Shumikhin, "Stenogramma," 290–92; Shumikhin, "Pis'ma narkomam," 69, 71.

57. Bonch-Bruevich to Karl Pauker, January 25, 1934, OR RGB, f. 369, k. 187, d. 17, "Pis'ma v OGPU, 1933, 1934, b.d," *ll.* 28–30.

58. Quoted in Bonch-Bruevich to Lavrentii Beria, June 28, 1939. Reproduced in Shumikhin, "Dnevnik Mikhaila Kuzmina," 143.

59. Bonch-Bruevich to Gorb, February 4, 1934, OR RGB, f. 369, k. 187, d. 17, "Pis'ma v OGPU, 1933, 1934, b.d.," *ll.* 31–34; Bonch-Bruevich to Yagoda, February 10, 1934, OR RGB, f. 369, k. 187, d. 17, *l.* 36.

60. Letter to Yagoda, February 10, 1934, OR RGB, f. 369, k. 187, d. 17, "Pis'ma v OGPU, 1933, 1934, b.d.," *ll.* 36–40.

61. Shumikhin, "Stenogramma," 292.

62. Quoted in Shumikhin, "Pis'ma narkomam," 72.

63. Bonch-Bruevich to Bubnov, May 20, 1934, OR RGB, f. 369, k. 181, d.4, "Pis'ma Bubnovu, 1934 mai," *ll.* 32–33. Document partially published in Shumikhin, "Pis'ma narkomam," 72.

64. Bonch-Bruevich to Gorb, April 23, 1934, OR RGB, f. 369, k. 187, d. 17, "Pis'ma v OGPU, 1933, 1934, b.d.," *l.* 47; Bonch-Bruevich to Bubnov, June 14, December 28, 1934, OR RGB, f. 369, k. 181, d. 5, "Pis'ma Bubnovu, 1934 iiun'–iiul'," *l.* 15, and OR RGB, f. 369, k. 181, d. 6, "Pis'ma Bubnovu, 1934 avgust–dekabr'," *l.* 50.

65. Gorb was shot in 1937. On Gorb and his fate, see *Razvedka i kontrrazvedka v litsakh*, 122. By the time Bonch-Bruevich wrote to Beria, almost all of those involved in the GLM imbroglio and the question of Dzhunkovsky's memoirs had been executed—Agranov, Bubnov, Yagoda, and Pauker, as well as Vladimir Fedorovich himself.

66. Bonch-Bruevich to Beria, June 28, 1939, cited in Shumikhin, "Dnevnik Mikhaila Kuzmina," 142–43.

67. Patricia Kennedy Grimsted, *Archives and Manuscript Repositories in the USSR: Moscow and Leningrad* (Princeton, NJ: Princeton University Press, 1972), 28.

68. For the further adventures of Dzhunkovsky's materials that were taken from Pushkin House and moved to Moscow in December 1929, see Gosudarstvennyi arkhiv Rossiiskoi Federatsii, *Putevoditel'*, vol. 1, *Fondy gosudarstvennogo arkhiva Rossiiskoi Federatsii po istorii Rossii XIX–nachala XX vv.*, ed. Gregory L. Freeze and S. V. Mironenko (Moscow: Izdatel'stvo Blagovest, 1994), xiii–xv.

69. One of the earliest works to cite materials from Dzhunkovsky's archives was V. S. Diakin, *Russkaia burzhuaziia i tsarizm v gody pervoi mirovoi voiny (1914–1917)* (Leningrad: Nauka, 1967).

70. This according to Peregudova and Panina's introduction to Dzhunkovsky, *Vospominaniia*, 1:26.

71. Bonch-Bruevich's salary as director of GLM was five hundred rubles per month. GARF, f. 629 (Gosudarstvennyi literaturnyi muzei), op. 1, d. 9, "Otchet muzeia o rabote za iiul'—dekabr' 1933 goda," *l.* 10. In a conversation in the spring of 2003 Ninel Abramovna Stechkina, the daughter of Narkom A. L. Gilinsky, stated that his monthly salary was also five hundred rubles.

72. Nadezhda Shebasheva and Evgeniia Makarenko to Joseph Stalin, December 14, 1937. Document supplied by Anastasia Dunaeva, January 7, 2010.

73. Liubimova and Golovkova, "Butovo—Russkaia golgofa."

74. Stalin, *Mastering Bolshevism*, 21–22.

75. Service, *Stalin*, 350.

76. "Operativnyi prikaz narodogo komissara vnutrennikh del, No. 00447, July 30, 1937," in Mark Iunge and Rol'f Binner, *Kak terror stal "bol'shim,"* 84–93.

77. *Butovskii polygon*, 8:130–31.

78. Shearer, *Policing*, 286–87.

79. GARF, f. R-10035, d. P-74952, *ll.* 7–8. Documents supplied by Anastasia Dunaeva. See also her book *Reformy politsii*, 302.

80. GARF, f. R-10035, d. P-74952, *ll.* 10, 13; Dunaeva, *Reformy politsii*, 303; Zhirnov, "Protsedura," 2; Liubimova and Golovkova, "Butovo—Russkaia golgofa."

81. Shearer, *Policing*, 355.

82. Shebasheva and Makarenko to Stalin, letter in GARF, f. R-10035, d. P-74952, *l.* 28, supplied by Anastasia Dunaeva. See also her *Reformy politsii*, 303.

83. GARF, f. R-10035, d. P-74952, *l.* 15, supplied by Anastasia Dunaeva. See also her *Reformy politsii*, 303.

84. GARF, f. R-10035, d. P-74952, *l.* 18, supplied by Anastasia Dunaeva. See also her *Reformy politsii*, 303.

85. Zhirnov, "Protsedura."

86. Ivanov-Razumnik, *Memoirs*, 312–13.

Conclusion

1. Quoted in Dunaeva, *Reformy politsii*, 298.

2. 2 Timothy 4:6–7.

3. Daly, *Watchful State*, 224.

4. Richard Robbins, "His Excellency the Governor: The Style of Russian Provincial Governance at the Beginning of the Twentieth Century," *Imperial Russia, 1770–1917: State, Society, Opposition; Essays in Honor of Marc Raeff*, ed. Ezra Mendelsohn and Marshall S. Shatz (DeKalb, IL: Northern Illinois University Press, 1988), 76–92.

5. Tumanova, "A Conservative in Power."

6. Kulikov, *Biurokraticheskaia elita*, 13–14. For much of the nineteenth century, this term "serving intelligentsia" was applied chiefly to lower-level bureaucrats and the zemstvo Third Element. Kulikov believes that by the beginning of the twentieth century the bureaucratic elite should be seen as belonging to the intelligentsia.

7. Developments ably discussed and analyzed by Wortman, *Legal Consciousness*; Lincoln, *Vanguard of Reform*.

8. Dowler, *Russia in 1913*, esp. 190–232.

Glossary

***burzhui*:** A bourgeois; a member of the privileged classes
***byvshii chelovek; byvshie liudi*:** A former person; former people; *ci-devant*
Cheka (chrezvychainaia komissiia): Extraordinary commission (Soviet secret police)
d. (*delo*): Archival file
***druzhnnik (i)*:** Militiaman
***dvorianstvo*:** The nobility; gentry
f. (*fond*): Archival collection
GLM: State Literary Museum
GPU (Gosudarstvennoe politicheskoe upravlenie): State political administration (Soviet secret police)
***gradonachal'nik*:** City commandant
***gubernator*:** Provincial governor
***guberniia; gubernia*:** Province
INO (Inostrannoe otelenie): Foreign department
intelligent(y): Member(s) of the intelligentsia
Ispolkom: Executive committee of the Soviet
Kadets; KDs: Constitutional Democrats
KRO (Kontrrazvedivatel'nyi otdel): Counter-intelligence department
kulak: Prosperous peasant
***l.* (*list*):** Folio, page
***lishenits; lishentsy*:** A person or persons deprived of voting rights
mir: Peasant land commune
MVD (Ministerstvo vnutrennikh del): Ministry of Internal Affairs
***nachal'nik gubernii*:** Provincial governor
***narod*:** The common people
***narodnik(i)*:** Russian populist(s)
NKVD (Narodnyi komissariat vutrennikh del): People's Commissariat of Internal Affairs (Soviet secret police)
OGPU (Ob"edinennoe gosudarstvennoe politicheskoe upravlenie): United State Political Administration (Soviet secret police)

Okhrana; *okhranka*: Tsarist security police
***okhranniki*:** Those who serve in the tsarist security police
OO (okhrannoe otdelenie): Security bureau
***otdel*:** Department
***otdel'nyi vid na zhitel'stvo*:** Passport permitting a woman to live apart from her husband
***pokrovitel'stvo*:** Protection, patronage
***provokator*:** Secret police agent; agent provocateur
RSDRP; SDs: Russian Social Democratic Labor Party; Social Democrats
***sotrudnik*:** Agent; worker
Sovdepiia: Pejorative term for Soviet territory
Sovnarkom (Sovet narodnikh komissarov): Council of People's Commissars
***spets*:** Specialist
SRs: Socialist Revolutionaries
starets: Venerated holy person
Stavka: Supreme Headquarters
troika: Three man judicial tribunal
***uezd*:** County
***uprava*:** Zemstvo executive board
Vecheka (Vserossiiskaia chrezvychainaia komissiia): All-Russian Extraordinary Commission (Soviet secret police)
***vitse-gubernator; "vitse"*:** Provincial vice-governor
***volost'*:** Canton
Zemgor: Union of zemstvos and towns
***zubatovshchina*:** The Zubatov experiment; "police socialism"

Bibliography

Dzhunkovsky's Memoirs

Vladimir Dzhunkovsky was his own Boswell, and his voluminous memoirs are the indispensible source for any account of his life. For the historian and biographer, memoirs are always suspect to a degree, and questions of the writer's veracity must always be kept in mind. In the main, however, Dzhunkovsky's recollections are remarkably accurate. This is because he not only wrote his memoirs from memory but also was able to use his enormous personal archive. Thus he could quote directly from the many original documents he possessed. There are, to be sure, places were Dzhunkovsky's memory fails or when he gets dates wrong, but these are relatively rare. There remain some matters in dispute—questions concerning Roman Malinovsky and Rasputin—but many reputable historians such as Anastasia Dunaeva, Zinaida Peregudova, and Isaak Rozental accept most of Dzhunkovsky's accounts. The biggest problem in the memoirs is not what Dzhunkovsky writes but, rather, his silences on many personal matters and his refusal to discuss the failings of members of the royal family and of people he loved. And of course, his memoirs end with the beginning of 1918, and the biographer must reconstruct the last twenty years of Dzhunkovsky's life unguided by the subject.

Archival Sources

Bakhmeteff Archive, Columbia University (BAR)
- N. N. Kisel-Zagorianskii
- V. F. Malinin
- K. N. Mandrazhi
- G. M. Sadovskii
- K. V. Semchevskii
- F. V. Shlippe
- Soiuz Pazhei

Gosudarstvennyi Arkhiv Rossiiskoi Federatsii (GARF)
- Chrezvychainaia sledstvennaia komissiia (1467)
- V. F. Dzhunkovskii (826)
- Gosudarstvennyi literaturnyi muzei (629)
- Kantseliariia tovarishcha ministra vnutrennikh del V. V. Dzhunkovskogo (270)
- Narodnyi komissariat iustitsii RSFSR (A-353)
- Nikolai II (601)
- P. P. Stremoukhov (R-6546)

Gosudarstvennyi tsentral'nyi teatral'nyi muzei im. Bakhrushina. Otdel rukopisei (GTsTM)
- V. F. Dzhunkovskii (91)

Hoover Institution Archives (HIA)
- Grand Duchess Kseniia Aleksandrovna Papers
- Robert H. Bruce Lockhart Papers
- Okhrana Collection
- Russian Pictorial Collection
- B. K. Shebeko Collection

Edward Ellis Smith Collection
N. Sviatopolk-Mirskii Collection
Alexandre Georgievich Tarsaidze Collection
Natalie Grant Wraga Papers
Ryszard Wraga Papers
Rossiiskaia gosudarstvennaia biblioteka. Otdel rukopisei (OR RGB)
V. D. Bonch-Bruevich (369)
Izdatel'stvo M. i S. Sabashnikovykh (261)
S. D. Urusov (550)
Rossiiskii gosudarstvennyi arkhiv sotsial'no-politicheskoi istorii (RGASPI)
F. E. Dzerzhinskii (76)
V. I. Lenin (2)
Sekretariat V. I. Lenina (5)
Rossiiskii voenno-istoricheskii arkhiv (RGVIA)
15-aia Sibirskaia strel'kovaia diviziia (2527)
5-ii Armeiskii korpus (2189)
Posluzhnye spiski ofitserov (409)
3-ii Sibirskii korpus (2280)
8-aia Sibirskaia strel'kovaia diviziia (2520)

Books, Articles, and Dissertations

Abraham, Richard. *Alexander Kerensky: The First Love of the Revolution.* New York: Columbia University Press, 1987.

Akademiia nauk SSSR. Institut istorii. *Istoriia Moskvy v shesti tomakh.* Moscow: Izdatel'stvo Akademii Nauk SSSR, 1955.

Akademiia nauk v resheniiakh politburo TsKRKP (b)-VKP (b), 1922–1952. Moscow: Rosspen, 2000.

Alexander, Grand Duke of Russia. *Once a Grand Duke.* New York: Farrar and Rinehart, 1932.

Alexopolous, Golfo. "The Ritual Lament: A Narrative of Appeal in the 1920s and 1930s." *Russian History/Histoire Russe* 24, nos. 1–2 (Spring–Summer 1997): 117–29.

Alexopolous, Golfo. *Stalin's Outcasts: Aliens, Citizens and the Soviet State, 1926–1936.* Ithaca, NY: Cornell University Press, 2003.

Anan'ich, B. V., and R. Sh. Ganelin, eds. *Nikolai Vtoroi: Vospominaniia, dnevniki.* St. Petersburg: Pushkinskii fond, 1994.

Anan'ich, B. V., R. Sh. Ganelin, and V. M. Paneiakh, eds. *Vlast' i reformy: Ot samoderzhavnoi k sovetskoi Rossii.* St. Petersburg: Dmitrii Bulanin, 1996.

Anan'ich, B. V., R. Sh. Ganelin, et al. *Krizis samoderzhaviia v Rossii, 1895–1917.* Leningrad: Nauka, 1984.

Andreeva, N. "Pribaltiiskie nemtsy i pervaia mirovaia voina." In *Problemy sotsial'no-ekonomicheskoi istorii Rossii XIX–XX vekov. Sbornik statei pamiati Valintina Semenovicha Diakina i Iuriia Borisovicha Solov'eva*, edited by V. S. Diakin and Iu. B. Solov'ev, 461–72. St. Petersburg: Aleteiia, 1999.

Andreeva-Bal'mont, E. A. *Vospominaniia.* Moscow: Izdatel'stvo imeni Sabashnikovykh, 1997.

Andreevskii, G. V. *Moskva 29–30ye gody.* Moscow: Informpoligraf, 1998.

Andrew, Christopher, and Oleg Gordievsky. *KGB: The Inside Story of Its Foreign Operations from Lenin to Gorbachev.* New York: HarperCollins, 1990.

Andrew, Christopher, and Vasili Mitrokhin. *The Sword and the Shield: The Mitrokhin Archive and the Secret History of the KGB.* New York: Basic Books, 1999.

Anikst, Ol'ga. "Vospominaniia o Lenine." In *O Lenine: Vospominaniia*, edited by N. L. Meshcheriakov, 4:87–95. Moscow: Gos. izdatel'stvo, 1925.

Antonov, Vladimir, and Vladimir Karpov. *Tainye informatory Kremlia: Vollenberg, Artuzov i drugie.* Moscow: Geia, 2001.

Applebaum, Anne. *Gulag: A History.* New York: Doubleday, 2003.

Arkhiv akademika S. F. Platonova v otdele rukopisei rossiiskoi natsional'noi biblioteki. Katalog: vyp

1. Materialy k biografii, memuarnye materialy, raboty i issledovaniia, materialy k rabotam. St. Petersburg: Izdatel'stvo rossiskoi natsional'noi biblioteki, 1994.

Arutiunov, G. A. *Rabochee dvizhenie v Rossii v period novogo revoliutsionnogo pod'ema, 1910–1914 gg.* Moscow: Nauka, 1975.

Ascher, Abraham. *P. A. Stolypin: The Search for Stability in Late Imperial Russia.* Stanford, CA: Stanford University Press, 2001.

Ascher, Abraham. *The Revolution of 1905.* 2 vols. Stanford, CA: Stanford University Press, 1988–1992.

Avrekh, A. Ia. "Chrezvychainaia sledsvtennaia komissiia vremennogo pravitel'stva: Zamysel i ispolnenie." In Akadeniia Nauk SSSR Institut istorii, *Istoricheskie zapiki,* 118:72–101. Moscow: Nauka, 1990.

Avrekh, A. Ia. *Tsarizm i IV Duma, 1912–1914 gg.* Moscow: Nauka, 1981.

Baedeker, Karl. *Russia with Teheran, Port Arthur and Peking: A Handbook for Travellers.* Leipzig: Karl Baedeker, 1914.

Bailey, Geoffrey. *The Conspirators.* New York: Harper and Brothers, 1960.

Bakhrushin, Iu. A. *Vospominaniia.* Moscow: Khudozhestvenniia literatura, 1994.

Baliazin, Vol'demar N. *Imperatorskie namestniki pervoprestol'noi, 1709–1917.* Moscow: Izd. Tverskaia 13, 2000.

Ball, Alan M. *And Now My Soul Is Hardened: Abandoned Children in Soviet Russia, 1918–1930.* Berkeley: University of California Press, 1994.

Bal'mont, K. D. "Skvoz' stroi (Pamiati Nekrasova)." In K. D. Bal'mont, *Solnechnaia priazha: Stikhotvoreniia. ocherki.* Moscow: Detskaia literatura, 1989.

Beletskii, S. P. "Vospominaniia." In *Arkhiv Russkoi revoliutsii,* 12:5–75. Moscow: "Terra" Politizdat, 1991.

Belov, S. V. *Knigoizdateli Sabashnikovy.* Moscow: Moskovskii rabochii, 1974.

Belyi, Andrei. *Nachalo veka.* Moscow-Leningrad: n.p., 1933.

Berezhkov, V. I., and S. V. Pekhereva. *Zhenshchiny-Chekisty.* St. Petersburg: Izd. dom "Neva," 2003.

Blackstock, Paul W. *The Secret Road to World War Two: Soviet versus Western Intelligence.* Chicago: Quadrangle Books, 1969.

Blok, Aleksandr A. *Zapisnye knizhki, 1901–1920.* Moscow: Izd-vo khudozhestvennoi literatury, 1965.

Bogdanovich, A. V. *Tri poslednikh samoderzhtsa.* Moscow: Novosti, 1990.

Bokhanov, A. N. *Rasputin: Anatomiia mifa.* Moscow: ATS Press, 2000.

Bokhanov, A. N. "Velikii kniaz' Sergei Aleksandrovich." In *Rossiiskie konservatory,* edited by A. N. Bokhanov. Moscow: Russkii mir, 1997.

Bonnell, Victoria E. *Roots of Rebellion: Workers' Politics and Organizations in St. Petersburg and Moscow, 1900–1914.* Berkeley: University of California Press, 1983.

Bradley, Joseph. *Muzhik and Muscovite: Urbanization in Late Imperial Russia.* Berkeley: University of California Press, 1985.

Brooks, Jeffrey. *When Russia Learned to Read: Literacy and Popular Literature, 1861–1917.* Princeton, NJ: Princeton University Press, 1985.

Brook-Shepherd, Gordon. *The Iron Maze: The Western Secret Services and the Bolsheviks.* London: Macmillan, 1998.

Bulatsel', P. F. *Bor'ba za pravdu.* Moscow: Institut russkoi tsivilizatsii, 2010.

Burbank, Jane. *Intelligentsia and Revolution: Russian Views of Bolshevism, 1917–1922.* New York: Oxford University Press, 1986.

Butovskii poligon, 1937–1938. Kniga pamiati zhertv politicheskikh repressii. Edited by E. A. Baikov. 8 vols. Moscow: "Al'zo," 1997–2004.

Cassiday, Julie A. *The Enemy on Trial: Early Soviet Courts on Stage and Screen.* Dekalb: Northern Illinois Press, 2000.

Castiglione, Baldesar. *The Book of the Courtier.* Edited by Daniel Javitch. New York: Norton, 2002.

Chamberlin, William Henry. *The Russian Revolution, 1917–1921.* 2 vols. Princeton, NJ: Princeton University Press, 1987.

Che-Ka: Materialy po deiatel'nosti chrezvychainykh komissii. Berlin: Novaia Rossiia, 1922.

Chernyshevsky, Nikolai. *What Is to Be Done?* Translated by Michael R. Katz. Ithaca, NY: Cornell University Press, 1989.

Costello, John, and Oleg Tsarev. *Deadly Illusions.* London: Century, 1993.

Crane, Stephen. *The War Dispatches of Stephen Crane.* Edited by R. W. Stallman and E. R. Hagemann. New York: New York University Press, 1964.

Dadygina, T. V. "100-letie otechestvennoi voiny 1812 g. v foto—i kinodokumentakh." *Otechestvennye arkhivy* 5 (1992): 86–91.

Daly, Jonathan W. *Autocracy under Siege: Security Police and Opposition in Russia, 1866–1905.* DeKalb: Northern Illinois University Press, 1998.

Daly, Jonathan W. *The Watchful State: Security Police and Opposition, 1906–1917.* DeKalb: Northern Illinois University Press, 2004.

Delo provokatora Malinovskogo. Moscow: Respublika, 1992.

Dmytryshyn, Basil, ed. *Imperial Russia: A Source Book, 1700–1917.* 2nd ed. Hinsdale, IL: Dryden, 1974.

Dnevniki imperatora Nikolaia II. Moscow: "Orbita," 1991.

"'Dokladnaia zapiska' V. F. Dzhunkovskogo 9 noiabria 1929 g. A. S. Enukidze o svoem arkhiva, khranivshemsia v Pushkinskom dome." In Rossiiskaia Akademiia Nauk, Arkheograficheskaia komissia, *Arkheograficheskii ezhegodnik za 2001 god,* 413–20. Moscow: Nauka, 2002.

Dolgopolov, Nikolai. "Ot Savinkova do Ramzaia: Osen' rezidenta." *Moskva* 3 (2004): 163–202.

"'Dostoinstvo vlasti trebuet ne mstit' a razobrat' vinovnost' kazhdogo': F. V. Dubasov o dekabr'skom vooruzhennom vosstanii 1905 g. v Moskve." *Istoricheskii arkhiv* 5–6 (1998): 80–102.

Dowler, Wayne. *Russia in 1913.* DeKalb: Northern Illinois University Press, 2010.

Dunaeva, Anastasiia Iu. "Mezhdunarodnye kul'turnye sviazi veks prosveshcheniia v sud'be Dzhunkovskikh i Rashetov." In *Mir i novoe vremia: Sbornik materialov dvenatsatoi vserossiiskoi konferentsii studentov, asperantov i molodykh uchenykh po problemam istorii mezhdunarodnykh otnoshenii XVI–XX vv.,* edited by Nikolai Vlasov, 176–81. St. Petersburg: Sankt-Peterburgskii gosudarstnennyi universitet, 2009.

Dunaeva, Anastasiia Iu. *Reformy politsii v Rossii nachala XX veka in Vladimir Fedorovich Dzhunkovskii.* Moscow: Ob"edinennaia redaktsiia MVD Rossii, 2012.

Dunaeva, Anastasiia Iu. "V. F. Dzhunkovskii i Operatsiia 'Trest': Mify i dokumenty." In *Mir i novoe vremia. Sbornik materialov odinnadtsatoi vserossiiskoi nauchnoi konferentsii studentov, aspirantov i molodykh uchenykh po problemam mirovoi istorii XVI–XXI vv.,* edited by Nikolai Vlasov, 187–89. St. Petersburg: Sankt-Peterburgskii gosudarstvennyi universitet, 2009.

XX vek: Khronika moskovskoi zhizni, 1901–1910 gg. Edited by S. G. Muranov, A. S. Roshchina, et al. Moscow: Mosgorarkhiv, 2001.

XX vek: Khronika moskovskoi zhizni, 1911–1920 gg. Moscow: Mosgorarkhiv, 2002.

Dzhunkovskii, V. F. *Vospominaniia.* Vols. 1 and 2. Moscow: Izdatel'stvo im. Sabashnikovykh, 1997.

Dzhunkovskii, V. F. *Vospominaniia (1915–1917).* Vol. 3. Moscow: Izdatel'stvo im. Sabashnikovykh, 2015.

Dzhunkovskii, Vladimir F. "Koronatsionnye torzhestva 1896 goda v Moskve: Iz 'zapisok' generala V. F. Dzhunkovskogo." *Otechestvennaia istoriia* 4 (1997): 13–24.

Dziak, John J. *Chekisty: A History of the KGB.* New York: Ballantine, 1988.

Elwood, Ralph C. "The Malinovskii Affair: 'A Very Fishy Business.'" *Revolutionary Russia* 11, no. 1 (June 1998): 1–16.

Elwood, Ralph C. *Roman Malinovsky: A Life without a Cause.* Newtonville, MA: Oriental Research Partners, 1977.

Emmons, Terrence, and Wayne S. Vucinich, eds. *The Zemstvo in Russia: An Experiment in Local Self Government.* Cambridge: Cambridge University Press, 1982.

Engel, Barbara Alpern. *Breaking the Ties that Bound: The Politics of Marital Strife in Late Imperial Russia.* Ithaca, NY: Cornell University Press, 2011.

Engelstein, Laura. *Moscow, 1905: Working-Class Organization and Political Conflict.* Stanford, CA: Stanford University Press, 1982.

Field, Daniel. *The End of Serfdom: Nobility and Bureaucracy in Russia.* Cambridge, MA: Harvard University Press, 1976.

Figes, Orlando. *Natasha's Dance: A Cultural History of Russia.* New York: Henry Holt, 2002.

Figes, Orlando. *A People's Tragedy: A History of the Russian Revolution.* New York: Viking Press, 1997.

Filipova, T. A. "Liberal'no-konservativnyi sintez i mentalitet elita (Rossia v epokhu pozdnei imperializma)." In *Actio Nova 2000*, edited by A. I. Filiushkin, 409–25. Moscow: Globas, 2000.

Filipova, T. A. "Liberal'no konservativnyi sintez (popytka khronopoliticheskogo analiza)." In *Russkii liberalizm. Istoricheskie sud'by i perspektivy*, edited by V. V. Shelokhaev, 201–9. Moscow: Rospen, 1999.

Finkel, Stuart. "An Intensification of Vigilance: Recent Perspectives on the Institutional History of the Soviet Security Apparatus in the 1920s." *Kritika: Explorations in Russian and Eurasian History* 5, no. 2 (Spring 2004): 299–320.

Fitzpatrick, Sheila. *The Commissariat of Enlightenment: Soviet Organization of Education and the Arts under Lunacharsky, October 1917–1921.* Cambridge: Cambridge University Press, 1970.

Fitzpatrick, Sheila. *Everyday Stalinism—Ordinary Life in Extraordinary Times: Soviet Russia in the 1930s.* New York: Oxford University Press, 1999.

Fitzpatrick, Sheila. *Tear Off the Masks! Identity and Imposture in Twentieth-Century Russia.* Princeton, NJ: Princeton University Press, 2005.

Fleishman, Lazar'. *V tiskakh provokatsii: Operatsiia "Trest" i russkaia zarubezhnaia pechat'.* Moscow: Novoe literaturnoe obozrenie, 2003.

Florinsky, Michael T. *The End of the Russian Empire.* New York: Collier Books, 1961.

Frieden, Nancy M. *Russian Physicians in an Era of Reform and Revolution, 1856–1905.* Princeton, NJ: Princeton University Press, 1981.

Fuhrmann, Joseph T. *Rasputin: A Life.* New York: Praeger, 1990.

Fuhrmann, Joseph T. *Rasputin: The Untold Story.* Hoboken, NJ: John Wiley and Sons, 2013.

Fuhrmann, Joseph T., ed. *The Complete Wartime Correspondence of Tsar Nicholas II and the Empress Alexandra, April 1914–March 1917.* Westport, CT: Greenwood Press, 1999.

Fuller, William C., Jr. *Civil-Military Conflict in Imperial Russia, 1881–1914.* Princeton, NJ: Princeton University Press, 1985.

Fuller, William C., Jr. *The Foe Within: Fantasies of Treason and the End of Imperial Russia.* Ithaca, NY: Cornell University Press, 2006.

Galvazin, Sergei. *Okhrannye struktury Rossiiskoi imperii: Formirovanie apparata, analiz operativnoi praktiky.* Moscow: Kollektsiia "Sovershenо sekretno," 2001.

Gatrell, Peter. *Russia's First World War: A Social and Economic History.* London: Pearson Education, 2005.

Geifman, Anna. *Thou Shalt Kill: Revolutionary Terrorism in Russia, 1894–1917.* Princeton, NJ: Princeton University Press, 1993.

Geifman, Anna, ed. *Russia under the Last Tsar: Opposition and Subversion, 1894–1917.* Oxford: Blackwell, 1999.

Gerson, Lennard. *The Secret Police in Lenin's Russia.* Philadelphia: Temple University Press, 1976.

Gerua, B. V. *Vospominaniia o moei zhizni.* 2 vols. Paris: Voenno-istoricheskoe izdatel'stvo, 1969.

Gippius, Zinaida. *Dnevniki.* 2 vols. Moscow: NPK "Intelvak," 1999.

Gladkov, Teodor. *Nagrada za vernost'—kazn'.* Moscow: Tsentrpoligraf, 2000.

Gleason, William. *Alexander Guchkov and the End of the Russian Empire.* Philadelphia: American Philosophical Society, 1983.

Golinkov, D. L. *Krushenie antisovetskogo podpol'ia v SSSR.* 3rd ed. 2 vols. Moscow: Politizdat, 1980.

Golitsyn, S. *Zapiski utselevshego: Roman.* Moscow: Orbita, 1990.

Gosudarstvennost' Rossii: Slovar'-spravochnik. 5 vols. Moscow: Nauka, 1996–2005.

Got'e, Iurii Vladimirovich. *Time of Troubles: The Diary of Iurii Vladimirovich Got'e.* Edited and translated by Terence Emmons. Princeton, NJ: Princeton University Press, 1988.

Grabbe, Paul. *Windows on the River Neva.* New York: Pomerica Press, 1977.

Graham, Loren R. *The Soviet Academy of Sciences and the Communist Party, 1927–1932.* Princeton, NJ: Princeton University Press, 1967.

Grand Duchess George of Russia. *A Romanov Dairy: The Autobiography of HI & RH Grand Duchess George.* New York: Atlantic International, 1988.

Grant, Natalie. "Deception on a Grand Scale." *International Journal of Intelligence and Counterintelligence* 1, no. 4 (1986–1988): 51–78.

Grant, Natalie. "The Trust." *American Intelligence Journal* 12, no. 1 (Winter 1991): 11–15.

"Gubernator pristroilsia." *Bezbozhnik* (February 2, 1929): 3.

Gurko, V. I. *Features and Figures of the Past.* Stanford, CA: Stanford University Press, 1939.

Gutnov, Dmitrii. "Moskovskii gubernator V. F. Dzhunkovskii i organizatsiia iubileinykh borodinskikh torzhestv 1912 g." At http://gutnov.ucoz.ru/publ/.

Haimson, Leopold H., ed. *The Politics of Rural Russia, 1905–1914.* Bloomington: Indiana University Press, 1979.

Haimson, Leopold H. "The Problem of Social Stability in Urban Russia, 1905–1917." *Slavic Review* 23 (December 1964): 619–42; 24 (March 1965): 1–22.

Haimson, Leopold H. "'The Problem of Social Stability in Urban Russia on the Eve of War and Revolution' Revisited." *Slavic Review* 59 (Winter 2000): 848–75.

Hamm, Michael F., ed. *The City in Late Imperial Russia.* Bloomington: University of Indiana Press, 1986.

Hardeman, Hilde. *Coming to Terms with the Soviet Regime: The "Changing Signposts" Movement among the Russian Emigrés in the Early 1920s.* DeKalb: Northern Illinois University Press, 1994.

Haslam, Jonathan. *Near and Distant Neighbors: A New History of Soviet Intelligence.* New York: Farrar, Straus and Giroux, 2015.

Herlihy, Patricia. *The Alcoholic Empire: Vodka and Politics in Late Imperial Russia.* Oxford: Oxford University Press, 2002.

Hingley, Ronald. *The Russian Secret Police: Muscovite, Imperial Russian and Soviet Political Security Operations.* New York: Simon and Schuster, 1970.

Iartsev, A. A. *Senat i zemstvo: Administrativnaia iustitsiia i mestnoe samoupravlenie v dorevoliutsionnoi Rossii, 1864–1890.* Kaliningrad: Tipografiia "Iskra," 2008.

Iunge, Mark, and Rol'f Binner. *Kak terror stal "bol'shim": Sekretnyi prikaz no. 00447 i tekhnologiia ego ispolneniia.* Moscow: Ario-XX, 2003.

Ivanov-Razumnik, R. V. *The Memoirs of Ivanov-Razumnik.* Translated by P. M. Squire. London: Oxford University Press, 1965.

"'Izmeneniia pasportnoi sistemy nosiat printsipal'no vazhnyi kharakter.' Kak sozdavalas' i razvivalos' pasportnaia sistema v strane." *Istochnik* 6 (1997): 101–21.

Izmozhik, V. S. *"Chernye kabinety": Istoriia Rossiiskoi perliustratsii, XVIII–nachalo XX veka.* Moscow: Novoe literaturnoe obozrenie, 2015.

Jackson, A. V. Williams. *From Constantinople to the Home of Omar Khayyam: Travels in Transcaucasia and Northern Persia for Historic and Literary Research.* New York: Macmillan, 1911.

Jakobson, Michael. *Origins of the Gulag: The Soviet Prison Camp System, 1917–1934.* Lexington: University of Kentucky Press, 1993.

Jansen, Marc. "The Bar during the First Years of the Soviet Regime: N. K. Muravyov." *Revolutionary Russia* 11, no. 2 (1990): 211–23.

"Kak zhil v Moskve i rabotal V. F. Dzhunkovskii." *Vechernie izvestiia,* January 29, 1913, 3.

Kassow, Samuel D. *Students, Professors and the State in Tsarist Russia.* Berkeley: University of California Press, 1989.

Khutarev-Garnishevskii, Vladimir V. "Osinoe gnezdo provokatsii: Politicheskii sysk v armii v preddverii pervoi mirovoi." *Rodina* 9 (2010): 120–23.

Khutarev-Garnishevskii, Vladimir V. "Otdel'nyi korpus zhandarmov i organy Departamenta politsii MVD: Organy Politicheskogo syska nakanune i v gody Pervoi mirovoi voiny, 1913–1917 gg." Avtoreferat disertatsii. Moscow, 2012.

Kimmerling, Elise. "Civil Rights and Social Policy in Soviet Russia, 1918–1936." *Russian Review* 41, no. 1 (January 1982): 24–46.

Kir'ianov, Iu. I. "Maiskie besporiadki 1915 g. v Moskve." *Voprosy istorii* 12 (1994): 137–50.

Klement'ev, Vasilii F. *V bol'shevitskoi Moskve, 1918–1920*. Moscow: Russkii put', 1998.

Knox, Alfred. *With the Russian Army, 1914–1917*. 2 vols. London: Hutchinson, 1921.

Kobiakov, Sergei. "Krasnyi sud: Vpechatleniia zashchitnika v revoliutsionnykh tribunalakh." In *Arkhiv russkoi revoliutsii*, 7:246–75. Moscow: Terra, Politizdat, 1991.

Kokovtsov, V. N. *Iz moego proshlogo: Vospominaniia, 1903–1919*. 2 vols. Moscow: Nauka, 1992.

Koni, A. F. *Sobranie sochinenii*. 8 vols. Moscow: Iuridicheskaia literatura, 1966.

Kotkin, Stephen. *Stalin*. Vol. 1: *The Paradoxes of Power, 1878–1928*. New York: Penguin Press, 2014.

Kozhevnikov, M. V. *Istoriia sovetskogo suda, 1917–1956*. Moscow: Izd-vo iuridicheskoi literatury, 1957.

Krasnaia kniga VChK. 2 vols. Moscow: Izd. politicheskoi literatury, 1989.

Krasnov, Vasilii. *Khodynka: Ocherki ne do smerti rastoptannogo*. Moscow: Gosudarstvennoe izdatel'stvo, 1926.

Kropotkin, Peter. *Memoirs of a Revolutionist*. New York: Dover, 1988.

Kucherov, Samuel. *Courts, Lawyers and Trials under the Last Three Tsars*. New York: Praeger, 1953.

Kucherov, Samuel. *The Organs of Soviet Administration of Justice: Their History and Operation*. Leiden: Brill, 1970.

Kulikov, S. V. *Biurokraticheskaia elita Rossiiskoi imperii nakanune padeniia starogo poriadka (1914–1917)*. Riazan: P. A. Tribunskii, 2004.

Kupriianovskii, P. V., and N. A. Molchanova. *Poet Konstantin Bal'mont: Biografiia. Tvorchestvo. Sud'ba*. Ivanovo: Izd. "Ivanovo," 2001.

Kurlov, P. G. *Gibel' imperatorskoi Rossii*. Moscow: Sovremennik, 1992.

Kuskova, Ekaterina. "Peters i Dzhunkovskii (Iz vospominanii)." *Poslednye novosti* 6117 (December 24, 1937): 2.

Lapovok, Ia. S. "50 let v efire." At http://www.cqham.ru/ualfa_bio.htm/.

Lauchlan, Iain. *Russian Hide-and-Seek: The Tsarist Secret Police in St. Petersburg, 1906–1914*. Helsinki: Vammala, 2002.

Lazarev, K. "Aleksandr Dmitrievich Samarin (1868–1932) v vospominaniiakh ego docheri Elizavety Alexandrovny Samarinoi-Chernyshevskoi." *Pamiat'* 3 (1980): 329–73.

Leggett, George. *The Cheka: Lenin's Political Police*. Oxford: Clarendon Press, 1981.

Leonov, V. P., and Zh. I. Alferov, eds. *Akademicheskoe delo, 1929–1931 gg.: Dokumenty i materialy sledstvennogo dela, sfabrikovannogo OGPU. Vyp. 1. Delo po obvineniiu akademika S. F. Platonova*. St. Petersburg: Biblioteka Rossiiskoi Akademii Nauk, 1993.

Levin, Aleksey E. "Expedient Catastrophe: A Reconsideration of the 1929 Crisis at the Soviet Academy of Science." *Slavic Review* 47, no. 2 (1988): 261–79.

Levin, Alfred. "The Shornikova Affair." *Slavonic and East European Review* 21 (November 1943): 1–18.

Lieven, Dominic. *Nicholas II: Twilight of the Empire*. New York: St. Martin's Griffin, 1993.

Lieven, Dominic. *Russia's Rulers under the Old Regime*. New Haven, CT: Yale University Press, 1989.

Lincoln, W. Bruce. *The Great Reforms: Autocracy, Bureaucracy, and the Politics of Change in Imperial Russia*. DeKalb: Northern Illinois University Press, 1990.

Lincoln, W. Bruce. *In the Vanguard of Reform: Russia's Enlightened Bureaucrats, 1825–1861*. DeKalb: Northern Illinois University Press, 1982.

Lincoln, W. Bruce. *In War's Dark Shadow: The Russians before the Great War*. New York: Dial Press, 1983.

Lincoln, W. Bruce. *Passage through Armageddon: The Russians in War and Revolution, 1914–1918*. New York: Simon and Schuster, 1986.

Lincoln, W. Bruce. *Red Victory: A History of the Russian Civil War*. New York: Simon and Schuster, 1989.

Lindenmeyr, Adele. "Building Civil Society One Brick at a Time: The People's Houses and Worker Enlightenment in Late Imperial Russia." *Journal of Modern History* 84 (March 2012): 1–39.

Litvin, A. L. *Krasnyi i belyi terror v Rossii, 1918–1922 gg.* Kazan: Tatarskoe gazetno-zhural'noe izdatel'stvo, 1995.

Liubimova, K., and P. Golovkova. "Butovo—Russkaia golgofa—Kaznennye generaly." At http://www.martyr.ru/content/view/8/18/.

Lobanov-Rostovsky, A. *The Grinding Mill: Reminiscences of War and Revolution in Russia, 1913–1920.* New York: Macmillan, 1935.

Lockhart, Robert H. Bruce. *Memoirs of a British Agent.* London: Putnam, 1932.

Lohr, Eric. *Nationalizing the Russian Empire: The Campaign against Enemy Aliens during World War I.* Cambridge, MA: Harvard University Press, 2003.

Lubianka 2: Iz istorii otechestvennoi kontrrazvedki. Moscow: Izd-vo "Mosgorarkhiv," 1999.

Lur'e, F. M., and Z. I. Peregudova. "Tsarskaia okhranka i provokatsiia." *Iz glubiny vremen* 1 (1992): 51–83.

Lyandres, Semion. "Conspiracy and Ambition in Russian Politics before the February Revolution of 1917: The Case of Georgii Evgen'evich L'vov." *Journal of Modern Russian History and Historiography* 8 (2015): 99–133.

Lyandres, Semion. *The Fall of Tsarism: Untold Stories of the February Revolution.* Oxford: Oxford University Press, 2013.

Madariaga, Isabel de. *Russia in the Age of Catherine the Great.* New Haven, CT: Yale University Press, 1981.

Mager, Hugo. *Elizabeth, Grand Duchess of Russia.* New York: Caravel and Graf, 1998.

Maier, N. "Sluzhba v komissariate iustitsii i narodnom sude." In *Arkhiv russkoi revoliutsii* 8:56–109. Moscow: Terra, 1991.

Makarevich, Eduard. *Vostok-zapad: Zvezdy politicheskogo syska. Istorii, sud'by, versii.* Moscow: Terra-knizhnyi klub, 2003.

Malinin, V. F. "Zabastovka vodoprovoda v Moskve: Iz vospominanii o 1905 gode." Manuscript in the Malinin Collection, BAR.

Malmstad, John E., and Nikolay Bogomolov. *Mikhail Kuzmin: A Life in Art.* Cambridge, MA: Harvard University Press, 1999.

Manning, Roberta T. *The Crisis of the Old Order in Russia: Gentry and Government.* Princeton, NJ: Princeton University Press, 1982.

Marie, Grand Duchess of Russia. *Education of a Princess: A Memoir.* New York: Viking Press, 1931.

Marshall, Alex. "Russian Military Intelligence, 1905–1917: The Untold Story behind Tsarist Russia in the First World War." *War in History* 11, no. 4 (2004): 393–423.

Martynov, A. P. *Moia sluzhba v otdel'nom korpuse zhandarmov.* Stanford, CA: Hoover Institution Press, 1973.

Martynov, P. I. "Otchet o zabastovochnom dvizhenii sredi rabochikh promyshlovo-zavodskogo raiona bakinskogo gradonachal'stva za period vremeni s 28-go maia po 8-e iiulia 1914 goda." Published by S. Sef in *Proletarskaia revoliutsiia* 7, no. 54 (July 1926): 227–59.

Massie, Robert K. *Nicholas and Alexandra.* New York: Dell, 1967.

Matthews, Mervyn. *The Passport Society: Controlling Movement in Russia and the USSR.* Boulder, CO: Westview Press, 1993.

McKee, Arthur. "Taming the Green Serpent: Alcoholism, Autocracy, and Russian Society, 1881–1914." Ph.D. diss., University of California, Berkeley, 1997.

McReynolds, Louise. *Russia at Play: Leisure Activities at the End of the Tsarist Era.* Ithaca, NY: Cornell University Press, 2003.

Mehlinger, Howard D., and John M. Thompson. *Count Witte and the Tsarist Government in the 1905 Revolution.* Bloomington: Indiana University Press, 1972.

Melancon, Michael. *The Lena Goldfields Massacre and the Crisis of the Late Tsarist State.* College Park, TX, 2006.

Melancon, Michael. "Unexpected Consensus: Russian Society and the Lena Massacre, April 1912." *Revolutionary Russia* 15, no. 2 (2002): 1–52.

Mel'gunov [Melgounov], Sergei P. *The Red Terror in Russia.* London: J. M. Dent, 1926.

Meshcherskaya, Ekaterina. *A Russian Princess Remembers: The Journey from Tsars to Glasnost.* New York: Doubleday, 1989.

Moskovskii al'bom: Vospominaniia o Moskve i moskvichakh. Edited by Iu Aleksandrov, V. Enisherlov, and D. K. Ivanov. Moscow: Izd. zhurnala Nashe nasledie, 1997.

Moskovskii arkhiv: Istoriko-kraevedicheskii al'manakh. Vol. 2. Edited by E. G. Boldina and M. M. Gorinov. Moscow: Mosgorarkhiv, 2000.

"Nachalo 'dela' Akademii nauk: Stenogramma zasedaniia osoboi komissii Narkomata RKI SSSR 24 oktiabria 1929 g." *Istoricheskii arkhiv* 1 (1993): 79–109.

Nemirovich-Danchenko, Vladimir. *My Life in the Russian Theater.* Translated by John Cournos. London: Geoffrey Beles, 1937.

Nikulin, L. V. *Mertvaia zyb': Roman khronika.* Moscow: Voennoe izd-vo Ministerstva oborony, 1965.

Nikulin, L. V. *The Swell of the Sea.* Springfield, VA: National Technical Information Service, 1972.

Ocherki istorii rossiiskoi vneshnei razvedki. Edited by E. M. Primakov. 6 vols. Moscow: Mezhdunarodnaia otnosheniia, 1996.

Oktiabr'skaia revoliutsiia i armiia (25 oktiabria 1917 g.–mart 1918 g.) Sbornik dokumentov. Edited by L. S. Gaponenko. Moscow: Nauka, 1973.

Okunev, N. P. *Dnevnik moskvicha, 1917–1924.* Paris: YMCA Press, 1990.

"'Ostalos' eshche nemalo khlama v liudskom sostave.' Kak nachinalos' 'delo Akademii nauk.'" *Istochnik* 3 (1997): 105–26; 4 (1997): 103–19.

Otchet moskovskogo stolichnogo popechitel'stva o narodnoi trezvosti za 1904 g. Moscow: Pechatnaia S. P. Iakovleva, 1905.

Padenie tsarskogo rezhima: Stenograficheskie otchety doprosov i pokazanii dannykh v 1917 g. v chrezvychainoi sledstvennoi komissii vremenogo pravitel'stva. Edited by P. E. Shchegolev. 7 vols. Leningrad: Gos. izdatel'stvo, 1924–1927.

Paléologue, Maurice. *An Ambassador's Memoirs.* Translated by F. A. Holt. 3 vols. New York: George H. Doran, n.d.

Papchinskii, A., and M. Tumshis. *Shchit raskolotyi mechom: NKVD protiv VChK.* Moscow: Sovremennik, 2001.

Pares, Bernard. *The Fall of the Russian Monarchy: A Study of the Evidence.* New York: Knopf, 1939.

Pavlov, D. B. "Tribunal'nyi etap sovetskoi sudebnoi sistemy, 1917–1922 gg." *Voprosy istorii* 6 (2007): 3–16.

Pechenuk, Volodimir. "Temperance and Revenue Raising: The Goals of the Russian State Liquor Monopoly." *New Zealand Slavonic Journal* 1 (1980): 35–48.

Perchenok, F. F. "Delo Akademii nauk i velikii perelom v sovetskoi nauke." In *Tragichskie sud'by: Repressirovannye unchenye Akademii nauk SSSR. Sbornik statei.*, edited by V. Kumanev. Moscow: Nauka, 1995.

Peregudova, Z. I. *Politicheskii sysk Rossii, 1880–1917.* Moscow: Rosspen, 2000.

"Perepiska pravykh i drugie materialy ob ikh deiatel'nosti v 1914–1917 godakh." *Voprosy istorii* 1 (1996): 113–33; 3:142–65; 4:135–55; 8:78–100; 10:119–43.

Peris, Daniel. *Storming the Heavens: The Soviet League of the Militant Godless.* Ithaca, NY: Cornell University Press, 1998.

Petrov, N. G. *Bol'sheviki na zapadnom fronte: Vospominaniia.* Moscow: Gosurdarstvennoe izdatel'stvo politicheskoi literatury, 1959.

Pipes, Richard. *The Russian Revolution.* New York: Vintage Books, 1991.

Pipes, Richard, ed. *The Unknown Lenin: From the Secret Archive.* New Haven, CT: Yale University Press, 1996.

"Pis'ma K. D. Bal'monta k V. F. Dzhunkovskomu." In *Konstantin Bal'mont, Marina Tsvetaeva i khudozhestvennye iskaniia XX veka. Mezhvuzovskii sbornik nauchnykh trudov,* 2:61–65. Ivanovo: Ivanovskii gosudarstvennyi universitet, 1996.

Platonov, O. A. *Ternovyi venets Rossii: Istoriia masonstva, 1731–1995.* Moscow: "Rodnik," 1995.

Platonov, O. A. *Zhizn' za tsaria (Pravda o Grigorii Rasputine).* St. Petersburg: Voskresenie, 1996.

Plekhanov, A. M. *VChK-OGPU, 1921–1928 gg.* Moscow: X-History, 2003.

Podorozhnyi, N. E. *Narochskaia operatsiia v marte 1916 g. na russkom fronte mirovoi voiny.* Moscow: Gos. voennoizdatel'svo Narkomata oborony, 1938.

Popov, A. L. *Iz istorii zabastovochnogo dvizheniia v Rossii nakanune imperialisticheskoi voiny: Bakinskaia zabastovka 1914 g.* Leningrad: Gosudarstvennoe izdatel'stvo, 1925.

Priklonskii, D. *Biografiia tainogo sovetnika S. S. Dzhunkovskogo.* St. Petersburg, 1840.

Prologue to Revolution: Notes of A. N. Iakhontov on the Secret Meetings of the Council of Ministers, 1915. Edited and translated by Michael Cherniavsky. Engelwood Cliffs, NJ: Prentice Hall, 1967.

Queen Marie of Roumania. *The Story of My Life.* London: Cassell, 1934.

Rabochee dvizhenie v Azerbaidzhane v gody novogo revoliutsionnogo pod'ema (1910–1914 gg.): Dokumenty i materialy. 2 vols. Baku: Izd. AN AzSSR, 1967.

Radzinsky, Edvard. *The Rasputin File.* New York: Doubleday, 2000.

Raeff, Marc. *Michael Speransky: Statesman of Imperial Russia, 1772–1839.* The Hague: Martinus Nijhoff, 1957.

Rayfield, Donald. *Stalin and His Hangmen: The Tyrant and Those Who Killed for Him.* New York: Random House, 2004.

Razgon, Lev. *True Stories.* Translated by John Crowfoot. Dana Point, CA: Ardis, 1997.

Razvedka i kontrrazvedka v litsakh: Entsiklopedicheskii slovar' rossiiskikh spetsluzhb. Edited by A. Dienko. Moscow: Russkii mir, 2002.

Reichman, Henry. *Railway Men and Revolution: Russia, 1905.* Berkeley: University of California Press, 1987.

Rendle, Matthew. *Defenders of the Motherland: The Tsarist Elite in Revolutionary Russia.* Oxford: Oxford University Press, 2010.

Revoliutsiia 1905–1907 gg. v Rossii: Dokumenty i materialy. Nachalo pervoi russkoi revoliutsii, ianvar'–mart 1905 goda. Edited by E. V. Illeritskaia, N. S. Trusova, A. A. Novosel'skii, and L. N. Pushkarev. Moscow: Izdatel'stvo Akademii Nauk SSSR, 1955.

Revoliutsiia 1905–1907 gg. v Rossii: Dokumenty i materialy. Vysshii pod"em revoliutsii 1905–1907 gg.: Vooruzhennye vosstaniia, noiabr'–dekabr, 1905 goda. 2 vols. Edited by A. L. Siderov. Moscow: Izdatel'stvo Akademii Nauk SSSR, 1955.

Revoliutsionnoe dvizhenie v russkoi armii (27 fevralia–24 oktiabria 1917 goda): Sbornik dokumentov. Edited by L. S. Gaponenko. Moscow: Nauka, 1968.

Rimlinger, Gaston V. "Autocracy and the Factory Order in Early Russian Industrialization." *Journal of Economic History* 20 (March 1960): 69–91.

Robbins, Richard G., Jr. "Building Vladimir Dzhunkovskii's Memory Palace: The Curious Fate of His Archive and Memoir." *Journal of Modern Russian History and Historiography* 4 (2011): 1–30.

Robbins, Richard G., Jr. *Famine in Russia, 1891–1892: The Imperial Government Responds to a Crisis.* New York: Columbia University Press, 1975.

Robbins, Richard G., Jr. *The Tsar's Viceroys: Russian Provincial Governors in the Last Years of the Empire.* Ithaca, NY: Cornell University Press, 1987.

Robbins, Richard G., Jr. "Vladimir Dzhunkovskii: Witness for the Defense." *Kritika: Explorations in Russian and Eurasian History* 2 (Summer 2001): 635–54.

Robbins, Richard G., Jr. "Was Vladimir Dzhunkovskii the Father of the 'Trust'? A Quest for the Plausible." *Journal of Modern Russian History and Historiography* 1 (2008): 113–43.

Robien, Louis de. *The Diary of a Diplomat in Russia.* Translated by Camilla Sykes. New York: Praeger, 1970.

Robinson, Paul. *Grand Duke Nikolai Nikolaevich: Supreme Commander of the Russian Army.* DeKalb: Northern Illinois University Press, 2014.

"Rodoslovnye: Dzhunkovskie." At http://www.MTU-NET.ru/sherbach/rodoslov/djun.html/.

Root, G. Irving. *Battles East: A History of the Eastern Front in the First World War.* Baltimore, MD: Publish America, 2007.

Rossiia 1913 god: Statistiko-dokumental'nyi spravochnik. St. Petersburg: Izdatel'stvo Russko-Baltiiskii informatisonnyi tsentr, 1995.

Rozental', I. S. "Eshche raz o dele provokatora Malinovskogo." *Voprosy istorii KPSS* 5 (1989): 103–17.

Rozental', I. S. *Moskva na pereput'e: Vlast' i obshchestvo v 1905–1914 gg.* Moscow: Rospen, 2004.

Rozental', I. S. *Provokator Roman Malinovskii: Sud'ba i vremia.* Moscow: Rospen, 1996.

Rozental', I. S. "Stranitsy zhizni generala Dzhunkovskogo." *Kentavr* 1 (1994): 90–99.

Rozental', I. S. "Zlopoluchenyi portret: Sto let 'grozy dvenadtsatogo goda' i general Dzhunkovskii." *Sovetskii muzei* 4 (1992): 39–41.

The Russian Provisional Government, 1917: Documents. Selected and edited by Robert Paul Browder and Alexander F. Kerensky. 3 vols. Stanford, CA: Stanford University Press, 1961.

Ruud, Charles A., and Sergei A. Stepanov. *Fontanka 16: The Tsars' Secret Police.* Montreal: McGill-Queen's University Press, 1999.

Sabashnikov, M. V. *Zapiski Mikhaila Vasil'evich Sabashnikova.* Moscow: Izdatel'stvo imeni Sabashnikovykh, 1995.

Sablinsky, Walter. *The Road to Bloody Sunday: Father Gapon and the St. Petersburg Massacre of 1905.* Princeton, NJ: Princeton University Press, 1976.

Savinkov, Boris. *Izbrannoe.* Leningrad: Khuzdozhestvennaia literatura, 1990.

Savinkov, Boris. *Memoirs of a Terrorist.* Translated by Joseph Shaplen. New York: A and C Boni, 1931.

Schapiro, Leonard. *Rationalism and Nationalism in Russian Nineteenth-Century Political Thought.* New Haven, CT: Yale University Press, 1967.

Schlögel, Karl. *Moscow, 1937.* Translated by Rodney Livingstone. Malden, MA: Polity Press, 2012.

Schneer, Matthew. "The Markovo Republic: A Peasant Community during Russia's First Revolution, 1905–1906." *Slavic Review* 53, no. 1 (Spring 1994): 104–19.

Schneiderman, Jeremiah. *Sergei Zubatov and Revolutionary Marxism: The Struggle for the Working Class in Russia.* Ithaca, NY: Cornell University Press, 1976.

Sellers, Edith. "The Russian Temperance Committees." *Contemporary Review* 82 (December 1902): 866–79.

Serkov, A. I. *Istoriia russkogo masonstva, 1845–1945.* St. Petersburg: Izdatel'stvo im. N. I. Novikova, 1996.

Serkov, A. I. *Russkoe masonstvo, 1731–2000: Entsiklopedicheskii slovar'.* Moscow: Rospen, 2001.

Service, Robert. *Lenin: A Biography.* Cambridge, MA: Harvard University Press, 2000.

Service, Robert. *Stalin: A Biography.* Cambridge, MA: Harvard University Press, 2005.

Shaumian, S. G. *Izbrannye proizvedeniia.* 2 vols. Moscow: Gosudarstvennoe izdatel'stvo politicheskoi literatury, 1957–1958.

Shearer, David R. *Policing Stalin's Socialism: Repression and Social Order in the Soviet Union, 1924–1953.* New Haven, CT: Yale University Press, 2009,

Sheremeteva, O. G. *Dnevnik i vospominaniia.* Moscow: Indrik, 2005.

Shevelev, L. E. *Chinovnyi mir Rossii, XVIII–nachalo XX v.* Saint Petersburg: Izkusstvo-SPb, 1999.

Shevliakov, A. S., ed. *Otechestvennye konstitutsii (1918–1993) Istoriia. Dokumenty. Voprosy.* Tomsk: Izdatel'stvo nauchno-tekhnicheskoi literatury, 1998.

Shilov, D. N. *Gosudarstvennye deiateli rossiiskoi imperii, 1802–1917: Bibliograficheskii spravochnik.* St. Petersburg: Dmitrii Bulanin, 2001.

Shipov, D. N. *Vospominaniia i dumy o perezhitom.* Moscow: Rospen, 2007.

Shklovsky, Victor. *A Sentimental Journey: Memoirs, 1917–1922.* Translated by Richard Sheldon. Ithaca, NY: Cornell University Press, 1970.

Shumikhin, S. V. "Dnevnik Mikhaila Kuzmina: Arkhivnaia predystoriia." In *Mikhail Kuzmin i russkaia kul'tura XX veka: Tezisy i materialy konferentsii 15–17 maia 1990,* edited by G. A. Morev, 139–45. Leningrad: Sovet po istorii mirovoi kul'tury AN SSSR, 1990.

Shumikhin, S. V. "Pis'ma narkomam." *Znanie-sila* 6 (1989): 69–74.

Shumikhin, S. V., ed. "Stenogramma obsledovaniia tsentral'nogo muzeia khudozhestvennoi literatury, kritiki i publitsistika komissiei kul'tpropa TsKVKP (b) 28 aprelia 1934 g." *Tynianovskii sbornik* 4 (Riga: Zinatne, 1990): 290–317.

Sledstvennoe delo Patriarkha Tikhona: Sbornik dokumentov po materialam tsentralnogo arkhiva FSB RF. Moscow: Pamiatniki istoricheskoi mysli, 2000.

Smirnov, A. F. *Gosudarstvennaia Duma Rossiiskoi imperii, 1906–1917: Istoriko-pravovoi ocherk.* Moscow: Kniga i biznes, 1998.

Smirnov, I. L. *"Markovskaia respublika": Iz istorii krest'ianskogo dvizheniia 1905 v moskovskoi gubernii.* Moscow: Moskovskii rabochii, 1975.

Smirnova, T. M. *"Byvshie liudi" sovetskoi Rossii: Strategii vydvizheniia i puti integratsii, 1917–1936 gody.* Moscow: "Mir istorii," 2003.

Smirnova, T. M. "Sotsial'nyi portret 'byvshikh' v Sovetskoi Rossii, 1917–1920 (Po materialam registratsii 'lits byvshego burzhuaznogo i chinovnogo sostoianiia' osen'iu 1919 v Moskve i Petrograde)." In *Sotsial'naia istoriia. Ezhegodnik 2000*, edited by K. M. Anderson, L. I. Borodkin, and A. K. Sokolov, 87–126. Moscow: Rospen, 2000.

Smith, Douglas. *Former People: The Final Days of the Russian Aristocracy.* New York: Farrar, Straus and Giroux, 2012.

Smith, Douglas. *Rasputin: Faith, Power, and the Twilight of the Romanovs.* New York: Farrar, Straus and Giroux, 2016.

Smoliarchuk, V. I. *Anatolii Fedorovich Koni.* Moscow: Nauka, 1981.

Sovet ministrov rossiiskoi imperii v gody pervoi mirovoi voiny. Bumagi A. N. Iakhontova (Zapiski zasedanii i perepiska). St. Petersburg: Izdatel'stvo Dmitrii Bulanin, 1999.

Spence, Richard. *Boris Savinkov: Renegade on the Left.* Boulder, CO: Westview Press, 1991.

Spence, Richard. "Russia's 'Operatsiia Trest': A Reappraisal." *Global Intelligence Monthly* 1, no. 4 (April 1999): 19–23.

Spence, Richard. *Trust No One: The Secret World of Sidney Reilly.* Los Angeles: Feral House, 2003.

Spiridovich, A. I. *Velikaia voina i fevral'skaia revoliutsiia.* New York: Vseslavianskoe Izdatel'stvo, 1960.

Stalin, Joseph. *Mastering Bolshevism.* San Francisco: Proletarian Publishers, n.d.

Stalin, Joseph. *Works.* 13 vols. Moscow: Foreign Languages Publishing, 1953.

Steevens, George W. *With the Conquering Turk: Confessions of a Bashi-Bazouk.* New York: Dodd, Mead, 1897.

Stone, David R. *The Russian Army in the Great War: The Eastern Front, 1914–1917.* Lawrence: University Press of Kansas, 2015.

Stone, Norman. *The Eastern Front 1914–1917.* London: Penguin Books, 1998.

Swift, E. Anthony. *Popular Theater and Society in Tsarist Russia.* Berkeley: University of California Press, 2002.

Telitsyn, V. L. "Dzhunkovskii, Stepan Stepanovich." In *Othechestvennaia istoriia. Istoriia Rossii s derevneishikh vremen do 1917 goda. Entsiklopediia*, edited by V. A. Ianin, M. Ia. Volkov, and V. V. Zhuralev. Moscow: Nauchnoe izdatel'stvo Bol'shaia Rossiiskaia Entsiklopediia, 1996.

Thurston, Robert W. *Liberal City, Conservative State: Moscow and Russia's Urban Crisis, 1906–1914.* Oxford: Oxford University Press, 1987.

Tikhmenev, N. P. *General Dzhunkovskii v ostavke.* Petrograd: n.p., 1915.

Titov, Iu. M. *Razvitie sistemy sovetskikh revoliutsionnykh tribunalov.* Moscow: RIO VIuZI, 1987.

Tolf, Robert W. *The Russian Rockefellers: The Saga of the Nobel Family and the Russian Oil Industry.* Stanford, CA: Hoover Institution Press, 1976.

Tolz, Vera. "The Formation of the Soviet Academy of Sciences: Bolsheviks and Academics in the 1920s and 1930s." In *Academia in Upheaval: Origins, Transfers and Transformations of the Communist Academic Regime in Russia and Eastern Europe*, edited by Michael David-Fox and György Peteri, 39–71. Westport, CT: Bergin and Garvey, 2000.

Trubetskoi, S. E. *Minuvshee.* Paris: YMCA Press, 1989.

Tucker, Robert C. *Stalin in Power: The Revolution from Above, 1928–1941.* New York: Norton, 1990.

Tumanova, Anastasia S. "A Conservative in Power: Governor N. P. Muratov." *Russian Studies in History* 52, no. 3 (Winter 2014–2015): 38–55.
Tumshis, M. A. *VChK: Voina klanov: Lubianka bez retushi.* Moscow: Iauza EKSMO, 2004.
Tyrkova-Williams, Adriana. *From Liberty to Brest-Litovsk: The First Year of the Russian Revolution.* London: Macmillan, 1919.
Ugrimova, T. A., and A. G. Volkov, eds. *"Stoi v zavete svoem": Nikolai Konstantinovich Murav'ev, advokat i obshchestvennyi deiatel': Vospominaniia, dokumenty, materialy.* Moscow: AMA Press, 2004.
Urusov, S. D. *Zapiski: Tri goda gosudarstvennoe sluzhby.* Moscow: Novoe literaturnoe obozrenie, 2009.
Uskov, Vladimir A., and Kseniia V. Poroshina. "Gosudarstvennoe upravlenie v usloviiakh sotsial'noi neopredelennesti: Rol' V. F. Dzhunkovskogo." *Sotsial'no-ekonomicheskie iavleniia i protsessy* 10, no. 8 (2015): 200–206.
Vaksberg, Arkady. *Stalin's Prosecutor: The Life of Andrei Vyshinsky.* Translated by Jan Butler. New York: Grove Weidenfeld, 1991.
Vasil'chikova, L. L. *Ischeznuvshaia Rossiia: Vospominaniia kniagini Lidii Leonardovnoi Vasil'chikova, 1886–1919.* St. Petersburg: Peterburgskie sezony, 1995.
Vazhenin, A. G., and P. V. Galkin, *Moskovskoe zemstvo v nachale XX veka: Iz opyta regional'nogo samoupravleniia.* Moscow: Moskovskii gosudarstvennyi oblastnoi universitet, 2004.
Venturi, Franco. *Roots of Revolution: A History of Populist and Socialist Movements in Nineteenth-Century Russia.* Translated by Francis Haskell. New York: Knopf, 1960.
Verner, Andrew M. *The Crisis of the Russian Autocracy: Nicholas II and the 1905 Revolution.* Princeton, NJ: Princeton University Press, 1990.
Voeikov, V. N. *S tsarem i bez tsaria: Vospominaniia poslednogo dvortsovogo komendanta gosudaria imperatora Nikolaia II.* Moscow: Voennoe izdatel'stvo, 1995.
Voitsekhovskii, S. L. *Trest: Vospominaniia i dokumenty.* London, Ontario: Zaria, 1974.
Voloshina-Sabashnikova, M. V. *Zelenaia zmeia: Istoriia odnoi zhizni.* St. Petersburg: Andreev i sinov'ia, 1993.
"Vstrecha v stavke. Nikolai II i A. D. Samarin. Iiun' 1915 g." *Istoricheskii arkhiv* 2 (1996): 176–86.
Vysotskii, Sergei. *Koni.* Moscow: Molodaia gvardiia, 1988.
Wagner, William G. *Marriage, Property and Law in Late Imperial Russia.* Oxford: Oxford University Press, 1994.
Waldron, Peter. *Between Two Revolutions: Stolypin and the Politics of Renewal in Russia.* DeKalb: Northern Illinois University Press, 1998.
Walkin, Jacob. *The Rise of Democracy in Pre-revolutionary Russia: Political and Social Institutions under the Last Three Tsars.* New York: Praeger, 1962.
Warwick, Christopher. *Ella: Princess, Saint and Martyr.* London: John Wiley and Sons, 2006.
Wcislo, Francis W. *Reforming Rural Russia: State, Local Society and National Politics, 1855–1914.* Princeton, NJ: Princeton University Press, 1990.
Weiner, Douglas R. "Dzerzhinskii and the Gerd Case: The Politics of Intercession and the Evolution of 'Iron Felix' in NEP Russia." *Kritika: Explorations in Russian and Eurasian History* 7, no. 4 (Fall 2006): 759–91.
Weissman, Neil B. *Reform in Tsarist Russia: The State Bureaucracy and Local Government, 1900–1914.* New Brunswick, NJ: Rutgers University Press, 1981.
Wheatcroft, S. G. "The 1891–92 Famine in Russia: Towards a More Detailed Analysis of Its Scale and Demographic Significance." In *Economy and Society in Russia and the Soviet Union, 1860–1930: Essays for Olga Crisp,* edited by Linda Edmondson and Peter Waldron, 44–64. New York: St. Martin's Press, 1992.
Wildman, Allan K. *The End of the Russian Imperial Army.* 2 vols. Princeton, NJ: Princeton University Press, 1980–1987.
Wolfe, Bertram D. *Three Who Made a Revolution: A Biographical History.* New York: Cooper Square Press, 2001.

Wood, Elizabeth A. *Performing Justice: Agitation Trials in Early Soviet Russia.* Ithaca, NY: Cornell University Press, 2005.

Wortman, Richard S. *The Development of a Russian Legal Consciousness.* Chicago: University of Chicago Press, 1976.

Wortman, Richard S. *Scenarios of Power: Myth and Ceremony in Russian Monarchy.* 2 vols. Princeton, NJ: Princeton University Press, 1995–2000.

Wraga, Richard. "Cloak and Dagger Politics." *Problems of Communism* 10, no. 2 (1961): 56–59.

Wraga, Richard. "Eshche o 'Treste.'" *Vozrozhdenie* 11 (September–October 1950): 136–43.

Wraga, Richard. "Trest." *Vozrozhdenie* 7 (January–February 1950): 114–35.

Yaney, George. *The Systematization of Russian Government: Social Evolution in the Domestic Administration of Imperial Russia, 1711–1905.* Urbana: University of Illinois Press, 1973.

Yaney, George. *The Urge to Mobilize: Agrarian Reform in Russia, 1861–1930.* Urbana, 1982.

"'Zachislit' za VChK vpred' do osobogo rasporiazheniia.' Delo V. F. Dzhunkovskogo v moskovskoi taganskoi tiurme." Compiled by A. N. Semkin. *Otechestvennye arkhivy* 5 (2002): 79–98.

Zaionchkovskii, A. M. *Mirovaia voina, 1914–1918 gg.* 2 vols. Moscow: Voenizdat, 1938.

Zalesskii, K. A. *Pervaia mirovaia voina: Biograficheskii entsiklopedicheskii slovar'.* Moscow: Veche, 2000.

"Zameshannykh nemtsev arestovat' . . . anglichan ne trogat." *Otechestvennye arkhivy* 6 (2008): 84–97.

Zdanovich, A. A. *Organy gosudarstvennoi bezopasnosti i krasnaia armiia: Deiatel'nost' organov VChK-OGPU po obespecheniiu bezopasnosti RKKA (1921–1934).* Moscow: Prodiuserskii tsentr' "Iks-Istorii" Kulikovo pole, 2008.

Zhirnov, E. "Protsedura kazni nosila omerzitel'nyi kharakter." *Komsomol'skaia pravda* (October 28, 1990): 2.

Index

Note: Page numbers in *italics* refer to figures.